DICK B

365 DAYS OF LIVING AND DYING WITH JESUS

LIVE | DEAD

Joy

MY HEALTHY CHURCH

Published by My Healthy Church
1445 North Boonville Avenue
Springfield, Missouri 65802

Cover design and interior design by Prodigy Pixel www.prodigypixel.com

Unless otherwise specified, Scripture quotations used in this book are from The New King James version®. © 1982 by Thomas Nelson, Inc. Used by permission. All rights reserved.

Scriptures marked NIV are taken from the Holy Bible, New International Version®. , NIV®. Copyright © 1973, 1978, 1984, 2011 by Biblica, Inc. ™ Used by permission of Zondervan. All rights reserved worldwide. www.zondervan.com. The "NIV" and "New International Version" are trademarks registered in the United States Patent and Trademark Office by Biblica, Inc.™

ISBN: 978-1-62423-171-1

Printed in the United States of America

17 16 15 14 • 1 2 3 4 5

--- ALL PHOTOGRAPHY COURTESY OF THINKSTOCK ---

Page 4–5 Heckepics/iStock	Page 114 GillianHolliday/iStock	Page 264 Zhuzhu/iStock
Page 11 Mr_Khan/iStock	Page 137 Oversnap/iStock	Page 275 SafakOguz/iStock
Page 12 Photochecker/iStock	Page 142 Hansjoerg Richter/iStock	Page 276 Pavelgr/iStock
Page 13 Hani Jamjoom/iStock	Page 143 Nirian/iStock	Page 277 Svetlana Privezentseva/iStock
Page 16 SZE FEI WONG/iStock	Page 147 Byelikova_Oksana/iStock	Page 283 Nicholashan/iStock
Page 21 Mtcurado/iStock	Page 148 Selimaksan/iStock	Page 293 Gururugu/iStock
Page 28 David Evison/iStock	Page 171 Fotoduki/iStock	Page 306 CharlesGibson/iStock
Page 30 AndreaAstes/iStock	Page 175 Heckepics/iStock	Page 308 Nico Smit/iStock
Page 41 yavuzsariyildiz/iStock	Page 176 Donyanedomam/iStock	Page 309 IPope/iStock
Page 42 Prill Mediendesign & Fotografie/iStock	Page 177 Kasto80/iStock	Page 313 ImpaKPro/iStock
Page 46 Jk78/iStock	Page 183 Sherman2013/iStock	Page 325 CRSHELARE/iStock
Page 47 Typhoonski/iStock	Page 184 Altin Osmanaj/iStock	Page 336 Kailash Soni/iStock
Page 53 Mustafa6noz/iStock	Page 191 Perseomed/iStock	Page 341 Jelena Jovanovic/iStock
Page 57 MartinM303/iStock	Page 197 Eric Limon/Hemera	Page 342 Luciano Mortula/iStock
Page 61 Kadmy/iStock	Page 208 LisaStrachan/iStock	Page 343 Dima266f/iStock
Page 76 Silverjohn/iStock	Page 209 Artpritsadee/iStock	Page 346 Calypte/iStock
Page 77 Photochecker/iStock	Page 210 Thottungal Oamkumar/iStock	Page 356 Fotoember/iStock
Page 82 LeeCraker/iStock	Page 232 Keith Levit/Keith Levit Photography	Page 374 Inigofotografia/iStock
Page 87 Lola Aykutoglu/iStock	Page 241 Benstevens/iStock	Page 375 Montreehanlue/iStock
Page 104 Mariusz Prusaczyk/iStock	Page 242 Nataliafrei/iStock	Page 390 Arman Zhenikeyev/iStock
Page 109 Dkgilbey/iStock	Page 243 Alexey Bykov/iStock	Page 401 Mathess/iStock
Page 110 Pniesen/iStock	Page 253 Ibrakovic/iStock	Page 407 Urf/iStock
Page 111 G_jee/iStock	Page 255 Amamara Ali/Hemera	

TO

———————

MOM AND DAD
FOR TEACHING ME TO ABIDE IN JESUS

FOR

———————

MY BELOVED SONS, LUKE AND ZACK,
WHO WILL GO FAR BEYOND US

Conte

7   INTRODUCTION

9   TWELVE KINGDOM
PRAYERS TO PRAY OVER
UNREACHED PEOPLE
GROUPS (UPG)

13   JANUARY

47   FEBRUARY

77   MARCH

111   APRIL

143   MAY

177   JUNE

209   JULY

243   AUGUST

277   SEPTEMBER

309   OCTOBER

343   NOVEMBER

375   DECEMBER

413   ABOUT THE AUTHOR

INTRODUCTION

THEY CALLED IT THEIR "EIGHT TO TEN."

*M*om and Dad devoted the prime hours of their morning to lingering with Jesus. They each took their Bible, journal, devotional reading, and a cup of coffee out into the equatorial garden to spend extravagant time with Jesus. You could set your clock by it. This was the foundation of who they were and everything they did. I learned from my parents that the source of all fruitfulness in life is the ongoing presence of Jesus—present through His Word and prayer.

When I was seven years old, my father challenged me to read through the Bible every year. I did so and have continued to do so for the past thirty-five years. Bible reading and reflection form the core of my "abiding time."

I wrote this devotional over a period of one year from January 1 to December 31, 2013. The daily meditations are summaries of my daily abiding time. I wrote this devotional for my sons, but I hope that you will benefit from it as well. Each day includes readings from three chapters of the Old Testament, one chapter from Psalms, one chapter from the Gospels, and one chapter from Acts or the Epistles of the New Testament. The meditations will be most helpful if you follow the suggested readings.

My wife, Jennifer, and I minister in the Muslim world with the Live Dead community. This simply means we are committed to church planting among unreached people through multinational teams. The people groups remaining to be reached with the gospel are found in challenging contexts. We have to "live dead" if they are to cross over into eternal life.

Living dead is not original or unique to us. Christians across time have been called to the crucified life. Looking to Jesus, we stumble in their footsteps—both grinning and grimacing as He stamps His image upon us. Hopefully, this daily devotional will encourage you to do the same.

LIVING DEAD IS A GREAT JOY FOR US, AND—IF WE WILL BE FAITHFUL—IT WILL ALSO BE A JOY FOR THE ETHNOLINGUISTIC PEOPLE GROUPS CHRIST CAME TO REDEEM.

TWELVE KINGDOM PRAYERS

The daily entries in this devotional each highlight an unreached people group for whom you can pray. These people groups are drawn from areas in the world where Live Dead currently has church planting teams (Africa and Eurasia). The statistics are drawn from the Joshua Project. The prayers included are called "kingdom prayers" as they are biblically based. The best way to have prayer answered is to pray what God wants us to pray. We do that by praying the injunctions of the Bible. Each daily devotion includes one kingdom prayer for you to pray over the UPG listed. Feel free to pray all twelve kingdom prayers over the UPG. In this case, we suggest a one-minute prayer for each of the twelve kingdom prayers for a total of twelve minutes of prayer over that UPG.

For example, if the daily featured UPG is the Rashaida of Sudan, Eritrea, and Saudi Arabia, you can:

1. Pray for laborers.
Jesus told us to pray that the Lord would raise up laborers (hard workers) for the harvest fields. Pray that God would raise up missionaries from all over the world to plant the church together among the Rashaida (Matt. 9:37–38).

2. Pray for the conviction of sin.
A person is saved only through the knowledge of his sinful state and the subsequent repentance and turning to Jesus. Pray that the Rashaida would feel and know the burden of sin and come to Jesus for forgiveness and salvation (Matt. 11:28–30).

3. Pray for the cross to be unveiled.
False religions and deceptive ideologies have blinded men and women throughout the world to the truths of the gospel. Please pray that God would unveil the cross and would remove the veil on the minds and spirits of the Rashaida (2 Cor. 3:16–17).

4. Pray for faith and against fear.
The Bible says that God has given His followers a spirit of power. Pray that believers among the Rashaida would be set free from a spirit of fear and would boldly proclaim the truth of the gospel (2 Tim. 1:6–8).

5. Pray for the Word of God to rise.
God's Word is so much more powerful than anything people can say; it is a mighty lion that needs to be unleashed. Please pray for the Word of God (in written, oral, musical, and dramatic forms) to be translated and to rise among the Rashaida (Isa. 55:10–11).

6. Pray that the Spirit will be poured out on all flesh.

God promised to pour out His Spirit on all flesh, men and women, young and old, rich and poor. Please pray that God would pour out His Spirit on the Rashaida, that they would see dreams and visions of Jesus, and that they would be powerfully saved and empowered to be His witnesses (Joel 2:28–32).

7. Pray that Jesus would unite the body of Christ.

Jesus wants His followers to be one. Please pray that God would unite the body of Christ. Pray that Christians from around the world would work together to reach the Rashaida and that the Rashaida would be joined to the body of Christ (John 17:20–23).

8. Pray for good soil.

Pray that the hearts of the Rashaida would be like good soil, ready to hear the gospel and respond (Matt. 7:1–8; 18–23).

9. Pray for peace.

The Bible tells us to pray for the peace of Jerusalem (Ps. 122:6) and to pray for all people (1 Tim. 2:1–4). Pray that the Rashaida would experience peace not only in their nation but also in their hearts. Pray for the peace that results when men and women are reconciled with God (John 14:27). Pray for men and women of peace among the Rashaida (Luke 10:6).

10. Pray for bold proclamation.

Pray that believers among the Rashaida would proclaim the message of the gospel clearly, making the most of every opportunity God places before them (Col. 4:2–5).

11. Pray against works-based salvation and legalism.

Pray that the Rashaida will understand that hope for forgiveness and acceptance with God is available only through Jesus' work on the cross (1 Cor. 1:18).

12. Pray for joy in persecution.

Church history tells us that the church grows the most when persecution is present. Pray that the believers among the Rashaida will endure persecution in a Christlike manner and will give their lives for the sake of the gospel if necessary (1 Peter 2:21–23).

We are looking for Live Dead advocates for unreached people. A Live Dead advocate is one who prays these twelve prayers daily for UPGs and gathers others to pray with them, one who joins us in our twelve monthly fasts, and one who supports Live Dead church-planting efforts at $12 per month.

FOR MORE INFORMATION VISIT WWW.LIVE-DEAD.ORG
AND CLICK ON THE ADVOCACY TAB.

We pray for JOY

11

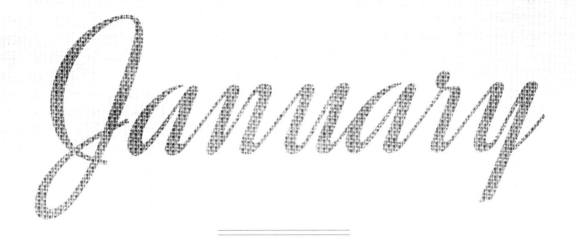

January

"OH, THAT I HAD A THOUSAND LIVES AND A
THOUSAND BODIES! ALL OF THEM SHOULD BE DEVOTED TO NO
OTHER EMPLOYMENT BUT TO PREACH CHRIST TO THESE DEGRADED,
DESPISED, YET BELOVED MORTALS."

—*Robert Moffat*

JANUARY 1: DIVINE DIVISION

GENESIS 1-3; PSALM 1; MATTHEW 1; ACTS 1

*J*esus is constantly pruning us. He loves us so much that He constantly takes the initiative through His Spirit to remove from us what He hates that we might blossom in the things He loves. It is a mistake to think His discipline is seasonal for He is a constant gardener. Mortification (the weakening of sin in us) is the work of the Holy Spirit. As John Owen said, "He works in us and with us—not against us, or in spite of us, or without us."[1] The beginning of a new year affords a fresh start, but let us base all our commitments on the understanding that unless Jesus does the work in us, our intentions are in vain.

God hovers over our form and deformity. It is His intention to bring light to what is dark in us. He intends to separate out the darkness, to do the fine surgery that divides those aspects of our character and nature that disgust Him from those that bring Him glory. He does this that we might produce fruit, fruit that lasts. This divine division is both beautiful and costly. It cost Him sweat and blood; it will likely cost us similarly. We may not like what Jesus cuts away from us. We may not appreciate what He by His Spirit births in us either—but both should be embraced without fear. The God who is with us conceives and births strange and unprecedented things.

Without abiding in Jesus we can do nothing. This means spending daily extravagant blocks of time in His presence and ongoing communion with Him. Our responsibility is to position ourselves where Jesus can flood us with mercy. We start with desperation. There must be an inner cry for help, based on the realization that we need certain things pruned out of our lives and other things grafted in. This desperation helps us to be disciplined, discipline then yields desire, and desire bears delight. When we delight in Jesus—when He is all that thrills and fuels us—we have the means to represent Him well among all the peoples of the earth. Clothed in Him, we have His power and His character. It is a winsome combination.

ALGERIAN MUSLIMS OF ALGERIA (23,851,000; 0.9% EVANGELICAL)

PRAY THAT GOD WOULD RAISE UP MISSIONARIES FROM ALL OVER THE WORLD TO PLANT
THE CHURCH TOGETHER AMONG ALGERIANS
(MATT. 9:37).

*W*e have reduced worship to what we like. One key to experiencing the ongoing presence of Jesus is to worship Him in the way He wants to be worshiped. God did not respect Cain's worship. (The implication is that HIS worship was not costly enough.) Cain essentially killed his brother Abel over worship. Herod killed innocent children when the sages worshipped Jesus. True worship not only costs us something (we give from our treasures), it also costs something of those close to us.

Many people resent God's preferences for worship. Nations also resent the rule of God; they do not want to worship Him in the way He directs. Collections of people want to worship God according to their own customs and preferences, outside the super-exaltation of the divine Son. He who sits in the heavens laughs at this shortsighted rebellion. Every tongue will worship Jesus eventually. The only question is whether we do that joyfully (even if sacrificially) now or fearfully at the last day.

God has highly exalted Jesus that we might worship Him, that all peoples might worship Him. Peter's sermon in Acts 2 was attended by Iranians, Iraqis, Egyptians, Kurds, Libyans, and others who now are considered Muslim peoples. In the midst of perversity (Cain, Noah's contemporaries, Herod, and our own continually evil hearts), God goes to war, and He wars by demanding worship on His terms (Gen. 6:5).

God's expectation of worship is that it costs us something. It also costs something of those who love us and whom we love. He expects us to lay our treasures at His feet. He expects us to walk against the flow of perversity in our day. He expects us to open our mouths and praise Him loudly—even when we do not feel like it . . . especially when we do not feel like it. Praise that costs us something is worship Jesus is pleased to receive. Crucial to walking in the unmitigated presence of Jesus is the ongoing battle with ourselves to worship Jesus on His terms.

ADYGHE MUSLIMS OF TURKEY (646,000; 0.0% EVANGELICAL)

PRAY THAT THE ADYGHE WOULD FEEL AND KNOW THE BURDEN OF SIN AND WOULD COME TO JESUS FOR FORGIVENESS AND SALVATION (MATT. 11:28-30).

JANUARY 3: THE ARK OF REPENTANCE

GENESIS 7–9; PSALM 3; MATTHEW 3; ACTS 3

*K*nowing that the thoughts and imaginations of people are only evil, all the time, God decided to destroy the earth. The wrath of God was poured out through the flood—the fountains of the deep and the windows of heaven unleashed His anger. Noah and his family survived by remaining in the ark for over one year. All other flesh died.

All sin has to go. Mortification is not selective. We cannot think God can be appeased by our efforts to eradicate one bad habit, one tendency to temptation, or one besetting sin. All our sin must be crucified. We cannot diffuse the wrath of God by partial or conditional surrender. All must be laid on the altar. God's fountains and windows will be unleashed in total war against the total person. We often think of repentance in terms that are specific and momentary. God wants us to live a *life* of repentance.

John the Baptist understood the stakes and warned the religious pretenders against the "wrath to come." Only repentance saves us—a repentance that is ongoing and active. Peter, in his Acts 3 sermon, insisted that all "repent and be converted." As we practice ongoing humility and change, Jesus helps us turn away from our iniquities.

Total mortification seems unrealistic. John Owen reminds us: "It is man's duty to mortify sin, but not in his own way. The Spirit alone mortifies sin in believers. He has promised to do it, and all other means without Him are empty and vain."[2] Only by the ongoing humility of living in the ark of repentance can we position ourselves under the reforming and renewing hand of God. Let us not think we can repent over select sins alone. Let us live fully aware of our sinful natures while equally aware that God fully forgives our sin. We must ever sense the waves crashing against the "ark" in order to appreciate its sanctuary.

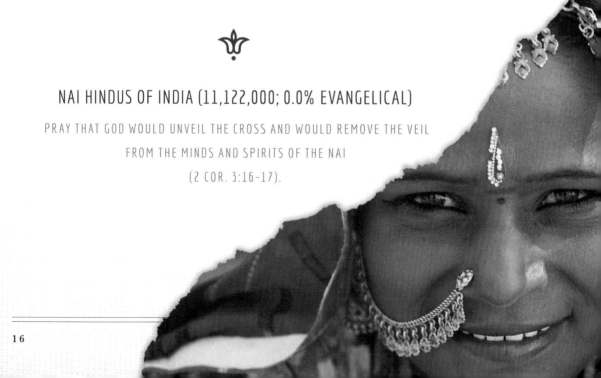

NAI HINDUS OF INDIA (11,122,000; 0.0% EVANGELICAL)

PRAY THAT GOD WOULD UNVEIL THE CROSS AND WOULD REMOVE THE VEIL
FROM THE MINDS AND SPIRITS OF THE NAI
(2 COR. 3:16–17).

A creative God delights in His diverse creation: Arabs in the desert sipping mint tea; pale, skirted, alpha males in Scotland downing haggis; Latinos in temperate climes drinking mate; Nilotic Africans chugging curdled milk. God delights in them all and has apportioned them a place geographically and culturally. God created the people of this world "according to their languages, in their lands, according to their nations" (Gen. 10:31–32).

Rather than worship God, people decided to worship themselves by "making a name." Our jealous God does not tolerate worship of the unworthy, and so the only One worthy intervened. He inserted language differentiation and scattered the people groups across the earth. Not content to leave His people divided and devalued, as soon as He scattered them (Gen. 11), God revealed to Abram His plan to bless all peoples on earth. Abram would be blessed so that through his seed (Jesus, Gal. 3:16) all the people of the earth would be blessed.

In the fullness of time, Jesus was born and lived in Galilee of the Gentiles (Matt. 4:15–16) so those living in darkness might come to the light. Jesus established His right to rule and described the endgame: "This gospel of the kingdom will be preached in all the world as a witness to all the nations, and then the end will come" (Matt. 24:14). Revelation 5:9 gives us a sneak peak of our forever: every tribe, tongue, people, and nation in worship of Jesus.

We are not the only ones to know this. Every demon in hell fights against the supremacy of Jesus. It was the declared deity of Jesus through His resurrection that inflamed religious leaders in Acts 4. Setting the model for all antichrist ideologies to follow, they tried to muzzle Christ's followers from teaching or preaching in His name. This denial of Christ's eminence—His deity—is transparent. The forces of our age are continually "against His Christ . . . against Your holy Servant Jesus" (Acts 4:26–27).

There are only two groups of people in the world: those who worship the divine Christ and those who rebel against Him. Like Abram, let us be people who leave what we know for what is uncomfortable. Let us make our way to the peoples who refuse to worship Jesus, pitch our tent, build our altars, and call on the name of the Lord. He will look on all threats against us and grant us boldness to speak His Word. We and the nations will be shaken.

NGAZIDJA MUSLIMS OF COMOROS (382,000; 0.2% EVANGELICAL)

PRAY THAT BELIEVERS AMONG THE NGAZIDJA WOULD BE SET FREE FROM A SPIRIT OF FEAR OF WHAT MAY COME AND WOULD BOLDLY PROCLAIM THE TRUTH OF THE GOSPEL

(2 TIM. 1:6-8).

JANUARY 5: RIGHTEOUSNESS AND FEAR

GENESIS 13–15; PSALM 5; MATTHEW 5; ACTS 5

*F*riendship with God is not like other friendships. While it is true that Abram was the friend of God, we should not glibly sing "I am a friend of God" without due consideration of Genesis 15:12. When God met with Abram, it was an experience of "horror and great darkness." What makes our relationship with God sublime is the juxtaposition of reverent fear and intimacy.

We cannot approach God cavalierly. He is the Father God to whom we can run and cling, yet He is also the possessor of heaven and earth. How does this strange combination play out in our daily walk with the God we can approach, the God who terrifies?

For Abram the progression went like this: God spoke . . . then Abram believed and obeyed. God was so pleased that Abram believed that He counted the belief as righteousness. In other words, when we believe God is who He says He is and we believe He will do what He has promised to do, He is so pleased with us that He considers us in right-standing friendship with Him. When we are in friendship with God, He rewards us by shielding us. He rewards His friends with Himself—a deep fullness and satisfaction that only He can bring.

Blessed are the people who long (hunger and thirst) for this righteousness, this right standing with God— for they will be full . . . of Him! The reward of righteousness is not an external trophy but a deep, inward fulfillment and satisfaction. All other pleasures and achievements do not penetrate the depth of the soul like righteousness does, for righteousness makes us friends with God.

If we do not fear the Lord or we presume on His friendship or we lie to the Holy Spirit (Acts 5:3–9) or we do not hold God in awe—we will experience the unshielded horror of God's majesty. It will scare us to death. It is much better to be God's friend than His enemy.

IRAQI MUSLIMS OF IRAQ (16,661,000; 0.2% EVANGELICAL)

PRAY FOR THE WORD OF GOD IN WRITTEN, ORAL, MUSICAL, AND DRAMATIC FORMS TO BE
TRANSLATED AND TO RISE AMONG THE IRAQI
(ISA. 55:10-11).

JANUARY 6: SUBMISSION
GENESIS 16-18; PSALM 6; MATTHEW 6; ACTS 6

*H*agar bore Ishmael (meaning "God hears") who is considered the father of Arab Muslims. The term *Islam* means "submission" or "subjugation," and Hagar was told to submit to Sarah. Hagar responded by identifying the Angel of the Lord as the God she had seen, the One who saw and heard her anguish. How sweet the double comfort that God has heard the anguish of the 1.6 billion children of Ishmael and that He calls them to the freedom of submitting to His Christ. We tend to laugh at the impossible promises of God, rather than glory in what is possible. May we, too, submit ourselves with joy to the promised destiny of millions of Muslims.

More than 4,000 minarets rise above the city of Cairo. With five prayer calls a day, this amounts to over 20,000 public, daily mournful petitions rending the sky. Will not "the God who hears and sees" look down in pity on these who are sorely deceived? Can we but lift our voice to God, who hears our voice and will receive our prayers (Ps. 6:9)? How unfortunate are these sons of Abraham whose twisted truth is a double bind. Light that is in us as darkness is a great evil (Matt. 6:23).

Doctrine matters. Truth and clarity about the deity of Christ are crucial. Because twisted light is such a tactic of the Fallen Angel, we cannot subscribe to postmodern thinking when it elevates the journey (the process) regardless of the starting point. We must have men and women who continually dedicate themselves to prayer and to the ministry of the Word (Acts 6:4). We must have men and women who unceasingly speak the truth about Jesus in the power of the Spirit (Acts 6:13). We must have men and women who realize that to do so will bring stones down on their heads and joy into their hearts.

We must submit ourselves to the divine Jesus and shamelessly insist that others do so as well.

CHAR AIMAQ MUSLIMS OF AFGHANISTAN (299,000; 0.0% EVANGELICAL)

PRAY THAT GOD WOULD POUR OUT HIS SPIRIT ON THE CHAR AIMAQ PEOPLE. PRAY THAT THEY WOULD SEE DREAMS AND VISIONS OF JESUS AND WOULD BE POWERFULLY SAVED AND EMPOWERED TO BE HIS WITNESSES
(JOEL 2:28-32).

JANUARY 7: MORTIFICATION

GENESIS 19-21; PSALM 7; MATTHEW 7; ACTS 7

*M*ortification is the process by which God progressively weakens the power of sin in our lives. God initiates this grace, but He expects our participation. The weakening of sin's death grip requires both an act of God and the unrestrained obedience of each person.

God, because of the mercy with which He loves us, will take us by the hand and walk us away from disaster (as He did for Lot in Genesis 19:16). Mercy keeps us from what we deserve. As long as we hold on tight and keep walking, we won't get vaporized into a pillar of salt. God, because of His unmerited kindness, withholds us from sinning (as He did for Abimelech in Genesis 10:6) and from touching what or whom we should not.

I thank God that He takes the initiative to help me in my temptations. I may always look back (as Lot's wife did) to my own destruction, but escape is not only possible but orchestrated (and sometimes enforced) by God's great mercy.

In the divine nature, mercy is always balanced by wrath. God is angry with the wicked every day (Ps. 7:11). The wicked are twofold: the unrepentant in outright rebellion who are unprotected from God's wrath and those under the blood who are covered and protected but who battle against indwelling sin. The repentant are still wicked in heart, thought, and deed—they are simply counted righteous because of the prevailing blood of Jesus. God's wrath then is directed at the wicked portion of my heart. He will judge it. God's mercy in judgment is to expose what is wicked in me, divide it out of me, and destroy it.

We are told not to judge one another (Matt. 7:1) because we all have wicked hearts. Because God's wrath will divide out my wickedness and destroy it, I must be careful that I view others in the same Calvary light. I must not only see their sins, I must accept that the mercy that covers me covers them as well. A soft heart toward others represents God's perspective toward ourselves and ensures His kind dealings with our folly. Only when we have a merciful perspective that is reflective of the Father's heart does He trust us to be rulers and judges of others (Acts 7:27). And God's judgment always leads to deliverance (Acts 7:35).

Mortification is freedom.

MAPPILA MUSLIMS OF INDIA (8,986,000; 0.0% EVANGELICAL)

PRAY THAT CHRISTIANS FROM AROUND THE WORLD WOULD WORK TOGETHER TO
REACH THE MAPPILA AND THAT THE MAPPILA
WOULD BE JOINED TO THE BODY OF CHRIST
(JOHN 17:20-23).

JANUARY 8: COSTLY WORSHIP

GENESIS 22-24; PSALM 8; MATTHEW 8; ACTS 8

*I*saac was not the first son God asked Abraham to surrender. Abraham had already grieved the loss of Ishmael, a pain worse than death. God called Isaac "your only one," a reference to the most important person in Abraham's life, his future, his hope, his joy, his treasure. This is true worship—to give up that which costs us everything.

When we seek to move past singing and verbal praise as our standard for worship to offering up what is most precious, it is imperative to remember that God gives what it hurts most to return. Isaac was the miracle baby, the child who brought laughter, and the shame buster. God gave Isaac, and God asked for Isaac back. We do not have to manufacture costly worship. We simply return to Jesus the most precious thing (or persons) that He has loaned to us. Our God will provide for Himself our costly worship.

Costly worship delights the heart of God. Not because He is twisted and derives His greatest joy from our deepest sorrows, but because when we give up what is precious to us we declare to Jesus: "*You* are most precious. *You* are above all others."

When we delight the heart of God, He blesses us. His blessings are not to be confused with or limited to possessions or persons. His blessings are an invitation into His person, character, and purposes. He blesses us by using us to bless the nations. A supreme reward for costly worship is participation in God's grand mission to be worshiped by every people group on earth. Our blessing is to be a blessing to all nations. Our reward for costly worship is participation in the divine nature and mission of God.

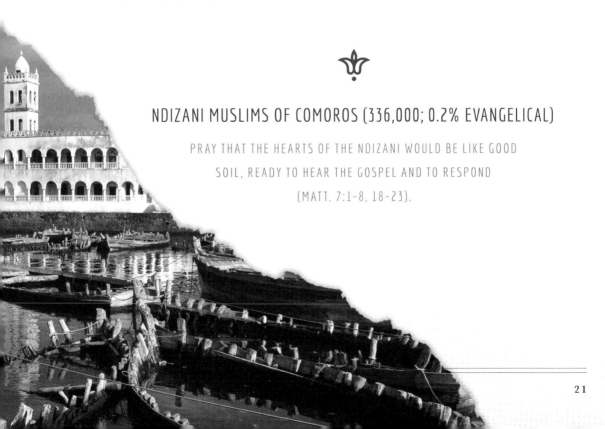

NDIZANI MUSLIMS OF COMOROS (336,000; 0.2% EVANGELICAL)

PRAY THAT THE HEARTS OF THE NDIZANI WOULD BE LIKE GOOD
SOIL, READY TO HEAR THE GOSPEL AND TO RESPOND
(MATT. 7:1-8, 18-23).

JANUARY 9: CALLING BEFORE CLEANSING

GENESIS 25-27; PSALM 9; MATTHEW 9; ACTS 9

*J*esus calls us before He cleanses us. We have this mistaken notion that we must prepare ourselves for service—that our usability influences God's selection. This is true neither for salvation nor for service. God calls sinners to repentance—not those who suppose themselves righteous. God called Matthew the tax collector on a seeming impulse. Matthew responded, in his unconverted mess, and Jesus formed and discipled him along the way.

Usability has much more to do with obedience than giftedness. Obedience even precedes character. If we will obey Jesus, trust Him enough to say "Yes Lord," and trust that He sees in us something we have not exhibited, this is enough for Him to begin to forge our character. First is obedience, second character, and third competency.

What God has done for us, we should expect Him to do for others. Like Ananias, we hold the sins of a "Paul" against him. We doubt the call of God on the life of one who has erred. But would God treat Paul differently than Matthew? Why do we expect God to have less grace on others than He has had on us? Let us trust God to choose His vessels. Then let us lay down our lives to bless them, pray for them, and rejoice over them when they exceed us in usefulness to the kingdom.

A true test of Jesus-like character is when we sincerely rejoice at the advancement of others in the kingdom and at the increase of their usability. After Ananias prayed for Paul, we never hear of him again in the Scriptures. Paul's ministry profile soared while Ananias disappeared. May we not only rejoice, like John, in the increase of Jesus and our own decrease (John 3:30), but let us also rejoice when Jesus increases in our peers.

SYRIAN MUSLIMS OF SYRIA (14,448,000; 0.1% EVANGELICAL)

PRAY FOR THE PEACE THAT RESULTS WHEN MEN AND WOMEN ARE RECONCILED WITH GOD
(JOHN 14:27). PRAY FOR MEN AND WOMEN OF PEACE
(LUKE 10:6) AMONG THE SYRIANS.

JANUARY 10: DISAPPOINTMENT'S DESTINY

GENESIS 28-30; PSALM 10; MATTHEW 10; ACTS 10

*J*acob was married to four women, three of whom he did not choose. Rachel missed out on her own wedding and was barren because her rival was unloved. Leah, perhaps most disappointed of all, was given to someone who loved another.

Leah longed to be loved. She tried so hard to win her husband's affection. If only she could produce sons—then her husband would love her, then she would be appreciated, then she would be wanted. None of her efforts to please others were accomplished, and in the end her disappointment led her to God's intended destiny: praise. At the end of futile efforts to please others comes the realization that what we should have been doing all along is praising the Lord.

It is not only futile to live a life that seeks the approval of others, it is also wicked. "The wicked in his proud countenance does not seek God; God is in none of his thoughts" (Ps. 10:4). It is sobering to realize that our pursuit of affirmation from people is wickedness. It is sin to be more concerned what people think of us (even good people, even fathers and mothers, brothers and sisters) than what God thinks of us. God must be in our thoughts. When we do not live for His approval, we sin wickedly.

This is what it means to live a life worthy of Jesus (Matt. 10:37). We live most concerned about honoring Him, dedicated to winning His approval. Jesus has to be supreme in our affections, confessions, and attentions. When we stop trying to please others—when we care first for what Jesus thinks, and we constantly confess Christ above man or woman—we join Leah in praise. Our lives declare, *"Now, we will praise the Lord."*

FIROZKOHI MUSLIMS OF AFGHANISTAN (296,000 MUSLIMS; 0.0% EVANGELICAL)

PRAY THAT BELIEVERS AMONG THE FIROZKOHI WOULD PROCLAIM THE
MESSAGE OF THE GOSPEL CLEARLY AND WOULD MAKE THE MOST OF EVERY
OPPORTUNITY GOD PLACES BEFORE THEM
(COL. 4:2-5).

JANUARY 11: NOT WORTHY

GENESIS 31-33; PSALM 11; MATTHEW 11; ACTS 11

*G*od is not a genie we can summon to fulfill our wishes. We so quickly fall into spiritual entitlement and forget that we are "not worthy of the least of all the mercies and of all the truth which You have shown" (Gen. 32:10). Entitlement is ugly in any manifestation but especially so when we think God owes us something. The raw reality is that we do not deserve any of His mercies or truth. He is worthy, and for His pleasure we were created. He is not created for our will or whim.

We really have only two rights. We have the right to be called the children of God, and we have the right to be filled with the Holy Spirit. We can stand on those two promises from our good Father in heaven. But we do not deserve blessing. We do not deserve healing. We do not deserve forgiveness. We do not deserve deliverance. We do not deserve favor or revelation or provision or any of the great mercies God lavishes on us. We certainly do not deserve the haven of His unmitigated presence. As soon as we think we are worthy, that we deserve His mercy and truth, something is corrupted in our spirit. When we demand God's favors—when we think or act in an entitled way—we are just ugly and wicked.

John the Baptist, greatest of those born of women, stumbled on this point because he was disappointed that Jesus did not act as John thought He would or should. An early indicator of spiritual entitlement is when we are disappointed with God. Who are we to expect God to work according to our preferences? Every mercy and truth received should be recognized as undeserved favor rather than every disappointment considered justice withheld.

Unchecked spiritual entitlement leads us to think we are more worthy than others. This ultimately leads to the arrogant idea that others do not deserve the mercy we have received. Such arrogance makes us impenitent. The sad irony of spiritual entitlement is that it leads to spiritual death and God's judgment. How much better to be a Barnabas and rejoice at the grace of God poured out on others. How much safer to walk with the limp of Jacob and recognize we are not worthy of the least of God's mercies.

PASI HINDUS OF INDIA (7,524,000; 0.0% EVANGELICAL)

PRAY THAT THE PASI WILL UNDERSTAND THAT HOPE FOR FORGIVENESS
AND ACCEPTANCE WITH GOD COMES ONLY THROUGH
JESUS' WORK ON THE CROSS
(1 COR. 1:18).

JANUARY 12: WRONG RIGHTNESS

GENESIS 34-36; PSALM 12; MATTHEW 12; ACTS 12

*W*ho would have thought that Shechem the fornicator would turn out to be the good guy? Simeon and Levi were technically right to be outraged at the dishonor done to Dinah their sister, but they defended the family honor in such a way that made Jacob "obnoxious among the inhabitants of the land" (Gen. 34:30). In Matthew 12, the Pharisees were technically right about honoring the Sabbath but functionally wrong about dishonoring people. Their misguided and self-righteous application of principle led them to mistreat others as part of the process of feeling good about themselves.

What is most interesting about self-righteousness is its lethal nature. Simeon and Levi slaughtered an entire community. The Pharisees "went out and plotted against [Jesus], how they might destroy Him" (Matt. 12:14). Being wrong-right not only destroys others, it ends up suicidal, for when the light that is in us is darkness, how great is that darkness (Matt. 6:23).

What is most sobering about self-righteousness is that it is a double slayer. It attacks another at injury to itself. Jealousy leads us to demonize others, even friends and colleagues. When we start to look for the sins and mistakes of others, two tragedies occur. First, we find sins and expose them, often through gossip and slander, rather than allow love to cover a multitude of sins. Second, by being a critic—a flawed critic—we remove ourselves from God's covering of our flaws. We forfeit immunity, and the ultimate result is disastrous self-injury.

I consider the most terrifying verse in all Scripture to be Matthew 12:36: "But I say to you that for every idle word men may speak, they will give account of it in the day of judgment." Most of our idle words criticize others while hypocritically praising (directly or indirectly) ourselves. Even if there is some basis for criticism, this is wrong-rightness and it is most foolish. When we take credit for the gifts and favors of God (another face of hypocrisy), when we self-righteously destroy others, we ingest worms into our spirits (Acts 12:23) and doom ourselves to a painful and ignoble end. Hypocrisy (wrong-rightness) kills us from the inside out.

SWAHILI MUSLIMS OF EAST AFRICAN COAST (4,770,000: 0.2% EVANGELICAL)

PRAY THAT THE BELIEVERS AMONG THE SWAHILI WILL ENDURE PERSECUTION IN A CHRISTLIKE MANNER AND WILL GIVE THEIR LIVES FOR THE SAKE OF THE GOSPEL IF NECESSARY (1 PETER 2:21-23).

JANUARY 13: GUILT-BASED THEOLOGY OF SIN

GENESIS 37-39; PSALM 13; MATTHEW 13; ACTS 13

*H*ow can I do this great wickedness, and sin against God?" Joseph asked when he was tempted by Potiphar's wife (Gen. 39:9). David, after sinning against Uriah, his own honor and family, and even against Bathsheba, made this startling confession in Psalm 51:4: "Against You [God], You only, have I sinned!"

The Christian theology of sin is guilt-based. Even if no one else knows what we have done, even if the sin is internal, it is damning, for we have offended the holiness of God. Pre-Christian (Judaic) and post-Christian (Islamic) theologies of sin are much more shame-based. Sin is most heinous when its effects ripple out among the community and insult the honor of those related to the sinner. The more people the action negatively affects, the more serious the sin.

A holy God, however, is just as insulted by secret sins, for all sin is under His wrath. Our internal accommodations of sin (pride, lust, attitude, jealousy, etc.) are just as offensive to God as our errant external actions. The internal concessions are the root; the external actions are the fruit. We are in a daily mortal struggle. We are in a boxing match that does not end until death. Sin seduces us moment by moment: "Come and lie with me!" We must not only say no repeatedly, holding up our prayer-gloved hands, we must also keep moving our feet away from the barrage of sin's fists so we are not even near temptation. Sometimes we also have to leave what is rightfully ours and just flee.

Let us not be the fools who critique the outward failings of those around us without acknowledging that our inward sins are just as ugly, just as lethal. We must be committed to a lifelong boxing match of resisting an untiring foe. "He did not heed her, to lie with her or to be with her" (Gen. 39:10). God is so pure that my internal sins, the sins that do not involve or shame anyone else, are enough to condemn me to judgment.

MOROCCAN MUSLIMS OF MOROCCO (14,448,000; 0.01% EVANGELICAL)

PRAY THAT GOD WOULD RAISE UP MISSIONARIES FROM ALL OVER THE WORLD TO PLANT THE CHURCH TOGETHER AMONG MOROCCANS
(MATT. 9:37).

*T*here are three spirits that plague humanity. These are the spirits of *I know, I can,* and *I will.* Somehow we have swallowed the lies that we know better than God does, we can do things in our own strength, and what we want is most important. We think we understand what needs to be done, and we think we have the resources to force our will on our reality.

Joseph understood that "interpretations belong to God" (Gen. 40:8). He said, "It is not in me [to interpret]; God will give Pharaoh an answer of peace" (41:16). The sooner we come to terms with our complete inability to know or solve or achieve or produce in our own strength, the happier and safer we will be. It is the fool who says, by self-sustained thinking and action, that there is no God (Ps. 14:1). The unflinching testimony of Scripture points out that you and I are that fool. No one does good . . . all have turned aside . . . together all err . . . no one fully relies on the Lord—no, not anyone.

We castigate atheists for their theoretical disavowal of the Creator but functionally live just like them. When we depend on our own wisdom, our own strength, and our own willpower (and all of us repeatedly do), we are the fools who say with our lives, "There is no God!"

It does not help that people love to worship people. A person would much rather glorify himself or another person than the Lord of hosts. Paul and Barnabas were used by God to give an answer of peace to a cripple. His healing made the mob delirious, and Paul and Barnabas had to tear their clothes and cry out in order to avoid unmerited praise. They later reported correctly "all that God had done *with* them" (Acts 14:27, italics added). We are the tools—God uses us or not as He wills.

Let us not be Christian fools who live as if there were no God. Let us with Joseph, Paul, and Barnabas recognize that it is not in us to help or to save. What is in us is limited and downright embarrassing; it only leads to death and sorrow. What is in God is beautiful and life-giving. God chooses to act *with* us—God gives the answers of peace.

ANSARI MUSLIMS OF PAKISTAN (4,174,000; 0.0% EVANGELICAL)

PRAY THAT THE ANSARI WOULD FEEL AND KNOW THE BURDEN OF SIN AND WOULD COME
TO JESUS FOR FORGIVENESS AND SALVATION
(MATT. 11:28-30).

JANUARY 15: HONOR AND HUMILIATION

GENESIS 43-45; PSALM 15; MATTHEW 15; ACTS 15

*G*od sent Joseph unexpectedly into slavery, and God elevated him, just as unexpectedly, to the palace. Both the humiliation of the pit and the honor of the palace ultimately saved lives. God's humiliations and God's honors in our lives have the same intent: to save all peoples for His glory. We, therefore, can embrace them both for they are means not ends. The sting of humiliation cannot hurt us for we know that God's fame among the nations is at play. The allure of honor cannot corrupt us, for we realize that God has made us "lord of all Egypt" (Gen. 45:9) for the express purpose of saving many lives.

To navigate the pitfalls of both humiliation and honor, we must speak truth to ourselves (Ps. 15:2, 5). People who speak truth to themselves are immovable. It is crucial to be self-aware. We are both vile and redeemed, and both realities must be understood. When we know we are redeemed, then humiliation is an honor. When we know we are wicked, honor humbles us. The only way to stay fastened to the immovable Rock is to see ourselves in both lights.

When we see ourselves correctly, we ask for help. In Matthew 15:25, a woman of Tyre and Sidon begged Jesus to help her demonized daughter: "Then she came and worshiped Him, saying, 'Lord, help me!'" Asking for help is worship! When we declare that we are unable, we humble ourselves. When we declare that Jesus is completely able to handle all things, we honor Him. Jesus is given worth. Self-reliance is idolatry because it honors the self—it attributes worth to the self.

God plucks young men and women from obscure pits and places them in palaces. God sets the unexpected as lord over Egypt. God takes unusual figures like Paul and uses them as apostles to the nations. He takes the ones who can handle both honor and humiliation and "treats those two impostors just the same."[3]

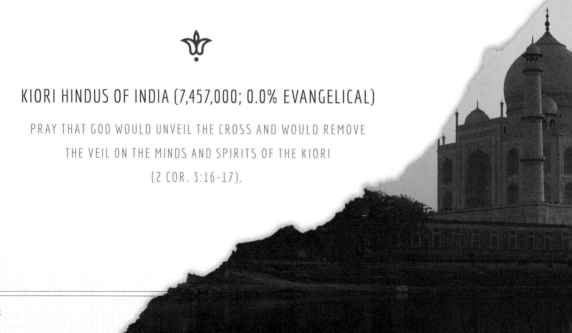

KIORI HINDUS OF INDIA (7,457,000; 0.0% EVANGELICAL)

PRAY THAT GOD WOULD UNVEIL THE CROSS AND WOULD REMOVE
THE VEIL ON THE MINDS AND SPIRITS OF THE KIORI
(2 COR. 3:16-17).

JANUARY 16: THE DIVINE NO

GENESIS 46–48; PSALM 16; MATTHEW 16; ACTS 16

*D*avid blessed the Lord who gave him "counsel . . . in the night seasons" (Ps. 16:7). God is faithful to lead us, to guide us, and to give us advice even when the decision is not a straightforward one. In Acts 16, the divine no was just as much a part of God's guidance as the heavenly yes. Paul and Timothy tried to preach in Asia but the Holy Spirit did not allow it (Acts 16:6). They next attempted to minister in Bithynia (16:7) but that, too, the Spirit did not allow.

God is just as good to us in His denials as He is in His approvals. The denials of God are immeasurable mercies. If God answered all our prayers with a positive response, how miserable we would be. Thank heaven that heaven says no! Negations, restrictions, refusals, denials, and rejections are all divine mercies. May we be as thankful when God says no as when He says yes.

When we learn to allow Jesus to choose for us, we enter into a new plane of joy and safety. David wrote, "You will show me the path of life; in your presence is fullness of joy" (Ps. 16:11). Submitting to God's restrictions keeps us in life. Staying in the life of Jesus grants us the joy of Jesus. Let us rejoice when the divine Jesus denies our heartfelt requests. He knows best how to keep us in joyful life.

A fruitful pastor I know keeps a job description from God in his desk. The job description is eight pages long—every page completely blank. He has signed it on the bottom of the last page. Periodically, he pulls it out and reminds himself that God has the authority and absolute right to fill in those pages as He wills.

God can sustain us in a hostile environment, shielding us from abuse. God can also lead us through the valley of the shadow of death. It is His choice. God can exalt us before humanity. He can also invite us into His humility and shame. He gets to write the story. When we accept His divine denials as well as His divine approvals, we embrace His authorship of our lives. When we let Jesus write our stories, we can be assured of His ongoing, joy-filled presence. Joy in the presence of Jesus is far better than the bitterness of getting our own way as a result of wayward prayers.

SOMALI MUSLIMS OF EAST AFRICA (10,080,000, 0.0% EVANGELICAL)

PRAY THAT BELIEVERS AMONG THE SOMALI WOULD BE SET FREE
FROM A SPIRIT OF FEAR OF WHAT MAY COME AND WOULD BOLDLY
PROCLAIM THE TRUTH OF THE GOSPEL
(2 TIM. 1:6-8).

JANUARY 17: DEPRESSED DEVILS

GENESIS 49-50; PSALM 17; MATTHEW 17; ACTS 17

*H*ow frustrating it must be to be the Devil. Whatever he means for evil (Gen. 50:20), God has the ability to turn for good. Time after time they have blown out the victory cigars in hell at the realization that certain defeat has once again been grasped from the jaws of victory. "This just in: The cross is still bloody, but the blasted tomb is now empty!" God's unmatched ability to turn the schemes of the Enemy into the good of the saints has made both the Devil and demons insecure. Poor devils, their only certainty is defeat. God's faithfulness has robbed them of their parties.

We should not assume, however, that man has no part to play in God's interventions. When evil surrounds us, we must long for deliverance. John Owen reminds us: "Longing, breathing, and panting after deliverance is a grace in itself, having a mighty power to conform the soul to the likeness of the thing longed for."[4] When evil seduces us, we have to run away like Joseph. We must purpose with the psalmist, "I have purposed that my mouth shall not transgress. . . . I have kept away from the paths of the destroyer" (Ps. 17:3–4). When we play our part, God confronts the Devil and casts him down. Jesus then keeps us as the apple of His eye, sheltered under His wings (Ps. 17:8).

When we think too highly of ourselves, we stumble and are vulnerable to the evil of our Enemy. Too much belief in self leads to powerlessness. We often wonder why we cannot cast out demons (Matt. 17:16). It is because we are too fond of our dignity and not dependent enough on Jesus. Some things He alone can do. Some things we cannot do unless we are willing to fail or to appear foolish. Even if it is done through us, it still has to be Jesus who casts Satan down. It is the lowly and faith-filled follower who makes the Devil depressed.

SAUDI MUSLIMS OF SAUDI ARABIA (12,041,000; 0.1% EVANGELICAL)

PRAY FOR THE WORD OF GOD IN WRITTEN, ORAL, MUSICAL, AND DRAMATIC FORMS TO BE
TRANSLATED AND TO RISE AMONG THE SAUDI
(ISA. 55:10-11).

JANUARY 18: HE KNOWS OUR SORROWS

EXODUS 1-3; PSALM 18; MATTHEW 18; ACTS 18

*I*n His nontransferable attributes—omniscience, omnipresence, omnipotence—the God of the Bible and the God of the Qur'an are remarkably similar. Yet similarities quickly cease when we consider the nature of a God who would come near, a God who would become flesh. Muslims consider the incarnation despicable. It behooves us to consider their horror, for the immeasurable horror of the incarnation heightens its wondrous beauty to us.

It is despicable to Muslims to think that God took the form of His creation. God cried, God pooped, God got tired, God was tempted, God died—these are progressively unfathomable. We can only begin to comprehend this tragic humiliation of God if we ask, *"Why on earth, why in heaven, did He humble Himself so horribly?"*

God tells us why: "I . . . have heard their cry because of their taskmasters, for I know their sorrows. . . . So I have come down to deliver them . . ." (Ex. 3:7–8). The God who dwells outside of time knows our pain because He lived it. God's knowledge of our bitter encounters with sorrow are not limited to theory or to the observation of a protected angelic form touring this holocaust museum we call earth. He came down and lived here as one of us. "Man of sorrows, what a name, for the Son of God who came."[5]

Jesus experientially feels our pain. Betrayal? That spike has already been pounded through His wrist. Loneliness? That lash has whipped His back more than once. Loss of a loved one? He has wept at cemeteries. Sickness? "Surely He has borne our griefs and carried our sorrows. . . . He was wounded for our transgressions, He was bruised for our iniquities . . . and by His stripes we are healed" (Isa. 53:4–5). Rejected? The Father turned His head away.

Because God knows how miserable sorrow is, He comes down to help us. A God who is only transcendent cannot be empathetic. A transcendent God who humbles Himself to share in our sorrows can only be loved and worshiped. God hears our cry from His temple. Our cries come before Him, even to His ears, and He rends the heavens and comes down (Ps. 18:6–8). "I know that sorrow!" He says. "I, too, cried."

AVAR MUSLIMS OF AZERBAIJAN (51,000; 0.0% EVANGELICAL)

PRAY THAT GOD WOULD POUR OUT HIS SPIRIT ON THE AVAR PEOPLE. PRAY THAT THEY WOULD
SEE DREAMS AND VISIONS OF JESUS AND WOULD BE POWERFULLY SAVED AND
EMPOWERED TO BE HIS WITNESSES
(JOEL 2:28–32).

JANUARY 19: ALL IN

EXODUS 4-6; PSALM 19; MATTHEW 19; ACTS 19

*G*od is not reluctant to kill those whom He calls. In one of the more puzzling turns of biblical events, God called Moses to go to Egypt on a rescue mission and then "on the way . . . the LORD met him and sought to kill him" (Ex. 4:24). Tracing backwards from the intervention of Zipporah (she circumcised her son and threw the bloody foreskin at Moses' feet) helps us identify and understand the offense. Evidently Moses was not in full compliance with the Abrahamic covenant.

God demands *all.* Those who are called must give everything. We are masters of the partial surrender. We excel at giving Jesus almost everything. Yet to hold something back is to doom both our calling and our long-term health. God sets impossible and costly terms for following Him. It is impossible for a camel to go through the eye of a needle (Matt. 19:25–26). It is impossible to come into the kingdom on our own terms. Inevitably, our terms are that we give God almost everything but retain control of the one thing most precious to us. God puts His finger on the one thing we won't surrender and says, "You have to be all in. That retention scuttles the whole covenant. Yes, I have called you, but I will discard you if you do not surrender all."

The cost of a calling is not only one for leaders to count. Moses' son certainly had an abrupt introduction to the communal cost of God's call—it was his blood that saved the day. Those who would emerge from slavery must participate in the cost and escape under duress. Deliverance for both deliverer and escapee is a painful process, not an immediate translation to a trouble-free station. In the process of deliverance, things often get worse before they get better. "Anguish of spirit and cruel bondage" (Ex. 6:9) often restrict us from hearing and receiving what would help us to life.

Those who agree to deliver others while working under God's authority must realize they cannot do this with secret faults or presumptuous sins (Ps. 19:12–13). Presumptuous sins anger God, and secret faults destroy us from the inside out. We may continue for a short season in a public role (while being presumptuous in sin and hiding secret faults), but there will be no transformative power to our words or witness. External words and appearances without internal purity and truth only leave us naked and wounded, vulnerable to the demonic powers (Acts 19:16). Anything less than *all* for Jesus leads to our death—even on the road to deliver others. When God calls you, if you are not "all in," you are not in at all.

SONAR HINDUS OF INDIA (7,199,000; 0.0% EVANGELICAL)

PRAY THAT CHRISTIANS FROM AROUND THE WORLD WOULD WORK TOGETHER TO REACH THE SONAR AND THAT THE SONAR WOULD BE JOINED TO THE BODY OF CHRIST (JOHN 17:20-23).

JANUARY 20: SPIRIT-LED DEATH

EXODUS 7–9; PSALM 20; MATTHEW 20; ACTS 20

*A*s people of the Spirit, we love new initiatives. We love it when the Spirit breathes new life. We love it when the Spirit gives fresh insight. We love it when the Spirit begins something refreshingly different and unique. We are comfortable and desirous of the Spirit-led life, quick to embrace the power, guidance, deliverance, and liberty the Spirit gives—but we are slow to accept that the Spirit also leads us to death.

Spirit-Led Restrictions (Acts 20:22). Paul announced that he was headed to Jerusalem, "bound in the spirit." It was not security police, oppressive government, terrorist kidnappers, or poor leadership that made Paul's world small. The life-giving Spirit of God provided the limitations. God prevented Paul from any other option. The Spirit's leading was so clear and so restricted that Paul felt bound to obey it.

Spirit-Led Uncertainty (Acts 20:22). Paul obeyed this narrow guidance of the Spirit, "not knowing the things that [would] happen to [him] there." The same Spirit who reveals and illumines also keeps us in the dark. The Spirit of God is under no obligation to explain all He has in mind. Our partnership with the Holy Spirit is not egalitarian. We often forget that the Spirit is part of the Godhead, so we treat Him more like a buddy than deity. We must surrender our demand to know what and why and submit to the restrictions of the Spirit without insisting on details.

Spirit-Led Suffering (Acts 20:23). One thing Paul knew for certain was that "chains and tribulations" awaited him. Like Jesus, who knew that He was compelled to go to Jerusalem where betrayal, condemnation, mocking, scourging, and crucifixion awaited (Matt. 20:17–19), Paul had one assurance: The Spirit was unerringly leading him to face a future of suffering.

Remarkably, Paul proclaimed that none of these things (restrictions, uncertainty, and suffering) moved him (Acts 20:24). Instead, these deaths gave him joy as he finished his race and testified to the gospel. All who follow Jesus must come to terms with the Spirit leading them to death: the death of self-will, which leads to the deliverance of others. We do not live to be served but to serve and to give our lives for the ransom of others (Matt. 20:28). If we will do this joyfully, we will indeed be baptized with the baptism of Jesus.

YEMENI OF DJIBOUTI (68,800; 0.0% EVANGELICAL)

PRAY THAT THE HEARTS OF THE YEMENI WOULD BE LIKE GOOD SOIL,
READY TO HEAR THE GOSPEL AND TO RESPOND
(MATT. 7:1–8; 18–23).

JANUARY 21: UNDER THE BLOOD

EXODUS 10-12; PSALM 21; MATTHEW 21; ACTS 21

*W*hen I was a child, my parents taught me to "plead the blood." Essentially this meant to resist the forces of oppression and evil that would come against my body, soul, or mind by reminding them (and myself) that I was under the protection of Jesus. In demonic encounters, we pray in the Spirit, we pray with understanding, and we cover ourselves with the blood of Jesus. This sounds strange but what it means is to invoke the protective shield that Jesus offers. When we are "under the precious blood," we are safe. No weapon formed against us can prosper. The biblical origin of this phrase is, of course, the Exodus Passover. God's people were told to apply the blood of a lamb or goat to the doorposts and lintels of their homes. God told them, "When I see the blood, I will pass over you" (Ex. 12:13).

It is interesting and still appropriate that, for us, "pleading the blood" has come to mean spiritual warfare and prayer that resists the attacks of the Devil and preserves us from his evil intentions. We forget that the blood of the Passover lamb originally protected the people of God from the wrath of God. The blood of the lamb protects me from God!

Just as truth without mercy kills, mercy without truth corrupts. Let us not forget that God's holiness and purity demand the death of all who sin, which means all who are born, not just the firstborn of the wicked. I *and* my sons deserve to die. The blood of Jesus shed on the cross protects us from the justice of God, which demands our death. To "stay under the blood" is to stay protected from the wrath of God. It is the mercy of God that keeps us immovable, rooted in safety (Ps. 21:7).

Let us not be like fools who venture into sin, outside the covering blood of Jesus. We really have only two options: (1) stay broken and humble under the blood of Jesus, conscious that we are sinners who deserve death (Matt. 21:44; falling on the cornerstone), or (2) have the wrath of God fall on us and grind us to powder. It is right to "plead the blood." It is imperative to "stay under the blood"—not just in resistance and repulsion of evil but in order to be protected from God's righteous wrath. We're "under the blood, the precious blood, under the cleansing, healing flood; keep [us], Savior, from day to day; under the precious blood."[6]

TUNISIAN MUSLIMS OF TUNISIA (9,969,000; 0.0% EVANGELICAL)

PRAY FOR THE PEACE THAT RESULTS WHEN MEN AND WOMEN ARE
RECONCILED WITH GOD (JOHN 14:27). PRAY FOR MEN AND WOMEN OF
PEACE (LUKE 10:6) AMONG THE TUNISIANS.

JANUARY 22: THE COMFORTS OF SLAVERY

EXODUS 13–15; PSALM 22; MATTHEW 22; ACTS 22

S lavery has its securities. For example, when Moses led God's people out of bondage, suddenly they had to fend for themselves. Water was hard to come by in the desert, and at least back in Egypt there were onions and garlic. With Pharaoh's armies pressing in, the people complained: "Because there were no graves in Egypt, have you taken us away to die in the wilderness? . . . Is this not the word that we told you in Egypt, saying, 'Let us alone that we may serve the Egyptians'?" (Exod. 14:11–12). Some people prefer the small world of a prison, where at least they get three free meals a day.

Kenneth Bailey points out that Jesus addressed a similar question when He met blind Bartimaeus:[7] "What do you want me to do for you?" (Mark 10:51). Jesus obviously knew the man was blind, so in effect He was saying, "If I deliver you from the slavery of blindness, you can no longer beg for a living. Food will not be dropped in your outstretched hands; you will have to work for it. Do you really want the challenges of being free?"

We often love our chains. We hold on to our aches and pains because they earn us sympathy. We hold on to our anger and jealousy because they serve as fuel and motivation. We hold on to the blankets of our insecurities because they warm us in some strange and twisted way. To be free from what enslaves us brings us to the wall of the Red Sea, and we exchange the comforts of slavery for the challenges and responsibilities of freedom.

Interestingly, if we can press on, the boundaries become walls of protection. The sea that restricted the escaping Israelites became "a wall to them on their right hand and on their left" (Ex. 14:22). It became their protection from the enemy. Our walls of protection are somewhat different. Praise is our protection. When we exalt the one who is "fearful in praises" (15:11), we engage a spiritual secret: Praise brings victory and deliverance. From the despair of being forsaken (Ps. 22:1), the psalmist acknowledged the holiness of God. The psalmist declared that God is enthroned in the praises of His people (22:3) and that He delivers those who trust in Him. If slavery (oppression, rejection, trouble) leads us to praise, we have the comfort of knowing that God will deliver us. Praise is our comfort in trial.

BALKAN GAGAUZ TURKISH, YORUK OF TURKEY (414,000 MUSLIMS; 0.0% EVANGELICAL)

PRAY THAT BELIEVERS AMONG THE BALKAN GAGAUZ TURKISH WOULD PROCLAIM THE MESSAGE OF THE GOSPEL CLEARLY AND WOULD MAKE THE MOST OF EVERY OPPORTUNITY GOD PLACES BEFORE THEM
(COL. 4:2–5).

JANUARY 23: ABIDING FOR OTHERS

EXODUS 16-18; PSALM 23; MATTHEW 23; ACTS 23

The best thing we can do in church planting among unreached people is to abide in Jesus. This is true whether we are a minister or a mother or a follower of Jesus who desires to make disciples. When we "stand before God for the people" (Ex. 18:19), we do more for those we seek to bless than any other frenetic activity or ministry on their behalf. Extravagant daily time with Jesus—in His Word and in His presence through prayer—is the single most productive thing we can do. It is the most effective way to bless others.

Moses was worn weary by the demands of life and ministry. His father-in-law, Jethro, told him something similar to what Jesus told Martha and everyone like her, "You are distracted with much serving, but one thing is needed" (Luke 40:40–42). When we stand before God for the people, several important things happen: (1) Those we lead and serve learn to rely on God for themselves; (2) Jesus gives us the wisdom for the "hard cases" (Ex. 18:26); and (3) we do not burn out but are able to endure (18:23). The long-term well-being of both ourselves and our disciples is predicated on our daily abiding—standing before the Lord for the people. When we abide with Jesus, we bless others.

A restored soul (Ps. 23:3) results from continually abiding in the house of the Lord (v. 6). Restored souls do not fall into sin or depression. A passion for holiness is only supported and sustained by a disciplined process of abiding. It is not emotion that keeps us pure, nor is it unrefined desire that keeps us from sin. Only the disciplined rhythm of a life consecrated to be with God morning by morning, day by day, week by week, month by month, year by year—continually standing before God—keeps us from falling. We position ourselves for God's protection by giving Him extravagant time each day. When this becomes our daily practice and priority, it is not only "the people" who are blessed—we, too, are preserved and sustained. Abiding in Jesus is the primary way we survive and thrive.

KASHMIRI MUSLIMS OF INDIA (7,151,000; 0.0% EVANGELICAL)

PLEAD THAT THE KASHMIRI WILL UNDERSTAND THAT HOPE FOR
FORGIVENESS AND ACCEPTANCE WITH GOD IS ONLY AVAILABLE
THROUGH JESUS' WORK ON THE CROSS
(1 COR. 1:18).

JANUARY 24: WE REVERE SO WE DO NOT FEAR

EXODUS 19-21; PSALM 24; MATTHEW 24; ACTS 24

*T*he paradoxes of God are His graces, for they enable our limited understanding to wrestle with His immeasurable transcendence. God's ways are so far above our ways—theory is not sufficient for comprehension—that we must experience the paradoxes of God in order to apprehend them.

Deliverance Is a Person, Not a Place. In Exodus 19:4, God reminded Moses, "I bore you on eagles' wings and brought you to Myself." While it is true that he and God's people had left Egypt behind, the desert was not much more accommodating. Moses and company learned experientially that God was their refuge—not a new location that replaced another. Thousands of Christians through history have experienced this same truth. They were not relieved of poverty, healed, released from prison, or rescued from the lion's mouth—but they found refuge. God brought them to Himself, whether their external conditions changed or not.

Revelation Comes Through Trial as Well as Triumph. God told Moses that He would come to him in the "thick cloud" (Ex. 19:9). Isaiah spoke of the Valley of Vision, the restricted-view areas that help one see. We learn more about ourselves and our Creator when we are under duress than we do in comfort. Prosperity tends to make us wander; persecution often drives us to the arms of Jesus.

We Approach God Boldly and Cautiously. "Do not fear," Moses told the people. "God has come to test you . . . that His fear may be before you, so that you may not sin" (Ex. 20:20). On one hand, only "he who has clean hands and a pure heart" (Ps. 24:4) can ascend to the hill of the Lord. On the other hand, "The vilest offender who truly believes, that moment from Jesus a pardon receives."[8] God the Father is approachable. He welcomes with open arms those who come penitent. However, those who approach the "mountain of God" (Ex. 19:12) cavalierly will be put to death.

When we fear the Lord with humble reverence and honor, we fear Him appropriately. This fear protects us from His holy wrath, and we can approach the throne of grace fearlessly to find help in our time of need. We revere the Lord, so we do not have to fear Him.

AFAR OF DJIBOUTI (416,000; 0.0% EVANGELICAL)

PRAY THAT BELIEVERS AMONG THE AFAR WILL ENDURE PERSECUTION IN A CHRISTLIKE MANNER AND WILL GIVE THEIR LIVES FOR THE SAKE OF THE GOSPEL IF NECESSARY (1 PETER 2:21-23).

JANUARY 25: FARTHER UP AND FURTHER IN

EXODUS 22–24; PSALM 25; MATTHEW 25; ACTS 25

*M*y favorite book among C. S. Lewis' Chronicles of Narnia is *The Last Battle*. In the final chapter, as the Narnians explore Aslan's country, they find that the farther they travel, the broader and more beautiful the land. God's concentric circles expand the closer you press to the center.[9] The Narnians exhort one another to press on and up to "higher ground"[10] in joyful, non-competitive discovery as they race one another.

But not all things of the Lord can be pursued in community. In Exodus 24, Moses ascended the mountain of God with the elders of Israel and Joshua. There they "saw God" and even "ate and drank" with Him (v. 11). Staggering! How wonderful that communal interaction must have been. But God had a further invitation for just Moses and Joshua: "Come up to me . . . and be there" (v. 12). Moses and Joshua climbed farther up, and the glory of the Lord descended on the mountain as they lingered in God's presence (vv. 13–15).

On the seventh day, God called Moses alone out of the cloud, and Moses communed with God for forty days and forty nights (v. 18). No companion traveled with Moses to that place of intimacy. Some things of the Lord cannot be experienced corporately. Some things, Jesus tells us, should be told to no person, no spouse, no child, no friend. Some intimacies are intended just for the partakers.

Some things of the Spirit are not to be shared. The lesson of the wise virgins in Matthew 25:9 is that oil is not to be given to others at a cost to your own supply. This sounds counter to laying down your life for others, but Jesus never intends for us to sacrifice intimacy with Him in the pursuit of helping others. He sets this boundary clearly: We must at all costs preserve a personal intimacy with Jesus, even if that pursuit means we refrain from helping or serving others. Why? Because if we are not intimate with Jesus (if we run out of oil), we will have nothing transformative to give to others.

The best thing I can do in my service to others is to abide with Jesus. When I preserve my personal intimacy with Him, I serve those around me best. My intimacy with Jesus gives me the right—and the authority—to exhort others to rush "farther up and further in."

PERSIAN MUSLIMS OF IRAN (29,000,000; 0.09% EVANGELICAL)

PRAY THAT GOD WOULD RAISE UP MISSIONARIES FROM ALL OVER THE WORLD TO PLANT THE CHURCH TOGETHER AMONG THE PERSIANS (MATT. 9:37).

*W*e all betray Jesus in one way or another (Matt. 26:31). If we are all Spartacus, we are all Judas as well. Jesus lives with our continual collective betrayal—we betray Him with our kisses, and we betray Him with our loud protestations of supposed fidelity. When we brazenly approach His presence to betray Him, He sees right through our hypocrisy and asks, "Friend, why have you come?" (26:50). We shudder at those who spat in His face, beat Him, and struck Him with the palms of their hands (26:67) without realizing that by our actions we have cursed and sworn, "I do not know the man!"

It is a mystery that God receives our worship at all. We betray Him and worship Him in alternating whimsy. The great heart of God alone can endure our instability. Yet when we worship (and our worship can be as genuine as our betrayal), God is big enough and glad enough to receive it. It is true that we can wound and betray Jesus, but it is equally true that we can genuinely minister to Him. When we pour out costly fragrant oil (26:7), when we give to Jesus extravagantly, He is delighted and lets everyone know.

Jesus' accommodation of our frequent betrayals does not mean He endorses or accepts them. He longs for us to minister to Him constantly. Often we approach worship to receive—peace, healing, help—and He is gracious to meet us. We forget that we really can bless the Lord! We really can make Jesus happy. We really can minister to Him. And we can do this continually—if we will.

Aaron and his sons tended the light of the lampstand from morning to night (Ex. 27:20–21). The psalmist endeavored to go about God's altar in innocence as he "loved the habitation of [God's] house and the place where [God's] glory dwells" (Ps. 26:8). When we approach worship from the perspective of what we can give extravagantly to God rather than receive from Him, He speaks to us from the mercy seat (Ex. 25:22). Our reward is to break our alabaster treasures and lavishly pour them out on Him. Even with Jesus, it is in giving that we receive.

SAUDI-HIJAZI MUSLIMS OF SAUDI ARABIA (9,077,000; 0.1% EVANGELICAL)

PRAY THAT THE SAUDI-HIJAZI WOULD FEEL AND KNOW THE BURDEN OF SIN AND WOULD COME TO JESUS FOR FORGIVENESS AND SALVATION (MATT. 11:28-30).

*O*ne theory of leadership presents three concentric circles. The innermost circle is labeled "Control," the middle circle is labeled "Influence," and the outermost circle is labeled "Concern." The theory posits that we should spend eighty percent of our energy and time on what we can control. As we spend energy on what we can control, we are better able to influence what we cannot control and speak to areas of concern.[11] Unfortunately, here in the Arab world and in much of life, so many things are out of our control. Psalm 27 gives us insight into where we can expend our energy.

I Will Not Fear (vv. 1–3). Turbulence makes me nervous, and I have to fly continually. We worry about our children's health, danger, political insecurity, harm, sickness, or thieves who barge into our bedroom at night bearing knives and bats. But there are even more insidious fears—the ideologies of our day are coercive and intimidating. We can determine that we will not give in to the spirit of fear for "the LORD is [our] light and salvation" (v. 1).

I Will Abide (vv. 4–5). I am in control of my schedule. I determine when I go to bed and when I rise. In a biographical sermon on George Whitefield, John Piper[12] said that Whitefield went to bed at the stroke of nine o'clock, even if he had guests and they were in mid-sentence. You and I can decide how much time we spend in the presence of Jesus.

I Will Praise (vv. 6–7). The text references "sacrifices of joy." It is costly praise that delights Jesus. There is no inappropriate time to praise Him. Psalm 34:1 states, "I will bless the LORD at all times; His praise shall continually be in my mouth." The context is the time David pretended to be mad as he scratched the gates of Gath with drool in his beard.

I Will Seek (v. 8). I will be insatiable for Jesus.

I Will Trust (vv. 9–10). Change, betrayal, and death will only drive me to Jesus. Persecution will make me better, not bitter.

I Will Learn (vv. 11–12). My enemies will be my tutors. My irritants will be lessons. I will pray mercy on those who do me harm.

I Will Believe (vv. 13–14). My work will be to "believe in Him who was sent"—Jesus.

On Columbus' journey to America, when dissent arose among the crew as the journey grew long, it is purported that he wrote in his diary: "Sailed on." I will sail on. I will believe that Jesus is worth any price and that God will win in the end. Jehovah will have the final say.

My heart says of you,
"Seek his face!" Your face,
LORD, I will seek.

PSALM 27:8, NIV

LEBANESE MUSLIMS OF TURKEY (1,124,000; 0.1% EVANGELICAL)

PRAY THAT GOD WOULD UNVEIL THE CROSS AND THAT THE VEIL ON THE MINDS AND SPIRITS OF
THE LEBANESE WOULD BE TAKEN AWAY (2 COR. 3:16–17).

JANUARY 28: GOD INSURANCE

EXODUS 31-33; PSALM 28; MATTHEW 28; ACTS 28

*W*e can no less handle God's goodness than we can His wrath. From my youth I have loved the hymn, "He Hideth My Soul." The chorus rejoices, "He hideth my soul in the cleft of the rock that shadows a dry, thirsty land; He hideth my life in the depths of His love, and covers me there with His hand."[13] Moses was covered by God's hand, from God—from God's goodness!

In Exodus 33, Moses asked to see God's glory. God explained that His glory is His grace and mercy applied as He wills—outside of man's consent (vv. 18–19). God then revealed His goodness to Moses, but God only revealed His "back"—protecting Moses from the full revelation of God's goodness by hiding Moses in the cleft of the rock. If God were to reveal all of His goodness to us, we would explode. This reality is justification for heaven: The goodness of God is so great that for all eternity He can progressively reveal Himself and there will be no end to His revelation. The wonder of eternity is not endless time. It is the unending revelation of the goodness of God!

We must never lose reverence for being protected from God by God. The blood of the Passover lamb protected the Israelites from the wrath of God. It was God's destroying angel who saw the blood and passed over the guilty. The Israelites were no better than the Egyptians—they just had God insurance. Let us retain a wonder that God, who has every right to destroy us, also makes a way for us to enter His presence.

Entering His presence, let us not forget that His goodness is so eternally great that it, too, can destroy us. God will eternally, progressively reveal His goodness to us. What joy this gives us for heaven!

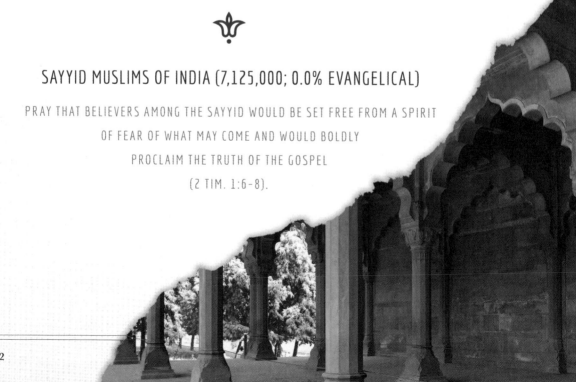

SAYYID MUSLIMS OF INDIA (7,125,000; 0.0% EVANGELICAL)

PRAY THAT BELIEVERS AMONG THE SAYYID WOULD BE SET FREE FROM A SPIRIT
OF FEAR OF WHAT MAY COME AND WOULD BOLDLY
PROCLAIM THE TRUTH OF THE GOSPEL
(2 TIM. 1:6-8).

JANUARY 29: MERCY AND TRUTH

EXODUS 34-36; PSALM 29; MARK 1; ROMANS 1

*T*ruth without mercy kills. Mercy without truth corrupts. Intimacy in relationship is impossible without large doses of both. Chuck Miller points out that with grace alone you can have friendship—but you cannot have intimacy.[14] Only when truth and grace intertwine do friendships and marriages become intimate.

Church-planting teams in the Muslim world are often organized around memorandums of understanding, or MOUs. These charters lay out the values, vision, and guidelines for the teams so new members can determine whether or not they want to join. These MOUs are covenantal. In Exodus 34:27, God made a covenant with His people through Moses and said, "According to the tenor of these words I have made a covenant with you and with Israel." The point is not rigid legalism. The point is the spirit of the communication—understandable only because Moses was intimate with God (forty days and nights without water, soaking up God's presence, face-glowing understanding). God spoke mercy and truth to Moses—not just rules and regulations—and Moses grasped the spirit, or tenor, of God's words.

MOUs are not the point. They are a starting place for those who do not know us. The point is intimacy derived over time from liberal application of both mercy and truth. When my team knows me, the MOU is no longer necessary. Intimacy reveals a person's will better than a charter. Knowing who our authority is helps us know what pleases that person, and this confidence is our counsel.

Moses appealed endearingly to God: "Let my LORD, I pray, go among us, even though we are a stiff-necked people" (Ex. 34:9). God—giver of mercy and truth—knows that we need both. Since He is patient enough to travel with us on our faltering journeys, let us likewise journey with others—despite their imbalances one way or the other—and give what we have received. God walks with us. He gives grace and truth. We have intimacy with Him, and in that intimacy is joy. Let us walk with others with the same shining face.

OMORO, HARARGHE MUSLIMS OF ETHIOPIA (4,892,000; 0.1% EVANGELICAL)

PRAY FOR THE WORD OF GOD IN WRITTEN, ORAL, MUSICAL, AND DRAMATIC FORMS TO BE
TRANSLATED AND TO RISE AMONG THE OMORO, HARARGHE
(ISA. 55:10-11).

JANUARY 30: JOY IN THE MOURNING

EXODUS 37–39; PSALM 30; MARK 2; ROMANS 2

*W*e have the misguided conception that joy and sorrow are opposites. Joy may well come in the morning (Ps. 30:5), but it also comes in the "mourning." When God takes the "u" out of mourning, it can lead to dancing (30:11). Unfortunately, there is often too much "you" (and me) in our mourning, which is self-pity—and self-pity is a joy quencher.

William Hentry Temple Gairdner was a missionary in Cairo at the turn of the twentieth century with the Church Missionary Society. His best friend was a man named Douglas Thornton. Gairdner and Thornton—though polar opposites—were fast friends and indivisible colleagues. They trusted and depended on each other. When Thornton died (in his early thirties), Gairdner was at his bedside. The presence of Jesus was so strong in that little room that Gairdner, despite his sorrow, could not help but rejoice. Immediately after Thornton went to be with Jesus, Gairdner slipped out of that room and realized: "Joy and sorrow are not antithetical; they mingle together all our lives long."[15]

William Blake (1757–1827) said it well in his poem "Auguries of Innocence":[16]
> *Man was made for joy and woe;*
> *And when this we rightly know,*
> *Thro' the world we safely go.*
> *Joy and woe are woven fine,*
> *A clothing for the soul divine.*
> *Under every grief and pine*
> *Runs a joy with silken twine.*

Very few of us live with unmitigated joy or sorrow. The normal Christian experience includes equal measures of both. We have the promise before us of an eternity without tears of sorrow, but our present reality must include suffering and pain. The wonder of Jesus is that He makes this fellowship sweet. When we endure trials and disappointments with our eyes on Him, He has the capacity to give us a measure of His joy—even in tragedy.

With my own eyes I have seen this. I have seen a family rejoice in spite of the sorrow that their father languishes in prison. I have seen a mother praise God even when her child suddenly died. I have felt in my own heart an intimacy with Jesus—a joy inexpressible and full of glory—when I have turned my disappointments over to Him. There is joy in both the morning and the mourning.

YEMENI MUSLIMS OF NORTHERN YEMEN (11,939,000; 0.0% EVANGELICAL)

PRAY THAT GOD WOULD POUR OUT HIS SPIRIT ON THE YEMENI PEOPLE. PRAY THAT THEY WOULD BE POWERFULLY SAVED AND EMPOWERED TO BE HIS WITNESSES (JOEL 2:28–32).

*H*ow hungry we are for the manifest presence of Jesus. We read about the cloud descending and the glory filling the tabernacle (Ex. 40:34), a glory so great that not even Moses—who was accustomed to the presence of God—could enter. We long for this. We sit in pedestrian church services and small groups, tasting His presence, but sensing there is so much more on the other side of the veil. How our hearts long for the empowered presence of Jesus.

Over and over again, the text of Exodus 40 repeats that the tabernacle was prepared as "God had commanded Moses." Decorations, clothing, positioning, composition, materials, ritual cleansing—everything was done exactly as God wanted. Then the succinct "So Moses finished the work" (v. 33). Only after studious preparations did the presence of God descend.

Preparedness is mutual. Psalm 31:19 tells us that God has stored up and prepared goodness for us! His goodness is hidden "in the secret place of [His] presence" (v. 20). We prepare for what God has prepared for us—the life that issues from being with Him.

Jesus takes the initiative for this impartation. "He called to Him those *He Himself wanted*" (Mark 3:13, emphasis added). What a comfort that as we prepare to meet with Jesus, all along He has been preparing to meet with us. As we obey explicitly what He tells us to do and cleanse our hearts through repentance and humble ourselves, He wants to meet with us. I can hardly believe it. He wants me! He wants me to be with Him (3:14). Oh what wonder! In His forbearance, He has "passed over my sins" (Rom. 3:25) and called me to be with Him, in the glory of His presence.

I prepare to receive what Jesus has prepared for me—a direct impartation of Himself from His glorious presence. By being in His presence, I am prepared to go out into the world and preach in power. Jesus called to Himself those He wanted (Mark 3:13) and appointed them to be with Him (v. 14) that He might send them out to preach and to have power (v. 15). The imparted presence of Jesus is never to be selfishly hoarded—it is always given to be released. When we commit our spirits into His hand (Ps. 31:5), He commits His Spirit to ours—and commissions us to bear the glory of His presence everywhere.

BALOCH MUSLIMS OF EASTERN PAKISTAN (7,012,000; 0.0% EVANGELICAL)

PRAY THAT CHRISTIANS FROM AROUND THE WORLD WOULD WORK TOGETHER
TO REACH THE BALOCH AND THAT THE BALOCH WOULD BE JOINED
TO THE BODY OF CHRIST (JOHN 17:20-23).

February

"I HAVE BUT ONE PASSION—IT IS HE, IT IS HE ALONE.

THE WORLD IS THE FIELD AND THE FIELD IS THE WORLD; AND

HENCEFORTH THAT COUNTRY SHALL BE MY HOME WHERE I CAN BE

MOST USED IN WINNING SOULS FOR CHRIST."

—Count Zinzindorf

FEBRUARY 1: LIFESTYLE REPENTANCE

LEVITICUS 1-3; PSALM 32; MARK 4; ROMANS 4

*T*he Old Testament law required frequent sacrifices for sin. In part this was because the blood of animals could not cleanse the conscience, but it also pointed to the ongoing need of every individual to repent. We have turned repentance into an event, a periodic turning from ourselves and our wickedness. While it is not wrong to periodically examine ourselves, it is better to live a lifestyle of repentance.

The psalmist points out that the person whose transgression is forgiven—whose sin is covered, whose spirit has no deceit—is blessed (Ps. 32:1). On the contrary, those who live with hidden sin feel old and tired (vv. 3–4). Nothing saps the life out of us more than pretending to be something we are not, such as bearing the agony of guilt on the inside with plastic smiles plastered on the outside. Sin ages us.

When we confess our sins (v. 5) and pray to God in a time when He can be found—and incidentally that time is whenever we pray (v. 6)—He becomes our hiding place (v. 7). Think of it: Ongoing confession of sin is our preservation. It keeps us young. Lifestyle repentance keeps us from trouble, surrounds us with deliverance, and gives us energy. A soft heart before Jesus—a heart that lives repentance, and a spirit that knows there is nothing kept secret "but that it should come to light"—is a liberated heart (Mark 4:22). Oh the joy of continual confession, continual turning from self and sin to the Savior.

Let us not be a people whose ritual repentance inoculates us from the intimacy of lifestyle repentance. Soft spirits, ever tender to the small promptings and rebukes of the Holy Spirit, are a delight to God. He graciously accepts our large confessions, our seasonal turnings—but He delights when we constantly turns to Jesus. Day by day, moment by moment, let us live a life of repentance. Let us live addicted to repentance.

MAHRATTA HINDUS OF INDIA (6,894,000; 0.0% EVANGELICAL)

PRAY THAT THE HEARTS OF THE MAHRATTA WOULD BE LIKE GOOD SOIL, READY TO
HEAR THE GOSPEL AND TO RESPOND
(MATT. 7:1-8, 18-23).

*P*ride keeps us off our knees. We seek to position ourselves in a place of strength, having believed the lie that personal high ground protects us. We forget that deliverance does not result from personal strength (Ps. 33:16–17) but from dependency on Jesus. The sooner we humble ourselves and realize that everyone must beg, the safer we are.

Demons Beg. When Jesus confronted demonic powers, they immediately knew they were over-matched and began to whine. We look at the intimidating powers at work around us—both ideologically and coercively—and we shudder, cowed by their evil strength. Let us, rather, picture them groveling before Jesus (Mark 5:12).

Leaders Beg. Jairus, influential in the synagogue (Mark 5:22), fell at Jesus' feet. He did not care what his peers thought. He was so desperate for help that he, too, groveled. When our pride keeps us from begging, it also keeps us from miracles. One reason people in the West do not see as many miracles as people in the Global South is because we in the West are too refined to beg. If you are too proud to beg for yourself, will you at least beg for others?

Humble Followers Beg. The woman with the issue of blood was lowly enough to fall at Jesus' feet (Mark 5:33) and tell Him the whole truth. "Here it is, Jesus—all my dirty laundry, laid out for you and everyone else to know." Repeatedly in the Scriptures the most powerful deliverances resulted from the most public confessions. Bringing our weakness into the public light is often the only way to private joy.

There is one more category of beggars in this Mark 5 text: "Then they began to plead with Him to depart from their region" (v. 17). This is one of the saddest verses in the Bible. They preferred their pigs over the presence of Jesus. We all beg—we either beg Jesus to help us or we beg Him to leave us. The latter is sheer folly, the former the greatest wisdom. May Jesus make us wise, wise enough to beg.

OROMO, JIMMA MUSLIMS OF ETHIOPIA (2,759,000; 1.2% EVANGELICAL)

PRAY FOR THE PEACE THAT RESULTS WHEN MEN AND WOMEN ARE
RECONCILED WITH GOD (JOHN 14:27). PRAY FOR MEN AND WOMEN OF PEACE
(LUKE 10:6) AMONG THE OROMO, JIMMA.

FEBRUARY 3: BREATH PRAYER

LEVITICUS 7–9; PSALM 34; MARK 6; ROMANS 6

From the fourth to the sixteenth century, Christians prayed what they called "breath prayers." The idea was to spend some time in reflection in order to identify what your heart really longed for from God. What did your spirit cry out for? What were you desperate to receive from Him? The prayer was encapsulated in a short sentence of seven to nine syllables. Each Christian prayed this prayer numerous times a day. They picked an event that happened frequently during the day, and every time that event occurred, they lifted up their prayer to the Lord. Initially, these prayers felt somewhat academic and dry, but over the weeks and months of discipline, they became more natural. As months became years, the prayers moved into the subconscious levels and people prayed them reflexively—even in their sleep! These prayers became as natural and regular as breathing.[1]

Abiding in Jesus essentially means to lavish extravagant daily time on Him. This is enjoyed in two primary ways: (1) a fixed block of time repeated daily at the same time that is spent in Bible reading, prayer, and other spiritual disciplines, and (2) all-day, continual communion. Breath prayers are a way to abide in an ongoing manner.

When I was eighteen years old, I attended a watch-night service. This is what we used to call the prayer meeting on the evening of December 31, when we gathered to pray in the New Year. At this particular prayer meeting, someone passed around a little box of Scripture verses. Each person took a card and prayed that Scripture for the rest of the year. The verse I selected randomly that night has become my life verse: "The LORD is near to those who have a broken heart, and saves such as have a contrite spirit" (Ps. 34:18).

From that verse I derived my breath prayer. The great longing of my heart is that I will be near to Jesus and He to me. If I have that, I have all. Taking that verse and the second verse of "Away in a Manger," I daily try to pray, "Be near me, Lord Jesus."[2]

Jesus invites us to abide with Him. If we do, He promises that we will bear fruit (other disciples, in the John 15 context) and they, in turn, will abide. Central to abiding with Jesus is communing with Him all day long. Breath prayers help us abide in Him. Let us breathe to Jesus the desires of our hearts.

TIHAMI MUSLIMS OF YEMEN (4,630,000; 0.0% EVANGELICAL)

PRAY THAT BELIEVERS AMONG THE TIHAMI WOULD PROCLAIM THE MESSAGE
OF THE GOSPEL CLEARLY AND WOULD MAKE THE MOST OF EVERY
OPPORTUNITY GOD PLACES BEFORE THEM
(COL. 4:2–5).

FEBRUARY 4: UNCLEAN ABOMINATIONS

LEVITICUS 10-12; PSALM 35; MARK 7; ROMANS 7

*S**ome Things Are an Abomination to People.*** Leviticus 11 runs through a litany of things that defile. The law was given, in fact, to help people distinguish between the clean and unclean (Ex. 11:46–47). Basically, there are three sources of evil: the unholy troika of Devil, world, and flesh. Jesus points out that what defiles us is neither the Devil nor the wickedness of the world around us. What defiles us, what is an unclean abomination, is what comes out of our own hearts (Mark 7:15).

Evil thoughts? Unclean. Adulteries? Abomination. Fornications? Unclean. Murders? Abomination. Thefts? Unclean. After considering this list you may feel pretty good about yourself—but that, too, is abominable. Jesus' list in Mark 7:21–23 continues: Covetousness? Unclean. Wickedness? Abomination. Deceit? Unclean. Lewdness? Abomination. Jealousy? Unclean. Blasphemy? Abomination. Pride? Unclean. Foolishness? Abomination. With Paul we acknowledge that sin has produced all manner of evil desires in us (Rom. 7:8), has deceived us (v. 11), and has produced death in us (v. 13).

I once heard a speaker explain that one form of Roman capital punishment was to handcuff a corpse to the back of a prisoner. Back to back, chained at the wrists and ankles, the condemned person had to carry a decomposing body wherever he went. The rotting flesh of the defiled body infected the prisoner and eventually killed him. This is a vivid illustration of our agonizing cry joined to Paul's: "Who will deliver [us] from this body of death?" (v. 24) The answer is simple, of course. Jesus does all things well (Mark 7:37). When we ask Him, He casts the evil, the indwelling sin (Rom. 7:20), out of us.

*S**ome Things Are an Abomination to God.*** If we do not come to Jesus, continually begging for imparted holiness, another death descends upon us. Aaron's sons offered strange fire before the Lord. Unconfessed evil lurked in their hearts. They presumed they could lead the people and minister without being covered in God's holiness. As a result, they died before the Lord—never to be mourned by Aaron and his remaining sons (Lev. 10:4–7).

The difference between Paul and Aaron's sons (both public ministers, anointed for broad ministry) was that Paul confessed the evil in his heart and begged Jesus for holiness. Aaron's sons tried to cover their evil. Sin that is kept in the dark is an abomination to God. It is the secret, unconfessed sin that destroys.

HAZARA MUSLIMS OF AFGHANISTAN (2,932,000; 0.03% EVANGELICAL)

PLEAD THAT THE HAZARA WILL UNDERSTAND THAT HOPE FOR FORGIVENESS AND
ACCEPTANCE WITH GOD IS ONLY THROUGH JESUS' WORK ON THE CROSS
(1 COR. 1:18).

FEBRUARY 5: GATEKEEPERS

LEVITICUS 13-15; PSALM 36; MARK 8; ROMANS 8

*T*he reach of sin is staggering. If you let it in, sin will run wild, attack your vulnerable places, and destroy your vulnerable ones. That is why God deals with it so ruthlessly. The Levitical laws on leprosy seem ludicrous: so detailed and extreme. Yet God was simply communicating that the law of the leper is similar to the law of sin: leprosy, like sin, can affect those who come in contact with it. Similarly, cleansing from sin is not to be confused with forgiveness. Forgiveness is instantaneous; cleansing requires a process.

We love to quote the "no condemnation" promise of Romans 8:1, but we need to remind ourselves that the promise is conditional. "There is therefore now no condemnation to those who are in Christ Jesus, *who do not walk according to the flesh,* but after the Spirit" (emphasis added). Walking in the Spirit is a process that demands time and intentionality. We are not condemned *if* we go through the process of being sanctified. It is only when we walk in God's light that we are free from the insidious spread of sin. It is only in His light that we see light (Ps. 36:9).

It is far better to put energy into prevention rather than cure. Sin is so destructive that though both forgiveness and cleansing are possible, they come at great cost—a cost often borne by the innocent as well as the guilty. It is for this reason that we must be gatekeepers. We must stand at sin's port of entry and bar it from coming in. Everyone is responsible for his own choices, yet leaders are culpable when they open the door to destruction.

My Greek grandmother was a medium before she came to Jesus. She could see into the spirit world—both angelic and demonic. After she gave her life to Jesus, He appeared to her in a vision, put His hand on her head, and pulled what seemed to be a "shroud" off of her. It was as though a veil was lifted off her soul. From that time, she could no longer see into the spirit world—good or bad. Her daughter and grand-daughter, however, both have keen spiritual discernment. It sounds crazy, but one day before I was born, my mother passed by a room where my older sister was watching television. There happened to be some horror commercial on at that time, and my mother had a vision of demonic forces reaching out from the television in an attempt to influence and even conquer my sister's mind.

The things we allow into our homes affect our children—even before they can comprehend language. Sin spreads. Evil is ravenous. Without seeing demons under every chair, let us at least recognize ubiquitous demonic ambition. Let us not allow evil to run riot in our spheres of influence (among our vulnerable ones) through negligence because we let it in our minds, onto our computers, or into our homes.

GADARIA HINDUS OF INDIA (6,350,000; 0.0% EVANGELICAL)

PRAY THAT BELIEVERS AMONG THE GADARIA WILL ENDURE PERSECUTION IN A CHRISTLIKE
MANNER AND WILL GIVE THEIR LIVES FOR THE SAKE OF THE
GOSPEL IF NECESSARY (1 PETER 2:21-23).

A dispute arose among Jesus' followers regarding which of them would become the greatest. We all have a little bit of Absalom in us—angling for the throne, sizing up our competition, hoping to be first in line to succeed the current authority. Jesus steps into the midst of our scheming and tells us, "If anyone desires to be first . . . he shall be last" (Mark 9:35). The *"anyone"* refers, of course, to *everyone.* We all want to be first in one manner or another, but there can be only One above all others. Jesus is not implicitly commending the means to emerge greater than others. He is indirectly pointing out that there can be only One who is first: Himself. When we strive to be first, we are, in fact, striving to be God. That is His place, and His alone.

The way to deal with our ambition to be God is, first, to be like Him. This seems theoretically counterintuitive, but it is simple functionally. As modeled by Jesus, God cares for the weak and insignificant. In our attempt to be like Him, if we put the needs of those we consider inferior above ourselves, we will both succeed and fail. In our success, we will begin to acquire His character, and His character will give us such delight in serving that we will forget about being primary. In our failure, we will acquire humility, and that humility will reveal the folly of our original ambition—being primary. So humility also helps us realize and embrace the comfort of being the creation without the pressure of being the Creator. Giving up greatness is both security and rest.

Pride (the mother of all sins) is, for the most part, subtle in its initial forays into our spirit. I lead a great team here in Egypt. I rejoice to see them thrive and grow, to pass me in their abilities in Arabic, cultural adaptation, and church-planting. Sometimes I feel like a commander surrounded by incredible generals. The problem is that I become bossy. I forget to be polite or thankful, and I relish sitting on my missiological perch as the voluble "know-it-all." When I am not careful, I easily slip into my god-fantasy of being first among equals. To be like Jesus is not to be Jesus, the only One who is first, but to relish being great-less, the last among equals.

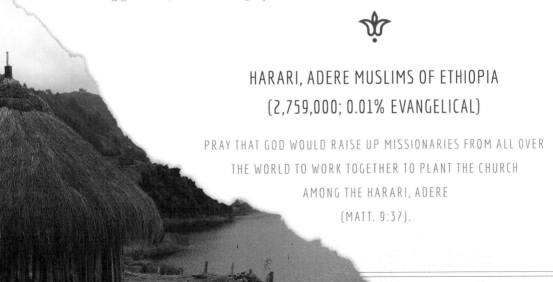

HARARI, ADERE MUSLIMS OF ETHIOPIA
(2,759,000; 0.01% EVANGELICAL)

PRAY THAT GOD WOULD RAISE UP MISSIONARIES FROM ALL OVER
THE WORLD TO WORK TOGETHER TO PLANT THE CHURCH
AMONG THE HARARI, ADERE
(MATT. 9:37).

FEBRUARY 7: PERSECUTION INHERITANCE

LEVITICUS 19-21; PSALM 38; MARK 10; ROMANS 10

*J*esus promises that whoever has left family, houses, and lands for His and for the gospel's sake, will receive in this life all that and more—one hundred times more, in fact (Mark 10:29–30). This is certainly true in frontier missions. Those who leave home and hearth to plant the church where it has not been planted enter a brotherhood that is surprisingly joyous and tender. Arab, African, Asian, American, and Anglo come together to form a family as loving as it is varied. To consider only the reward of those who leave their homelands and families is to consider only half the truth. Jesus also said that those who follow Him to where He is not known will receive all the above *"with persecutions."*

Our inheritance is to suffer together. Those who bear the name of Jesus beyond the borders of safety are granted the honor of facing trials together. How blessed it is to suffer together. This is our sacred communion, it is our heritage, and it is our joy. There is something twisted about Western believers only sending money and prayer to those under pressure and persecution. When we do this, we not only misrepresent Jesus (who suffered outside the camp with and for His brethren), we also communicate the false idea that our lives are more precious than theirs—they are expendable and we are pampered. Tragically, too, we miss out on a treasured inheritance: the joy of suffering with others. The fellowship of our Lord's sufferings demands participation, not empathetic observation.

Suffering together unifies the body of Christ. Suffering together does more to build trust and reconciliation than a thousand seminars. Suffering together beautifies the church and prepares Christ's bride for His return. Suffering together glorifies Jesus. Suffering together ultimately leads to unleashed life.

"As the Master shall the servant be, and pierced are the feet that follow Me."[3] Jesus was betrayed; so will we be. Jesus was condemned; so will we be. Jesus was delivered up; so will we be. Jesus was mocked; so will we be. Jesus was scourged; so will we be. Jesus was spit on; so will we be. Jesus was killed; so will we be. Jesus rose again; so will we. And when that rising is multiethnic, it cannot be attributed to the fortune of man or the arbitrary luck of context. Only a joined persecution can give unquestioned glory to the Father. Only multicultural persecution leads to the obedience of all nations.

SOUTH AZERBAIJANI MUSLIMS OF IRAN (14,000,000; 0.09% EVANGELICAL)

PRAY THAT THE SOUTH AZERBAIJANI WILL FEEL AND KNOW THE BURDEN OF SIN AND WILL COME TO JESUS FOR FORGIVENESS AND SALVATION (MATT. 11:28-30).

*G*od warned Aaron and his sons not to profane His holy name by what they dedicated to Him in worship (Lev. 22:1). To give God what is less than our best is an insidious form of cursing. What we dedicate to God can insult Him. The blasphemous curse of our day is to give God what offends Him because it is less than our best—our leftover energy and attention, the scraps of our time, or what we cannot give to someone else. The Scripture warns that those who worship cavalierly will be put to death (Lev. 24:16).

The Profanity of Worship Mixed with Sin. Spiritual death is a process. God is repulsed when we habitually approach His altar with unconfessed sin. When we make a habit of lifting our hands, singing, or praying in the Spirit from a lifestyle of unconfessed or habitual sin, we commit spiritual suicide. Over time, we become numb to the convictions of the Spirit. We develop spiritual calluses and dichotomize our sin out of our worship. This leads to the unpardonable sin: We no longer hear the promptings of the Spirit. Without that sensitivity to hear, we have no faith (Rom. 10:17, "faith comes by hearing"). Without faith it is impossible to please God because we have lost the capacity to obey.

The Profanity of Worship Mixed with Materialism. Jesus cleansed the temple (Mark 11) for two reasons, and one of those reasons was the profanity of a materialistic approach to worship. The Western church is particularly guilty of this with our million-dollar facilities and fashion-show Sunday mornings. The Global South in its poverty is also suspect. A materialistic approach to worship is demonic and profane. Jesus, in effect, cursed the temple. His atoning death and resurrection make ritual sacrifice unnecessary, and He is intolerant of buildings for buildings' sake.

The Profanity of Worship That Omits Missions. The second reason Jesus cleansed the temple was because it had lost its missions priority. The buyers and sellers had set up camp in the Court of the Gentiles—the venue ordained for the nations to worship Jehovah. Jesus was furious at this profanity and thundered, "My house shall be made a house of prayer for *all nations*," (Mark 11:17) directly referencing Isaiah 56:7. When we approach congregational worship without a priority on giving the gospel to all people groups, we curse God, and He will bring a curse back. People, churches, ministries, and denominations that worship profanely (without incorporating God's desire to be glorified by all ethnolinguistic peoples) curse Him. He will not tolerate this profanity. He will tear down every stone of every edifice that curses Him.

JEW, ISRAELI, AND SABRA JEWS OF ISRAEL (4,430,000; 0.04% EVANGELICAL)

PRAY THAT GOD WOULD UNVEIL THE CROSS AND WOULD REMOVE THE VEIL ON THE MINDS AND SPIRITS OF THE JEWS, ISRAELIS, AND SABRA JEWS (2 COR. 3:16-17).

FEBRUARY 9: APPROPRIATELY AGAINST

LEVITICUS 25–27; PSALM 40; MARK 12; ROMANS 12

A fallacy has crept into our thinking that has affected our witness. We no longer think it appropriate to be against something. We think we must only concentrate on the good things of the gospel and believe that speaking positively is enough to overcome evil. Romans 12, the same chapter that tells us a renewed mind transforms us (v. 2), instructs us to think soberly not haughtily (v. 3), encourages us not to set our mind on high things (v. 16), and instructs us that non-hypocritical love hates evil.

The sacrifice that delights God is our proclamation of good news with unrestrained lips (Ps. 40). We declare His faithfulness, we do not to conceal His lovingkindness, and we say continually "The LORD be magnified!" (v. 16). The point is not that we are to witness always to the positive things of God—the point is that we are to witness always to *the character of God*. God hates evil and is against anything twisted and unholy. A vital part of witness is to declare what God is against as well as what He is for. There can be no good news outside the context of bad news. There is no redemption outside the fall.

God's covenant (Ex. 26:13 and following) appointed terror, punishment, plagues, fury, destruction, and abhorrence to those who disobeyed. This is the context for His great and merciful patience (Lev. 26:40–44). Jesus Himself used a polemic approach. He frequently spoke against what He disagreed with. In Mark 12:12, He spoke a parable *"against* them" (emphasis added). In Mark 12:27, Jesus informed His examiners: "You are . . . greatly mistaken!" Over and over Jesus spoke against evil.

Chapter 12 of Romans exhorts us to overcome evil with good (v. 21). Let it sink into our spirits that flattery, deceit, passive-aggressive behavior, manipulation, fear, self-preservation, disingenuous answers, and false identity are all tools of Satan. We do not overcome evil by being false, fearful, or faithless. We overcome evil by speaking the truth of God's character—proclaiming both what He is for and what He is against. We speak truth; truth that is merciful, gracious, kind, firm, strong, corrective, and life-giving. Part and parcel of being for Jesus is publicly standing with Him on what He is against.

AWAN MUSLIMS OF PAKISTAN (5,058,000; 0.0% EVANGELICAL)

PRAY THAT BELIEVERS AMONG THE AWAN WOULD BE SET FREE FROM A SPIRIT OF FEAR OF WHAT MAY COME AND WOULD BOLDLY PROCLAIM THE TRUTH OF THE GOSPEL (2 TIM. 1:6–8).

FEBRUARY 10: RIGHTEOUS SUFFERING

NUMBERS 1-3; PSALM 41; MARK 13; ROMANS 13

*M*uch of the pain we experience in life is a result of our own folly. Our pride, selfishness, insecurity, sin, ambition, jealousy, and pride lead us down painful paths. There is a pain, however, that is undeserved. Nothing hurts quite as much as having colleagues and friends think you are "toxic." To have them whisper against you (Ps. 41:7), to treat you as if an evil disease clings to you (v. 8), to have your own "familiar friend, in whom [you] trusted . . . lift up his heel against [you]" (v. 9). Social leprosy does not numb, it stings like little else.

It is a deep wound to be misunderstood, mistrusted, doubted, questioned, slandered, and falsely accused. It hurts when you cannot explain what really happened and must quietly bear some undeserved scarlet letter. These deep wounds are opportunities—opportunities to enter the fellowship of Jesus' sufferings.

When we suffer unjustly, we gain intimacy and union with Jesus. When we experience betrayal like Jesus did, we feel what He felt. If we respond in the way He responded (He opened not His mouth), we can experience a deep reward. But do not confuse the painful wounds of righteous suffering with the surface scratches that result from our own folly, stubbornness, and flesh. All too often we lick our scratches in self-pity, scratches we earned because of our own poor choices.

Let us not confuse the hurt that arises from our sin, and the deep wounds that result from the sin of others. Only the grief of being "toxic to others" because we are righteous before God can lead to the deepest intimacy with Jesus and the sweet sorrow of righteous suffering. There is a big difference between the bitter consequences of stupidity and selfishness and the character-changing agony of suffering for Jesus.

KACHHI HINDUS OF INDIA (5,829,000; 0.0% EVANGELICAL)

PRAY FOR THE WORD OF GOD IN WRITTEN, ORAL, MUSICAL, AND DRAMATIC FORMS TO
BE TRANSLATED AND TO RISE AMONG THE KACHHI
(ISA. 55:10-11).

FEBRUARY 11: EXTRAVAGANCE

NUMBERS 4-6; PSALM 42; MARK 14; ROMANS 14

*A*t the house of Simon the leper, a woman broke an alabaster box of costly oil and extravagantly anointed Jesus with it (Mark 14). Many who observed her offering thought it a waste. Jesus thought differently. What the woman spent on Jesus, at cost to herself and seeming waste to others, He considered so precious that He prophesied: "Wherever this gospel is preached in the whole world, what this woman has done will be told as a memorial to her" (v. 9).

What is our primary role in preaching the gospel in all the world? Extravagant time with Jesus! Jesus says of this woman's lavish outpouring: "She has done a good work for Me" (v. 6). First, we lavish extravagant daily time on Jesus (what He considers our work), then we go into the world to bear witness to what God has done in Christ. We are so wrongheaded in our approach to life and ministry. We are doggedly determined to work for Jesus while forgetting that witness must follow worship. We will not be remembered for what we have done. Like the woman of extravagance, what will affect people is whether or not we have lavished consistent attention on Jesus. When we get the sequence right (first lavishing extravagant daily time on Jesus), He works through us in ways that would not be possible otherwise, and whatever is accomplished has His incontrovertible stamp on it.

Interestingly, the text continues, "Then Judas Iscariot, one of the twelve, went to the chief priests to betray Him to them" (v. 10). Later Judas betrayed Jesus with a sign of intimacy, a kiss (v. 45). A chief way we betray Jesus is with false intimacy. Some of those who are most offended by extravagant intimacy with Jesus are the ones who maintain a surface intimacy with Him. Task-oriented, efficient, hard-working individuals sometimes struggle with the seeming passivity of abiding in Jesus. While some of their concerns have merit (we can be guilty of "spiritual gluttony" as the church fathers called it), the danger for the movers and shakers is that their lives will be forgettable because they never learned to abide (lavish extravagant daily time) in Jesus.

The chief end of man is "to glorify God, and to enjoy Him forever."[4] When we prioritize Jesus by lavishing extravagant daily time on Him, He ensures there is a gospel result. The best thing we can do for unreached people is to abide in Jesus. It is the first thing we must do so that all nations will be fulfilled in the eternal worship of Jesus, and it is the primary thing we are called to in life, service, and mission. If we get that right, we can go from that place of extravagance into all the world and make disciples of every *ethne*.

RASHAIDA MUSLIMS OF SUDAN (98,000; 0.0% EVANGELICAL)

PRAY THAT GOD WOULD POUR OUT HIS SPIRIT ON THE RASHAIDA AND THAT THEY WOULD SEE
DREAMS AND VISIONS OF JESUS. PRAY THAT THEY WOULD BE POWERFULLY SAVED
AND EMPOWERED TO BE HIS WITNESSES
(JOEL 2:28-32).

FEBRUARY 12: PATIENCE AND COMFORT

NUMBERS 7–9; PSALM 43; MARK 15; ROMANS 15

*I*n Romans 15:1, Paul exhorted believers to bear with the scruples of the weak, to not please themselves. In verse 2, he instructed believers to please their neighbors for their good. Love is doing what is best for our neighbors, regardless of the cost to us—or them. The point is edification, not the pleasure of the process. Our model is Christ (v. 3), who "did not please Himself" but bore reproach for others.

A Roman who watched Jesus die became convinced of His divinity (Mark 15:39). It is important that we die well. To live dead is to live a life that dies progressively. For the Christian, death is a daily process, not a one-time event. Paul knew what this meant, testifying, "I die daily" (1 Cor. 15:31).

The Patience and Comfort of the Scriptures (Rom. 15:4). When we "die daily" by laying down our lives for others, this leads to hope. This is what the Scriptures teach us. The lives of our forerunners in the faith demonstrated that the deepest satisfaction is linked to the costliest sacrifice. The lives that were poured out for others were most rewarded with the presence of Jesus. The history of faith gives us hope, for a precedent is established that guarantees blessing to the lowly.

The Patience and Comfort of God (Rom. 15:5). This Scriptural promise is based in the character of God. Time works for God. He is not subject to the laws and restraints of time. The Author of time commands and demands its servitude. Time is, therefore, on the side of the righteous. We can die daily because we know that time (God's servant) will ultimately bring life and comfort.

The Patience and Comfort of the Body (Rom. 15:5–6). Because God is patient with us and assures us in His Word that comfort results from patience, we can be patient with one another. We can lay down our wills for one another because the character of God has been demonstrated through history, and we are connected to that living history. I can die daily for my brother because Jesus died eternally for me. I can be patient with my sister, and she with me, because God has been patient with us. We can hope to see endless life on the other side of daily death because God purposed resurrection after crucifixion. If God could patiently endure the agonizing death of His Son for the joyous comfort on the other side, then surely I can put up with some relatively minor irritants for the good of the body and for the sake of my brother.

PALESTINIAN MUSLIMS OF THE WEST BANK AND GAZA (3,878,000; 0.05% EVANGELICAL)

PRAY THAT CHRISTIANS FROM AROUND THE WORLD WOULD WORK TOGETHER TO REACH THE PALESTINIANS AND THAT THE PALESTINIANS WOULD BE JOINED TO THE BODY OF CHRIST (JOHN 17:20–23).

FEBRUARY 13: PROPHETHOOD OF ALL BELIEVERS

NUMBERS 10-12; PSALM 44; MARK 16; ROMANS 16

*O*ne of the many reasons God gives the Holy Spirit is to help us bear the burdens of leadership (Num. 11:17). Moses was overwhelmed by the needs of a complaining people, worn out by their incessant demands for former comforts. God responded by spreading His Spirit among seventy elders . . . and those closest to Moses reacted.

The Purist. Joshua was worried about authority. He did not want the unapproved people to move in the gifts of the Spirit, so he told Moses to make the unsanctioned people stop prophesying. Moses' response is priceless: "Oh that *all* the LORD's people were prophets and that the Lord would put His Spirit upon them" (Num. 11:29, emphasis added). Joel repeated this desire when he prophesied that the Spirit would be poured out upon all flesh in the last days. Moses was not threatened when God used others to communicate. This is true leadership of the Spirit: to genuinely rejoice when God speaks through others, unthreatened and unconcerned about being replaced as God's spokesman.

The Pretenders. Aaron and Miriam were worried about authority. They did not think that Moses alone had heard from God and, offended by his choice of a Sudanese wife, saw an opportunity to criticize. Their offense probably had some grounds (no second-wife scenarios, even in the Old Testament, end well), but the point was not Moses' flaws, it was their presumption. Even while we should not restrict others from being used by the Spirit, we should not assume our own worth or intrinsic right to prophesy. Moses again was unconcerned, and God intervened to rebuke Aaron and Miriam. Once more, Moses responded in humility and prayed for his sister to be healed.

It is easy in this narrative to condemn Aaron and Miriam, but the point of the text is that Joshua, like Aaron and Miriam, was wrong. There are two equal and opposite errors when it comes to the prophethood of all believers. One (Joshua's) is to be protective, possessive, defensive, and overly worried about the abuse of spiritual gifts. The other (Aaron's and Miriam's) is to take offense when our flawed friends move in the gifts of the Spirit and, as a result, to miss hearing what God says through them.

The prevention and cure for these twin mistakes is humility. Moses modeled it for us. He was neither worried about the young prophets nor defensive at the criticism of his peers. He allowed God to defend him (which God is skilled at doing), and he encouraged a liberal spreading and sharing of the Spirit. May we likewise encourage and empower all God's people to be prophets. May we be humble enough to hear the Spirit from the young and from flawed friends. This humility legitimizes the Spirit to speak through us—for we, too, are equally flawed.

RAKHSHANI MUSLIMS OF PAKISTAN (379,000; 0.0% EVANGELICAL)

PRAY THAT THE HEARTS OF THE RAKHSHANI WOULD BE LIKE GOOD SOIL, READY TO HEAR THE
GOSPEL AND TO RESPOND (MATT. 7:1-8, 18-23).

FEBRUARY 14: ONLY BELIEVE

NUMBERS 13-15; PSALM 45; LUKE 1; 1 CORINTHIANS 1

*M*oses did not send the twelve spies into Canaan in order to find out whether conquest was possible. He sent them to discover how God would do the impossible. The point was not the giants or the challenges—the point was the glory of God. The glory of the impossible is God's alone. The more improbable the conquest, the clearer it is that God did it. God was, in fact, giving His people the privilege of an impossible assignment—that they might revel in His glorious deliverance. Joshua and Caleb got the point, "[The giants] are our bread, their protection has departed from them" (Num. 14:9), but the other spies failed—they failed to believe.

Belief delights the heart of Jesus. Disbelief is doubly dangerous. We not only reject God, but He rejects us (v. 34). If belief makes God deliriously happy, disbelief makes Him blazing mad. Disbelief leads to complaint, complaint leads to rebellion, rebellion leads to God's wrath, and consumed carcasses littering a wilderness (v. 29).

Jesus is looking for individuals who will believe Him for impossible things. When Jesus discovers the man or woman who trusts Him enough to believe for what is impossible, He is thrilled. He entrusts His Spirit and His unlimited power to those simple enough to say: "Yes, Lord, let it be in the world, according to Your Word." The mountain movers are the grasshoppers who believe. John reminds us that our work is to believe. Let us work hard at believing.

BRAHMIN KANAUJIA HINDUS OF INDIA (5,640,000; 0.0% EVANGELICAL)

PRAY FOR THE PEACE THAT RESULTS WHEN MEN AND WOMEN ARE
RECONCILED WITH GOD (JOHN 14:27). PRAY FOR MEN AND WOMEN OF
PEACE (LUKE 10:6) AMONG THE BRAHMIN KANAUJIA.

FEBRUARY 15: GOD'S SIGN IS GOD

NUMBERS 16–18; PSALM 46; LUKE 2; 1 CORINTHIANS 2

*A*n angel gave the shepherds in the field proof of God: "This will be the sign to you: You will find a Babe wrapped in swaddling clothes and lying in a manger" (Luke 2:11). What is the sign that God is with us? *God with us!* God did not leave the guarantee of His presence to a miracle or metaphysical idea. He came down and dwelt among us. We saw Him, we touched Him, we heard Him, we laughed with Him, and we interacted with Him. Through the apostles, we touched the very God of very God. He proved that He is with us by being with us. God is His own sign.

People demand a sign. Ideologies compete in the theoretical arena. Religions strive to outdo each other with works—all in an effort to prove that God is with them. Our sign is simply this: God came down and dwelt among us, and we beheld His glory.

Why do we foolishly strive for evidence of God outside of God? He hears our silly requests for proof and says, "I will give you better than academic proof—I will give you experiential proof." We ask for evidence; God gives the eternal. Our folly is that even when God shows Himself on offer, we still insist on secondary tiers of evidence (circumstantial).

The psalmist understood that the proof of God *for* us is God *with* us: "God is our refuge and strength, a *very present* help in trouble" (Ps. 46:1, emphasis added). As God is His own sign through the incarnation, so must we be His living signs among the nations. We are to be their present (bodily) help in time of trouble. It is a shame to the gospel that reporters and humanists are more intrepid than missionaries. Newspersons and do-gooders often lay down their lives in Afghanistan and Somalia more quickly than the heralds of the King.

God's sign is His incarnate Son suffering with and for mankind. We are to participate in that incarnation by being the present, bodily signs of Jesus in the hell-holes of the earth. In order to stop the plague, Aaron ran with the healing censor and stood "between the dead and the living" (Num. 16:47–48). Christ in us is the only preserving agent available to this world. Let us be the signs of His love. Let us run into the midst of all plagues, stand between the dead and the living, and point to Jesus—the God who became man, the God who is His own sign.

SHAKIA MUSLIMS OF SUDAN (825,000; 0.05% EVANGELICAL)

PRAY THAT BELIEVERS AMONG THE SHAKIA WOULD PROCLAIM THE MESSAGE OF THE GOSPEL CLEARLY AND WOULD MAKE THE MOST OF EVERY OPPORTUNITY GOD PLACES BEFORE THEM (COL. 4:2–5).

FEBRUARY 16: GOD IS OUR INHERITANCE

NUMBERS 19-21; PSALM 47; LUKE 3; 1 CORINTHIANS 3

*M*oses hit a rough patch. In short order his sister died (Num. 20:1), there was no water for his massive congregation (v. 2), and his followers gathered and complained against him (v. 3). Initially, he handled the situation well, falling on his face and experiencing the glory of the Lord (v. 6). Moses listened to God, but made one tragic adjustment to God's instructions by striking the rock rather than speaking to it. God gave the people water but denied Moses the Promised Land. At first blush it seems that God was too harsh. A little more information gives a better perspective.

No One Is Allowed to Rebel. God explained His rationale later in the narrative when He said that Aaron would not enter the Promised Land because "both of you rebelled against My word" (v. 24). No one can disobey God's word . . . not missionaries, not ministers, not Moses. When we meet with God, when we have responsibility to lead others into the presence of God, when God speaks to us, we must obey what He tells us. We have to get the how, when, and what right regardless of who we are—or face the consequences.

Nothing Should Point Others to Us. Paul explained to the Corinthians that we are but messengers through whom others believe (1 Cor. 3:5). When God's messengers participate in God's message in a way that draws attention to themselves, God is offended. God told Moses to speak to the rock— instead, Moses struck it. On the surface this seems innocuous, but God wants the primary communication of His message to come through speaking as our actions can detract from the source. Of course, we have seen equally offensive examples of the opposite—the abuse of hypocritical words without loving actions. Yet, God insists that the focus of any act or speech be on Him alone.

When our actions (even in the attempt to communicate God's message) convey the idea that we are the source or the answer, this steals glory from God, and He does not tolerate such lechery. To the simple, striking the rock might have indicated that Moses was the source of the miracle. Speaking rather than striking would have removed Moses one half-step from the miracle and provided confirmation that God had done this. God punished Moses because Moses acted in the flesh when he knew better. And yes, the more spiritual authority you have, the more you must obey God implicitly.

No Inheritance Matches God Himself. Moses' primary passion was not to cross a river and die fulfilled. Moses' all-consuming desire was to be in God's presence. Pitching a tent in the Promised Land would never fulfill Moses—his only joy was God. Success in ministry is not the goal. God is the goal—and that is what God gave to Moses.

BERBER, KABYLE MUSLIMS OF ALGERIA (3,461,000; 2.0% EVANGELICAL)

PLEAD THAT THE BERBER, KABYLE WILL UNDERSTAND THAT HOPE FOR FORGIVENESS AND ACCEPTANCE WITH GOD IS AVAILABLE ONLY THROUGH JESUS' WORK ON THE CROSS (1 COR. 1:18).

FEBRUARY 17: THE PRECIOUS WORD

NUMBERS 22–24; PSALM 48; LUKE 4; 1 CORINTHIANS 4

Perversity of Our Words. You do not want God as an opponent. Balaam clearly heard from God the first time: He was not to go with Balak's lackeys (Num. 22:13). But after repeated requests and appeals to Balaam's vanity, he looked for a way to compromise. He went to Balak, verbally maintaining the high ground even as his donkey carried him toward disaster. God considered this compromise perverse (v. 32). We cannot endeavor both to obey God and to gain honor and riches. To compromise the message is to choose God as an enemy. Even stupid donkeys recognize this as folly.

Provision of God's Word. God supplies the seed both for eating and sowing. He put words in Balaam's mouth (vv. 38; 23:5, 12, 16). As long as we are more afraid of people than of God, we will be guilty of Balaam's error: compromise for personal comfort. This compromise will always lead to disaster. God supplies what we must say. We need not stress about content and can devote our energies to obedience. As long as we fear God more than people, He will continue to provide what we should say.

Protection of God's Word. God's sword can both block and thrust. God's Word is both what we speak on offense and how we protect ourselves on defense. When Satan tempted Jesus (Luke 4), Jesus repeatedly referred to the Word. One of the premier ways to protect ourselves from temptation (vulnerability to sin) is to memorize the Word of God and to quote it out loud in times of duress.

Proclamation of God's Word. Jesus quoted Isaiah in a passage that is often used to promote a social gospel (Luke 4:18–19). The verbs Jesus chose to highlight, however, are *preach, heal, proclaim, set at liberty,* and *proclaim.* The priority is on proclamation with an implication that healing and deliverance come from the spoken word. As much as we do not like to hear it (and as much as speaking has been abused), God still ordains that we communicate the gospel primarily through preaching. Faith *still* "comes by hearing, and hearing by the word of God" (Rom. 10:17).

Power of God's Word. Proclamation is valid only if done with power and authority. "What a word this is!" remarked Jesus' hearers when He spoke with power and authority (Luke 4:36). By His words, Jesus rebuked both demons (vv. 35, 41) and sickness (v. 39). Little in the world is as tedious as hypocritical words—which are powerless. Paul reminds us that "the Kingdom of God is not in [an empty] word but in power" (1 Cor. 4:20).

Parameters of God's Word. There are boundaries in life, even boundaries to our thinking. God's Word gives us the "riverbanks" of our thoughts. Some things should not be asked; some things should not be considered. We are to learn "not to think beyond what is written" (1 Cor. 4:6). How precious that God's Word both gives life and keeps us from death.

NORTH IRAQI MUSLIMS OF TURKEY (516,000; 0.1% EVANGELICAL)

PRAY THAT BELIEVERS AMONG THE NORTHERN IRAQIS WILL ENDURE PERSECUTION
IN A CHRISTLIKE MANNER AND WILL GIVE THEIR LIVES FOR THE SAKE OF THE
GOSPEL IF NECESSARY (1 PET. 2:21–23).

FEBRUARY 18: GOD'S ZEAL

NUMBERS 25-27; PSALM 49; LUKE 5; 1 CORINTHIANS 5

Zeal for Holiness. Sexual sin led the people of God into idolatry (Num. 25:1–2). While all sin is heinous, there is something about sexual sin that perverts from the inside out and affects others. Eleazar the High Priest acted ruthlessly against sexual sin. He put a spear through the offending couple, stopped the plague, turned back God's wrath, and was rewarded with God's covenant of peace (v. 12). The New Testament version of this zeal is found in 1 Corinthians 5 where Paul instructed, "In the name of the Lord Jesus Christ . . . deliver such a one to Satan for the destruction of the flesh . . . " (v. 4). Those in authority must deal harshly with sexual sin. We must be ruthless, zealous with God's zeal against any sexual impurity in our own lives.

Zeal for Praise. In his book *The Insanity of God*, Nik Ripken tells of a Russian pastor who was unjustly imprisoned for seventeen years. In his cell, every dawn of those seventeen years, the pastor rose, stood at attention on his bed, raised his hands toward heaven, and sang to God at the top of his lungs. Fellow prisoners mocked him, but he sang on, zealous to greet each new day with praise to Jesus. After seventeen years, his captors marched him to a place of execution. All the prisoners stood at attention in their cells and sang out this pastor's song of praise to the heavens. Not knowing how to respond, the communist authorities released him.[5] We must be dedicated, zealous with God's zeal, for praise. "The upright shall have dominion . . . in the morning" (Ps. 49:14).

Zeal for the Impossible. Jesus told Simon and his colleagues to "launch out into the deep and let down your nets for a catch" (Luke 5:4). Having fished all night, Simon knew that history was against him, but he agreed to cast the nets because Jesus asked. When Simon attempted what he knew was impossible, the harvest exceeded his ability to conserve—so he called in other partners to help. When God gave the impossible, Simon was awed and horrified that God would use such sinful vessels and would visit them in person. Our zeal for the impossible is only maintained in purity if we are both awed and horrified that God would use us to do the impossible. The impossible will not happen without humility and without dependence on one another. These seem to be God's requirements for overwhelming breakthrough.

Zeal for God's Presence. How did Jesus respond to healings, miracles, power unleashed, and the resulting fame and recognition? He "withdrew into the wilderness and prayed" (v. 16). We cannot sustain zeal for God, nor steward it wisely, if we are not often in His presence. The zeal of God is His to give, to steward, and to renew. Only as we spend daily extravagant time abiding with Jesus will God's zeal bring us life rather than destruction.

DOSADH HINDUS OF INDIA (4,956,000; 0.0% EVANGELICAL)

PRAY THAT GOD WOULD RAISE UP MISSIONARIES FROM ALL OVER THE WORLD TO WORK TOGETHER TO PLANT THE CHURCH AMONG THE DOSADHS (MATT. 9:37).

FEBRUARY 19: WEAPON OF MASS DESTRUCTION

NUMBERS 28-30; PSALM 50; LUKE 6; 1 CORINTHIANS 6

*O*ut of the abundance of the heart [the] mouth speaks" (Luke 6:45) and, unfortunately, missionaries often speak scathing destruction. Attila the Hun was wimpy compared to what Christians sometimes speak. Our tongues set all kinds of forests on fire (James 3:5)—and we do it so sweetly. Four misuses of the tongue disqualify us from declaring the statutes of the Lord (Ps. 50:16): we give our mouths to evil (v. 19); our tongues speak deceit (v. 19); we speak against our brother (v. 20); and we slander our mother's son (v. 20).

Christ-followers can be some of the best liars when they exaggerate and subtly shade the truth to their own advantage. Disciples can be the most competitive, vindictive, slanderous, and gossipy of all God's creations—and feel good about it. The danger for the proclaimer is the unrighteous use of the tongue. A mouth framed for the glory of God can also be used to carve up brothers and sisters.

Words that destroy—especially words that destroy brothers and sisters, the innocent, and the vulnerable—are nothing like God. We think He is altogether like us (v. 21), but He is altogether different in His life-giving words. Our destructive words, spoken from our deceptively destructive hearts, are the opposite of holiness—they are evil. The opposite of evil words are words of praise. God says, "Whoever offers praise glorifies Me," (v. 23). Praising God and encouraging others is the opposite of tongue death—these are mouth-to-life resuscitation.

Because words are powerful and a priority means of communication, they are dangerous. We communicate the gospel by preaching, for that is how faith comes. Faith does not come by doing—not according to the Scriptures. Faith does not even come by loving—not according to the Scriptures. Faith comes by hearing, and hearing by the Word of God (Rom. 10:17). Hypocritical words are so heinous and empty words so vain precisely because anointed words have such power to change lives.

The antidote for evil words is not action without explanation—it is the foolishness of preaching that brings life. There is a clear biblical priority on the proclamation of the gospel, and for this reason the Devil goes to great lengths to discredit all proclaimers. The goal of the Enemy is not to kill us but to silence us—for in silencing us, he aims to render God mute. When we live in an ungodly way, we do the Devil's work for him and silence ourselves. Words intended to bring life deafen the hearer, damage the speaker, and discredit the Giver.

NUBIAN MUSLIMS OF SUDAN (248,000; 0.0% EVANGELICAL)

PRAY THAT THE NUBIANS WOULD FEEL AND KNOW THE BURDEN OF SIN AND WOULD COME TO JESUS FOR FORGIVENESS AND SALVATION (MATT. 11:28-30).

FEBRUARY 20: SUBMISSIVE AUTHORITY

NUMBERS 31-33; PSALM 51; LUKE 7; 1 CORINTHIANS 7

*J*esus encountered a Roman centurion, a man with at least one hundred direct reports (Luke 7). Through his understanding of submission, this Roman authority exhibited more faith than anyone Jesus had met. "I also am a man placed under authority," he said (v. 8). "Say the word, and my servant will be healed" (v. 7). When we submit to Jesus, we prove that we trust Him.

Effectual authority is derived from submission. In order to have life-transforming authority, you need to be submitted to authority. Anyone can be a tyrant, but only the submitted lead others to life. Counterintuitively, we gain authority by submitting to authority. Authority does not result from dominance (that is bullying) or power (that is extortion). Authority comes from submission and trust in God. Jesus' power resulted from His submission to the Father. Our power results from the depth of our submission to Jesus. That depth is tested by how well we submit to our earthly, imperfect authorities. When we submit to our authorities, we prove that we trust Jesus.

We demonstrate our faith by how we submit to earthly authority. Do we believe that God is sovereign? Did He place these fallen humans over us? In mission and ministry, an array of men and women who walk with a limp will lead us. Do we trust that God can speak to them about us? It is a trust issue—not so much trusting them to hear God as trusting Him to overcome their liabilities and use their strengths for our well-being. This takes faith—not faith out in the merry ether but faith on the muddy fields of our daily lives and decisions.

This trust requires brokenness and a belief that God, not my immediate authority, is the principle actor in my life. Faith understands that authority in my life is there only because there is someone above that person and so on all the way up the authority chain to the ultimate and perfect authority of God. When we trust God, we can trust our human authority. This trust is linked to brokenness, for brokenness bestows the grace to submit to others. Brokenness is a strong, protective force. When we are broken before God, He acts in all His power (Ps. 51:17). Our protection and defense are all about Him. The contrite and humble in heart trust that God will defend them in the highest court. There is rest and safety in that belief. There is also blessing to those under our authority for they, too, will experience God's justice and protection through our hands—as we lead with submitted authority.

MOOR MUSLIMS OF MOROCCO (3,057,000; 0.0% EVANGELICAL)

PRAY THAT GOD WOULD UNVEIL THE CROSS AND WOULD REMOVE THE VEIL ON THE MINDS AND SPIRITS OF THE MOOR (2 COR. 3:16-17).

FEBRUARY 21: AFRAID OF JESUS

NUMBERS 34-36; PSALM 52; LUKE 8; 1 CORINTHIANS 8

*E*verybody is afraid of Jesus; some just do not know it yet. If you are not afraid of Jesus, you either have not seen Him as He is or you are stupid—or maybe both. In Luke 8 we have a litany of people who were terrified of Jesus. Their fear caused different reactions.

The disciples initially feared they would perish in the raging sea, but when Jesus calmed the waters, they become more afraid of Him than the storm. "Who can this be? For He commands even the winds and water, and they obey Him!" (v. 25) Greater fears overcame lesser fears.

Next, the demons joined the disciples in fearing Jesus. A legion of evil spirits trembled before Him (v. 28) and begged Him not to torment them before their time. The demons were terrified of Jesus and His authority to condemn them to the abyss before their time.

The denizens of Gadarene joined the fearful queue. They feared Jesus would take away their source of income. They preferred their pigs to the Prince of Life and Provision. Their fear of what Jesus would do to them caused them to drive Him away (v. 37).

A daughter fell at Jesus' feet, afraid of what her plea might cost her (v. 47). Her fear of sickness and death led her to approach the Lord, and her faith was rewarded with healing.

Disciples, demons, denizens, and daughters were all afraid of Jesus, as they should have been. If we are not afraid of Jesus, we have misunderstood Him. The point is not fear—that is common to all who encounter Him. The point is whether or not that fear drives us close to Him or drives Him away from us. The choice is determined by the greatest fears in our lives. If our greatest fears revolve around security, self-preservation, and safety, then Jesus makes us uncomfortable because His presence seems to undermine our efforts at stability. If our greatest fears are sin and being separated from His presence, then our intimidating encounters with Him lead us to pursue Him, no matter the cost.

If you are not afraid of Jesus, you should be. If you are afraid of Jesus, that fear should draw you closer to Him. It seems counterintuitive, but fear can lead to faith. Perfect love casts out lesser fears and teaches us to embrace the appropriate fear of the Lord who commands waves, demons, and sickness to do His bidding. Do not be afraid to fear Jesus.

RIND MUSLIMS OF PAKISTAN (773,000; 0.0% EVANGELICAL)

PRAY THAT BELIEVERS AMONG THE RIND WOULD BE SET FREE FROM A SPIRIT OF FEAR OF WHAT MAY COME AND WOULD BOLDLY PROCLAIM THE TRUTH OF THE GOSPEL

(2 TIM. 1:6-8).

FEBRUARY 22: DEATH ACCOMPLISHED

DEUTERONOMY 1-3; PSALM 53; LUKE 9; 1 CORINTHIANS 9

*A*s Jesus prayed, His face was altered (Luke 9:29). Moses and Elijah, glorified by death, appeared to Jesus and spoke to Him about "His decease which He was about to accomplish" (v. 31). Jesus descended the mountain, once again encouraged to die well.

Death—the last enemy—is intimidating. We dread it, fear it, and clutch at the last vestiges of our pitiful earthly life in panic. Those who have gone before us in the faith remind us that death is something to be attained. It is our final earthly accomplishment.

How well Satan has convinced us of the superiority and finality of this boring temporal existence. Our spirits have become clouded and our eyes blurred. We have forgotten that we are sleeping, that these are the shadowlands and we live dimly. We have forgotten that we are limited by flesh, sin, and the Devil. For those submitted to Jesus, physical death is but ultimate spiritual birth. It ushers us into the unmitigated presence of Jesus. Physical death is our ticket home.

Physical death is not the only accomplishment to be gained, however, for in this temporal life we also have the possibility of dying to self. It is the fool who lives without consulting God or who tries to die to self in his or her own power (Ps. 53:1). God wants to give us the promised land of a life lived for others, but we must go in and possess it. In this battle to die to self, God will go before us, He will fight for us, He will carry us, and He will search out a place for us (Deut. 1). But the promised land of self-denial still requires our belief (that it is truly a place of refuge) and our action. Unbelief in God is betrayal. We must believe there is joy and liberty in dying to self if we are going to stand in that territory and possess it.

When we die to self, we begin to wake up to heavenly joys. There is resurrection life that can only be experienced on the other side of death. The eternal fulfillment of this will only be realized when we cross Jordan for ourselves, but God in His mercy allows us a foretaste. Dying to self gives us an appetizer of the glorious joy that will be ours forever when we awake from this earthly slumber. It is a preview, if you will, of the joy set before us. Therefore, dying to self is not an accomplishment in the merit badge sense. It is its own reward, for it gives us a taste of heaven. Do not starve your soul by being reluctant to die.

BANIA AGARWAL HINDUS OF INDIA (4,908,000; 0.0% EVANGELICAL)

PRAY FOR THE WORD OF GOD IN WRITTEN, ORAL, MUSICAL, AND DRAMATIC FORMS TO BE
TRANSLATED AND TO RISE AMONG THE BANIA AGARWAL
(ISA. 55:10-11).

FEBRUARY 23: THE PRIMACY OF HEARING

DEUTERONOMY 4-6; PSALM 54; LUKE 10; 1 CORINTHIANS 10

*T*o listen is to live (Deut. 4:1). When we cultivate the ability to hear Jesus, this "is our wisdom" (v. 6). Listening to Jesus is a discipline, a spiritual muscle that is strengthened by exercise. Hearing is part and parcel of the greatest commandment: *"Hear,* O Israel, and be careful to observe it [Deut. 6:3]. . . . *Hear,* O Israel: The LORD our God, the LORD is one" (v. 4, emphasis added). The first imperative of the Great Commandment is "Hear!"

Jesus speaks to us in various ways, some of them surprising. The things that Jesus speaks to us are enough. We do not have to seek frantically for other input. "These words the LORD spoke to all your assembly, in the mountain from the midst of the fire, the cloud, and the thick darkness, with a loud voice; and He added no more" (Deut. 5:22). I love the parameter of Moses' reminder: "He added no more." We do not need extra. God has spoken to us through His Word and in these last days through His Son. We do not depend on others. Jesus is the beloved Word of God—we hear Him!

Jesus loves it when we listen to Him. We are so distracted with serving that sometimes we forget to listen to Him (Luke 10:40). He reminds us that "one thing is needed"—the thing that Mary chose to do: sit at Jesus' feet and *hear* His word (v. 39). To hear is to be near.

Jesus loves it when we listen to Him because it means we are coming close to Him intentionally, tuning out other voices to concentrate on His. Some of the voices we need to tune out belong to other disciples. Sometimes we need to turn off the worship music, close the devotional, put away the commentary, ignore the podcast, drape a towel over the television, and sit at Jesus' feet—just to hear Him.

Go ahead now and listen to Jesus. Make it a habit to hear. To hear is to be near. God's presence is His power. Close this book . . . shut off the electronic device . . . turn off your music—sit down at the feet of Jesus, just you and your Bible, and listen. This is the one thing you need.

BEJA MUSLIMS OF SUDAN (1,949,000; 0.0% EVANGELICAL)

PRAY THAT GOD WOULD POUR OUT HIS SPIRIT ON THE BEJA PEOPLE AND THEY WOULD SEE DREAMS AND VISIONS OF JESUS. PRAY, THAT THEY WOULD BE POWERFULLY SAVED AND EMPOWERED TO BE HIS WITNESSES

(JOEL 2:28-32).

FEBRUARY 24: THE WEAK CHOICE

DEUTERONOMY 7-9; PSALM 55; LUKE 11; 1 CORINTHIANS 11

To live among Arabs is to fall in love with them. Loving Arabs opens you to both their joys and their prejudices. You cannot linger long with the Arabs before experiencing their opinionated passion about the Jewish people. Years ago, when my wife and I were commissioned by our home church to reach out to Muslims, a Messianic pastor gave us our first Arabic Bible and exhorted us: Those who work with Muslims should frequently pray for the Jewish people; those who work among Jews should consistently pray for the Arabs.

Neither arrogance on the part of the Jews and their devoted supporters nor angst on the part of Arabs and their friends is mitigated when we understand the circumstances of God's choosing: "The LORD did not set His love on you nor choose you because you were more in number than any other people, for you were the least of all peoples" (Deut. 7:7). God chose the Jewish people because they were the smallest and weakest. They are similar to the turtle found perched on a fence post, hard-shell belly on the flat top of the wooden post, legs waggling in the air. The only way the turtle got there was for someone to place it there.

We often play soccer in the cool Cairo nights. We rent a small, synthetic-grass field, turn on the lights, and enjoy "the beautiful game." Last night we were playing, and one player was considerably superior to all of us. We kept changing the teams, giving him the weaker and weaker players. To our frustration, he continued to win, making anyone who played with him better, including a six-year-old boy.

God stood on the court of history and surveyed those who could play alongside Him. He looked over the strong, capable, and obvious choices. Then His eyes went to the most insignificant people He could find— and that is who He picked. He wanted the weaklings for His team, and the reason is simple: All the glory would go to Him. When God assembles a team of insignificant people and wins with them, it is pretty obvious who is responsible for the victory.

Those of us who are passionate for God's purposes with the Jewish people can be encouraged, for in them we have the pristine example of how God uses the foolish things of the world to shame the wise, the weak things to conquer the strong. Those of us passionate about God's promises to the Arabs can likewise rejoice (and relax), for His decision to choose the Jews does not diminish the worth of the Arabs. His choice of the Jews is not about them; it is about Him. If God can use them, He can certainly use you and me. If God can use the insignificant, intimidated Jewish people to win fame for His name, He can certainly use the larger, stronger peoples of the earth for that same eternal glory.

YEMENI MUSLIMS OF YEMEN (6,072,000; 0.0% EVANGELICAL)

PRAY THAT CHRISTIANS FROM AROUND THE WORLD WOULD WORK TOGETHER TO REACH THE YEMENI AND THAT THE YEMENI WOULD BE JOINED TO THE BODY OF CHRIST (JOHN 17:20-23).

FEBRUARY 25: BATTLE PRAISE

DEUTERONOMY 10-12; PSALM 56; LUKE 12; 1 CORINTHIANS 12

*O*ur spiritual battle is to the death. When we represent Jesus among the nations, we stand for Him against all presumptive authorities and demonic powers. We would be fools to think we can do this in framework of peace. Jesus, after all, came to bring "fire on the earth" (Luke 12:49) and not peace "but rather division" (v. 51). Our battle is to the death.

In our ceaseless battle we have one key weapon of renewal—praise. Because the pressure will never stop, because the evil hordes will keep on pressing, it is imperative that we learn to refresh while we fight. Battle praise does this for us. "He is your praise . . . who has done for you these great and awesome things" (Deut. 10:21). He is also our praise who will do more. Praise is not just post-victory. Praise is something we express in the midst of warfare. When we praise—as we swing our swords— we act in faith, and faith always delights the heart of Jesus.

Praise should be our lifestyle, not relegated to the high moments of victory parades. Praise should be part of our normal life, part of our battle, part of our reaction to every circumstance. When we praise in suffering, when we praise in prison, when we praise in sickness, when we praise in disappointment, when we praise in tragedy, when we praise in pain—we fight at a turbo level. When we praise despite all outward and inward resistance, we penetrate the highest levels of worship. With our praise we say to the Enemy: "Is that all you've got?" As Jesus said, they may kill the body, but what more can they do (Luke 12:4)? If prison and torture and death elicit praise from both the departed and those who faithfully remain, what more can the Devil do?

In our ceaseless battles, let us join the psalmist and declare over and over again: We will praise His word (Ps. 56:4, 10); we will render praise (v. 12); and we will do so in trial and at trials, in courts and in confession. Denial of Jesus at any level is blasphemy against the Holy Spirit, so we resolve and vow that we shall ever open our mouths and declare that Jesus is the Son of God. Our confession before men will be praise to God the Son, praise to God the Spirit, and praise to God the Father. There is a battle for our praise. Praise is the battle. Let us be vigilant that our praise will always, ever, go to Jesus.

ARAIN MUSLIMS OF PAKISTAN (9,867,000; 0.0% EVANGELICAL)

PRAY THAT THE HEARTS OF THE ARAIN WOULD BE LIKE GOOD SOIL,
READY TO HEAR THE GOSPEL AND TO RESPOND
(MATT. 7:1-8, 18-23).

*T*he biblical optimist realizes that Scripture has a fairly dim view of unredeemed humanity. People are prone to wander, and they tend to self-destruct. Though God's people remain as preserving salt, trouble will increase until Jesus returns in glory. Wheat and tares will grow together until the end, but Jesus is coming back because people have made a mess of things and will continue to do so. In this milieu of a decaying world, terrible things will happen. When bad things happen, we need to ask the right question. Jesus' point in Luke 13:1–5 is startling. He said that we all deserve to be tortured and have towers fall on us. The question is not why bad things happen to good people; the point is that we all deserve tragedy. The real wonder is that good things happen to any of us, wicked as we are.

While it is true that sickness is a bond from Satan (v. 16) and evil manifests itself against us in diverse ways, it is also true that in select cases we embrace and pursue what is difficult for the glory of God and for the gospel of Jesus Christ. When Jesus was warned to flee Herod, he reminded that old fox that resurrection was the destiny and the cross a necessary tool. We, too, must each press toward our Calvary. In the event that we are the hunted and evil is the aggressor, the Scriptures give us hope. The writer of Psalm 57 described being swallowed up, set on fire, hunted by spears, stabbed with sharp swords, and bowed down by assault. Evil does hunt us—doggedly. In these moments we have essential recourse.

Take Shelter. We make our refuge under the shelter of God's wings until the calamities pass by (Ps. 57:1). There is a land of Goshen. There is a place of quiet rest. There are times when we are covered and protected. There are moments for wise withdrawal and waiting out the storm in a protected place.

Stay Steadfast. At other times our shelter is the presence of Jesus, and we experience His dynamic reality in the course of prison, suffering, sickness, loss, and grief. In these moments, His love within helps us not to be provoked and not to think evil but to bear all things, to believe all things, to hope all things, and to endure all things (1 Cor. 13:4–5, 7). Love is magnified under pressure. Love from above holds us steady in tragedy. The real proof of the people of God is the love that is released from our lives when we are crushed.

Sing. When we are hunted, it unsettles our pursuer if we sing. Who sings, who praises as they flee for their lives? Who whistles in the night when the monsters close in? Singing under pressure does two things in the spirit realm: It declaws the Enemy (he does not know how to handle a person who praises under duress), and it magnifies God. When we sing while we are hunted, God is exalted above the heavens and glorified above all the earth (Ps.57:11).

BOYA HINDUS OF INDIA (3,871,000; 0.0% EVANGELICAL)

PRAY FOR THE PEACE THAT RESULTS WHEN MEN AND WOMEN ARE RECONCILED WITH GOD (JOHN 14:27). PRAY FOR MEN AND WOMEN OF PEACE
(LUKE 10:6) AMONG THE BOYAS.

FEBRUARY 27: PROPHETIC LEGACY

*T*he Bible says we should desire to prophesy (1 Cor. 14:1). It demystifies prophecy and frames it in terms of encouragement and edification of the church. We are, in fact, exhorted to excel in edifying those who belong to Jesus (v. 12). Interestingly, this means we are to work hard at exercising and improving the prophetic gifts we should all seek. There is a discipline, an order, and a growth cycle to prophecy. Prophecy is not the proprietary domain of the wild and woolly. All of God's people should seek to prophesy. We should seek to excel in edifying and encouraging one another.

Paul concluded in 1 Corinthians 14:15–19 that he *would* pray in the Spirit (to build up his inner man) and he *would* prophesy (to edify and encourage the people of God). Our conclusion must be the same: we will pray in the Spirit privately and we will increasingly prophesy in public. In the ordered life of the body of Christ, prophecy is evidence that God continues to visit His people.

There is an active component to prophecy. We should eagerly bless others through encouragement and edification. We should enter a friend's home, walk into a Bible study, and prepare for regular worship service with the intention that the Spirit will speak through us. Rather than participate in communal worship with a view to receive, we need to attend business meetings and family devotions with the intention to open our mouths and allow Jesus to speak through us. When we actively look for someone to edify, we take the lower place. When we wait for others to encourage us, when we hold our tongues that others may use theirs to praise us, we ascend to the higher place (Luke 14:10–11). When we lay down what others think of us in order to build up the body of Christ, we humble ourselves and delight the Giver of the Spirit.

Salt that has lost its flavor is useless (v. 34). Likewise, the disciple who has ceased to bless others verbally is useless. Prophecy (edification and exhortation) does not preclude acts of service, but all believers are to exercise a verbal gift. Edification and exhortation do not preclude rebuke or prediction either, but the wise prophet is selective and occasional in those aspects of prophecy and concentrates on what will encourage and edify.

As prophets, all believers should open their mouths in an orderly manner and encourage and edify the body of Christ. We should desire this gift. We should discipline ourselves to actively use this gift. We should learn from the Holy Spirit and spiritual elders how to grow in this gift. Perhaps most importantly, we need to remember that the prophet who speaks his own words will die (Deut. 18:20). Let our prophetic legacy be a trail of people encouraged to love and obey Jesus—not the tragedy of unfulfilled words from a soiled mouth and a hypocritical heart.

FUR MUSLIMS OF SUDAN (962,000; 0.0% EVANGELICAL)

PRAY THAT BELIEVERS AMONG THE FUR WOULD PROCLAIM THE MESSAGE OF THE GOSPEL CLEARLY AND WOULD MAKE THE MOST OF EVERY OPPORTUNITY GOD PLACES BEFORE THEM

(COL. 4:2–5).

FEBRUARY 28: JESUS, VERY GOD OF VERY GOD

DEUTERONOMY 19-21; PSALM 59; LUKE 15; 1 CORINTHIANS 15

*T*o downplay the deity of Jesus is to be a false witness. We cannot pretend not to know what we know. The clear revelation of Scripture, the self-testimony of Christ, the witness of the Holy Spirit, and the affirmations of the apostles and church fathers all contribute to our clear understanding and the irrefutable evidence that Jesus is God.

Romans 1:4 reminds us that Jesus "was declared to be the Son of God with power according to the Spirit of holiness, by the resurrection from the dead." It is true that the title "Son of God" has connotations of kingly power and rule over the nations while the title "Son of Man" (the preferred term Jesus used to describe Himself) has connotations of deity (as introduced in Daniel). It is also undeniable that the resurrection proved the deity of Jesus. People can die; only God can die and rise again.

The focus of the apostles' teaching was on the resurrection. Why? Atonement is possible only if Jesus is God, and the resurrection proved that He is God. If Christ is not risen, if He is not God, then our preaching is empty and our faith in vain. If Christ is not risen, then both our faith and our witness are futile (1 Cor. 15:14–17).

It has become popular to downplay the deity of Jesus in witness. This is a tragic and costly error. Contrary to current opinion, Jesus did not downplay His divinity. He constantly emphasized it. He forgave sin, He overruled natural law (walked on water, calmed storms, multiplied bread), and declared Himself equal to God. People hated Him and killed Him for His claims of deity. To downplay the deity of Jesus in witness, even to Muslims . . . especially to Muslims . . . is false witness.

Do not be embarrassed by the mystery of Jesus as fully man and fully God. All false religions stumble on the nature of Christ. There is only one God. There is only One who has been fully man and fully God. This is the gospel that saves. First Corinthians 15:1–7 declares that Christ died for our sins according to the Scriptures (only man can die). He was buried. He rose the third day according to the Scriptures (only God can rise from the dead). He was seen by Cephas, then by the twelve. After that He was seen by over 500 brethren at once, by James, by the apostles, and by Paul. We too—born out of time—must testify unashamedly that Jesus is God.

MAZANDERANI, TABRI MUSLIMS OF IRAN (4,115,000; 0.0% EVANGELICAL)

PLEAD THAT THE MAZANDERANI, TABRI WILL UNDERSTAND THAT HOPE FOR FORGIVENESS AND ACCEPTANCE WITH GOD IS AVAILABLE ONLY THROUGH JESUS' WORK ON THE CROSS (1 COR. 1:18).

March

"*I USED TO THINK THAT PRAYER SHOULD HAVE
THE FIRST PLACE AND TEACHING THE SECOND. I NOW FEEL IT
WOULD BE TRUER TO GIVE PRAYER THE FIRST, SECOND, AND THIRD
PLACES AND TEACHING THE FOURTH.*"

—*James O. Fraser*

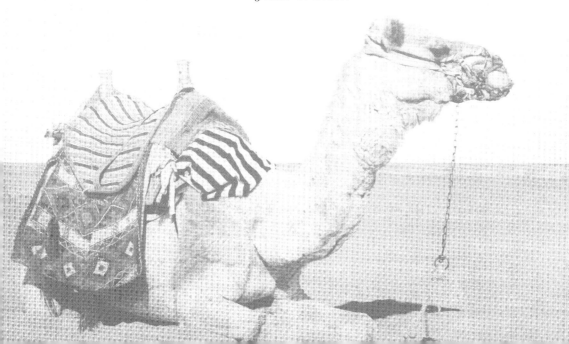

MARCH 1: ANATHEMA

DEUTERONOMY 22-24; PSALM 60; LUKE 16; 1 CORINTHIANS 16

Somewhere along the way, Jesus acquired fuzzy status. A misconception crept into the church—and was embraced by the world—that regulated Jesus to a likable, people-pleasing, everyone's-kind-uncle figure. An honest reading of Scripture shows Jesus to be very different, very divisive, very dangerous, and very difficult to get along with . . . *on our terms.*

In Psalm 60 God chose some to be helmets (Ephraim), some to be lawgivers (Judah), and some to be bedpans (Moab). A thrown shoe is the highest insult in the Middle East, and God cast His shoe over an entire civilization: Edom. In Luke 16:15 Jesus declared: "What is highly esteemed among men is an abomination in the sight of God." Jesus clearly pointed out that hell is real and hot—three times He described the "torment" of Hades (Luke 16:23, 24, 28). Deuteronomy 22:5 reveals that God considers gender blending an abomination. Deuteronomy 23:1–4 shocks us by pointing out that an inclusive God barred the emasculated, illegitimate, and foreigner from His holy place. Our good and gracious God throws the words *abomination* and *anathema* (accursed) around pretty freely.

Jesus divides, provokes, insults, challenges, criticizes, rebukes, judges, condemns, destroys, and acts in a thousand other ways that are not inclusive, kind, soft, gentle, or accommodating. Of all the harsh and shocking actions of Jesus, one of the most arresting is this assertion: If you do not love Jesus, you are accursed (1 Cor. 16:22). The God who can turn curses into blessings (Deut. 23:5) can certainly take our blessings away and turn them into curses—and it seems He does so when we do not love Him.

The troubling and awe-inducing aspects of God diminish neither His goodness nor His greatness. Because God is unapproachable (wrapped in impenetrable light), the incarnation is stronger, not weaker, and pure . . . not sullied. Because God is just, exclusive, holy, righteous, and holds impossible standards, His embrace and forgiveness is deeper, wider, fuller, and more marvelous . . . not less. Because God is love, His hatred for sin is just and righteous . . . not hypocritical or twisted.

Because we are cursed, doomed, tortured, tormented, and condemned when we do not love Jesus, when we *do* love Him it is all the more sweet, rewarding, and fulfilling. Curses and blessings complement each other in the sense that they make each other stronger. Strange as it seems, just as there is a promised curse on those who do not love Jesus, there is an equally fierce opposite: Those who love Him are and will be magnificently blessed. Let us stay on the Godward side of *anathema.*

SHILHA, SOUTHERN MUSLIMS OF MOROCCO (3,023,000; 0.1% EVANGELICAL)

PRAY THAT THE BELIEVERS AMONG THE SHILHA WILL ENDURE PERSECUTION IN A CHRISTLIKE MANNER AND WILL GIVE THEIR LIVES FOR THE SAKE OF THE GOSPEL IF NECESSARY (1 PETER 2:21-23).

MARCH 2: COLLECTIVE SUFFERING

DEUTERONOMY 25–27; PSALM 61; LUKE 17; 2 CORINTHIANS 1

*R*ecently, I was in Jordan near the border with Syria, where I listened to an Arab in Bedouin garb play the American tune "Yankee Doodle Dandy" on Scottish bagpipes while standing in an ancient Roman amphitheater. Today I am in Tunisia thinking about my Sudanese and international friends who are gathered in Ethiopia to listen to the Holy Spirit. More than 100 of these colleagues have been kicked out of Sudan over the past three months. It is reported that almost fifty Sudanese are currently imprisoned in Khartoum, and some of them have been shamefully treated and abused.

Jesus never intended for us to suffer alone. We may not be able to cross oceans or deserts and sit in lonely cells with colleagues, but we can traverse that distance spiritually and bear the burdens of our brothers in prayer. Knowing that they do not agonize alone empowers followers of Jesus under duress to bear unimaginable suffering. Collaborative suffering is bearable suffering.

Knowing from Scripture and from history that others have suffered and blossomed in pain is necessary preparation for our own trials. We can shore up our souls for trouble by reading and meditating on how those who have gone before us found strength to glorify Jesus before snarling beasts and men. The trials of others help us, and our trials, in turn, help others. "Blessed be . . . the God of all comfort, who comforts us in all our tribulation that we may be able to comfort those who are in any trouble, with the comfort with which we ourselves are comforted by God" (2 Cor. 1:3–4). Paul went on to explain that both sufferings and consolations abound in Christ, and because there is a collective experience of both, there is endurance for salvation and consolation.

If our collective prior suffering helps those now under pressure, their current anguish also comforts us. Our suffering helps others. When my Sudanese brothers and sisters suffer, it draws me to them. It puts my marginal trials in perspective and gives me courage for my challenges. God, too, participates in collaborative suffering—primarily because He suffered for us but also by allowing suffering so "that we should not trust in ourselves, but in God who raises the dead" (2 Cor. 1:9). When our hearts are overwhelmed, God leads us to Himself, the rock that is higher than us (Ps. 61:2). Suffering collectively teaches the body of Christ to depend on Him and to anticipate life from death. Suffering is intended to be redemptive, and suffering for the gospel always results in unreached people responding to the gospel.

AZERBAIJANI, AZERI TURK MUSLIMS OF AZERBAIJAN (278,000; 0.15% EVANGELICAL)

PRAY THAT GOD WOULD RAISE UP MISSIONARIES FROM ALL OVER THE WORLD TO PLANT THE CHURCH TOGETHER AMONG AZERBAIJANI, AZERI TURKS (MATT. 9:37).

MARCH 3: OVERWHELMED

DEUTERONOMY 28-30; PSALM 62; LUKE 18; 2 CORINTHIANS 2

Overwhelmed by Evil. I am looking out my window at an Arabian city of millions, wondering how on earth the Devil's lies have become so strong here. Our work takes my wife and me from Arabian city to Arabian city, and we are provoked and overwhelmed at the magnitude of the lost, the strength of the binding chains. The Devil is so good at lying—he twists everything. Every good and pure aspect of life, of thinking and of doing, has some perversion of the Evil One. His lies come at us in unceasing waves, pounding our minds, hearts, and souls. We must become adept at recognizing his lies.

The only way not to be overwhelmed by the continual and convincing lies of the Devil is to become an expert in truth. Truth has to be experienced relationally. Theory and intelligence will not protect us from the genius of the Devil's deception—he is too wickedly wise for us. Our only hope is to experience the Truth: Jesus. Only by obeying, loving, and clinging to the Truth (God Himself) can we survive the battering of ubiquitous lies (Deut. 30:20).

Overwhelmed by God. In truth, Jesus is constantly intense. At first blush, encounters with God in the flesh are more overwhelming than encounters with the Devil. God, too, is unreasonable in His expectations and demands. God's claims about Himself, God's expectations of us, God's requirements of obedience, and God's standards and impossibilities all overwhelm (Luke 18:27). We often feel like the young ruler who could not live up to Jesus' expectations, and in that discouragement we open ourselves up for more of the Devil's trickery as he hisses, "That is right. You cannot possibly have faith, stay pure, remain obedient. You might as well not try."

We simply cannot do or be what Jesus wants us to do or be. We have tried and failed too many times. May we simply sit at His feet and quietly wait for His help (Ps. 62:1, 5). May we learn that He is our source—not in the sense of getting supplies from Him (as if He could be reduced to a warehouse) but of getting *into* Him. We fall into Him, and there we find our supply. The only way we will not be overwhelmed by life, sin, and the Evil One is if we are overwhelmed by the goodness and truth of Jesus.

KALAL MUSLIMS OF INDIA (3,795,000; 0.0% EVANGELICAL)

PRAY THAT THE KALAL WOULD FEEL AND KNOW THE BURDEN OF SIN AND WOULD COME
TO JESUS FOR FORGIVENESS AND SALVATION
(MATT. 11:28-30).

Encircled. Moses entrusted his legacy to a song. Recounting the journey from death and bondage to life and freedom, he realized that what people sing they remember. His song reminds God's people that though we wander through much of life insecure without guarantees of health, happiness, or even liberty, we do not wander alone or unprotected. God sees and finds us in desert lands, in howling wildernesses (Deut. 32:10). The great lesson of Zacchaeus is not that he sought, ran, and climbed (Luke 19:3–4), but that the Son of Man sought and saved him (Luke 19:10)! God seeks us out that He might have mercy on us.

Overshadowed. David had a similar experience, both of deliverance under duress and a musical response. David wandered in the deserts of Judea, fleeing from those who sought his life. Uncomfortable, unsettled, navigating his own howling wilderness, he, too, sought, rose early, and longed for God in a dry and thirsty land (Ps. 63:1). David, too, discovered in his seeking that the great Hound of Heaven had been seeking him . . . and God is the better seeker. "Because You have been my help, therefore, in the shadow of your wings, I will rejoice" (v. 7).

In this context of being hunted, of weary wandering through howling deserts, David joined Moses in singing and penned the chorus: "Thy lovingkindness is better than life . . . my lips shall praise You. . . . My mouth shall praise You with joyful lips" (vv. 3, 5). David learned to sing in the desert—a song of being overshadowed by God in the midst of trial. David essentially realized that the joy of being in God's presence brings the deepest satisfaction. Nothing compares to being encircled and overshadowed by God.

We all wander through deserts. We all have circumstances beyond our control and comfort. God seeks us out in our distress and overshadows us. He encircles us with His presence. Our part is to open our mouths and declare to Him and the watching world that His presence is our reward, our sustenance, and our joy. Often, our faith declaration precedes the feeling and the experience. Yet we delight the heart of God when we anticipate His encircling and overshadowing. Let our joyful lips encourage mournful hearts. Let our praise open our spiritual eyes to understand that He has sought us out and protected us.

MASALIT MUSLIMS OF SUDAN (357,000; 0.0% EVANGELICAL)

PRAY THAT GOD WOULD UNVEIL THE CROSS AND WOULD REMOVE THE VEIL ON THE MINDS AND SPIRITS OF THE MASALIT (2 COR. 3:16-17).

MARCH 5: DYING SWEET

DEUTERONOMY 33-34; PSALM 64; LUKE 20; 2 CORINTHIANS 4

*I*f anyone had the right to be a little bombastic in a farewell address, it was Moses. This man was kind of intimidating. Not everyone talked to God face to face, stared down the strongest powers of earth, and was used by God in "mighty power and great terror" (Deut. 34:12). Moses had every right to do a Jacob thing (Gen. 48) and insert several curses on "his sons" in his final blessings. But he did not. Moses ended sweet.

Moses got to the end of life with his eyes clear and his natural vigor undimmed. He had outlasted those younger. He had kept unbroken fellowship with God through trials while others floundered. Moses could easily have gone out bitter. After all, because he got angry at the rascals, he was barred from the culminating stage of the journey—crossing Jordan. But Moses, about to die, poured out the most gracious of blessings and hopes. Let Reuben live! Let Judah's hands be sufficient for him! Let Benjamin be sheltered all day long and carried on the shoulders of God! Let Joseph be given the precious things of heaven! Let Zebulun (going out) and Issachar (staying home) rejoice! Let Gad have a lawgiver's reserved portion! Let Dan spring like a young lion! Let Naphtali be satisfied with favor, full of the blessings of the Lord! Let Asher be favored by his brothers with strength to match his days! Let the everlasting arms be under Jeshrun as God rides the heavens to help (Deut. 33:5–27)! There was no bitterness in Moses to seep out at the end of his life. All that was left was blessing.

Moses got stronger in spirit even as his physical life came to an end. Jesus wants to manifest His life in us by the way we die, by the way we carry burdens. Like Moses, Jesus wants us to get sweeter and sweeter as we get older—to have this stark contrast between our diminishing physical ability and an ever-sweetened spirit. We have crosses, sickness, trials, and burdens, and we always carry them as a living display of the rising life of Jesus in our mortal bodies, even as we are poured out and worn down. The outward flesh perishes while the inward spirit is renewed daily and soars. Jesus is glorified when we die sweet.

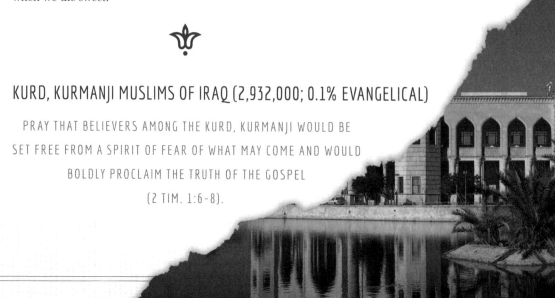

KURD, KURMANJI MUSLIMS OF IRAQ (2,932,000; 0.1% EVANGELICAL)

PRAY THAT BELIEVERS AMONG THE KURD, KURMANJI WOULD BE
SET FREE FROM A SPIRIT OF FEAR OF WHAT MAY COME AND WOULD
BOLDLY PROCLAIM THE TRUTH OF THE GOSPEL
(2 TIM. 1:6-8).

MARCH 6: FUNERAL AWAKENING

JOSHUA 1-3; PSALM 65; LUKE 21; 2 CORINTHIANS 5

*I*n this last phase of the last days, the powers of the heavens are being shaken (Luke 21:26), and God's witnesses will increasingly face suffering and death. This is a great opportunity for witness (vv. 13–15). What we know is that as the gospel advances into the heart of Islam, fear will grow in the ranks of the wicked, and fear will lead them to dreadful, horrific acts. What is not known is how we will react to the increase of violence and martyrdom. Will the church advance despite or because of the loss of our loved ones? Or will tragedy make us fear and flee?

God preaches a simple and profound funeral message to Joshua: "Moses My servant is dead. Now therefore, arise, go over this Jordan, you and all this people" (Josh. 1:2). As missionaries increasingly die for Jesus, incredible pressure will mount on their sending bases and organizations. Family, media, internal pressure, blame, lawsuits, grief, anger, and fear will all collude to scream: "Pull back, exercise caution, do not deploy to war zones. Do not send young families in harm's way. Wait, delay, the cost is too great to press on." We must understand the cost is too great *not* to press on. God intends the death of missionaries to be a rallying call for more to go where those have died. The funerals of our friends serve to remind us of their passions and to awake in us the longing to share their obedient joy.

God told Joshua to be strong and courageous, to obey God's Word and call. "Moses is dead, Joshua, so now it is time to cross Jordan, advance, run to the battle. His death is your call to action, your call to press on, and your call to take the ground Moses only saw." If we do not press on past the death of our pioneers, we insult their lives and waste their deaths. If we pull back when our pioneers fall, we trample their memory and dishonor their sacrifice. There can only be one response at missionary funerals: a challenge to wake up and run to the frontier.

Moses is dead. Abraham is dead. Ezra is dead. John is dead. Peter is dead. Paul is dead. Augustine is dead. Aquinas is dead. Francis is dead. Luther is dead. Lull is dead. Carey is dead. Taylor is dead. Livingstone is dead. Studd is dead. Zwemer is dead. Elliot is dead. McGavran is dead. Winter is dead. Hogan is dead. It is time to rise and cross the Jordan they have led us to. Our pioneer missionaries are going to die. Let us determine now that when they fall, our response will be to commission a dozen more to take their place. When our heroes die, we won't send flowers. We will commemorate their lives and deaths with the only gift they really want: We will send our sons and daughters to press on in their place.

TAIMANI MUSLIMS OF AFGANISTAN (592,000; 0.0% EVANGELICAL)

PRAY FOR THE WORD OF GOD IN WRITTEN, ORAL, MUSICAL, AND DRAMATIC FORMS TO BE TRANSLATED AND TO RISE AMONG THE TAIMANI (ISA. 55:10-11).

MARCH 7: ABIDING STRATEGY

JOSHUA 4–6; PSALM 66; LUKE 22; 2 CORINTHIANS 6

*S**trategy Follows Abiding.*** When Joshua met the commander of the Army of the Lord, he tried to recruit Him (Jesus) onto the team (Josh. 5). Pre-incarnate Jesus told Joshua, "I am not for you or against you, for that is the wrong question; the real question is whether you will worship me." We should not ask God to bless our strategy; rather, we should fall at His feet and worship. Strategy comes from worshiping, from falling prostrate at the feet of the Lord of angel armies. What are our battle instructions? "Take off your shoes, for you are in the presence of the Holy One." How do we prepare for battle? We fall on our faces before Jesus and we worship.

Worship opens a strategic channel to us from the war room of heaven. Worship unites us to the heart of God and illumines our minds to think His thoughts. Thinking His thoughts allows us to understand His strategy. This sequence is important. There is a vast difference between asking Jesus to bless *our* plans and falling at His feet so we can hear *His*. Our strategy comes from abiding at His feet in worship.

Victory Follows Praise. As we wait at the feet of Jesus for instructions, a counterintuitive command sinks into our spirit: Worship and praise are not only battle preparations, they are battle instructions. Worship not only precedes battle, and praise not only follows battle, but worship and praise *are* the battle. When we praise the Lord, we war with "nuclear" weapons. Sure, we swing the sword of practical physical action—but the grand weapons of our warfare are not carnal, tangible, or concrete. The big booms of spiritual warfare are invisible even while they are audible. Praise is the victory! After Joshua worshipped, the Lord revealed a battle strategy to conquer Jericho: march in circles, blow brass, and shout out praise. This is not something Joshua would have conceived in a thousand war councils.

The beauty of praise as a primary weapon is that everyone can wield it. You do not have to be strong, wise, seasoned, or esteemed. You do not have to be healthy, rich, educated, or acclaimed. All you have to do is open your mouth and repeat back to Jesus who He has revealed Himself to be. As we exalt, magnify, extol, sing, praise, and adore *out loud* the precious nature of Jesus, the arsenal of heaven is unleashed and battles are won. Let us be faithful warriors today. Let us lift up the weapon of praise (fueled by the armory of abiding) and go to war.

DHANUK HINDUS OF INDIA (3,767,000; 0.0% EVANGELICAL)

PRAY THAT GOD WOULD POUR OUT HIS SPIRIT ON THE DHANUK PEOPLE AND THAT THEY WOULD SEE DREAMS AND VISIONS OF JESUS. PRAY THAT THEY WOULD BE POWERFULLY SAVED AND EMPOWERED TO BE HIS WITNESSES
(JOEL 2:28–32).

MARCH 8: GLORIOUS CONFESSION

JOSHUA 5–8; PSALM 67; LUKE 23; 2 CORINTHIANS 7

*W*hen Achan sinned, Moses strangely exhorted him to "give glory to the LORD God of Israel and make confession to Him" (Josh. 7:19). Achan had sinned grievously and would die for his sin because his disobedience brought disaster on the congregation. Yet there was still a place to glorify God by admitting his sin. God is glorified in many ways, and one is when we confess our sins. When we confess our sins, we bring them into the light, and light—truth—is the exclusive domain of God. Truth honors God.

Jesus' self-confession of deity and authority likewise was glorious. Pilate asked Jesus: "Are You the King of the Jews?" Jesus confessed, "It is as you say" (Luke 23:3). Jesus continually and progressively bore witness to Himself. There is no shame in God declaring to be God. We need not wince when we read that Jesus bore witness of Himself. This is the right of deity. People look foolish when they exalt themselves, but God is diminished when He does not. It is glory for God to declare His own name.

Our glory is in confessing that we are *not* God. When we, criminals that we are, admit that we are justly condemned (Luke 23:40–43), we glorify God by participating in His truth. There is no shame in accepting and proclaiming our true human nature. This, too, is our glory. Likewise, when fallen people confess that Jesus is God—as in Luke 23:47: "Certainly this was a righteous Man"—He is glorified.

Second Corinthians 7:9–11 explains the benefit of confession: It brings our weakness and depravity and sin into the light. There is an appropriate sorrow both for us and for those who are affected by our sin. When we sorrow in a godly manner, we repent. Repentance leads to redemption and redemption to relief. Verse 11 is a bolt from heaven: "For observe this very thing, that you sorrowed in a godly manner: What diligence it produced in you, what clearing of yourselves. . . ."

Sin breeds sorrow. When that sorrow leads to confession, it is godly. Confession results in clearing. How glorious it is to be free from guilt and shame. The Devil's lie is that hiding sin holds shame at bay. The truth is that unconfessed sin is raging sin, and it destroys from within. Confessed sin opens the portals of heaven into our darkness, and the result is that light and glory overwhelm the shame. Confession is our glory, for it lifts our heads and eradicates shame. It is glorious to confess sin. It is glorious to confess who Jesus is. It is glorious for Jesus to bear witness of Himself. Let us not miss out on the glory of confession.

TIGRE MUSLIMS OF ERITREA (1,322,000; 0.05% EVANGELICAL)

PRAY THAT CHRISTIANS FROM AROUND THE WORLD WOULD WORK TOGETHER TO REACH THE TIGRE
AND THAT THE TIGRE WOULD BE JOINED TO THE BODY
OF CHRIST (JOHN 17:20–23).

MARCH 9: COUNTERINTUITIVE BATTLE

JOSHUA 9-12; PSALM 68; LUKE 24; 2 CORINTHIANS 8

The Labor of Surprise. "Joshua therefore came upon them suddenly, having marched all night from Gilgal" (Josh. 10:9). Sudden victories are set up by intense labor behind the scenes—often for prolonged periods. In order to be positioned for surprising success, Joshua and his army had to march through the night. We cannot expect victory without labor. No battle is won in our sleep. Battles are won only if we are willing to put in the hard nights' work of long marches, to fight tired. Just as we should not expect victories to come to us without labor, we should recognize that the "sudden" victories of other people are possible because of their long travail or the travail of their predecessors.

The Primary Warrior. It is easy to think that our labor determines our victory. While it is true that Joshua and company marched all night and swung their swords around in the trenches, it is equally true that the Lord routed (v. 10), the Lord delivered (v. 12), and the Lord fought for them (v. 14). In the end, an act of God (hailstones) killed more people than the Israelites killed with their swords. We participate in our battles in the sense that the Lord is the primary warrior. We are not the center of our own wars. God does the heavy fighting. We go into battle confident that He is on our side and, as we emerge in victory, it is imperative that we be just as assured He won the battle for us.

The United Enemy. The more forces that combine against you, the better it is for you. In Joshua 11:5, we read that multiple kings gathered together, united to fight against the people of God. We tend to be overwhelmed by one enemy, but God has a habit of multiplying our enemies. This is a blessing in disguise. We should rejoice and take courage when our enemies multiply; it saves us time . . . as God will defeat them all at once. Joshua conquered the land city by city, but at times God brought all his enemies together so Joshua could strike a wider blow. The more forces that combine against us, the better it is for us. God will save us time and will glorify Himself by overcoming combined enemy attacks.

The Time to Attack. There is rarely a bad time to go on the offensive. Attacking when the enemy least expects it never hurts. During the American Civil War, General Ulysses S. Grant distinguished himself from other Union generals as he often attacked immediately after a setback or stalemate. He was not necessarily smarter than other generals, but he was certainly braver. The Devil does not expect us to witness when under interrogation. Demons do not expect us to praise Jesus when they intrude. The coercive forces of government and ideology do not expect us to bless and serve when they oppress. Evil does not expect us to stand firm when we are sick, attacked, or maligned. The time to attack is when we are under pressure. Praise, blessing, and thanks . . . when we offer these despite the advance of the Enemy, we stun the powers of evil into powerlessness.

LEBANESE MUSLIMS OF LEBANON (2,821,000; 0.5% EVANGELICAL)

PRAY THAT THE HEARTS OF THE LEBANESE WOULD BE LIKE GOOD SOIL, READY TO HEAR THE GOSPEL AND TO RESPOND (MATT. 7:1-8; 18-23).

*H*eavenly rights do not match human rights. When we consider what the Scripture says about our rights, we find that little aligns with our assumptions. There are only two primary rights we can cling to biblically: the right to be called a child of God and the right to be filled with the Holy Spirit.

The Right to Be Called a Child of God. "But as many as received Him, to them He gave the right to become the children of God" (John 1:12). When we pick up the cross to follow Jesus, we forfeit many other rights. We give up the right to be liked and respected. We give up the right to be rich and comfortable. We give up the right to be safe and secure. We give up the right to be praised and paraded. We give up the right to our own wills and preferences. We give up the right to be free from shame, suffering, and death. We have no right to this life. We have no right to pain-free service. We do not even have a right to victory or success. On one hand, we stand in faith with Caleb and request "give me this mountain" (Josh. 14:12) for "it may be that the LORD will be with me" and help me conquer. Or maybe His will is that I die trying.

The Right to Be Filled with the Holy Spirit. John the Baptist understood completely his limited rights and role. He knew he was to bear witness to Jesus and to lead people to baptism: "I indeed baptize you with water, but He will baptize you with the Holy Spirit" (Mark 1:8). Jesus said in Luke 11:13, "If you then, being evil, know how to give good gifts to your children, how much more will your heavenly Father give the Holy Spirit to those who ask Him!" We have the right to ask the Father for the Holy Spirit. This right is linked to Fatherhood and thus to the right to be called His child. As our Father, He delights to give us the Holy Spirit. The Scripture is clear that the Spirit is given multiple times. Paul told the Ephesians to "be filled with the Spirit"—present continuous tense (Eph. 5:18). The same collection of disciples who were filled with the Holy Spirit in Acts 2:4 were filled again with the Spirit in Acts 4:31. Subsequent fillings of the Holy Spirit are both our right and our necessity. We desperately need to be filled and refilled with the Holy Spirit. Thanks be to Jesus, He grants us this right.

BALOCH, WESTERN MUSLIMS OF TURKMENISTAN (36,000; 0.0% EVANGELICAL)

PRAY FOR THE PEACE THAT RESULTS WHEN MEN AND WOMEN ARE RECONCILED WITH GOD (JOHN 14:27). PRAY FOR MEN AND WOMEN OF PEACE (LUKE 10:6) AMONG THE BALOCH.

MARCH 11: CAPTIVE THOUGHTS

JOSHUA 16–18; PSALM 70; JOHN 2; 2 CORINTHIANS 10

The charge to bring "every thought into captivity to the obedience of Christ" (2 Cor. 10:5) is not written in the context of internal purity or vain personal imaginations. Captive thoughts are those connected to arguments and high things that exalt themselves against the knowledge of God in spiritual warfare. In other words, our noncarnal weapons of war, which pull down strongholds, are mighty to attack and capture the ideologies that are antichrist.

Islam is, in essence, an antichrist religion. Every Muslim would be shocked and even offended at that statement for they claim to love and honor Jesus. Yet the central component of Islam is *Tawheed*—the unity of God. More simply put: the disavowal of the deity of Christ. You cannot be a Muslim and believe that Jesus is God. You cannot be a Christian if you do not confess that Jesus is God. Islam is an offense to Jesus because it denies His rightful place as King of Kings, Lord of Lords, very God of very God. Jesus is an offense to Islam because He claims to be divine.

The Muslim creed *(shahada)* is composed of two parts: "There is no God but God," and "Muhammad is the prophet of God." Liberal Christians swallow both, rationalizing that Muhammad led Muslims out of polytheism to monotheism. Uninformed Christians question the clause regarding the universal prophethood of Muhammad but accept the "no God but God" component. The reality is that the Islamic creed is a denial of Trinitarian monotheism and is simply stating: "Jesus is not God." This is a thought that must be taken captive.

Islam is not the first or only antichrist ideology. Secular humanism is just as fanatic in its denunciation of the deity of Jesus. The denial of the divine nature of Christ is a primary reason for these two competing ideologies, which differ dramatically on abortion, homosexuality, alcohol, and human rights, to tolerate and even complement each other. Both reject the deity of Jesus.

We not only defend the deity of Jesus by maintaining our firm belief and worship of Him despite mockery, slander, and scorn; we also aggressively attack the false thought by constantly proclaiming who Jesus claimed to be. We cannot respond to this arrogant and rebellious rejection of Christ's deity by embarrassment or concession. We cannot respond in self-censorship by removing familial language from our texts, being reluctant to pray in Jesus' name, or reticent to proclaim Jesus in all His glorious Lordship. We take evil thoughts about Jesus captive—an evil thought is anything that diminishes Christ's deity—by constantly, boldly proclaiming: *Jesus is God!*

BRAHMIN-GAUR HINDUS OF INDIA (3,412,000; 0.0% EVANGELICAL)

PRAY THAT BELIEVERS AMONG THE BRAHMIN-GAUR WOULD PROCLAIM THE MESSAGE OF THE GOSPEL CLEARLY AND WOULD MAKE THE MOST OF EVERY OPPORTUNITY GOD PLACES BEFORE THEM (COL. 4:2–5).

MARCH 12: CONSTANT CONFLICT, CONSTANT CARE

JOSHUA 19-21; PSALM 71; JOHN 3; 2 CORINTHIANS 11

We want to go to war without having to fight. We seek to conquer enemy territory without engaging the enemy. We rush to battle hoping we will not have to strike too many blows or receive any in return. We have such a sissified view of spiritual struggle. Why are we so surprised at demonic counterattacks? We press into holiness, we forge forth to the frontier, and at the first resistance we stop stunned. Whoever told us the road to storm the gates of hell was carpeted? Whoever promised the fight would be fair? Whoever promised the Geneva Conventions apply to the Devil? We have such a sheltered view of kingdom advance. War always means wounds, blood, and death. There is no letup in the conflict, and there is no cease-fire in this most demanding of all campaigns—the super-exaltation of Jesus among every people.

Satan will continue to deceive as an angel of light, but we will continue to join Paul in stripes above measure, frequent prisons, deaths often, whippings, beatings with rods, perils, robbers, false brethren, weariness, toil, sleeplessness often, hunger, thirst, fasting, cold, and nakedness (2 Cor. 11:14, 23–27). These, too, are promises of Scripture. The future for us, until Jesus comes, will be continual conflict, resistance, and battle. All praise to Jesus then, for His "continual" promises. Psalm 71 gives us these assurances:

God Is Our Continual Refuge. "Be my strong refuge, to which I may resort continually" (v. 3). We have a constant shield, an impenetrable umbrella. Over and over again we can run to God for shelter. The war does not cease, but neither does our refuge. Our refuge is a person, not a place, and thus our refuge is mobile. Our refuge goes with us into prison and into trial and into torture and past the gates of death to eternal refuge on the other side.

God Is Our Continual Strength. "I will go in the strength of the Lord God" (v. 16). Our renewable energy supply is inexhaustible. The eternal energy of God refuels us. We can never empty His supplies. We simply return to Him over and over again to be strengthened. God's strength will outlast the Enemy's attacks.

God Is Our Continual Comfort. You "comfort me on every side" (v. 21). There are many sides that need comfort: Yesterday a precious Egyptian brother was tortured and killed in Libya because he would not deny his faith in Jesus. Today his family needs comfort. Other constant pains, losses, and worries need healing. God has the capacity to comfort us continually. He has more bandages than the Enemy has arrows.

Conflict with the Enemy and comfort from God are both continual. However, we, too, have a continual role to play. *We must continually proclaim praise to God.* The psalmist exhorts us to praise all the days from our youth to the present (vv. 8, 15, 17, 24). Our response to God's continual care in the face of the Enemy's constant attack is continual praise.

SILTI MUSLIMS OF ETHIOPIA (1,155,000; 0.5% EVANGELICAL)

PLEAD THAT THE SILTI WILL UNDERSTAND THAT HOPE FOR FORGIVENESS AND ACCEPTANCE WITH GOD IS AVAILABLE ONLY THROUGH JESUS' WORK ON THE CROSS (1 COR. 1:18).

MARCH 13: SPENT

JOSHUA 22–24; PSALM 72; JOHN 4; 2 CORINTHIANS 12

*W*isely, Paul did not flaunt his heavenly experience to the Corinthians (2 Cor. 12). He reveled instead in the paradoxes of the gospel. God gives thorns to keep us humble (v. 7); He also gives sufficient grace (v. 9); His strength is made perfect in our weakness (v. 9); and limitations make us powerful (v. 9).

Biblically, suffering is a gift. It is granted to us both to believe on and suffer for the name of Christ. Thorns are given. We do not accidentally step on our designated thorns—God lovingly selects them for us. Our thorns are handpicked, God-made, and uniquely designed to keep us humble. Gifts are intended to be cherished, and if God is the giver, then our thorns should be precious to us. Behold what manner of love the Father has lavished on us that He grants us the thorny means to stay lowly.

Grace, too, is a gift. Grace gives us the capacity to survive, to endure, and to complete our work. God does not intend for us to arrive at the end of the journey fresh and energetic. He intends for us to die tired, to get to heaven with an empty tank and a depleted bank account. Paul told the Corinthians, "I will very gladly spend and be spent for your souls" (v. 15). Grace helps us motor through the finish line . . . take a few more breaths on the cross . . . and lay down our wills one more time. Grace gives us the sufficiency to complete what is painful, to be poured out and spent—to the last drop.

If we think that finishing strong means we have reserve energy at the end, then we must rid ourselves of that notion. Long-distance runners use everything up—they finish strong by completing the task exhausted. Their completeness is in their weakness. We have not arrived at Christian maturity until we have learned to live weak. The complete Christian is the perpetually weak, non-self-reliant one. Being poured out fulfills us. In God's mysterious ways, our limitations are what complete us. When lowliness has ushered in grace, grace helps us empty ourselves, and when we are empty, we are most powerful. Indeed, God builds His greatest works on our emptiness. It is our lowliness not our greatness that endears us to the people we love and serve.

BERBER, IMAZIGHEN MUSLIMS OF MOROCCO (2,497,000; 0.07% EVANGELICAL)

PRAY THAT THE BELIEVERS AMONG THE BERBER, IMAZIGHEN WILL ENDURE PERSECUTION IN A CHRISTLIKE MANNER AND WILL GIVE THEIR LIVES FOR THE SAKE OF THE GOSPEL IF NECESSARY (1 PETER 2:21–23).

MARCH 14: OBEDIENCE IS THE VICTORY

JUDGES 1-3; PSALM 73; JOHN 5; 2 CORINTHIANS 13

*W*hen God's people entered the Promised Land, they found it difficult to completely overcome and remove all the pagan inhabitants. God sovereignly allowed some of their adversaries to linger. These people were left unconquered in the land so that God "might test Israel by them, to know whether they would obey the commandments of the LORD" (Judges 3:4). God's tests measure our levels of obedience.

Obedience is not the byproduct of faith. The reason that obedience is better than sacrifice is because obedience is the highest form of victory, the purest expression of faith. Obedience is the desired product—it is the goal. God is after the victory of obedience. He is not so concerned with how victories are won. After all, He can win them in many different ways. He is more concerned that we win victories in the way He prescribes. He is not so concerned with what victories are won. After all, He can win by losing—He can be glorified by death on a cross, weakness, foolishness, and limitations. He is more concerned that the victories won are won in the way He instructs.

We pass God's tests by obedience not by performance. God is not measuring us by how much or how little we accomplish; He is measuring us by how much of our hearts He controls. He identifies His measure of control by how quickly and how thoroughly we obey Him. To obey is better than sacrifice. To obey is better than accomplishment. To obey is better than victory—for obedience *is* the victory, not just the means of victory.

When we understand that obedience is the victory, this brings tremendous relief. The pressure of performance is lifted as we realize that God does not measure us by how many Muslims we bring to faith. He measures how quickly and joyfully we obey Him. Because our obedience is the victory, it leads to the obedience of others. The writer of Romans mentioned three times that the goal of God is to bring the nations (all people groups) to "the obedience of faith." To say that obedience is the victory is not to say that we relinquish the goal of seeing saved and discipled Muslims in vibrant communities of faith. The obedience of the missionary is linked to the obedience of faith of the nations. Obedience is the means to mission. As we obey, others will be saved and discipled. Obedience lifts the pressure of performance even while it guarantees God's results—for He desperately wants to see the lost found and nurtured.

BARWALA MUSLIMS OF PAKISTAN (491,000; 0.0% EVANGELICAL)

PRAY THAT GOD WOULD RAISE UP MISSIONARIES FROM ALL OVER THE WORLD TO PLANT THE CHURCH TOGETHER AMONG THE BARWALA

(MATT. 9:37).

MARCH 15: BELIEF

*I*t is impossible to please both God and man (Gal. 1:10). To be a God pleaser is out of fashion. "Christianity," G. K. Chesterton said, "is always out of fashion because it is always sane; and all fashions are mild insanities."[1] The Scripture is clear: Without faith it is impossible to please God, because He who comes to God must *believe* that He is, and that He rewards those who trust Him (Heb. 11:6). The most sane thing we can do is also the most unpopular—to believe.

Belief Is Our Work. Jesus (in John 6:29) said: "This is the work of God that you believe in Him whom He sent." Belief is hard work. Everything around us attacks our faith. Circumstances, rival ideologies, false religions, lack of requested proof, the success of our enemies—all combine like allied kings against the people of God. Demons and demigods consort against us, and we must realize that, like Sisera, God deploys enemies against us so He can deliver them into our hands (Judges 4:7). Our response to the challenge is primarily to believe. Plunked down here in the middle of the Arab world, I must *believe* that God is going to be exalted by every unreached people on earth. This is my primary work, my labor, and my assignment. This is the work of God—that I believe in Jesus and that I believe Jesus will reign everywhere, among all peoples.

Belief Is Our Drink. When I believe Jesus, I never thirst (John 6:35). There is an interesting link between satisfaction and belief. The human heart is insatiable when it desires anything other than Jesus. We have infinite capacity to be dissatisfied—it is one of the few ways we are unlimited. But when we believe Jesus, we are at peace and we lose the unending drive for contentment. Believing satisfies . . . believing is our happy, settled home.

Belief Is Our Life. "This is the will of God. . . . Everyone who sees the Son and believes in Him may have everlasting life, and I will raise him up at the last day" (John 6:39–40). Belief is my eternity. It is by believing that I secure heaven. Jesus wants me to believe, because believing is my ticket to eternal everything. This belief is not a random optimism. It is not a sincere fixation on what is false. Belief is only life when it is connected to Jesus, and it must be a specific belief that Jesus is the Christ, the Son of the living God (v. 69). There is no eternal security outside of a devoted belief that Jesus is God.

PINJARA HINDUS OF INDIA (3,272,000; 0.0% EVANGELICAL)

PRAY THAT THE PINJARA WOULD FEEL AND KNOW THE BURDEN OF SIN
AND COME TO JESUS FOR FORGIVENESS AND SALVATION
(MATT. 11:28–30).

MARCH 16: FRONTIER FAITH

JUDGES 7-9; PSALM 75; JOHN 7; GALATIANS 2

*C*utting the frontier takes a unique, forged faith. Those who camp next to hell still live in the flesh and pursue heaven's aims from the flawed position of the fallen. They live a life in the flesh by faith (Gal. 2:20). Frontier faith has these essential components:

Reduction. A few well-trained and humble warriors are better than a large, arrogant army (Judg. 7:2). God can and will only use those who give Him all the glory. He occasionally reduces His forces to guarantee that the victories earned are so improbable as to be attributed only to Him. Gideon's army was reduced from 32,000 to 300—less than 1 percent of the original force actually won the victory. This minority used its smallness shrewdly (7:17) by employing strategic thinking. Smallness is no excuse for stupidity.

Fearlessness. We must understand that enemy forces feed on and are fed by fear. Fear inside errant ideologies is what drives them and energizes them. Gideon was allowed to sneak into the Midianite camp in order to hear their fear (Judg. 7:10–13). The enemy realized that a rolling barley loaf would "tumble" into town and knock down their tents. We are that barley loaf—we clumsily roll down a hill in all our weakness, and God amazingly uses us to defeat His enemies. False ideologies intrinsically know they cannot win. What are we afraid of then? Let's roll!

Emulation. "Look at me and do likewise; watch . . . and when I come to the edge of the camp you shall do as I do," Gideon said in Judges 7:17. Frontier faith has to be modeled by leadership. We cannot stand at the back of our armies, safely ensconced on our horses while keeping our boots clean and our swords sheathed. We have to press to the edge of the enemy camp and say, "Follow me as I follow Christ. Follow me as I follow Paul. Follow me as I follow Lull, Martyn, Carey, Taylor, Elliot, and Townsend. Do what I do, live and fight in faith on the edge with me." As Amy Carmichael, missionary to India, said: "It must always be 'come,' never 'go.'"

Proclamation. We have to make some frontier noise. The enemy is not intimidated by whispers. It is the shouting, the breaking of pitchers, the blowing of trumpets, the sudden light in the darkness that surprises and routs the enemy (Judg. 7:18–20). We have to open our mouths despite the risks and the superiority of the foe. It is the unexpectedly bold proclamation that strikes fear into the heart of our Enemy.

HASANIA MUSLIMS OF SUDAN (601,000; 0.1% EVANGELICAL)

PRAY THAT GOD WOULD UNVEIL THE CROSS AND WOULD REMOVE THE
VEIL ON THE MINDS AND SPIRITS OF THE HASANIA
(2 COR. 3:16-17).

MARCH 17: THE MISERY OF GOD

JUDGES 10-13; PSALM 76; JOHN 8; GALATIANS 3

*J*ust because God is eternal does not mean He is invulnerable. The fact that God is outside of time makes His misery all the more horrific. The agony of the cross was felt before the creation of the world ("the lamb slain from the foundation of the world" Rev. 13:8) and will be felt long after the re-creation. An eternal God bears eternal wounds. The body of the resurrected Jesus yet bears His scars.

God Is Miserable When His People Sin. It grieves the heart of God when His people follow false gods. This misery is compassionate because He knows that sin destroys from the inside out. He knows that sin cannot make us happy or fulfilled. When He sees us choose what will destroy us, He suffers. Eli Gautreaux points out that "when a child is lost, it is the father who suffers."[2] Anyone who has lost a child in a shopping mall or other public place can identify with the agony of the heavenly Father when His children wander away foolishly.

God Is Miserable When His People Suffer. In Judges 10, God's people repented of their sin and idolatry, put away their foreign gods, and served the Lord. The Bible then says of the Lord: "And His soul could no longer endure the misery of Israel" (Judg. 10:16). God enters the misery of His people. It is said that a parent is only as happy as his or her most unhappy child. God the Father is not restricted to human emotions, but this paternal grief originates in Him! God is miserable when His children are miserable—such is the extent of His care. The Devil would lie to us and tell us that God is distant and unconcerned. No! When we suffer, God cries with us.

God Is Miserable When His People Sacrifice to Him What He Does Not Want. The shocking story of Jephthah's daughter in Judges 11 is a prime example of humanity giving God what makes God miserable. Jephthah rashly declared that he would sacrifice the first thing that greeted him out of his house if God granted victory in battle. Jephthah's precious daughter came rejoicing out of the house to embrace her father—and Jephthah ultimately sacrificed her "to God." God did not want this sacrifice. It grieved Him. God is miserable when we sacrifice our families and children to Him in the name of ministry. Self-flagellation, legalism, offerings, or sacrifices made from guilt—all make Jesus unhappy.

What makes Jesus supremely happy is when His people repent of sin, trust Him in suffering, and give Him what He wants: obedience, praise, and faith. Let us not contribute to the misery of God. Let us rejoice His heart by giving Him what He wants.

AZERI TURK MUSLIMS OF IRAQ (2,031,000; 0.2% EVANGELICAL)

PRAY THAT BELIEVERS AMONG THE AZERI TURKS WOULD BE SET FREE FROM A SPIRIT OF FEAR OF WHAT MAY COME AND WOULD BOLDLY PROCLAIM THE TRUTH OF THE GOSPEL (2 TIM. 1:6-8).

MARCH 18: SPIRIT HUNGER

JUDGES 14-16; PSALM 77; JOHN 9; GALATIANS 4

*O*ften our theoretical knowledge of God laps our experience. This seems to be particularly true of our knowledge of God the Spirit, when our heads become stumbling blocks to our hearts. We cognitively admit that the Holy Spirit is a person in the triune godhead, but we live as though there are only two members in the godhead. Comfortable with the Father and the Son, we are not quite sure how to interact with the Spirit beyond perfunctory levels. Galatians 4:6 reveals that God has sent forth the Spirit of His Son into our hearts by which we cry, "Abba, Father". It is the Spirit of the divine Son in me who calls out to the divine Father that He send the divine Spirit. All three persons of the Trinity work together, indivisibly, to fill God's children with God's Spirit.

The tragedy is that, like Sampson (Judg. 16:20), we often do not know that the Lord has departed from us. The Spirit moved upon Samson as a lad (13:25); the Spirit came mightily upon him and he tore a lion apart (14:6); the Spirit of the Lord came mightily upon him and he killed thirty people (14:19); and when the Philistines came against him, the Spirit rose up within him and he slayed 1,000 men (15:14–15). If it is unfortunate never to walk in the fullness of the Spirit, but it is tragic to have the Spirit come mightily upon you and then lose that empowerment due to poor choices and associations. Samson experienced the power of the Spirit working through him, then he grieved the Holy Spirit, and the Spirit departed without Samson realizing it.

The baptism of the Holy Spirit is based on the concept of subsequence. Those who believe that the only work of the Spirit occurs at salvation and those who believe that the work of the Spirit culminates in Spirit baptism share the same error. Both limit the work of the Spirit.

The work of the Spirit is "already and more." Yes, the Spirit indwells us at salvation. Yes, the Spirit overshadows us and fills us and empowers us. Yes, this filling of the Spirit is to be repeated and repeated and repeated. Yes, we can grieve the Spirit and have God's power removed from us, and yes, this can happen without our realizing it.

The presence of Jesus (Ps. 77:13) is my answer—not facts. My answers do not come from information or facts, but from the person of Jesus. When Jesus (who is Truth) is present, *I am answered!* Similarly, the presence of Jesus is my strength. When I am devoted to the presence of Jesus and I seek *Him,* His strength comes upon me through His Spirit. If I violate His private, intimate, exclusive terms as Samson did, I grieve His Spirit, and the Spirit's power is lifted from me. While we are never outside God's love, we can lose His trust and consequently His power.

BASHKIR MUSLIMS OF UZBEKISTAN (50,000; 0.5% EVANGELICAL)

PRAY FOR THE WORD OF GOD IN WRITTEN, ORAL, MUSICAL, AND DRAMATIC FORMS TO BE TRANSLATED AND TO RISE AMONG THE BASHKIR
(ISA. 55:10-11).

MARCH 19: DOUBLY HELD

JUDGES 17–18; PSALM 78; JOHN 10; GALATIANS 5

*D*riving all these years in Africa and the Arab world has shown me that sheep are much dumber than goats. Sheep will wander right in front of oncoming traffic. Goats have the good sense to avoid cars. When you are speeding down the road and see a goat (distinguishable by the tail that sticks up as opposed to the sheep, whose tail hangs down), you know that you can keep speeding. If you see a sheep, you must proceed with caution. Being a dumb sheep myself, I am thankful for a Shepherd who lays down His life for me and whom I can know (John 10:14). What a marvel! I—dumb sheep that I am—can know the Good Shepherd, know His voice, and have access to His presence. He leads me safely, so I do not fear (Ps. 78:52).

Both my hands are held. I am as secure as a little child holding the hands of two strong parents. That child can walk anywhere—through Cairo traffic, along cliffs, beside crashing waves, over thorns and thistles, on hot cement or frozen sidewalks. That child can run freely in green pastures or be lifted up cliffs, hoisted over crevices or guided over train tracks. The Father holds one hand, the Son the other, and the Spirit guides me along. Most comforting of all is that I am doubly held. John 10:28 reminds that no one can snatch me out of Jesus' hand, and John 10:29 states that no one can snatch me out of the Father's hand.

This is what it means to "walk in the Spirit" (Gal. 5:16, 25). We do not walk alone; both our hands and our hearts are held. The triune God walks with us. We war by the Spirit (v. 17), we are led by the Spirit (v. 18), and we bear fruit by the Spirit (v. 22), all with both our hands held. We are guided and enabled, even propelled through these processes of life by the Father, the Son, and the Spirit.

Sometimes a child is restrained by those who hold his hands. "For we through the Spirit, eagerly wait" (Gal. 5:5). We are so used to thinking of the Spirit in terms of movement and propulsion, that we forget that the same Spirit who raised Christ from the dead also led Him to, and sustained Him on, the cross. The Spirit helps us wait. The Spirit empowers us to suffer. The Spirit bears us across the threshold of death and into the presence of Jesus. Waiting, suffering, dying—all are works of the Spirit. He never stops holding our hands. When Jesus said that no one takes us out of His or the Father's hands, He meant *no one* and *nothing*. Nothing can break the double handhold of God. Nothing can break God's grip on me. Nothing can drive my Good Shepherd away. I am safe. I am doubly held.

BRAHMIN, SANADHYA HINDUS OF INDIA (3,166,000; 0.0% EVANGELICAL)

PRAY THAT GOD WOULD POUR OUT HIS SPIRIT ON THE BRAHMIN, SANADHYA PEOPLE AND THAT THEY WOULD SEE DREAMS AND VISIONS OF JESUS. PRAY THAT THEY WOULD BE POWERFULLY SAVED AND EMPOWERED TO BE HIS WITNESSES

(JOEL 2:28–32).

MARCH 20: BLOOD AND TREASURE

JUDGES 19-21; PSALM 79; JOHN 11; GALATIANS 6

*O*ne of the most troubling narratives in Scripture is that of the Levite and his concubine in Judges 19–21. Why did a Levite have a concubine anyway? In a bizarre series of events, a gang of male Benjamites wanted to rape the Levite. Instead, his host offered both his virgin daughter and the Levite's concubine. In the end, the Levite thrust his concubine outside and she was gang raped all night. She died and her body was cut in pieces and sent throughout Israel. Who needs Hollywood! Repulsed, the people of Israel sent an army to punish the tribe of Benjamin, who would not discipline their lewd and violent own. Then the story gets really challenging.

The tribe of Benjamin (the bad guys and only 26,000 in number) defeated Israel (the good guys and 400,000 in number), killing 22,000 of them. The people of Israel encouraged themselves (Judg. 20:22), wept before the Lord until evening, and asked counsel of the Lord. God told them to keep attacking, and their obedience was rewarded by 18,000 more of their number being killed. Stunned, the people sat before the Lord until evening, crying, fasting, offering sacrifices, and asking counsel again. Once more God told them to attack, and when they did, thirty more of the good guys were slain before the battle ultimately turned.

The turning of the nations always requires the blood of the saints. Caiaphas was correct: It is expedient for one man to die for the people (John 11:50). Tertullian was correct: The blood of the martyrs is the seed of the church. The Scriptures are correct: "God is not mocked; for whatever a man sows, that he will also reap" (Gal. 6:7). If we sow our sons and daughters for the glory of God in the cause of missions, we will reap a harvest of souls among the nations . . . *if we do not lose heart.* God will not be mocked—He will respond to the death of His saints by a harvest among unreached peoples. The challenge does not lie in God's commitment to this promise but in our willingness to let our loved ones die. Jesus loved Lazarus, but He lingered when He heard He was sick and let him die—for the glory of God (John 11:4).

For God to be glorified among all peoples of the earth, not only must missionaries be willing to die, but senders (pastors, families, mission agencies) must be willing to send them to their deaths. I have no worries about the willingness of the soldiers to go to battle. I wonder if the senders will shoulder the crushing responsibility of sending more of their beloved to perish. We must trust Jesus enough to believe that He will not be mocked. We must love the nations enough that we absorb painful losses and continue to commission. And we must be strong enough to resist not only the arrows of our enemies but the wrath and pain of our friends. Let us resolve now that this war for precious souls is worth our blood and treasure.

ZARAMO MUSLIMS OF TANZANIA (918,000; 0.70% EVANGELICAL)

PRAY THAT CHRISTIANS FROM AROUND THE WORLD WOULD WORK TOGETHER TO REACH THE ZARAMO AND THAT THE ZARAMO WOULD BE JOINED TO THE BODY OF CHRIST (JOHN 17:20-23).

MARCH 21: IN CHRIST

RUTH 1-4; PSALM 80; JOHN 12; EPHESIANS 1

*W*illiam Borden is buried in Cairo. On his tombstone is written: "A man in Christ." Borden was only twenty-five when he died. He was studying Arabic to be better prepared to reach Muslims in China. He also happened to be the heir to the Borden estate—famous for their milk products. A graduate of Yale and Princeton, Borden walked away from fame and fortune to give his life for the glory of God among those who had never heard. He is most famous for a life summed up in his own words: *No Reserves, No Retreat, No Regrets.*[3]

John 12:24 reminds us that our death is our fruit. Hating our life is how we preserve it (v. 25). Our purpose is not to be saved from trouble: "What shall I say? Father, save Me from this hour?" *No!* Rather, "glorify Your name." (v. 27) God is magnified through a life that seems to lose everything. The reality is that a "grain of wheat" has to die first, and then Jesus calls it out of the tomb, raises it from the dead, empowers it to bear witness and, as a consequence, the world goes after Jesus (v. 17). The real question then is this: "Have you died yet?"

We are so focused on living that we forget that the highest form of life is resurrection life and that this life is only entered into by dying. A crucified life is not only judgment on the world; it is witness to that same world. A crucified life points to the victory of Jesus on the cross. His death resulted in "the ruler of this world" being cast out (John 12:31). The cross was the great exorcism of history: The cross unseated the demonic powers, and the crucified life is an irritating reminder to the Devil that he has been thrown down. When followers of Jesus die to themselves, they stick it in the eye of the Devil and remind him that Jesus is life and has won.

And to what end? Ultimately the glory of God, but attending the elevation of God is our encouragement. When we die to self, according to Ephesians 1, we are blessed in Jesus (v. 3); chosen in Jesus (v. 4); adopted by Jesus (v. 5); accepted by Jesus (v. 6); redeemed in Jesus (v. 7); purposed in Jesus (v. 9); gathered together in Jesus (v. 10); inheritors in Jesus (v. 11); blessed by trust in Jesus (v. 12); empowered by faith in Jesus (v. 15); and have knowledge in Jesus (v. 17). We cannot afford *not* to die!

Borden realized this secret and died immensely wealthy—a man in Christ . . . possessor of all things. Oh, the joy of dying to our pitiful, miserable, limited smallness in all things and rising to the life of *everything* supplied to us in Christ.

SHAWIYA MUSLIMS OF ALGERIA (1,961,000; 0.0% EVANGELICAL)

PRAY THAT THE HEARTS OF THE SHAWIYA WOULD BE LIKE GOOD SOIL,

READY TO HEAR THE GOSPEL AND TO RESPOND

(MATT. 7:1-8, 18-23).

*S*amuel ministered to the Lord before Eli (1 Sam. 2:11); ministered before the Lord as a child (v. 18); grew in stature and favor before God and man (v. 26); and again ministered to the Lord before Eli (3:1)—all before God called him. Samuel's call is intriguing for two reasons: He ministered to the Lord before knowing the Lord, and he was called before he had a revelation of the Word.

It is possible to have ministered for many years to and before the Lord without knowing Him. We should be both sobered and encouraged by this. Sobered, for all of us are capable of hollow service, and encouraged, for there is more of Jesus for us to know. God calls us out of ministry to Himself. Too many of us seek to hear God's call to the ministry, while God is more interested in calling us out of self-centered ministry to Himself. We are doubly blind, for not only are we serving Him powerlessly, but we do not even realize the folly of our ways. We teach and preach the Word, but we do not know it for we do not constantly, conscientiously obey it.

God called Samuel while the boy was ministering. The one whose name means "God hears" was able to hear God despite the clutter of service. "Here I am!" It is imperative that those who serve Jesus keep telling Him they are available. "Here I am, Jesus! Just as willing to obey today as I was yesterday. Here I am, Jesus! Just as willing to lose everything today as when I was young! Here I am, Jesus! Just as willing to follow you to the cross as when I first believed. Here I am, Jesus. Here I am!"

Do not be satisfied with your level of obedience, sacrifice, giving, or hearing. Strain in the Spirit to listen to the voice of the Lord. He may call you while you are ministering. If you will hear and obey, like Samuel, you will grow and the Lord will be with you. He will not let any of your words fall to the ground. I am sick of my own powerless words, and I detest standing in front of a congregation and knowing that my words are void of any transformative power. I am ashamed that my words fall to the ground more often than not—impotent and weak. I long to speak the life-giving words of Jesus. I long for God to reveal Himself to me in a fresh, burning reality (1 Sam. 3:21).

I rejoice that there is more of God to know. I rejoice that a powerless, forgettable ministry is not God's intention for me nor is it my destination. I rejoice that God is calling me away from perfunctory ministry into the knowledge of Himself. I rejoice that there is more of God and more of His Word to give me life. "Speak, LORD, for Your servant hears!" (v. 9)

BHIL MUSLIMS OF PAKISTAN (388,000; 0.0% EVANGELICAL)

PRAY FOR THE PEACE THAT RESULTS WHEN MEN AND WOMEN ARE RECONCILED WITH GOD (JOHN 14:27). PRAY FOR MEN AND WOMEN OF PEACE (LUKE 10:6) AMONG THE BHILS.

MARCH 23: INGLORIOUS

1 SAMUEL 4–6; PSALM 82; JOHN 14; EPHESIANS 3

*I*n 1 Samuel 4, the Philistines captured the ark of God. Israel had gone to war against the Philistines. They knew they needed help and they knew that God dwelt above the cherubim, so they had brought Him along (v. 4). They shouted, and the earth shook. The Philistines heard the report and, knowing they were up against a formidable foe ("God has come into the camp!" v. 7), exhorted each other to "be strong and conduct yourselves like men . . . and fight" (v. 9). If it's good for the goose (enemies of God), that sure seems like good advice for the gander (His people as well).

The battle took place and, stunningly, God lost. The ark was captured, Eli fell over backward, and Phineas' wife gave birth to a son and called him "Ichabod"—the glory has departed.

We need to give our fathers and mothers in the faith more credit. Eli did not mourn the slaughter of his sons, and he really did not care about a box. The anguish was not that God had been captured (nestled in among the cherubim), because that is impossible. The anguish was that God was gone. The only way the enemies could have captured the ark was if God's presence had left. God had left His people. This is functional hell—the absence of the presence of God. Eli and his daughter-in-law were astute enough to realize the implications of a captured ark: God was no longer with Israel. The glory had departed; they were in hell.

The Hebrew word for glory *(khavod)* has a sense of "weight" in the meaning. There is a heaviness to the presence of Jesus. When Jesus is present in power, you feel Him. You sense in your spirit when God is pleased, when He is moving, when He is speaking, and when He is present. Eli carried a double anguish. Not only had God departed (and His people were in functional hell); Eli realized that he was partially liable for God's absence. His unrestrained sons had led the people astray (1 Sam. 2:24). They had made the Lord's people transgress.

Functional hell is the absence of the presence of God. Pity the men or women who bear liability for the absence of God due to their sins or because they led others to sin. Let us not be the damned who are responsible for the absence of God—this is the opposite of mission. Real mission is to bear the weight of the presence of Jesus to people who know it not. Anti-mission is to grieve the Spirit of God by our sin and cause Him to abandon us to a deserved hell. Mission is glorious. Anti-mission is inglorious hell.

RAJPUT, CHAUHAN HINDUS OF INDIA (3,111,000; 0.0% EVANGELICAL)

PRAY THAT BELIEVERS AMONG THE RAJPUT, CHAUHAN WOULD PROCLAIM THE MESSAGE OF THE GOSPEL CLEARLY AND WOULD MAKE THE MOST OF EVERY OPPORTUNITY GOD PLACES BEFORE THEM (COL. 4:2–5).

*T*he entire history of God's people reveals unfaithfulness. Even mighty Samuel could not keep his flock (or his sons) from sin. Often we glamorize the Ebenezer stone as a commemoration of man's faithfulness—"Thus far the LORD has helped us" (1 Sam. 7:12). We read into the text that God's people had been faithful over long periods, therefore He had helped them. In reality, the people had been idolatrous for twenty brutal years. For twenty years, the ark of God sat in Kirjath Jearim while God's people served foreign gods and goddesses.

Samuel confronted the people, they repented, and he offered a sacrifice. In the middle of Samuel's sacrifice the enemy attacked: God thundered, confused the enemy, and Israel overcame them. It is intriguing that God confused their enemy when they sacrificed. It is important that Samuel set up the Ebenezer stone in this context.

The people of Israel did not have a legacy of faithfulness. They had only just reconciled with God. At the very moment God acted on their behalf, He also forgave them for years of idolatry. He intervened the instant He forgave. The Ebenezer stone was just as much a testament to the people's waywardness as it was to God's faithfulness. Samuel erected the stone as a reminder of the constant need for God's help. The Ebenezer stone reminds us that we, too, are prone to wander, yet God has helped us. He has helped us when we did not deserve it. He has helped us when our legacy was shameful, and He has helped us when we repented. An Ebenezer stone reminds us that we continually need help for we are continually stupid.

A continual reminder of our folly should not discourage us, and it will not discourage us, as long as we understand that God will continually help us if we ask Him to. In effect, Samuel was saying: "God delivered you when you did not deserve it. You have not deserved it; you do not deserve it; you will never deserve it. This is the nature of God. He is faithful when we are faithless. He does not change. *Live every moment dependent on Him.*"

Ebenezer stones help us remember that we are continually craven and God is constantly good; therefore, we are completely dependent on Him to help us. Initial deliverance, ongoing provision, and subsequent victories are all acts of God. He always rescues the humble. He never rescues the proud.

ORMA MUSLIMS OF KENYA (69,000; 0.0% EVANGELICAL)

PLEAD THAT THE ORMA WILL UNDERSTAND THAT HOPE FOR FORGIVENESS
AND ACCEPTANCE WITH GOD IS ONLY AVAILABLE THROUGH JESUS' WORK ON THE CROSS
(1 COR. 1:18).

MARCH 25: LEADERSHIP DESERVED

1 SAMUEL 10-12; PSALM 84; JOHN 16; EPHESIANS 5

*C*hurches, mission agencies, and nations all ultimately end up with the leadership they deserve. We love to blame our leaders for the plight of our institutions while failing to recognize that we are our own leaders—the elected official is just a reflection of the collective moral standing. We cannot blame a wicked leader for the plight of a nation—the leader is usually an elevated reflection of that nation.

In Jesus, leadership selection is more about God than man. Human leadership selects the one who best reflects the human group. In spiritual leadership, God selects the unexpected person and shapes that individual to reflect the divine nature. God puts the most unlikely people in authority and then gives them what they need to lead well. If you have been chosen to lead through a God-honoring process, it is probably because you have a significant liability and the Lord desires to reveal His greatness through your smallness. Leadership appointment should always humble us.

Saul certainly had some charisma and leadership qualities, most of which seemed to be external (tall, strong, and handsome), yet he had obvious insecurities that led him to hide in the baggage, intimidated at the thought of responsibility. Samuel prophesied to Saul that the Spirit of the Lord would come upon him, that he would be turned into another man, and God would be with him (1 Sam. 10:6–7). God indeed gave Saul another heart. The Spirit did indeed descend on him, and he graciously lead a glad people (11:15). At the beginning of Saul's reign, God was glorified. There is an anointing for leadership. When God chooses a leader, He chooses one with evident flaws so His grace might be just as evident, and all the glory would go to God.

When leaders forget that their unworthiness is covered by God's provision, their insecurities get the better of them and they lash out at those around them who seem threatening. Saul fell into this pit concerning David. Saul did not remember that God had chosen him to lead largely because he was incapable. It is our inadequacies that most clearly display the glory of God through His Spirit. Let us not forget that insufficiency is our greatest qualification for leadership.

LIBYAN MUSLIMS OF LIBYA (1,857,000; 0.2% EVANGELICAL)

PRAY THAT THE BELIEVERS AMONG THE LIBYANS WOULD ENDURE PERSECUTION IN A CHRISTLIKE MANNER AND WOULD BE WILLING TO GIVE THEIR LIVES FOR THE SAKE OF THE GOSPEL IF NECESSARY (1 PETER 2:21-23).

MARCH 26: SPIRITUAL INTENSITY

1 SAMUEL 13–15; PSALM 85; JOHN 17; EPHESIANS 6

S piritually Pugnacious. Jonathan is my all-time favorite Bible character. I love him for many things, not least of which is his glad desire to abdicate the throne for his buddy from the poor side of town. Jonathan did not want to sit on the throne, he wanted to fight. It was not a matter of if, the only question was where. "It may be the LORD will work for us," (v. 6) he told his armor bearer, and off they climbed to take on superior odds. God wants to instill that fighting spirit in us. Let us determine that it is not a matter of if, it is just a matter of where. This was the belief of Hudson Taylor in frontier mission: The fight for unreached people is academic; the only deliberation is where Jesus wants us to do it.[4] Let us end like Jonathan did—swinging the sword to the end. He never lost his fighting spirit.

Spiritually Passionate. We often think of Samuel as soft, perhaps because we first meet him as the little son of gentle Hannah. Samuel was anything but stoic. He grieved and cried all night over Saul (1 Sam. 15:11), then told Saul to "shut up" (v. 16)! He picked up a sword and hacked Agag into pieces (v. 33), then retreated out of public service and mourned for Saul (v. 35). Samuel was not a meek man. He rocketed to the extremes of passion: from grief and tenderness to violent zeal and action. In God, and in God's representatives, mercy and truth must meet (Ps. 85:10). Mercy without truth corrupts; truth without mercy kills. We are not created to be neutral. Our balance comes through passion rightly applied in opposite directions.

Spiritually Prioritized. Many people think of the apostle Paul as a small-framed intellectual who wasn't good at sports so he retreated to his books and ended up a genius. He may or may not have been able to bash an Agag to death with a rolled-up Torah, but he sure could take a punch. Whatever his physical stature, he was single-minded in spirit. In Ephesians 6:18, he exhorted his disciples to keep praying in the Spirit. Why? Because he wanted to speak "boldly, as [he] ought to speak" (Eph. 6:19–20). Paul's priority was church planting. He focused on preaching and teaching in order to make disciples. He gathered those disciples in churches, appointed elders, and kept moving. Paul felt compelled to open his mouth at great cost to his person in order to proclaim the gospel. ("Woe is me if I preach not the gospel!") This was his priority and passion, and for it he paid every price.

Jesus wants us to be intense. Following Jesus is not for the balanced—not if balance means timidity and not if a zero-sum effect cancels out complementary truths. Let us embrace the fullness of a radical allegiance to Jesus in all things.

BOSNIAK MUSLIMS OF TURKEY (100,000; 0.0% EVANGELICAL)

PRAY THAT GOD WOULD RAISE UP MISSIONARIES FROM ALL OVER THE WORLD TO PLANT THE CHURCH TOGETHER AMONG THE BOSNIAKS

(MATT. 9:37).

MARCH 27: DEATH GAIN

1 SAMUEL 16-18; PSALM 86; JOHN 18; PHILIPPIANS 1

*J*esus, "knowing all things that would come upon Him, went forward" (John 18:4) to drink the cup the Father gave Him (v. 11). He accepted that it was expedient for one man to die for the people (v. 14). If it takes one missionary (or more) to die that every unreached people group on earth be reached with the gospel, this is a worthwhile and affordable expense. This is an expediency we can, and must, embrace. The peoples of the world are worth immeasurably more: the death of God's own Son. If many missionary deaths are gently graphic reminders of the supreme sacrifice for sin—we will gladly pay them. Oh the joy of the martyr and the rescued people when they reunite around the eternal throne in worship! Missionary deaths will seem a glorious bargain for such a yield, and we will wonder that we were so reluctant to pay more.

Mission to Muslims will increasingly be based on prison, suffering, and martyrdom. Our chains will bring an opportunity for the defense and confirmation of the gospel (Phil. 1:7). Our chains are Christ's will, and they serve for the furtherance of the gospel (v. 13). Frankly, God will send us to prison so that His love may be displayed to those who persecute us. His gospel, set on trial, will shine. Our prisons will be God's show-room—He will illuminate them as hostile people shuffle through, as if to say, "Look what the gospel can do!" When we suffer gloriously, when we embrace prison, when we stop fleeing contexts of violence and die well among our brothers, we will inspire confidence. Our commitment to suffering will make the "brethren . . . much more bold to speak the word without fear" (v. 13). In the moment of testing, as well as before the trial, our fearlessness of death and suffering is proof to the enemies of the gospel that the truth is found in Jesus.

Suffering is a gift God gives to His people that they continually refuse to open (v. 29). Suffering is as much a gift as salvation. Suffering and death are personal gain, for they promote us to the presence of Jesus. There is a sweet communion with Jesus available only to those who suffer for His name. Eternal, unequaled sweetness waits for us in heaven. This being true, why are Christians so reluctant to go there? Suffering and death are corporate blessings because Jesus never wastes a martyr's death—it is expedient for one (or more) missionary to die for unreached people. Oh the joy of participating in all nations worshipping Jesus—by life and by death. Knowing this, let us go forward and drink our cup.

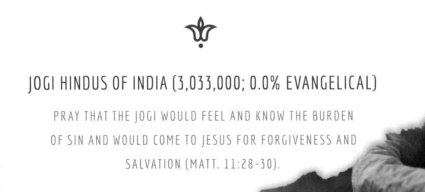

JOGI HINDUS OF INDIA (3,033,000; 0.0% EVANGELICAL)

PRAY THAT THE JOGI WOULD FEEL AND KNOW THE BURDEN
OF SIN AND WOULD COME TO JESUS FOR FORGIVENESS AND
SALVATION (MATT. 11:28-30).

MARCH 28: GETHSEMANE, GABBATHA, GOLGOTHA

1 SAMUEL 19-21; PSALM 87; JOHN 19; PHILIPPIANS 2

ethsemane: What Is Your Cup? Jesus did team meetings, and He often did them at Gethsemane Gardens—He was a fan of the outdoors. The secret police crashed the meeting, and Jesus asked them what they wanted. In one of the more comical passion incidents, Jesus identified Himself, and the scary bad guys collapsed on the ground in a heap. I can hear the clatter of dropping shields and swords. The bravest of the bunch seemed to be Peter, who ambitiously hacked off an ear, only to be restrained by Jesus. "Shall I not drink the cup which My Father has given Me?" Jesus asked (John 18:11).

We all have a cup to drink. Let us step forward to drink it, and may the calm resolve with which we swallow our suffering point directly to Jesus.

Gabbatha: Who Is Your Caesar? Jesus was taken before Pilate, who was confused about who was judge and ruler. Pilate found no fault in Jesus (John 19:4), never realizing that it was not Jesus who was on trial. The fool judged God and looked the worse for it. The people also erred, saying, "He ought to die" (v. 7)! Ironically, they were right in their wrongness—the Prince of Life did have to die that they might live, but it was not what He deserved. The fools got one thing right, however, a central point that sages of our day tend to avoid: Jesus did claim to be God (v. 7), and for this claim He was crucified.

A final and enduring folly is to forget who really holds the power. Pilate had power because God gave it to him. Christians should not forget that God in His sovereign wisdom empowers evil rulers for His purposes. There is only One who sits on the eternal judgment seat, and we will be condemned or rewarded based solely on whether we bowed the knee and confessed that Jesus Christ is God.

Golgotha: Where Is Your Center? In the call to a crucified life, there is the sinister danger of making ourselves the center of our own crucifixions. Even in death, even in suffering, even in sacrifice, and especially in dying to self, Jesus must be the center. Too often we accept suffering for the attention it draws to us. Jesus must be the center of our demise. If we are the center, we are not dying—no matter the depth of our pain. Death to self must result in the disappearance of the vessel and the illumination of the treasure within.

We have to die to live dead. If our identity comes from pioneer mission, risk for God, or the respect and applause of supporters who are impressed with our valiant deeds, then we have put ourselves in the center of Calvary, and we have blasphemed. Jesus has to be the center, not just in our living, but also in our dying.

GUHAYNA MUSLIMS OF SUDAN (1,943,000; 0.0% EVANGELICAL)

PRAY THAT GOD WOULD UNVEIL THE CROSS AND WOULD REMOVE THE VEIL ON THE MINDS AND SPIRITS OF THE GUHAYNA (2 COR. 3:16-17).

MARCH 29: IN DEFENSE OF AUTHORITY

1 SAMUEL 22-24; PSALM 88; JOHN 20; PHILIPPIANS 3

*T*he best way to respond to unjust attacks from an authority figure is to defend that leader. God will take care of your defense (1 Sam. 24:12). David moved from forest to desert as he ran for his life from Saul, and he spent his time defending Saul's people from Saul's enemies. David never took Saul on as an enemy; rather, he fought his leader's battles, even when his leader was trying to kill him. The Christlike way to respond to an insecure leader is to continue to do that leader's work, even while that leader is trying to remove you. Another way is to care for those under the leader, not as David's son Absalom did, in order to take the leader's place, but as David did, who served the people because it was the right thing to do.

Gene Edwards, in his book *A Tale of Three Kings*, points out the correct response to ungodly or insecure leadership as he contrasts the reactions of Saul, David, and Absalom.[5] Jonathan, too, must be considered, for there is an auxiliary role to be played when authority is being misused. Jonathan—rightful heir to Saul's throne—recognized that God had chosen someone other than himself for leadership. Secure leaders willingly abdicate the place they have been groomed for to the one prepared by God. He is not bound by our mechanisms of selection, and the secure leader gladly bows to His wisdom. Not only did Jonathan accept God's choice (and his own demotion), he genuinely advocated for David to Saul.

David teaches us to submit. He considered Saul his master and the leader anointed by God, even when Saul wanted to kill him (1 Sam. 24:6). By his negative response, Saul teaches us not to be insecure and to groom young leaders to replace us. Absalom, the anti-David, shows us the danger of ambition. Jonathan teaches us how to surrender titles and defend others.

There comes a time when every leadership team discusses potential leaders. Inevitably, there are concerns or doubts about the suitability of an emerging leader. Someone in the inner circle needs to speak up for that young person. A Jonathan on the leadership team (potentially the one with the most to lose) must defend the young leader. How it pleases the Lord when we cede our place to someone He has chosen. It takes a special security to recognize that He has chosen another person to take your place and to rejoice in it.

Jonathan is a biblical hero because he did what few in his day or ours are willing to do, and he rejoiced in it. He displayed incredible spiritual security and authority by defending others—at cost to himself. David also defended himself by risking his life for others. When leadership doubts or questions us, let us respond in the spirit of Jonathan and David—linked spirits because they understood authority so magnificently.

NAJDI BEDOUIN MUSLIMS OF SYRIA (1,520,000; 0.0% EVANGELICAL)

PRAY THAT BELIEVERS AMONG THE NAJDI BEDOUIN WOULD BE SET FREE FROM A SPIRIT OF FEAR OF WHAT MAY COME AND WOULD BOLDLY PROCLAIM THE TRUTH OF THE GOSPEL (2 TIM. 1:6-8).

*W*hen we follow Jesus, it is easy to follow men. David was chosen and anointed and would be established by God (Ps. 89:18–24), but there was trial before the exaltation. He threatened those in leadership (Saul), and those who opposed his ascent to responsibility insulted him (Nabal). David had no trouble realizing that he should not strike Saul, for he had the good sense to know that God would either kill Saul or Saul would die in battle or Saul's day would come (1 Sam. 26:10). David's passion, however, blinded him to the same reality from fools. Abigail stepped in and saved the day, and David responded: "Blessed be the LORD God of Israel, who sent you [Abigail] this day to meet me! And blessed is your advice, and blessed are you . . ." (1 Sam. 25:32–33)! No matter how shamefully we are treated, there is no reason to strike out at the people above us or below us for God will beat down our foes (Ps. 89:23).

In the end it does not matter what others do, even what they do to us—we must simply follow Jesus (John 21:19, 22). In the end it is not about leading, it is about following. When we follow hard after Jesus, others will follow along with us. The ambition to lead is common and is not without godly impulse. We must remember, however, that the best leaders are those who follow Jesus. Our authority over others is sourced in our submission to Jesus. Only the submitted are fit to lead. This is, in part, what Paul referred to in Philippians 4:12 when he said: "I know how to be abased, and I know how to abound." The context refers to contentment in poverty or wealth, but it can also apply to leading and following—both are sources of contentment for they are indivisibly linked. We only lead well when we follow hard after Jesus. Whether there is a dearth of popular support or we are lauded to the heavens, we discount them both, for the point is not our elevation or demotion. The point is our proximity to Jesus. When we follow hard after Him, we are oblivious to both praise and scorn. We have one fixation—staying on His heels.

There is something magnetic about those devoted to following Jesus. Those who follow hardest most naturally lead. Their lives say with Paul's that "the things which you learned and received and heard and saw in me, these do" (Phil. 4:9). When we follow Jesus, it is easy for others to follow us. If you have natural leadership abilities and a godly desire to lead, the best way to cultivate that gift (and leadership is a gift God gives) is to devote yourself to following Jesus.

AZERBAIJANI MUSLIMS OF NORTHERN AZERBAIJAN (8,352,000; 0.17% EVANGELICAL)

PRAY FOR THE WORD OF GOD IN WRITTEN, ORAL, MUSICAL, AND DRAMATIC FORMS TO BE
TRANSLATED AND TO RISE AMONG THE AZERBAIJANI
(ISA. 55:10–11).

MARCH 31: DURESS AND DELIVERANCE

1 SAMUEL 28-31; PSALM 90; MATTHEW 1; COLOSSIANS 1

*W*hen you live in the Arab world you become the proverbial orange stepped on by an elephant—whatever is in you gets squashed out. There remains no dignity, no mask, no pretense. Duress exposes what is in us, what we have carefully covered. We need Cairo (or Khartoum, Peshawar, Jakarta, Mogadishu, Istanbul, etc.) much more than it needs us. Extreme contexts and cities put a slow, building pressure on us, and, over time, what is inside our hearts is exposed for all to see. This is a supreme gift. Those who repent for what is in their hearts are reconstructed and rise again to abundant life and ministry. Those whose shame cannot be overcome by their desire for wholeness limp along in life—never experiencing the fullness of God. In His mercy, He does not regulate this deconstruction and reconstruction experience to those who work in pioneer contexts. The frontier has the tendency to accelerate and magnify the process.

Duress alone does not guarantee growth. Suffering makes some people better and some people bitter. Trials make some shine and others sour. Trauma and trouble lead some to magnify God and others to draw attention to themselves. Fear and impatience made Saul break his own convictions about consulting mediums (1 Sam. 28), and grief caused David's men to want to stone him (1 Sam. 30:6).

The emotions that trials awaken in us accentuate the fragility of our hearts. They also remind us who we are without Jesus. We do not judge those who falter under duress for we all stumble in one way or another. When we are broken and exposed as frauds, we have only love and understanding for those on a similar path. We also have great hope and joy for we know where it can lead them—to liberty, life, and happiness.

Before the Spirit of God came upon Saul, he was an insecure and timid layperson. God's Spirit transformed this weakling into a great leader who won battles and prophesied. When Saul disobeyed the Lord, God's favor was lifted and Saul was exposed—a pitiful sham. What makes David exemplary, and why he is called a man after God's own heart, is how he responded to duress. When his enemies plundered his home and abducted his family, and his followers shouted for mutiny, he wisely reacted in two ways: He cried his eyes out, and he strengthened himself in the Lord. David's duress led him to God.

Duress is a gift. It is a great freedom to have nothing to hide. God's deconstruction is one of His greatest mercies. On the other side of exposure is freedom, life, and the liberty of being wholly in the light. We can concentrate on discovering Jesus, not on covering shame.

LUNIA HINDUS OF INDIA (2,995,000; 0.0% EVANGELICAL)

PRAY THAT GOD WOULD POUR OUT HIS SPIRIT ON THE LUNIA PEOPLE AND THAT THEY WOULD SEE
DREAMS AND VISIONS OF JESUS. PRAY THAT THEY WOULD BE POWERFULLY SAVED
AND EMPOWERED TO BE HIS WITNESSES (JOEL 2:28-32).

[Be] strengthened with all power according to his glorious might so that you may have great endurance and patience.

COL. 1:11 NIV

April

"IF YOU ARE SICK, FAST AND PRAY;

IF THE LANGUAGE IS HARD TO LEARN, FAST AND PRAY;

IF THE PEOPLE WILL NOT HEAR YOU, FAST AND PRAY,

IF YOU HAVE NOTHING TO EAT, FAST AND PRAY."

—*Frederick Franson*

APRIL 1: PUBLIC SHAME

2 SAMUEL 1-3; PSALM 91; MATTHEW 2; COLOSSIANS 2

*O*n the day when we remember fools, it is good to note just whom the cross shames. Colossians 2 reminds us that the cross was a public spectacle, a public triumph over principalities and powers. What seemed to be the humiliation of God was in fact His ultimate victory. Oh, the horror of being Satan! Think of the hate and rebellion that led him to scheme and connive to embarrass Jesus in the public view. Think of the organizational energy that seethed and glowered and rose in expectation as Jesus stumbled to Golgotha. Think of the surge of evil joy that rose in demonic hearts as Jesus writhed naked, tortured for all to see.

Think of the bolt of terror that flashed across the Devil's mind as the earth shook and he sensed that something was wrong. Then, Jesus marched into hell, seized the keys of death, burst out of the tomb, ascended to the Father, and unleashed the Spirit. The Devil realized he had been mocked, exposed, and revealed—not only as a fraud but as incredibly stupid. How it must have irked him, who prides himself on his intellect, to be so publicly outwitted and humiliated.

Furious at his impotency to thwart the plan of God and frantic in the knowledge he has lost and soon will be destroyed, the Enemy of our souls frantically looks for others he can drag into his pit. Sure, our world is marred by evil and tragedy, and the attacks of evil seem overwhelming, but we must understand that the ferocity of the attacks indicate that our foe is mortally wounded. The Devil is drowning and wildly clutching others to drown with him. We would be fools to expose ourselves cavalierly to the last scratching of Satan. He has one breath left, and that one is running out.

When we understand that Jesus has made a public spectacle of the Devil, this gives us the patience to endure the Devil's last, desperate assault. We know his time is limited, so when he hurls himself at our bodies, souls, and spirits, we simply take shelter in the secret place of the Almighty. We allow God's angels to take charge over us and bear us up. We revel in the reality that we are answered, accompanied, delivered, honored, satisfied, and saved (Ps. 91:15).

A proper understanding of the public spectacle of the cross helps us remember that Satan's humiliation spurs him to a last, frantic attack. This attack is dangerous, because a dying foe is the most desperate, but by the same token a dying attack cannot last forever. The wise follower of Jesus hunkers down in the shadow of the Almighty, presses into the storm behind the divine shield accompanied by angel hosts, and advances to celebrate the victory of Jesus. It is the Devil who is the Easter fool.

MOORISH MUSLIMS OF MURITANIA (3,004,000; 0.07% EVANGELICAL)

PRAY THAT CHRISTIANS FROM AROUND THE WORLD WOULD WORK TOGETHER TO REACH THE MOORS AND THAT THE MOORS WOULD BE JOINED TO THE BODY OF CHRIST (JOHN 17:20-23).

APRIL 2: MORE UNDIGNIFIED

SAMUEL 4-6; PSALM 92; MATTHEW 3; COLOSSIANS 3

*C*ount Zinzendorf said, "I have one passion, and it is Him and only Him."[1] When Jesus is our consuming passion, our dignity becomes less important to us. We might even dance through the streets in our underwear like King David.

David's exuberant worship is all the more remarkable because of his status. Kings are poised, calm, and measured. When necessary, David was all of those things, but the dignity of office took second place to the ruling passion of his life—intimate union with God. If our goal is to be respected by others, we act, proclaim, and missionize dignified. If the goal is to enjoy God and exalt Him eternally, we abandon dignity.

It Was Before the Lord. David's wife, Michal, was not impressed with his exuberant worship. She was born in purple, was used to the palace, and was sure of the bounds of propriety. She knew that kings did not act like other people. She knew kings acted to please people. However, David knew nothing of the sort. Pleasing people was the farthest thing from his mind (which in part makes a great leader). He simply wanted to rejoice in God, and whatever he did was not for Michal or the people or the servant girls—it was for God. Those who fear God most fear people the least.

I Will Be More Undignified Than This. There are no dignity limits for the worshiper, only obedience and intimacy. David was committed to an ongoing pursuit of God. His rejoicing in God was not a performance or an embarrassing emotional reaction. David's undignified reveling in God was the norm, and he was committed to super-exalting the Lord everywhere . . . always . . . no matter what anyone thought. The point is deity, not dignity. If we are not overwhelmed, we have not been in God's presence.

I Will Be Humble in My Own Sight. The person who has no reputation to protect is the most free. What a luxury not to care what people think of us. "Praise and blame equally are nothing to him who is dead and buried with Christ," Father Macarius said.[2] When we do not take ourselves too seriously, we have the most latitude in life and service. We are equally happy to be lauded or derided—both fall on deaf ears. We are equally pleased to wash toilets or lead kingdoms—both are an inconsequential joy. If loss of dignity is the price we pay for intimacy with Jesus, so be it. The loss is gain.

BEDOUIN, TAJAKANT MUSLIMS OF ALGERIA (1,488,000; 0.0% EVANGELICAL)

PRAY THAT THE HEARTS OF THE BEDOUIN, TAJAKANT WOULD BE LIKE GOOD SOIL, READY TO HEAR THE GOSPEL AND TO RESPOND (MATT. 7:1-8, 18-23).

APRIL 3: CARRIED CONTINUALLY

2 SAMUEL 7-9; PSALM 93; MATTHEW 4; COLOSSIANS 4

*G*od took David from the sheepfold to make him ruler. The Lord was with David and preserved him wherever he went (2 Sam. 7:9; 8:6; 8:14). God carried David continually.

There is an ongoing tension in our hearts—that of continually needing God's help even as we continually resent it or are reluctant to accept it. I often feel guilty that I need Jesus. I do not want to bother Him. On one hand, I know that I desperately need Him and cannot live without Him. On the other hand, my pride and insecurity make me reluctant to ask for His help. My pride keeps me from calling on Jesus because I want to achieve things by my own strength so I might receive honor. My insecurity keeps me from calling on Jesus because I do not feel worthy to approach Him, and insecurity is just a subtle form of pride. It is humbling to be dependent on someone, and no one wants to be a burden to others. Something inside a proud heart does not want to be an ongoing liability. To be the dependent recipient of ongoing grace requires a fortified humility.

The wonder is that God delights to be our source and constant supply. Our continual dependency seems like an imposition to us, but it is engineered by Him. He made us to be dependent on Him. He delights to carry us, to hold us together, to give us breath, and to provide constant care. Because we are finite and the dependency of others drains us, we assume our constant needs must weary God. While we love and revel in His ongoing care, the parts of our nature that are not crucified recoil in shame at the idea that we need His benevolence. We love His help and are embarrassed by His help at the same time.

Jesus wants us to believe that it is His joy to carry us and that He delights in being our constant provider. He wants us to believe that we are not a burden to Him, that it is His joy to shepherd us. He wants us to believe that our dependence on Him is not irksome or displeasing, that He revels in it. He is honored by our dependence on Him. God's joy is that we eternally need His supplies. Our joy is that He eternally supplies our needs.

JHALAWAN MUSLIMS OF PAKISTAN (733,000; 0.0% EVANGELICAL)

PRAY FOR THE PEACE THAT RESULTS WHEN MEN AND WOMEN ARE RECONCILED
WITH GOD (JOHN 14:27). PRAY FOR MEN AND WOMEN OF PEACE
(LUKE 10:6) AMONG THE JHALAWANS.

APRIL 4: EXCEEDINGLY GLAD

2 SAMUEL 10-12; PSALM 94; MATTHEW 5; 1 THESSALONIANS 1

How sweet it is to suffer and die. The crucified life has so much joy. If only we could trust Jesus, take Him at His word and embrace dying daily, we would be enriched. Yet it is difficult for us to believe that joy and sorrow are companions.

We spend incredible emotional energy at the thought of opposition or rejection. We avoid conflict and affliction, blind to the reality that the Word is often received "*in* much affliction, with the joy of the Holy Spirit" (1 Thess. 1:6, emphasis added). We are more familiar with the sobriety of the Spirit than with His joy, and we force a dichotomy where there is none: pain and joy, sorrow and joy, difficulty and joy, hardship and joy, poverty and joy, suffering and joy, sickness and joy, death and joy. Jesus told us, "Blessed are those who are persecuted . . . revile[d] . . . maligne[d]. . . . *Rejoice and be exceedingly glad . . .*" (Matt. 5:10–12, emphasis added).

We tell ourselves that joy comes despite affliction. Jesus tells us that joy comes because of affliction. We tell ourselves that joy helps us overcome rejection. Jesus tells us that rejection is a joy. We tell ourselves there is joy on the other side of persecution. Jesus tells us that joy swells in trials. We segregate joy and pain. Jesus unites them, and we discover in the multitude of our anxieties that His "comforts delight our souls" (Ps. 94:19). Some depths of joy are only discovered in the valley of shadows. Some delights are only magnified when we live in anxious times or places.

It is a mistake to pity those who surrender all they know and the securities they enjoy for the insecurities and instabilities of pioneer missions. An appropriate response when friends and family leave home to move to Somalia, Afghanistan, Syria, or Yemen with their vulnerable children is godly jealousy. Joyous intimacies are available only to those who forsake all for Jesus. Do not mourn for those imprisoned—envy them, for Jesus floods them with exceptional joy in His presence. Do not anguish over those who are sick or widowed—they gain a unique intimacy with Jesus. We do not pray trouble on our friends, but neither should we mindlessly pray them out of it. Their suffering may be divinely mandated to grace them with exceeding joy. Whatever steps bring us closer to Jesus are joyful ones.

MALLAH HINDUS OF INDIA (2,966,000; 0.0% EVANGELICAL)

PRAY THAT BELIEVERS AMONG THE MALLAH WOULD PROCLAIM THE MESSAGE OF THE GOSPEL CLEARLY AND WOULD MAKE THE MOST OF EVERY OPPORTUNITY GOD PLACES BEFORE THEM (COL. 4:2-5).

APRIL 5: PLEASING GOD

2 SAMUEL 13-15; PSALM 95; MATTHEW 6; 1 THESSALONIANS 2

*I*t is impossible to please everyone, so you might as well please Jesus. It is a fallacy to think that people will like you for preaching the gospel. Every person needs to be affirmed, respected, and admired, but proclaiming the gospel does not satisfy these needs—not from people, at least. The gospel brings as much ire and anger as it does acceptance. Paul knew this and reminded the Thessalonians that despite suffering and setback he had spoken the gospel to them "in much conflict . . . not as pleasing men . . . neither at any time did we use flattering words . . . nor did we seek glory" (1 Thess. 2:2–6).

According to Jesus, the kingdom of God is not all-inclusive. Matthew 6 talks of food, drink, and clothing, and then instructs us to "seek first the kingdom and His righteousness, and all these things shall be added to you" (v. 33) If they are to be *added,* they cannot be essential parts of the kingdom. The kingdom is foundational, but it is not us nor is it what we do. Paul told the Thessalonians that the gospel had been preached. Not only was the gospel shared but "also our own lives" (1 Thess. 2:8). Again, our lives are not the gospel—they are something in addition to the primary communication of what Jesus has done.

To draw a line between the kingdom of God inside of us and food and clothing, or between the proclaimed gospel and shared lives, is not to diminish either. We are to live blamelessly and to walk worthy of the gospel and the kingdom (1 Thess. 2:11–12), but the Bible refuses to equate the internal kingdom and external living or the message and the missionary. Because we love to be liked, much of what we offer to a broken world is based, in part, on their acceptance of us for what we do. In John 10:33, Jesus' attackers told Him: "For a good work we do not stone You, but for blasphemy, and because You, being a Man, make Yourself God." They appreciated Jesus for the physical acts of mercy and provision He offered—they hated Him for His verbal truth, for His claim to be God.

If you want to be true to the kingdom and to the gospel, be prepared to be resented. Doing good in order to be liked and seen by men is its own reward (Matt. 6:1–5). If we want to please God, we must declare that Jesus is God. This is a message resented by both Muslims and secularists and most everyone else as well. A steady proclamation of Jesus as God leaves no room for any other ideology; it is a mutually exclusive claim that demands all worship and allegiance. A commitment to the deity of Jesus is a commitment to scorn. To please God is to disappoint people. To lift up the divine Christ despite pressure and scorn, suffering and trial, is to please God.

FULA JALON, PULAAR, AND FULANI MUSLIMS OF GUINEA (4,351,000; 0.0% EVANGELICAL)

PLEAD THAT THE FULA JALON, PULAAR, AND FULANI WILL UNDERSTAND THAT HOPE FOR
FORGIVENESS AND ACCEPTANCE WITH GOD IS AVAILABLE ONLY THROUGH JESUS'
WORK ON THE CROSS (1 COR. 1:18).

*W*hen Jesus is the source of our affections, we are convinced that He is worthy of all things. He is worthy of our lives, our deaths, our hopes, and our worship. Jesus is worth dying for. He is worth suffering for. We should not be shaken by our sufferings and trials, for "we are appointed" to glorify Jesus in them (1 Thess. 3:3). We are appointed to worship Jesus in *all* things.

Constant Worship (Ps. 96:2). The good news of God's salvation is to be proclaimed from day to day. We worship by lifting our voices in lands of oppression and by magnifying the Lord. We worship by declaring that Jesus is God, in the teeth of ideologies that angrily and actively oppose Him. We must constantly lift our voices and declare the worth of Jesus through worship. But worship is not just devotional—worship is evangelistic. We worship day by day when we witness. When Jesus is so important to us that we constantly tell others how wonderful He is, this, too, is worship.

Global Worship (Ps. 96:3, 7, 10). We are to proclaim the glory of God among the nations. Families of peoples are to give to the Lord glory and strength. We are to say among the nations "the Lord reigns." The people of God are to proclaim the Word of God by the Spirit of God among all ethnolinguistic people. Our goal is the global worship of Jesus by every tongue and tribe. Our goal is that every known tongue will be well represented around the eternal throne. Our local worship will be complete only when people around the globe worship Jesus as God.

Holy Worship (Ps. 96:9). The beauty of holiness is both a place and a condition. Post-Pentecost, the Holy Spirit was unleashed on the world. The purpose of the rent veil in the temple was not to allow the nations of the world to rush into a tiny physical space but to symbolize the release of the Spirit in movable temples throughout the world. The Spirit of God is holy, and God's moveable temples must be holy. When we worship in holiness, it is a beauty that people recognize and God endorses. No man or woman is perfect, but when we stand to extol God—having nothing between us and others or between us and our Lord—there is a special beauty that pleases Him and nourishes others.

We are appointed to worship. We were created to worship, all the time, everywhere. When our worship leads to affliction, then let affliction magnify our worship. Let not affliction silence us or sully our praise. Let affliction be the instrument to broadcast the worth of Jesus in all things.

GILAKI MUSLIMS OF IRAN (4,112,000; 0.0% EVANGELICAL)

PRAY THAT THE BELIEVERS AMONG THE GILAKI WILL ENDURE PERSECUTION IN A CHRISTLIKE MANNER AND WILL GIVE THEIR LIVES FOR THE SAKE OF THE GOSPEL IF NECESSARY (1 PETER 2:21-23).

APRIL 7: SORROW SWALLOWER

2 SAMUEL 19-21; PSALM 97; MATTHEW 8; 1 THESSALONIANS 4

*Y*esterday, a good friend told me that he has been unfaithful to his wife. He has not lived up to God's will for sexual purity. He has not possessed his own vessel in honor, and he has not obeyed God's call to holiness (1 Thess. 4:3, 4, 7). We grieve with him and his family. In no position to cast stones, we sorrow.

The Scriptures contain an extraordinary injunction about sorrow. We are to sorrow as people who have hope (v. 13). I love the reality in which God works. Faith never denies facts, and salvation does not make us immune to sorrow. Our sins and the sins of others are incredibly painful. Yet, as we stagger under the consequences of our own stupidity or are stricken by the selfishness of others, we are told to sorrow in hope. This is not a glib exhortation. Jesus has authority to call us to hope on the other side of pain because He rose from the grave after the agony of the cross. Resurrection life means there is something for us on the other side of sorrow. Sin causes anguish, yet Jesus exhorts us to writhe in hope.

Jesus took our sin upon Himself—He is the great sin swallower. He also took our sickness upon Himself—He is the great sickness swallower. If Jesus can swallow sin and sickness, He can certainly swallow our sorrow. He takes our infirmities and carries them (Matt. 8:17). He absorbs our sins, our sickness, our sorrow—He is the sorrow swallower. When we are wounded, deeply wounded, it is foolish to tell ourselves not to reel or agonize. Our only recourse is to remind ourselves that Jesus will swallow our sorrow. You will not always hurt. Your wound will scar and you will carry that forever (Jesus had scars on His glorified body), but one day your sorrow will be swallowed. Where does your pain, sickness, and sorrow go when Jesus swallows it? It is nailed to His cross, where the nails pierced through His hands.

The agony of sexual sin is twofold: To the betrayed spouse it is heart piercing, and unfathomable sorrow descends. We shouldn't say much to that person, just hug them tight and pray that they may sorrow in hope. To the betrayer we also turn in love. They have their own agony and crushing judgment, and lectures are no kindness. We embrace them also and long for them to believe that God swallows our sorrow and brings life from death.

BERBER, RIFI MUSLIMS OF MOROCCO (1,402,000; 0.03% EVANGELICAL)

PRAY THAT GOD WOULD RAISE UP MISSIONARIES FROM ALL OVER THE WORLD TO PLANT
THE CHURCH TOGETHER AMONG THE BERBER, RIFI
(MATT. 9:37).

APRIL 8: DELIGHTED IN

2 SAMUEL 22-24; PSALM 98; MATTHEW 9; 1 THESSALONIANS 5

*I*t is difficult for most of us to believe that God delights in us. We can accept that He forgives us, because He is magnanimous. We can accept that He provides for us, because He is generous. We can even accept that He loves us, because He is big enough to condescend and love what is unlovable. We tell ourselves that love is clinical, a decision. Delight is spontaneous joy, and there is nothing about us that would cause God spontaneous joy. We can accept other great acts of God because we recognize they originate from who He is. When we consider that God delivers us because He delights in us (2 Sam. 22:20), we shift the eternal equation and make ourselves the center of the question. We think we need to earn God's joy. Yet, if He forgives, provides for, and loves us out of who *He* is, why should He shift and delight in us because of who we are? He does not; God delights in us because of who He is. If God delighted in us because of who we are, this would put unbearable pressure on us to be delightful (which we could never be).

The fact that we are delivered because God delights in us increases the majesty of God and propels us to glorious liberty. The pressure is gone. The pressure to perform, the pressure to be perfect, and the pressure to be worthy are all gone. Rather than try to deserve the delight of God, we revel in the wonder of His delight and live thankful. Certainly, we want to be disciplined, consecrated, and intentional, but living this way because of God's pleasure is entirely different than living this way to earn His pleasure.

God delights in us because He knows we bear His nature. He delights to see Himself in us. Yes, we are fallen . . . yes, we are marred . . . yes, we are foolish . . . but He sees past our folly. He remembers what the first Adam was like before the fall and how we carry his genes. He also knows what the second Adam has done for us in allowing converted men and women to partake in the divine nature. God sees past the tarnish to the treasure within Himself. These are strange and glorious realities. God delights in me because of who He is, not because of who I am!

God's delight becomes the source of our strength, our power, and the gentleness that makes us great. In ourselves, we cannot do anything glorious, but the glorious God who lives within us shares His nature with us. Due to His indwelling, we live under His delight and with His powerful favor to bless others. God's delight is the gift that keeps on giving: delight breeds delight. When God delights in us, we delight in Him and we become the delight of others who are drawn to the God who lives within us. How delightful to be God's delight!

KUR GALLI MUSLIMS OF AFGHANISTAN (285,000; 0.1% EVANGELICAL)

PRAY THAT THE KUR GALLI WOULD FEEL AND KNOW THE BURDEN OF SIN AND WOULD COME TO JESUS FOR FORGIVENESS AND SALVATION (MATT. 11:28-30).

APRIL 9: COUNTED WORTHY

1 KINGS 1-3; PSALM 99; MATTHEW 10; 2 THESSALONIANS 1

*O*f all the things Jesus is against, one of the more surprising is temporal peace. Jesus did not "come to bring peace but a sword" (Matt. 10:34). Jesus brings division to families and societies. When we follow Jesus we are divided from our lives and united with Him. In this upside-down kingdom, suffering is only bestowed on the worthy (2 Thess. 1:5). You have to be counted worthy to suffer for God's kingdom; you have to be counted worthy of His calling. History has judged those who suffer to be either wicked or unfortunate. Yet heaven decrees it an honor to suffer when we suffer for Jesus' sake. Not everyone is given the high privilege of deep suffering.

Second Thessalonians 1 tells us that our endurance in suffering is manifest evidence of the righteous judgment of God. God will trouble those who trouble us (v. 6), and when Jesus comes He will give rest to those who are troubled, (v. 7). When we face trials, sufferings, and tribulation with a quiet peace, our endurance shouts a message in the spirit realm: "God will vindicate me. God will have vengeance on you."

We sit calmly in the courtroom of earth for we know final judgment awaits, and we will be declared innocent. Prison, scorn, abuse—all are the pompous and impotent theatrics of the evil "prosecuting attorney." He may seem impressive, his case may seem airtight, and the galleries may grin and gloat. But our immovability in the dock is unsettling to our foes and assuring to our friends. "Why aren't they worried?" the observers ask. "What do they know that we do not know?"

We know that the Judge of all the earth will do right. We know that "the name of our Lord Jesus Christ [will] be glorified in [us,] and [we] in Him" (v. 12). Pity the fools who are so excited at our trial. No matter the fabricated or factual evidence against us, we have an advocate in the heavens and the judge happens to be our Father. He has whispered to us His final decision. We sit peaceably, absorb the abuse, and endure the scorn with a quiet serenity that unnerves our accusers. Our worthy suffering points to the ultimate righteous judgment of God. "Do all the injustice to us you will," we say, "for there is a God in heaven who sees all and will judge you. Our peace under pressure is a warning. We are not alarmed, and therefore you should be."

Knowing how it ends reminds us that righteousness will not be fully implemented until "the Lord Jesus is revealed from heaven with His mighty angels, in flaming fire taking vengeance" (vv. 7–8). We probably will not see justice in our day. We will not see righteousness descend like rain as long as the earth is under human responsibility. Justice and righteousness will not come from man—they will come on that last great day when Jesus comes in furious power. It will be the first day of eternal justice.

MEGH HINDUS OF INDIA (2,913,000; 0.0% EVANGELICAL)

PRAY THAT GOD WOULD UNVEIL THE CROSS AND WOULD REMOVE THE VEIL ON THE MINDS
AND SPIRITS OF THE MEGH (2 COR. 3:16-17).

APRIL 10: POOR PREACHING

1 KINGS 4-6; PSALM 100; MATTHEW 11; 2 THESSALONIANS 2

*J*esus' primary way of dignifying the poor was by preaching to them. He looked beyond socio-economic status and treated every human equally. In fact, His interaction with the poor is notable for what He did *not* do. He did not maintain a feeding program. He did not organize social institutions. He did not concentrate on the political or economic injustices of the day. Jesus dealt with sin, and He found it equally prevalent among the poor and the rich. He placed no priority on the poor. To say that "the ground at the foot of the cross is level" means the poor have no special salvific considerations.

People have always been offended by the equality of all persons before God. A twisted sort of pride views the poor as advantaged before God. Yet neither God nor sin is any respecter of persons, and Jesus' earthly ministry was devoted to one primary task: saving sinners. Jesus sent a message back to John, "The poor have the gospel preached to them. And blessed is he who is not offended because of Me" (Matt. 11:5–6). The hubris of the rich elevates the needs of the poor because it makes the rich feel superior and self-satisfied to be the solution. Jesus said that the primary solution for poverty is to preach sin and the Savior. The poor have one advantage: they are not ashamed to admit they need help. The best thing we can do for them is to tell them about Jesus. Blessed is the person, whether rich or poor, who is not offended at Jesus' priority: the eternal soul.

When we make soul winning a priority this does not delegitimize caring for people's bodies and minds. Those who struggle with the language of priority when it comes to holism usually do not struggle with the concept of priority in other spheres of life. Does anyone resist the priority we have in our relationship with God over loved ones and friends? Prioritizing my walk with Jesus makes me a better husband, father, and friend. I love others best by loving Jesus first. The same principle applies to holism. We care best for the totality of humanity's needs by prioritizing care for their souls. The insertion point is arbitrary (sometimes you bind up wounds before you open your mouth), but the priority on addressing sin in the heart and offering heaven as the eternal home remains.

BAMBARA MUSLIMS OF MALI (4,379,000; 0.016% EVANGELICAL)

PRAY THAT BELIEVERS AMONG THE BAMBARA WOULD BE SET FREE FROM A SPIRIT OF FEAR OF WHAT MAY COME AND WOULD BOLDLY PROCLAIM THE TRUTH OF THE GOSPEL (2 TIM. 1:6-8).

APRIL 11: GLORY CLOUDED

1 KINGS 7-9; PSALM 101; MATTHEW 12; 2 THESSALONIANS 3

*D*avid lifted a cry of longing for us all: "Oh, when will You come to me?" (Ps. 101:2). We know we belong to Jesus, yet we long for more of Him. We struggle with the "plague" of our own hearts (1 Kings 8:38). Our sin and flesh cloud our spirits and make it seem that God is remote, clouded, veiled. Hunger for God is itself a grace for it is God who "inclines our hearts to Himself" (1 Kings 8:58). Our hearts are often blurred by self and sin, yet we long for Jesus to come to us in renewed vitality. What a wonder that God puts the desire for Himself within us. We do not have to manufacture passion, for we only pervert it when we try. Rather, by faith we trust that God will give us a desire for more of Him and will fulfill that desire.

When we honestly and humbly hunger, pray, confess His name, and turn from our sin, then God in heaven hears, forgives, teaches, and delivers. The affliction God sends on our souls due to our sin is a precursor to hunger. God often has to withhold His sweet presence in order for us to hunger for Him. He does not do this capriciously; our folly requires it. Nothing makes us hunger for the master's table like wallowing in the mire with pigs for a while. God helps us hunger for Him by allowing us to experience how unsatisfying everything else is.

When Solomon dedicated the temple, the glory cloud of God's presence filled the temple and the priests could no longer minister. The presence of God was so thick that the priests paused to enjoy it. Often, we are so busy trying to manufacture God's presence that we fail to recognize and participate in it. The goal of the priests was not to minister ritually but to prepare a place for God's presence. Their ministry was fulfilled, not interrupted, when God manifested His presence.

In our lives, families, and teams, we must remember that the goal is the manifest presence of Jesus. We can become so busy being busy that the revealed presence of Jesus seems like a delay. We forget that the goal is not ministry that works toward the presence of Jesus. The goal is the presence of Jesus. Oh, that God would interrupt our efforts to enter His presence by manifesting His presence, and that we would have the wisdom, when that happens, to drop everything and enjoy it! The goal is not church or singing or preaching—these are all means toward His presence. When the presence of Jesus manifests, enjoy it! Stop singing, worshiping, preaching, praying, ministering, talking . . . stop everything and linger in the glory cloud—the tangible presence of Jesus.

ALAWITE MUSLIMS OF SYRIA (1,311,000; 0.01% EVANGELICAL)

PRAY FOR THE WORD OF GOD IN WRITTEN, ORAL, MUSICAL, AND DRAMATIC FORMS TO
BE TRANSLATED AND TO RISE AMONG THE ALAWITE
(ISA. 55:10-11).

APRIL 12: SUPER G'S

1 KINGS 10-12; PSALM 102; MATTHEW 13; 1 TIMOTHY 1

*F*or being the wisest man ever to live, Solomon sure was stupid. He did not heed God's warning about marrying those of disparate faiths. Instead, he "clung to them in love" (1 Kings 11:2), and "when Solomon was old . . . his wives turned his heart after other gods" (v. 4). The common pitfalls of men in every age are money, sex, and power, or as they are also known: the gold, the girls, and the glory.

There is something beautiful about Isaac being a one-woman man. Polygamy (even among the patriarchs) brought nothing but trouble. Solomon, with 1,000 women to please and be pleased by, made himself vulnerable over and over until his folly breached even his unprecedented wisdom. I am sure, in his intelligence, that he had strong reasons for his accommodations. After all, who can argue with the wisest man? But he was still stupid. Too many girls, too much gold, too much self-glory—all made even the wisest man a fool.

Rather than living for girls, gold, and glory, which destroy, God calls us to live for glory, grace, and gospel, which give life. When our motivation for life and mission is the weight of the presence of Jesus, this is life-giving and life-spreading. Instead of a lust for flesh, we have a raging passion to exalt God and to see every tongue worship Him. The fire still rages in our breasts but not to please our bodies or make much of the opposite sex—we live to make much of God! Grace keeps us humble. Conscious that God has given us what we do not deserve, we hold possessions and authority lightly, eager to give them away. The gospel points everything to Jesus. We are not the gospel and what we do is not the gospel. The gospel is what God has done, is doing, and will do in Christ. The gospel keeps us Christocentric. When Christ is the focus of our affections and attentions, we are not wooed by gold, girls, or self-glory. Christ is so much brighter, purer, and higher.

Wealth, education, and social status do not protect us from folly. Our world lauds those who make money, earn fame, and capture beautiful spouses. God's Word reminds us that anything outside the glory of God, the grace of the cross, and the gospel of Jesus Christ is folly. Girls, gold, and self-glory destroy. God's glory, grace, and gospel bring life *and* wisdom.

CHHIMBA MUSLIMS OF PAKISTAN (408,000; 0.0% EVANGELICAL)

PRAY THAT GOD WOULD POUR OUT HIS SPIRIT ON THE CHHIMBA PEOPLE AND THAT THEY WOULD SEE DREAMS AND VISIONS OF JESUS. PRAY THAT THEY WOULD BE POWERFULLY SAVED AND EMPOWERED TO BE HIS WITNESSES (JOEL 2:28-32).

APRIL 13: GRACE AND MERCY

1 KINGS 13–15; PSALM 103; MATTHEW 14; 1 TIMOTHY 2

*T*he real question in life is not "Why do the innocent suffer?" but "Why does a holy God with such unattainable standards of purity allow anyone to live?" The Scriptures make it clear that no one is good—no one is righteous. This truth comes as a shock to us for we have been brainwashed into believing we are good, innocent, and undeserving of the wrath of God. From the perspective of a holy, majestic God, we are all vile, reprehensible, and deserving of judgment and hell.

When tragedy strikes we should not wail "why us?" but should marvel that God's wrath is not poured out in greater measure. When earthquakes, wars, and tsunamis happen we question why God "allows" such things. We should shudder at such catastrophes for the reality is that we deserve these and worse. God's mercy is all that stands between us and His justice. God is just to strike us. The wonder is that He does not.

Who is this God who does not strike me every time I sin? Who is this God who, in grace, gives me joy, love, and eternal friendship? Who is this God who, in mercy, withholds sickness, wrath, and judgment? Who is this God who gives heaven and withholds hell? Who is this God who gives what I do not deserve and withholds what I do? Is this God's usual way of dealing with people? The staggering answer to this last question is *yes!* God's character is one of mercy and grace, truth and judgment. His mercy holds back His wrath, but both will ultimately be complete, for they are indivisible.

What about innocent babies? There are none. There is only mercy. Just because a baby black mamba snake is cute, does not mean the DNA of death is not deeply embedded in his soul. Sin is deeply embedded in the human race, latent in even the cutest newborn. God's grace gives heaven to those who die before an accountable age, for while we believe in original sin, we do not believe in original guilt. God's mercy withholds hell from the infants who die before they are able to repent from their sin (inherited and chosen). God is great enough to grant grace and mercy to the undeserving, but let us be under no illusion: No one is innocent, no one deserves grace, no one deserves mercy—not even a newborn. Babies go to heaven on God's merit, not their own.

TAMIL MUSLIMS OF INDIA (2,881,000; 0.0% EVANGELICAL)

PRAY THAT CHRISTIANS FROM AROUND THE WORLD WOULD WORK TOGETHER TO REACH THE TAMIL AND THAT THE TAMIL WOULD BE JOINED TO THE BODY OF CHRIST

(JOHN 17:20–23).

APRIL 14: STANDING IN HIS PRESENCE

1 KINGS 16–18; PSALM 104; MATTHEW 15; 1 TIMOTHY 3

*A*mong their other qualifications, overseers are qualified to teach (1 Tim. 3:2). Deacons are to hold the mystery of the faith with a clear conscience (v. 9). Disciples are to have enough internal fortitude not to be bothered by offending religious powers (Matt. 15:12–14), and God's intention is to make "His ministers a flame of fire" (Ps. 104:4). To represent God is to be able and willing to minster both His love and His rebuke. It is difficult for us to get the balance right. We are either too soft, which leads to corruption, or too harsh, which crushes.

Gabriel informed Zacharias that he would be mute for a season. Elijah told King Ahab that there would be no rain for three years. What gives angels, prophets, and ministers the right and the balance to dispense judgment? What keeps us from erring on the side of frustrated harshness when we encounter disbelief or outright evil? One thing: abiding in the presence of Jesus.

Gabriel said to Zacharias: "I am Gabriel, who stands in the presence of God, and was sent to speak to you. . . ." (Luke 1:19–20). Elijah said to Ahab: "As the Lord God of Israel lives, before whom I stand . . ." (1 Kings 17:1). The only way the oracles of God get His judgment and His mercy right is by faithfully standing in His presence. We cannot glibly pronounce pardon and blessing, nor rashly spout prophetic judgment without abiding in the presence of Jesus. Quick blessing or reactionary condemnation both are equally misrepresentative of Jesus when they do not issue from a life that is saturated in the presence of God.

The stakes are too high to be cavalier with our pronouncements. It is imperative, both for our souls and those to whom we minister, that ministers of the gospel be people of God's presence. When we are patient in His presence, we learn how He deals with people. We do not rush to judgment. We do not look with human eyes. We wait for His perspective, and then we announce it. We may not enjoy what we have to say (and the prophet who enjoys pronouncing disaster is as suspect as the minister who affirms when God condemns), but our affinity with the message is secondary. What is primary is that we have stood attentively in the presence of Jesus, then bolted to pass on His decisions as soon as He bids us do so.

FULAKUNDA, PEUL, FULANI, AND PULAAR MUSLIMS OF GUINEA BISSAU (295,000; 0.0% EVANGELICAL)

PRAY THAT THE HEARTS OF THE FULAKUNDA, PEUL, FULANI, AND PULAAR WOULD BE LIKE GOOD SOIL, READY TO HEAR THE GOSPEL AND TO RESPOND (MATT. 7:1-8, 18-23).

APRIL 15: DOCTRINE MATTERS

1 KINGS 19-21; PSALM 105; MATTHEW 16; 1 TIMOTHY 4

*I*t is increasingly common to relegate doctrine to secondary importance. In the church and in mission, we are bombarded with messages of journey, relationship, and process—as if journeys do not need maps, relationships do not have guidelines, and process is without benchmarks. Biblical teaching (right thinking about God and the world) is more necessary than ever. Wrong thinking about Jesus and His plans in the world is offensive to Christ (Matt. 16:23). Jesus reserved some of His strongest verbal attacks for those near to Him who misunderstood and tried to dissuade Him from His purposes.

To forfeit doctrine by relegating it to a place of unimportance is a critical error. According to Paul, demons have doctrines (1 Tim. 4:1). Demonic ideologies are very much at work crafting their messages artfully, expounding their worldview, and pressing their thinking. When we do not stand up for right thinking about God and His truth, we allow demonic doctrines a free hand. We must resist demonic doctrines from without and from within the church. Jesus warned us to beware of the doctrine from within that is religious, hypocritical, and legalistic (Matt. 16:12).

Good doctrine empowers and gives life. We can be "nourished in the words of faith and of the good doctrine" as we "give attention to reading, to exhortation, to doctrine." As we "take heed to [ourselves] and to the doctrine," we will "save both ourselves and those who hear us" (1 Tim. 4:6, 13, 16). Doctrine matters because it nourishes and saves us, and it saves those who hear us. Sound teaching leads to life! Sound teaching, the bread of heaven, satisfies God's people (Ps. 105:40). God's people cannot live on sugar nor can they live on medicine. They need the meat and potatoes and vegetables and fruit of the whole counsel of God.

In our pursuit of good doctrine, we must be careful not to think we alone have it. God's people need all of God's people to understand the Bible and the nature of God. We need our African brothers to tell us that the prosperity gospel is demonic. We need our Chinese sisters to tell us that suffering is normal. We need our Latino friends to remind us to depend on the Holy Spirit. We need Americans to underline the value of consistent devotion to the Word. We need Europeans to show us how the gospel can ride on the arts.

We may be tempted to say with Elijah: "Oh Lord, I alone am left!" I am the only one with good doctrine (1 Kings 19:10, 14). But God says: "Nonsense, I have reserved thousands of others for Myself who have not bowed the knee to demonic thinking. Why not link with them? Be strengthened by them. Be balanced by them." Doctrine does matter, and we need the full-orbed perspective of the global body of Christ in order to get it right.

GYPSY, HALEBI MUSLIMS OF EGYPT (1,279,000; 0.0% EVANGELICAL)

PRAY FOR THE PEACE THAT RESULTS WHEN MEN AND WOMEN ARE RECONCILED WITH GOD
(JOHN 14:27). PRAY FOR MEN AND WOMEN OF PEACE (LUKE 10:6)
AMONG THE GYPSY, HALEBI.

*W*ise people learn to love their critics, for critics often speak a measure of truth. We need to be secure enough to absorb the sting of truth even when it is barbed with envy. The wise person swallows the truth and spits out the malice. We can learn about ourselves from our critics as they are often more ready to speak truth to us than our friends. When we carefully consider the accusations of our enemies, we often find fact mingled with animosity—and we are wise to extract the metal from the ore.

Speaking truth that is unpopular is just as difficult as gleaning truth from our adversaries. Ahab resented Micaiah (1 Kings 22) because the prophet continually told the king what the king did not want to hear. It is wearisome to bring the minority report—as much for the speaker as for the listener. The danger for the listener is to stop listening and miss hearing truth. The danger for the speaker is to stop speaking and miss telling truth. A special stamina is required when unpopular truth is needed: stamina of both hearing and speaking. The gospel is not popular. The good news starts off as bad news. We tell people they are bound for hell, justly condemned on account of their own sins. We call people to change and to repent. The direct implication is that they are wrong, foolishly so—and no one likes to be called a fool.

Truth-telling is fraught with danger. When we tell the truth, we risk ridicule, rejection, and persecution. These dangers are temporal, no matter how much they sting, while the risks of not telling the truth are eternal. We must have the discipline both to tell the truth and to listen to the truth—especially when it is inconvenient or troublesome.

Truth-telling has some parameters. To spout facts without any consideration for the listener can be as counter-productive as not speaking at all. Paul exhorts Timothy (1 Tim. 5:1–2) to exhort rather than rebuke older men as fathers, younger men as brothers, and younger women as sisters. A pompous, self-righteous approach to truth makes our wisdom sound like a lie. Only God speaks truth from a position of moral superiority. Weeping prophets are more understandable than shouting ones—even when they proclaim the same message. As Samuel Hugh Moffett said, "We are but beggars telling other beggars where to find bread."[3]

DHOBI MUSLIMS OF PAKISTAN (1,065,000; 0.0% EVANGELICAL)

PRAY THAT BELIEVERS AMONG THE DHOBI WOULD PROCLAIM THE MESSAGE OF THE GOSPEL CLEARLY AND WOULD MAKE THE MOST OF EVERY OPPORTUNITY GOD PLACES BEFORE THEM (COL. 4:2–5).

APRIL 17: GODLY CURSING

2 KINGS 1-3; PSALM 107; MATTHEW 18; 1 TIMOTHY 6

*E*lisha was on his way to Bethel when some young people mocked him and his bald head (nothing is new under the sun). "So he turned around and looked at them, and pronounced a curse on them in the name of the Lᴏʀᴅ" (2 Kings 2:24). He gave a curse in the name of the Lord? We do not usually associate cursing and the Lord—but two mama bears mauled forty-two youths for their irreverence.

Godly cursing is not profane or vulgar. It pronounces discipline and consequences for those who act inappropriately. Jesus taught this in Matthew 18:15–17 when He explained how to correct an errant friend. If the friend does not respond to private, plural, and then church correction, the friend is to "be to you like a heathen and a tax collector." Again, these are not words we usually associate with Jesus, but there they are—the "cursing" (consequences) of God for those who act inappropriately.

Scripture is clear that God is merciful, He expects us to be merciful, and He gets irritated when we are not (Matt. 18:34). So godly "cursing" must be infrequent and applied cautiously. All the same, there is a time to pronounce the wrath of God and the consequences of sin. This, too, is in the spirit of Jesus. We generally interpret the verses about two or three gathering and agreeing on earth in Jesus' name as referring to "receiving" (vv. 19–20). To ask "in Jesus' name" is to ask in His Spirit for things He wants. When we ask for what He wants, of course He delights to answer. That is why praying Scripture is so important and so potent. When we pray Scripture, we know we pray what God wants and are certain He will answer our requests. However, to ask for what Jesus wants must also occasionally include God's "curses"—His punishment and consequences on those who act inappropriately.

There is great power when we come together, agreeable to one another and to the Spirit of Jesus. This double harmony between the supplicants themselves and the supplicants and the Savior provides authority to ask boldly and protection from asking wrongly. When the body agrees that God's consequences should be requested, this protects the individual from vendettas or revenge. God's consequences are intended to heal. They are, by design, both a last resort and a final reach of love. Let us be honest and loving enough with one another to declare and enact God's consequences for inappropriate behavior.

ASSAMESE MUSLIMS OF INDIA (2,739,000; 0.0% EVANGELICAL)

PRAY THAT THE ASSAMESE WILL UNDERSTAND THAT HOPE FOR FORGIVENESS AND ACCEPTANCE WITH GOD IS AVAILABLE ONLY THROUGH JESUS' WORK ON THE CROSS (1 COR. 1:18).

APRIL 18: THE HONOR OF BEING SELF-SUFFICIENT

2 KINGS 4–6; PSALM 108; MATTHEW 19; 2 TIMOTHY 1

*J*esus is pleased by those who give without a whiff of entitlement. When Elisha asked how he could return thanks to the Shunammite noble woman for her hospitality, she responded, "I dwell among my own people" (2 Kings 4:13). This was not a pompous comment. It was a cultured and dignified way to say: "I do not need subsidy or pandering. I am blessed by the Lord, and it is my honor to bless others. I did not give in order to receive; I gave because I wanted to and because I could." People who are self-sufficient like this please Jesus. They desire nothing for their ministry.

Gehazi had a completely different perspective on ministry. Elisha grew old and had nothing material to show for many years of service. Gehazi had even less. Perhaps Gehazi thought: *What is in it for me? How will I survive when Elisha is gone? It is all very well for him to fix poisonous stews with flour and multiply twenty loaves of barley bread to feed 100 men. But I can't do that, so who will take care of me and my family when Elisha is gone?* Elisha provided a glimpse into Gehazi's thinking when he asked, "Is it time to receive money and to receive clothing, olive groves and vineyards, sheep and oxen, male and female servants?" (2 Kings 5:26). Evidently, Gehazi had some retirement plans in mind. He had served Elisha faithfully for years and it was time for him to be rewarded.

But Gehazi's thinking was faulty. As a result, Naaman's leprosy descended on him—a judgment that seems harsh to us. Why should a little self-preservation deserve generations of shame? In an honor-and-shame culture, the greed or other sin of one person never affects just that person. When Gehazi asked for monetary reward after Elisha had refused it, he made both Elisha and God look petty. Gehazi sullied the honor of prophet and potentate by reducing them to "for hire" practitioners. In the eyes of the Syrians, his actions reduced God to a charlatan who performed a service for a monetary reward. Something precious was lost.

There is another danger in accepting benefits for ministry. John Woolman points out that honorariums often buy our silence, or at least our censored speech: "Sometimes, when I have felt truth lead to it, I have found myself disqualified by a superficial friendship."[4] May the prophetic voice never be extinguished because we accept some kindness, some unintended bribe that limits our ability to speak the pure Word of God. May greed never make us leprous—unfit to serve the Lord or His sheep.

WOLOF MUSLIMS OF SENEGAL (5,007,000; 0.0% EVANGELICAL)

PRAY THAT THE BELIEVERS AMONG THE WOLOF WILL ENDURE PERSECUTION IN A CHRISTLIKE MANNER AND WILL GIVE THEIR LIVES FOR THE SAKE OF THE GOSPEL IF NECESSARY (1 PETER 2:21-23).

APRIL 19: IT IS ONLY DEATH

2 KINGS 7–9; PSALM 109; MATTHEW 20; 2 TIMOTHY 2

Four leprous men of Israel made three profound statements. The first was: ***"Why are we sitting here until we die?"*** (2 Kings 7:3). The Syrians had surrounded the city, the people were starving, and the lepers came to the conclusion that they had another option. They did not need to sit around and wait for death. They concluded: *We are going to die anyway. We might as well die actively rather than passively.* Coming to this happy conclusion, they trotted off to plunder the deserted camp. There is something repulsive about the inward-focused retirement plans of a person who is basically waiting to die. How Jesus delights over senior citizens who spend their golden years "plundering" the nations through prayer, visitation, and outreach.

The second penetrating statement was: ***"If they kill us, we shall only die"*** (2 Kings 7:4). The question is, "What is so bad about death?" Lazarus could speak to this issue for he was a member of a very exclusive club. Plenty of people since Nicodemus have been "born again," but Lazarus was one of a handful who have "died again." If "to be absent from the body is to be present with the Lord" (2 Cor. 5:8), then when Lazarus died the first time, he was in the unmitigated presence of God—what wonder! And what a shock to be called back to a stinky grave and a sin-filled earth. I am confident Lazarus longed for death the rest of his life. I am also confident that death did not scare him. More than the rest of us, Lazarus knew that life on earth is merely a dream and heaven is our home. In a pioneer ministry fraught with risk to life and security, this reality comforts us: "If they kill us, we shall only wake up in the presence of Jesus!" What is so bad about that? It is hard to intimidate or silent someone who is not afraid of death, who even longs for it.

Third, the lepers realized: ***"We are not doing right. This day is a day of good news, and we remain silent. If we wait until morning light, some punishment will come upon us"*** (2 Kings 7:9). The lepers had found food and supplies and had begun to bury them, storing up necessities for their future. They realized that this was sin. They also realized the urgency to share saved supplies. Those who survive until that great morning of re-creation amply supplied but neglect to share the message with starving cities will earn one thing: punishment. It is criminal for Jesus' followers, who are amply supplied, to sit in holy huddles while vast collections of people have no access to or news about the Living Bread. Let us do right. Like lepers with a renewed lease on life, let us rush to the cities and call out to the gatekeepers that there is life, deliverance, and hope.

KUWAITI MUSLIMS OF KUWAIT (1,169,000; 1.0% EVANGELICAL)

PRAY THAT GOD WOULD RAISE UP MISSIONARIES FROM ALL OVER THE WORLD TO PLANT
THE CHURCH TOGETHER AMONG THE KUWAITI
(MATT. 9:37).

*J*ehu is not known for a balanced lifestyle. His driving was aggressive; he was ruthless (2 Kings 10:7); sarcastic (v. 9); zealous for God (v. 16); devious (vv. 18–19); violent, and severe (v. 24). He killed Ahab's seventy sons by cutting their heads off, forty-two of Ahaziah's sons just for being friendly with their cousins, and all the prophets of Baal. The Scripture commends him for his violent acts.

We must be careful when applying Old Testament violence to this age of grace. On the one hand, God does not change. God is still "angry at the wicked every day," and Jesus will still come with a "robe dipped in blood." Hell is still real, and those who rebel against God by rejecting the amnesty offered in the cross will suffer there forever. On the other hand, the New Testament and the teachings of Jesus clearly show us that the kingdom of God does not advance by coercion.

There is something degenerate about loving violence. Paul lists "brutal" as an indicator of a wayward heart (2 Tim. 3:3). To enjoy watching or causing others to be hurt is to be like the Devil. He kills and destroys. Cultures that promote violence in their media, entertainment, and practice are wicked. To enjoy watching violence is the spirit of antichrist. Obviously, violent acts are sometimes necessary to protect the innocent, but they must never be enjoyed and ever regretted.

The true follower of Jesus willingly suffers violence but does not enjoy watching it. This is the great litmus test of our hearts: If we are willing to suffer, if we accept this guarantee of suffering with relish (2 Tim. 3:12), we share in Jesus' heart to lay down our lives for others. However, if we enjoy watching others suffer, even under the guise of entertainment, there is something not Christlike in our hearts.

We need redeemed Jehu's among the followers of Jesus. We need radicals. We need those willing to do violence to their own wills. We need those who will embrace suffering for the sake of the gospel. We need those who are imbalanced, as long as they are weighted toward exalting Jesus among the nations.

Paul's life seemed to attract violence: He was beaten with rods, with whips, and with stones. He was shipwrecked, mocked, imprisoned, and repeatedly abused. Yet he could testify, "And out of them all, the Lord delivered me!" (2 Tim. 3:11) God's deliverance usually takes us through by grace, not by evacuation. Paul went to his eternal sanctuary when his head was cut off. The only violence that should attract us is that of suffering for Jesus in order to spread the gospel to the uttermost parts of the earth.

DHUND MUSLIMS OF PAKISTAN (593,000; 0.0% EVANGELICAL)

PRAY THAT THE DHUND WOULD FEEL AND KNOW THE BURDEN OF SIN AND WOULD COME
TO JESUS FOR FORGIVENESS AND SALVATION
(MATT. 11:28-30).

APRIL 21: ENDING WELL

2 KINGS 13-15; PSALM 111; MATTHEW 22; 2 TIMOTHY 4

*W*e know Paul's summary of his life: "I have fought the good fight, I have finished the race, I have kept the faith," (2 Tim. 4:7). Let us not forget that his head was chopped off. Ending well has nothing to do with going to heaven healthy. One of the clearest mockeries of the prosperity "gospel" is 2 Kings 13:14: "Elisha had become sick with the illness of which he would die."

That great lion of God, Elisha, made the Jordan part, cleansed the water source of a city, called bears out of the woods to discipline rude youths, predicted victories through music, performed miracles with oil, raised a young boy from the dead, purified poisonous stew, fed a hundred men on pitiful rations, healed a Syrian from leprosy, floated a metal ax head, struck an army blind, prophesied bread from the windows of heaven, and called down fire from heaven. Yet this same man of power and faith got sick and died a slow, painful death. A terminal illness ended the life of the most faith-filled and powerful man of that day. The dry bones of this same man raised another man from the dead.

Ending well has nothing to do with dying rich, being respected by people, or slipping peacefully from sleep to the heavens. You may die with all the external trappings of peace, but peaceful passage has historically happened at the stake, on the cross, and in physical agony on a sickbed. If God mandated that Elisha cross over to eternal health on the bridge of terminal illness, how dare we presume that Christians will be spared the burdens of sickness, suffering, or trial?

Further, it is a travesty for any follower of Jesus to arrive at the end of their race with strength to spare. We are to be poured out, spent, and exhausted on the gospel. "Nothing in our hands we bring"[5] refers to eternity as much as it does to salvation. We came naked, we will leave naked; so we might as well pour out all we have for the glory of God.

Does God want everyone healthy and provided for? Ultimately, yes—in heaven. Temporally, the prophets died sick, apostles had their heads chopped off, and the Messiah writhed naked on a cross. All ended superbly well. All remained faithful until the end of the beginning, and all passed victorious into eternal life. Faith is not about money and wealth. Faith is about trust in Jesus—trust that He is real, worth suffering for, worth being sick for, worth being in prison for, and worth dying for. We end well when we carry the supremacy of Jesus' worth all the way to heaven—no matter how our sojourn on earth ends.

DARZI HINDUS OF INDIA (2,712,000; 0.0% EVANGELICAL)

PRAY THAT GOD WOULD UNVEIL THE CROSS AND WOULD REMOVE THE VEIL ON
THE MINDS AND SPIRITS OF THE DARZI
(2 COR. 3:16-17).

*D*isobedience is linked to disbelief. When you stop believing, you stop obeying. I obey Jesus because I trust Him. I trust that Jesus is good, pure, wise, and *right*. When I trust God is doing the right things for His glory and for my good, then I obey Him readily. When I doubt that He is good or that what He ordains for me will work toward good, I obey Him grudgingly. When we stop believing in the essential goodness (rightness) of God, we start rejecting His counsel. When we reject His counsel, we become like the God-hating fools around us—for that is what underlies disobedience: a hatred of God. As it did Israel in 2 Kings 17, rejecting God's counsel leads us to self-destruction, sacrificing our children, and selling ourselves to do evil, which has the implicit, if unspoken, intent of making God angry.

This decadent progression is sure: from living to make God glad, to existing to provoke His anger. This is the Devil's fate, and a lack of belief leads us to act like him. Trust in who God says He is and what He tells us to do makes us like Jesus. There is no treading water. The current of fallen Eden pulls us away from trust. We must fight to trust! We cannot mix trust with fear of rulers, peers, or colleagues. In truth, we cannot fear the Lord unless we fear Him alone. Jehovah will not be one of many gods. He will not even be the greatest of many. He must be worshiped alone. In 2 Kings 17:41, when the people enacted partial reform, they "feared the LORD, yet served their carved images." Partial faith is not faith at all—it is disbelief. "The mighty God, the maker of heaven and earth, will not be one of many treasures, not even the chief of all treasures. He will be all in all or He will be nothing."[6]

The Devil ceaselessly tries to undermine our trust in Jesus. He hates those who trust God, for our trust in God reminds the Devil that he did not trust and now suffers the consequences. Further, the Enemy knows that our trust is both his undoing and our deliverance. Trust in Jesus defeats the schemes of evil. Active, energetic, faithful belief in God does the greatest damage to the Devil's plans. This is why he does everything he can to undermine our trust in Jesus.

When the Devil mutters in our ears like the lying Assyrian at the gates, we need to hold our peace and answer him "not a word" (2 Kings 18:36). We do not engage in a battle of wits with the Devil—we battle at the level of our wills. Ignoring his attempts to undermine our trust in Jesus, we resolve not to give him energy or attention. We give *all* our trust, *all* our obedience, *all* our strength, and *all* our thinking to Jesus. We defeat the Devil by believing and obeying God.

ARAB, SHUWA, AND BAGGARA MUSLIMS OF CHAD (1,720,000; 0.0% EVANGELICAL)

PRAY THAT BELIEVERS AMONG THE ARAB, SHUWA, AND BAGGARA WOULD BE SET FREE FROM A SPIRIT OF FEAR OF WHAT MAY COME AND WOULD BOLDLY PROCLAIM THE TRUTH OF THE GOSPEL (2 TIM. 1:6-8).

APRIL 23: TAKE ROOT DOWNWARD

2 KINGS 19-21; PSALM 113; MATTHEW 24; TITUS 2

*W*e too easily forget who builds the church. Missionaries do not build the church. Money does not build the church. Programs do not build the church. Methods do not build the church. Indigenous leaders do not build the church. Miracles do not build the church. Witness does not build the church. Not even our prayers build the church because prayer is something we do and we do not build the church. Only Jesus builds the church! When we try to build the church, we build it to defend. When Jesus builds His church, He builds it to attack. Jesus' church is militant—it batters down the gates of hell. The most important lesson a church planter can latch onto is to stop trying to build the church. If God builds the church, who can be against it?

Of course we witness, of course we plan, of course we pray, of course we disciple, of course we learn a foreign language and spend our lives—even suffer—for the church that Jesus builds. Of course we shed our blood, leave our homes, speak a foreign tongue imperfectly, experience disease and discomfort, and struggle through stress and oppression that the church might be built, but we do so knowing that Jesus is the master builder. We do the grunt work of pushing a wheelbarrow around. More often than not, we do the work no one will ever see. We long for the church to be planted—and because we do, we take root downward.

In 2 Kings 19:30, Isaiah assured Hezekiah that God would rescue Judah from the Assyrians and that the remnant would "again take root downward, and bear fruit upward." A second lesson for church planters is that we must dig down to build up. Abiding in Jesus is integral to church planting. Spending extravagant and intimate time with Him on a daily basis is the hidden foundation that supports disciples growing together. Jesus builds His church with living stones, yet we are surprised to arrive in our fields of service and find that we are stones, not masons.

We come to the mission field with great expectations of how we will build God's church, only to have Jesus grab us, whack off some unnecessary flesh, pound us into a shape He can use, and stick us underground as one small part of the foundation. Then He covers us up with dirt. We are stunned—we came to be mighty builders. Instead, God deconstructs us and uses us to play a hidden part that others will never see or praise.

When Jesus has a collection of living stones He has pressed into useable shape, He often hides them in the earth and makes them strong enough to bear the weight of His church. What is our part? We take root downward . . . we excel in the hidden process of becoming like Jesus. We dig deep, that we might bear fruit heavenward.

JEBALA MUSLIMS OF MOROCCO (1,130,000; 0.02% EVANGELICAL)

PRAY FOR THE WORD OF GOD IN WRITTEN, ORAL, MUSICAL, AND DRAMATIC FORMS TO BE TRANSLATED AND TO RISE AMONG THE JEBALA (ISA. 55:10-11).

APRIL 24: INCONSEQUENT CONSEQUENCES

2 KINGS 22-24; PSALM 114; MATTHEW 25; TITUS 3

*J*esus' opinion is the only one that matters. My good friend Omar Beiler puts it this way: "Don't give other people free rent in your head." We can spend inordinate energy worrying what others think of us, rather than simply doing what God wants of us. The longer we live, the more difficult decisions become. When faced with a choice, choose to delight in delighting Jesus. Let the only energy you exert after you have made a difficult and potentially unpopular choice be celebration energy as you rejoice in pleasing Jesus.

Tender hearts do what is right regardless of the consequences. Josiah was like no king before or after him in his reckless pursuit of holiness. He radically removed all traces of false worship (2 Kings 22). We should be as relentless in purging our hearts and lives of any trace of idolatry. The remarkable aspect of Josiah's reforms, however, is that he undertook them regardless of the outcome for himself or his nation. Huldah, the prophetess, told Josiah that because of his tender heart, humble spirit, and godly sorrow (2 Kings 22:19), he would escape judgment. She also said that the nation had accumulated too much guilt for God to relent of judging them (v. 17). Josiah made the radical reforms anyway. The point was not consequences but doing what pleased God. May we be just as radical, unconcerned about consequences, and devoted to pleasing Jesus.

God wants to make us His sanctuary and dominion (Ps. 114:2). When we are temples purified for His indwelling, when we are so completely under His control that it can be said we are His "New Dominion," the Lord is greatly pleased and we are easy for Him to use. We find this condition joyful, for faithfulness to Jesus not only pleases Him, it makes us happy. My joy is found in being faithful (Matt. 25:21). When I am faithful to Jesus, my wife, my family, and my friends, an inevitable byproduct is great joy in my soul. It is in my best interest to be completely faithful, for my faithfulness brings joy to everyone, myself included! Faithfulness makes me happy.

Joy is found in doing what is right in Jesus' eyes. When we scurry around, frantically trying to please others, it robs us of joy, and we are never at rest. When we devote ourselves to pleasing Jesus regardless of the consequences, joy fills His soul and ours.

DUNGAN MUSLIMS OF KYRGYZSTAN (59,000; 0.0% EVANGELICAL)

PRAY THAT GOD WOULD POUR OUT HIS SPIRIT ON THE DUNGAN PEOPLE AND THAT THEY WOULD SEE DREAMS AND VISIONS OF JESUS. PRAY THAT THEY WOULD BE POWERFULLY SAVED AND EMPOWERED TO BE HIS WITNESSES (JOEL 2:28-32).

APRIL 25: ACTIVE BETRAYAL

2 KINGS 25; PSALM 115; MATTHEW 26; PHILEMON

We all betray Jesus—all the time. Matthew 26:25 puts the action of Judas in the present active sense: "Then Judas, who was betraying Him." If you resist the claim that we all actively betray Jesus, there is something of Peter lurking inside you. "Even if all are made to stumble because of You, I will never be made to stumble" (v. 33). Poor fool. Peter eventually swore that he did "not know the Man" (v. 72). The super-spiritual among us are the ones who give Jesus away with a kiss. (Beware the dramatic professions of allegiance in yourself and others.) It is better to be silent and sober when we realize that "all the disciples forsook Him and fled" (v. 56).

In Africa and the Middle East, food is often served from a common platter or bowl. A way to honor another person is to reach into the bowl, choose a choice piece of meat or vegetable, and hand it to a friend. In Ethiopia, they place the morsel directly in your mouth. Some scholars say this is what Jesus did: He reached into the bowl, selected a choice piece of food, looked Judas in the eye, and extended one more opportunity to him: "Judas, I love you. I love you to the end. I know who you are and what you are about to do. Judas, I give you one more chance." Jesus extended grace.

When we take communion in remembrance of Jesus, we remember with Peter "the word of Jesus" and we weep (v. 75). Communion reminds us that we actively betray our Lord. Communion forces us to admit that not only were we once sinners saved by grace, we continue to sin and continue to be saved by grace. Despite all our covenants and promises and efforts and resolutions, we actively betray Jesus. That is not the wonder. The wonder is that in the Lord's Supper, Jesus reaches into the bread of His torn body, stretches across time and sin, extends mercy, looks us in the eyes, and says: "This is My body. Take, eat!" We are Judas. Jesus loves us still and offers us a chance to turn from our betrayal and be forgiven.

When Judas betrayed Jesus, he also broke brotherhood and betrayed his friends. Our sin always affects others and is usually against others. This is why we are instructed not to take communion when our hearts are not right with our friends. Communion allows us repeated opportunities to repent and to be forgiven—by our brothers and sisters. Communion is also a prime time to forgive, to be like Philemon and release a past wrong. It is incumbent on us, as active betrayers whom Jesus forgives again and again, to forgive those who have betrayed us . . . again and again.

MUSAHAR HINDUS OF INDIA (2,674,000; 0.0% EVANGELICAL)

PRAY THAT CHRISTIANS FROM AROUND THE WORLD WOULD WORK TOGETHER TO REACH THE MUSAHAR AND THAT THE MUSAHAR WOULD BE JOINED TO THE BODY OF CHRIST (JOHN 17:20-23).

APRIL 26: LIFE BY PROXY

1 CHRONICLES 1-3; PSALM 116; MATTHEW 27; HEBREWS 1

*J*im Elliot and his four friends who died taking the gospel to an unreached tribe in Ecuador had no idea how many people would be called into missions as a result of their sacrificial deaths.[7] Our deaths, too, can have a profound effect on others. Our deaths even have resurrection power.

When Jesus "yielded up His spirit" (Matt. 27:50), verses 51 and 52 tell us that the "veil of the temple was torn in two from top to bottom; and the earth quaked, and the rocks were split, and the graves were opened; and many bodies of the saints who had fallen asleep were raised." It is fascinating to note that the *death* of Jesus raised these saints—not His resurrection. When we lay down our spirits, something happens in the unseen realm that gives life to the dead. Death of will or body in the name of Jesus always gives life. We bring more life by dying than by living.

Church history records seasons of martyrdom, and I am convinced we are entering one such season. Yet common to all ages is the call to a crucified life—death to self. The principle of yielding up our spirits so others can be raised from the dead is always efficacious. As a father of strong teenage boys, I am learning that sometimes yielding to their opinion gives them life. As a husband, it is often in my best interest to yield to the preferences of my wife. As she feels honored and cherished, she delights to yield to me. As I yield to my leaders and to those who follow me, something about my death gives them life, and I am ultimately the benefactor of that life. Most importantly, as I yield to Jesus, things in my soul that are dead rise from the ashes. Yielding our spirits brings life from death—to others and to ourselves.

In the mysterious plan of God, our yielded spirits impact those with whom we are not intimate. The saints who rose from their graves when Jesus died did not know Him. The text indicates that random men and women were raised from their graves. Jesus' yielded spirit unleashed the presence of God, and this irresistible power jerked decayed flesh out of tombs. When we die to self, when we yield our spirit in total surrender to God, something in the spirit realm is unleashed—and it has life-giving force. The stakes are too high not to die. Our deaths unleash power. Our yielded spirits give life to others—both near and far.

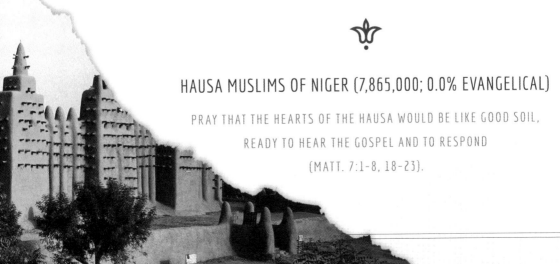

HAUSA MUSLIMS OF NIGER (7,865,000; 0.0% EVANGELICAL)

PRAY THAT THE HEARTS OF THE HAUSA WOULD BE LIKE GOOD SOIL,
READY TO HEAR THE GOSPEL AND TO RESPOND
(MATT. 7:1-8, 18-23).

APRIL 27: MISSION STATEMENT

1 CHRONICLES 4-6; PSALM 117; MATTHEW 28; HEBREWS 2

*J*esus has all authority on heaven and earth. Because He is supreme, it is fitting that He gives us orders. Every Christian should live and die under these commands:

Go. In the original Greek, this word conveys the sense of "as you are going." It implies movement and flexibility. Jesus wants His followers to have a peripatetic gene—spiritually if not physically. We should be ever moving and seeking: "Who has not heard? Where has the gospel not gone? Where does the church not exist?" Jesus never intended for His followers to settle down into comfort or self-absorption. If the eyes of the Lord rove to and fro around the earth seeking the lost, so must ours.

Disciple. Wherever we go, we must make followers of Jesus. Matthew 28:19 qualifies who we should disciple: all nations. The Jesus follower must have a clear focus on the ethnolinguistic peoples who have not heard about Him. Reaching unreached peoples is not the exclusive responsibility of frontier missionaries. Every believer is responsible to participate in the endeavor to see every tongue and ethnicity represented around the throne (Ps. 117; Rev. 5:9).

Baptize. Water baptism is a public declaration that we belong to Jesus. Spirit baptism empowers us to public witness—it affects our speech and propels us to invite others into the body of Christ. The Bible makes no allowance for private faith. Jesus is too precious to hoard. To follow Jesus must include a public stand with Him and His body. The Great Commission and secret belief are mutually exclusive. We must pursue a full-orbed Trinitarian encounter: Father, Son, and Holy Spirit.

Teach. We are to teach disciples "to observe all the things" that Jesus commanded (Matt. 28:20). Doctrine matters, and obedience matters. It is not enough to be familiar with the Word of God. We need to know and obey the Word of God. Every aspect of the disciple's life must be conformed to what the Bible teaches. We must help one another understand and apply the Bible in our daily lives. If we do not obey what Jesus says in His Word, we are not converted. We cannot be disciples if we do not obey.

Abide. In reciprocal living, if Jesus is with us always, even to the end of the age, we must be with Him. All the activities mentioned above require that we spend daily time in His presence and walk with Him all day long. We cannot expect to represent Jesus well if we are not intimate with Him, both in intentional daily blocks of time and ongoing communion. As my dear friend John York once stated: "There is no 'go' (into all the world) without 'lo' (I am with you always)." Go! Disciple! Baptize! Teach! Abide! We have our orders. What are we waiting for?

SOMALI MUSLIMS OF YEMEN (1,032,000; 0.02% EVANGELICAL)

PRAY FOR THE PEACE THAT RESULTS WHEN MEN AND WOMEN ARE RECONCILED WITH GOD (JOHN 14:27). PRAY FOR MEN AND WOMEN OF PEACE (LUKE 10:6) AMONG SOMALI.

*I*n 1 Chronicles 9 we read that gatekeeping was a trusted office. Faithful men who lived around the temple were responsible to preserve holy worship. Tasks varied—some cleaned, some sang, some cooked ("the trusted office over the things that were baked in the pans," v. 31)—but they all united in two main goals: keep evil out and usher people into God's presence.

The official office of gatekeeping has passed away but the spiritual function remains. Those in spiritual leadership still function as gatekeepers. They are responsible to keep evil out of a team, family, or congregation even while welcoming them into God's presence. When a leader allows sin into his life, it runs amuck among his followers and destroys the vulnerable ones. Spiritual leaders are held to a higher standard because when they lapse, the damage is not limited to their souls—it affects those whom they have led. Do not deceive yourself. The evil you let into your heart will leap from you to your vulnerable ones.

The obligations of a leader do not excuse the followers. Each person is responsible before God to enter His presence. Praise gets you in; unbelief keeps you out.

"Open to me the gates of righteousness; I will go through them, and I will praise the LORD. This is the gate of the LORD" (Ps. 118:19–20). We can learn something from Muslims in this regard. One ubiquitous expression that Muslims use is "Al Hamdu Lilah!" It means "Praise be to God." Muslims declare this when they are happy or when they are sad. It can be the answer to most any question. If the unconverted can continually proffer praise, how much more should those who have been brought near by the blood of Jesus? We should lift constant praise to Jesus, not just in worship settings but in the marketplace—where we spend most of our time. The person who constantly praises the Lord constantly walks in His presence. Let verbal praise be the punctuation of a life that continually magnifies the Lord—out loud!

"So we see that they could not enter [His rest] because of unbelief" (Heb. 3:19). If praise keeps us pressing toward God's presence, unbelief drives us away. When we believe, we extol. When we do not believe, we cease declaring the manifold majesties of Jesus. When we stop verbally exalting Jesus, something in our spirit withers and shrinks. Verbal witness is crucial—not just for the listener but for the speaker. As we constantly exalt Jesus, it builds our faith. Praise and proclamation draw us into His presence. A muted Christianity is a starving Christianity—and it will eventually die. The primary indicator of unbelief is a lack of praise and verbal exaltation of Jesus. Gatekeepers, let us keep the sin out and draw the seeking heart in through praise.

GEORGIAN ORTHODOX OF TURKEY (20,000; 1.0% EVANGELICAL)

PRAY THAT BELIEVERS AMONG THE GEORGIANS WOULD PROCLAIM THE MESSAGE OF THE GOSPEL CLEARLY AND WOULD MAKE THE MOST OF EVERY OPPORTUNITY GOD PLACES BEFORE THEM (COL. 4:2–5).

APRIL 29: FAITHFUL AFFLICTION

1 CHRONICLES 10-12; PSALM 119; MARK 2; HEBREWS 4

*I*n tenderness, God afflicts us or allows us to be afflicted. The severe mercies of the Lord come to us in many forms, and one of them is affliction. Psalm 119:75 states: "In faithfulness You have afflicted me." God's faithfulness is not only expressed in blessings that bring us joy. His faithfulness is also revealed through circumstances that bring us pain. Soul surgeries and spiritual spankings lovingly give life. Psalm 119:67 and 71 say: "Before I was afflicted I went astray, but now I keep your word. . . . It is good for me that I have been afflicted, that I may learn Your statutes." We should welcome affliction as one of God's professors—it teaches us His Word and His ways. Affliction makes us like Jesus. He, too, knew the pain and promise of being afflicted by God. Working for Jesus in pioneer contexts places us in the path of these common afflictions.

Betrayal. Many times the people you help, who share a meal with you, who pray, cry, laugh, and serve with you, will turn against you. Sometimes this betrayal is as drastic as reporting you to the security police. Other times it is as stinging as gossip behind your back. Serving Jesus in radical obedience inevitably means disappointing others—and sometimes the disappointed are those closest to you. Out of their disappointment they lash out, and little is as painful as the unloving wounds of a friend. Affliction at the hands of friends and colleagues can cut the most; therefore, it has the greatest potential to teach. It is deep surgery.

Loss. At times, God allows possessions, freedoms, health, strength, dignity, even ministry to be stripped from us. Some of my friends have lost all their worldly belongings, their innocence, their opportunities for service, their ministries, their health, their homes, their keepsakes . . . and they felt each loss deeply. When all is stripped away, we must answer one question: Is Jesus enough? Is Jesus truly all that "satisfies and thrills our souls"?[8] If we hold on to Jesus, secure in the knowledge that He is holding on to us, then the affliction of loss reminds us just how sweet He is.

Death. Oh for the vision to see death as God's faithful affliction! In an increasingly rebellious world, violent assault, rape, murder, and martyrdom are increasingly common. These travesties have never ceased, but for a season the West has been shielded from them in terms of suffering for Jesus. That season is ending. We now must join our brothers and sisters from around the world who have not been sheltered. Our comfort in these afflictions is this: "Your word has given me life!" (Ps. 119:50) In the midst of great suffering and even physical death, God's tender mercies, carried to us by His Word, give us life.

RAJPUT MUSLIMS OF INDIA (2,493,000; 0.0% EVANGELICAL)

PLEAD THAT THE RAJPUT WILL UNDERSTAND THAT HOPE FOR FORGIVENESS AND ACCEPTANCE WITH GOD IS AVAILABLE ONLY THROUGH JESUS' WORK ON THE CROSS (1 COR. 1:18).

APRIL 30: INADEQUATE CONSENSUS

1 CHRONICLES 13-15; PSALM 120; MARK 3; HEBREWS 5

*I*t does not matter how much effort you put into good things. It does not matter how many people are involved. It does not matter how much professional advice you solicit. It does not matter how much consensus you build. If you do not repeatedly consult the Lord about the proper order, He will break out against you (1 Chron. 15:13).

David consulted his junior and senior leaders, he consulted the priests and Levites, he took a plebiscite and was assured of the popular support of the people—but David did not consult the Lord. As a result, Uzza died, and the incredible national mobilization, planning, celebration, and extravagance came to nothing—in fact, it ended abruptly. God does not care about disappointing our celebrations even when the party is for Him. His parties must be celebrated in His ways, otherwise He doesn't come.

Sandwiched between the two attempts to bring the ark home (one ended in failure and one in joy) was a breakthrough victory over the Philistines. The remarkable thing about David was his alacrity in learning. Immediately after failing to consult the Lord on a domestic decision, he faced a national emergency. He consulted the Lord about what to do and won a great victory (1 Chron. 14:11). It is remarkable that David consulted the Lord again and did not assume that God's methods are formulaic and can be repeated without His approval.

We are incapable of thinking like God. Our natural minds are so limited in contrast to His unlimited wisdom. Prayer is the only way to protect ourselves from our own faulty assumptions. Turning to God for His counsel to learn His orders and His way is just as important on the heels of victory as it is in times of duress. Phillip Henry, father of renowned Bible commentary author Matthew Henry, stated it well. Two of his children were deathly sick, and as he wrestled in prayer for their healing, he wrote: "If the Lord will be pleased to grant me my request this time concerning my children I will not say as the beggars at our door used to do, 'I'll never ask anything of him again.' But on the contrary, He shall hear oftener from me than ever; and I will love God the better, and love prayer the better, as long as I live."[9]

God loves for us to consult Him over and over. As soon as we stop consulting Him, we start making deadly mistakes. God's insistence on prayer is for our own good. He knows the harm we inflict on ourselves without His counsel. To gather all the wisdom of godly friends and neglect the opinion of God is catastrophic. Only one opinion matters, and we must solicit the divine will over and over again—lest we die.

PULAAR, TUKULOR, AND FULANI OF MAURITANIA (190,000; 0.21% EVANGELICAL)

PRAY THAT THE BELIEVERS AMONG THE PULAAR, TUKULOR, AND FULANI WILL ENDURE PERSECUTION IN A CHRISTLIKE MANNER AND WILL GIVE THEIR LIVES FOR THE SAKE OF THE GOSPEL IF NECESSARY (1 PETER 2:21-23).

May

"I TELL YOU, BRETHREN, IF MERCIES AND IF JUDGMENTS DO NOT CONVERT YOU, GOD HAS NO OTHER ARROWS IN HIS QUIVER."

—*Robert Murray M'Cheyne*

MAY 1: SOUL IMMUNITY

1 CHRONICLES 16–18; PSALM 121; MARK 4; HEBREWS 6

*O*bedience gets harder. As we progress in faith, obedience becomes more costly, not less. As we hear and obey, there is more for us to surrender (Mark 4:24). God's priority is the preservation of the soul. F. W. Boreham wrote: "God is as sensitive to any injury done to the soul as I am to the apple of my eye."[1] God does not maintain the same caution for our bodies. He will afflict our bodies if it will protect or heal our souls. He will not sacrifice the soul for the sake of the body. This priority does not mitigate the importance of the body. It bluntly reminds us that losing a piece of our bodies is not equal to losing a piece of our souls.

The Bible repeatedly refers to divine protection. God reminded David in 1 Chronicles 16:21–22 that "He permitted no man to do [His people] wrong. . . . 'Do not touch My anointed ones, and do My prophets no harm.'" God preserved David wherever he went (18:13). Psalm 121 promises help from the Lord, protection from stumbling, shade, and preservation from all evil—going and coming. The Bible just as repeatedly records how God's people suffered incredibly. There are twin scriptural truths here and neither negates the other: We have incredible immunity and protection until our time, *and* it is normal to suffer for the gospel of Jesus Christ.

Knowing that we are indomitable—untouchable unless God decides otherwise—gives us great boldness to advance in the world without fear. Knowing that we are destined to suffer for His name gives us great assurance in trial, for we recognize that it has been allowed by an all-knowing, all-loving Father. However, it is important to note. God promises that evil has no right to touch our souls no matter what it does to our bodies. "The LORD shall preserve you from all evil; He shall preserve your soul" (Ps. 121:7). We must understand this promise in spiritual terms, as all men have been marred and scarred by evil. Hebrews 6:19 reminds us that our hope is "an anchor of the soul, both sure and steadfast, which enters the Presence behind the veil." We have full soul immunity from evil. We have unbroken refuge in the presence of God because of what Jesus has done for us. For now, we have only seasonal body immunity. In this life, followers of Jesus will get sick, suffer, and die. Only our glorified bodies will be fully immune from the effects of sin.

OMANI MUSLIMS OF OMAN (996,000; 1.2% EVANGELICAL)

PRAY THAT GOD WOULD RAISE UP MISSIONARIES FROM ALL OVER THE WORLD TO
PLANT THE CHURCH TOGETHER AMONG THE OMANI
(MATT. 9:37).

*D*avid sinned: He stayed home from the war, he crowned himself, and he numbered his armies in pride. All this was done around the time he slept with another man's wife, then murdered him—a man who just happened to be one of his mighty men. As a result of David's sin, God's judgment descended and God destroyed 70,000 innocent men. (First Chronicles 21 implies that the census brought judgment, but one sin often entangles us in another.) Sin—pride, in particular—always destroys both the proud individual and other innocents nearby. God stopped His destroying angel over Jerusalem—an angel that David, the elders, and even a curious fellow named Ornan could see. Ornan turned with his sons and saw the angel. His sons were terrified, but Ornan "continued threshing wheat" (1 Chron. 21). When David offered to buy Ornan's land, Ornan offered it for free, then went further: "Look, I also give you the oxen for burnt offerings, the threshing implements for wood, and the wheat for the grain offering: *I give it all*" (v. 23, emphasis added).

There is something endearing about the simple totality of Ornan's response. He was a hardworking farmer on the edge of the city, focused on threshing his wheat. He was completely dedicated to the task, and not even God's avenging angel hovering over his head could distract him! His boys ran for cover, but Ornan gave a Smith Wigglesworth-like shrug and kept threshing. (Wigglesworth reportedly awoke one night to see the Devil standing across the room. He said, "Oh, it's only you," and turned over to go back to sleep.)[2] David appeared before Ornan and requested land for the sacrifice. Ornan had not sinned so it was not his problem, but when he participated, he was all in. Land, oxen, tools, wheat—"Here you go, Lord, have it all."

Jesus loves all-or-nothing people like Ornan. It is lukewarm people who make Him retch. One endearing trait of missionary kids is that they find it hard to be hypocrites. They either serve God with all their hearts or they run from Him with all their strength. Jesus appreciates the clarity of their resolve and, of course, prefers they run to Him. In God's sight, half measures are no measures at all. If you are going to serve Jesus, there is only one way: all in. We do not serve Him one poker chip at a time. We shove our land, animals, tools, and harvest into the middle of the table and say, "Jesus, I give it all!"

GUJAR MUSLIMS OF PAKISTAN (4,298,000; 0.0% EVANGELICAL)

PRAY THAT THE GUJAR WOULD FEEL AND KNOW THE BURDEN OF SIN AND WOULD COME TO JESUS FOR FORGIVENESS AND SALVATION (MATT. 11:28-30).

MAY 3: DEATH PREPARATION

1 CHRONICLES 22-24; PSALM 123; MARK 6; HEBREWS 8

*G*od did not allow the "man after His own heart" to build the temple, for that man had too much blood on his hands. Nonplussed, David in effect said, "If I can't build it, I will make sure my sons can!" So he assembled unfathomable resources for Solomon and those who would follow. First Chronicles 22:5 tells us that "David made abundant preparations before his death." The generous and wise steward cares primarily for what his descendants will experience.

David's greatest legacy, however, was not silver, gold, cedar, and carved stone. First Chronicles 23:5 tells us that David made 4,000 instruments for giving praise. He instructed some of the Levites "to stand every morning to thank and praise the LORD, and likewise at evening" (v. 30). Long after David died, these instruments helped worshipers to magnify the Lord. Three thousand years later we still sing David's songs and have not improved on the simple depth of their content. David prepared worship for us! Long after the temple was destroyed and the golden utensils melted down in Babylon, David's songs of praise still echo from every corner of the earth.

I can best prepare for death by aiding worshipers who will outlive me. This starts with my sons. The best legacy I can leave them is the knowledge, capacity, and desire to praise the Lord. Who knows what the saints can see from heaven, but if the praise of my boys from earth is mingled with mine from around the throne, my soul will be satisfied. I am not satisfied, however, if that praise comes only from my biological progeny. My hope, and God's intention, is that each one of us leave a legion of people to praise after us.

Praise does not die with the decay of our earthly temples. When we receive our glorified bodies, our hands will be raised without flagging and our tongues lifted without ceasing to magnify the Lord. If we have prepared well, those who endure on earth will also praise, and they will hail from every tribe, tongue, people, and nation. There is no better way to prepare to die than to spend every resource equipping all people to praise Jesus.

BRAHMAN AND BHUMIHAR HINDUS OF INDIA (2,460,000; 0.0% EVANGELICAL)

PRAY THAT GOD WOULD UNVEIL THE CROSS AND THAT HE WOULD REMOVE THE VEIL ON
THE MINDS AND SPIRITS OF THE BRAHMAN AND BHUMIHAR
(2 COR. 3:16-17).

MAY 4: JESUS IS WORTHY OF DESIRE

1 CHRONICLES 25-27; PSALM 124; MARK 7; HEBREWS 9

I feel the pull of addiction. When I awake, my smart phone seduces me as emails sweetly call. My computer embraces me and will not let me go. There is a compulsion in my being, a lust to answer emails, a passion to rise and rush into the arms of my betrayer. Why don't I desire Jesus like this? Why do we not awake with purified lust?

Perverted lust has become so rampant in our world that we forget it is good to sing lustily. We forget that desire is purified or sullied by its object, not by its intrinsic function. Why don't we lust after God? If we have wanderlust, why do we not have God-lust—why are we not men and women whose guiding passion is the manifest presence of Jesus?

Mark 7:37 reminds us that Jesus does all things well. This includes His intentional design of desire. God made us to desire Him, and He is worthy of our desire! If we do not desire Jesus, we cannot expect Muslims to hunger for Him. If we do not desire Jesus, why should Arab or any people forsake their abusive lovers for Him? If Jesus is not the desire of His church, how can we possibly believe that He will be the desire of the nations?

Desire cannot be manufactured. When we try, it leads to legalism. Jesus grants us the desire to desire Him. It is enough for Him that we desire to desire Him. In His great mercy, when He hears one of His children humbly ask for a heart to desire, He is satisfied and grants that heavenly spark. I know what it is to lust. All men and women have felt the surge of desire for things that will ultimately betray them. Jesus wants to grant us God-lust: a fire in our souls to desire Him, Him alone, and more of Him. Jesus delights to answer the desperate plea to desire Him, as He knows that God-lust fulfilled is beautiful, satisfying, and life-giving.

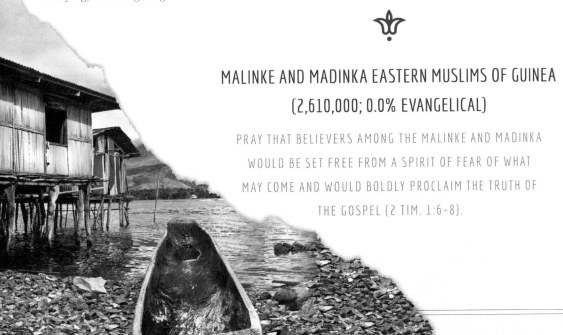

MALINKE AND MADINKA EASTERN MUSLIMS OF GUINEA
(2,610,000; 0.0% EVANGELICAL)

PRAY THAT BELIEVERS AMONG THE MALINKE AND MADINKA
WOULD BE SET FREE FROM A SPIRIT OF FEAR OF WHAT
MAY COME AND WOULD BOLDLY PROCLAIM THE TRUTH OF
THE GOSPEL (2 TIM. 1:6-8).

MAY 5: I AM HIS FOOTSTOOL

1 CHRONICLES 28-29; PSALM 125; MARK 8; HEBREWS 10

*D*avid called the temple "the footstool of our God" (1 Chron. 28:2), and Solomon asked rhetorically, "Will God really dwell with man?" (2 Chron. 6:18) God never intended for the temple to be a cage to contain Him for human observation and entertainment. The image of a footrest is more appropriate.

Will God really dwell *in* us? Oh the wonder of this "hope of glory." Yet we cannot think that God's indwelling means His containment. God ordains suffering as one means to ensure He is never restrained. Under no circumstances and in no prisons will Almighty God be confined.

Hebrews 10:20 says the veil is Christ's flesh. The temple veil was torn to unleash the presence of God on the world. Pentecost was made possible by Calvary. When the incarnate God was torn apart on the cross, this allowed for His presence to be unleashed among the nations. The nations must have Calvary if they are to have Pentecost, and so must we. When life rips apart our God-dwelt bodies, something of the fragrance of Jesus is released in the world. We, too, are a veil, and when we are torn for Jesus' sake, some fragrance in the spirit realm wafts to unreached peoples.

Jesus is worthy of our suffering. It is worthwhile to suffer for Him, for when we do, this releases the Spirit. We should understand suffering as an ongoing "fellowship," not a one-time event that earns a "persecution badge." The Western approach to suffering is to go through one traumatic experience, write a book about it, join the church lecture-circuit, and lap up respect and honor.

A suffering lifestyle does not reject days of preparation, celebration, or restoration. A suffering lifestyle is not self-flagellation or dour endurance. A suffering lifestyle is a joyful life, one that is willing to be torn so that Jesus might be unleashed on the world. If you do not have joy in your suffering you are not suffering God's way. You are just miserable.

SOUTHERN MUSLIM KURDS OF IRAN (3,400,000; 0.01% EVANGELICAL)

PRAY FOR THE WORD OF GOD IN WRITTEN, ORAL, MUSICAL, AND DRAMATIC FORMS TO BE TRANSLATED AND TO RISE AMONG THE SOUTHERN KURDS (ISA. 55:10-11).

MAY 6: CRYING BY FAITH

2 CHRONICLES 1-3; PSALM 126; MARK 9; HEBREWS 11

The things we do not ask for define us. Solomon did not ask for riches or honor or fame, and consequently was granted them all. In Mark, Jesus repeatedly asked those He healed and helped not to share news about Him. This seems strange to us and counter to God's own goal of giving all people an opportunity to repent. Yet, again and again Jesus instructed followers and disciples not to spread His fame. This request reinforced His passion to go to the cross, for He knew that fame would hinder His purpose. He did not come to be popular—He came to die. If riches, honor, and fame worked against Jesus' calling, why do you think they will not work against yours? Perhaps it is because your goal is to live. But your goal should be to die. That is what Jesus models for us: death to self, death to sin, death that brings life to others. By faith we understand that God brings life through death and that we do not start living until we die.

Hebrews 11:6 reminds us that it is fitting to desire our heavenly home. This, too, is faith—to trust that what lies ahead of us is where we really belong and that it is much fuller than anything we enjoy now. This trust allows us to endure great hardship. By faith we are tortured. By faith we are mocked. By faith we are scourged. By faith we are tested. By faith we wander destitute. All these sufferings we embrace joyfully for we are walking toward home. The Scripture says the world is not worthy of those who understand this simple truth. Conversely, we are not enamored of the world. We know there is a much better reality prepared for us. By not asking for peace, pleasure, and safety in this world, we are pleading for it in the next—trusting that our heavenly home has all the amenities God has planned for us to enjoy.

Our misunderstood striding through life is not a headlong rush to leave others behind and enter paradise alone. This faith-walk is intrinsically bound to inviting others to come with us. "He who continually goes forth weeping, bearing seed for sowing, shall doubtless come again rejoicing, bringing his sheaves with him" (Ps. 126:6). There are peripatetic purposes in our wandering this earth: (1) to continually weep over those who are asking for and frantically seeking the wrong things; (2) to continually cast God's Word invitation before them; and (3) to continually gather the nations for a group entrance into heaven. This is not easy—it is brutally, tearfully laborious. But if we are faith-full, if we trust, if we are willing to invest in some tears, we will laugh all the way to heaven. Our tears are an investment that will yield the joy of a group entrance into heaven.

JORDANIAN MUSLIMS OF JORDAN (992,000; 0.3% EVANGELICAL)

PRAY THAT GOD WOULD POUR OUT HIS SPIRIT ON THE JORDANIAN PEOPLE AND THAT THEY WOULD SEE DREAMS AND VISIONS OF JESUS. PRAY THAT THEY WOULD BE POWERFULLY SAVED AND EMPOWERED TO BE HIS WITNESSES (JOEL 2:28-32).

MAY 7: DESPISING SHAME

*L*ooking to Jesus helps us be ashamed of shame. When our eyes are fixed on ourselves, we notice our nakedness. We blush and construct awkward, fig-leaf clothing. When we are oblivious to ourselves, it is hard to be ashamed. Shame is directly connected to self-consciousness. We were designed to live God-conscious lives, for there is no shame in Him. It is not so much that God wants us to stop thinking highly or lowly of ourselves—He wants us not to think of ourselves at all, but to fix our eyes and attention on Him.

A naked baby can saunter into a room shamelessly, for not only does the child not notice (or know) she is naked—she also does not know that we know she is naked. There is no shame for there is no self-consciousness. We despise shame by being radically God-conscious. "Since my eyes were fixed on Jesus, I've lost sight of all beside—so enchained my spirit's vision, looking at the Crucified."[3] Eyes fixed on Jesus leads to shameless hearts.

Jesus endured the cross, endured hostility from sinners, and even endured the chastening of God—all which brought intense shame—for the joy set before Him, for what He could "see" (Heb. 12). Yes, part of that joy was the redemption of humanity, but textually, Jesus' joy was connected to sitting down at the right hand of the Father. God is the joy of God. An eternal God was not incomplete before the creation and redemption of humanity. God delights in God, and the joy set before Jesus that empowered Him to endure horrific shame was the joy of union with the Father. If Jesus' antidote to shame was the delight of intimacy with the Father, then ours must be the same.

Just because we despise shame does not mean we will escape shame. As we draw closer and closer to the return of Jesus, we will increasingly be the blight and bane of the world. We will face more shame, not less. It will become less and less respectable to be a devoted follower of Jesus. Our future guarantees more scorn, more abuse, more disdain, and more shame . . . not less. We despise shame, not by avoiding it but by ignoring it as we fix our eyes on Jesus. Looking to Jesus clothes us, for when our eyes are fixed on Him, He clothes us with His righteousness. He covers all our shame.

When we have sinned and shamed ourselves and our loved ones, there is only one recourse. It is not to look at ourselves or those who look at us in our misery—it is to fix our eyes on Jesus, to walk toward Him and let His eyes cover us.

GUJJAR MUSLIMS OF PAKISTAN (2,077,000; 0.0% EVANGELICAL)

PRAY THAT CHRISTIANS FROM AROUND THE WORLD WOULD WORK TOGETHER TO REACH THE GUJJAR AND THAT THE GUJJAR WOULD BE JOINED TO THE BODY OF CHRIST (JOHN 17:20-23).

MAY 8: FASTING AND FEASTING

2 CHRONICLES 7-9; PSALM 128; MARK 11; HEBREWS 13

A deep bass note of humility resounds through all biblical prayers. These prayers teach us how men and women should approach God, whether in triumph or tragedy: from a position of respect and reverent awe. Most modern feasting and fasting have lost this lowliness. Solomon dedicated the temple, and the people enjoyed a great feast culminating in a sacred assembly. After they observed fire come down from heaven and the glory descend on the temple, they "bowed their faces to the ground on the pavement, and worshiped and praised the LORD" (2 Chron. 7:3). In this context, the people returned to their tents . . . "joyful and glad of heart for the good that the LORD had done" (v. 10). It was a context of deep devotion.

When we feast, it is usually to celebrate ourselves (a graduation, a promotion, an accomplishment, a birth, a marriage). We tend to celebrate what we have done; so both fasting and feasting have lost any semblance of humility. Praise should not center on what God has helped us to accomplish. Pure praise is a declaration of what God has done in spite of us (Heb. 13:15). Praise does not flow out of our abundance or largesse. Praise—when it is precious to Jesus—flows out of our lack and our need.

Immediately after this great God-centered feast at the temple dedication, God gave this conditional promise: "If My people . . . will humble themselves, and pray . . . I will hear from heaven" (2 Chron. 7:14). All too often our prayers are whiny, demanding, or conditional: "Jesus, *if* you deliver me, I will serve you." There is an underlying arrogance in our prayers, an arrogant assumption that God must cater to us. If He does not act when, where, or how we demand, He is suspect. We approach prayer like a patron at a fast-food restaurant. We know what we want and we want it quickly—and woe to the adolescent deity who gets our order wrong, does not give us enough ketchup, or serves us lukewarm fries.

A second arrogance we carry into prayer is the expectation that God will forgive us when we have not forgiven others—when we retain resentment and hurt. Mark 11:25–26 reminds us that if we have "anything against anyone," we should forgive that person so our Father in heaven can forgive us. Few are the followers of Jesus who approach public or private prayer without harbored grievances against others. We approach the throne of grace gracelessly. We desire for ourselves what we will not grant to others. We want undeserved mercy without having to give it. This attitude is repulsive to the Lord of mercy, and it is a primary reason our prayers are hindered. Prayer and praise, fasting and feasting must have an underlying, unbroken humility—otherwise they are ineffectual.

MURAO HINDUS OF INDIA (2,384,000; 0.0% EVANGELICAL)

PRAY THAT THE HEARTS OF THE MURAO WOULD BE LIKE GOOD SOIL, READY
TO HEAR THE GOSPEL AND TO RESPOND
(MATT. 7:1-8, 18-23).

MAY 9: GODLY DIVISION

2 CHRONICLES 10-12; PSALM 129; MARK 12; JAMES 1

A change of leadership can lead both to unity and to schism. Rehoboam inherited some followers who were a little disgruntled, but he had the opportunity to win them over (2 Chron. 10:7). Unfortunately, he took the poor advice of younger advisors and lost ten of the twelve tribes of Israel. (Thank the Lord for the wise gray-heads among us!) He mustered an army to subdue the rebellion, but God said: "You shall not go up to fight against your brethren . . . for this thing is from Me" (2 Chron. 11:4).

We know that God is not for rebellion and that He prefers brothers to be unified, so this must have been His accommodation to the stubbornness of the people. It would have been better if Rehoboam had won over the disgruntled . . . if Abraham's and Lot's herders had gotten along . . . if Jacob had not deceived Esau . . . if Paul and John Mark had resolved their differences—but when God's children cannot reach an optimal agreement, He is *not* in favor of war.

There is a godly dignity in conceding to our brothers and sisters after we have made a wrong choice. In life and ministry, we constantly encounter second-best choices—both our own and others'. Redemption often depends on the reaction of the one insulted or offended. Division becomes bitter when the wronged party reacts to the poor choice of a brother by "going to war." There is a better way to win our brother: aid him in his poor choice. People often make choices out of selfishness and fear. A wise response is akin to that of Gamaliel—acceptance. If this thing is of God, it will last; if it is not of God, it will fade.

We can even go one step farther. This is the Jesus way: We can help those who make a poor choice or at least a choice that does not sit well with us. We can offer our love and support and encouragement. It does not matter that they did not consult us. It does not matter that they chose to distance themselves, and it does not matter that they set up camp in "our" territory (though we often forget who this earth belongs to anyway). When we bless and serve and supply their needs—when we decide "not to go to war against them,"—God often turns the scenario into something mutually life-giving. It is an incredibly joyous experience to bless the disagreeable choices of others.

Humility increases when we bless those who make choices that pain us. When brothers and sisters leave for another ministry, team, or church across town . . . when new ministries move in and siphon off "our" people . . . when alliances break down and collaborations falter . . . we have an incredible opportunity to accept these events in the spirit of Jesus. When the unity of believers is threatened, the way to be reunited is to serve and love and encourage each other.

SONINKE MUSLIMS OF MALI (9,969,000; 0.0% EVANGELICAL)

PRAY FOR THE PEACE THAT RESULTS WHEN MEN AND WOMEN ARE RECONCILED WITH GOD (JOHN 14:27). PRAY FOR MEN AND WOMEN OF PEACE (LUKE 10:6) AMONG THE SONINKE.

*E*vidently, Martin Luther was not impressed with the book of James, allegedly calling it "the epistle of straw." James's contention that faith alone cannot save (James 2:14) seems to run counter to the whole Reformation message. James and Luther are probably still hashing it out over a cup of coffee and have come to some heavenly agreement. In my view, James simply said the following:

Faith (noun) ***Works*** (verb, "labors"). James pointed out that Christianity is not the lazy person's way to heaven. We cannot say "I believe" and then sit back and live a lazy, carnal life. In this sense, belief is insufficient as "even the demons believe—and tremble" (James 2:19). Faith is not a mental assent to what Jesus has done or who Jesus is. Faith is an active response to what God has done. James put it this way: "Faith was working together with [Abraham's] works, and by works faith was made perfect" (v. 22). Faith sweats. Faith walks through the trenches of life and exerts energy in response to what God has initiated. Faith goes to doctors. Faith drinks boiled water. Faith buys life insurance. Faith does not deny facts and does not lazily depend on God.

Faith (adjective) ***Works*** (noun). Paul shared James' thinking of works done in faith. When he wrote 1 Thessalonians 1:3, he commended the church in Thessalonika for their "work of faith." Some things are done in trust. We step out actively without guarantee or insurance. We build arks, we leave our home-lands, we step onto the water, we pray for the sick—all these and many more are works done in faith. There is a beautiful union between God's promises and our actions. The follower of Jesus is constantly doing things (works) by faith (trusting while not knowing).

Faith (noun) ***Works*** (verb, "succeeds"). On this partnership of faith and works, Luther and James invite Abraham to their table and drink their coffee together. Faith succeeds. James put it this way: "Abraham believed God, and it was accounted to him for righteousness. And he was called the friend of God" (James 2:23). When we trust Jesus, we obey Him. His is the greater work, but we have a part to play: We trust and obey. When we do, faith is complete, all things are possible, and we are considered friends of God. There is no greater success or reward.

ARAB MUSLIMS, GULF OF UNITED ARAB EMIRATES (923,000; 0.0% EVANGELICAL)

PRAY THAT BELIEVERS AMONG THE ARABS WOULD PROCLAIM THE MESSAGE OF THE GOSPEL CLEARLY AND WOULD MAKE THE MOST OF EVERY OPPORTUNITY GOD PLACES BEFORE THEM (COL. 4:2-5).

MAY 11: LOYAL LOYALTY

2 CHRONICLES 16–18; PSALM 131; MARK 14; JAMES 3

*I*t is incredibly difficult to finish well. Our final views of Noah, Lot, Gideon, Samson, Eli, David, and even Solomon, for all his wisdom, are less than ideal. Asa is one of the most troubling of the lot. For thirty-six years he faithfully followed the Lord and even defeated a million-man army from Sudan. But after thirty-six years, he turned to the Syrians for help against Israel, and God rebuked him: "For the eyes of the LORD run to and fro throughout the whole earth, to show himself strong on behalf of those whose heart is loyal to Him" (2 Chron. 16:9a).

God is eager to act on our behalf, but His one requirement is loyalty—unflinching loyalty to the end. You would think thirty-six years of loyalty would earn Asa a mulligan, but no. "You have done foolishly; therefore from now on you shall have wars" (v. 9b). It is a fearful thing to fall from the hands of a loving God. Thirty-six years of loyalty could not carry Asa past treason—for that is what happens when we stop trusting the Lord. Something profound shifted in Asa. He began to treat truth-tellers poorly, and he oppressed the people (v. 10). He became diseased in his feet, "yet in his disease he did not seek the LORD, but the physicians" (v. 12). Even a funeral bed filled with spices and fragrant ointments could not cover up the stench of a life that rotted at the end (v. 14).

Jehoshaphat, Asa's son, at first seemed to take notice. He walked before the Lord like David (17:3), and God established his kingdom (v. 5). Jehoshaphat delighted in the ways of the Lord (v. 6) and sent teachers with the law throughout the kingdom (vv. 7, 9). As a result, God protected him from his enemies (v. 10). Our loyalty is our protection. But that loyalty must endure to the end—and it must be comprehensive. Jehoshaphat married Jezebel's daughter (!) and went to war as Ahab's ally (and almost died). Then Jehu confronted him: "Should you help the wicked and love those who hate the LORD? Therefore the wrath of the LORD is upon you" (19:2). Add Jehoshaphat's name to the list of those who stumbled at the end. Comprehensive loyalty includes having the same enemies God has. We cannot befriend the people God is against. We cannot be mostly loyal—not even for thirty-six years. God has to have *all* our trust, *all* our lives.

Because comprehensive loyalty is so rare, God seeks it out, and when He finds it, He shows Himself strong on behalf of the loyal person. My heart trembles at the biblical record. If these incredible men, who were far wiser, godlier, and stronger than I, could not be enduringly loyal, how can I be? My heart is also stirred: "Jesus, help me be that exceptional fool: stubborn enough to trust you with all my heart . . . for all things . . . for all my days."

HAJAM MUSLIMS OF PAKISTAN (1,897,000; 0.0% EVANGELICAL)

PRAY THAT THE HAJAM WILL UNDERSTAND THAT HOPE FOR FORGIVENESS AND ACCEPTANCE WITH GOD IS AVAILABLE ONLY THROUGH JESUS' WORK ON THE CROSS (1 COR. 1:18).

MAY 12: IN PRAISE OF PRAISE

2 CHRONICLES 19-21; PSALM 132; MARK 15; JAMES 4

*S*ome battles are won only by praise. Better said, the battle is often for our praise. Will we praise the Lord in the face of adversity and challenge? If the Devil can steal our praise or corrupt it, he has accomplished his ends—no matter the external results. This is why prison, sickness, trial, and even death are so misleading. The point in trial is not external deliverance or relief, but praise that rises from our hearts to heaven. Praise is the victory.

Praise Confuses the Enemy. As Jehoshaphat led his armies in praise (2 Chron. 20:22), this confused his enemies and they started attacking each other. When we are under demonic pressure and evil surrounds us, the best thing we can do is attack it with verbal praise. Yes, our battle praise should be verbal. It starts in our hearts but should come boldly out of our mouths. Both enemies and friends need to hear us exalt Jesus in the midst of trial. Evil forces do not know what to do with those who praise the Lord under duress. Our soul enemies do not know what to do when the darker the cloud we experience, the louder we praise.

Praise Encourages Friends. When others hear us praise God in our difficulties, it helps them get their eyes off themselves and their challenges. A main strategy of Satan is to get us to fixate on ourselves, our needs, our hurts, our grievances, our challenges, our sickness, or our injustices. When we praise despite our difficulties, others take note, and it helps them lift their eyes off themselves and direct their praise to the Lord.

Praise Brings Joy to the Person Who Praises. Most wonderful of all, praise brings joy to the person who praises. When we praise the Lord—when we lift our voices and from glad hearts magnify and extol Him—something grows in our spirits. God designed us to be satisfied in Him alone. When we are and we express it, we reap the benefit. A soul-joy swells within us, and we feel peace, contentment, and rest.

Everyone can praise God. Praise grows with pressure, with age, with limitations, and with problems. The older, sicker, more confined we become, the more we can (and should) praise the Lord. Praise is our battle cry. The more the Enemy throws at us, the more we praise the Lord. Praise is our right, and it is our joy. Let us never, ever surrender our praise.

BEDAR HINDUS OF INDIA (2,280,000; 0.0% EVANGELICAL)

PRAY THAT THE BELIEVERS AMONG THE BEDAR WILL ENDURE PERSECUTION IN A CHRISTLIKE MANNER AND WILL GIVE THEIR LIVES FOR THE SAKE OF THE GOSPEL IF NECESSARY (1 PETER 2:21-23).

MAY 13: COUNSELED TO DEATH

2 CHRONICLES 22-24; PSALM 133; MARK 16; JAMES 5

Bad Counsel. This is the season when we celebrate Mother's Day, and Athaliah might win the prize for worst mother of all. Ahaziah came to the throne by default when Arab raiders killed his older brothers. As his reward, he inherited counselors from the dark side. His mother "advised him to do wickedly" (2 Chron. 22:3), and the house of Ahab "were his counselors after the death of his father, *to his destruction*" (v. 4, emphasis added). Sometimes the ones closest to us do us the most harm. This is tricky because the ones closest to us know us best, love us most, and often can provide the best help. But we must be careful, for they can also counsel us to death.

Good Counsel. When King Ahaziah died, the evil queen grandmother grabbed power for six years until brave Jehoiada (the priest) "strengthened himself" (23:1) and established Joash as a seven-year-old king. "Joash did what was right in the sight of the LORD, all the days of Jehoiada the priest" (24:2). Jehoiada counseled Joash to life. We all need elder brothers and sisters in the faith to walk us through the treacheries of life. We are wise when we recognize that youthful zeal needs the tempered patience of age. When the strength and vitality of youth combine with the wisdom of experience, we forge formidable teams. When young leaders do not revere and listen to the gray-headed among them, they do so at their own peril.

When Jehoiada died, Joash reverted to his father's mistake of listening to clever idiots, and "wrath came" (v. 18). Within a year, Joash was killed by his own advisors, and Judah and Jerusalem were defeated by a smaller army (vv. 24–25). Be careful who you listen to! The advice of some of your best friends could kill you!

Great Counsel. When Joash began to go astray, "the Spirit of God came upon Zechariah" (24:20), and he rebuked the king and the people for their folly. In the end, we must listen to the Holy Spirit. He is our wonderful Counselor. It is true that the wisdom of age can aid us. It is true that in the multitude of counselors there is wisdom, but human advice only supplements God's advice. We need to learn to listen to Him. The voice from heaven on the Mount of Transfiguration said it more precisely: "This is My beloved Son. Hear Him!" (Mark 9:7)

The better part of wisdom is to take counsel from friends (and enemies), then put that advice to the side while you listen to the Holy Spirit. God the Holy Spirit is, after all, omniscient. He knows what to do. The Spirit is our primary counselor. Let us not be the fools who do not listen to Him. Let us be most eager for His counsel—in issues great and small.

MANDINGO, MADINKA MUSLIMS OF GUINEA BISSAU (195,000; 0.006% EVANGELICAL)

PRAY THAT GOD WOULD RAISE UP MISSIONARIES FROM ALL OVER THE WORLD TO PLANT THE CHURCH TOGETHER AMONG THE MANDINGO, MADINKAS (MATT. 9:37).

MAY 14: DANGEROUS QUESTIONS

2 CHRONICLES 25; PSALM 134; LUKE 1; 1 PETER 1

*I*n Luke 1, we encounter two seemingly similar questions with two very different results. When the angel told Zacharias that his aged wife would have a son, he asked: "How shall I know this? For I am an old man, and my wife is well advanced in years" (Luke 1:18). For his question, he was struck dumb—unable to speak. A few verses later, when the angel told a young virgin girl that she would become pregnant by the power of the Holy Spirit, she asked, "How can this be, since I do not know a man?" (v. 34). For her question, she was considered most favored among women.

It is not that God cannot handle our questions. He is not threatened by our inquiries; He is not impatient or unwilling to respond to the confusion of His naïve children. Yet this text clearly shows that some questions make God angry and others please Him. There was a difference between Zacharias' question and Mary's question. In Zacharias' case, the angel said, you "did not believe my words which will be fulfilled in their own time" (v. 20). To Mary, the angel said, "Blessed is she who believed, for there will be a fulfillment of those things which were told her from the Lord" (1:45). Belief sanctifies our questions.

Jesus loves those who believe. He loves belief. Trust that arises from our puny hearts pleases God. Conversely, lack of belief ticks Him off—especially when He finds it among those who have walked with Him for a long time and should know better. The difference in the responses of Zacharias and Mary is highlighted by the fact that Zacharias was a godly man who had walked in righteousness for years—he, of all people, should have believed. Mary was a teenager who had no tenured intimacy with God—she, of all people, had reason not to believe.

God can handle our questions when we ask them believing. "God, you have said this, so I know it will happen. It is, however, such a ridiculously impossible prediction, I am just dying to know—how in the world are you going to do it?" God loves those types of questions and rewards the faith behind them. He is not so enthused with those who know Him best and trust Him least. Those who have walked with Jesus should be cautioned—He expects you to trust Him. Bring Him your questions in belief; those are the questions He delights to answer. He will answer your doubt-based questions, too, but those answers are not so much fun to receive.

BEDOUIN MUSLIMS OF EASTERN BEDAWI EGYPT (902,000; 0.0% EVANGELICAL)

PRAY THAT THE BEDOUIN OF BEDAWI WOULD FEEL AND KNOW THE BURDEN OF SIN AND WOULD COME TO JESUS FOR FORGIVENESS AND SALVATION
(MATT. 11:28-30).

MAY 15: LOWLY AND SAFE

2 CHRONICLES 26–27; PSALM 135; LUKE 2; 1 PETER 2

*U*zziah was a Renaissance man. He "did what was right in the sight of the Lord (2 Chron. 26:4). He sought God (v. 5); defeated enemies (v. 6); became exceedingly strong (v. 8); loved the soil (v. 10); equipped soldiers who "made war with mighty power" (v. 13); made inventive weapons of war (v. 15); and his "fame spread far and wide, for he was marvelously helped [by the LORD] till he became strong" (v. 15). Then he entered the temple to burn incense . . . and God struck him down. He became a leper and lived in isolation until he died.

Pride destroyed Uzziah. "But when he was strong his heart was lifted up, to his destruction" (v. 16). It is exhilarating to be used by God. When He courses through our speech, touches through our hands, blesses through our gifts, it is life-giving and marvelous. It feels so *good* to be used for good by a good God. But when He uses us, we face two pitfalls: The most obvious is to think any good extended was sourced in us. This is blatant pride. The second and more sinister pitfall is the one that ensnared Uzziah, who erred in an act of worship.

Uzziah's arrogant spirituality was infused with an assumption of spiritual authority. Just because God helps us in one area, does not mean we have license in others. Uzziah had good counselors, he had a legacy of seeking the Lord, and he had a record of successes. But his victories worked against him as he slipped into spiritual pride—a pride that became evident in the way he worshiped. It was not a bad thing to offer incense to the Lord in the temple, but this was not Uzziah's job. Success tempts us to over-run the boundaries God has set for us, forgetting that we should not use our liberty as a "cloak for vice" but as bondservants of God (1 Peter 2:16).

God used His freedom to wrap Himself in swaddling clothes. This is God's sign: humility. Because Jesus clothed Himself in humility, this must be the prominent mark of His representatives—especially as they are marvelously helped. How rare it is to see a man or woman grow more humble the more victories they win. How common it is for pride to mark our worship. Woe to those who use public places of worship as a theatre for themselves, who assume a spiritual role God did not give them. How beautiful it is when godly men and women win victories in God, then sit back quietly and let others offer incense.

HAZARA MUSLIMS OF AFGHANISTAN (2,932,000; 0.03% EVANGELICAL)

PRAY THAT GOD WOULD UNVEIL THE CROSS AND WOULD REMOVE THE VEIL ON THE MINDS AND SPIRITS OF THE HAZARA (2 COR. 3:16–17).

MAY 16: SUBMIT—"EVEN IF"

2 CHRONICLES 28-30; PSALM 136; LUKE 3; 1 PETER 3

*J*esus ascended into heaven and now sits at the right hand of God with angels, authorities, and powers subject to Him (1 Peter 3:22). It is on this authority that He asks us to submit to Him. Jesus, who submitted completely to the will of the Father, has every right to ask us for our submission.

Peter instructed wives to submit to their husbands (v. 1), *even if* some do not obey the Word. He went on to teach that there is incorruptible beauty in a gentle and quiet spirit, which is very precious to God (v. 4). The beauty of a quiet spirit is not limited to women. Strong men can have this incorruptible grace, too. There is little as masculine as a compassionate, tenderhearted, courteous Christian man whose spirit is tender and gentle, quiet and firm (v. 8). A man secure in the mercy and kindness of God is a pillar of strength and the backbone of society. These giants o faith are always subject to authority. The strongest men and the bravest and wisest women are those who have learned the secret of submission. While submission makes us strong, rebellion makes us weak.

Rebels are those who have insight, capacity, leadership skills, abilities, natural gifts, wisdom, and charisma, and refuse to submit those gifts to the governance of those in authority over them. Leaders rebel. Peter reminds us that this submission is not predicated on the worth of the leader above us. Often we will be asked to submit to those less able than ourselves in some arenas, but the point is not the person, his abilities, or his deficiencies—the point is whether or not we submit "even if." We prove our strength by our submission; rebellion only proves and reveals our weakness.

In the Godhead there is order within union, leadership within equality. There is also order within the home. When the husband fails to lead his family in a Christlike manner, all kinds of wounds emerge. The strong husband, however, will be wise enough to know when to yield to the wisdom of his wife and even of his children. Similarly, the wise wife will respect and submit to her husband, even if he is deficient in faith or conduct (based on biblical standards), and thereby become increasingly beautiful. We all become stronger the more we submit to the authority God has placed over us. We also become more beautiful.

KHATIK HINDUS OF INDIA (2,057,000; 0.0% EVANGELICAL)

PRAY THAT BELIEVERS AMONG THE KHATIK WOULD BE SET FREE FROM A SPIRIT OF FEAR OF WHAT MAY COME AND WOULD BOLDLY PROCLAIM THE TRUTH OF THE GOSPEL (2 TIM. 1:6-8).

MAY 17: KNOWING WHEN TO DIE

2 CHRONICLES 31-33; PSALM 137; LUKE 4; 1 PETER 4

*H*ezekiah began his reign as a humble king. He sought God with all his heart and, as a result, he prospered (2 Chron. 31:21). Faced with overwhelming odds, he joined with Isaiah to cry and pray (32:20), and the Lord fought for him against "the arm of flesh" (v. 8). The Lord "guided on every side . . . and gave them rest" (v. 22). Then Hezekiah became terminally ill and begged for more time to live, so God granted him fifteen additional years. Tragically, somewhere in those fifteen years, Hezekiah lost his humility—"his heart was lifted up; therefore wrath was looming over him and over Judah and Jerusalem" (v. 25). Evidently, God "withdrew from him, in order to test him, that He might know all that was in his heart" (v. 31). It is a shame that Hezekiah did not know when to die. During his extended years, Manasseh was born, who later seduced the people "to do more evil than the nations whom the LORD had destroyed" (33:9), and Hezekiah fell into sin and put the people at risk of God's wrath. Three sobering applications stand out from Hezekiah's extended life.

You Can Live Too Long. Leaders who do not recognize when it is time to step away from leadership can do much damage. They hold on to power and position longer than God intends. How life-giving it is when leaders recognize their time to step down, release the reins of authority, and pass the baton graciously to others. Those who stay too long in leadership give birth to "children" who introduce all kinds of evil.

Humility Lost Is Wrath Incurred. God used Hezekiah wondrously when he thought little of himself. Yet, he gave in to the common temptation to think God's employment of him made him special. His pride subjected him and his followers to the wrath of God. I have sympathy for those who begin as evil and eventually repent (as Manasseh did) and sadness for those who begin well, live well, then stumble at the finish. Something about lost humility after a life of blessing seems to irritate God so much that His punishment for the offense is extreme. He places maximum value on sustained humility—it is precious to Him.

God Withdraws to Test Us. Our omniscient God certainly knows what is in our hearts. His withdrawal is intended as mercy. It lets us see what is in our hearts. When God removes blessing, protection, and anointing, this is both a mercy and an invitation. When we realize the vileness of our hearts, He wants us to humble ourselves once again and depend on Him.

Physical death is actually an awakening to what we have lived for. If we have lived for ourselves, we will awaken to judgment. If we have lived for Jesus by humbly living for others, we will awaken to reward. God help us know when to die. God help us awake to the things in our lives that are horrific to Him. God help us die humble.

FULAKUNDA, PULAAR, AND FULANI OF SENEGAL (1,693,000; 0.0001% EVANGELICAL)

PRAY FOR THE WORD OF GOD IN WRITTEN, ORAL, MUSICAL, AND DRAMATIC FORMS TO BE
TRANSLATED AND TO SPREAD AMONG THE FULAKUNDA, PULAAR, AND FULANI
(ISA. 55:10-11).

MAY 18: THE END IS NEAR

2 CHRONICLES 34–36; PSALM 138; LUKE 5; 1 PETER 5

*J*osiah reigned in Judah and ushered in radical reforms. He attacked idolatry with fury. He broke, made into dust, scattered, burned, broke down, beat into powder, or cut down with swords all relics, people, and rituals associated with pagan worship (2 Chron. 34:4–7). After he found the lost book of the law, Josiah spoke with Huldah, the prophetess. She told him that, despite his zeal, it was too late for Israel to escape the wrath of God. The people had been wicked for so long that God's wrath would "be poured out on this place, and not be quenched" (v. 25). A few kings later this final destiny was assured, for the nation had "mocked the messengers of God, despised His words, and scoffed at His prophets, until the wrath of the LORD arose against His people, *till there was no remedy*" (36:16, emphasis added). There was a point of no return. In spite of His infinite patience, God's holiness limited what He could overlook.

Cartoonists have long marked the crazed prophet who walks the streets with signs pronouncing the end of the world. The problem is, they are right—the prophets that is. Every day brings us closer to cosmic judgment. It is foolish theology that claims we will clean up this world and present it sparkling to our returning King. Despite all the external advances of society, people's hearts continue to mock, despise, and scoff at Jesus—and there is no remedy. Jesus is coming in furious glory, and our only hope is to be sheltered from His wrath by His blood.

Josiah's example helps us tremendously here. God told him: "Because your heart was tender, and you humbled yourself before God when you heard His words against this place and against its inhabitants, and you humbled yourself before Me, and you tore your clothes and wept before Me, I also have heard you. . . . Surely I will gather you . . . to your grave in peace" (34:27–28).

Psalm 138:6 reminds us that God regards the lowly but distances Himself from the proud. First Peter 5:5 confirms that God resists the proud but gives grace to the humble. It behooves us to advance to the end of this earth with humility, a tender heart, and anguish over God's judgment. We work furiously to the end, hoping to save one more brand from the burning, even while we long for the end to come and to be gathered to our rest.

TURKMEN MUSLIMS OF IRAN (2,300,000; 0.05% EVANGELICAL)

PRAY THAT GOD WOULD POUR OUT HIS SPIRIT ON THE TURKMEN AND THAT THEY WOULD SEE DREAMS AND VISIONS OF JESUS. PRAY THAT THEY WOULD BE POWERFULLY SAVED AND EMPOWERED TO BE HIS WITNESSES (JOEL 2:28–32).

MAY 19: HEDGED IN

EZRA 1-3; PSALM 139; LUKE 6; 2 PETER 1

*S*ocial media reveals both too much and too little. On the one hand, every banality is self-disclosed to a voyeuristic world. On the other hand, our true selves are buried beneath layers of self-absorption. Psalm 139 unveils the joys of being fully known. God has searched and known us (v. 1). He knows when we sit up, get up, and what we think (v. 2). He knows where we go and when we lay down, and He knows all our ways (v. 3). He knows every idle word that has rolled off our tongues (v. 4). Most marvelous of all, He has "hedged [us] behind and before, and laid [His] hand upon [us]" (v. 5). This, indeed, is too wonderful to believe.

Because God Knows Us, We Do Not Need for Others to Know Us. Much of the frenzy of modern self-disclosure stems from the insecurity of being anonymous. Our culture makes much of those who make much of themselves. When no one bothers to exalt us, we feel driven to self-promotion. We present it under the guise of family activities or hobbies or humor, but it is actually a cry: "See me! Know me! I am of worth, too! I have something to contribute!" These pathetic cries for attention are not necessary if we are secure in being known by Jesus. When we understand that Jesus knows us intimately and loves us deeply—despite what He knows about us—this alleviates any need to be known and exalted by others.

Because God Knows Us, We Keep No Secrets. There is a fine pivot point here. To say we should keep no secrets is not to encourage the constant self-revelation of banalities. It simply means that in relationships with God and others, we have nothing to hide. We have no skeletons in the closet, we have no lies to lie about, and we have nothing false or shameful to conceal. To be secret-less is to be at peace always, never fearful that someone will discover something negative about us. God knows it all. We have brought everything into His light so we are impervious to scorn or blame. This is a great freedom. This is the secret of a powerful life.

Because We Are Hedged In, We Are Free. Most people resent God's boundaries, fearing that restraint removes freedom. The opposite is true. Only those who embrace the limits of God have rest, joy, and freedom. To have no boundaries is to be in the prison of insecurity and doubt. When God hedges us in from behind, we have the assurance that we will not falter, fail, or return to our vomit. When God hedges us in before, we have the assurance that we will not go outside of His will or His pleasure. We can run, abandoned and protected. There are no cliffs to fall off.

How marvelous it is to be completely known and completely surrounded by God. This is what it means to be free.

BEDOUIN MUSLIMS OF JORDAN (780,000; 0.01% EVANGELICAL)

PRAY THAT CHRISTIANS FROM AROUND THE WORLD WOULD WORK TOGETHER TO REACH THE BEDOUIN AND THAT THE BEDOUIN WOULD BE JOINED TO THE BODY OF CHRIST (JOHN 17:20-23).

*T*attletales often have golden tongues. When the adversaries of the children of the captivity offered to help build the temple (Ezra 4:1), Zerubbabel saw through the ruse and refused their help. The rascals then wrote to Artaxerxes, "because we receive support from the palace, it was not proper for us to see the king's dishonor" (v. 14) and succeeded in shutting down the work on the temple: "Thus the work of the house of God . . . ceased" (v. 24). In the short term, the bad guys often win. The micro view concedes that evil wins some battles, while the macro view asserts that God always triumphs.

Haggai and Zechariah stepped into the breach and prophesied Zerubbabel into action. This is the context for the marvelous verses in Zechariah 4:6–7: "This is the word of the LORD to Zerubbabel: 'Not by might, not by power, but by My Spirit,' says the LORD of hosts. 'Who are you, O great mountain? Before Zerubbabel you shall become a plain! And he shall bring forth the capstone with shouts of 'Grace, grace to it.'" The temple was rebuilt, the capstone was put in place, the opposition was overcome, and Zerubbabel pushed through the micro setback and won the macro victory. Back to Ezra 6:16: "the descendants of the captivity celebrated the dedication of this house of God with joy."

Samuel Zwemer, "The Apostle to Islam," knew the reality of long-term victory despite short-term defeats better than anyone. In 1911 he wrote:

> "Frequent set-backs and apparent failure never disheartened the real pioneer. Occasional martyr-doms are only a fresh incentive. Opposition is a stimulus to greater activity. Great victory has never been possible without great sacrifice. . . . Does it really matter how many die or how much money we spend in opening closed doors, and in occupying the different fields, if we really believe missions are warfare and the King's glory is at stake? War always means blood and treasure. Our only concern should be to keep the fight aggressive and to win victory regardless of cost or sacrifice. The unoccupied fields of the world must have their Calvary before they can have their Pentecost."[4]

Working in the Arab world teaches you to have a macro view of life. If you look at each day's labor with a microscope, the results drive you to despair. Arabic comes pitifully slowly, disciples are made with agony, colleagues falter, governments shake, and progress, if measurable at all, seems to be backward. Instead, you need to look at the larger view. Look back over the last years to consider what God has done, then look forward to all He has promised to do—now the picture is much brighter. All of us have lost battles, all of us bear scars. Failure does not surprise us or discourage us. We simply fall forward, dust ourselves off, and rise to battle on, for we know how this ends: God wins.

HEMSHIN MUSLIMS OF TURKEY (20,000; 0.0% EVANGELICAL)

PRAY THAT THE HEARTS OF THE HEMSHIN WOULD BE LIKE GOOD SOIL, READY TO HEAR THE GOSPEL AND TO RESPOND (MATT. 7:1-8, 18-23).

MAY 21: UNHOLY MATRIMONY

EZRA 7–10; PSALM 141; LUKE 9; 2 PETER 3

*S*ix times in two chapters, Ezra commented that the hand of the Lord was upon him. God miraculously provided for temple reconstruction and furnishings and ensured the safe delivery of resources through hostile lands. Ezra arrived in Jerusalem exhilarated at God's unmerited favor. Euphoria quickly descended into horror, however, as Ezra discovered that the grace given for escape, enlightenment, and a measure of revival in bondage (Ezra 9:8) was in jeopardy because God's people had married pagan wives. Ezra understood that the nation's plight of exile and punishment could be traced back to unholy matrimony—when Solomon's foreign wives introduced idolatrous worship in the heartland. Though it seems like a minor offense, Ezra saw the ultimate implications and was devastated. He prayed, confessed, wept, tore his robe, plucked out his beard, sat down astonished, fell on his knees, and spread out his hands to God. "Here we are before You, in our guilt, though no one can stand before You because of this," he moaned (v. 15).

Ezra, with the consensus of the leaders, took radical steps. He conducted a careful review, and all who had married pagan women, including those who had children, ended that alliance. Only this costly action turned away God's fierce wrath (10:14).

A common lie of the Enemy is that success allows fudging. When we experience the hand of the Lord and our ministry grows, our influence increases, and our giving to missions expands, the Devil whispers that we can visit Delilah. We marry inappropriate spouses. We partner with those who are proud. We take help from those who are vain. We compromise principles for comfort, ease, or personal profit. All these are unholy alliances. They may seem like minor compromises initially, but the Ezra in us knows that ultimately they are deadly, costly, and abhorrent to God. We cannot be too careful of our alliances—either in life or in ministry.

More to the point, if we align with those who are not godly or we take support from those who are immoral—no matter their public reputation—we are in danger of judgment and great punishment. We have no biblical recourse other than godly sorrow and the painful severance of any association with these people. I am not referring to those who are married to ungodly spouses. I am referring to those in ministry who partner with ungodly people. At whatever cost to public ministry, we must maintain private purity.

DOM HINDUS OF INDIA (2,249,000; 0.0% EVANGELICAL)

PRAY FOR THE PEACE THAT RESULTS WHEN MEN AND WOMEN ARE RECONCILED WITH GOD (JOHN 14:27). PRAY FOR MEN AND WOMEN OF PEACE (LUKE 10:6) AMONG THE DOM.

We often hear the phrases, "What we do flows out of who we are" or "who we are is more important than what we do." This is wrongheaded thinking—not because doing is more important than being, but because it imposes a false dichotomy. You cannot be without doing.

God Is What He Does; He Does What He Is. God is good because He does good. God is love because He loves. God is merciful because He acts mercifully. God is a giver because He gives. It seems simplistic, but in essence you cannot be something without doing it. God is love because in the Trinity, Father, Son, and Spirit actively love one another and their love spills out over all creation. God is light because His radiance emanates from Him proactively, and there is no passive darkness about Him at all (1 John 1:5). God is love and light because He loves and lights.

Man Is Because of Who God Is and What God Does. My doing does not flow out of my being, because I am not love; I am not light. Anything good I do flows out of God's being and doing. I exist because God made me. Anything noble or righteous I do is because God has empowered me to do it. What naturally flows out of me is corrupt and vile. If I love, it is certainly not because I am inherently loving—it is because God is and does love, and His love resides *and* acts through me. We are told in Scripture to "be doers of the Word" (James 1:22). Jesus encouraged a lawyer to live by doing love: "Do this [love God and neighbor] and you will live" (Luke 10:28). We cannot *be* love without *doing* love. We become loving by acting out the love of God. We become who God wants us to be by doing what He commands us to do. Yes, God changes our hearts, but we participate in the process through acts of obedience. Without active obedience, there is no lasting transformation.

One Thing Is Needed. Being and doing are codependent. Mary sat at Jesus' feet and heard His word, while Martha was distracted by much serving. Jesus reminded Martha that one thing in the midst of a worried and troubled world is needed: actively abiding in Jesus (Luke 10:38–42). Abiding is not "being"—not if being means passive nothingness. Abiding is actively lingering in the presence of Jesus and actively obeying Him in all that we do. Jesus said that the one necessary thing is to prioritize Him, to spend extravagant and ongoing communion with Him.

If we are not with Jesus constantly, then we are doing without being—and as the world has ever realized, this only leads to emptiness.

KANEMBU MUSLIMS OF CHAD (822,000; 0.0% EVANGELICAL)

PRAY THAT BELIEVERS AMONG THE KANEMBU WOULD PROCLAIM THE MESSAGE OF THE GOSPEL CLEARLY AND WOULD MAKE THE MOST OF EVERY OPPORTUNITY GOD PLACES BEFORE THEM (COL. 4:2–5).

MAY 23: UNDER AUTHORITY

NEHEMIAH 4-6; PSALM 143; LUKE 7; 1 JOHN 2

*T*o place ourselves under authority is to exhibit great faith. In Luke 7, a soldier demonstrated what it means to trust: "Say the word, and my servant will be healed" (v. 7). Jesus is impressed by the person who does not whine, does not doubt, and does not even need a personalized home visit. Jesus is delighted by hearts that simply trust Him. When we submit all we are and have to Him, He considers this the greatest manifestation of faith. We exhibit our love for Jesus by taking Him at His word, by not demanding proof and by not bothering Him. Sometimes our prayers are just whining, and God rejoices when His children make a habit of not whining. Faith is not restricted to the miraculous. Great faith is displayed by ordinary, daily obedience.

Ongoing faith submits to the commands of Jesus—without discussion, without argument. John equated this discipline with knowledge of God. "By this we know that we know Him, if we keep His commandments" (1 John 2:3). Obedience is our epistemology. It is how we know that we know Jesus—our alacrity to do what He wants us to do. Steeped in self-centeredness, people want God to please them, forgetting that we exist to please Him. A primary way to please God is to trust Him. When we obey Him immediately and joyfully, we bring Him great pleasure. He rewards us for trusting Him both by answering our prayers and confirming within our spirits that we know Him. Obedience becomes a source of great joy and comfort. By obeying Him we have trusted Him . . . by trusting Him we have pleased Him . . . by pleasing Him we have felt His pleasure . . . and His pleasure is life to our souls.

The two most practical ways we exhibit our trust of Jesus is by (1) obeying His Word and by (2) obeying those He has placed in authority over us. We need not worry about abuse, for there is inbuilt protection in the order of these twin authorities. We obey earthly authorities as long as their instruction does not contradict the authority of the Word of God. Obedience-based discipleship is the only true discipleship. The Word of God does us no good if we do not obey it. Our faith is manifested and grown when, on a regular basis, we obey what we read daily in the Bible. Our faith is proved and refined as we submit to those God has placed in authority over us. By continually submitting to God's Word and God's authorities, we are protected and we enjoy His deep pleasure.

BEDOUIN MUSLIMS, GULF OF UNITED ARAB EMIRATES (763,000; 0.0% EVANGELICAL)

PRAY THAT THE BEDOUIN WILL UNDERSTAND THAT HOPE FOR FORGIVENESS AND ACCEPTANCE WITH GOD ARE AVAILABLE ONLY THROUGH JESUS' WORK ON THE CROSS
(1 COR. 1:18).

MAY 24: THE SORROW AND JOY OF THE SCRIPTURE

NEHEMIAH 7–9; PSALM 144; LUKE 11; 1 JOHN 3

*I*n order to contextualize prayer, we need a biblical precedent. When Ezra read the Scripture, the people stood, then lifted their hands, then bowed their heads and worshipped the Lord with faces to the ground (Neh. 8:5–6). Today, Muslims imitate these same forms of prayer. When teaching former Muslims to pray, we can show them that their external forms have precedent in the Scriptures. It makes them glad to know that God can redeem an external form and infuse it with His Spirit.

The Scriptures, however, often start by making us feel poorly about ourselves. In Ezra's day, "all the people wept, when they heard the words of the Law" (Neh. 8:9). The role of the Scripture is first to deconstruct—both the Muslim and us. We are not good, we are not wise, we are not deserving, and our hearts are sinful. Our initial approach to Scripture and to the revelation of God should be one of misery, because Scripture first reveals how far short of God's image we fall. His Word first breaks us down then puts us back together.

Once we realize how far we are from God's nature, we can be renewed by the joyful hope of the Scriptures. Ezra comforted the wailing community: "Do not sorrow, for the joy of the LORD is your strength" (v.10). God's Word also reminds us of His manifold mercies (9:19), and that He has given His good Spirit for our instruction (v. 20). We approach the Scriptures with both sobriety and gaiety: sober, for God's Word is relentless and ruthless in exposing our sins . . . and joyous, for it continually reminds us of His great love and provision.

Morning by morning, evening by evening, we place ourselves under the correction and construction of Scripture. How foolish to neglect this great refreshing. What joy, what strength is derived from this ongoing feast. The joy of the Lord is directly connected to our submission to His Word. The Scripture becomes the source of our joy. The Scripture becomes the text of our witness. The Scripture becomes the content of our prayers. As we allow God's Word to mold us and motivate us, this builds us up and brings us joy. The Bible is given to us to make us cry. It is also given to us that we might rise from our sorrow and laugh, that we might be filled with the exuberance of God. His Word fuels us with a riotous joy that propels us into all the world.

HERKI MUSLIMS OF TURKEY (38,000; 0.0% EVANGELICAL)

PRAY THAT THE BELIEVERS AMONG THE HERKI WILL ENDURE PERSECUTION IN A CHRISTLIKE MANNER AND WILL GIVE THEIR LIVES FOR THE SAKE OF THE GOSPEL IF NECESSARY (1 PETER 2:21-23).

MAY 25: THE BLESSING OF CURSE

NEHEMIAH 10-11; PSALM 145; LUKE 12; 1 JOHN 4

Scripture has an awe-inspiring holism concerning the character of God. It does not let us emphasize one aspect of His character to the detriment of a complementary attribute. It does not let us arrive at a zero-sum effect with mercy canceling out judgment or blessing removing cursing. Scripture pounds out the reality that "the Lord is gracious and full of compassion, slow to anger and great in mercy. The Lord is good to all, and His tender mercies are over all His works" (Ps. 145:8–9). This is irrevocably true, just as it is also true that those who do not obey God will fall under His curse, His wrath.

It is true that the servant who knows his master's will and does not "prepare himself or do according to His will, [will] be beaten with many stripes" (Luke 12:47). It is just as true that God will bless and reward the servant who does His will. The kindness that leads us to repentance is often the kindness of discipline and rebuke. Scripture insists on a full revelation of the nature of God. Jesus came as Savior of the world (1 John 4:14), yet His said, "I came to send fire on the earth, and how I wish it were already kindled!" (Luke 12:49). He came to bring peace to men of goodwill (2:14), yet He said, "Do you suppose that I came to give peace on earth? I tell you, *not at all*, but rather division" (Luke 12:51, emphasis added). We do God no favors by trying to reconcile these incredible realities. Their truth is heightened by their opposition.

God manifested love by sending His only Son as propitiation for our sins (1 John 4:10). The term *propitiation* means "to appease." God's love—expressed on the cross—appeases God's wrath. Both God's anger and love are real, and they accent rather than neutralize each other. John tells us that if God so loved us by absorbing wrath, "we also ought to love one another" (v. 11).

We should love each other in the same wrath-absorbing manner that God has loved us. When, at great cost, we absorb the negative results of a loved one's error, we love that person as Christ loved us. When we throw ourselves in front of the bus rather than throw a colleague or friend under it, we are "as He is . . . in the world" (v. 17). When we absorb wrath for others, we know we abide in God (v. 13) and He in us, because His Spirit is active in us. When we love one another in this costly way, God abides in us (v. 12).

The follower of Jesus is willing to suffering unjustly for others: to suffer that Muslims would know Jesus . . . that colleagues would not be ashamed . . . to cover the mistakes of others. This is the love of God. We experience what it means to be cursed for others, and we take on the nature of God.

KANDU HINDUS OF INDIA (2,057,000; 0.0% EVANGELICAL)

PRAY THAT GOD WOULD RAISE UP MISSIONARIES FROM AROUND THE WORLD TO PLANT THE CHURCH AMONG THE KANDU (MATT. 9:37).

MAY 26: LIFESTYLE REPENTANCE

NEHEMIAH 12-13; PSALM 146; LUKE 13; 1 JOHN 5

*P*ilate evidently had a nasty side. In Luke 13:1–5 we read that he slaughtered some worshipers at the temple and mixed their blood with the sacrifices they had brought to offer. Nasty. Jesus referenced this tragic event alongside the misfortune of the tower of Siloam falling upon and crushing eighteen "innocent" bystanders. Jesus gave a surprising comment on these two shocking occurrences: Those who suffered deserved what they received.

First John 5:16 reminds us that there is a sin leading to death, and the corpus of Scripture clarifies that we have all committed it. Jesus' troubling point is that we all deserve to have our blood mingled with our sacrifices, and we all deserve towers to fall on our heads. The point in question is not why a good God allows bad things to happen to good people. The real question is why a good God allows good things to happen to bad people and restrains His own wrath. You and I are shockingly evil in God's sight. Jesus goes on to tell us that unless we repent, we will likewise perish (Luke 13:3, 5).

Those who call us to repentance do us a tremendous favor. We have grown accustomed to being told that we are not so bad, that we are not heinous, filthy, and repugnant before God. We need modern prophets like Nehemiah who will lovingly contend with us and curse us, strike some of us and pull out our hair, make us swear by God that we will not allow anything to defile us (see Neh. 13:25). How loving are they who declare the gate narrow! Those who preach a tolerant gospel hate our souls. There is no lasting love or concern in their message, and we should not venerate those who do us so much damage.

A clear-eyed view of human nature calls for a lifestyle of repentance. It is not enough to have seasonal wrestling with a realization of our fallen state, though that is healthy and appropriate, and should happen minimally every time we remember the Lord's death in communion. We must live sorry for our sins and thankful for the cleansing blood. Repentance literally means a turning from sin to Jesus, and we should live with turned hearts. Our hearts and minds should be daily, constantly turning from the sin that so easily entangles us to the Savior who so completely frees us. Moment by moment we should be repenting— turning to Jesus. Let us live a lifestyle of repentance, always conscious and sorry for our ugliness, always thankful and amazed at God's generous mercy that beautifies the humble.

ZERMA, DYERMA MUSLIMS OF NIGER (3,037,000; 0.001% EVANGELICAL)

PRAY THAT THE ZERMA, DYERMA WOULD FEEL AND KNOW THE BURDEN OF SIN AND WOULD COME TO JESUS FOR FORGIVENESS AND SALVATION (MATT. 11:28-30).

MAY 27: THE DOCTRINE OF CHRIST

ESTHER 1–3; PSALM 147; LUKE 14; 2 JOHN

*C*hurch history is replete with those inside the flock who have misrepresented or misunderstood Christ. The Scripture minces no words: "Whoever transgresses and does not abide in the doctrine of Christ does not have God" (2 John 9). If you do not think correctly about Jesus, you do not have God! To abide in the doctrine of Christ does not mean merely to agree with His thinking. It means to think correctly about Him . . . to place Him at the absolute center of worship. Anything less than the radical exaltation of Jesus above all things is wrong. It must always be all about Jesus.

Not content to stop there, John exhorted believers to deal ruthlessly with those who pretend to follow Christ but do not think correctly about Him. If anyone comes into our midst who does not exalt Jesus, we are not to receive that person into our houses or even greet him (v. 11). God is not tolerant if tolerance is "the virtue of a man without convictions" as G. K. Chesterton once said.[5] God gets downright narrow when it comes to our thinking, believing, and teaching about Jesus. Those who deny the full humanity and full deity of Jesus are nothing less than antichrists. Our view of Jesus is not graded on a percentage basis—it is either right or wrong. It is a true or false test, and either you get Jesus right (fully God, fully man) or you get Him all wrong. If someone comes into our team, our church, our midst with a faulty view of Jesus, we must not give them a voice or influence. They cannot be part of us if they are wrong or flippant about Jesus. This does not apply to the lost—we expect and allow them to get Jesus wrong, for if they are seeking Him, He will set them right. This applies to any who would exert influence within the body of Christ. Those with faulty doctrine about Jesus are under no conditions to be given a pulpit whether private or public.

Getting Jesus right is more than doctrinal purity; it must include unflinching obedience. To abide in the doctrine of Christ is to honor Him in our thoughts, to magnify Him with our mouths, and to obey Him with our wills and bodies. Getting Jesus right is to think what He thinks, think right about who He is, and then to act as He directs. Anything else is counter to Him, and anyone counter to Him is an antichrist.

BAHRAINI OF BAHRAIN (732,000; 1.4% EVANGELICAL)

PRAY THAT GOD WOULD UNVEIL THE CROSS AND WOULD REMOVE THE VEIL
ON THE MINDS AND SPIRITS OF THE BAHRAINI
(2 COR. 3:16–17).

MAY 28: AGAINST THE LAW

ESTHER 4-6; PSALM 148; LUKE 15; 3 JOHN

*O*ur palaces cannot protect us. There is no retreat from the advance of evil, for evil breeds within and cannot be barred by physical gates. Mordecai warned Esther: "Do not think in your heart that you will escape in the king's palace any more than all the other Jews. For if you remain completely silent at this time . . . you and your father's house will perish" (Esther 4:13–14). Our countries cannot protect us from the advance of Islam. Homeschooling does not protect us from worldliness. The church bubble does not protect us from humanism. If we are not proactive, we will perish.

God's directions may require that we act contrary to convention at cost to ourselves. Esther realized this when she sent a message to her cousin Mordecai saying, "I will go to the king, which is against the law; and if I perish, I perish" (v. 16). When salvation is on the line, God's law trumps the laws of earth. We do not stop witnessing in Muslim contexts even if that violates a law. We do not stop giving out Bibles in communist countries even if that violates a law. We do not stop calling sin what it is in the West even if that violates emerging hate-speech laws. We do not make our survival the aim even if our actions jeopardize our position or our safety. If we perish, we perish. We take our objections to the powers that be, even if our objections are against protocol—even if by objecting we die.

We think that mission is only for the salvation of others, which it certainly is, but our own souls are also at stake. To not obey God's great desire is to damage our own hearts. We disobey at peril to our own spirits and our own houses. When we disobey, God is not at a disadvantage because relief and deliverance will arise from another place (v. 14). When we disobey, we are disadvantaged.

GAHLOT MUSLIMS OF PAKISTAN (412,000; 0.0% EVANGELICAL)

PRAY THAT BELIEVERS AMONG THE GAHLOT WOULD BE SET FREE FROM A SPIRIT OF FEAR OF
WHAT MAY COME AND WOULD BOLDLY PROCLAIM THE TRUTH OF THE GOSPEL
(2 TIM. 1:6-8).

MAY 29: PRESERVED

ESTHER 7-10; PSALM 149; LUKE 16; JUDE

*J*esus knows how to protect us. He protects us from the Devil, from our enemies, and from ourselves.

Protected from the Devil. Jude reminds us to let God rebuke the Devil (Jude 9). Some people today see demons under every bed, and some do not see them at all. We are called to navigate the two extremes—to recognize that there is warfare at the unseen level but not to fall in love with the idea of being at war. When Satan marshals evil against us, we do not pompously rebuke him or his minions, for in our own strength they are stronger than we are. When under attack, we stay in the shadow of the cross. We station ourselves under the prevailing blood, and we say: "Devil, you may be stronger than I am, but you are much, much weaker than Jesus is, so take your accusation to Him. He will rebuke you. He will justify me."

Protected from Our Enemies. Esther and Mordecai learned that when the Lord rebukes the devourer, what seems like disaster is turned to triumph. "On the day that the enemies of the Jews had hoped to overpower them, the opposite occurred, in that the Jews themselves overpowered those who hated them" (Esther 9:1). Something within us should leap when we are sentenced to death, thrown into prison, accused and slandered, resisted and opposed. The more dangerous and damaging the threat, the more excited we should be for Jesus has the unparalleled ability to take certain doom and transform it to glorious triumph. Impossibilities should be our bread and butter. God is nowhere proved as glorious as when He snatches life and victory from the jaws of certain death: The greater the challenge, the greater the opportunity for God's glory.

Protected from Ourselves. Of all our enemies, the most insidious one lies within. It is our own sin that most often topples us. What agony we collectively experience when one of our own hoists themselves on their own pikestaff as a result of foolish and fleshly choices. How prone we are to self-destruction. How few there are who finish well. Into this fear steps our wonderful Jesus who is able to keep us from stumbling and is able to present us faultless with exceeding joy (Jude 24). What tremendous hope this gives us. It is possible to run this race of faith without being destroyed by my own flesh. Jesus is able to protect me from myself. Oh, thanks be to God our Savior! Glory, majesty, dominion, power both now and forever! Jesus is able to keep me from falling!

BHAR HINDUS OF INDIA (2,006,000; 0.0% EVANGELICAL)

PRAY FOR THE WORD OF GOD IN WRITTEN, ORAL, MUSICAL, AND DRAMATIC FORMS TO BE TRANSLATED AND TO RISE AMONG THE BHAR

(ISA. 55:10-11).

MAY 30: GOD'S ADVERSITY

JOB 1–3; PSALM 150; LUKE 17; REVELATION 1

*G*rief and worship are complementary. We treat them as opposites when in reality they coexist. "Job arose, tore his robe, and shaved his head; and he fell to the ground and worshiped" (Job 1:20). We tend to separate our times of loss and pain from our times of praise and worship. Job modeled for us the coexistence of grief and worship, saying, "The LORD gave, and the LORD has taken away. Blessed be the name of the LORD" (v. 21). Even in his agony he reminded his wife: "Shall we indeed accept good from God, and shall we not accept adversity?" (2:10). Times of grief are incredible opportunities for worship, neither mutes the other.

To accept the adversity that God allows is problematic for us and would be questionable if it were not so clearly spelled out in Scripture. God says to Satan concerning Job: "He is in your power. . . . He is in your hand" (1:12, 2:6). God put His choice servant in the hand and under the power of Satan. He allowed Satan to afflict Job. This allowance was not without hedges: "only do not lay a hand on his person" (1:12) but "spare his life" (2:6). All the same, God's man was put in the hands of Satan to be afflicted.

When Jesus trusts us enough to allow Satan to afflict us, it raises the question whether we trust Jesus enough to be afflicted. In God's view, trust is not percentage based. We either trust or we do not. We cannot partially trust; we have to be all in. In Luke 17:5–10 the disciples asked for increased faith. Jesus pointed out that even a little faith can do the impossible, like cast a tree into the sea. He seems to have been implying the comprehensive nature of trust. We cannot trust Him partially—it must be all or nothing. Or better said, the faith that pleases God is an all-encompassing, comprehensive faith. It is a faith that accepts adversity as well as good from God because it trusts that God has a good reason to allow both.

We tend to want increased faith so we can do great things and get great recognition. Jesus wants us to have faith to trust Him enough to do small things, difficult things, so He gets great glory. By faith, we do all things that we have been commanded to do (17:10), in other words we accept the adversity of God, knowing we are "unprofitable" servants. Faith is not about us. Faith is our trust that all things revolve around God and He can turn both good and adversity toward His fame.

SONINKE, SARAKOLE MUSLIMS OF MAURITANIA (188,000; 0.15% EVANGELICAL)

PRAY THAT GOD WOULD POUR OUT HIS SPIRIT ON THE SONINKE, SARAKOLE AND THAT THEY WOULD SEE DREAMS AND VISIONS OF JESUS. PRAY THAT THEY WOULD BE POWERFULLY SAVED AND EMPOWERED TO BE HIS WITNESSES (JOEL 2:28–32).

MAY 31: UNGODLY COUNSEL

JOB 4-6; PSALM 1; LUKE 18; REVELATION 2

*B*ad advice can come from good people. Psalm 1:1 points out the obvious: The man who does not walk in the counsel of the ungodly is like a tree. The less obvious is that we should also avoid the ungodly counsel of the righteous. Job's friends are great examples of good men who gave suspect advice. On the surface, Job's counselors spoke truth, even truth that is quoted elsewhere in Scripture: "Do not despise the chastening of the Almighty, for He bruises, but He binds up; He wounds, but His hands make whole. . . . You shall be hidden from the scourge of the tongue" (Job 5:17–18, 21). These are good words, but they were totally inappropriate in the context of Job's experiences. We can give and receive truth at the wrong time, in the wrong way. The truisms of Job's friends brought no help or relief. Godly counsel cannot simply be true—it must also be timely and kind. Sometimes the kindest speech is silence, and the kindest friends let those who are suffering vent without holding their anguished words against them (6:26).

In Luke 18, another desperate man received bad advice. A blind man sat outside Jericho. He heard that Jesus was coming, and he began to call out for help. Those who went before Jesus basically told the blind man to shut up, "but he cried out all the more, 'Son of David, have mercy on me!'" (Luke 18:39). The urgency and agony of the plea caught Jesus' attention. He stood still and took the time to deliver. There are times in all our lives when need overcomes propriety. Good friends counsel moderation or restraint. In that moment we must ignore the ungodly counsel of godly men and adopt the bulldog determination of the importunate. We must beware both the ungodly counsel of the wicked and the ungodly counsel of the righteous.

In the same vein, we must beware what kind of counsel we give to others. We, too, are more than capable of handing out foolish advice. Job's friends were not bad men, and they loved Job deeply, yet they completely missed what God intended. The human tendency is to be too hard on the things God allows and too soft on the things God despises. It is a sin to allow evil influence to spread (Rev. 2:20), just as it is a sin to disallow God's righteous acts to run their painful course. We should not be quick to truncate what an ever-wise God is doing, nor too slow to stand up to what an ever-holy God hates. We need God's discerning help to keep us from receiving or giving ungodly counsel. The only way to walk this path is to delight in His counsel day and night (Ps. 1:2). God just does not think like we do.

BERBER MUSLIMS, NORTHERN SHILHA OF ALGERIA (715,000; 0.005% EVANGELICAL)

PRAY THAT CHRISTIANS FROM AROUND THE WORLD WOULD WORK TOGETHER TO REACH THE BERBER AND THAT THE BERBER WOULD BE JOINED TO THE BODY OF CHRIST (JOHN 17:20-23).

That all of them may be one,
Father, just as you are in me and
I am in you. May they also be in
us so that the world may believe
that you have sent me.

JOHN 17:21 NIV

June

———

"DO NOT THINK ME MAD. IT IS NOT TO MAKE MONEY THAT I
BELIEVE A CHRISTIAN SHOULD LIVE. THE NOBLEST THING A MAN
CAN DO IS JUST HUMBLY TO RECEIVE AND THEN GO
AMONGST OTHERS AND GIVE."

—David Livingstone

JUNE 1: "NO OTHER PLEA"

JOB 7-9; PSALM 2; LUKE 19; REVELATION 3

*O*ur best righteousness is perverse before God. Job understood this: "Though I were blameless, it would prove me perverse" (Job 9:20). Job's friends decided that his anguish was due to his sin. On the one hand Job agreed, yet in despair he pointed out that no one can be blameless before God. He uttered a touch of pre-Calvary hopelessness, or better said . . . a-Calvary darkness. Though Job conceded that people cannot be righteous before God, something in his spirit reached for the cross.

Though on this side of Calvary we see more clearly, our spirits likewise reach for the cross. We, too, know that we cannot make ourselves good, and that people—at their best—are still perverse by the measure of God's holiness. We have but one line to stutter before His throne: "I need no other argument, I need no other plea. It is enough that Jesus died, and that He died for me."[1]

Job knew it, even though he could not quite see the solution as we can. He knew that God is the only hope for salvation. If God wants to find fault with people, He certainly can. Job astutely pointed out: "If it is a matter of strength, indeed He is strong; and if justice, who will appoint my day in court?" (v. 19) It is not as if we have a case to make. We cannot take on God's legal system and hope to win. We do not belong in the same universe with Him—much less have the right to consider ourselves equal adversaries in a court of law. "He is not a man as I am, that I may answer Him, and that we should go to court together" (v. 32).

So we find ourselves like Job—grasping. Job sensed deep in his soul what has been graciously revealed to us. The most perfect person is vile before a holy God, and if God wants to pick a fight with us, it is no contest. Job, however, did not have the luxury of seeing a mediator (v. 33). We sing back to Job and in doing so, sing to ourselves. We sing not from pride but from mutual relief, for God has introduced an unexpected Deliverer into our hopeless case. We were alone in the dock, the gavel descending to pound out our deserved sentence of death, when the courtroom doors burst open and an unexpected Savior exploded into the room. The watching cosmos fell quiet, and we who were guilty fell on our knees and whispered, "For my pardon this my plea—nothing but the blood of Jesus."[2]

KHARRAL MUSLIMS OF PAKISTAN (412,000; 0.0% EVANGELICAL)

PRAY THAT THE HEARTS OF THE KHARRAL WOULD BE LIKE GOOD SOIL, READY TO HEAR THE GOSPEL AND TO RESPOND (MATT. 7:1-8, 18-23).

JUNE 2: AUTHORITY TO NOT ANSWER

JOB 10-12; PSALM 3; LUKE 20; REVELATION 4

*J*esus is under no obligation to answer our questions. The only ones compelled to give answers are those inferior to the questioner. Those in authority can choose "if" and "how" they answer questions. When a superior detects a poor attitude or a challenge behind the inquiry, the superior has every right to remain silent.

Job, in his agony, asked God "Why?" (Job 10:2, 18) Job understood that God had made him and was subsequently unmaking him, but Job did not understand the "why." He understood the process but not the point. Why, God? All things are in Your hand; why have You allowed (or caused) such suffering? Unlike the cavalry of Tennyson's Light Brigade, we are not bound to the unthinking, unquestioning posture: "not for them to reason why."[3] God is big enough to answer our questions, even to welcome them. For God it is not a matter of asking why, it is a matter of attitude and authority.

In Luke 20, those who desperately wanted to protect their manufactured authority, and who were insecure about the unnatural authority they felt Jesus had acquired, approached Him with a question. They wanted to know who had given Him the right to exercise power. This type of question, which was rooted in a desire to be in control, was unacceptable to Jesus, and He refused to answer it. He rejected the premise of the question: that He was in any way under the authority of people. When we approach God from an attitude of control, He does not tolerate the question—for we have no right to resist His absolute right to reign. When we approach Him in brokenness, from a desire to understand, He graciously says, "Come up here, and I will show you things" (Rev. 4:1). The self-disclosure of God is connected to our humility. He takes the initiative to explain things to us when we are lowly. When we are demanding, He lets us simmer down for a season. He is not an almanac or a search engine—at our beck and call for answers. He has all authority, even the authority not to answer us.

In this context of authority, Jesus revealed two options for us: We can either be broken, or we can be ground to powder (Luke 20:18). Our pride leads us to hunt for other results, but there are none. The Lord of Glory welcomes questions from a broken heart. He crushes questions intended to challenge or control. Be careful not only *what* you ask but *how* you ask.

HAJAM MUSLIMS OF INDIA (1,867,000; 0.0% EVANGELICAL)

JUNE 3: PROVERBS OF ASHES

JOB 13-15; PSALM 4; LUKE 21; REVELATION 5

*G*od is perturbed with empty words, not because words are unimportant but because they are so important. Words have the power to break hearts and to give life. God has chosen to communicate largely through words, to create through His Word, and to spread the good news primarily through words.

We live in an increasingly shallow age where hollow words are nothing new. Many scholars think that Job is chronologically the first book in the Scriptures. Way back then Job scolded his verbose friends: "Your platitudes are proverbs of ashes" (Job 13:12). While we can use words to unpack complex concepts, we can also use them to reduce profound truths to flippant ditties. American spirituality tends to reduce massive realities about God into little rhyming phrases—cute but eventually repulsive. Arius, 256–336 AD, was a priest in Alexandria, Egypt, who spread heresy that God was superior to Jesus mainly through cute, rhyming songs.[4] God calls us to a simplicity that does not reduce His character to formulas. Our challenge is to articulate His complexities as best we can without speaking platitudes that we have not experienced. Truths we parrot to others that we have not lived are proverbs of ashes.

One essential mark of human words is their short shelf life. Words sourced in human wisdom quickly sour or fall to the ground. What seems cute or catchy, if repeated often enough, becomes irritating. By contrast Jesus says, "Heaven and earth will pass away, but My words will by no means pass away" (Luke 21:33). Because God's words are powerful and permanent, we do well to sing, pray, and preach them—literally. What better way to pray than to pray Scripture? When we pray Scripture, we know we are praying God's will, and our prayers are guaranteed to be answered. When we sing Scripture, we sing God's own passions back to Him, and we experience His pleasure and presence. When we preach Scripture, we speak timeless truth that is supported by the authority of the Eternal One.

When Jesus baptizes us with His Spirit, it always affects our mouths. In an age where technology has empowered more empty words than ever before, our words must be distinctive—lest we merely add to the babble. Jesus promised: "I will give you a mouth and wisdom which all your adversaries will not be able to contradict or resist" (Luke 21:15). We need to speak proverbs that are anointed speech, not ashes.

SUSU MUSLIMS OF GUINEA (1,203,000; 0.0% EVANGELICAL)

PRAY THAT BELIEVERS AMONG THE SUSU WOULD PROCLAIM THE MESSAGE OF THE GOSPEL CLEARLY AND WOULD MAKE THE MOST OF EVERY OPPORTUNITY GOD PLACES BEFORE THEM (COL. 4:2-5).

JUNE 4: SHATTERED AND SHAKEN

JOB 16-18; PSALM 5; LUKE 22; REVELATION 6

*O*ur pretension wounds the Savior. Those who pretend to abide in Him while their hearts and actions are treacherous inflict the most pain on His sacred heart. May God keep us from being men and women who linger long with Him in His Word and His presence while hearing little and changing less. When people are wounded, they strike; when Jesus is hurt, He heals.

We all betray Jesus. Peter in the end was no different from Judas. Woe to those who think they can be loyal to Jesus in their own strength. Peter, who claimed he would endure prison and death for Christ (Luke 22:31–34), faltered at the accusation of simple peasants. We all have treacherous hearts and in our natures we are all cowards. None of us can stand for Jesus in our own strength. Those who were "slain for the word of God and the testimony they held" (Rev. 6:9) did so through God's grace.

Jesus promised a woe on those who betray Him: not punishment from God, but the agony of realizing that one had what was pure, sublime, and supreme yet threw it away. This, too, is a mercy, a calling to return humbly to the One we have despised. Thanks be to God whose kindness leads Him to intervene in our lives, to deconstruct us that He might build us up again. Job experienced this loving deconstruction. "He has shattered me," Job said. "He also has . . . shaken me to pieces" (Job 16:12–14). Job had to be broken down in order to be built up in God's image.

One of God's harshest punishments is to leave us alone, for when we are left to ourselves and our own wisdom we self-destruct. God's interventions are His greatest mercies. We complain and strive when God breaks us, but without these painful processes we would speed toward the disaster of self-rule. How beautiful are the breakings of God. These are the consolations of God (15:11): that in His mercy He loves us enough to shatter us. That is why we declare steadfastly with Job, "Though He slay me, yet will I trust Him" (13:15).

PASHTUN MUSLIMS OF IRAN (2,130,000; 0.0% EVANGELICAL)

PRAY THAT THE PASHTUN WOULD UNDERSTAND THAT HOPE FOR FORGIVENESS AND ACCEPTANCE WITH GOD IS AVAILABLE ONLY THROUGH JESUS' WORK ON THE CROSS (1 COR. 1:18).

JUNE 5: THE LANGUAGE OF WEEPING

JOB 19-21; PSALM 6; LUKE 23; REVELATION 7

*G*od's children are often asked to bear unimaginable pain. The problem of evil is not, for us, a theoretical exercise. Instead, we wonder why bad things happen to good people, even going so far as to blame God—ignorantly, sinfully—for our troubles: "Know then that God has wronged me, and has surrounded me with His net" (Job 19:6). More than that, we wonder why good things happen to bad people: "Their houses are safe from fear, neither is the rod of God upon them" (Job 21:9).

In the midst of indescribable tragedy we have two comforts. First, God speaks the language of tears. We do not have to articulate our agony. We do not have to be coherent. We do not have to make sense. We do not have to be composed or "holy." We wail, and He understands us for on the inside He also weeps. How so? By taking on mortal flesh and suffering on the Cross, the Son of God experiences our pain and our sorrow as His own.

Second, at some point in our weeping Jesus calls us softly as He called Mary. Blinded by grief and tears, we do not recognize Him. So He stands and waits and cries along with us, softly calling again. As we listen to Jesus weep, something in our own brokenness is soothed. We understand that Jesus has experienced more pain than we have—His own, ours, and that of the whole world. Then, like Job, something rises in our spirits. It starts small but ever rises: "I *know* that my Redeemer lives, and He shall stand at last on the earth; and after my skin is destroyed, this I know, that in my flesh I *shall* see God" (Job 19:25–26, emphasis added). My tears are mingled and then lost in His. He wipes them away by swallowing them up in Resurrection victory (Rev. 7:17).

As mortals, bound by time, we consider Christ's agony on the cross to be confined to one day. And yet, God, who is outside of time, knew from the foundation of the world that the Lamb would be slain. The Son of God, who knew no suffering in eternity, entered time with the foreknowledge and intent to suffer for us. Our suffering overtakes us like a thief in the night. The Lamb of God was not taken by surprise, however. From all eternity, from the moment He was born in Bethlehem, Calvary was ever before Him.

What kind of God is this? What kind of God does this . . . for us?

PUNJABI MUSLIMS OF SAUDI ARABIA (697,000; 0.0% EVANGELICAL)

PRAY THAT THE BELIEVERS AMONG THE PUNJABI WILL ENDURE PERSECUTION IN A CHRISTLIKE MANNER AND WILL GIVE THEIR LIVES FOR THE SAKE OF THE GOSPEL IF NECESSARY (1 PETER 2:21-23).

JUNE 6: ANGER AND JUDGMENT

JOB 22-24; PSALM 7; LUKE 24; REVELATION 8

*T*he fall of humanity has spoiled many good things of God, among them anger and judgment. For us, these two words have a negative connotation. We equate *anger* with sin and *judgment* with punishment. Yet a perfect, eternal God is always good, and His goodness is not bound by the fall of humanity. Ergo, if God is angry and if He judges, there must be attending, inherent goodness in it.

The psalmist calls for the anger and judgment of the Lord to rise. "Arise, O LORD in your anger. . . . Rise up for me to the judgment You have commanded" (Ps. 7:6). Afraid and confused about the nature of God's anger, we ignore it or hide from it. Cowed by a misunderstanding of the wrath of God, we are embarrassed that He does not control His temper. But God is altogether "unique, and who can make Him change?" (Job 23:13). There is an aspect of God that appropriately terrifies us (v. 16). God would not be God if He did not scare us witless. This "just judge . . . is angry with the wicked every day" (Ps. 7:11). It is shameful for us to be ashamed of God's anger. Rather than apologize for His anger, we need to embrace it and warn others of it.

Likewise, God's judgments are love. We shudder at His judgments for we misunderstand them. Judgment is a high form of mercy. When God judges us, He divides out our sin. Judgment is divine surgery. God carefully puts us on the operating table of love, searches out the gangrene in our spirits, and carefully cuts it out. Of course there is pain, both in the process and the recovery, but it is the pain of life, of being loved. God loves us enough to cut out the things that are killing us. Only a fool would be ungrateful to the surgeon who has saved his life by cutting out a malignant tumor! Yet we continually whine at God's judgments, at the very acts that save us from ourselves.

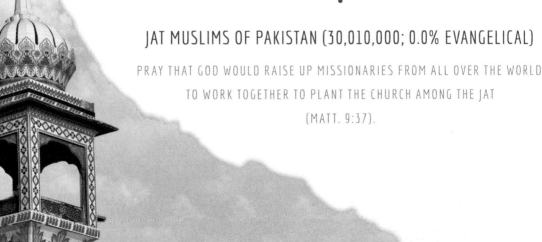

JAT MUSLIMS OF PAKISTAN (30,010,000; 0.0% EVANGELICAL)

PRAY THAT GOD WOULD RAISE UP MISSIONARIES FROM ALL OVER THE WORLD TO WORK TOGETHER TO PLANT THE CHURCH AMONG THE JAT (MATT. 9:37).

JUNE 7: KNOW THYSELF

JOB 25–27; PSALM 8; JOHN 1; REVELATION 9

K*now Who God Is.* All lies are based on a distortion of who God is. Conversely, all truths are based in the reality of who He is. We know ourselves by knowing Him. Though the things we know of God are the "mere edges of His ways" and we only hear "a small whisper of Him" (Job 26:14), it is enough to provide clarity about ourselves. By knowing that God is grace and truth, the Lamb who takes away the sins of the world, and the King (John 1), we correctly come to terms with who we are.

Know Who You Are Not. We know who we are by first knowing who we are not. John the Baptist clearly understood who he was not. He declared that he was not the Messiah, was not Elijah, and was not the Prophet (John 1:19–23). John had no illusions of grandeur or ambitions to be more than who he was—a voice bearing witness. Homespun wisdom tells us there are two essentials in identity: There is a God, and we are not Him. It seems simplistic, but we could avoid many problems and much pain if we would let God reign without meddling in His business.

Know Who You Are. Jesus knows who we are before we do. He saw Nathanael before Philip called him (John 1:48). Jesus gives us the right to become children of God (v. 12). We actually have very few rights according to Scripture, and what rights we do have are connected to sonship. We have the right to be called the children of God, which gives us the right to be filled with the Holy Spirit. These are the only rights we need for they define who we are—and they are enough.

Know Who You Will Become. Jesus beams upon us: "You are Simon, you shall be called Cephas" (John 1:42). Jesus sees both who we are and who He will help us become. We can be content in the now to be a child of God; we can take comfort "that I, a child of hell, should in His image shine!"[5] Jesus wants to stamp His character deep upon our lives. We are safe because we are in His family, but safety is not the same as satisfaction. We must yearn, long for what we shall be: like Him! This is the most marvelous of mysteries.

KAIBARTTA HINDUS OF INDIA (1,854,000; 0.0% EVANGELICAL)

PRAY THAT THE KAIBARTTA WOULD FEEL AND KNOW THE BURDEN OF SIN
AND WOULD COME TO JESUS FOR FORGIVENESS AND SALVATION
(MATT. 11:28–30).

*J*esus does not need me or my service. He does not even need my witness. John puts it this way: "[Jesus] had no need that anyone should testify of man, for He knew what was in man" (John 2:25). My testimony does not improve or disparage God's character. He is who He is regardless of me. He existed before any person, and the actions or inactions of any person have no effect whatsoever on His character. He does not need our approval; He does not even need our worship. He does not need the worship of the nations. God is not more fulfilled when the peoples praise Him. He is eternally satisfied in Himself. He does not need our flimsy praise—but He ordains and commands it.

Command Before Call. The fact that God does not need our help in no way undermines the involvement of people in mission. He commands to go into the world and bear witness of Jesus. God's command precedes His call. In our individualized world, we have placed great importance on a personal call, but our obedience is more important. God has given orders, and a "call" simply provides the clarification of those orders. God directed Paul to bear witness to the Gentiles before Paul was invited to Macedonia. We can twist our calling into an excuse to do what we want, where we want but obedience is primary.

Call Before Character. Once we have settled forever that God has our unquestioned obedience, we are yielded and flexible to be deployed and redeployed as He sees fit. He may assign us to the home front, the supply lines. He may ask us to pioneer or to administer. He may move us around freely. This understanding of the calling is a collective one. God uses us as He deems best. God does not cast around for men and women of the highest integrity and then select them. (He knows all our hearts, and they are not pretty). He appoints us and then through the process shapes His character in us.

Character Before Competence. Some people approach mission service with a resume in hand. God smiles politely and sets our natural gifts aside until He has formed His character in us. He does not waste our natural abilities, but they are the least important variable in the process. Before we can excel in our gifting, we must glow with His nature. God really can use anyone in missions—the genius and the simpleton and everyone in between. There are one-talent and five-talent laborers, the number of talents is not the point.

We are not needed. We are commanded. When we comply, we receive clarity (call). After our call, God goes to work on our character. After He deconstructs and reconstructs, He adds His anointing to our competencies, and we are, at last, suitable to be His tools.

FULANI, MAASINA MUSLIMS OF MALI (1,201,000; 0.0% EVANGELICAL)

PRAY THAT GOD WOULD UNVEIL THE CROSS AND WOULD REMOVE THE VEIL ON THE MINDS AND SPIRITS OF THE FULANI, MAASINA (2 COR. 3:16-17).

JUNE 9: STAYING GREEN

JOB 31-33; PSALM 10; JOHN 3; REVELATION 11

*J*ob made a covenant with his eyes not to look upon a young woman (Job 31:1). He knew that our human hearts tend to walk after our eyes (v. 7) and are prone to lead us to destruction and disaster (v. 9). God watches what we watch (v. 4); He sees all our ways. I left Cancun, Mexico, yesterday, where skimpy bathing gear leaves little to the imagination, and am sitting in the London airport on my way back to Cairo, where ladies covered in burqas abound. But whether in Cancun or Cairo, my heart remains the same. I must intentionally stay in covenant with my eyes, and with the One who gives sight.

Dr. Mark Laser of Faithful and True Ministries presents a color code to help us with covenant and confession regarding sexual purity.[6]

Red represents the blatant sin issues: pornography, adultery, and lust. (This is a list of the most common issues but is not an exhaustive list). These actions violate covenant and must involve confession, repentance, and discipline.

Yellow represents actions that are not necessarily sinful, but make us vulnerable to disobedience and sin (red issues). For example, I am too hypocritical to walk into an airport bookstore and browse through a pornographic magazine, but I am tempted to walk through that same bookstore, pick up a novel, and flip through the pages hoping to "stumble upon" a saucy section. That bookstore is a yellow for me. There is nothing inherently wrong with an airport bookstore, but if it places me in a position of vulnerability, I must avoid it. Another example would be browsing the Internet late at night when you are tired and everyone else is sleeping. Fatigue makes you vulnerable—it is a yellow zone.

Green refers to positive actions that keep us far from vulnerability: faithfully abiding in Jesus; daily lingering in His Word and presence; going to bed early; a regular exercise program; weekly dates and consistent intimacy with your spouse; being accountable to someone; and practicing a habit of transparency that brings all things into the light.

We tend to think of confession as primarily focused on the red zone. The discipleship process helps us live in the green zone and bring confession to the yellow zone. By the Spirit's help we do not live in the reds, and we bring the yellows into the light. When we meet with our accountability partner we need to confess things we do that put us in vulnerable positions. Ultimately, as we mature and establish patterns of holiness, we even need to confess where we are not proactive in the green zone. Alan Johnson, a friend and colleague who lives in Bangkok, Thailand, has shared with me the reality of living in a sex-trade city. He points out that we need more than covenant eyes. We need a covenant life: our whole being (mind, body, soul) in the green, the proactive holiness of all things in the light, all things in love, and all things in liberty.

URDU MUSLIMS OF SAUDI ARABIA (647,000; 0.0% EVANGELICAL)

PRAY THAT BELIEVERS AMONG THE URDU WOULD BE SET FREE FROM A SPIRIT OF FEAR OF WHAT MAY COME AND WOULD BOLDLY PROCLAIM THE TRUTH OF THE GOSPEL (2 TIM. 1:6-8).

JUNE 10: OUTLASTING THE DEVIL

JOB 34-36; PSALM 11; JOHN 4; REVELATION 12

*O*ne of the best ways to defeat your enemies is to outlive them. Enemies have a way of self-destructing if you give them enough time—time is always on the side of the righteous. The good news is that we will be standing long after our common Enemy and accuser is thrown into the pit. Revelation 12 reminds us that the Devil is both a deceiver and an accuser, and because his time is short, his wrath is great (v. 12).

The Devil has no patience due to the fact that he has limited time. He knows Jesus has already won. In frenzied despair the Devil tries to destroy as many people as possible. I picture it as a one-breath frenzy. God has thrown him into the deep end of the cosmos' swimming pool, and he has one breath to do damage. The implication is that by patience we possess our souls. In that frantic death-shake, the Devil does not have time for long engagements. When we hold steady against his lies and attacks, he is compelled to move on to someone more vulnerable. As soon as he sees that we will not yield to his accusations and temptations, he despairs and moves on. For sure, he cycles back at a more opportune time and the battle is rejoined, but one of our surest defenses against a strong foe is to remind him we are protected by God, who is stronger. We do not take lightly this death attack, for it is fierce; yet we know we can outlast it if we hold steady.

Rather than flee trouble, we stand against it. "In the LORD, I put my trust; how can you say to my soul, 'Flee . . .?'" (Ps. 11:1). When we flee in the face of adversity, we put others at risk for we leave vulnerable ones exposed. We need to stand in the gap, slam our shepherd's staff down on the bridge like Gandalf, and shout: *"You shall not pass!"* When we resist and outlast the enemy, we save not only ourselves but our little ones as well. Patience is a primary weapon, and patience is not passive. It is impossible to defeat a foe who will not quit, who can endure abuse, and who absorbs punishment knowing that every blow received drains the limited supply of the attacker. We stand there, actively absorbing whatever is launched against us, because God has let us understand that the arsenal of evil is limited and cannot be replenished.

JATT MUSLIMS OF PAKISTAN (568,000; 0.0% EVANGELICAL)

PRAY FOR THE WORD OF GOD IN WRITTEN, ORAL, MUSICAL, AND DRAMATIC FORMS TO BE TRANSLATED AND TO RISE AMONG THE JATT

(ISA 55:10-11)

JUNE 11: GRAVE LISTENERS

JOB 37-39; PSALM 12; JOHN 5; REVELATION 13

*I*n John 5, Jesus established His credentials. He declared Himself equal with God (v. 18); declared He gave life (v. 21); asserted that all judgment is given to Him (v. 22); demanded that everyone should honor Him (v. 23); and proclaimed He had life in Himself (v. 26). Upon these assertions He then announced: "The dead will hear the voice of the Son of God and . . . will live. . . . The hour is coming, in which all who are in the graves will hear [My] voice and come forth" (vv. 25, 28, 29).

Living in the Arab world does wonders for a person's faith. I have just come back from Mexico where hundreds of South Americans filled an auditorium and flooded the air with exuberant praise and prayer. Rapturous worship ascended to the heavens. I stepped off the plane into a Muslim city of twenty-five million and wondered if the Arab praise will ever rival that of our Latino brothers and sisters. Jesus assures us it will.

Now, we see only a painful trickle of Arab Muslims enter the kingdom. The work is so slow, the ground so resistant, and the enemies so organized. Death holds tightly to its victims. Jesus sees the imminent hour we can hardly believe will happen—when Arab Muslims will hear His voice, rise from the bondage and chains of Islam, and live! Our reality now is backbreaking labor for unsteady fruit. Our soon-to-be-future is abundant harvest, net-breaking fish, and more Arab Muslims flooding into the kingdom than we know how to deal with. Men and women will come in groups, morning and night, hungry for Jesus . . . desperate for the Bible . . . longing to be discipled.

In context, John 5 refers to a physical resurrection, but the principle involved is that Jesus is God and has the power to bring life from the dead. He resurrects dead dreams, dead relationships, dead hopes, and dead longings. He can take what the Enemy has crushed and breathe back into it God-filled life. When we walk by cemeteries, we should get excited: Think of the living who will burst forth from those earth beds in glory! When we walk in Muslim cities, something in our spines should tingle as we think of the men and women Jesus is going to call into life. These "living dead" will hear His voice, and they will rise to life in Him. Jesus will call them out of the deadness of Islam into the glorious liberty of being sons and daughters of God. And because God's heart is great and generous, it will not be a few—God will call millions of Muslims to life.

If all things were easy and possible, God would be redundant. By definition God requires impossibilities. Bringing the dead to life? That is easy for God . . . and just about to happen.

BELDAR HINDUS OF INDIA (1,797,000; 0.0% EVANGELICAL)

PRAY THAT GOD WOULD POUR OUT HIS SPIRIT ON THE BELDAR AND THAT THEY WOULD SEE DREAMS AND VISIONS OF JESUS. PRAY THAT THEY WOULD BE POWERFULLY SAVED AND EMPOWERED TO BE HIS WITNESSES (JOEL 2:28-32).

JUNE 12: THE CURE FOR SELF-RIGHTEOUSNESS

JOB 40-42; PSALM 13; JOHN 6; REVELATION 14

*F*rançois Fénelon described the root of self-righteousness. He said that we "start to mistreat the people we are secretly jealous of. Jealousy, hidden in your deepest inner folds, exaggerates the least faults of others. Then come the disguised criticisms. You deceive yourself in order to justify yourself. . . . Your self-interest hides in a million clever disguises. There is no end to the excuses we will come up with. . . . Even your outrage at the faults of others is a great fault. Don't you see your own wretchedness? It would certainly level your self-righteousness to the ground."[7]

The life of Job illustrates both the descent into self-righteousness and the recovery. After he sputtered out all the reasons why he was good and did not deserve to suffer, God confronted him directly by asking a series of questions. God pointed out that Job's excuses were an attempt to correct God (Job 40:2). This metaphysical slap across the divine face stunned Job into silence, and he said: "Behold I am vile. . . . I lay my hand over my mouth. I have uttered what I did not understand . . . therefore I abhor myself and repent in dust and ashes" (v.4, 42:6).

Self-righteousness is tricky because it is equal parts flesh and righteousness. Usually we are partially correct about something, but our attitude toward others is wrong. We speak out of place, we assume as unbecoming posture, and we correct or judge our leaders when we should just shut up and let God work things out. At other times, friends or colleagues misunderstand or abuse us as Job's friends did, and we join our error to theirs by despising them for hurting us.

Job's story demonstrates how to escape from the deluded prison of self-righteousness. First, we have to see ourselves clearly and repent of what we see. Like Job, we need to clap our hands over our mouths, admit to God and ourselves that we are idiots, and be genuinely sorry for our presumption. Second, we need to forgive those who have offended or insulted us. "The LORD restored Job's losses when he prayed for his friends" (42:10). We must be careful that forgiveness does not renew a cycle of self-righteousness: *I am better than you, so I forgive you.* When we forgive out of the shame of being an idiot and in the joy of being forgiven ourselves, this severs the root of self-righteousness.

MINYAK-MANJACO MUSLIMS OF GUINEA BISSAU (158,000; 0.008% EVANGELICAL)

PRAY THAT CHRISTIANS FROM AROUND THE WORLD WOULD WORK TOGETHER TO REACH THE MINYAK-MANJACO AND THAT THE MINYAK-MANJACO WOULD BE JOINED TO THE BODY OF CHRIST (JOHN 17:20-23).

JUNE 13: THE UNPOPULAR JESUS

PSALM 14; ISAIAH 1-3; JOHN 7; REVELATION 15

*W*hen Jesus has been universally liked, He has been misunderstood. The Muslim Jesus, the secular Jesus, the liberal Jesus look little like the historical Jesus.

Jesus the Hated. The people hated Jesus because He testified that their works were evil (John 7:7). In today's world, He would be castigated for pointing out the evils of society. Jesus spoke boldly and clearly the uncompromised doctrine of the Father (vv. 16, 26). Because He pointed out the evils of society when it was unpopular to do this, people considered Him a "hater." To be like Jesus is to speak out against evil and to be hated. Striving to be liked and respected by the world, whether our own culture or the culture we are trying to evangelize, is errant—if we would be like Jesus.

Jesus the Demonized. When Jesus spoke against sin the people complained (John 7:12). They were perturbed enough to make a shocking accusation: "You have a demon!" (v. 20) Jesus' ministry was revolutionary to the point that some thought Him wicked. We are warned in Scripture that something is amiss when all people speak well of us. Yet our hearts crave to be admired. To be like Jesus is to be so contrary to conventional wisdom that people think we are evil!

Jesus the Divider. "There was a division among the people because of Him" (John 7:43). We mistakenly think that Jesus always unites people. The reality is that Jesus constantly divides people. Because He is truth, and because truth is unyielding and must conquer, those who submit to truth unite with Jesus and those who resist truth unite against Him. Unity is a noble goal, but not at the expense of truth. The reality of Jesus is that division follows in His wake. We are not used to thinking of Him in those terms, but if we are to be like Jesus, we, too, will be divisive when it comes to truth. It is a false expectation to think that all people can be united.

The historical and present Jesus is not the nonoffensive people-pleaser that many reduce Him to. Those who diminish Him in this way resent His divine right to rule and to define truth. They are not His friends—they are rebels with gilded tongues. We must reconcile ourselves to the reality that to follow Jesus means that we, too, must speak out against evil, be hated, be thought demonic, and be polarizing. Any other expectation is wayward.

QASHQAI MUSLIMS OF IRAN (1,780,000; 0.0% EVANGELICAL)

PRAY THAT THE HEARTS OF THE QASHQAI WOULD BE LIKE GOOD SOIL,
READY TO HEAR THE GOSPEL AND TO RESPOND
(MATT. 7:1-8, 18-23).

JUNE 14: BEAUTIFUL JUDGMENT

PSALM 15; ISAIAH 4-6; JOHN 8; REVELATION 16

*O*ur rebellious hearts hate to be judged. Ostensibly it is because we claim the judge cannot know our hearts. In reality, men and women resent judgment because they know they are guilty . . . and they hate for their hearts and sins to be revealed. By definition, divided hearts are partially errant, so when our hearts are on trial they reveal something ugly. That is why God's judgment is priceless: it burns away the evil parts of our hearts without harming the good.

When God judges, He divides our hearts from that which is unholy and in the process He is exalted. The revelation of our evil exalts God, not because He feels good about pointing out our shame but because He wants to make us like Himself. When He judges us, our ugliness is burned away and we start to look beautiful. Judgment, when accepted, purifies and makes holy. To be holy is to be like God and to bring Him honor. Judgment is a win-win proposition: We are beautified, and God is glorified.

God's judgment is freeing. The cross is the great gavel of God. When He pounded Christ's cross into the ground, He planted the instrument of His judgment of sin. God judged (divided out) sin on the cross. Under the judgment of God we are safe and protected. The cancer that was killing us from the inside has been removed. Isaiah exulted in the reality of this beautiful judgment. After revealing that God had washed away sin by the spirit of judgment and burning, he declared in the next verses: "For over all the glory there will be a covering. . . . There will be a tabernacle for shade in the daytime from the heat, for a place of refuge, and for a shelter from storm and rain" (Isa. 4:5–6) The beautiful judgment of God provides our covering.

> Beneath the cross of Jesus I fain would take my stand,
> The shadow of a mighty rock within a weary land;
> A home within the wilderness, a rest upon the way,
> From the burning of the noontide heat, and the burden of the day.[8]

KURD, SORANI MUSLIMS OF IRAQ (630,000; 0.01% EVANGELICAL)

PRAY FOR THE PEACE THAT RESULTS WHEN MEN AND WOMEN ARE
RECONCILED WITH GOD (JOHN 14:27). PRAY FOR MEN AND WOMEN OF
PEACE (LUKE 10:6) AMONG THE KURD, SORANI.

JUNE 15: THE FULLNESS OF JOY

PSALM 16; ISAIAH 7-9; JOHN 9; REVELATION 17

*A*n Egyptian believer was in our home last night. He has served four years as a missionary in Libya and has been arrested three times—the last arrest led to an extended time in prison where he was beaten severely multiple times. On one occasion they tied his hands up to a rafter above his head, put a blindfold on him, stuffed his mouth with a dirty rag, and put a gun to his head. "Any last requests?" they sneered. Our brother nodded his head, and they removed the rag and freed his hands. "I want to pray," he said, and immediately did so. "Thank you Lord that my life is in your hands. Amen." He finished his brief prayer, plucked the rag out of the surprised guard's hand, and stuffed it back into his mouth. Stunned at his fearlessness, the guard beat him mercilessly and called others to join in the beating.

Psalm 16 describes passages through hell. Every saint will eventually pass through one or more hellish situations. "Therefore my heart is glad, and my glory rejoices; my flesh also will rest in hope. For You will not leave my soul in Sheol, nor will You allow Your Holy One to see corruption" (vv. 9–10). This promise to the Messiah has currency for us. The psalmist goes on to say: "You will show me the path of life; in Your presence is fullness of joy; at Your right hand are pleasures forevermore" (v. 11). Somehow people believe the lie that the highest earthly pleasures involve ease and comfort. This may be true for heaven, where evil is banished, but on earth, where evil abounds, the greatest joys are found in the presence of Jesus regardless of physical conditions.

Christian joy in this temporal world does not depend on health, wealth, or lack of suffering. Mysteriously, the richest humans are currently the least happy, and the suffering church is much more joyful than the prosperous one. Christian joy comes from the certainty that we will be delivered one day and from the expansive pleasure of suffering with Jesus any day. When we suffer for Jesus because we stand for Him or share Him with a fallen world, divine energy and comfort are poured into our spirits. It is not rational and it is not transferable. It is the unique and special privilege of those who have tearfully trodden the path of suffering. To suffer with Jesus is to know that "the lines have fallen" for us "in pleasant places" (v. 6). Jesus is ever before us, at our right hand, and we shall not be moved (v. 8). We can then be in prison . . . beaten . . . yet with aplomb stick the gag back in our mouths and with a blindfolded twinkle say: "Go ahead: Shoot me. I am my Beloved's and He is mine, and His banner over me is love." (Song 2:4)

JHINWAR MUSLIMS OF PAKISTAN (630,000; 0.01% EVANGELICAL)

PRAY BELIEVERS AMONG THE JHINWAR WOULD PROCLAIM THE MESSAGE OF THE GOSPEL CLEARLY AND WOULD MAKE THE MOST OF EVERY OPPORTUNITY GOD PLACES BEFORE THEM (COL. 4:2-5).

JUNE 16: VINDICATION AND SATISFACTION

PSALM 17; ISAIAH 10–12; JOHN 10; REVELATION 18

*I*n the eighteenth and nineteenth centuries, personal insults required "satisfaction." Satisfaction was linked to vindication. When a person felt that someone had assaulted his personal honor, a friend would arrange a duel and those involved would settle the matter by violence. In our day, we are just as concerned with vindication and will violently protest our innocence when we believe we have been wronged. Very little energizes us like the desire to clear our names, to prove that we are right. We will not rest or be satisfied until we have proved ourselves true.

Leaving aside the fact that we are all deeply flawed and are never completely without fault, vindication does not come from our activity. The psalmist wrote: "Let my vindication come from Your presence" (Ps. 17:2). It is inevitable that we will be misunderstood. It is inevitable that we will offend or disappoint others. Invariably, when we try to clear our names we only muddy the water. God invites us to let Him defend us. We are not even supposed to attend our own court case. Jesus invites us to rest in His presence while He rises to our defense. We find a similar promise in Isaiah 10:27: "The yoke will be destroyed because of the anointing oil." It is not my effort that vindicates or breaks through oppression and confusion—it is the active work of God to clarify and free.

Jesus did not open His mouth when He was on trial. He could have vindicated Himself before Herod and Pilate, but He chose not to. Jesus invites us into His own character, into the satisfaction of being like Him. "I shall be satisfied when I awake in Your likeness" (Ps. 17:15). When we are insulted or maligned, vindication and satisfaction come from sheltering in the presence of Jesus and being conformed to His image. The time we most want to defend ourselves is the time we should intentionally retreat to the presence of Jesus, shut our mouths, and let Him use the uncomfortable and embarrassing circumstances to stamp His image deeply upon us.

BANIA, KOMTI HINDUS OF INDIA (1,762,000; 0.0% EVANGELICAL)

PRAY THAT THE BANIA, KOMTI WILL UNDERSTAND THAT HOPE FOR FORGIVENESS AND ACCEPTANCE WITH GOD IS AVAILABLE ONLY THROUGH JESUS' WORK ON THE CROSS
(1 COR. 1:18).

JUNE 17: JESUS THE FIERCE

PSALM 18; ISAIAH 13-15; JOHN 11; REVELATION 19

*M*uch has been written about and taught on the subject of servant-leadership. The hyphenation of the term is indicative of problematic thinking. In the Bible no such concept exists as relates to Jesus. There is leadership and there is servanthood. Both are real, and both complement each other by being different, not by being conjoined. Today Jesus is heralded as the great servant-leader, which is nonsense. Jesus *is* the leader. We are the servants. The tremendous power in Jesus girding Himself with a towel and washing His disciples' feet was precisely this: He is *not* our servant—He is our leader. He is King of Kings and Lord of Lords. That is why His serving us is an unthinkable aberration. God does not exist to serve us. When we get to heaven, Jesus will not serve us—we will serve Him eternally! Do we really think He will be running around eternity, girded with a towel and washing the feet of the redeemed?

Revelation 19:11–16 unveils who Jesus is. He judges and makes war in righteousness (v. 11). He has eyes like a flame of fire, searing into and through the souls of humanity (v. 12). He has a robe dipped in blood, the evidence of dead enemies slain by God's anger (v. 13). He will strike the nations and rule them with a rod of iron (v. 15). He treads the winepress of the fierceness and wrath of Almighty God! (v. 15) He is King of Kings and Lord of Lords (v. 16). Does this describe a servant? This authoritative Jesus before whom elders and living creatures fall and worship is no servant.

A high view of Jesus heightens the wonder of the incarnation and the cross. We cannot truly appreciate the lowliness and sacrifice of God if we do not start with the reality of His majesty and absolute authority. Jesus is King, and we tremble before Him. It is horrific to think of Jesus serving us, yet this is what we have reduced Him to: a genie who answers our prayers and washes our feet. God have mercy on us all. The incarnation of God should be agony for us. It is so painfully out of character for Him that this is its glory and wonder. How dare we approach the incarnation casually, without a sense of grateful horror.

TUKULOR, PULAAR MUSLIMS OF SENEGAL (988,000; 0.0% EVANGELICAL)

PRAY THAT THE BELIEVERS AMONG THE TUKULOR, PULAAR WILL ENDURE PERSECUTION IN A CHRISTLIKE MANNER AND WILL GIVE THEIR LIVES FOR THE SAKE OF THE GOSPEL IF NECESSARY (1 PETER 2:21-23).

JUNE 18: TRUTHFUL LIAR

PSALM 19; ISAIAH 16-18; JOHN 12; REVELATION 20

*T*hree times in Revelation 20 John referred to the Devil as a liar, a deceiver of nations (v. 3). Being very good at what he does, the Devil is canny enough to mix a fair amount of truth in his deception. After all, the best lies are based on a truth and have the ability to appeal to our emotions as well as our intellect.

Christian mission to Muslims hinges on how this non-Christian religion is evaluated. If your perspective is that Islam, while disagreeable, is redeemable, you approach the Qur'an and the ideology from a fulfillment model: You start with what the Muslim believes and lead him or her to a more biblical understanding over time. If your starting point is that the Devil skillfully wrapped a grand lie in small truths, then you advocate discontinuity: You insist on a clean break with Islam and the beginning of a new life in Christ.

The genius of the Devil is his ability to take wicked concepts and wrap them in partial truths. It is dangerous—if not foolish—to reach back into an integrated lie to rescue small truths if their reason for being has always been to obfuscate the deception. It is sheer madness to look into an antithetical text for proofs of your faith because this undermines your own source of authority while giving credence to the opposing scripture.

Not all lies are equal. Some lies are more insidious than others. There are lies in Judaism, yet the Old Testament is inspired. There are deceptions in Catholicism, yet the Catholic scripture includes the God-breathed New Testament. What distinguishes Islam from either of these religious ideologies is that its authoritative text denies the deity of Christ—vehemently. It is impossible to reach into Islamic revelation to build a Christological case. You cannot take a text that lies about Jesus, forcefully claiming He is not God, to prove that He is God. Yes, there are small truths in the Qur'an. Yet if they were placed there with the intent to deceive, we would be foolish to start with the Qur'an when trying to introduce a Muslim to Jesus.

In contrast to texts that deceive, Psalm 19:7-11 reminds us that the law of the Lord is perfect, sure, right, pure, clean, true, sweeter than honey, able to warn us, and a reward to those who keep it. John 1 reminds us that Jesus is the eternal Word of God, and John 14 assures us He is truth—there is no deceit in Him at all. All descriptions of who Jesus is (the most crucial clarification in history) must be based on a source that is completely true—big Truths wrapped in bigger Truths surrounded by only Truth. There must be no lie in our truth.

BEDOUIN, SANUSI MUSLIMS OF LIBYA (616,000; 0.0% EVANGELICAL)

PRAY THAT GOD WOULD RAISE UP MISSIONARIES FROM ALL OVER THE WORLD TO WORK TOGETHER TO PLANT THE CHURCH AMONG THE BEDOUIN, SANUSI (MATT. 9:37).

JUNE 19: HEALED BY STRIKING

PSALM 20; ISAIAH 19–21; JOHN 13; REVELATION 21

*W*e are not the first to promise to live dead, and we are not the first to fail. Peter promised the Lord: "I will lay down my life for Your sake" (John 13:37) moments before denying Jesus three times. All who attempt to live the crucified life fail—many times. To live dead is to keep crawling back on the altar every time you fall off. Jesus graciously restored Peter, and He will graciously restore us. All things will be made new (Rev. 21:5), even our dedication. When we commit to follow Jesus radically and we fail, we are sorely tempted to stop trying. Jesus is honored when we fall and rise to try again. He is delighted to fulfill our petitions and to answer us in the day of our trouble (Ps. 20:1). We just do not expect Him to help us by striking us.

In Isaiah 19, the Lord promised to send a Savior to Egypt and Sudan. God promised that He would be known in Egypt. Immediately after the promises to these now Muslim nations the text says: "And the LORD will strike Egypt, He will strike and heal it" (v. 22). This was right before God said, "Blessed is Egypt My people" (v. 25). God's means of helping people, of revealing Himself, includes striking them so they will turn to Him and be healed. Surrounded by examples of abuse and poor fatherhood, something in us recoils at the thought of being struck by the heavenly Father. For many of us, beatings, whether physical or emotional, do not draw us closer to the abuser or lead to any kind of healing. We respond to striking by recoiling into a defensive posture.

God strikes us to get our attention. Jesus struck Peter with one glance, and Peter wept. Out of that shame and sorrow, he received restoration and healing. The severity of God's strike depends on the thickness of our skulls and our spirits. When we are soft toward Him, all He needs to do is look at us to get our attention. When we are recalcitrant and disobedient, sometimes He has to whack us upside the head with a club of grace. The intention is the same: to turn our attention to Him so He can remove the sin, pride, error, or falsehood and bring healing.

It should not surprise you that the direct result of promising Jesus to live dead is your failure to do so. When we commit to follow Jesus sacrificially, all hell breaks out against us and our flesh joins the uprising. We fail numerous times, or we succeed in part and grow a pompous spirit. God in His mercy strikes us, gains our attention, then lovingly heals and sets us free.

KABARDIAN MUSLIMS OF TURKEY (1,053,000; 0.0% EVANGELICAL)

PRAY THAT THE KABARDIAN WOULD FEEL AND KNOW THE BURDEN OF SIN AND WOULD
COME TO JESUS FOR FORGIVENESS AND SALVATION
(MATT. 11:28–30).

*E*ternity is the triune God. Without beginning or end, a community of love has always existed and will eternally exist: one God—three persons outside of time—who have loved each other forever. God invites us into that community, into that eternal love. God has placed something deep within us that knows there is a reality deeper and sweeter than whatever good we now enjoy. When we are filled with God's Spirit, we have an innate sense that He has possessed us for something more. We long for home, a home prepared for us where we will see His face directly, where there is no night, and where we will revel in the glory of the triune God (Rev. 22).

While we wait for this unfettered glory, God uses us as glory pegs. Isaiah prophesied what God would do with Eliakim: "I will fasten him as a peg in a secure place, and he will become a glorious throne to his father's house" (Isa. 22:23–24). Essentially, God said that though Eliakim was small and unrecognized, he would be established firmly as a hidden peg on which to hang glorious things.

This is God's intention for us while we wait for the full manifestation and enjoyment of His eternal glory. He wants to establish us securely in order to hang His glory on us. We are to be the small, forgotten peg that displays the glory of God. We are not the royal robe, but without our unseen steadiness, the glory robe would fall to the floor, crumpled. Not many begin Christian service with the ambition to be a hidden peg, completely obscure. When we have pegged well, no one can see us, no one even knows we are there—all they can see is God's glory.

There is no higher calling than to be an obscure peg—securely fastened to God's wall—that helps to display His glory. A faithful peg that is true to its assignment is not seen . . . and does not care. The highest joy for glory pegs is to go unnoticed even as God uses them to display His glory.

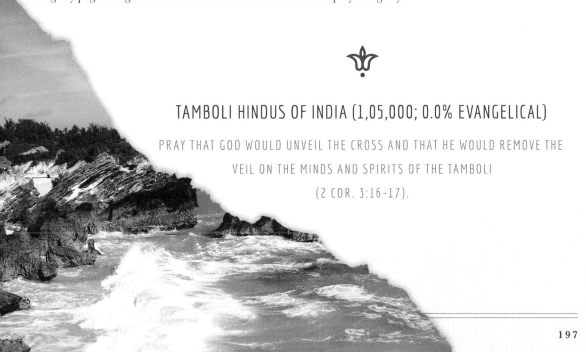

TAMBOLI HINDUS OF INDIA (1,05,000; 0.0% EVANGELICAL)

PRAY THAT GOD WOULD UNVEIL THE CROSS AND THAT HE WOULD REMOVE THE VEIL ON THE MINDS AND SPIRITS OF THE TAMBOLI
(2 COR. 3:16-17).

JUNE 21: GOD'S FIERY CENTER

PSALM 22; ISAIAH 25-27; JOHN 15; ACTS 1

*G*od said: "Fury is not in Me" (Isa. 27:4). The fire at God's center is one of love, not wrath. Yes, it is true that "God is angry at the wicked every day" (Ps. 7:11). Yes, wrath and mercy meet at the cross. Yes, sinners are in the hands of an angry God, precariously in danger of hell. Yet none of these truths diminish the reality that God is love—He is motivated by love, and love undergirds everything about Him, even His wrath. God is not energized by anger. The fire in God is a passionate love. God's mercy, His love in action, crowns and connects all His ways. His anger is just because He is love.

There are times when those who follow God should be angry. There are temples to cleanse, hypocrites to call out, innocent children to defend, justice to advance, and lies and perversity to attack and even kill. If our fiery center is anything but love (even if it is justice, truth, cause, outrage, need), we will eventually lose our balance and become like those we strive against. We must learn to follow Jesus in striving *for* those with whom we disagree—and this can only be done if the fire that rages within us is one of love. God designed us to be passionate, emotional creatures. Our balance comes from being extreme in opposite directions, not from a cancelation of qualities that makes us boring and lifeless.

We can be on fire and at peace at the same time. To be passionate and extreme is not to be out of control. The husband who loves his wife exuberantly to the end of his days is to be commended, not mocked. His passion requires disciplined and sustained faithfulness. God has promised to keep in "perfect peace" those whose minds are stayed on Him (Isa. 26:3). A mind fixed on Jesus controls the fire that burns within. A mind and will subject to God's Word rejoices at the great treasure therein, and "great peace have those who love Your law, and nothing causes them to stumble" (Ps. 119:162, 165). Those who abide in God's Word abide in His love—and the result is joy (John 15:11).

We are not called to have anger at our center; we are called to be on fire. We should be the most active, passionate, extreme people on the planet. When our fire is sourced in love, when it is governed by the peace that comes from obeying God's Word, the result is not only joy for us but for all around us—for all whom we touch. The fire within us sets others aflame. John Wesley allegedly said something that puts it well: "Do all the good you can, by all the means you can, in all the ways you can, in all the places you can, at all the times you can, to all the people you can, as long as you ever can. . . . Catch on fire with enthusiasm, and people will come for miles to watch you burn."[9]

MABA MUSLIMS OF CHAD (20,000; 0.0% EVANGELICAL)

PRAY THAT BELIEVERS AMONG THE MABA WOULD BE SET FREE FROM A SPIRIT OF FEAR OF WHAT MAY COME AND WOULD BOLDLY PROCLAIM THE TRUTH OF THE GOSPEL (2 TIM. 1:6-8).

JUNE 22: TONGUES OF MEN AND ARABS

PSALM 23; ISAIAH 28-30; JOHN 16; ACTS 2

*T*he core of Pentecostal doctrine is *subsequence*. Pentecostals believe that what happened in Acts 2 and following was normative but was not salvation. It is a normal biblical experience to have a fresh encounter with Jesus by His Spirit. It is a normal biblical experience for our encounters with the Spirit to affect our tongues. When we encounter the Spirit of Jesus—over and over again after we are saved—it always affects our tongues. We prophesy, we speak the Word of God with boldness, and we speak in tongues. There is no indication in the Scriptures that you can have an experience with the Spirit and it not affect your tongue.

When the Spirit fell at Pentecost on those who were already in relationship with Jesus and already had the Spirit of God within them, they began to speak in tongues—they uttered, with the Spirit's help, languages of the known world. Notice where the nations listed in Acts 2 are located today: Parthians, Medes, and Elamites are Iranians; Mesopotamia is Iraq; Judea is the West Bank; Cappadocia, Pontus, Asia, Phrygia, and Pamphylia are all in Turkey; Egypt; Libya; Cretans; and Arabs. With the exception of Crete, all the people mentioned in Acts 2 are now under the domineering thumb of Islam. It is time for them to experience a *new* Pentecost.

The primary evidence of Pentecost is not what my tongue does or does not say—it is whether or not every tongue confesses Jesus as Lord. Let us not fixate on initial physical evidence of the outpoured Spirit but be consumed with the ultimate physical reality of every people from every nation lifting their hands in worship, bending their knees in honor, and using their tongues to magnify the precious name of Jesus.

We can pray in the Spirit to our hearts' content around air-conditioned altars, but unless our tongues are lifted in prayer and proclamation in the streets of Riyadh, Jeddah, and even Mecca itself, then we of all people are the most babbling. Saudi Arabia, Libya, Egypt, Turkey, Iran, and the West Bank of Palestine were represented at the original Pentecost outpouring. At that time they received the former rain, but at present they are bone dry. Once more God is waiting for some of His children to speak both the words of the Spirit and the tongues of Arabs.

BALOCH SOUTHERN MUSLIMS OF UNITED ARAB EMIRATES (578,000; 0.0% EVANGELICAL)

PRAY FOR THE WORD OF GOD IN WRITTEN, ORAL, MUSICAL, AND DRAMATIC FORMS TO BE TRANSLATED AND TO RISE AMONG THE BALOCH
(ISA. 55:10-11).

JUNE 23: REFRESHING REPENTANCE

PSALM 24; ISAIAH 31–33; JOHN 17; ACTS 3

*I*t is astonishing to think that Jesus prays for us (John 17:20). He prays that we would be united in the Godhead that the world might believe in Jesus (v. 21). Our unity with one another and thus, our fruitfulness in mission depends on being individually united with God. There can be no endued fellowship in reaching the nations if our hearts are not right with Jesus. In Acts 3:26 we read that Jesus blesses us by turning us away from our iniquities. Repentance toward God opens our hearts to one another and brings refreshing to the world.

Our sin toward God causes us to sin against one another. When we reduce sin to an act against people, we dilute it. We must admit the full reality of sin and repent in order to be at peace with God and with others. Joseph recognized this when Potiphar's wife tempted him: "How can I do this great wickedness, and sin against God?" he asked (Gen. 39:9). David, after committing murder and adultery, said to God: "Against You, You only, have I sinned" (Ps. 51:4). We cannot deal with sin, even the "smallest" sin, until we admit it is a grievous insult against a holy God. A guilt-based theology of sin recognizes that sin is horrible, even if it does not affect any other human or creature. Hidden, private sins are just as damaging to our souls as outward, public transgressions. A shame-based theology of sin ranks sin according to its effect on others but does not take God's holiness seriously.

We can take no comfort that our sins are hidden in our minds or hearts. Just because our failings are private does not mean they are blotted out. There is only one way for our ugly private acts to be stricken from God's record: "Repent therefore and be converted, that your sins may be blotted out, so that times of refreshing may come from the presence of the Lord" (Acts 3:19). Many followers of Jesus conceal and carry private sins for years, even decades—and all the time that private failure eats away at their spirits. The passage of time does nothing to diminish the internal decay. Unconfessed sin dulls the presence of God.

Oh, the liberty and refreshing freedom we feel when absolutely nothing is covered in our hearts! When we are at liberty with God—when we experience the internal refreshing that results from repenting of *all* private sin—we are most suited to be unified with our brothers and sisters in God's mission.

KAMBOH MUSLIMS OF PAKISTAN (792,000; 0.0% EVANGELICAL)

PRAY THAT GOD WOULD POUR OUT HIS SPIRIT ON THE KAMBOH PEOPLE AND THAT THEY
WOULD SEE DREAMS AND VISIONS OF JESUS. PRAY THAT THEY WOULD BE
POWERFULLY SAVED AND EMPOWERED TO BE HIS WITNESSES
(JOEL 2:28–32).

A favorite tactic of the Devil is to use fear to shut the mouths of Christians. Our Enemy will issue threats from multiple sources in his repeated attempts to limit our verbal witness of Christ. Satan is more concerned about muzzling verbal witness than sabotaging acts of compassion, because the recipients can interpret acts of compassion as they wish. A bold, unapologetic witness of Jesus as the only means of salvation does not allow this latitude. How do we witness boldly when we are threatened? The Scriptures give us clear instruction:

Do Not Dignify the Threat by Responding to It. In Isaiah 36:21, when Sennacherib threatened the work of the Lord, God's people "held their peace and answered him not a word." We receive threats often in the Arab world either by phone, by text, or in person. Our first response is not to respond . . . not to be blackmailed . . . not to change anything about who we are or what we do. We act as if the threat does not exist. Bullies hate to be ignored.

Defuse the Threat by Becoming More Bold. When the authorities arrested Peter and John and instructed them not to speak in the name of Jesus, they responded by going to prayer with friends: "Now Lord, look on their threats, and grant to Your servants that with all boldness they may speak Your word" (Acts 4:29). The result was a shaking, a filling of the Holy Spirit, and speaking the Word with boldness (v. 31). How frustrating for the Devil when his attempts to silence us drive us closer to Jesus—for more of His Spirit and for greater boldness.

Determine That Obedient Boldness Is Worth the Consequences. Boldness does not guarantee immunity—it promises more resistance. "Jesus, therefore, knowing all things that would come upon Him, went forward . . ." (John 18:4). While we keep our eyes on the Lord who can pluck us "out of the net" (Ps. 25:15), we know that bearing witness of Jesus always meets resistance. Jesus knew this but went forward anyway. He even said, "I spoke openly to the world . . . and in secret I have said nothing" (John 18:20).

The obedient follower of Jesus cannot escape threats. In the context of His public speaking, Jesus said, "For this cause I have come into the world, that I should bear witness to the truth" (v. 37). What is true for Jesus is true for us: *For this cause we go into every part of the world, that we should bear witness to the truth.* The Devil's primary aim is to silence us. Our primary obedience is to boldly proclaim Jesus as Lord and Savior.

KHANDAIT HINDUS OF INDIA (1,689,000; 0.0% EVANGELICAL)

PRAY THAT CHRISTIANS FROM AROUND THE WORLD WOULD WORK TOGETHER TO REACH THE KHANDAIT AND THAT THE KHANDAIT WOULD BE JOINED TO THE BODY OF CHRIST (JOHN 17:20-23).

JUNE 25: THE JOYS OF THE EARTH

PSALM 26; ISAIAH 37–39; JOHN 19; ACTS 5

*B*efore "the things of earth . . . grow strangely dim,"[10] we who walk this fallen planet would be wise to enjoy its joys. Unusual as it sounds, there are some privileges on earth we can never enjoy in heaven: deliverance, praise in pain, and suffering shame for Jesus' sake.

Deliverance. When anything threatens God's people, He considers it as a reproach against Himself (Isa. 37:14, 23). God intervenes and saves us for His name's sake. In other words, attacks against God's people are insults against God, for the attacker is purporting that He cannot defend His own. He steps in and proves otherwise. Our rescue then is never about us—we are not the center of our deliverance. Rescue gives glory to the rescuer. Our salvation makes God look good. In heaven we celebrate this wonder retrospectively. On earth we are privileged to see God magnify Himself through our deliverance.

Pain Praise. There is a type of praise that is only possible this side of the grave. "Death cannot praise You!" is how Isaiah 38:17 puts it. There is a praise that can only ascend from earth. It is the agonized praise that rises from the midst of prison, sickness, trial, tragedy, loss, weariness, and pain. Heaven does not know this praise because that is where all the thorns are taken away and burned forever. As long as we live on earth, we are privileged to offer agonized praise—pain praise is precious to Jesus. Heaven's praise is pure and complete; earth's praise is raw and in process. Heaven's praise is from what is sure and seen; earth's praise is by faith in the midst of danger and despair. One day we will praise from eternal safety and final deliverance, but on earth we have the opportunity to delight God's heart by praising from our pain. We join Hezekiah in saying, "The living man, he shall praise You, as I do this day" (v. 19).

Suffering Shame. In heaven there will be no tears or embarrassment. The apostles rejoiced that they were counted worthy to suffer shame for Jesus' name (Acts 5:41). What an honor to be an associate of Jesus and to receive a tiny portion of the scorn He endured for us. Gladly we will be free of shame one day but, in the meantime, we count it a privilege to suffer for Jesus. It is a priceless opportunity and a passing one. Let us enjoy the joys of earth while they are available. We can offer earthly struggle as precious praise to Jesus in a way that is not possible in heaven. We do not glorify evil, pain, or shame—these are bad things. We simply decide that bad things can help us glorify Jesus. Therein is double delight—God's and ours.

SONGHAI-KOYRABORO MUSLIMS OF NIGER (871,000; 0.001% EVANGELICAL)

PRAY THAT THE HEARTS OF THE SONGHAI-KOYRABORO WOULD BE LIKE GOOD SOIL, READY TO HEAR THE GOSPEL AND TO RESPOND (MATT. 7:1–8, 18–23).

JUNE 26: EXCHANGED STRENGTH

PSALM 27; ISAIAH 40-42; JOHN 20; ACTS 6

*W*e are not supposed to come to the end of our lives with excess energy. We are purposed to be poured out as an offering. What a shame if we enter heaven with resources of any kind in reserve, having failed to pour out all our being and possessions for Jesus and the gospel. If a long-distance runner gets to the end of the race with energy abounding, he has not run wisely. When we run to win, we use all our resources, saving enough only for one last burst at the end. Running in this manner invites both the criticism of friends and the astonishment of enemies. Some will think we run too fast, while others will condemn us for pacing too slow. No outward observer can fully know our inward obedience. We must keep plodding according to the inward rhythm of the Spirit, determined never to stop but to spend and be spent for the gospel. A determination like this inevitably pushes us to the edge of what is possible. Soldiers, athletes, and farmers do some of their most important work when they are stretched to their limits and are tired.

Isaiah 40:31 is a great comfort to those who purpose to live tired in the service of the King. What keeps God's long-term runners steady when youths around them faint with weariness and young men utterly fall? "Those who wait on the LORD shall renew their strength." The Hebrew root of *renew* has strong implications of "exchange." Those who abide in Jesus exchange their strength for His. In the midst of our constant struggle, when we take time on a daily basis to linger with Jesus—to give Him extravagant time—He exchanges strengths with us. This is the secret of living and dying tired. Jesus takes our pitiful, receding, limited strength and in return gives us His! He gives divine energy to those who wait on Him. He takes our fatigue, our weariness, our discouragement, and our fading energy and exchanges it with His empowered life force.

Jesus expects us to eat right, sleep well, and be consistent in physical exercise. His divine energy is not a magic pill that covers our stupidity or neglect. But even when we are disciplined in these practical areas of life, the demands of ministry and service are unyielding. The only way to push through the inevitable fatigue that accumulates on body and soul is to wait on the Lord. Abiding in Jesus has ramifications on the whole person—body, mind, and spirit. When abiding becomes the anchor of our rhythm, we learn the skill of resting while we labor . . . of steadily putting one foot after the other . . . burning up our resources even as we are steadily and divinely supplied. Abiding gives us the wisdom to calibrate our journey perfectly so that we burst through the final tape consumed yet conquering.

BERBER, TEKNA MUSLIMS OF MOROCCO (557,000; 0.0% EVANGELICAL)

BERBER, TEKNA MUSLIMS OF MOROCCO (557,000; 0.0% EVANGELICAL) PRAY FOR THE PEACE THAT RESULTS WHEN MEN AND WOMEN ARE RECONCILED WITH GOD (JOHN 14:27). PRAY FOR MEN AND WOMEN OF PEACE (LUKE 10:6) AMONG THE BERBER, TEKNA.

JUNE 27: CREATED FOR GLORY

PSALM 28; ISAIAH 43-45; JOHN 21; ACTS 7

*D*eep within every person is the desire for significance. We want our lives to matter, to count for something. It is a comfort to realize that God has created us for glory—not our own. The desire to be glorified is wayward, but the desire for God to be glorified in us is true. He chose us for this very purpose (Isa. 43:7). He created us to bring Him glory.

The quest to glorify God without glorifying ourselves is a delicate one. We carry both motives deep within. We genuinely want to see Jesus exalted in all the earth, even while we wrestle down our desire to share in that glory—even indirectly. We make all kinds of promises to Him and break most of them along the way. He is not overly impressed with our promises; He knows how prone we are to break them.

Peter stood in for us all—promising to die with Jesus only moments before denying him publicly. Post-resurrection, Jesus asked Peter: "Do you *agape* Me?" Peter responded: "Lord, You know that I *phileo* You." Jesus was asking Peter: "Do you love Me with the love that will sacrifice all, that will give up all glory and will be satisfied to be nothing that I might be everything?" Peter responded: "Jesus, You know my folly. You know I have brotherly affection for you. You know my love is as weak as it is real. You know I still want to share in Your glory." Jesus asked again: "Do you *agape* Me?" Peter responded: "Lord, you know I only *phileo* You." And then the dagger: "Peter, do you only *phileo* Me?" And Peter in honest grief admitted: "Lord, You know all things—You know I only *phileo* You." Loving Peter and his broken honesty, Jesus then said, "Follow Me" (John 21:15–19).

To get us to the place where we are ready to give Him all the glory, Jesus has to break us down. The first step is for us to admit that we live very much for our own glory—no matter who we are or how humble we appear. Once we are shamed (and often it takes a public failure even to be aware how glory-covetous we are), we can back away from empty promises and say to Jesus: "You know my divided heart. You know how I long for my own glory next to Yours. Jesus, have mercy on me. I will not make empty promises. I will just try to obey." If we can get there—willing to obey, willing to be led by others, willing to follow Jesus uniquely and simply—then He can be glorified in us. Jesus only trusts the broken with His glory.

KARAKALPAK MUSLIMS OF UZBEKISTAN (522,000; 0.0% EVANGELICAL)

PRAY THAT BELIEVERS AMONG THE KARAKALPAK WOULD PROCLAIM THE MESSAGE OF THE GOSPEL CLEARLY AND WOULD MAKE THE MOST OF EVERY OPPORTUNITY GOD PLACES BEFORE THEM (COL. 4:2-5).

JUNE 28: END FROM THE BEGINNING

PSALM 29; ISAIAH 46-48; MATTHEW 1; ACTS 8

*F*our air force helicopters just flew over our apartment and tanks are deployed around the city—it is another normal day in the Middle East where instability is the norm. In these last days it is futile to wait for the pristine moment to move, live, or speak for Jesus if we restrict that moment to external peace. The gospel has ever advanced under pressure, and our day is no exception.

God alone knows the end from the beginning, His counsel shall stand, and He shall do all His pleasure (Isa. 46:10). He rules on the earth. Not only does He know all that goes on but He determines everything for His purposes. He intervenes in our affairs for His own sake. He has mercy on us and refines us for His own name's sake, not for ours (Isa. 48:9–10)! What He ordains in the realms of the earth is not primarily for us. We are not the center—it is for Him. Millions can demonstrate in the streets, soldiers can posture, politicians can predict, but all are pawns, at best, in the great battle of the heavens, and that is a battle God has already won.

When the people killed Stephen at the consent of Paul (Acts 8), a great lamentation followed. The church was widely persecuted and scattered; the authorities dragged men and women off to prison. "Therefore," the text says, "those who were scattered went everywhere preaching the word" (8:4). God, whose counsel will stand, who knows the end from the beginning, also knows how each local and global conflict will end before it begins. We can take great comfort in conflict knowing that God will ensure His own interests. Though we do not know all of God's goals, there are a few that are consistent in Scripture and redemption history:

God Always Glorifies Himself. The point of God's intervention in human folly is not that He aligns with one side or the other. There are no good guys compared to God. He cares only for the defense and honor of His name. We do not pray for or against rebels or regimes, for to do so would be to pray from a faulty human perspective. We pray: "Father, glorify Your name and however You choose to do that is fine with us." By deliverance or death, by peace or by war, by us or without us . . . nothing matters save that God is proved holy.

God Always Beautifies the Gospel. I often wonder why God allows false religions to thrive and spread. The answer is still a mystery to me, but one thing is sure—falsehood cannot help but beautify the gospel. False religions serve as a foil to make the gospel shine. War, disaster, trouble, and tragedy all serve as spotlights that elevate the only hope for humanity: what God has done in Christ. Bad news makes good news all the sweeter.

TELI MUSLIMS OF INDIA (1,638,000; 0.0% EVANGELICAL)

PRAY THAT THE TELI WOULD UNDERSTAND THAT HOPE FOR FORGIVENESS AND ACCEPTANCE WITH GOD IS ONLY AVAILABLE THROUGH JESUS' WORK ON THE CROSS (1 COR. 1:18).

JUNE 29: JOY COMES IN THE MOURNING

PSALM 30; ISAIAH 49–51; MATTHEW 2; ACTS 9

*W*eeping may endure for a night, but joy comes in the morning. . . . You have turned for me my mourning into dancing" (Ps. 30:5, 11). When the wise men saw the star stop over the house where Jesus lay, they rejoiced with exceedingly great joy and fell down and worshiped (Matt. 2:10–11). Joy comes from being where Jesus is and from worshipping Him. We experience Jesus . . . we worship . . . we *joy.* Jesus tends to be most clearly revealed in difficult circumstances. In trials, everything false is burned up leaving only what cannot be destroyed. The longer the trial, the more temporary things are removed until only Jesus remains. Because difficulty makes Jesus real to us, it is no surprise that joy comes in the "mourning."

The Devil is an irritable fellow, and joy frustrates him. His ongoing resentment of Jesus is fueled by the joys of Jesus and His people. Evil responds to great joy with great wrath—every male toddler in Bethlehem was viciously killed and the mothers of Ramah wept, lamented, and wailed, unable to be comforted. Because joy is so precious to the saints and so repugnant to the Devil, we should never take it for granted nor think it is automatic. Joy is something to fight for, something to choose and receive. Joy and woe are finely interwoven, and we must deliberately latch hold of joy when it is tied to sorrow. We *will* rejoice in God our Savior, even when we know our souls will be pierced. We rejoice despite sorrow, not because we are immune to suffering but because we rejoice by faith.

When we refuse to let the Devil steal our joy, Jesus turns our mourning into dancing. Faith never denies facts, so rejoicing in trial never means we live idealistically or in denial. There are chains, there are captives, but we rejoice in the presence of Jesus made real through difficulty. Joy is the advance messenger that heralds deliverance. When God's people rejoice on a broken earth, they anticipate the ultimate fulfillment when "the ransomed of the LORD shall return, and come to Zion with singing, with everlasting joy on their heads. They shall obtain joy and gladness. Sorrow and sighing shall flee away" (Isa. 51:11).

The presence of Jesus unleashes joy. Sometimes joy is most keenly felt when all insulators are swept away by trial, difficulty, and suffering. When pain has rendered meaningless all our supports, comforts, and even our friends, there is One whom we cannot dismiss. Jesus stands faithful in the rubble of our ruined lives. He alone can bear great wounds and retain a twinkle in His eye without any measure of twistedness. In those seasons, let us look into His sparkling eyes and choose His joy. Let joy come in the "mourning."

MANDINKA, MANDINGO MUSLIMS OF GUINEA BISSAU (16,000; 0.003% EVANGELICAL)

PRAY THAT BELIEVERS AMONG THE MANDINKA, MANDINGO WILL ENDURE PERSECUTION IN A CHRISTLIKE MANNER AND WILL GIVE THEIR LIVES FOR THE SAKE OF THE GOSPEL IF NECESSARY (1 PETER 2:21-23).

JUNE 30: THE BAD GOOD NEWS

PSALM 31; ISAIAH 52-54; MATTHEW 3; ACTS 10

*T*he good news is bad to the one who enjoys sin or embraces deception, for the opening word of the gospel is "Repent!" (Matt. 3:1–2) John the Baptist, Jesus, Peter, Stephen, Paul, and all biblical preachers had one thing in common: They told people they were wrong, so the people disliked them. Our calling is to be another voice to point out that humanity is sinful and only God can save. People often reject the "glad tidings of good things" (Isa. 52:7) because they are devoted to doing bad things. The good news is only good if people want to be rescued. If they do not think they are errant, then the good news is insulting.

The psalmist said that he was a reproach among all his enemies and especially his neighbors (Ps. 31:11). We live with the tension of wanting to be liked while being obedient proclaimers. A worldview driven by cultural anthropology leads people to make concessions to culture in order to be accepted. Missional living guided by biblical theology leads people to prioritize the King's message, which inevitably makes a majority of the populace dislike them. This tension cannot be reconciled without heresy, so it must not be reconciled. A priority on proclamation does not mean the messenger's supreme goal is to be disliked—that is sheer folly. It does mean that the messenger's supreme goal is to be faithful to the difficult and glorious message no matter the cost. The message ultimately is the problem because people resent its opening line: *Repent!* Implicit in the call to repent is the unyielding reality that people are wrong and must turn from their sin. No one welcomes this message.

The good news is as astounding as the bad news is troubling. "And the Lord has laid on Him the iniquity of us all. . . . Yet it pleased the Lord to bruise Him" (Isa. 53:6, 10). As the hymn says, "And can it be that I should gain an interest in the Savior's blood? Amazing love, how can it be that Thou, My God, should die for me?"[11] Two uncomfortable truths make up the good news: Everyone is a sinner, and God died for everyone's sin. The good news is weird and wonderful. Our role is to witness to the mystery. If we are but a voice for the marvelous, it does not matter what others think of us. We are not the point of the gospel. If our voice is rejected or silenced, another voice will rise, for the power is not in our voice, the power is in the message.

NUBIAN, KUNUZ MUSLIMS OF EGYPT (504,000; 0.0% EVANGELICAL)

PRAY THAT GOD WOULD RAISE UP MISSIONARIES FROM ALL OVER THE WORLD TO WORK TOGETHER TO PLANT THE CHURCH AMONG NUBIAN, KUNUZ (MATT. 9:37).

July

"FROM MY MANY YEARS OF EXPERIENCE I CAN UNHESITATINGLY SAY
THAT THE CROSS BEARS THOSE WHO BEAR THE CROSS."

—Sadhu Sundar Singh

JULY 1: GUILELESS

PSALM 32; ISAIAH 55–57; MATTHEW 4; ACTS 11

*T*here is something winsome about the person with no guile. We are impressed by the intelligent, awed by the strong, drawn to the attractive, amused by the witty, but the person without guile makes us feel safe. Psalm 32:2 reminds us that the person without deceit is blessed. This blessing comes primarily from being accepted by God and trusted by people. God loves the guileless for they make no attempt to deceive Him. The intelligent and strong of the world use their gifts to try to cover their weaknesses—which before omnipotent God makes them look ridiculous. Persons without guile make no attempt to cover weaknesses, motives, sins, or struggles and in that raw honesty they make themselves endearing to God and to others. There is a humility about the guileless that God loves: "For thus says the High and Lofty One who inhabits eternity, whose name is Holy: 'I dwell in the high and holy place with him who has a contrite and humble spirit, to revive the heart of the humble'" (Isa. 57:15).

There is a vast difference between hidden sin and covered sin. Hidden sin is unconfessed, and carrying it continually drains the life out of us (Ps. 32:4). Covered sin is confessed sin, and because it is confessed and repented of, God carries and covers it, allowing the confessor to walk in liberty. The guileless tend to be quick to repent. The guileless are not less sinful than the hypocritical (there is no second-rate sinner, we all share the title of chief); they are just more forthright about their failings. When we share our victories, we introduce a spirit of competition. When we share our failures, we introduce a spirit of compassion.

The longer we walk in the light, the more important it is that we have no guile—and the harder it is to be guileless. We love new believers for they are transparent about their sin and their candor is refreshing. But accumulated years in the faith tend to add layers of guile to the soul. Jesus is pleased with the long-term guile-free. Both guile and transparency are learned behaviors. Let us determine to be increasingly contrite, lowly, and guileless. What a glorious way to live and die—free from all sin and pretense!

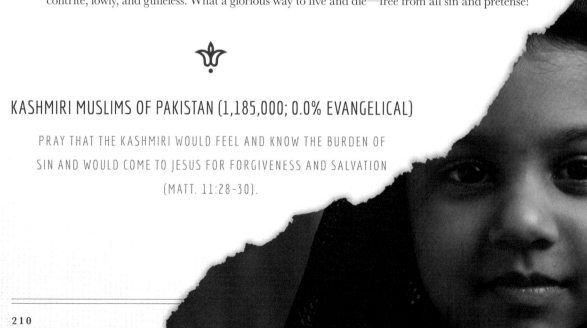

KASHMIRI MUSLIMS OF PAKISTAN (1,185,000; 0.0% EVANGELICAL)

PRAY THAT THE KASHMIRI WOULD FEEL AND KNOW THE BURDEN OF
SIN AND WOULD COME TO JESUS FOR FORGIVENESS AND SALVATION
(MATT. 11:28-30).

JULY 2: INSTITUTIONAL COMPASSION

PSALM 33; ISAIAH 58-60; MATTHEW 5; ACTS 12

*G*od has a habit of asking us to do impossible things, things that are not natural to us: like turning the other cheek, giving generously to the one suing us, walking an extra mile for the sake of the oppressor, giving to all who ask us, being perfect as our Father in heaven is perfect (Matt. 5:38–48). What God asks of us is only possible through a new nature, a nature given by God's Spirit, a nature that partakes of the divine. It is not in the human constitution to be like God consistently. We handle the discrepancy between God's expectations and our human capacity by diluting the request to a manageable level.

Take compassion and justice for example. We can handle a cause. We can handle organizing justice into a march, a monthly donation, or a two-week trip to Haiti. We can manage compassion by sponsoring an orphan, sending used clothes to Africa, or dropping some coins in the countertop charity box. We can write articles and give speeches for the grander causes and then, satisfied, retreat to the comfort and cleanliness of our protected suburban lives. But this is not doing the impossible, and God—even when justice and compassion are concerned, especially when justice and compassion are concerned—still desires the impossible.

Isaiah 58 instructs us to loose the bonds of wickedness, to undo the heavy burdens, to let the oppressed go free, to break every yoke, to share bread with the hungry, to cover the naked, and to bring the poor who are cast out into our house (vv. 6–7). We have selectively interpreted these injunctions at the corporate, macro level. We love institutional compassion because it lifts a load of guilt off our shoulders and makes us proud of our benevolence.

But Isaiah was writing to individuals. Macro justice and compassion can only be sustained if they are built on a million applications at the micro level. We are not to buy the homeless man a sandwich, pat him on the back, and leave him to his park bench. We are to *bring him into our house*. We are to get close and personal with poverty and injustice. We are to leave our ivory palace, give up our majesty, and follow Jesus to live right in the inner city—or invite the inner city right into our guest room. Compassion and justice are most beautiful at the personal, micro level and most distorted at the public, institutional macro level. Impossible justice and compassion are what is required of us, not the halfway step of institutional benevolence.

MOGHAL MUSLIMS OF INDIA (1,624,000; 0.0% EVANGELICAL)

PRAY THAT GOD WOULD UNVEIL THE CROSS AND WOULD REMOVE THE VEIL ON THE MINDS AND SPIRITS OF THE MOGHAL (2 COR. 3:16-17).

JULY 3: STAYING LITTLE

PSALM 34; ISAIAH 61-63; MATTHEW 6; ACTS 13

*J*ohn the Baptist is one of my favorite Bible characters because he stayed little all the way to the end. Luke recorded this rare feat in Acts 13:25: "As John was finishing his course, he said, 'Who do you think I am? I am not He. . . . There comes One after me, the sandals of whose feet I am not worthy to loose.'" John's example runs counter to many biblical leaders, some of them prominent. Samuel rebuked King Saul: "When you were little in your own eyes, were you not head of the tribes of Israel?" (1 Sam. 15:17). Something happens to us during our Christian walk that agitates against staying little. Unfortunately, as soon as we start to get "too big for our boots," we also begin to distance ourselves from Jesus. He loves the humble: "The LORD is near to those who have a broken heart, and saves such as have a contrite spirit" (Ps. 34:18). God tends to distance Himself from those who stray toward arrogance and self-sufficiency. There are two steps we can take to stay little: (1) clothe ourselves with praise of God and (2) be generous in forgiveness.

Clothed with Praise. Praise is a garment (Isa. 61:3). When we are "ever praising Him," we are robed in praise—it covers us. Self-praise tends to disrobe us and reveal our shameful nakedness. When we constantly point others to Jesus by praising Him, not only does He loom large but we stay small. Praise is a protection against pride, for we cannot both magnify ourselves and God. When we consistently invite others to "exalt His name together" (Ps. 34:3), it is impossible to puff up with pride. We stay little by constantly verbalizing that God is big.

Generous in Forgiveness. When we think we are something, when we are infected by the "I am somebody" spirit, we take offense easily. "How dare that person insult me or question my decision?" we ask ourselves. Offense and hurt rise quickly when we are not broken and contrite before the Lord. Little children do not take offense because they are not big enough in their own eyes to be insulted. We stay little by constantly forgiving those who hurt us. Anyone can be hurt; only those "too big for their boots" can be insulted. If you have felt the sting of insult, it is an indication that pride is mingled with your humility, and your primary recourse is to forgive the insult. Forgiveness keeps us lowly. Forgiveness reduces our injuries and makes us insult-proof. Forgiveness keeps us small, for we are not important enough to be insulted.

ZAGHAWA MUSLIMS OF CHAD (108,000; 0.0% EVANGELICAL)

PRAY THAT BELIEVERS AMONG THE ZAGHAWA WOULD BE SET FREE FROM A SPIRIT OF FEAR OF WHAT MAY COME AND WOULD BOLDLY PROCLAIM THE TRUTH OF THE GOSPEL (2 TIM. 1:6-8).

*G*od's highest joy is in Himself. He did not need to create people in order to be complete. In the eternal fellowship of the Trinity that precedes finite humanity, there is love, joy, and peace to overflowing. What a wonder, then, that God delights in people and that He will joy in His people (Isa. 65:19). Not only does God delight in us, He takes pleasure in the defense of our success. Psalm 35:27 refers to our enemies who are frustrated (thwarted by God) in their attacks against us. The psalmist announced: "Let them say continually, 'Let the LORD be magnified who has pleasure in the prosperity of His servant.'" This is somewhat heady territory—to have the joy of God over our lives, to have His obvious pleasure in us to the extent that even our adversaries marvel at His goodness. An obvious question is presented: Do the manner and means of our successes reveal to our enemies that God triumphed and not we? If we are not careful, we slip into self-congratulation rather than join our enemies in marveling at the greatness of God.

There is one sure way our victories can point to Jesus rather than to us: when we succeed in the face of obstacles large enough to ensure that our success could never have resulted from our abilities. Impossibilities are great friends of Christians. Without Goliath there would have been no David. We need to be challenged by impossible people and circumstances so it is clear that God has done the work. If we constantly overcome small hurdles, we inevitably appear to be self-sufficient. The humility of the believer demands impossible assignments. To ever succeed in our own strength is poison to our souls. To be overwhelmed is a blessing—overwhelmed not only by the giants without but within. The giants of our flesh bring us back to confession. We repent to God with Isaiah: "You are indeed angry, for we have sinned—in these ways we continue; and we need to be saved. . . . But now, oh LORD, You are our Father; we are clay, and You our potter; and we all are the work of Your hand" (Isa. 64:5, 8). The challenge of enemies without and within provides a service for us: it reminds us that "we all are the work of His hands."

It is not enough for us to recognize that our prosperity comes from a wondrous God who rejoices over us. We must live in such a manner that our enemies also recognize His mighty hand. This requires not one giant but a lifetime of impossibilities. Only those who continually slay impossible giants can amaze their enemies into magnifying the Lord. Our ongoing impossibilities are fodder for worship.

BERBER, UREGU MUSLIMS OF MOROCCO (446,000; 0.0% EVANGELICAL)

PRAY FOR THE WORD OF GOD IN WRITTEN, ORAL, MUSICAL, AND DRAMATIC FORMS TO BE TRANSLATED AND TO RISE AMONG THE BERBER, UREGU
(ISA. 55:10-11).

JULY 5: ARTIFICIAL INTELLIGENCE

PSALM 36; JEREMIAH 1-3; MATTHEW 8; ACTS 15

*W**hat Makes a Person Wicked?*** Psalm 36 describes the wicked as a person who does not fear (respect, reverence, awe) God (v. 1); who is proud of his sin and hatred (v. 2); and who ceases to be wise and do good (v. 3). Intelligence is not wisdom, for the wicked can be very clever. Wisdom does what is right for others at cost to oneself. Intelligence tends to do what is best for one's own interests regardless of the cost others bear. The wicked person also lies (v.3), schemes, and does not hate evil (v. 4).

What Makes a Person Godly? In contrast to the evil intelligence and selfish actions of the wicked, a godly person lives out mercy, faithfulness, righteousness, and wise judgments (v. 5). Those who act like God in this manner enjoy the following benefits: the lovingkindness of God, protection under the shadow of His wings, provision and abundant satisfaction by the fullness of His house, and pleasures from the rivers of God. (vv. 6–8) Only a fool would live and act in a way that denies him these benefits—which leads to a disturbing question:

What Causes the Godly to Be Wicked? The psalmist identifies two primary foes. These foes lead to thinking and acting wickedly. One foe is internal, "the foot of pride," and the other is external, "the hand of the wicked" (v. 11). To be proud about being righteous is wicked. It is alarmingly easy for thankfulness of God's goodness to slide into the delusion that we have merited His favor. As soon as we think God has blessed us because, in some small way, we deserve it or because we are better than others, we think wickedly. The wisdom of the righteous reminds them that they are prone to be wicked.

Christians are fairly well versed in the dangers of pride. Our more subtle enemy is the bitterness that results when the wicked attack us. When the hand of the wicked comes against us, our latent wickedness prompts us to respond in kind. It is both possible and attractive to respond to evil in an evil manner. However, the godly must exert intentional discipline not to respond to evil with evil, for the tool overwhelms the master; and it is impossible to do wicked acts (even in self-defense) without becoming wicked at heart. May we diligently and vigilantly respond to evil with good—this is a primary indicator of the godly. It is the character of the God of the Bible to love those who wound Him. No other god loves like this.

KAZAKH MUSLIMS OF KAZAKHSTAN (9,832,000; 0.06% EVANGELICAL)

PRAY THAT GOD WOULD POUR OUT HIS SPIRIT ON THE KAZAKH PEOPLE AND THAT THEY WOULD SEE DREAMS AND VISIONS OF JESUS. PRAY THAT THEY WOULD BE POWERFULLY SAVED AND EMPOWERED TO BE HIS WITNESSES (JOEL 2:28-32).

"Trust in the LORD . . . and dwell in the land. . . . Delight yourself also in the LORD, and He shall give you the desires of your heart" (Ps. 37:3–4). As God directs His people, He expects them to do the dangerous work of trusting Him and remaining rooted in troubled environments. Evil and instability make the gospel look good. Our primary desires should not be for a better life and a secure environment—but for the Lord. When we delight in Jesus, we want what He wants. Our passions align with His, and we discover that we no longer want what we thought we wanted. When we delight in Jesus, we desire what He wants to give us—Himself. When we desire Jesus, all other desires fade, for we find them increasingly distasteful. All that will fully satisfy is more of Him.

A Desire for Blamelessness Leads to Peace (Ps. 37:37). A desire for Jesus includes a desire to be like Him—and He gives us this desire. We no longer care what others think; we long to be blameless before God. The desire to be blameless before God brings us great peace, for we no longer strive for the applause of others. *Reputation* becomes a dirty word to us because it implies that we have judges other than Jesus. When we desire to be blameless, we unexpectedly enter a world of rest where we no longer strive for the approval of others.

A Desire for Righteousness Leads to Strength in Troubled Times (Ps. 37:39). When we long for Jesus, we understand that fellowship with Him includes right standing with others. We cannot be intimate with Jesus when we are at odds with either friend or foe. Jesus demands that we live at peace with everyone as much as it lies within our power to do so. He rises to the defense of those who hold no grudges. He stands up in recognition of those who forgive their persecutors. The righteous still have enemies, but when those enemies attack, their bite has no killing venom. The righteous have the internal emotional strength to shake serpents off into the fire. The forgiver is always the strongest person in the company.

A Desire for Trust Leads to Deliverance (Ps. 37:40). Trust is not automatic; we do not naturally trust. We ask Jesus to help us trust. "Lord, I believe; help my unbelief" is our constant plea. We desire to trust Jesus, and He honors that desire. When we delight in Him, He is delighted that we ask for trust, so He grants it and proves His delight by delivering us. Trust is what makes the believer fearless.

KHATI HINDUS OF INDIA (1,596,000; 0.0% EVANGELICAL)

PRAY THAT CHRISTIANS FROM AROUND THE WORLD WOULD WORK TOGETHER TO REACH THE
KHATI AND THAT THE KHATI WOULD BE JOINED TO THE BODY OF CHRIST
(JOHN 17:20-23).

JULY 7: DO NOT PRAY

PSALM 38; JEREMIAH 7-9; MATTHEW 10; ACTS 17

*B*ecause wrath and mercy meet in Jesus, we do not have an accurate understanding of Him if we make no place for wrath. To remove wrath from God is to reduce God's nature, and that is blasphemy. Jeremiah was probably stunned when God said: "Do not pray for this people, nor lift up a cry for them, nor make intercession to Me; for I will not hear you" (Jer. 7:16). There is a point where mercy must be justified by wrath; a point where brothers must be handed over to Satan for the saving of their souls (1 Cor. 5:5); a point where we stop trying either practically or spiritually to help—for our help is getting in the way of what God is trying to do.

In Jeremiah's context the people had crossed the red line for three primary reasons: ongoing disobedience, blatant hypocrisy, and child sacrifice. When those in covenant with God make a habit of disobeying Him, of singing His praise in church while serving their flesh elsewhere, and of sacrificing their children to advance themselves, God pours out His fury (Jer. 7:20). The sins of sixth-century Israel are eerily similar to the sins of God's people today. We are no better than our forefathers, and we will not escape a similar fate. Mercy triumphs through judgment. There can be no mercy without wrath, and some maladies are so severe that the only way to cure them is to expose them to God's fury. One of the most difficult and needed responses of love might be to step back from helping, stop praying people out of trouble, and allow their utter end to force a new beginning.

Non-prayer is not only a rough Old Testament method. In the New Testament Jesus declared: "Do not think that I came to bring peace on earth. I did not come to bring peace but a sword" (Matt. 10:34). Jesus was referring to contention within the family. Some relationships cannot be reconciled until both parties embrace truth and justice. When we pray, we are seeking resolution to a problem. We pray about problems; we praise about victories. Jesus reminded us that some problems should not be resolved—for the cost of their resolution can only be accomplished by some injury to the character and truth of God. His character must remain more important than the resolution of conflict. We must learn to trust Him to work through wrath. He knows that war and wrath are a last resort but a necessary one. Peace and resolution are not the primary aim of the follower of Jesus; our primary aim is the defense and advance of His holy name. We must have the spiritual fortitude to allow others to suffer—and to live with the tension it causes within us—that they might be redeemed and God's character preserved. Sometimes godly obedience is in *not* praying, in *not* seeking peace.

LURI MUSLIMS OF IRAN (2,600,000; 0.0% EVANGELICAL)

PRAY THAT THE HEARTS OF THE LURI WOULD BE LIKE GOOD SOIL, READY TO HEAR THE GOSPEL AND TO RESPOND (MATT. 7:1-8, 18-23).

JULY 8: RUNNING WITH HORSES

PSALM 39; JEREMIAH 10-12; MATTHEW 11; ACTS 18

*A*t first glance it seems that David sprang from nowhere to defeat Goliath. The Sunday school chorus "Only a Boy Named David" is running through my head right now—but little boys do not kill lions and bears. Even if David was young in age when he ran toward the giant of Gath, he was not young in battle experience. Large victories are the result of many small ones, and David had learned to overcome fear and contend with danger progressively. There were undoubtedly skirmishes with boisterous rams, sneaking serpents, cunning foxes, and various other predators that prepared him to battle big bears and large lions.

It is foolish for us to think of reaching an entire Muslim people group if we are reluctant to talk to our neighbors about Jesus. Missionaries of all nationalities are prone to dream of nations and tribes coming to Jesus, yet falter in evangelizing the merchant in the store across the street from their apartment. It is folly to think we will suddenly start evangelizing the lost abroad when we do not evangelize them in our home culture. "If you have run with the footmen, and they have wearied you, then how can you contend with horses? And if in the land of peace, in which you trusted, they wearied you, then how will you do in the floodplains of the Jordan?" (Jer. 12:5) If in our "land of peace" (where we are comfortable, fluent, and credible) we do not live a holy life, do not burn with active passion to reach the lost, and do not proclaim Christ as Lord of all, how will we do these things in the "floodplains" of the Arab world? We will not.

In Christian service and in missions, great victories are based on due process. We rightly desire the fruit we see in the ministries of great men and women of faith, but we are, at worst, reluctant to put down similar roots, and at best, naïve about what it costs to do so. Running "with footmen" requires the basic spiritual fitness of being able to thrive over the long term in difficult contexts. Essentially this is abiding missions—the ability to dig our own spiritual wells and to drink from them day after day, year after year, in a city or desert or environment that wants to see us falter. If we cannot abide with Jesus, we cannot expect to see His church planted among resistant peoples. We cannot skip the discipline or the time necessary to train to run with the infantry. The core competence of God's army is to place one foot in front of the other while abiding in Him. Only as we use this weapon faithfully can we mount the war horse of church planting to clash with our determined foe. If we do not abide at home, it is the deepest delusion to think we will abide on the field.

QATARI MUSLIMS OF QATAR (356,000; 0.0% EVANGELICAL)

PRAY FOR THE PEACE THAT RESULTS WHEN MEN AND WOMEN ARE RECONCILED WITH GOD (JOHN 14:27). PRAY FOR MEN AND WOMEN OF PEACE (LUKE 10:6) AMONG QATARIS.

JULY 9: GOD'S MOUTH

PSALM 40; JEREMIAH 13-15; MATTHEW 12; ACTS 19

The cost of being God's spokesperson is as high as the privilege is sweet. Jeremiah said, "Your words were found, and I ate them," and "Your word was to me the joy and rejoicing of my heart" (15:16). But in the very next verse, he lamented that he "sat alone because of [God's] hand" (v. 17). We tend to forget that heaven is the minority destination, the way is narrow, and few are those who find their way to life (Matt. 7:13–14). Accordingly, when we speak the Word of God faithfully, we will find ourselves somewhat lonely. Speaking God's Word compels us to say unsettling things—even to people we love. Intimates applaud as long as we direct God's exhortations toward "the other," but being God's mouthpiece requires that we speak without prejudice—even toward family and friends. God's prophets tended to live lonely, misunderstood lives.

God requires that His spokespersons share His passions. We find this both a blessing and a burden. It is a privilege to feel what God feels. He does not want us to be mechanical messengers—He wants us to share in the emotion of the message. Jeremiah is known as the weeping prophet because he did not deliver messages of judgment callously. He entered into the anguish of God. If we enjoy pronouncing judgment, we are acting in the flesh and do not understand what it costs the Father to admonish His children. God's mouthpieces do not tend to be composed, refined, and clinical. They tend to be ragged and raw—undone by the message they give.

God requires that His spokespersons have ruthless purity: "If you take out the precious from the vile, you shall be My mouth" (v. 19). Because of the sacredness of the message, God demands a pure spokesperson. Human nature being what it is, no messenger is perfect. That is why God relentlessly purifies His messengers. God employs an unyielding, unrelenting process to make holy those who would speak holiness. He will not accept a dissonance between the content of His message and the character of His messengers. There is an obvious gap between the two, but all who would speak for God must realize that He will narrow that gap aggressively in a lifelong cycle of strenuous sanctification. He will give further messages to those who submit to the refining processes; He will release those who resist to follow an easier path—but without the painful joy of speaking authoritatively for Him. Which leads us to one of the most terrifying passages in all of Scripture, Matthew 12:36–37: "But I say to you that for every idle word men may speak, they will give account of it in the day of judgment. For by your words you will be justified, and by your words you will be condemned."

KHATRI MUSLIMS OF PAKISTAN (1,034,000; 0.0% EVANGELICAL)

PRAY THAT BELIEVERS AMONG THE KHATRI WOULD PROCLAIM THE MESSAGE OF THE GOSPEL CLEARLY AND WOULD MAKE THE MOST OF EVERY OPPORTUNITY GOD PLACES BEFORE THEM (COL. 4:2-5).

*J*eremiah warned "cursed is the man who trusts in man" (17:5) and contrasted the fool who trusts in man with the sage who trusts in God (v. 7). The person who trusts in God will be "like a tree planted by the waters" that does not "fear when heat comes" (v. 8). What is striking about this passage is the next verse: "The heart is deceitful above all things, and desperately wicked: who can know it?" (v. 9) Why does God warn about our treacherous hearts immediately after promising stability and strength to the person who trusts in Him? The answer is disturbingly simple: We all are marred and prone to trust ourselves. Or more directly said—we all are idiots.

It is not popular to point out that men and women—even godly ones—have a propensity toward wickedness. While it is true that those who have trusted in Christ have a new nature and our sin is covered by grace, it is also true that the old nature is yet with us and will be until our final liberation from this earth. Hypostatic union is the doctrine that Jesus Christ was one person with two natures—fully man and fully God. The same principle applies to us—we are one person with two natures: fully redeemed and fully fallen. By implication then, to trust in God fully means we must wholly distrust ourselves. We partake of the divine nature, even while we continue to live in the miry clay of a fallen world. The new creation is in constant battle with the old. We continue to sin even as we live forgiven, and the person who thinks he or she is without sin is a misguided fool. Yet the person who thinks he or she will ever be bound by sin has misunderstood the present and eternal liberation of the gospel.

In this context we find Jeremiah's remarkable object lesson at the potter's house. "The vessel that he made of clay was marred in the hand of the potter; so he made it again into another vessel" (18:4). It is no shame to confess that even as believers in the hands of Jesus, we are still prone to sin and to submit to the treachery of our hearts. We are marred in His wonderful hands, not because His hands are unsteady but because our clay is wobbly. This sobering reality should not discourage us, for though we are marred, we are in the Potter's divine hands and He will skillfully *make us again into another vessel*. What a marvelous Jesus! He lovingly shapes us from glory to glory. We live neither with the false assumption that we are sinless and perfect, nor with the despair of being ever bound by sin. We are at once both treacherous and being made true.

MAL HINDUS OF INDIA (1,574,000; 0.0% EVANGELICAL)

PRAY THAT THE MAL WILL UNDERSTAND THAT HOPE FOR FORGIVENESS AND ACCEPTANCE WITH GOD ARE AVAILABLE ONLY THROUGH JESUS' WORK ON THE CROSS (1 COR. 1:18).

JULY 11: THE BURDEN OF THE LORD

PSALM 42; JEREMIAH 19-21; MATTHEW 14; ACTS 21

*E*ven prophets want to be liked. We interpret "His word in my heart like a burning fire shut up in my bones" of Jeremiah 20:9 in a positive light. We envision a prophet bubbling with all the precious promises of God who could not wait to encourage the faithful. The reality was that Jeremiah could not stop pronouncing doom and gloom on his own countrymen—and it became a problem for him. If we strip away the polite veneer of the text, Jeremiah was saying: "It stinks to be a prophet!"

There is a reason the prophets called their messages "a burden." There is a reason John the Baptist was beheaded (Matt. 14:1–12). There is a reason those who declare the "whole counsel of God" (Acts 20:27) are few and far between. It is a difficult thing to be the messenger of an angry God. Jeremiah felt this tension. He felt that God had coerced him (Jer. 20:7); that the cost of God's Word was reproach and daily derision (v. 8), mocking, and friends waiting for him to stumble (v. 10). Jeremiah felt his role was only labor, sorrow, and shame. He longed to speak something light and fluffy. "Just once, Lord," he cried. "Just once, could I be the good guy?"

One fortunate day Jeremiah had his chance. King Zedekiah sent messengers asking for a word from the Lord: "Perhaps the LORD will deal with us according to all His wonderful works" (21:2).The fire rose within Jeremiah's heart and, despite his own wishes, this was essentially the message for Zedekiah: God will turn back our weapons of war and fight against us with anger, fury, and wrath. Man and beast will die. God will not spare or have mercy or pity. He who fights for freedom will die. God has given the city to Babylon. And the only one who will survive is the one who defects to the enemy (21:4–11). "Oh by the way, have a nice day and thanks for dropping by!"

Nobody likes to be the bad guy all the time, and if someone enjoys that prophetic role, they are probably masquerading—a self-appointed prophet in the flesh. We know of Jeremiah as a weeper; his prophecies cost him something. If God's Word is not costing us something, if we are never reluctant to be His spokespersons, we are either not hearing Him clearly or not obeying Him fully. We must dispense the whole counsel of God. People cannot live on just sugar and medicine—they need living bread.

NUBIAN, FEDICCA-MOHA MUSLIMS OF EGYPT (334,000; 0.0% EVANGELICAL)

PRAY THAT BELIEVERS AMONG THE NUBIAN, FEDICCA-MOHA WILL ENDURE PERSECUTION IN A CHRISTLIKE MANNER AND WILL GIVE THEIR LIVES FOR THE SAKE OF THE GOSPEL IF NECESSARY (1 PETER 2:21-23).

JULY 12: THE WORSHIP OF ASKING FOR HELP

PSALM 43; JEREMIAH 22-24; MATTHEW 15; ACTS 22

*T*he primary message of prophet and apostle is "repent." It is not a popular message, nor is it a discriminating one, for it is preached to both believer and unbeliever. Jesus taught that what comes out of the heart and passes through the mouth is what defiles a person (Matt. 15:11, 18). According to Jesus, this is what is naturally in my heart: evil thoughts, murders, adulteries, fornications, thefts, false witness, and blasphemy. Not very pretty; and let us be brutally honest with ourselves—these things are still in our hearts even after we are saved.

That is why, morning by morning, we must go to Jesus and repent, why we must ask for His cleansing daily. In the night, in my sleep, my soul accumulates filth. If my dreams, which emanate from my heart, were broadcast to the world, it would be ugly, scandalous viewing. I must live a vibrant, daily experience of repentance. I am "prone to wander." I am "prone to leave the God I love." I need Jesus more today than I did yesterday. The message of the Scripture (mouthed by prophet and apostle, pastor and evangelist) is refreshingly simple and steadfast. It is proclaimed to both unregenerate sinners and redeemed sinners. It is this: Repent! Turn! Moment by moment, day after day, turn to the Savior. Turn from the allure of the world and turn your eyes, heart, feet, and mind to Him.

As a man I am attracted by flesh. This is true for all men and women. Though men are more stimulated by physical images, women, too, are sexual creatures and are affected by what they see. My eyes are still drawn to both the beautiful and the provocative. It does not matter that I live in a Muslim city with a pretense of modesty, my eyes are still drawn to attractive women. Every day provides an opportunity to turn my eyes to Jesus. Everything I see gives me a choice—will I let my gaze linger on what feeds my corrupt heart, or will I turn my eyes to Jesus and fix my adoration and worship on Him?

In Matthew 15:21–28 we read the beautiful story of a woman of Tyre and Sidon who chose to fix her eyes on Jesus. She came to Him and "worshipped Him, saying, 'Lord help me'" (v. 25). Her plea for help was worship. When our eyes see fodder for our fallen flesh, we can worship Jesus by asking for help. Repentance is asking for help; turning to Jesus is worship. We are inundated by images crafted to destroy us. We must respond by worship—by turning to Jesus and asking for His help. This pleases Him, and it rescues us.

KHOJA MUSLIMS OF PAKISTAN (784,000; 0.0% EVANGELICAL)

PRAY THAT GOD WOULD RAISE UP MISSIONARIES FROM ALL OVER THE WORLD TO WORK
TOGETHER TO PLANT THE CHURCH TOGETHER AMONG THE KHOJA (MATT. 9:37).

JULY 13: WINNING ENEMIES

PSALM 44; JEREMIAH 25-27; MATTHEW 16; ACTS 23

*I*f you speak God's Word, you will have enemies. God instructed Jeremiah to "stand . . . speak . . . do not diminish a word" (Jer. 26:2). As a result of his fidelity to God's person and message, the people threatened to kill him: "When Jeremiah had made an end of speaking all that the LORD had commanded . . . the priests and the prophets and all the people seized him, saying, 'You will surely die!'" (v. 8) To be like Jesus is to have enemies (Matt. 16:21); to follow Paul as he followed Christ is to have people determined to kill us (Acts 23:21). There is a connection between faithful proclamation and resistance. The psalmist said: "You, through Your commandments, make me wiser than my enemies; for they are ever with me" (Ps. 119:98). Because of the Word of God, we will ever have enemies but because of the Word of God, we will ever triumph over them. We win our enemies by out-loving them, outlasting them, and out-longing them.

Out-Love Your Enemies. Love is the beautiful and unrivaled core of the gospel, for this is the essence of God. Since no enemy has the unmatched weapon of love, it is not really a fair fight. We would be foolish not to wield the one weapon for which our enemies have no defense.

Outlast Your Enemies. Time is always on the side of the righteous. Many accusations cannot and should not be dignified with a response. In the short term, we must be willing to be slandered and misunderstood. Time will prove us right. Often the best thing we can do is to "answer not a word," and plod on faithfully. Critics and envious colleagues have a way of removing themselves. If their hearts are wayward, they will not be able to conceal it forever. If your heart is pure, it will eventually be vindicated. By our patience we will possess our souls—and those of others.

Out-Long Your Enemies. Gospel work finds little room for sluggish mornings. Repeatedly through Scripture, God describes Himself and His messengers as those who "rise up early" to warn and admonish (Jer. 25:3–4, 26:5). Missionary biographies consistently reveal that those who dented the darkness with light rose early to linger long with Jesus. A pastor in Bangladesh, saved out of Islam, challenges his church to rise before the early Muslim call to prayer so that the first utterance directed heavenward in that "occupied territory" will be the super-exaltation of Jesus. His point is that in the race to evangelize the world, the one who wants it most will win.

Our enemies are ever with us. We might as well win them to Jesus.

BRAHMAN, RAHDI HINDUS OF INDIA (1,549,000; 0.0% EVANGELICAL)

PRAY THAT THE BRAHMAN, RAHDI WOULD FEEL AND KNOW THE BURDEN OF SIN AND COME TO JESUS FOR FORGIVENESS AND SALVATION (MATT. 11:28-30).

JULY 14: GLADNESS

PSALM 45; JEREMIAH 28-30; MATTHEW 17; ACTS 24

*G*ladness is derived from both love and hate. "You love righteousness and hate wickedness; therefore God, Your God, has anointed You with the oil of gladness" (Ps. 45:7). Our view of righteousness is often linked to austere puritan killjoys, which does both the Puritans and the Lord a great disservice. True joy results from loving what is right and hating what is wicked. This is the gladness of God.

It falls awkwardly on our ears to hear that hate contributes to joy. This is because we misunderstand and misuse the term *hate*. We understand hate to mean the opposite of love. But hate is not the opposite of love—apathy is. G. K. Chesterton put it this way: "The goodness of good things, like the badness of bad things, is a prodigy past speech; it is to be pictured rather than spoken. We shall have gone deeper than the deeps of heaven and grown older than the oldest angels before we feel, even in its first faint vibrations, the everlasting violence of that double passion with which God loves and hates the world."[2]

God loves and God hates—these passions complement each other. If God's beautiful and perfect character can combine both love and hate toward the single end of gladness, then so can our character. When rightly balanced and directed—loving what is right, hating what is wicked—the result is the anointed gladness of pure joy. To be for God includes being against what He is against. To be for God is to enter into His complementary passions, to love what He loves and to hate what He hates. This is what makes us glad. Conversely, loving sin and hating righteousness make us sad (Jer. 30:15). There is no joy among the wicked—not the deep gladness of the soul. The wicked only enjoy a fabricated and false joy that destroys them from the inside.

If loving righteousness and hating wickedness make both God and us glad, it stands to reason that some things should be hated. God hates divorce, and so should we. God hates injustice, and so should we. God hates deceit, and so should we. God hates the violent sacrificing of children, and so should we. It is difficult for us to find this enduring gladness, for we have a propensity to fall in love with hating. This warning, however, does not remove God's invitation and example. The deepest gladness—the gladness of God—perfectly combines love for what is right with hatred for what is wicked. These complementary passions spur each other on to the depths of joy. We should not be afraid or reluctant to pursue this great gladness of God.

BERBER, FILALA MUSLIMS OF MOROCCO (334,000; 0.0% EVANGELICAL)

PRAY THAT GOD WOULD UNVEIL THE CROSS AND THAT WOULD REMOVE THE VEIL ON THE MINDS AND SPIRITS OF THE BERBER, FILALA (2 COR. 3:16-17).

JULY 15: THE INSTABILITY OF THE NORMAL

PSALM 46; JEREMIAH 31-33; MATTHEW 18; ACTS 25

S ome of the most precious promises of Scripture are given in the context of duress and instability. We love the encouragement of the psalmist that God is our "refuge and strength" (Ps. 46:1–2), forgetting that it is war and conflict that demand such a refuge. We lack fear even as the mountains shake and the earth is removed, as the nations rage and as wars increase (vv. 6, 8). It is in times of war and shaking that we are to be still and know that He is God. These last days are going to be terror-filled. Instability will be the new normal. Economies will fail, nations disintegrate, civil wars abound, famine, death, and tragedy increase. This is the context in which God calls us to be still, to be at rest, and to know that He is God. Out of duress we are comforted, and in trial God reveals His will. While he languished in prison, Jeremiah gave this famous assurance: "Call to Me, and I will answer you, and show you great and mighty things, which you do not know" (33:3). Revelation comes most clearly to us when we are oppressed . . . when our normal is unstable . . . when external props are taken away and all we have left is Jesus. Then we discover that He is all we need—and all we want.

Offenses must come, Matthew reminds us (18:7), and we should rejoice in them because God's greatness is revealed just as much in times of trouble as in times of triumph. We need to treat those two impostors just the same. In this age there will be cycles of peace and war, with war becoming more and more frequent, finally culminating in our blessed hope—that glorious day when Jesus returns to kill death and establish eternal peace. As distress becomes the norm, we must learn to be at peace while the world is at war. Jeremiah reminds us of the essence of God: "For the LORD is good, and His mercy endures forever" (33:11). This primal goodness of God, His love-in-kindness, is revealed at all times. God is not silenced by war; on the contrary, war and trouble often amplify His voice.

Let us give up the futile search for havens of peace on this earth. Let us give up the hope of a utopian society in this life. Heaven cannot come to earth until this earth is recreated and evil is banished from human hearts. Until that day, which we fervently long for, God calls us to live at war. We are to live normally in cities and countries that are disintegrating about us and to exude an unnatural calm that will testify to the present and coming kingdom, and to God who is above all the messes of humanity. Instability is our new normal. Suffering is the lot of every follower of Jesus. Let us embrace it because the worse it gets, the sooner it will be over and the sooner Jesus will come to liberate all creation. Then, and only then, will peace be normal.

KUMHAR MUSLIMS OF PAKISTAN (3,245,000; 0.0% EVANGELICAL)

PRAY THAT BELIEVERS AMONG THE KUMHAR WOULD BE SET FREE FROM A SPIRIT OF FEAR OF WHAT MAY COME AND WOULD BOLDLY PROCLAIM THE TRUTH OF THE GOSPEL
(2 TIM. 1:6-8).

JULY 16: SETTING BROTHERS FREE

PSALM 47; JEREMIAH 34-36; MATTHEW 19; ACTS 26

*G*od spoke through Jeremiah to remind the Jewish people about literal slavery and its wickedness: "no one should keep a Jewish brother in bondage" (34:9) In our modern, refined, fallen state, we still enslave our brothers and sisters, only in more subtle ways. Subtle slavery is still anathema, and we must be vigilant against it—in ourselves.

Set Our Brothers and Sisters Free by Trusting Them. Members of God's family can be the harshest prison wardens. We keep those we know locked in the cell of the person they used to be. Members of God's family can often be the last to recognize God working in each other. We tend to deal with each other according to patterns from decades ago. This is bondage. We must trust that our brothers and sisters are growing in the Lord, growing in wisdom, and growing in capacity. When we trust them with responsibility, when we believe they can do something now that they failed in before, we inject them with life. Sometimes we have to set our brothers free by calling out of them something they do not see in themselves.

Set Our Brothers and Sisters Free by Forgiving Them. It is a cruel sentence to lock our brothers and sisters in the sins of their past. This is especially true when they have sinned against us. We can hold general public sins against others, but it is more common to hold smaller personal affronts—and to hold them fiercely. When we refuse to forgive offenses, we leave our brothers and sisters bound and, ironically, find ourselves chained along with them. For our good, as much as for theirs, we need to forgive offenses and choose not to react negatively. We must be especially careful not to pretend to forgive—to tell others we have forgiven them but keep their offenses bound in our hearts. When we make false claims of liberty, it offends God and He grants us in kind: "Behold, I proclaim liberty to you . . . to the sword, to pestilence, and to famine!" (Jer. 34:17)

Set Our Brothers and Sisters Free by Affirming Them. It is all too common in Christian circles to damn others by faint praise. We are masters of indirect assassination. Our careful pauses, our framed responses, all communicate that we have reservations about a brother or sister. We liberate our friends by praising them to others. Without being dishonest, we can extol their positive aspects. There are times for candor, but evaluation must be based on the foundation of encouragement. We liberate others when we genuinely affirm them before their peers. This is shackle-breaking speech, and it has a double reward: Sincere praise frees others and us, for we find that the more we affirm them, the more our hearts warm toward them, and the greater common liberty and dignity we all enjoy.

PAN HINDUS OF INDIA (1,534,000; 0.0% EVANGELICAL)

PRAY FOR THE WORD OF GOD IN WRITTEN, ORAL, MUSICAL, AND DRAMATIC FORMS TO BE TRANSLATED AND TO SPREAD AMONG THE PAN (ISA. 55:10-11).

JULY 17: EVIL EYES

PSALM 48; JEREMIAH 37-39; MATTHEW 20; ACTS 27

*A*ncient Egyptians painted two eyes on their boats to protect them from misfortune—a practice still common in the Mediterranean region. Many Muslims live in fear of the "evil eye"—a curse or difficulty brought on by the jealousy of another. The evil eye of jealousy is avoided by using a blue pendant charm (usually in the shape of a droplet or a hand) and by declaring whenever you compliment another, "This is what God has willed!" This proclamation proves you are not jealous because jealousy is what opens the door for the curse.

Followers of Jesus do not usually curse those who offend them, not directly, anyway. But we tend to be naïve about how jealous we are of others and how jealousy destroys all it touches. When workers in the field of labor who had "borne the burden and the heat of the day" (Matt. 20:12) were jealous that shorter-serving laborers were equally rewarded, Jesus responded: "Is your eye evil because I am good?" (v. 15) The unfortunate answer for us is that we, indeed, are often jealous of God's goodness toward others. There is a resident evil in us that, at worst, desires mercy for ourselves while denying it to others and, at best, demands that others pay their dues just as we have. God's goodness to others tends to make us look bad, for none of us are as liberal with mercy as He is.

Unlike Jesus, our mercy can be cruel. Sometimes we offer cures that are more damaging than the disease. Out of an insidious self-righteousness, we demand penance of others that Jesus did not require of us. In wisdom Jesus sometimes applies "a severe mercy," but even then He puts rags under our armpits so the rope that pulls us from our deserved mire does not wound us unduly (Jer. 38:12). We cannot forget that those of us who have known Christ the longest, have the greatest spiritual heritage, know the Word the best, and are the most disciplined in our spirituality are often the premier Pharisees of our day—with the greatest propensity to "evil eyes."

Muslims misunderstand one key aspect of jealousy—that jealousy does more damage to the one who covets than to the one who is envied. Jealousy is a fierce and crippling master. The psalmist prayed, "Let no iniquity have dominion over me" (Ps. 119:133). Jesus provides us the "double cure" of being protected from wrath and being inwardly pure. Jealousy is an internal malady that leads to ambition, insecurity, slander, and a host of other soul viruses. Jesus wants us to share in His goodness. He wants us to mature to the place where we genuinely rejoice in His generosity toward others. This is how the "evil eye" is shattered: not by charms, but by a charity that sincerely revels in God's lavish mercy to both friend and foe.

BERBER, WARAIN MUSLIMS IN MOROCCO (290,000; 0.0% EVANGELICAL)

PRAY THAT GOD WOULD POUR OUT HIS SPIRIT ON THE BERBER, WARAIN AND THAT THEY WOULD SEE DREAMS AND VISIONS OF JESUS. PRAY THAT THEY WOULD BE POWERFULLY SAVED AND EMPOWERED TO BE HIS WITNESSES (JOEL 2:28-32).

JULY 18: TO BE, NOT TO SEEM TO BE

PSALM 49; JEREMIAH 40–42; MATTHEW 21; ACTS 28

*U*nlike the pure Word of God (Ps. 119:140), people's words are fickle. When a snake bit Paul on the island of Malta (Acts 28:4–6), the natives of the island determined he was a criminal unworthy of living, only to change their minds and decide that he was a god when he remained unharmed. In Matthew 21:28–32, Jesus told a parable of two sons: one who vowed obedience and one who seemed to rebel. The one who seemed obedient—"I go sir!"—but was not, incurred Jesus' wrath. Jesus is not impressed with those who seem obedient; He loves those who *are* obedient.

Jeremiah ran into the same malady: people who professed a pledged obedience with no intention to obey. A frightened contingent approached the prophet and asked him to determine God's will for them, pledging: "Whether it is pleasing or displeasing, we will obey" (Jer. 42:6). Jeremiah took ten days to seek an answer from God (a lesson in itself) before he gave instructions—which the people disobeyed. Jeremiah called them out: "You were hypocrites in your hearts when you sent me to the LORD your God, saying, 'Pray for us to the LORD our God, and according to all that the LORD your God says, so declare to us and we will do it'" (v. 20). God wants us to actually be obedient, not to seem to be obedient. He is not interested in rubber-stamping the decisions we have made or in blessing what we have already done.

Ministers and missionaries are often prone to the malady of seeming to be obedient. Generally, I am not impressed with missionaries—mainly because I am one and I know how much hypocrisy and duplicity I carry in my own heart. We liquidate domestic assets, say good-bye to family and friends, and head to unfamiliar lands to labor in difficult languages. It seems impressive to the outside observer. Missionaries seem obedient. To the inward witness of the Spirit, however, both minister and missionary can harbor a multitude of small disobediences. Jesus is not impressed by fig trees without figs. For the followers of Jesus who project all the outward leaves of obedience but do not actually submit in a thousand daily ways (and therefore do not produce fruit)—Jesus unleashes His ire: "Let no fruit grow on you ever again" (Matt. 21:19). It is not enough to claim obedience; it is not enough to seem obedient. There must be the inner witness and resulting fruit of saying yes to Jesus all the time.

If obedience is a hundred-meter race, it is over the last few meters that Christians tend to falter. While the first steps of our obedience are verbal, the majority of our obedience is small, daily submitted actions. The most critical portion, and the most painfully difficult, takes place the last few meters. That is where our obedience is proved.

KURMANJI KURDS MUSLIMS OF TURKEY (8,058,000; 0.0% FVANGELICAL)

PRAY THAT CHRISTIANS FROM AROUND THE WORLD WOULD WORK TOGETHER TO REACH THE KURMANJI KURDS AND THAT THE KURMANJI KURDS WOULD BE JOINED TO THE BODY OF CHRIST (JOHN 17:20–23).

JULY 19: UNLIKENESS

PSALM 50; JEREMIAH 43–45; MATTHEW 22; ROMANS 1

*P*eople have an ongoing tendency to drag God down to their level. Historically they have done this crudely through idols of wood and stone. The more insidious contemporary perversion is an ideological assault on the deity of Jesus. We must constantly affirm that Jesus is fully man and fully God.

God's intimacy opens the possibility that we will abuse our familiarity with Him. Familiarity can breed the confidence to disagree with God, and in our disagreements we tend to err by thinking that He thinks as we do. God thunders into that assumption: "You thought that I was altogether like you; but I will rebuke you" (Ps. 50:21). A crude idol or a diminished Jesus (any detraction of His deity) are equally offensive and are based on our being "mistaken, not knowing the Scriptures nor the power of God" (Matt. 22:29). Just because God condescends to commune with us does not mean He is like us. Just because He has promised that we will be like Him does not mean that He will be like us. It is we who fall ashamed before God and align ourselves with the divine; He does not change or compromise.

Some stubbornness in our hearts compels us to attempt, generation after generation, to reduce God to being like us. Ironically, sometimes the intimacy He offers leads us to disrespect Him. We must hold intimacy and worship in a healthy tension, remembering that we worship God for all the ways He is *not* like us. If we worship Him for our perceived similarities, we are actually self-worshiping. There is a part of our spirit that knows—and we must continually allow our spirits to instruct our minds—that God is altogether unlike us!

When we do not glorify God and thank Him, this leads to foolish, darkened hearts (Rom. 1:21). When our hearts are darkened, God gives us over to uncleanness (v. 24) and debased minds (v. 28). A debased mind is simply where our thoughts automatically go without the safety of God's light and nature. If we have reduced God to an elevated form of ourselves, and if we worship that demigod, we eventually become like it—and it is tragically flawed.

God is so incredibly good and pure, so unlike us, that being in His presence should cause us to despise ourselves. We do not have to dig up personal negatives; we just have to recognize His majestic goodness. If we have lost a sense of our inferiority before Him, we have diminished His glorious beauty and probably think too much of ourselves.

RAJPUT, BAIS HINDUS OF INDIA (1,534,000; 0.0% EVANGELICAL)

PRAY THAT THE HEARTS OF THE RAJPUT, BAIS WOULD BE LIKE GOOD SOIL,
READY TO HEAR THE GOSPEL AND TO RESPOND
(MATT. 7:1–8, 18–23).

JULY 20: INWARD BEAUTY

PSALM 51; JEREMIAH 46-48; MATTHEW 23; ROMANS 2

*W*hile people praise external beauty, God praises inward purity. He is gently ruthless about cleansing His people, kindly severe in His pursuit to make us holy. Some of His methods are so mercifully brutal it seems as if His cleansing will be the end of us. Yet He assures us: "I will not make a complete end of you. I will rightly correct you, for I will not leave you wholly unpunished" (Jer. 46:28). It is a bit of a shock when we realize how much of our inner selves needs to end, how much needs to be corrected, and how much we can live without.

One basic thing we need to correct is our fixation on externals. Jesus calls those fixated on external appearances "fools and blind" (Matt. 23:17), and goes to great lengths to reorient us toward internal beauty. The biblical theology of sin helps us understand internal holiness. In contrast to Islamic theology, which is shame-based, a biblical understanding of sin is guilt-based. In shame-based theology, sin is increasingly horrible according to the number of people it affects. In guilt-based theology, sin is first and foremost grievous because it is an offense against God, even if no one knows. There are shocking examples of this in Scripture. When tempted by Potiphar's wife to sexual sin, which would have been an offense against Potiphar as well as Joseph's family, Joseph replied in Genesis 39:9: "How then can I do this great wickedness, and sin against God?" After sinning against himself, Uriah, Bathsheba, and the honor of the throne, David confessed to God: "Against You, You only, have I sinned, and done this evil in Your sight!" (Ps. 51:4) It is staggering to consider that God is so insulted by our sin that He considers lying, adultery, and murder—all of which affect other humans—primarily offenses against heaven.

According to Paul, we are all inexcusable (Rom. 2:1), for no matter how isolated we are from others we cannot escape our own sin natures. We were brought forth in iniquity, conceived in sin (Ps. 51:5), and our sin natures are repugnant to God. Therefore, any confidence in the flesh is, in effect, an exaltation of what is wicked, and this invites destruction (Jer. 48:42). Our only hope is to assume a posture that God accepts: a broken spirit, a contrite heart (Ps. 51:17), and a circumcised heart (Rom. 2:29). Even the will to repent comes from Jesus because it is the goodness of God that leads us to have contrite and broken hearts (v. 4). When we choose to live broken and lowly, when we choose to confess that the propensities of our natures are evil, and we choose to submit to God's beautification of our hearts, then we are blessed by His praise (v. 29). This more than compensates for the scorn of people. God displays the inward beauty of His children in the public halls of heaven.

AKHDAM MUSLIMS OF YEMEN (277,000: 0.0% EVANGELICAL)

PRAY FOR THE PEACE THAT RESULTS WHEN MEN AND WOMEN ARE RECONCILED WITH GOD (JOHN 14:27). PRAY FOR MEN AND WOMEN OF PEACE (LUKE 10:6) AMONG THE AKHDAM.

JULY 21: RESTING SMALL

PSALM 52; JEREMIAH 49-51; MATTHEW 24; ROMANS 3

*T*he entirety of God's Word is truth (Ps. 119:160). He invites us to fall in love with it all over again. A distinguishing mark of those who have suffered or are suffering is a renewed love for the Bible, which leads to a renewed love for Jesus. We do not worship God's words—we worship His incarnate Word. God's written Word is a constant reminder of how good and big He is and how fallen and small we are.

God committed His oracles to His people (Rom. 3:2): God is true and every individual a liar (v. 4). People by nature are deceivers, and God, by nature, is truth; the lying words of people only make the truth of God increase (v. 7). Our lying words, along with our lying lives, prove there is none righteous—no, not one (v. 10). Something in our hearts, even in those who have been redeemed, wants to cling to a little bit of our inherent goodness. We easily admit that we are sinners (there is evil in us), but it is much harder for us to admit that we are devoid of good (there is nothing good in us). This is a much harder sell, even for those who have been in Christ most of their lives. It is one thing to admit there is sin in our hearts, but another thing to confess that there is nothing good in our hearts at all. Christians excel at the former and falter at the later.

This is the "battle-ax" that God uses to break in pieces both nations and individuals (Jer. 51:20). We are to proclaim among the peoples that God is completely good while people are completely fallen (50:2). This is the "resting place" that God's people have forgotten (v. 6): how to stop trying to be good and to enter into the stress-free zone of being justified. Oh, what wonder when God's truths sink into our souls: (1) We are justified freely; (2) Jesus provided propitiation by His blood; and (3) God passed over our sin to demonstrate His righteousness. Jesus is both just and justifier (Rom. 3:24–26).

I love the Bible because it continually diminishes me and exalts the Lord. The Scriptures are an ongoing delight for they show that my insignificance is my rightful place. The smaller I am the bigger God is seen to be. My smallness magnifies God, for whatever is accomplished in my limited life is obviously a work of grace. The Scripture removes the pressure of success and the burden of ongoing accomplishment, for it teaches me to rest in being small that God might be great.

SORANI MUSLIMS OF AFGHANISTAN (238,000; 0.01% EVANGELICAL)

PRAY THAT BELIEVERS AMONG THE SORANI WOULD PROCLAIM THE MESSAGE OF THE GOSPEL CLEARLY AND WOULD MAKE THE MOST OF EVERY OPPORTUNITY GOD PLACES BEFORE THEM (COL. 4:2-5).

JULY 22: ONLY BELIEVE

PSALM 53; JEREMIAH 52; MATTHEW 25; ROMANS 4

When God's imperfect children dream about the evangelization of the world and the return of the King, they have but one hope: belief. When we look at the ideological giants who defiantly raise their heads against God and His Anointed One, and we compare their might to our weakness, our only recourse is to believe that God can use our insignificant strength to accomplish His great purpose. Our primary work in missions is to believe (John 6:29). Our righteousness (as that of Abraham's in Rom. 4:3–6) results from belief. Followers of the Crucified One must hold on to these basic beliefs resolutely:

We Believe Jesus Is God. Simple as it may sound, it is essential to believe and proclaim the deity of Jesus. As we draw closer to His return, this belief will continually come under assault. It is a high privilege to lift our voices in taxis and over tea to declare with power: Jesus is God!

We Believe Jesus Is Good. As martyrdoms rise and the innocent pay the price for others' obedience, we must hold on to the belief that God is good. We must believe not only that God is good in tragedy, but that He is good in dryness. Dryness can lead us astray. We must not relinquish the reality that God is a steady seeker and He takes the initiative for our abiding. The health of our spirits does not just rely on our discipline. Wonderful Jesus seeks us out (Ps. 119:176) and takes responsibility for our intimacy with Him. How wonderful to be yoked with Jesus—not just for ministry, but also for spiritual vitality.

We Believe Jesus Has Resurrection Power. Jesus not only rose from the dead, He continually raises others from the dead. "God . . . gives life to the dead and calls those things which do not exist as though they did" (Rom. 4:17). Surrounded by the Muslim masses throwing themselves over the cliffs of time into eternal hell, we must stand against that tide in belief. We must shout into the onrushing crowd: "I believe God will raise you from the dead!" We must stand in our cities, in our Muslim countries, and at the doors of our Muslim neighbors and believe for them . . . until they believe for themselves.

No one has the wisdom or power to force Muslim people or any people to Jesus, but we do have the gift of faith, and God wants us to exercise it. Our priority, our prime work, is to believe. We believe Jesus is God with all authority. We believe He uses that authority for good. We believe He is going to raise the dead. Lord, we believe!

AHAR HINDUS OF INDIA (1,494,000; 0.0% EVANGELICAL)

PRAY THAT THE AHAR WILL UNDERSTAND THAT HOPE FOR FORGIVENESS AND ACCEPTANCE WITH GOD IS AVAILABLE ONLY THROUGH JESUS' WORK ON THE CROSS (1 COR. 1:18).

JULY 23: MERCY CONTEXT

PSALM 54; LAMENTATIONS 1-3; MATTHEW 26; ROMANS 5

*I*n Bible interpretation, people often say that "context is king" or "a text without a context is a pretext." We weaken the effect of some of the most popular and comforting Scriptures when we take them out of their contexts. Lamentations 3:22–24 is a great example. We relish the idea that God's mercies keep us from being consumed, that His compassions fail not, and His faithfulness is great, but the power is diminished when we pluck those verses out of context.

We (Jerusalem, God's people) have sinned. We have betrayed God over and over. Because we did not consider our destiny, our "collapse was awesome" (Lam. 1:9). As a result, these righteous acts of God have followed: He has sent fire to our bones; He has spread a net for our feet; He has made our strength fail; He has trampled us underfoot; He has cast us down; He has swallowed us up; He has set us up as a target and pierced our kidneys; He has taunted us all day long; He has filled us with bitterness; He has broken out our teeth; He has removed our soul far from peace; and He has removed our strength and hope (Lam. 1–3).

God has done all this to me because *I have betrayed Him*. This is the context for: "Through the LORD's mercies we are not consumed, because His compassions fail not. They are new every morning; great is Your faithfulness" (Lam. 3:22–23). We need mercy for internal sin, not for external enemies. Oh, the depth of the riches and goodness of God! The depth of our depravity and the righteousness of God's punishing acts against us simply highlight the great mercy of Jesus. We cannot rush past our sin and shame to embrace mercy, for mercy is magnified by depravity. The Lord's mercy rises magnificently above the ugliness of our betrayals and is bestowed despite our failures. In order to comprehend the depth of God's love, we must honestly grapple with our wickedness and must feel the sting of God's judgment. Only then can we truly experience the depth of His mercy.

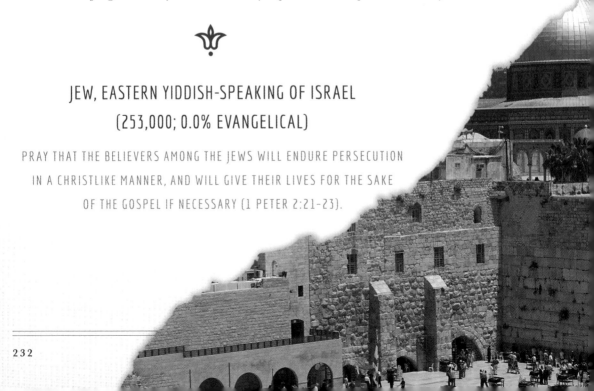

JEW, EASTERN YIDDISH-SPEAKING OF ISRAEL
(253,000; 0.0% EVANGELICAL)

PRAY THAT THE BELIEVERS AMONG THE JEWS WILL ENDURE PERSECUTION
IN A CHRISTLIKE MANNER, AND WILL GIVE THEIR LIVES FOR THE SAKE
OF THE GOSPEL IF NECESSARY (1 PETER 2:21-23).

JULY 24: SUSTAINED

PSALM 55; LAMENTATIONS 4–5; MATTHEW 27; ROMANS 6

*G*od intends for us not merely to survive but to thrive. As we draw ever closer to the return of King Jesus this will be more and more of a challenge. War, famine, sickness, trouble, and evil will all increase. It is the height of folly and requires a determined ignorance of history to think that life on earth will continually improve until Jesus comes. Redemption history is as bright as human history is doomed. As pressure increases and duress becomes normal, God's beautiful provision will sustain us joyfully until that glorious day when Jesus returns.

Sustained by Casting Burdens. Psalm 55:22 instructs us: "Cast your burden on the LORD, and He shall sustain you." In the Arab world it is common to see colleagues who kindly (but wrongly) carry the burden of missions on their shoulders. There are weights we were not built to shoulder. The pain, darkness, and depravity we encounter are too heavy for us to bear. It is wise, not irresponsible, to cast the burdens of each day onto Jesus. He promises to sustain us if we promise to cast accumulated heaviness onto Him. He is well able to carry the weight of the world.

Sustained by Praise. Jack Hayford's beautiful hymn "Exalt His Name Together" includes this encouragement: "Fall not beneath your burden, tho' tears your pathway dim, but praise the name of Jesus and be sustained in Him."[3] If casting burdens on Jesus is a defensive action that sustains us, praise takes us on the offensive. We attack the spirit of heaviness and oppression by praising God. It is crucial, it is critical, and it is imperative in times and places of darkness to open our mouths and praise Him. What we feel like does not matter, for it is not about our changing circumstances but about an all-glorious God. Praise sustains us because it reminds us and the circling demons of hell that God rules and He wins.

Sustained by the Word. When we do not know what to pray, we pick up the Bible and pray the Scriptures. When we do not know how to praise, we repeat back to God what He has said of Himself in His Word. When words fail us in counsel or witness, we quote the Scripture.

Sustained by Our Death. It sounds counterintuitive, but we "walk in newness of life" (Rom. 6:4) only after being buried with Christ in baptism. The crucifixion of the old nature (v. 6) frees us from sin. Death to sin makes us alive to God (v. 11). We are sustained by giving in to Jesus; for when we give up, He upholds us. It is sheer grace.

KURD, TURKISH-SPEAKING OF TURKEY (5,832,000; 0.0% EVANGELICAL)

PRAY THAT GOD WOULD RAISE UP MISSIONARIES FROM ALL OVER THE WORLD TO PLANT THE CHURCH TOGETHER AMONG KURDS (MATT. 9:37).

JULY 25: CELEBRATING THE TRINITY

PSALM 56; EZEKIEL 1-3; MATTHEW 28; ROMANS 7

*R*ebellion begins with a disbelief of who God is. If we really believe God is good, that He is in complete control, that He does all things well, that mercy crowns all His works, and that He knows what is best for us—if we really believe all these things—we will not resist or question Him. Non-Christian religions are rebellions against God because they disbelieve who He is according to how He is revealed in the Bible. Most rebellion is against who Jesus is, but rebellion against Father and Spirit are just as damaging. Islam, for example, is a direct rebellion against heaven, for it denies the deity of Jesus, the Fatherhood of God, and the indwelling fullness of the Holy Spirit. In interaction with those who disbelieve who God is, argument and apologetics are necessarily limited. The best thing we can do in the face of rebellion and unbelief is not to defend but to celebrate. God is most wondrously proclaimed when we exalt Him as God for us, God with us, and God in us.

God the Father Is for Me. Psalm 56:9 reminds us that enemies will be turned back "because God is for me." God created men and women to be His sons and daughters. A vacuum in the human spirit longs for the intimacy of a loving Father. We overcome the protestations of a Muslim against the Fatherhood of God by holy jealousy. We do not diminish the Fatherhood of God in our texts, experience, or evangelism. We celebrate and announce the glorious comfort of a heavenly Father. Our Muslim friends may object academically, but they cannot help but hunger to know God the Father, who is *for* them.

God the Son Is with Me. In Matthew 28:20 Jesus instructed us to go into all corners of the world to make disciples. God is with us, and if God is for us who can be against us (Rom. 8:31)? David Livingstone told a group of university students that this truth (Jesus is *with* us always) sustained him through the dangers and loneliness of his "exiled life." When he died, they found his corpse kneeling by his bed, his Bible open to Matthew 28:20. In the margin he had scrawled, "The word of a gentleman."[4]

God the Spirit Is in Me. In the midst of exile and astonishment, Ezekiel spoke several times of the Spirit of God entering him (Ezek. 2:2; 3:24). The Bible is replete with references to the indwelling Spirit. God *in* us is a marvel too wondrous for academic explanation. What the Muslim finds horrific should not cause embarrassment in our witness. Let us proclaim the mysterious wonders of God by celebrating what we are privileged to enjoy.

RAJPUT, RATHORE HINDUS OF INDIA (1,485,000; 0.0% EVANGELICAL)

PRAY THAT THE RAJPUT, RATHORE WOULD FEEL AND KNOW THE BURDEN OF SIN AND WOULD COME TO JESUS FOR FORGIVENESS AND SALVATION

(MATT. 11:28-30).

JULY 26: CRUSHING GOD

PSALM 57; EZEKIEL 4-6; MARK 1; ROMANS 8

*W*hile we cannot hurt God, we can crush His heart. This is a mystery. In one sense, He is above our sin and folly, immune to our attacks, and transcendent over our emotions and folly. In another sense, He came to earth, shared our sorrows, and felt keenly the nails through His flesh and our betrayals through His heart. We can crush the heart of God.

Adulterous Hearts. Ezekiel wrote this when God's fury was unleashed against His unfaithful people: "I was crushed by their adulterous heart which has departed from Me" (Ezek. 6:9). Little can compare to the pain of betrayal in a marriage. When a husband or wife breaks the exclusive and holy covenant with his or her spouse, it is a crushing blow unmatched by any other betrayal. If we, still being conformed into the image of God, can feel the pain of adultery, imagine what He must feel. He has emotions (we derive ours from Him) that are purer, higher, wider, and deeper than ours. His heart is so much bigger than mine; thus when I break His heart the damage and pain is unimaginable. Then consider that billions of people across time have crushed His heart time after time. What kind of God is this who can absorb so much pain and still be merciful to us?

Harlot Eyes. We wound God not only with acts of adultery but with our eyes, "which play the harlot" with idols (6:9). When a wife sees her husband's eyes wander to another woman, her heart is bruised. God, with His magnified emotions, feels that same rejection when we have unfaithful eyes. In lust we undress other idols, pant after money, fame, and power . . . even as we forget that God sees all. He sees what our unfaithful eyes wander after, and it hurts Him. When we cry with the psalmist, "turn away my eyes from looking at worthless things" (119:37), it should be because we realize that "eye-harlotry" not only destroys us, it also crushes almighty God.

Self-Loathing. In God's magnanimous heart He knows that our adultery and harlotry against Him also hurt us, and He longs for us to be pure for our own well-being. God knows that we will "loathe" ourselves for the evils that we commit "in all our abominations" (Ezek. 6:9). A much better choice is not to crush the heart of God, not to create pain for ourselves and our loved ones, but to delight God's heart and the hearts of those we love. Help us, Jesus.

BEDOUIN, ZIBAN MUSLIMS OF ALGERIA (231,000; 0.0% EVANGELICAL)

PRAY THAT GOD WOULD UNVEIL THE CROSS AND WOULD REMOVE THE VEIL ON THE
MINDS AND SPIRITS OF THE BEDOIN, ZIBAN
(2 COR. 3:16-17).

JULY 27: JUDGED AND REWARDED

PSALM 58; EZEKIEL 7–9; MARK 2; ROMANS 9

*W*e must not reduce God to a manageable deity by playing His complementary characteristics against themselves. Some of His characteristics are complementary, not contradictory. Because our minds so desperately and sincerely want to understand God, we reduce Him to a formula and end up with a zero-sum effect. Wrath and mercy are not contradictory, election and personal choice do not neutralize each other, and transcendence and immanence are glorious because they are equally real. Post-Reformation thinking (as a reaction to salvation by merit) has tended to diminish the biblical function of works.

Saved by Faith. Obviously no one can work their way to divine favor. When Jesus said He did not come to call the righteous but sinners to repentance (Mark 2:17), He meant that every person is a sinner and the self-righteous are blind to their needs. Romans 9:32 underlines the folly of striving to be accepted by God by any means other than faith. As long as we remember we are all sinners and continually need to trust Jesus to save us, we will be safe.

Judged by Works. The Bible is clear that while we are saved by faith, we are judged by works (Ezek. 7:4, 8–9). Works matter. It is not enough to be for God theoretically; we must be for Him functionally and against evil practically. In Ezekiel 9 we read the troubling vision of God destroying all those who do not mourn evil. We will be judged by what we do and what we do not do. Saving faith is not a pass to an easy, uninvolved life. We are responsible and required both to work for what is right and against what is wrong. Followers of Jesus should be the hardest-working people in the world. Laborers are those who sweat.

Rewarded by Works. Similarly, and on the positive side, we will receive rewards based on our works. Heaven does not seem to be democratic or egalitarian: There are levels of honor in eternity. Jesus was clear (Matt. 16:27), as is the entire New Testament, that He will reward His own according to their works. In one sense, our wages are all the same in the blessing of the eternal presence of Jesus. In another sense, rewards will be determined by how hard we worked for Jesus. This is another mystery that we cannot reconcile.

Let us be encouraged by the mercy of Jesus that saves us because we believe. Let us be sobered by the inevitable judgment and reward that is determined by what we actually do for Him. We work because we believe.

KYRGYZ MUSLIMS OF KYRGYZSTAN (3,854,000; 0.0% EVANGELICAL)

PRAY THAT BELIEVERS AMONG THE KYRGYZ WOULD BE SET FREE FROM A SPIRIT OF FEAR OF WHAT MAY COME AND WOULD BOLDLY PROCLAIM THE TRUTH OF THE GOSPEL (2 TIM. 1:6–8).

JULY 28: THE JOY OF HAVING ENEMIES

PSALM 59; EZEKIEL 10-12; MARK 3; ROMANS 10

*S*urrounded in his own home by those who would kill him, David made an intriguing request of God. David asked that his enemies be scattered—not slain—"lest my people forget" (Ps. 59:11). We need enemies!

God does not intend for us to lead a resistance-free life. We long to be free from oppression, but God's method of making us strong is to scatter our enemies that they might one day return. He does not slay them and remove them forever. If He removed all oppression, this would be a worse fate than repeatedly having to overcome aggressors and accusers. Those who resist us and attack us keep us dependent on God; they make us stronger. Oh, the blessedness of having enemies—they are the exercise weights of the soul, the resistance that builds our spiritual muscles. How thankful we should be to those who do not like us (even within the household of faith). How grateful we should be to those who attempt to assassinate us in character or body. They are friends to our soul.

Sir Alexander Fraser Tytler (1747–1813) was a Scottish jurist and historian. It is thought that he wrote in 1801: "The average age of the world's great civilizations has been 200 years. These nations have progressed through this sequence: from bondage to spiritual faith; from spiritual faith to great courage; from courage to liberty; from liberty to abundance; from abundance to selfishness; from selfishness to complacency; from complacency to apathy; from apathy to dependency; from dependency back to bondage."[5] What is true for nations is true for individuals. We do not stay on the mountaintop of faith, courage, and liberty. The irony is that in our fallen state (even post-conversion), God's blessings tend to make us complacent. We must be vigilant that they do not lead us away from Him.

Let us be deeply thankful for those who oppose us, especially within the faith. When friends seem like enemies, that is when we need them most. When a spouse disagrees with us, let us receive that opposition as a kindness, as the faithful wounds of a friend. When colleagues challenge or question us, let us consider their response as a mercy, not a threat. The resistance of our peers usually plays two roles: First, it challenges the sinful nature within us. We are all self-deceived to some degree. We need godly men and women who are brave enough and kind enough to stand up to us. Second, even when good friends misunderstand us, their objections are a kindness because their wounds turn us to Jesus.

GOSAIN IIINDUS OI INDIA (1,446,000; 0.0% EVANGELICAL)

PRAY FOR THE WORD OF GOD IN WRITTEN, ORAL, MUSICAL, AND DRAMATIC FORMS TO BE
TRANSLATED AND TO SPREAD AMONG THE GOSAIN
(ISA. 55:10-11).

JULY 29: THE DIVINE RESPONSE

PSALM 60; EZEKIEL 13-15; MARK 4; ROMANS 11

*S*o often, the demonic attack launched against us is this: "You are alone! No one really understands. No one has gone through what you have gone through." Variations on this lie include the temptation to think that we are exceptional, irreplaceable, and independent. Paul pointed out that Elijah fell into this trap: "I alone am left!" (Rom. 11:3). To this demonic thought God responded: "I have reserved for Myself seven thousand men who have not bowed the knee to Baal" (v. 4).

We Are Not as Alone as We Think We Are. Strong men and women of God are particularly vulnerable to the dangerous assumption that they are alone—an assumption laced with pride. In reality, the "I alone am left" feeling is based on a determination that we alone are the righteous defenders of truth and proclaimers of the gospel. Trouble, rejection, and persecution are common triggers that make us feel isolated, and if we are not cautious, the Devil can turn our isolation into pride. The divine response says, "I have many who have suffered for Me, who have stood up in times of pressure despite the cost. Be encouraged that others have stood before you and are standing with you now."

We Are Not as Exceptional as We Think We Are. When God uses us, the Devil tries to make us think that God can only use us. Paul gave a refreshing perspective on this: "Do not be haughty, but fear. For if God did not spare the natural branches, He may not spare you either (Rom. 11:20–21). No one is irreplaceable. We must not believe the lie that God needs us and that His work will suffer if we are not in the center of it. He alone is the center of all His works. He can use us or discard us as He sees fit. It is pure arrogance to assume He cannot work without us.

We Are Not as Independent as We Think We Are. A sneaky form of hubris for the follower of Jesus is a twist on what is beautiful. We sing, "I have decided to follow Jesus," and then add, "Though none go with me, I still will follow."[6] While the sentiment is noble, the reality is frail because none of us can follow Jesus by ourselves. He designed us to follow Him in community. We need each other. We cannot complete the pilgrimage alone. We need the contemporary body of Christ around us, and we need the truth and comfort of the historic body of Christ. When the Devil lies to us that we are alone, exceptional, irreplaceable, or independent, may we listen to the divine response within, a response sourced in the interdependence of the triune Godhead.

ARAB MUSLIMS OF IRAN (1,400,000; 0.1% EVANGELICAL)

PRAY THAT GOD WOULD POUR OUT HIS SPIRIT ON THE ARAB PEOPLE AND THAT THEY WOULD SEE DREAMS AND VISIONS OF JESUS. PRAY THAT THEY WOULD BE POWERFULLY SAVED AND EMPOWERED TO BE HIS WITNESSES (JOEL 2:28-32).

*G*od has always been open and honest with humanity. He has never changed the rules, and He has no moral surprises. From the beginning He explained clearly: "The soul who sins shall die" (Ezek. 18:4, 20). People have always known that God abhors what is evil and that He expects us to join Him in this revulsion (Rom. 12:9). People who accuse God of unfairness often justify sin under the guise of compassion for others. He sees right through the hypocrisy and reminds us: "Is it not My ways which are fair, and your ways which are not fair?" (Ezek. 18:29).

Because God is fair, each person must die for his sins. No one is more affected by this justice than God Himself. The sadness we feel at funerals originates in God's grief at those whose sin is their ruin (v. 30). Jesus weeping at Lazarus's grave is Jesus standing at every burial in tears. The wonder is not that people are punished, disaster happens, or tragedy strikes. The wonder is that God's mercy protects us from all kinds of nastiness. We all deserve a tortuous life and a horrific eternity, yet God has "no pleasure in the death of the one who dies" (v. 32). If only we could understand the anguish God feels for the consequences of His own fairness, we might in our childish way try to console Him. God pleads, "Get yourselves a new heart and a new spirit. For why should you die?" (v. 31) No one is more afflicted by justice than God Himself.

Ironically, God's fairness provides a means for us to escape what we deserve. His gracious compassion withholds deserved judgment. No one has a better claim to protest God's "unfairness" than the Devil. He knows that humanity deserves God's destroying anger and is continually frustrated that God's mercy triumphs over God's judgment. You can almost hear the demonic whine: *Hey! God, you are unfair! Your own laws demand you scorch the earth and all that dwell within it.* Unable to twist God's nature, the Devil wickedly turns on people and contorts the issue of fairness until they accuse God of unfairness for the suffering of the wicked. The real unfairness of the universe is that God allows rebellious people who have so grievously and continuously insulted Him to live and breathe—let alone have eternity.

We should fall on our knees daily and thank God that He is mercifully unfair toward us. It is not fair that God bears the brunt of sin. It is not fair that Jesus was nailed to a cross. It is not fair that humanity is allowed to rebel against God increasingly. It is not fair that He forgives wicked men and women. Praise and glory and honor and thanks to Jesus for His beautiful unfairness. It is our only hope.

SAHARAWI MUSLIMS OF MOROCCO (222,000; 0.0% EVANGELICAL)

PRAY THAT CHRISTIANS FROM AROUND THE WORLD WOULD WORK TOGETHER TO REACH THE SAHARAWI AND THAT THE SAHARAWI WOULD BE JOINED TO THE BODY OF CHRIST (JOHN 17:20-23).

JULY 31: LOVE PAINS

PSALM 62; EZEKIEL 19-21; MARK 6; ROMANS 13

*L*ove inflicts pain, even as it does no harm (Rom. 13:10). True love repeatedly disappoints, hurts, confronts, refuses, and disciplines. This is certainly how God has loved us, and we should not expect to love others without hurting them. Love hurts but does not harm. God's minister bears the sword but not in vain (v. 4) and with the hope that long-term health will come from short-term, faithful wounds.

God commanded Ezekiel to prophesy about a sharpened and polished sword (Ezek. 21). This sword of the Lord despised the scepter (v. 13), did double damage, slayed great men, and entered private chambers (v. 14). God told His ministers: Swords at the ready! Thrust right! Set your blade! Thrust left! Wherever your edge is ordered! (v. 16) God expects those who represent Him to courageously wield His Word.

We try too hard to soften God's truth. We know that we are to take up the sword of the Spirit, but we turn the sword into an instrument of gentleness. Under what pretense is a sword ever used for comfort? Even if the surgery is delicate, the knife still cuts and the sword still pierces. Various metaphors bring out the gentler aspects of God's Word (light, seed to the sower and bread to the eater, God made flesh), but these aspects complement rather than diminish the reality of God's Word as an instrument of war, attack, and offense. We use the truths of God, condensed by life and words, as attacking instruments that fear neither friend nor ruler, foe nor doubter. And we do this, the Bible says, knowing that "the day is at hand" (Rom. 13:11).

The closer we get to the return of Jesus, the more important it is that our words be precise, true, and to the point. Times of terror and emergency do not allow the luxury of patient love. In a crisis, the primary need is for immediate action and instruction. In that situation, we express love by shouting, shoving, pulling, pushing, pressing . . . not by a passive demonstration. Love speaks. Love shouts. Love goes red in the face and cares not for appearances, perceptions, and debate. Urgent times do not allow for the luxury of dialogue. When ships are sinking, those who care shout commands; they do not solicit feedback.

LAZURI MUSLIMS OF TURKEY (94,000; 0.2% EVANGELICAL)

PRAY THAT THE HEARTS OF THE LAZURI WOULD BE LIKE GOOD SOIL,
READY TO HEAR THE GOSPEL AND TO RESPOND
(MATT. 7:1-8, 18-23).

Truly my soul finds rest in God;
my salvation comes from him.
Truly he is my rock and my
salvation; he is my fortress, I will
never be shaken.

PSALM 62:1-2 NIV

August

"MISSIONS IS NOT THE ULTIMATE GOAL OF THE CHURCH.
WORSHIP IS. MISSIONS EXISTS BECAUSE WORSHIP DOESN'T."

—John Piper

AUGUST 1: BETTER THAN LIFE

PSALM 63; EZEKIEL 22-24; MARK 7; ROMANS 14

*G*od's lovingkindness is "better than life" (Ps. 63:3). This description of God's thoughts and actions toward us is so magnificent that it does not compare even to what we consider most precious. It is better than our highest reality and enjoyment. God's lovingkindness is better than food, better than peace, better than comfort, better than travel, better than sports, better than marriage, better than adventure, better than nature, better than every good thing we enjoy.

We cannot come into the fullness of Jesus' lovingkindness until we let go of the life we have made for ourselves (Ezek. 22:16). Life as we have designed it is still too affected by sin and self. A life that is "better than life" is only fully realized in heaven, but we can embark on it now as we live under the shadow of His wings (Ps. 63:7), where there is no iniquity and offense. We do not gain iniquity-free life by trying not to sin. We enter the better life not by trying to be good but by accepting what Jesus has done for us and using our energy to seek Him. It is impossible to run in two different directions at the same time. Those who run hardest after Jesus need not concentrate on running away from sin—you cannot run after Jesus and run after sin at the same time.

The following questions, based on Psalm 63, will help you decide if you are running toward "the better life" that Jesus intends for you:

Do Your Lips Praise Him? Praise is never intended to be internal. Do your lips cheer daily for magnificent, triumphant Jesus all day long? Does the earth hear your voice?

Do You Bless the Lord While You Live? While both praise and blessing can be verbal, blessing has a practical, experiential component. Do you ever embarrass Jesus by how you treat others? Or can He put you on a pedestal and expose your every movement and word to public scrutiny without damage to His reputation?

Is Your Soul Satisfied with Jesus? The evidence of soul satisfaction is practical simplicity. We do not need many clothes or books or toys or even friends. The better life is utterly outside what we possess or accomplish. The better life is satisfied with Jesus and without temporal clutter.

PULAYAN HINDUS OF INDIA (1,402,000; 0.0% EVANGELICAL)

PRAY FOR THE PEACE THAT RESULTS WHEN MEN AND WOMEN ARE RECONCILED WITH GOD (JOHN 14:27). PRAY FOR MEN AND WOMEN OF PEACE (LUKE 10:6) AMONG THE PULAYAN.

AUGUST 2: UNDERSTANDING THE WORD

PSALM 64; EZEKIEL 25-27; MARK 8; ROMANS 15

*G*eorge Herbert considered the Bible to be the storehouse and magazine of life and comfort. He said of the Scriptures that there the Christian "sucks and lives" and that from the Word we find precepts for life, doctrine for knowledge, examples for illustration, and promises for comfort.[1] These understandings are commonly known, but where Herbert serves us best is in his explanation of how to understand Scripture.

A Holy Life. Many people read the Bible but are unchanged by it for they do not read with a view to obedience. The Word is only transformative if we obey it (Ps. 119:9). While it is true that the hidden Word keeps us from sin, it is just as true that a holy life positions us to understand the Word. When we approach the Word free from habitual sin, we understand it better. Sin clouds our understanding and blinds us to what we read. A pure, humble spirit that approaches the Word is rewarded with illumination. Holiness sharpens our minds, while sin dulls our spiritual perception.

Prayer. In the West we tend to dichotomize prayer and Bible reading as if they were not connected. "Worship reading" was a phrase used at the beginning of the twentieth century to express the union of prayer and reading.[2] As we read the Scriptures, we should pause frequently and pray what the Scripture exhorts, praise God for the way Scripture reveals Him, and repent in the ways Scripture demands. Praying as we read opens the hidden Word to us.

Diligent Collation of Scripture with Scripture. In our hunger to receive guidance, we often contort the Scripture to suit our preferences. Our protection is in allowing Scripture to comment on Scripture. This is why scope of reading is important. When we read daily from the Old Testament, Psalms, Gospels, and Epistles, the Word explains and balances itself. "Whatever things were written before were written for our learning, that we through the patience and comfort of the Scriptures might have hope" (Rom. 15:4).

Commenters and Fathers. We have an incredible legacy in what one colleague calls the wisdom of "old dead guys." Every Christian should glean from the thinking and wisdom of the historic and global church. We understand the Lord better when He is described by other nationalities and other generations. It is our loss when we neglect to learn from those who live far from us or have gone before us.

JEBEL NAFUSAH MUSLIMS OF LIBYA (172,000; 0.0% EVANGELICAL)

PRAY THAT BELIEVERS AMONG THE JEBEL NAFUSAH WOULD PROCLAIM THE MESSAGE OF THE GOSPEL CLEARLY AND WOULD MAKE THE MOST OF EVERY OPPORTUNITY GOD PLACES BEFORE THEM (COL. 4:2-5).

AUGUST 3: AUDIBLE ARROGANCE

PSALM 65; EZEKIEL 28–30; MARK 9; ROMANS 16

*A*rrogance tends to be verbalized. While it is true that we can retreat into a haughty and condescending silence, for the most part we unveil our arrogance by what we say about ourselves and others. Arrogance is but a manifestation of insecurity, which functions on the premise that by putting others down we lift ourselves up. God absolutely hates arrogance, and He goes to great lengths to drive it out of His people. It is impossible to represent Jesus correctly from a prideful pulpit because pride distorts the image of God. Based on the premise that arrogance is insecurity in disguise, our insecurity tends to be verbalized in these primary ways:

Self-Serving Speech. Paul castigated those who with "smooth words and flattering speech deceive the hearts of the simple" (Rom. 16:18). When we use our verbal gifts to manipulate or distort truth, this is offensive to God. We may be golden-tongued and able to convince others, but Jesus is singularly unimpressed. Manipulators (even Christian ones) have learned to be wise in what is evil (v. 19), but there is nothing manipulative or deceptive about God. Paul gave the intriguing image of God crushing Satan under our feet in this context of deceptive speech (v. 20). Self-serving speech lifts up Satan, and Jesus does not tolerate this rebellion.

Speaking When We Should Be Silent. Much of our speech is foolish and contributes nothing of life to the hearer. Arrogance and insecurity cause us to blabber, while humility and security cause us to be comfortable in silence. Humility listens. The more humble we are, the more quickly we listen and the more hesitantly we speak. Jesus is absolutely thrilled with those who listen to Him more than they talk to Him. Somehow we have come to believe that prayer is best defined by talking to Jesus. How delighted He is with those who linger in His presence and say nothing and ask nothing but simply wait for Him to speak. We demonstrate humility in prayer by listening more than petitioning.

Defending Ourselves. Psalm 119:23 reminds us that the best response to the insecurity of others that is demonstrated by verbal attacks and criticism is to meditate on God's Word. Our natural inclination is to use words to defend ourselves. This, too, demonstrates insecurity. God wants us to feel secure enough in Him not to utter one word in self-defense. The more strenuously we defend ourselves, the more we show our insecurity and our arrogance.

LEZGIAN MUSLIMS OF AZERBAIJAN (184,000; 0.1% EVANGELICAL)

PRAY THAT THE LEZGIAN WILL UNDERSTAND THAT HOPE FOR FORGIVENESS AND ACCEPTANCE WITH GOD IS AVAILABLE ONLY THROUGH JESUS' WORK ON THE CROSS (1 COR. 1:18).

AUGUST 4: NO EXCUSES

PSALM 66; EZEKIEL 31–33; MARK 10; 1 CORINTHIANS 1

A muted prophet wrote one of the most well-known passages of Scripture concerning proclamation. God struck Ezekiel mute, and while Ezekiel could not speak, God reminded him that he was a watchman: "You shall hear a word from My mouth and warn them for Me" (Ezek. 33:7). It was only after this famous passage (on the blood-guilt one bears for not warning sinners of their peril) that God again opened Ezekiel's mouth (v. 22). God was saying: "There are no excuses—even the mute must shout out a warning!" God is so concerned about the welfare of the wicked (v. 11) that He removes any excuses from His messengers. All are expected to preach repentance, and an active obedience is always more difficult than a passive disobedience. It can be harder to fulfill *dos* than *do nots*.

When a rich young ruler asked Jesus what he should do, Jesus responded with five *do not* instructions—all of which were easily accomplished by this young man (Mark 10). In Christianity we tend to focus on what we should not do, and although that is right, it is a lower form of obedience. What Jesus really wants is our energetic obedience of the positive action that He requires. The rich young ruler had fulfilled what Jesus told him not to do, but the young ruler had not done what Jesus told him he *should* do. Jesus firmly and lovingly put His finger on the essential omission: the young man was hiding behind a low level of obedience. Jesus intentionally makes His requirements so lofty that no one can comply without divine help so that "no flesh should glory in His presence" (1 Cor. 1:29).

The narrative about the rich young ruler is about missions not money. Jesus told the young man to get rid of all his excuses—anything that would hinder him from taking up his cross and following Jesus. The verses following this charge explain that undertaking the impossible (giving up wealth, family, lands, security) for the sake of the gospel is not only possible with Jesus but will be rewarded (Mark 10:29). There are no excuses—not being mute, not being moneyed, not being a minority, not being marginalized. We must all breathe out loving warnings and invitations to those who are perishing. Never one to mince words, Jesus said that those who actively obey will be rewarded and that persecution is part of the reward (v. 30). There is a rich fulfillment (Ps. 66:12) for those who go through fire and water for Jesus. Some joys are found only on the other side of radical obedience and rigorous trial.

RAJPUT, PONWAR HINDUS OF INDIA (1,348,000; 0.0% EVANGELICAL)

PRAY THAT THE BELIEVERS AMONG THE RAJPUT, PONWAR WILL ENDURE PERSECUTION IN A CHRISTLIKE MANNER AND WILL GIVE THEIR LIVES FOR THE SAKE OF THE GOSPEL IF NECESSARY (1 PETER 2:21-23).

AUGUST 5: THE INITIATIVE OF GOD

PSALM 67; EZEKIEL 34–36; MARK 11; 1 CORINTHIANS 2

*O*ur Christian walk inevitably leads us through dry seasons. There are times when Jesus seems remote, and we can tell that we are not as intimate with Him as we once were. We want to abide in Him, to be renewed, to sense His intimate presence, but hard as we try, our hearts and spirits remain dry. It is of great comfort in seasons like this to be reminded that Jesus takes the initiative for our abiding, for our renewal. He compels us toward our own desires (Ps. 119:35). He takes responsibility to feed us and to make us lie down (Ezek. 34:15). The longings we faintly hold originate with Him, and He takes responsibility to renew us. Our revival does not depend on sheer effort or discipline.

The Great Shepherd is more concerned about our spiritual fatigue than we are. He is determined to give us "a new heart" and "a new spirit" (Ezek. 36:26–27). Most assuredly, He promises that He will *cause us* to walk in His statutes. He makes us walk in His ways, makes us lie down in green pastures, and initiates a new heart and spirit. All this is God's initiative—He who watches over our souls and promises "showers of blessings" (34:26). All this is wonderful. However it is critical to note that He renews us for His sake, not for ours.

God Revives Us for His Name's Sake. Ezekiel continually said that God's acts are not for us alone (36:21–23, 32). His acts toward us prove His character. Our renewal is not focused on us. God intends for it to magnify Himself, the One who has taken the initiative to revive unworthy and craven people. When others look at our lives and see joy "inexpressible and full of glory," the contrast between our capacity and our competence will be so stark that they will magnify God, who has obviously revived us.

God Revives Us for the Sake of the Nations. When God gives grace to impossible people in impossible situations, He intends for this to serve as an invitation to the nations. He wants them to see what He has done for the weak and to hunger for that same joyous deliverance. The nations will know that Jehovah is God when He is "hallowed in you before their eyes" (Ezek. 36:23). Our renewal is an advertisement of God to the nations: "The nations which are left all around you shall know that I, the LORD, have rebuilt the ruined places and planted what was desolate. I, the LORD, have spoken it, and I will do it" (v. 36). God renews us to magnify His own name and to allow our renaissance to be a testimony of His mercy to the peoples of the world.

BERBER, MOZABITE MUSLIMS OF ALGERIA (158,000; 0.0% EVANGELICAL)

PRAY THAT GOD WOULD RAISE UP MISSIONARIES FROM ALL OVER THE WORLD TO WORK TOGETHER TO PLANT THE CHURCH AMONG THE BERBER, MOZABITE (MATT. 9:37).

To live dead is to live in hope and to live very much alive. Those who die to themselves do so joyously for they believe that captivity will one day be led captive (Ps. 68:18). The second coming of Jesus is referred to as our "blessed hope" for it is the culmination of all our lesser hopes, the fulfillment of all our longings. However, we should be under no delusion about the days until our ultimate redemption—they are going to get darker and darker, and evil will become stronger and stronger.

Hope is going to become rare and precious. Christians who hope in themselves or their efforts at justice are going to be the most disappointed, for their hopes will be dashed. In these last days it will seem that evil is dominant, right up to the end. Ezekiel's prophecy to dry bones is a hope-themed proclamation. God explained the meaning of the dry bones and the reason for despair: "Son of man, these bones are the whole house of Israel. They indeed say, 'Our bones are dry, our hope is lost, and we ourselves are cut off!'" (Ezek. 37:11). Lost hope leads to death, despair, and dry bones. Hopelessness destroys. If we are to live we must retain hope. We must fight to hope, for when God opens our "graves" of hopelessness (v. 13) and puts His Spirit in us (v. 14) we find life and hope!

The darker life gets, the more joyful we Christians can become because we know something that others do not: "He is not the God of the dead, but the God of the living" (Mark 12:27)! Twice Mark pointed out that we are greatly mistaken (and damaged) when we opt for hopelessness. When we do not know the Scriptures (the promise of hope) or the power of God (the provision of hope), then death, disease, and disappointment are crippling. For the believer, impossible darkness and death are merely foils for the bright promises of God. Hope is what allows us to see beyond the horror of reality to our wonderful deliverance. Hope helps us say: "Death? Trouble? Anguish? Sickness? Trial? Pain? Suffering? We do not quake before these for we have hope that they will be destroyed. We have hope that dry bones will live. We have hope of a final, ultimate, eternal deliverance."

Hope does us one further service: It confronts and defeats the lie that the preponderance of life is unfortunate and it reminds us that even now, in Christ, we are incredibly favored. "Blessed be the LORD, who daily loads us with benefits" (Ps. 68:19). Pain and trouble are the anomaly; the goodness of God is the norm. Hope reminds us that even as we wait for final freedom, life in Jesus is incredibly sweet.

LOHAR MUSLIMS OF PAKISTAN (1,842,000; 0.0% EVANGELICAL)

PRAY THAT THE LOHAR WOULD FEEL AND KNOW THE BURDEN OF SIN AND WOULD COME TO JESUS FOR FORGIVENESS AND SALVATION (MATT. 11:28–30).

AUGUST 7: ENDURANCE IS WHAT WE DO

PSALM 69; EZEKIEL 40-42; MARK 13; 1 CORINTHIANS 4

*I*n our family we have three simple rules for our boys: love Jesus, do not whine, and do not quit. Implicit in the last two rules is the virtue of endurance. Though endurance is not often extolled as a virtue, to be a Christian is to endure. Our model for endurance is Christ Himself, who endured the cross. As Christians we need to remind ourselves continually who we are and what we do: We are people who endure. Endurance is the sign of a mature Christian. Those who are not deeply marked by Jesus do not have the capacity to endure. They give in or give up at the first sign of trouble or opposition.

Endurance is not unique to Jesus' followers. Many people who do not know Him endure incredible injustice, poverty, shame, and physical abuse. In order for our endurance to glorify God, it must often be a challenge that is impossible in our natural strength. What distinguishes Christian endurance from the endurance of non-Christians is the manner and the reason for our endurance. We can endure sickness with grace or we can grimace. We can bear sorrow with a frown or with favor. We can accept injustice in anger or peace. The follower of Jesus endures unimaginable things while remaining unbelievably calm. It is not our endurance that exalts Him—it is the manner in which we endure.

Christian endurance is also exceptional because we endure for a lofty reason. It is one thing to endure Arctic cold for the fame of being the first person to the North Pole. It is another thing to endure the heat of hell's opposition for the salvation of souls. Enduring the elements or the competition for fame and fortune do not compare to enduring shame and suffering for the sake of people's souls. Endurance for personal survival is not on the same level as endurance for the love of others. The greatest manifestation of endurance is one that suffers for the sake of one's enemies. First Corinthians 4:12 reminds us what we do in persecution: "Persecuted, we endure." Endurance is what we do. While it is true we endure for our personal dignity, for our families' honor, and for the good of the organization we represent, it is most true that we endure for the glory of God. We make God look good when we suffer well. We adorn the gospel when we endure for the truth. God's gospel is most beautified when we endure for the sake of our enemies.

AD-DHARMI HINDUS OF INDIA (1,331,000; 0.0% EVANGELICAL)

PRAY THAT GOD WOULD UNVEIL THE CROSS AND WOULD REMOVE THE VEIL ON THE
MINDS AND SPIRITS OF THE AD-DHARMI
(2 COR. 3:16-17).

AUGUST 8: NOT EVERYTHING IS SACRED

PSALM 70; EZEKIEL 43-45; MARK 14; 1 CORINTHIANS 5

*D*emocracy is a human idea, not a God idea. There is order in the Godhead, there are elders in heaven, and there are different rewards for different levels of obedience. In classical philosophy, justice was not understood as treating everyone the same. It was understood as treating people who were equals equally and people who were not equal unequally. In other words, the righteous were treated equally, but the unrighteous were not treated equally. God's view of justice is to treat everyone as they deserve (reward) and to treat everyone as they do not deserve (mercy).

In viewing everything as sacred, we must be careful lest we treat nothing as sacred. The God of the Bible is both omnipresent (steadily everywhere) and occasional (special and uncommon manifestations of His glory). Our union with God allows for both a constant abiding in Him and periodic intimacies that are rapturous to the soul. God's steady calming presence and His bursts of glory complement and heighten each other.

The Spirit of God took Ezekiel into the future to see the new temple. In the vision of God in Ezekiel 40, Ezekiel was interacting with God when, suddenly, a greater manifestation of God's presence caused Ezekiel to fall on his face (43:2–3, 44:4). Communion with God is interrupted by a greater surge of God. Walking with God is like swimming in the ocean at high tide—we are immersed and surrounded *and* huge waves come crashing over us periodically.

In Ezekiel 44:23, God told the prophet that His priests should "teach My people the difference between the holy and the unholy, and cause them to discern between the unclean and the clean." There is right and wrong, there is good and best, and there is holy and sacred. A postmodernist view of life tends to see no separation between sacred and secular, but this is not biblically accurate. There is holy, and there is Holy. We injure our souls when we reduce all interactions with God to one level, for we need both steady communion and blessed, overwhelming, sacred moments. We need to walk in holiness and purity before the Lord. We also need to have unique moments of His unveiled presence that send jolts of divine electricity down our spines, make our knees rattle, and cause us to fall prostrate on our faces before the God who overwhelms.

BAKHTIARI MUSLIMS OF IRAN (1,300,000; 0.0% EVANGELICAL)

PRAY THAT BELIEVERS AMONG THE BAKHTIARI WOULD BE SET FREE FROM A SPIRIT OF FEAR OF WHAT MAY COME AND WOULD BOLDLY PROCLAIM THE TRUTH OF THE GOSPEL (2 TIM. 1:6-8).

AUGUST 9: GLORIFY GOD IN YOUR BODY

PSALM 71; EZEKIEL 46–48; MARK 15; 1 CORINTHIANS 6

*E*very culture has blind spots. Some American Christians struggle to understand their European brothers and sisters who drink alcohol, do not spank their kids, and vote for Socialist or Green Party candidates. Some European Christians wonder how their American "cousins" can be saved and at the same time resist gun control, appear careless about conservation, and eat unhealthy foods.

Paul reminds us that both sex and food are good things (1 Cor. 6:13), but the follower of Jesus should not be brought under the power of any good thing other than Jesus (v. 12). We tend to vigorously uphold sexual morality while we frequently abuse the physical temple in which the Spirit of God resides. Both sexual immorality and gluttony are gross sins against our bodies (v. 18), and Jesus does not allow any master other than Himself to rule over us.

In some cultures in Africa, people admire a large body because it signifies wealth and status. The Bible, however, is supra-cultural and does not concede an unhealthy body to any culture. It does not excuse anyone for violating God's temple. Nutrition and exercise may not seem like spiritual topics, but they are. We are remiss if we are fat or lazy. To be clear: If we do not exercise or show restraint in our eating, we sin. There is something profoundly disturbing about an overweight missionary or preacher teaching about holiness, freedom, or deliverance when that person is so obviously under the power of "another." That person is not glorifying God in his body; he is under the power of something other than Jesus.

Sheer discipline or willpower cannot rescue us. We cannot conquer sexual sin and gluttony through effort alone. Those who are overweight and do not exercise are not bound in that condition for lack of trying to escape. There is a spiritual principle behind the cleansing of every temple. Paul put it this way: "God both raised up the Lord and will also raise us up by His power" (1 Cor. 6:14). This promise is in the middle of the passage on sex and food! We cannot conquer our physical addictions (whatever they are) without the same spiritual power that raised Jesus from the dead. This is stunning! God offers resurrection power to help us exercise and eat in a balanced fashion. How marvelous is this God of glory who empowers us both to die for Him among the nations and also to get up early to jog—that His temple might in all ways be adorned.

BERBER, ATTA MUSLIMS OF MOROCCO (135,000; 0.0% EVANGELICAL)

PRAY FOR THE WORD OF GOD IN WRITTEN, ORAL, MUSICAL, AND DRAMATIC FORMS TO
BE TRANSLATED AND TO RISE AMONG THE BERBER, ATTA
(ISA. 55:10–11).

AUGUST 10: MUSCULAR MISSIOLOGY

PSALM 72; DANIEL 1-3; MARK 16; 1 CORINTHIANS 7

*T*he church and the missions sending agency are the two great redemptive structures of God. They both evangelize and disciple, but they do so in different spheres. The church by nature is multifaceted, intended to represent the kingdom of God in a fully-orbed manner within society. The mission agency is to have one priceless vision: planting the church among people where it does not exist.

Both church and missions are to have a robust muscularity to their methods. Sometimes muscles are used tenderly, sometimes forcefully. The church nurtures, adopts, shepherds, teaches, cares, embraces, protects, conserves, and disciples. The church reveals the "tender mercies" of our God (Ps. 119:77). Men and women work within and from the church to express to all society the goodness and kindness of our gracious God. In contrast, missions takes new territory, boldly goes where there is none to nurture, advances through storm and enemy attacks, and marches all night long to battle all day for the King. Mission is singular in cause: win souls from among all peoples and establish them in churches. Mission is rough, aggressive, risk-prone, dangerous, raw, disturbing, and pioneer. Church and mission have an interdependence whose beauty is preserved by guarding their unique purpose.

God does not intend for missions to be soft and fuzzy. Missionary work should take on the powers of hell in places where the kingdom is most resisted and most unknown. In Daniel chapters 1–3, God's representatives manifested His glory among a darkened people (2:22). These men stood up to the rage and fury of a powerful pagan king (3:13). Full of fury (v. 19), the king condemned these proto-missionaries to a furnace (v. 27) because they had "frustrated the king's word and yielded their bodies that they should not serve nor worship any god except their own God" (v. 28). This is missions in its robust purity—standing against the powers of evil for the glory of God among all nations.

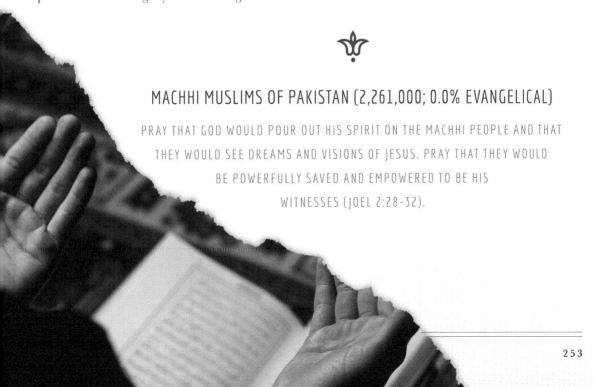

MACHHI MUSLIMS OF PAKISTAN (2,261,000; 0.0% EVANGELICAL)

PRAY THAT GOD WOULD POUR OUT HIS SPIRIT ON THE MACHHI PEOPLE AND THAT THEY WOULD SEE DREAMS AND VISIONS OF JESUS. PRAY THAT THEY WOULD BE POWERFULLY SAVED AND EMPOWERED TO BE HIS WITNESSES (JOEL 2:28-32).

AUGUST 11: HEAVEN RULES

PSALM 73; DANIEL 4-6; LUKE 1; 1 CORINTHIANS 8

*D*emocracy is a fallen, limited system. In the scope of eternity, democracy is a short blip on the radar, sandwiched with other fallen human constructs and bookended by the theocratic kingdom of God. Daniel knew this well and declared that "the Most High rules in the kingdom of men, gives it to whomever He will, and sets over it the lowest of men" (Dan. 4:17). In the days to come, democratic systems of government will wane on earth, giving way to their internal corruption. Before Jesus comes we are going to see various forms of totalitarian systems emerge and dominate. God is going to wean us from our reliance on democracy. This is too painful for us to consider, unless we run to God's sanctuary and understand that He controls both evil and righteous systems of rule (Ps. 73:16–17). These are heaven's rules of governance:

God Appoints and Dismisses Leaders. It may seem that elections and coups result from the work of people and people do play a part, but the Bible is clear that God appoints both good and bad leaders for His own purposes. When we struggle under our leaders, we can have double comfort: God appointed this leader (we are respectful) and God can remove this leader (we submit in hope). When God's purposes are accomplished, He removes poor leaders.

We Get the Leaders We Deserve. This unheralded principle of leadership holds true for countries as well as for churches and mission teams. Followers tend to complain and compare their leadership to others. They fail to see that honest people elect or are granted honest leaders and vice versa. Leaders almost invariably represent the culture and context from which they emerge. When we are unhappy with those who lead us, we must first examine ourselves. Men and women of integrity are ultimately rewarded with faithful and capable leaders. One of God's miracles is to reward good followers by shaping raw leaders into men and women who represent Him well to those they serve.

God Tends to Select the Lowliest to Lead. The world selects leaders according to perceived competence. God selects His representatives by character. He delights to seek out the humblest and lowest and by their elevation to glorify Himself. A humble teenage girl said it best: "He has scattered the proud in the imagination of their hearts. He has put down the mighty from their thrones and exalted the lowly" (Luke 1:51–52). We stand with Mary and magnify the Lord, rejoicing in God our Savior. He has done all things well, even setting up surprising people to lead us.

BAHT HINDUS OF INDIA (1,302,000; 0.0% EVANGELICAL)

PRAY THAT CHRISTIANS FROM AROUND THE WORLD WOULD WORK TOGETHER TO REACH THE BAHT AND THAT THE BAHT WOULD BE JOINED TO THE BODY OF CHRIST (JOHN 17:20-23).

AUGUST 12: FOR GOD'S SAKE

PSALM 74; DANIEL 7-9; LUKE 2; 1 CORINTHIANS 9

*G*od answers our prayers for His own sake. The heart of humanity longs to be the center of something, and the long journey to being like Jesus slowly helps us realize that only when God is the center of everything will we be satisfied. The phrase "for God's sake" has become an oath, a curse uttered in frustration. It is a vulgar cloaking of an eternal truth: All things, including answered prayer, are for the glory of God—not the glory of humanity. Everything that God does, He does for His own glory and purposes. Everything we do should also be for Him. The only reason this concept offends and unsettles us is because at our core we want to be the center of the universe. The sanctification process is a long lesson in embracing Jesus as the center.

We must learn to approach prayer for God's sake. Daniel said it well: "We do not present our supplications before You because of our righteous deeds, but because of Your great mercies" (Dan. 9:18). If we merit answers to our prayers, the answers are for our sakes. If we are completely undeserving of deliverance, the answers are for some reason other than our merit, and the only possible reason is to glorify God.

We must approach prayer knowing that any answer is for the sake of the supplier, not the supplicant. This is a difficult lesson for us: to make prayer God-centric in answer as well as in petition. We see a widow in need, a child with cancer, an impoverished people in darkness, and we pray as if they deserve deliverance. When we make the needy person the focus of the answer, we subtly shift God out of the center of answered prayer and insert ourselves, because any person in the equation ultimately represents us.

God revives us for His own sake. He heals that He might be glorified. He supplies that He might be worshiped. He forgives that He might be exalted. He delivers that He might be adored. He meets us that we might magnify Him. He acts to bring honor to His divine self, not to exalt man or woman. Let us stop approaching God for answers on behalf of ourselves. Let us learn to approach Him for the defense of His honor, for the glory of His name. Let us seek answered prayer for His sake.

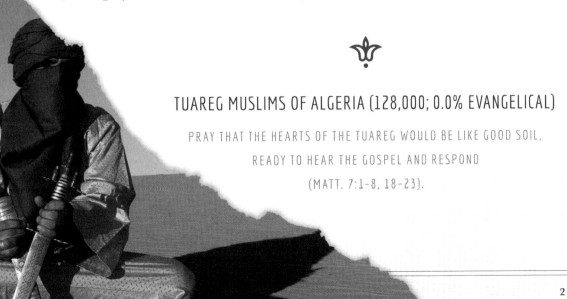

TUAREG MUSLIMS OF ALGERIA (128,000; 0.0% EVANGELICAL)

PRAY THAT THE HEARTS OF THE TUAREG WOULD BE LIKE GOOD SOIL,
READY TO HEAR THE GOSPEL AND RESPOND
(MATT. 7:1-8, 18-23).

AUGUST 13: GOD IS FAITHFUL

PSALM 75; DANIEL 10-12; LUKE 3; 1 CORINTHIANS 10

Trouble is normal for the dedicated Christian. If we continually experience long periods of quiet, it is because we are no threat to the Enemy. The biblical pattern for those in active obedience to God's will is prolonged seasons of trouble interspersed with short spurts of rest and renewal. We want it the other way around. We want long periods of rest with occasional battles, but this is not God's pattern. We need to station ourselves in the field and keep swinging our swords until they cleave to our hands. If even angelic warriors had to battle through to answered prayer, we should not think that we will accomplish anything lasting for the kingdom without great toil, sweat, and tears (Dan. 10:13).

God does not prove His faithfulness by His abundant provision (ease and safety) but by ongoing deliverance from sin, temptation, and the Devil. First Corinthians 10 reviews our colleagues who fell into sin before us. These men and women, much stronger than we, fell into lust, idolatry, sexual immorality, tempting Christ, and complaining. This did not please God so He scattered their bodies in the wilderness (v. 5). The Bible admonishes us that a life of struggle is our lot and provides a visual reminder of the bones of respected men and women scattered about us. What stops us from ending up like them? What sustains us in the never-ceasing battle against sin? Only this: God is faithful. He is faithful to help us escape sin. He is faithful to help us endure hardship. He is faithful to renew our spirits in the midst of conflict. He is faithful to give us joy on the weary journey.

God is faithful to lavish blessings on us, but we should remember that a war zone is no place for amenities. A great and glorious day is coming when our battle for holiness and for souls will end, when we will lay our weapons down. But that is then; now we war. Our present is an unceasing conflict, and we must learn to bless God for His faithfulness in the ongoing fight. He is faithful to keep us from falling, to keep us from the darts and arrows of the Devil, to keep us from bitterness of soul, to keep us from arrogant pride, to keep us from our own folly and the Devil's fury. God is faithful—and in our struggle He demonstrates that faithfulness by escape and endurance.

It is right to praise God for His provision and for His protection. The person who is no threat to evil finds himself praising God for material blessings, unaware that because he is no threat he has no trouble. The one who is hacking at the gates of hell is assaulted by all manner of darkness and finds himself thanking God for spiritual survival. God is faithful because He preserves our souls, not because He provides our toys.

PALLAR MUSLIMS OF PAKISTAN (701,000; 0.0% EVANGELICAL)

PRAY FOR THE PEACE THAT RESULTS WHEN MEN AND WOMEN ARE RECONCILED WITH GOD (JOHN 14:27). PRAY FOR MEN AND WOMEN OF PEACE (LUKE 10:6) AMONG THE PALLAR.

AUGUST 14: LIKE THE LOVE OF THE LORD

PSALM 76; HOSEA 1-3; LUKE 4; 1 CORINTHIANS 11

*N*ot many of us begin our career in missions by marrying a prostitute (Hosea 1:3). God does not ask of us what He asked of Hosea. Old Testament prophets had it rough: they had to walk around naked (Isa. 20:2); cook on dung (Ezek. 4:12); and not mourn a wife's death (Ezek. 24:16) . . . all while speaking the most unpopular messages. Not only did God ask Hosea to start his ministry by marrying a sullied woman, but he was to remain committed to her as she repeatedly cheated on him. God instructed Hosea: "Go again, love a woman who is loved by a lover and is committing adultery, just like the love of the LORD for the children of Israel, who look to other gods and love the raisin cakes of the pagans" (Hos. 3:1).

God obviously wanted Hosea to "feel" the things he preached. As Hosea felt the crippling blow of being betrayed by his wife, he entered into the passion of God. To be on the wrong end of adultery is to be shot by an emotional cannon—completely devastating and shattering. The God who created all and who is all powerful is wounded, shattered by our unfaithfulness. He is not immune to our betrayals and He feels our spiritual abandonment deeply. Only by experiencing a similar pain could Hosea fully communicate God's love.

As communicators of God's intentions we are invited, even instructed, to enter into His agonies. It is one thing to speak truth; it is another thing to live it. Those who live the realities they proclaim have a greater moral authority and anointing than those who are technically right but emotionally cold.

Not only must we come to terms with the agony of being betrayed, we must also grapple with the anguish of committing adultery ourselves—over and over again. The great God of the universe has humbly entered into an intimate relationship with His bride, yet we collectively and individually cheat on Him over and over again. We are serial adulterers. Every time we wince at the news of a friend who has fallen morally and broken a sacred vow, we should recoil at the horror of how many times we have done the same to God. He had the unquestioned authority to ask Hosea to go back to the betraying spouse because He has done the same with us over and over again. How marvelous is this love of God—a love that repeatedly seeks out prostitutes like you and me. This is the love He calls us to give to others. This is the love He calls us to live and to broadcast. How scandalous is love like this?

GANGAKULA HINDUS OF INDIA (1,286,000; 0.0% EVANGELICAL)

PRAY THAT BELIEVERS AMONG THE GANGAKULA WOULD PROCLAIM THE MESSAGE OF THE GOSPEL CLEARLY, AND WOULD MAKE THE MOST OF EVERY OPPORTUNITY GOD PLACES BEFORE THEM (COL. 4:2-5).

AUGUST 15: THE DECREASE OF INCREASE

PSALM 77; HOSEA 4–6; LUKE 5; 1 CORINTHIANS 12

*W*ealth and knowledge are dangerous. The smarter and richer people become, the more they tend to trust self and personal resources. "The more they increased, the more they sinned against Me" (Hos. 4:7). Jesus has no special priority for the economically poor; He came to save sinners, period. It is just that the poor are smart and simple enough to realize they need help. Poverty is a blessing in that it keeps us realistic about our needs. Wealth and power tend to subvert our continual dependence on God. As we get richer and smarter, we tend to become self-sufficient and dumber. Poor judgment and deceived thinking are the well-traveled paths of those without physical need. When the physical body is self-sufficient, the spirit thinks it is self-sufficient. Self-sufficiency of the spirit is sin because it is rebellion against the truth that people need God. The more capacity we have to care for ourselves the more we think we do not need God. Physical increase almost always leads to spiritual demise

God bothers to bless us, which is ironic. When a person is redeemed, he or she stops wasting life and resources, and there is a tangible and practical lift. As long as a person retains a God focus and a generous spirit, God continues to bless and provide, to channel His blessings through that person. God delights to shower blessings on us, and *prosperity* is a biblical word. God however defines prosperity holistically, and when He sees riches of the world diminishing the soul, He lovingly removes health and wealth to recover the soul. Sometimes God also removes health and wealth for His greater glory among the nations. You do not have to sin to be poor; God chose poverty for His beloved and sinless Son that humanity might have access to all the treasures of God. God sometimes asks His choicest servants to follow in the footsteps of lower-class Jesus. Simon, James, and John were blue-collar workers, and they "forsook all and followed Him" (Luke 5:11). Matthew was a white-collar tax collector, and "he left all . . . and followed Him" (v. 28).

We who are rich in this world should be thankful and generous . . . and warned. We should cast a dubious eye on our increase, for it could be our demise. The very provisions of God can lead us away from Him. We who are rich in this world should cast an envious eye toward those who live simply. They have the treasure and satisfaction of focused daily dependence on Jesus.

SOCOTRAN MUSLIMS OF YEMEN (120,000; 0.2% EVANGELICAL)

PRAY THAT THE SOCOTRAN WILL UNDERSTAND THAT HOPE FOR FORGIVENESS AND ACCEPTANCE
WITH GOD IS ONLY AVAILABLE THROUGH JESUS' WORK ON THE CROSS
(1 COR. 1:18).

*I*t seems unthinkable that we could handcuff God. How can the omnipotent God be limited? One of the mysteries of God is that He sometimes limits Himself to our expectations and requests. Matthew 13:58 says that Jesus "did not do many mighty works there because of their unbelief." It is not that God cannot act when people do not believe; it is that He chooses not to.

Unbelief Is Sin. A holy God cannot and will not partner with sin. He considers unbelief a flagrant rebellion, an insult. Psalm 78 tells us that "the LORD heard this and was furious . . . because they did not believe" and "they still sinned, and did not believe" (vv. 21–22, 32). The context refers to God's people, not pagans. This is about men and women in a covenant relationship with God. When God's people—including God's missionaries—do not believe Him, He gets furious. He considers unbelief in His followers as flagrant sin. It is more damaging than unbelief in the unregenerate. His followers know better. When we choose not to believe (and belief is a choice), we are like silly doves without sense (Hos. 7:11). We cannot harbor the sin of unbelief and expect God to act in power. We limit Him when we do not believe; our unbelief is effectual hate toward the lost. For when we do not believe, God does not act and the nations are not reached. Neither the saved nor the lost can afford unbelief.

Belief Is Love. Love "believes all things" (1 Cor. 13:7). When we love someone, we have no trouble accepting their word. Love takes the best possible meaning from every conversation. Love grants a benefit of the doubt. Love refuses to believe what it knows is contrary to the nature of the loved one. We love Jesus by believing Him. We know His character—we know He is faithful and we know we can trust Him even when He promises the most outlandish things or asks for the most impossible sacrifices. To love Jesus is to believe everything that He has said. Where He is loved, He acts. In the same way that He refuses to act where He is not loved, He delights to act where He is loved and trusted. In mission let us delight the heart of Jesus by loving Him enough to believe He will do extraordinary things. Our reward is that He will! Our belief in Jesus prompts Him to act among the nations. We can best love the lost by believing Jesus, for they will be the eternal benefactors of our belief.

MALLAH MUSLIMS OF PAKISTAN (356,000; 0.0% EVANGELICAL)

PRAY THAT THE BELIEVERS AMONG THE MALLAH WILL ENDURE PERSECUTION IN A CHRISTLIKE MANNER AND WILL GIVE THEIR LIVES FOR THE SAKE OF THE GOSPEL IF NECESSARY (1 PETER 2:21–23).

AUGUST 17: EDIFICATION OVER PROVOCATION

PSALM 79; HOSEA 8; LUKE 7; 1 CORINTHIANS 14

*C*lever, active Christians must be on guard that they do not fall in love with provocative ideas and bold actions. Through time, many saints fell out of love with Jesus as they fell in love with pioneering, cutting the frontier, or challenging the church to think. When our central aim becomes the provocation of the faithful, we "sow the wind and reap the whirlwind" (Hos. 8:7). It starts so nobly—God gives us a prophetic word that is fresh, new, sharp, and compelling. It is His choice thought for that day and time, and it helps and corrects His people. But it can become a drug to the speaker—for having been anointed to provoke God's people to truth once, there is both external and internal pressure to do so again. So the speaker begins to search for the next provocation, and the focus shifts from Jesus to complex thoughts and challenges. Falling in love with edgy ideas and complex challenges inevitably leads to falling out of love with Jesus.

There is a beautiful simplicity in God. Mystery does not have to be complicated. Our explanation is a person, not a precept. When Jesus comes to us, our minds and hearts are answered; when He speaks, something burns within us. He may or may not give us facts and reasons, and if He does not, it does not matter, for our surety is in Him not in details. Psalm 119:130 states: "The entrance of Your words gives light; it gives understanding to the simple." When Jesus speaks to us by His presence, things feel right. We may or may not be able to explain it, but our souls have rest when He is near. Provocation is not the standard means of feeding the flock; cultivating the presence of Jesus is. The presence of Jesus—His simple, blessed, matchless, incomparable presence—is what edifies us. It is what we feed on. His flesh is food indeed.

The great simplicities of God are found throughout the Scriptures. God told Hosea: "I have written for him the great things of My law, but they were considered a strange thing" (Hos. 8:12). People want complex theory; God gives simple reality. People want reasons; God grants His presence. The great things of God are considered strange and difficult, not because they are complex but because they are so delightfully simple. God is good. "But what about evil?" God is good. "But what about those who have never heard?" God is good. "Then why do the innocent suffer?" God is good. "Then what about sickness, injustice, and disaster?" Our questions are unending, and the kindest way God answers them is simply to overwhelm us with His presence.

HALWAI HINDUS OF INDIA (1,258,000; 0.0% EVANGELICAL)

PRAY THAT GOD WOULD RAISE UP MISSIONARIES FROM ALL OVER THE WORLD TO WORK TOGETHER TO PLANT THE CHURCH AMONG THE HALWAI (MATT. 9:37).

AUGUST 18: GRACE LABORS

PSALM 80; HOSEA 9; LUKE 8; 1 CORINTHIANS 15

*T*he work of missions is a marathon, not a sprint. Current strategies seem to emphasize the rapid expansion of the church, yet things that grow rapidly are not generally as sturdy as things that mature steadily over time. When quantity is praised above quality we adopt methods that yield the quickest and largest growth, with the repeated result of unhealthy, untenable communities of faith. Discipleship takes time. The growth process for both individuals and churches cannot be shortened without detrimental side effects. This is the oft-missed lesson of the parable of the sower in Luke 8.

In the parable, the Devil took away some seed before belief was born; some seed had no roots and fell to temptation; some seed was choked by cares, riches, or pleasures before it could bear fruit. Other seed fell on good ground, and those seeds heard "with a noble and good heart" and bore "fruit with *patience*" (Luke 8:15, emphasis added). Fruit requires patience. Discipleship is the mandate of every believer, but no disciple is shaped overnight. We must work patiently if we are going to see men and women conformed to the image of God's Son.

Paul reminds us in 1 Corinthians 15:10 that grace labors. God has labored over us. Think back over your own discipleship: How many sermons, how many mentors, how many friends, how many books, how many circumstances, how many years has God invested in you? Yet we are still so rough and in continual need of formation. How dare we think we can shorten the process of discipleship among unreached peoples! We must love the lost long enough to labor in grace for them and with them in the journey of discipleship. Though it may sound spiritual to say that it is enough for new believers to "have the Holy Spirit and the Bible," it is not true. Jesus' followers need each other in order to grow. We were not created to blossom in isolation.

Infant churches desperately need to be in communion with the global and historic church. Ironically, to "protect" nascent movements in the name of doctrinal purity is to doom them to heresy. It is our interaction with the body of Christ around the world and over time that helps us stay true. The body of Christ is designed to self-correct, and it needs all its members for this corrective process to be faithful. The Holy Spirit uses others to shape and correct us, and this is true both for individuals and communities. We must have the grace to be dedicated to one another over time and have the wisdom to choose strength and fruit over noise and fame.

BEDOUIN CHAAMBA MUSLIMS OF ALGERIA (115,000; 0.0% EVANGELICAL)

PRAY THAT THE BEDOUIN CHAAMBA WOULD FEEL AND KNOW THE BURDEN OF SIN AND WOULD COME TO JESUS FOR FORGIVENESS AND SALVATION (MATT. 11:28-30).

AUGUST 19: STEADFASTLY SET YOUR FACE

PSALM 81; HOSEA 10; LUKE 9; 1 CORINTHIANS 16

*O*ur Arab city was troubled this week: demonstrations turned ugly, rival factions of Muslims attacked each other, and violence erupted between security forces and civilians. The Christian minority was targeted, and many churches and Christian institutions were attacked. To live in the Arab world in our day is to experience both open doors and adversaries (1 Cor. 16:9). Interestingly, the most passionate calls for our team to evacuate come from our families and friends in the faith.

Jesus occasionally made a tactical retreat, but only in the context of steadfastly moving toward Jerusalem to die at the appointed time (Luke 9:51). Scripture, in fact, describes His death as something to be accomplished, not something to be avoided (v. 31). A subtle and emotional error has crept into the thinking of mission supporters—the error that the safety of the missionary is the highest goal of the sending church or agency. God sent Jesus to die, and He sends missionaries to follow in Christ's footsteps. Jesus instructs all who follow Him to deny themselves and take up their cross daily (v. 23), but bearing a cross is difficult when one is running *away from* Calvary. Jesus asks friends and family to bear the cost of sending loved ones into harm's way for the sake of the gospel. If mission in these last days falters, it will not be because missionaries are unwilling to die; it will be because senders are unwilling to commission them to suffer and die.

When the church sends God's servants into difficult, violent areas of ministry, it is a form of corporate praise. The Western church is losing the art of praise. We can sing, we can clap, but we are losing the gift of verbal, audible, personal, and unique glorification of Jesus—both in the church service and in the world. When we have the missional will to deploy and sustain our loved ones in chaotic and dangerous places, it is an intentional song of praise to the world and to the spiritual powers of destruction. This praise declares that Jesus is worth living for and worth dying for. The corporate willingness to send missionaries into danger for Jesus' sake is akin to standing up in the stadium of the world, thrusting the arms of the body of Christ into the air, and cheering at the top of our unified lungs for His advance across the field of time. It is senseless for the missionary to die due to politics yet in order to represent Jesus well, to encourage the brothers and sisters who cannot leave, and to make a praise statement to the world about the supremacy of Jesus missionaries (and their senders) must be determined to walk steadfastly toward their Jerusalem, not run away.

MEO MUSLIMS OF PAKISTAN (797,000; 0.0% EVANGELICAL)

PRAY THAT GOD WOULD UNVEIL THE CROSS AND WOULD REMOVE THE VEIL ON THE MINDS
AND SPIRITS OF THE MEO (2 COR. 3:16–17).

AUGUST 20: HEART CHURNS

PSALM 82; HOSEA 11; LUKE 10; 2 CORINTHIANS 1

*G*od invites us to join in His agony over lost people. Hosea 11 reveals the heart of a tender heavenly Father who draws with "gentle chords" and stoops to feed (v. 4). This Father, knowing that His errant children deserve banishment and exile, pleads with Himself: *How can I give them up? My heart churns within me; My sympathy is stirred.* (v. 8) When was the last time your heart churned because someone did not know Jesus?

When I first started to work among unreached people, I could not get away from the fact that everyone I saw was going to hell. I was a young man in Mauritania—the end of the earth—a country that was and is 99.99 percent Muslim. I entered into the anguished passion God feels for His lost loved ones. I prayed four hours a day; I wandered the streets weeping; I lost weight; and an intensity descended on my soul as my heart churned within me. My little human soul could not carry the weight of what I felt. I could not bear the emotional toll of so many lost people, so I compensated by ceasing to be moved at all. I was not designed to bear the weight of the world, so I coped by developing indifference.

Neither extreme honors the heavenly Father. We are not God, and we do not have the capacity to absorb the weight of human truancy. We do, however, bear the divine image, and God wants us to taste a little bit of His suffering for those who are lost. We should never get used to a Muslim funeral. When we stand over the graves of those who have gone to an eternity without Christ, something should pull our insides apart. If we cannot mourn for the world, let us at least dump ashes on our heads for our neighbors. We should not fabricate emotion; we should ask God to share a little of His. Let us not reduce God to a robot who does not feel the consequences of His own justice. Our emotions are sourced in God. He is passionate, capable of the highest joy and the deepest sorrow. To know Him is to share His passions, but how dare we think we know Him when we have become inured to people dying without Jesus.

The Father's heart is so tender that He "will not come with terror" (Hos. 11: 9). He will call sons and daughters "out of Egypt" (v. 1), and "His sons shall come trembling from the west; they shall come trembling like a bird from Egypt" (vv. 10–11). God asks us to let His lost ones know how terrible He feels at their disobedience. Luke 10:16 astoundingly reminds us that "he who hears you hears me." Can those who do not know Jesus hear the Father tearfully pleading through us?

BHARBHUNJA HINDUS OF INDIA (1,174,000; 0.0% EVANGELICAL)

PRAY THAT BELIEVERS AMONG THE BHARBHUNJA WOULD BE SET FREE FROM A SPIRIT OF FEAR OF WHAT MAY COME AND WOULD BOLDLY PROCLAIM THE TRUTH OF THE GOSPEL (2 TIM. 1:6-8).

AUGUST 21: SHAME'S REDEMPTION

PSALM 83; HOSEA 12; LUKE 11; 2 CORINTHIANS 2

*G*od's goal for shame is redemption. There is a prominent Coptic priest in the Middle East who is evangelical in his doctrine and practice. In his television program he uses shock and shame to draw the Muslims' attention to what their text and faith actually teach. (He is careful to use their own texts and theologians as his sources.) He does this intentionally, knowing that the initial reaction to his approach will be anger and hostility. Interestingly, he may be responsible for more Muslims coming into the kingdom than any other man in history. Many Muslims testify that their initial reaction to him and his message was one of fury because he exposed the inconsistencies and shameful aspects of their tradition. Then as they set out to prove he was wrong, they found he was right.

This is a microcosm of what God does for us. God brings to light the things that shame us in order that we might seek Him. Shame does not necessarily imply sin. Some things shame us that are not our fault. We may be bald, short, barren, have a high-pitched voice, or some other condition that is not a result of our rebellion but is embarrassing. Shame sometimes results from the actions of others: family, friends, organizations, or other proximate entities act in ways we do not approve or endorse. God uses both the shame of sin and of our connections to bring us to Himself. He does this by offering us a choice: Are we going to find our identity in Him and accept that He is good enough and big enough to cover our shame, or are we going to spend time and energy frantically trying to cover (or change) whatever embarrasses us? At the root of the issue is the level of consideration we give to what God thinks of us.

When sin is the cause of shame, God wants us to repent, to bring our sin and shame to Him, and to accept His forgiveness. Sin's effects cannot be covered, but one miracle of grace is that when we confess our sins Jesus removes our guilt and shame. We no longer care what others think about us. We deeply desire His acceptance, and when we find it, the sting of reproach fades away. There is deep joy in being beloved of God. When shame is caused by some factor not of our sinful choosing, we find that accepting who God has made us to be swallows up the disappointment of what we do not have or who we are not. The shame of lack is more than rewarded with the pride of having Jesus.

JERBA MUSLIMS OF TUNISIA (106,000; 0.1% EVANGELICAL)

PRAY FOR THE WORD OF GOD IN WRITTEN, ORAL, MUSICAL, AND DRAMATIC FORMS TO BE TRANSLATED AND TO SPREAD AMONG THE JERBA (ISA. 55:10–11).

AUGUST 22: DEATH'S GLORY

PSALM 84; HOSEA 13; LUKE 12; 2 CORINTHIANS 3

*P*ilgrimage is a good thing. Our ultimate destination of the unbroken and unrestrained presence of Jesus requires that we pass through the valley of death, not just its shadow. Heaven is real, and most of us are going to have to die to get there. Referring to heaven as "Glory" has fallen out of use, but perhaps we should revive the term. Going "from strength to strength" (Ps. 84:7) and "from glory to glory" (2 Cor. 3:18) is both cyclical and linear. Our renewed strength and refined glory have a destination—heaven!

Jesus instructed us not to be afraid of those who "kill the body, and after that have no more that they can do" (Luke 12:4). Fear of death is the most common and most senseless fear of Christians. But the great hope of what we will enjoy after physical death should make Christians the most fearless of God's creation. If the worst our enemies (sickness, age, tragedy, persecutors) can do to us is help us take that final step to glory, then we should thank them, not resent them. There is no need to fear or hate those who help us in our pilgrimage.

If the ministry of death is glorious and what is passing away was glorious then "what remains is much more glorious" (2 Cor. 3:7, 11). Referring to life as prone to nightmares does not diminish its beauty or the joys abundant in our pilgrimage, but it does remind us that life's passing glory is nothing compared to resurrection life, when death is plagued and the grave is destroyed (Hos. 13:14). We are not supposed to have an anxious mind about this world or the things in it, for this world will be taken away from us in a moment (Luke 12:20). Therefore, our diligence should be directed to being "rich toward God" (v. 21). Heart follows treasure (v. 34), and if our longing, hope, anticipation, and desire is to be with Jesus, then death is a good thing—it leapfrogs us toward what we want most.

While the process of being transformed into God's image by His Spirit is active in the present (2 Cor. 3:18), it is completed by death. This is why dying to self each day is so important and should cause us to rejoice. Daily deaths, common disappointments, little rejections, surprising rebukes, unexpected failures, and deserved discipline all are part of the "glory to glory" process. When something is taken away from us, such as pride or possessions, we should rejoice. People and circumstances that help us die to self are our friends. Our lives get better the more we lose them. We become stronger the more we die.

MIRASI MUSLIMS OF PAKISTAN (1,714,000; 0.0% EVANGELICAL)

AUGUST 23: PEACE'S KISS

PSALM 85; HOSEA 14; LUKE 13; 2 CORINTHIANS 4

*I*ntimate peace comes from being right with God and with others. When our relationships are harmonious, all hell can break out against us and we still have the internal fortitude to stand strong. In order for righteousness and peace to kiss, mercy and truth must also converge. The psalmist put it this way: "Mercy and truth have met together, righteousness and peace have kissed" (Ps. 85:10). Truth without mercy kills; mercy without truth corrupts. True peace is not attained without both truth and mercy.

In frontier missions the most common reason workers leave the field is conflict with team members, colleagues, or national leaders. It is not persecution or the scorn of the recalcitrant lost that keeps us up at night—it is the tension and friction between those who are yoked to us in ministry. The river of relational conflict has many streams: jealousy, insecurity, rebellious followers, arrogant leaders, competitive peers, diverse vision and personality, poor communication, and many other factors. Any number of issues can create conflict. Only with a wise blend of truth and mercy can our relationships be right and peaceful. Second Corinthians 4:2 gives us excellent counsel on how to preserve the intimacy of peace.

Renounce Hidden Things. Transparency is such a refreshing gift. We owe each other the honor of bringing our thoughts into the light. Because human nature tends to assume the worst or choose the worst possible meaning, we need to have conversations with one another that are grace-oriented in factual integrity. And we need to have these conversations quickly. Keeping short accounts is basic to peaceful relationships.

Do Not Walk in Craftiness. Unfortunately, Christians and Christian organizations are not immune to posturing and politics. Our relationships need to become simpler, not more complex. Much of what passes for relational skill is simply manipulation, and manipulation is the Devil's work. Being guileless is a lost discipline. We choose to be crafty when we could choose to be simple, unguarded, and vulnerable. This choice is costly, as the guileless are often misunderstood to be ambitious.

Do Not handle God's Word Deceitfully. Those who know the Word of God best are often those who twist it most skillfully. No minister of the gospel is exempt from wrenching a proof text out of context in self-defense. We must ruthlessly serve the Scriptures—not enslave them.

Peace is in our hands. If we walk in mercy and truth, peace will kiss us.

BRAHMIN, TELUGU HINDUS OF INDIA (1,128,000; 0.0% EVANGELICAL)

PRAY THAT CHRISTIANS FROM AROUND THE WORLD WOULD WORK TOGETHER TO REACH THE BRAHMIN, TELUGU AND THAT THE BRAHMAN, TELUGU WOULD BE JOINED TO THE BODY OF CHRIST (JOHN 17:20-23).

AUGUST 24: JOYLESS OR JOYFUL?

PSALM 86; JOEL 1; LUKE 14; 2 CORINTHIANS 5

*N*o one is as miserable as the half-hearted disciple. Missionaries, ministers, and Christians can be the most miserable of the joyless. Joy is linked to a united heart, and when the heart is divided joy withers away (Joel 1:12). When God is worshiped poorly, joy and gladness are cut off from the house of God (v. 16). Life is worship, and when ministry is half-hearted there is no joy in our labor and no joy in our times of corporate worship. Joy comes from robust, full commitments, not ordinary half measures. Joy comes from carrying your own cross and forsaking all you have (Luke 14:26–27, 33). Joy comes from a full, united heart.

Joy Comes from a United Heart (Ps. 86:11). Reverence has long been confused with sobriety. The reverent heart gives Jesus everything and is rewarded with bliss. Philip Doddridge put it this way: "Now rest my long-divided heart! Fixed on this blissful center, rest; here have I found, a nobler part. Here heavenly pleasures fill my heart."[3] Energy spent exalting self or enjoying sin to make ourselves happy is wasted energy, for it steadily saddens. A heart devoted to making God happy brings constant joy.

Joy Comes When We Praise with All Our Hearts (Ps. 86:12). A divided heart and a legalistic heart bear the same fruit: joylessness. Praise is the antidote to legalism. The joyous people in the Bible were always full of praise for God and His works. They praised with singing, psalms, dancing, clapping, shouting, drums, cymbals, and organs. It is hard to be dour, sour, and legalistic when your heart is devoted to praise.

Joy Comes from Seeking God with a Whole Heart (Ps. 119:10). The pursuit of God enriches us. Spiritual adrenaline kicks in when we follow the One who is the fountain of all joy. As we trace His steps we inhale His fragrance, and it intoxicates our spirits and makes us giddy at the soul level. His joy inexpressible and full of glory causes us to rejoice and makes us hungry for more.

Joy Comes from Hiding God's Word in Our Hearts (Ps. 119:11). The Devil twists obedience into a discipline performed for obscure reasons to little advantage. What a tragedy when we view obedience to God's Word as anything other than a means to joy. A warm rush of pleasure surges through our being when we obey God's Word. The more difficult the obedience, the more our soul rejoices. Obedience is joy, but in order for our "joy to be full" (John 15:11), we must wholeheartedly reverence, praise, seek, and obey our precious Jesus.

LAK MUSLIMS OF IRAN (1,250,000; 0.0% EVANGELICAL)

PRAY THAT THE HEARTS OF THE LAK WOULD BE LIKE GOOD SOIL,
READY TO HEAR THE GOSPEL AND TO RESPOND
(MATT. 7:1-8, 18-23).

AUGUST 25: LATTER RAIN

PSALM 87; JOEL 2; LUKE 15; 2 CORINTHIANS 6

*W*e all long for another great outpouring of the Holy Spirit. Though the church age was inaugurated at Pentecost when God unleashed the Holy Spirit in the world in a new and powerful dimension, we know that God has promised the former and latter rain (Joel 2:23). If Peter's Pentecost was the former rain, surely there is yet a latter rain to come—one last great universal outpouring of the Holy Spirit on all flesh. (v. 28) Before that great and terrible day of the Lord (v. 11), before Jesus comes back, there will be one more great shower of blessing, one more massive harvest of souls. Joel, however, reminds us that this outpoured Spirit is preceded by several critical factors: God's day of judgment (vv. 1, 11), God's people wholeheartedly returning to Him (v. 12), men and women who "rend [their] hearts and not [their] garments" (v. 13), communal fasts and sacred assemblies (vv. 15–16), and spiritual leaders who intercede (v. 17). We long for one last outpouring of the Spirit that results in spiritual harvest, but this is not something to wait for passively—it must be pursued.

All of God's people must come together for one final latter rain, yet spiritual leadership has a critical role to play. Joel puts it this way: "Let the priests, who minister to the LORD, weep between the porch and the altar" (v. 17). Having the position of a leader in missions tends to numb a person over time to an appropriate angst and longing for what the followers do not have. As we enter the presence of Jesus, do we weep for what we do not experience of Him? Are we heartbroken over the shallowness of our spiritual children? Great outpourings of the Spirit over history have always followed the anguished longing of intercessors for more of Jesus.

Outpourings of the Spirit always bring a heightened revelation and glorification of Jesus. The Spirit's work is to magnify Jesus. Mission ministry is revival's byproduct, not its goal. When the Spirit is unleashed, He glorifies Jesus. Baptisms of the Spirit are further steps into the knowledge of God, whereby Jesus becomes more real to the soul. When Jesus is real to us, that reality is so magnificent that we cannot contain it or restrict it to ourselves; we are compelled to tell others. The reason that outpourings (fillings, baptisms) of the Spirit always affect the tongue (boldness, prophecy, speaking in tongues, Spirit-empowered speech) is because Jesus has grown so large within us that we must either broadcast Him or burst. When we want Jesus for others so badly that we weep for it, God will "pity His people" (v. 18) and send the latter rain.

DHOFARI MUSLIMS OF OMAN (92,000; 0.4% EVANGELICAL)

PRAY FOR THE PEACE THAT RESULTS WHEN MEN AND WOMEN ARE RECONCILED WITH GOD (JOHN 14:27). PRAY FOR MEN AND WOMEN OF PEACE (LUKE 10:6) AMONG THE DHOFARI.

AUGUST 26: GODLY SORROW

PSALM 88; JOEL 3; LUKE 16; 2 CORINTHIANS 7

*T*here is a benefit to being separated from friends and loved ones. Jesus sometimes rotates our attention away from what is good to help us become spiritually mature. "Loved one and friend You have put far from me, and my acquaintances into darkness" (Ps. 88:18). Sometimes that good thing or good friend is returned; sometimes it is replaced with another good thing.

No infant enjoys being weaned. I was preaching in the bush of northern Kenya once and watched a tribal mother anoint her breast with cow manure in order to convince her insistent child not to suckle. The weaning worked but not without some wailing. God weans His children from good things to develop spiritual maturity but it is still not enjoyable. Obedient service to Jesus can take us away from our friends and family both physically and emotionally. Sometimes those closest to us do not understand our obedience (this was true for Jesus' family), which can cause them to distance themselves from us. We were intended to live in community, and when our obedience causes relational drift, God gives us new friends and spiritual families to embrace. The sorrow of loneliness purges, simplifies, and points us to Jesus.

Some lessons are learned only under duress. The psalmist prayed, "Make me understand the way of Your precepts" (Ps. 119:27). Behind the request was the recognition that we must often learn through adversity. Ease is good for many things but learning is not one of them. Loneliness positions us to hear from Jesus, away from the din of other voices. Paul stated that godly sorrow is "not to be regretted" (2 Cor. 7:10) because it produces benefits such as diligence, zeal, and vindication (v. 11). Loneliness can lead to focus, sanctification, channeled energy, renewed reverence, appropriate longing, passion, and ultimately the Lord's public endorsement. There is a time to be surrounded by family and friends, and there is a time to stand alone and be deepened by the sorrow of separation—both give life.

When obedience leads to loneliness, this leads to greater affection. Not only do we feel closer to Jesus when we feel farther from everyone else, but He has greater joy over the spiritual depth this develops in us. God cannot love us more, but He can have greater joy when our sorrow leads us to look, think, and act more like Him. It is by entering the loneliness of God that we encounter His companionship most deeply.

MOCHI MUSLIMS OF PAKISTAN (3,326,000; 0.0% EVANGELICAL)

PRAY BELIEVERS AMONG THE MOCHI WOULD PROCLAIM THE MESSAGE OF THE GOSPEL CLEARLY AND WOULD MAKE THE MOST OF EVERY OPPORTUNITY GOD PLACES BEFORE THEM (COL. 4:2-5).

AUGUST 27: UNPROFITABLE SERVANTS

PSALM 89; AMOS 1; LUKE 17; 2 CORINTHIANS 8

A word of thanks is misplaced when we give it to someone who is doing their duty for God. Jesus reminds us, "When you have done all those things which you are commanded, say, 'We are unprofitable servants. We have done what was our duty to do'" (Luke 17:10). The church makes a grave error when it lauds the obedience of the missionary over the faithfulness of the church layperson. When God's people laud each other for "crossing land and sea to make one convert" they not only misunderstand Christian obedience (precious regardless of geography), they also propel to folly the person who is thanked. For if a person is thanked often enough by others he begins to demand etiquette from God, and God refuses to be reduced to the civilities of His servants. God refuses to thank us for what He has commanded us to do.

Rather than thank us, Jesus invites us to share in the reproach He experiences. Our deep insecurity compels us to seek praise, while Jesus' complete security empowers us to open ourselves to scorn. We dread the reproach of people, and that is the reason so many Muslims who have trusted in Christ have come to Him through a dream or a vision. In order to follow Jesus, a Muslim must endure unimaginable lost. Loss of family, employment, shelter, esteem, children, nationality, and even life are not uncommon. Dreams and visions are more usual in the salvation journey of Muslims than signs and wonders. Muslims know God is all-powerful—they have no problem believing He can do anything—but they are not prepared to carry shame. People in Muslim cultures need reassurance that they will not walk through intense reproach alone. Many of them have come to the brink of redemption and hesitated because they could not bear the thought of the shame and reproach from the community. When Jesus appears to Muslims in visions, He assures them of His presence, not His power. He tells the seeker on the brink of unbearable scorn: "When you pass through the waters I will be with you. . . . When you walk through the fire you will not be burned" (Isa. 43:2).

God does not thank—He rewards. When we obey, which is simply our duty and nothing to be commended for, Jesus rewards us, inviting us into the reproach He experiences. Human wisdom seeks commendation. The beautiful lowliness of God embraces reproach.

HADI HINDUS OF INDIA (1,116,000; 0.0% EVANGELICAL)

PRAY THAT THE HADI WILL UNDERSTAND THAT HOPE FOR FORGIVENESS AND ACCEPTANCE
WITH GOD ARE AVAILABLE ONLY THROUGH JESUS' WORK ON THE CROSS
(1 COR. 1:18).

The quicker we surrender to Jesus, the better. Mercy, which is God's best for us no matter how much it hurts, is so satisfying if we will surrender to it. We tend to unwittingly fight God's mercy; we resist the very thing that would deliver and satisfy. The psalmist prayed: "Satisfy us early with Your mercy, that we may rejoice and be glad all our days!" (Ps. 90:14) So many disciples struggle to surrender to mercy. If only we could learn the benefit of early surrender: a deep gladness and relief of soul whereby Jesus has made us glad (v. 15). Gladness is something God does for us, not a pathetic effort on our part to be happy. When God makes us glad (v. 16), His glory makes us beautiful. When we try to make ourselves happy, we make ourselves ugly.

Mercy is accessed by surrender. God wants to help us by taking away whatever limits us. We tend to pour energy and hope into ministries or projects that eventually turn into self-made prisons. God wants to satisfy us with mercy by removing our idols, but we are reluctant to let go, for the comfort our "prison" affords us, for our invested sweat equity, and for the shame of a project closing before we planned. Jesus recognizes His competition in our hearts—the "one thing" more dear to us than He (Luke 18:22)—and He mercifully goes after that idol. The sooner we surrender, the better it will be—yet we foolishly prolong the struggle.

When we cry "Son of David, have mercy" (v. 38), it is a prayer of surrender: a prayer that asks God to remove the thing that hinders us and to bestow the thing that satisfies us. Both are mercies. We must surrender to both. To have gladness all our days we must surrender to God's mercy. Early in the day we should surrender poor attitudes. Early in life we should surrender control. Early in ministry we should surrender ambition. The earlier we surrender, the happier we will be. The most enduring prisons are the ones we build around ourselves. God, in His great mercy delivers us from the good things that bind us. It is a relief to surrender good dreams, well-intentioned ministries, and altruistic efforts to Jesus. Our satisfaction and gladness are not found in great accomplishment but in daily surrender.

BEDOUIN, LEVANTINE MUSLIMS OF SYRIA (88,600; 0.0% EVANGELICAL)

PRAY THAT THE BELIEVERS AMONG THE BEDOUIN, LEVANTINE WILL ENDURE PERSECUTION IN A CHRISTLIKE MANNER AND WILL GIVE THEIR LIVES FOR THE SAKE OF THE GOSPEL IF NECESSARY (1 PETER 2:21-23).

AUGUST 29: RUTHLESS JESUS

PSALM 91; AMOS 3; LUKE 19; 2 CORINTHIANS 10

*J*esus is ruthless. He must rule over all . . . all of me, all the earth, all creation, every atom, every galaxy . . . all things must be subject to Him. He is the constant potter, shaping, cleansing, straightening, completing, and steadily bringing us to fuller life by forming us into His image. He must have every part of us, and He is absolutely intolerant of any rebellion. We do not naturally want to be submissive (Luke 19:14), nor do we actually think we need to be. We tend to judge ourselves by ourselves (2 Cor. 10:12), something Jesus does not allow. He insists that we compare ourselves to Him.

Jesus Ruthlessly Exposes Pride. There are two warring convictions inside our hearts. The flesh insists that we do not need help, that we can make it in our own strength, that we really are not that bad, and that we deserve mercy and favor. The Spirit furiously refutes this self-deception and constantly convicts. The forces within us are angry with each other. D. L. Moody thought that a mad sinner was better than a sleepy one. Moody said of Naaman: "First he lost his temper, then his pride, then his leprosy."[4] This is often the journey to conversion. The ruthlessness of Jesus does not allow anyone to be self-satisfied.

Jesus Ruthlessly Forms the Divine Image. God is not a moderate. Moderation is praised as a virtue, but God is balanced by seemingly opposite passions: He is completely loving and completely just. He will ruthlessly break a person down and then, just as ruthlessly, build that person back up. God is forgiving and patient, slow to anger and abounding in mercy, *and* He also slays His enemies (Luke 19:27).

When Jesus sets to work on a person, He does not rest or cease but casts down every argument, brings every thought into captivity, and punishes all disobedience. God uses His authority for edification, not destruction (2 Cor. 10:8), but edification is often a painful process. Temples are not cleansed until things and people are driven out (Luke 19:45).

We Respond Radically. What God does in people's hearts is so profound that it forces the proclamation: "The LORD has spoken! Who can but prophesy?" (Amos 3:8). When God is at work, either we open our mouths and declare His glory, or the stones will cry out (Luke 19:40). We do not proclaim Him widely because we have not encountered Him powerfully. We are mute because we are moderate. When Jesus is joyfully received, we will respond immoderately like Zacchaeus (Luke 19:8). Biblical balance requires radical responses to Jesus. This is the peace of heaven (v. 38).

MOGHAL MUSLIMS OF PAKISTAN (1,097,000; 0.0% EVANGELICAL)

PRAY THAT GOD WOULD RAISE UP MISSIONARIES FROM ALL OVER THE WORLD TO WORK
TOGETHER TO PLANT THE CHURCH AMONG THE MOGHAL
(MATT. 9:37).

*P*eople love to worship—we were created for this purpose. Unfortunately, we often worship fool-ishly. We love rituals, rhythms, and regularity because they comfort us. Though God designed us to worship, He did not intend that we should glorify worship. Worship is a means to love and glorify Jesus; it is a means, not an end. When worship is worshiped, Jesus is diminished—and nothing must diminish the glory of God, not even worship.

"Come to Bethel and transgress," the prophet called. "At Gilgal multiply transgressions. Bring your sacrifices every morning, your tithes every three days. Offer a sacrifice of thanksgiving with leaven, proclaim and announce the freewill offerings; for this you love" (Amos 4:4–5). Amos pointed out that people have a tendency to fall in love with worship, which becomes sin.

When Worship Covers Rebellion, It Is Sin. We cannot live in unconfessed or habitual sin and then trot over to church or small group or family devotions to sing and lift our hands in praise without such hypocrisy damaging our souls and irritating Jesus. Sometimes the most pious people can be the most bitter. God is not impressed with those whose faithfulness in morning prayer and Bible reading is eclipsed only by their consistently poor attitude, assassinating tongue, or hidden hate.

When Worship Is Used as a Drug, It Is Sin. Worship is not supposed to make us feel good. While worship is certainly satisfying, if we make our satisfaction the aim of worship we have made it an idol. We have diminished the worth of Jesus and treated worship as an over-the-altar drug. Worship is not about us; it is about Jesus. If we worship only when we feel like it or in order to feel better, we demonstrate that Jesus is worthy only of occasional adoration. We are called to worship Jesus because of who He is, and the purest worship is not based on feelings or emotions. We worship because of who God is, not because of what we feel or hope to feel.

When Worship Is Used to Gain Attention, It Is Sin. Some people lift their hands, sing loudly, and jump around at the front of the church, or lead worship in such a way that the Father turns His head away. He is insulted when we offer to others what we should present only to Him. It is like a woman disrobing for someone besides her husband. On the other hand, some people refuse to lift their hands, to exercise a prophetic gift, or involve any of their emotions in worship. This, too, is sin. It is like a husband who refuses to show his wife affection because he is embarrassed for others to see how much he loves her.

TARKHAN SIKHS OF INDIA (1,089,000; 0.0% EVANGELICAL)

PRAY THAT THE TARKHAN SIKHS WOULD FEEL AND KNOW THE BURDEN OF SIN AND WOULD COME TO JESUS FOR FORGIVENESS AND SALVATION (MATT. 11:28-30).

AUGUST 31: ADORNED

PSALM 93; AMOS 5; LUKE 21; 2 CORINTHIANS 12

*H*oliness is beautiful, and God goes to great lengths to beautify His people. Lowliness is beautiful, and God uses extreme measures to help His people be lowly. Holiness and lowliness are insepa-rable; it is impossible to lack one and have the other. God uses unusual methods to keep us lowly. He sends thorns in the flesh and messengers of Satan to buffet us (2 Cor. 12:7), and He makes us weak in order to perfect His strength (v. 9). Lowliness seems to be untenable to a person who is naturally strong. It would be nice if we could trust our strengths, but human folly gets in the way so God must put limits on us. He guards our strengths by limiting their effectiveness. Usually this means we are missing a crucial piece of the puzzle, which God provides through someone we do not like or someone weak or someone surprising. Enforced dependency on others keeps us humble, and humility adorns us with God's beauty for He is eminently lowly.

Only the humble can stay holy. When we try to be holy through our own efforts this invariably leads to hypocrisy. Only those who know they cannot be holy in their own strength have any hope of it. In order for holiness to adorn God's house (Ps. 93:5), His people must recognize they are not holy and cannot make themselves so—holiness is a gift God gives to the humble. We sanctify ourselves (we discipline ourselves to stay away from what is vile), but our efforts simply position us before God for cleansing. He makes us holy; we cannot make ourselves holy. The beauty of human temples is based on their interiors (Luke 21:5); they are adorned from a purity that originates within. Nothing is as ugly as a beautiful woman or handsome man who acts vainly or selfishly. Nothing is as beautiful as a broken woman or man who is lowly and holy before Jesus.

In these last days, Jesus is determined to adorn His people. Beautification requires time, and for us it requires patience. We forget just how ugly we are, how deeply pride and sin are woven into our being and thinking. Jesus is committed to the beauty process, but it will be a painful one. We must want holiness badly enough to endure the scrubbing. Jesus promises that at the end of a patient process not a hair of our head will be lost (Luke 21:18). However, that promise is given with others: You will be persecuted and imprisoned (v. 12), you will be betrayed and killed (v. 16), and you will be hated by all (v. 17). The older we get and the more we suffer, the worse we look on the outside . . . but the more we shine on the inside.

BEDOUIN, RUARHA MUSLIMS OF ALGERIA (69,200; 0.0% EVANGELICAL)

PRAY THAT GOD WOULD UNVEIL THE CROSS AND WOULD REMOVE THE VEIL ON THE MINDS AND SPIRITS OF THE BEDOUIN, RUARHA (2 COR. 3:16-17).

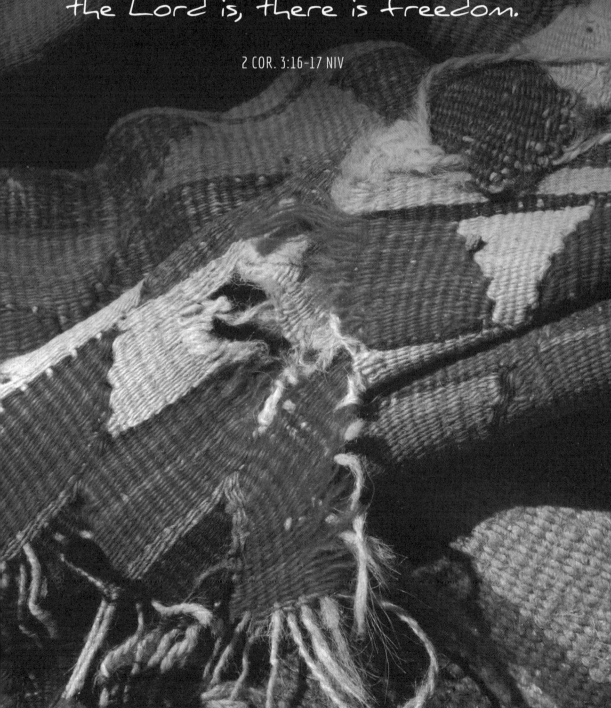

Whenever anyone turns to the Lord, the veil is taken away. Now the Lord is the Spirit, and where the Spirit of the Lord is, there is freedom.

2 COR. 3:16-17 NIV

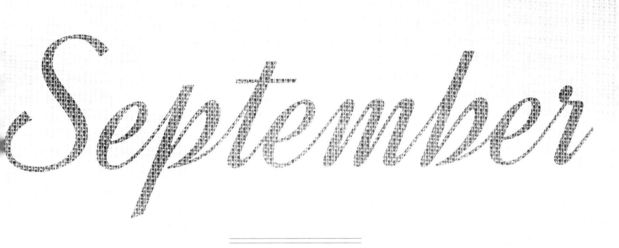

September

"GOD'S AUTHORITY ON EARTH ALLOWS US TO DARE TO GO
TO ALL THE NATIONS. HIS AUTHORITY IN HEAVEN GIVES US OUR
ONLY HOPE OF SUCCESS. AND HIS PRESENCE WITH US
LEAVES US NO OTHER CHOICE.

—*John Stott*

SEPTEMBER 1: SIFTED LIKE WHEAT

PSALM 94; AMOS 6; LUKE 22; 2 CORINTHIANS 13

*T*he expression "live dead" is just another way of saying "die to self" or "live a crucified life." To live dead is not new. We are simply applying the principle of self-denial in a frontier missions context. The problem with taking up the challenge to live dead is that all who do so fail, and fail miserably. Somehow, it is pompous to try to live the crucified life. Those who attempt to live dead must be vigilant that they do not start to think they are better than other believers. As soon as the crucified life becomes a competition, it is corrupted, and nothing stinks to high heaven as much as self-righteousness.

Those Who Think They Are the Greatest Fall the Hardest. Jesus' disciples had some basis for their assumptions of grandeur. After all, He had chosen them, He had used them in ministry (signs and wonders), they were more intimate with Him than anyone else on earth, and they had forsaken all to follow Him. Those who are intimate with Jesus and attempt to follow Him to the cross are the most susceptible to spiritual pride. The longer we attempt to live dead, the more prone we are to hypocrisy.

Those Who Make the Biggest Claims Fail Most Publicly. Peter declared his willingness to go to prison and die with Jesus on the same night he swore up and down that he did not know Jesus (Luke 22:33–34). Those who announce they are living the crucified life tend to disown Jesus by their bragging words, attitudes, and actions. Consecration claims make us vulnerable to the Devil's attacks. Jesus saw the discrepancy between Peter's boasts and his capacity and knew the Devil would press into that inconsistency in an effort to destroy Peter.

If it is dangerous to try to live dead, it is more dangerous not to try at all for fear of failing. Failing (a public exposure of our lack of righteousness) is intrinsic to living dead. Self-denial must include the public shame of being exposed for who we really are: stupid sinners, unable to make ourselves good. Those who want to avoid putting their weakness on display live a different form of pride, but it is still pompous. Those who attempt to live dead know they will fail miserably, even publicly, and that the humiliation of being inept and weak is part of the crucified life. It takes a unique form of courage to attempt something you know you will fail at, something that guarantees humiliation. The good news is that Jesus prays for us. If we are willing to be humiliated, He is willing to restore us and make our journey helpful to others. If we can live dead by failing, so can they.

MOHAJIR MUSLIMS OF PAKISTAN (428,000; 0.0% EVANGELICAL)

PRAY THAT BELIEVERS AMONG THE MOHAJIR WOULD BE SET FREE FROM A SPIRIT OF FEAR OF WHAT MAY COME AND WOULD BOLDLY PROCLAIM THE TRUTH OF THE GOSPEL (2 TIM. 1:6-8).

SEPTEMBER 2: UNPOPULAR

PSALM 95; AMOS 7; LUKE 23; GALATIANS 1

*W*here did we get the idea that the gospel makes people happy or that preaching God's Word pleases the unconverted? The gospel offends far more people than it delights. For the Good News to have relevance it must be contrasted with sin and judgment and the wrath of God. The gospel points out to every person that he is wrong and must change. This Word from heaven does not sit well with the arrogant of the earth. If God's voice hardens many hearts, what makes us think our voice will soften many hearts? "Today, if you will hear His voice: do not harden your hearts, as in the rebellion" the psalmist said (95:7–8). The implication is that God's voice makes many people rebellious. We assume it is enough for God to speak—it is not! People must respond, submit, and obey the Word of God . . . and most do not.

We who share the gospel must be committed to a life of human displeasure, satisfied that the delight of God far outweighs the scorn of people. As Paul reminded the Galatians, if in "this present evil age" we seek to please people we cannot be bondservants of Christ (1:4, 8–10). This pleasing or upsetting people is in the context of preaching a difficult gospel. When we consistently represent God, "the land is not able to bear all [our] words" (Amos 7:10), and we face incredible pressure not to prophesy in Bethel (v. 13), to regulate and moderate what we say. When we run into the anger of those who resent the Good News—and we will—we must be an Amos, not a Pilate. Amos responded to pressure by saying: "I was no prophet, nor was I a son of a prophet. . . . Then the LORD took me as I followed the flock, and the LORD said to me: 'Go, prophesy to My people Israel'" (vv. 14–15). And Amos did just that. On the other hand, Pilate responded to pressure by letting disgruntled people decide what he should do with Jesus (Luke 23:23–25). Do not let people tell you what to do with Jesus! Do not allow those who feel guilty and angry because of the gospel frame or alter your message.

Bearing the cross after Jesus (Luke 23:26) means, in part, that we must be hated as He was hated. We are separated and called through grace that He might be revealed in us (Gal. 1:16). That will make people mad. We must rid ourselves of the notion that preaching the gospel and bearing the image of Christ will make us popular. Those who faithfully steward the gospel will be polarizing and unpopular.

QASSAB MUSLIMS OF INDIA (1,087,000; 0.0% EVANGELICAL)

PRAY FOR THE WORD OF GOD IN WRITTEN, ORAL, MUSICAL, AND DRAMATIC FORMS TO BE TRANSLATED AND TO RISE AMONG THE QASSAB
(ISA. 55:10–11).

SEPTEMBER 3: JESUS THEORY

PSALM 96; AMOS 8; LUKE 24; GALATIANS 2

Abiding Helps Us Understand. While walking on the Emmaus road, two disciples discussed the strange events surrounding the death and resurrection of Jesus. "While they conversed and reasoned . . . Jesus Himself drew near and went with them" (Luke 24:15). The event is obviously literal, but it also has spiritual significance. Jesus does not abandon us in the reflective process; He walks with us as we wrestle with the difficulties of life in the faith. The Scriptures burn into our hearts as Jesus opens them to us (v. 32), but it is His presence that illumines our minds. Jesus revealed Himself to the two disciples "in the breaking of bread" (v. 35). They asked Him to abide with them (v. 29), and as a result they gained understanding.

Doubt Makes Us Foolish; Belief Makes Us Wise. The nonspiritual academic is at a disadvantage when his skepticism leads him to doubt. Today's hero is the one who doubts everything. Biblical heroes were those who trusted God for what they did not understand. Biblical mysteries are not things we cannot possibly understand; they are eternal and beautiful realities God gives by revelation. Biblically, doubt and skepticism are not virtues but are handicaps. The more we doubt, the more we become blind. The more we trust, the better we see. The burning presence of Jesus in our hearts clears the fog of wrong thinking in our heads and makes us wise.

A Jesus-centered epistemology (how we know what we know and distinguish justified belief from opinion) posits that wisdom and understanding are byproducts of intimacy, not intelligence. Wisdom through the ages is derived from the nearness of Jesus. When Jesus abides in us and we in Him, we have the resources to understand all things. Whether or not we draw from those resources is up to us. As we journey down our confusing roads, we have the opportunity to walk with Jesus. His presence empowers us to make sense of the world. Abiding in Him causes our hearts to burn, our eyes to be opened, and our understanding to be empowered. On the Emmaus road, the two travelers asked Jesus an unintentionally humorous question: "Are You the only stranger in Jerusalem, and have You not known the things which happened there in these days?" (24:18). Jesus must have smiled to Himself. Then, as now, He is actually the only one who *does* know—and it is by walking with Him that we come to understand.

KHORASANI MUSLIM TURKS OF IRAN (858,000; 0.0% EVANGELICAL)

PRAY THAT GOD WOULD POUR OUT HIS SPIRIT ON THE KHORASANI AND THAT THEY WOULD SEE DREAMS AND VISIONS OF JESUS. PRAY THAT THEY WOULD BE POWERFULLY SAVED AND EMPOWERED TO BE HIS WITNESSES (JOEL 2:28-32).

SEPTEMBER 4: UNDIGNIFIED

PSALM 97; AMOS 9; JOHN 1; GALATIANS 3

*U**ndignified for Jesus.** If mountains melt like wax in God's presence (Ps. 97:5), what makes us think we can restrain our emotions when He reveals Himself to us? Yet people today prize little as highly as public composure. God is not a fan of pride, whatever its disguise, and we can be proud of our restraint. It takes an uncommon lowliness to respond freely to God with our emotions. David was beloved of God for many things, unrestrained and emotional response in worship being one of them (2 Sam. 6:16).

Undignified for the Gospel. Bearing witness of Jesus often requires that we forfeit dignity. We have to be willing to lose face so that others might hear and understand who He is. He became a curse for us (Gal. 3:13), so why should we not be willing to become despised for the sake of others? If Jesus was willing to hang naked on a cross, a spectacle across time, should we not be willing to have our vulnerabilities, sins, and limitations exposed? Our tolerance for indignity is shockingly low. We love to help others from a position of strength, as a dignified benefactor. We are less willing to help from a position of weakness and shame.

Undignified for Ourselves. John the Baptist's confession of who he was not, "I am not the Christ" (John 1:20), was just as important as his confession of who he was, "a voice crying" (v. 23). Both confessions were lowly. It is not until we are comfortable with and thankful for our limitations that God empowers us to be used in our strengths. Our longing for significance so easily leads us to present ourselves as stronger than we really are. We covet the respect of our peers, and we fear they will reject or discard us if they know about our indignities. This pretense becomes a burden over time. It is a constant pressure to want others to think well of us and to think we are in control of life. It is excruciating when sins or circumstances strip away our veneer of capacity and our true, limited self is revealed. It is also liberating.

We need to be undignified for our own sakes. This frees us. When we have nothing to hide from others, we are invulnerable to the prison of their expectations. Walking in the light requires a life without secrets, a life that embraces indignity for the freedom we find on the other side of shame.

MAHRA MUSLIMS OF OMAN (66,600; 0.0% EVANGELICAL)

PRAY THAT CHRISTIANS FROM AROUND THE WORLD WOULD WORK TOGETHER TO REACH THE MAHRA AND THAT THE MAHRA WOULD BE JOINED TO THE BODY OF CHRIST (JOHN 17:20-23).

SEPTEMBER 5: TRUE FRIENDSHIP

PSALM 98; OBADIAH; JOHN 2; GALATIANS 4

*R*eal friends hurt each other. Paul asked the Galatians if he had become their enemy because he told them the truth (Gal. 4:16). Obadiah pointed out that brothers who do not help each other will be judged harshly by God and the opposite of the Golden Rule will kick in: If you do not help, you will not be helped (Obad. 11). Truth is a primary way faithful friends wound each other—it is help that hurts.

Enemies That Tell the Truth Serve as Friends. Jesus reminded us that something is wrong with us when everybody speaks well of us. The human psyche needs accusers as much as it needs supporters. An absence of either damages the soul. If no one around us opposes our ideas, we soon succumb to the delusion that all our ideas are wise and all our ways are wonderful. In the end, voices that cry out against us are voices of kindness. Often our enemies are more truthful than our friends. If we have the humility to listen to our critics, there is often truth, or a measure of truth, in their accusations. Wise people listen carefully to those who do not like them, to those who do not agree with them, for their observations can refine both their arguments and their character. Enemies serve us by attacking our weaknesses.

Friends Who Do Not Tell Us the Truth Serve as Enemies. We need friends who lovingly tell us what we do not know or cannot see about ourselves. Friends who leave us to our folly, in the end, hate us. If we do not love our friends enough to disagree with them, to confront them, then we have not loved them at all. If we do not tell our lost friends that they are lost, we have committed the most damaging of hate crimes. If friendship evangelism means that we do not speak truth about the gospel, hell, heaven, and repentance for weeks, months, and years, because we are waiting for "just the right moment," we have loved too little, not too much.

Telling people they have sinned and rebelled against God is love speech. The Devil bullies us into silence, twisting what is loving proclamation into "hate speech." But we must love the lost enough to withstand their anger at our observations. We must love both friend and enemy enough to bear their wrath. People do not enjoy being loved in this tough way; yet it is a necessary form of love that helps others despite their wrath. Real love wounds others in the short term for the hope of long-term life.

MUSSALI MUSLIMS OF PAKISTAN (2,321,000; 0.0% EVANGELICAL)

PRAY THAT THE HEARTS OF THE MUSSALI WOULD BE LIKE GOOD SOIL, READY TO HEAR THE GOSPEL AND TO RESPOND (MATT. 7:1-8, 18-23).

SEPTEMBER 6: BECOMING LESS

PSALM 99; JONAH 1; JOHN 3; GALATIANS 5

*G*od's presence compels, fuels, and demands mission. We cannot claim to be intimate with Jesus and not be passionately stirred for the nations. To know anything about Jesus is to know that He yearns to be glorified by every tribe, tongue, people, and nation. This knowledge is a fire of love because He knows our highest satisfaction is in His deepest praise. A Christian who is not burdened, prayerful, and agonized over people who do not know Jesus is an incomplete and shortsighted Christian.

In our folly we would rather relinquish God's presence than spread His love to those we fear or resent (Jonah 1). Jonah exemplifies a common adverse reaction toward those who resist Jesus. Yet Jesus is unwavering in His mission, and when we understand His aims while refusing to join with those aims we lose intimacy with Him. We experience a tempest in our souls (Jonah 1:12) and a disturbance in heaven. We would rather people refuse Jesus than suffer so they might receive Him.

In order for Jesus to increase we must decrease, but we are always reluctant to become less. Interestingly, we shrink in importance the more people come to know Jesus because the more our disciples know Jesus the less they need or notice us. Though this should cause us to celebrate, our natural selves do not like to be diminished. It is even possible that some of our reluctance to reach the unreached is because the more they are reached, the less we are needed. The more mature the indigenous church, the less-necessary the missionary. Contrary to what the Spirit intends, sending churches tend to laud frontier missionaries as heroic. We make missionaries bigger and bigger while God makes them smaller and smaller.

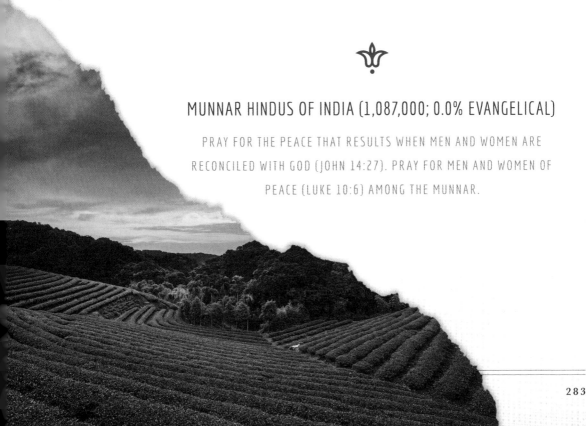

MUNNAR HINDUS OF INDIA (1,087,000; 0.0% EVANGELICAL)

PRAY FOR THE PEACE THAT RESULTS WHEN MEN AND WOMEN ARE RECONCILED WITH GOD (JOHN 14:27). PRAY FOR MEN AND WOMEN OF PEACE (LUKE 10:6) AMONG THE MUNNAR.

SEPTEMBER 7: GOD-MADE

PSALM 100; JONAH 2; JOHN 4; GALATIANS 6

We idolize ourselves. When we think we are "self-made," we have in effect created an idol of ourselves. Of all forms of idolatry, self-worship is the most foolish, for in worshipping self we "forsake our own Mercy" (Jonah 2:8). In other words, we forsake the mercy of God when we glorify ourselves. The Bible is clear that "it is He who has made us, and not we ourselves" (Ps. 100:3); yet we retain large dollops of pride that we are self-made men and women.

God Makes People. Paul wrote, "If anyone thinks himself to be something, when he is nothing, he deceives himself" (Gal. 6:3). We must come to terms with being nothing. We must understand that all the things we enjoy in life and ministry happen because God allows and empowers them. But because we are naturally goal-oriented and we love to measure outcomes, we attribute any good thing that happens in ministry, at least in part, to human effort. Jesus said He has sent us to "reap that for which [we] have not labored; others have labored, and [we] have entered into their labors" (John 4:38). In other words, "Others have done the hard work." Not only has God made us and made us fruitful, but others have made us fruitful as well; we benefit from the sweat and sacrifice of those who have gone before us.

People Unmake Themselves. As God deserves all the credit for establishing people, people deserve all the blame when they "unmake" what He has done. It is as inevitable as it is unfortunate that you and I are overtaken by our own trespasses (Gal. 6:1). We often interpret this verse as referring to grand moral failures, but it also includes pride, hatred, contentions, jealousies, outbursts of wrath, selfish ambitions, dissensions, envy . . . a multitude of less-obvious ugliness (5:19–20). We all unmake ourselves, which is why restoration by "the spiritual" (6:1) should be done gently. It is only a matter of time before we will unmake ourselves and will need a kind and understanding hand to help us up.

God Makes Solutions. God makes people . . . people makes messes . . . and God makes solutions. "The LORD . . . prepared a great fish to swallow Jonah" (Jonah 1:17). This fish was not prepared in a day. Years, possibly decades before Jonah needed help, God picked a little fish egg and sovereignly preserved it day by day, growing it into monstrous size for a specific, divine deliverance. God in His foreknowledge sees our future failings and has already planned our deliverance. We need not fret over our destiny or our deliverance for God has already prepared them both.

BAJELANI MUSLIMS OF IRAQ (58,500; 0.03% EVANGELICAL)

PRAY THAT BELIEVERS AMONG THE BAJELANI WOULD PROCLAIM THE MESSAGE OF THE GOSPEL CLEARLY AND WOULD MAKE THE MOST OF EVERY OPPORTUNITY GOD PLACES BEFORE THEM (COL. 4:2-5).

SEPTEMBER 8: DANGEROUS DECEIT

PSALM 101; JONAH 3; JOHN 5; EPHESIANS 1

*M*ore than fear, more than hate, and almost equal to pride, deceit is a hallmark of the Devil. In order to be completely free of the influence of the Father of Lies, we must be fundamentally and comprehensively true. For those who would bear the image of God, there can be nothing false or deceitful about us. God declares unequivocally through the psalmist: "He who works deceit shall not dwell within my house; he who tells lies shall not continue in my presence" (Ps. 101:7). Deceit banishes us from the presence of God. Followers of Jesus need to avoid all forms of deceit—even the subtle ones.

Exaggeration. Of all the forms of deception, exaggeration is the most common. Public speakers are so prone to this seduction. We hide behind all kinds of justification, excusing ourselves for speaking hyperbolically. We must come to grips with the reality that exaggeration weakens the truth, and over time it undermines the credibility of the speaker. Truth needs no assistance and no varnish. When we exaggerate, we use a tool of the Devil and we cannot assume that it will leave us unharmed.

Flattery. Insecurity has many forms and flattery is one of them. When we praise someone, it is often because we want to be praised. We compliment someone because we want the compliment returned. We praise because for we crave recognition. Self-deprecation is the twin sister of flattery and has the same intention. When we speak poorly of ourselves, it is usually because we long for someone to disagree and affirm us. The root of both flattery and self-deprecation is the desire to be praised. Both are untruthful, even if factual, for their intended outcome is counter to what they present. God has no use and no respect for either of these impostors.

Discrepancy. The psalmist vowed: "I will walk within my house with a perfect heart" (Ps. 101:2). How you deal with your spouse, children, family, and intimate friends is an indicator of your spiritual maturity. It is possible and prevalent for men and women to appear gracious, patient, kind, and respectful in public, while at home they are rude, impatient, mean, and demeaning. This is deceitful, and it is of the Devil. A person of truth is the same in private and public. The greater the discrepancy between our private and public lives, the more we are modeling ourselves after "the angel of light," who is the chief demon. To be like Jesus is to be completely true and to have nothing deceitful in us, about us, or coming out of our mouths.

PASHAYI, SOUTHEAST MUSLIMS OF AFGHANISTAN (192,000; 0.0% EVANGELICAL)

PRAY THAT THE PASHAYI WILL UNDERSTAND THAT HOPE FOR FORGIVENESS AND ACCEPTANCE WITH GOD IS ONLY AVAILABLE THROUGH JESUS' WORK ON THE CROSS (1 COR. 1:18).

SEPTEMBER 9: UNCHANGED

PSALM 102; JONAH 4; JOHN 6; EPHESIANS 2

*G*od does not change. His character does not evolve to accommodate the renaissance or relapses of people. He has ever been merciful and will ever be just. The seemingly harsh God of the New Testament is full of love and compassion. Gentle Jesus, who is coming back with a robe dipped in blood, will consign the wicked to eternal, unrelenting hell. It is the same God and it is the same glory. He will endure. He remains the same (Ps. 102:26). Intriguingly, people are just as offended at God's mercy as they are at His wrath.

Jonah was not fond of the Assyrians, and more than anything in the world he wanted God to destroy them for their heinous crimes. But Jonah, being a prophet, realized that God's center is love and mercy, and he was horrified (angered) at the thought of enemies being pardoned. "I know that You are a gracious and merciful God," Jonah pouted, "slow to anger and abundant in lovingkindness, One who relents from doing harm" (Jonah 4:2). If anyone deserved wrath, it was the Assyrian butchers, but Jonah knew and resented that God would lavish mercy on them.

God's mercy angers us. We have more twisted justice within us than we have Calvary love. God continually expresses mercy to us and we lap it up. At the same time, we do not want others to receive it. We judge others to be unworthy of His mercy. In some cases we would rather die than participate in giving His mercy to others (Jonah 4:3). The issue is not that we are unrealistic about the unconverted; it is that we are dishonest about ourselves. The Assyrians were brutally pagan, lewd, and violent. They deserved God's wrath, but that was not the point. The point was that in God's sight Israel was just as disgusting. We walk to the precipice of disaster if we resent the mercy God lavishes on the wicked for we, too, are wicked. God spares us by divine love.

An unchanging God continues to give mercy to wicked people. In the ages to come He will continue to show the "exceeding riches of His grace in His kindness toward us in Christ Jesus" (Eph. 2:7). Jesus is our peace (v. 14): He reconciles us and the Assyrians, us and the radical Muslim, us and the child abuser, us and the cannibal, us and the rapist—together by the same blood and by the same mercy. Let us rejoice that God would ransom those who have hurt us the most when they repent, for if He cannot have mercy on them He cannot have mercy on us. God does not change over time nor does He change over context. He is always just, always merciful.

BOHRA MUSLIMS OF INDIA (1,083,000; 0.0% EVANGELICAL)

PRAY THAT THE BELIEVERS AMONG THE BOHRA WILL ENDURE PERSECUTION IN A CHRISTLIKE MANNER AND WILL GIVE THEIR LIVES FOR THE SAKE OF THE GOSPEL IF NECESSARY (1 PETER 2:21-23).

SEPTEMBER 10: FOR OTHERS

PSALM 103; MICAH 1; JOHN 7; EPHESIANS 3

*M*uch of what God sovereignly allows or purposes in our lives is for the sake of others. He does not want us to hoard what He does in our lives. He works in us that He might work through us for the sake of others. He wants us to share our pain and our joy not secret them away. He uses our private and personal events to bless and encourage others. We do not need to share details or intimacies that He has reserved for Himself, but we do need to live transparently, an epistle to be read for the benefit of others.

Our Affliction Is for Others. The faithful affliction of God is a merciful kindness that results in our comfort (Ps. 119:74–76). God's tender mercy wounds us and helps to make our hearts blameless. Those who have been mercifully wounded by God are of great benefit to others, for they are softer, humbler, more compassionate, quicker to empathize, and more credible in comfort. When one of God's servants is faithfully afflicted, it is a joy for others to be around that person because only a wounded heart can share certain things that are unshakably true, deep, and lasting. When our lives are touched by God's loving discipline or His purposeful suffering, we can accept it with equanimity because we know it will not only benefit our souls but will also minister to others. Paul reminded the Ephesians: "Do not lose heart at my tribulations for you, which is your glory" (Eph. 3:13)! The cross we bear is not for our sakes alone but also for the sakes of others.

Our Grace Is for Others. Paul wrote to the Ephesians about "the dispensation of the grace of God which was given to me for you" (Eph. 3:2). God had given Paul a revelation into divine mysteries for the express purpose that he would spread these truths as far and wide as possible. When the Spirit reveals something to us, or God by His grace helps us understand a truth, this happens so we can share with others and help them along. We believe in the prophethood of all believers. We believe that what the Spirit reveals (vv. 4–5) should be shared with others both privately and publicly. We frequently grace others in private, but the spiritual gifts are grace gifts that have a significant public function. When we are abiding in Jesus together (family devotions, team meetings, church worship), the Spirit wants us to share grace among the family. When God's Spirit illumines us (with word, prophecy, tongue and interpretation, picture, impression, Scripture verse, or song) in corporate events, He wants us to pass that grace on to others. Glorifying Jesus is the heart of the outpoured Spirit. "The Spirit was not yet given, because Jesus was not yet glorified" (John 7:39). As we seek Jesus and His glory, He graces us with His presence, and grace received must be grace shared.

NAJDI BEDOUIN MUSLIMS OF JORDAN (57,900; 0.01% EVANGELICAL)

PRAY THAT GOD WOULD RAISE UP MISSIONARIES FROM ALL OVER THE WORLD
TO PLANT THE CHURCH TOGETHER AMONG THE NAJDI
(MATT. 9:37).

SEPTEMBER 11: UNIFIED PRISONERS OF THE LORD

PSALM 104; MICAH 2; JOHN 8; EPHESIANS 4

*W*e all serve someone. Those who serve sin and the Devil end up in bondage (John 8:34). Those who serve the Son end up free (v. 36). Paul was ridiculously happy to serve the Lord and considered himself the Lord's prisoner (Eph. 4:1). Imprisoned for and by and with Jesus is not only liberty, it is a calling. Humans do not send us to prison when we are sent for the gospel's sake, God calls us to prison. Therefore, our primary goal is to not escape from prison or seek deliverance from trouble or evacuate from countries that are disintegrating. Our goal is to glorify Jesus and walk worthy of His calling—the call to be His prisoner.

Because Jesus' followers are so reluctant to go to prison, we often fall into sin in order to avoid it. We lie . . . we compromise . . . we fear . . . we betray. Rather than answer the prison call joyfully, we run from it frantically, like Jonah ran from Nineveh. In the process, we hurt our brothers and sisters. We tend to focus on persecution stories that tell of the growth of the church and the maturity of the martyr, but persecution has made just as many Christians into failures as it has made into saints. External pressure and the threat of prison or persecution have turned many believers against each other, and the body of Christ has not helped. We consider persecution and prison exceptional. We either laud the ones who suffer for their exceptional faith or we criticize them for incurring the authorities' attention and wrath. The biblical reality is that suffering is neither heroic nor foolish—it is the Christian way. We should neither celebrate it nor recoil from it; we should simply do it for Jesus' sake.

Paul exhorted those who would be faithful prisoners of the Lord to "keep the unity of the Spirit in the bond of peace" (Eph. 4:3) and "the unity of the faith" (v. 13). The Devil knows that unity is crucial when Jesus' followers are under pressure so he uses pressure to divide believers. When Paul instructed believers not to let the sun go down on their wrath, nor to give place to the Devil (v. 26), it was in the direct context of being "members of one another" (v. 25) and in the immediate context of being the Lord's prisoner, maintaining unity, and "bearing with one another in love" (v. 2). Prison and persecution are biblical norms, and division is the typical human response. God's glory shines brightest when His "prisoners" unite in suffering. Unity is precious enough to fight for, to humble ourselves for, to give up our opinions for, and to suffer for. God uses suffering to bring His people together. He is glorified by united children, which is why the Devil does all he can to divide us.

PASHTUN, NORTHERN MUSLIMS OF AFGHANISTAN (6,600,000; 0.01% EVANGELICAL)

PRAY THAT THE PASHTUN WOULD FEEL AND KNOW THE BURDEN OF SIN AND WOULD
COME TO JESUS FOR FORGIVENESS AND SALVATION
(MATT. 11:28-30).

*W*e have no need to envy any mythical figures, past or present. Neither Ulysses nor Superman has anything on those who are filled with and controlled by the Spirit. Micah 3:8 reminds us that we can be filled with power, justice, and might in order to proclaim God's Word. A priority on verbal proclamation does not diminish the importance and necessity of complementary ministry, even as the priority on as a minister's relationships with God and family do not diminish the importance of that person's vocational activities.

In our obedience to proclaim the gospel to the uttermost parts of the earth, we will experience great resistance and suffering. On the way to fulfill his destiny, Joseph's feet were hurt with fetters, he was laid in irons, and "the word of the LORD tested him" (Ps. 105:18–19). All this is in the context of making "known His deeds among the peoples" (v. 1). The advance of the gospel not only includes but *requires* suffering, which makes God's promises all the more intriguing. He promises that He will not allow anyone to touch His anointed spokespeople, even that they will not suffer harm (vv. 14–15). This seeming dissonance (untouchable yet destined to suffer) is reconciled simply by this: We are indestructible until our time. Both promises of God are true—He will keep us and He will deliver us from trouble—but He will also allow us to hurt, perhaps to endure unimaginable horrors. Both promises should comfort us.

The Promises of Immunity Are Comforting. We can obey God's repeated order "not to fear" because we have superpower shields around our minds, bodies, and spirits. We are indestructible! We can live in the most chaotic countries, the most dangerous inner cities, among the most violent peoples, in the midst of civil war, disaster, and upheaval. We can charge these giants with a giggle because none of them can touch us! We can go to the hardest places with the most inflammatory message because God has guaranteed safe passage.

The Promises of Suffering Are Comforting. Even as God promises protection, He promises suffering. If at any time our immunity is lifted, we can endure the resulting agony with the assurance that He has allowed it to happen. We can be unshakable under duress knowing that a loving Father has allowed it and purposed it. He will take us through or take us to His heavenly home. Either way He will bring His people out "with joy" (v. 43).

RAJPUT, BHATTI HINDUS OF INDIA (1,062,000; 0.9% EVANGELICAL)

PRAY THAT GOD WOULD UNVEIL THE CROSS AND WOULD TAKE AWAY THE VEIL ON THE MINDS AND SPIRITS OF THE RAJPUT, BHATTI (2 COR. 3:16–17).

SEPTEMBER 13: WAR COUNSEL

PSALM 106; MICAH 4; JOHN 10; EPHESIANS 6

*I*n spiritual warfare we must be careful to wait for God's counsel. He wants to deliver us, but if we rely on our own wisdom He will send leanness to our souls (Ps. 106:15). If we will listen to Him in the midst of panic and pressure He promises to "teach us His ways" (Mic. 4:2) and to lead us out (John 10:3). God's counsel and commandments have promises attached to them (Eph. 6:2–3), and these promises are based on enduring principles of spiritual warfare.

Abide. "Be strong in the Lord and the power of His might" (v. 10). The reality of spiritual warfare is that Jesus fights for us from within us. As soon as we think we can take on evil powers and principalities we are doomed. The best way to resist the Devil is to be intimate with Jesus, whose glorious presence terrifies the Devil and his minions. We cannot battle evil unless we are deeply imbedded in Christ.

Prepare. "Take up the whole armor of God" (v. 13). We must train for spiritual warfare. It is foolish to spar with the Enemy unguarded and out of practice. If we do not have the discipline to eat right, exercise, and get up early to linger with Jesus, what foolish audacity makes us think we can battle evil powers in the spiritual realms? Wars are won on the training ground not on the battlefield. Spiritual wars are won before they are fought by those who are spiritually prepared and have multiple weapons. You may wield the sword with excellence, but if you leave your helmet at home you will not last long.

Fight. "Having done all . . . stand" (v. 13). When we are deep in Jesus and have built up our spiritual muscles, the next challenge is endurance. Most battles are not won quickly. We must stand in the breach "at all times" (Ps. 106:3), swinging away, repelling assault after assault. There are no short-cuts; there is nowhere to run. We must stand fast against wave after wave of evil attacks that rush against us. You will be disappointed if you expect short spiritual battles. Most spiritual battles take years, so God's people must stand indefatigable.

Trust. "Above all, [take] the shield of faith" (Eph. 6:16). In this passage of Ephesians 6, Paul repeatedly used strong language: *finally* be strong, *whole* armor, having *done all* stand, *above all* take up faith. In spiritual warfare, above all things we must trust. We must trust that Jesus will give us the endurance to fight on when no respite comes. We must trust Him to prepare us and train us for the challenges to come. We must trust Him to fight for us and from within us when we are overwhelmed and confused. We must trust that He will win.

ZOTT GYPSY MUSLIMS OF UNITED ARAB EMIRATES (56,800, 0.2% EVANGELICAL)

PRAY THAT BELIEVERS AMONG THE ZOTT GYPSIES WOULD BE SET FREE FROM A SPIRIT OF FEAR OF WHAT MAY COME AND BOLDLY PROCLAIM THE TRUTH OF THE GOSPEL

(2 TIM. 1:6–8).

SEPTEMBER 14: THE POWER OF THANKS

PSALM 107; MICAH 5; JOHN 11; PHILIPPIANS 1

The psalmist pleaded, "Oh, that men would give thanks to the LORD for His goodness!" (Ps. 107:8). As with many of God's instructions, giving thanks pleases Him while it also satisfies us. A beautiful mystery in our faith is that fulfillment and satisfaction are directly tied to obedience. The more we worship and give thanks, the more God satisfies our souls. Giving thanks may please the receiver, but it also satisfies the giver. It is important for us to learn the discipline of thanksgiving: We thank God in pleasant situations and we thank Him in adverse situations.

Thanks for Being Hungry. It is a gift of God to experience hunger. Fasting reminds us that only Jesus can satisfy. Daily bread for our bodies reminds us that only the "Bread of Heaven" can "feed us till we want no more"[1] (Ps. 107:9). In life we often find that good things have lost their luster and pleasures no longer allure. This is a gift of God, a message we should receive with thanks. Dissatisfaction is an appeal from heaven's throne for us to turn to the only One who can truly satisfy.

Thanks for Being Little. Micah prophesied that though Bethlehem was "little . . . yet out of you shall come forth to Me the One to be Ruler in Israel" (Mic. 5:2). We should give thanks for being insignificant and limited because God delights to use the weak things of the world to shame the wise. Being little positions us for His greatness. When we are little in our own eyes, mighty God comes forth to rule. He emerges from our weakness and our limitations.

Thanks for Being Sick. Jesus reminded His disciples that the terminal illness of a beloved friend was "not unto death, but for the glory of God" (John 11:4). Some sickness is prolonged so that Jesus might receive greater glory. Most sickness happens not a result of sin but because God wants to do something in the life of the infirm and in the lives of those around that person. When we approach sickness with genuine thanks, it startles both the evil principalities who perversely enjoy suffering and the unconverted who fear it.

Thanksgiving is one of the most underused of Christian weapons. We are moderately obedient to thank God for pleasant things, but woefully silent when we have the opportunity to thank Him for hunger, smallness, and sickness. There is much to be gained for our souls and won for the kingdom when we learn to give thanks in all things, for "this is the will of God in Christ Jesus" for us (1 Thess. 5:18).

PASHTUN, NORTHERN MUSLIMS OF PAKISTAN (23,102,000; 0.0% EVANGELICAL)

PRAY FOR THE WORD OF GOD IN WRITTEN, ORAL, MUSICAL, AND DRAMATIC FORMS TO
BE TRANSLATED AND TO SPREAD AMONG THE PASHTUN
(ISA. 55:10–11).

SEPTEMBER 15: RESURRECTION

PSALM 108; MICAH 6; JOHN 12; PHILIPPIANS 2

*O*ne of the ironies of the crucified life is that it can lead to arrogance. We can be so proud of our sacrifice that we nullify it. Jesus "humbled Himself" in obedience "to the point of death," and made Himself of no reputation (Phil. 2:7–8). In contrast, we often use humility to build our reputations. We want to be known for being unknown. There is a troubling tendency among ministers to use sacrifice and self-denial as a subtle way of "seeking [their] own" (v. 21), a ministerial ambition that needs to be throttled. As my friend Tim Decker wryly says, "We need to die to live dead!"

To appear to deny self and to actually crucify self are two different things. Micah was not impressed with those who were outwardly mortified and inwardly arrogant (6:8) and neither is Jesus. He does not want us to walk right up to the precipice of humility, only to falter through a half-death. Resurrection is real only if death is complete. Make no mistake, resurrection is the goal . . . not death. "Live dead" might be better phrased "live dead live." Crucifixion was not Jesus' ultimate goal—it was resurrection. The cross is meaningless without the empty tomb, even as the empty tomb is impossible without the cross. For Jesus, humility and lost reputation were not the final goal—even now He reigns in splendor, exalted over every principality and person. God's final goal was His own glory and the radiance of Jesus celebrated verbally and wholly by every people. The goal of "live dead" is life, not death. But we must die fully if we are going to live richly.

Many Jews believed in Jesus on account of the resurrection of Lazarus (John 12:11). Lazarus's death was not remarkable—all kinds of men and women died during the lifetime of Jesus. But the resurrection of Lazarus was revolutionary. "Therefore the people who were with [Jesus] when He called Lazarus out of his tomb and raised him from the dead, bore witness" (v. 17). Lazarus was not remarkable for his death but for his resurrection. Likewise, our resurrection will bear the grandest witness of Christ.

Many people can suffer and be afflicted, but few have the spiritual fortitude to die completely to self and rise in life and light and joy. Jesus is magnified most not when His children suffer but when they rise up after suffering sweet, gentle, joyous, merciful, forgiving, and kind. It is resurrection not crucifixion that brings Jesus the greatest glory.

RABARI HINDUS OF INDIA (996,000; 0.0% EVANGELICAL)

PRAY THAT GOD WOULD POUR OUT HIS SPIRIT ON THE RABARI AND THAT THEY WOULD SEE DREAMS AND VISIONS OF JESUS. PRAY THAT THEY WOULD BE POWERFULLY SAVED AND EMPOWERED TO BE HIS WITNESSES (JOEL 2:28-32).

SEPTEMBER 16: PUNISHMENT

*D*isciples of Jesus have lost the appreciation for punishment. Christianity is not a consequence-free zone, and grace does not preclude discipline. Even godly people need punishment from time to time, like good children in general. When something is taken away or denied or is painful, this teaches us a lesson. David and Moses are classic examples of beloved children whom God punished. Just because we have avoided eternal punishment does not mean we are exempt from temporal punishment when we sin. Sin continues to have consequences post-conversion, and a loving heavenly Father punishes His children—with the aim of restoration. Grace that is twisted to eliminate all punishment is a disfigured grace.

Micah conceded, "I will bear the indignation of the LORD because I have sinned against Him, until He pleads my case and executes justice for me" (7:9). Punishment is humbling for it reminds us not to have any confidence in the flesh (Phil. 3:3). It is also encouraging for it reminds us that God loves us so much He is determined to eradicate our sinful nature. Micah went on to say of God: "He will again have compassion on us, and will subdue our iniquities. [He] will cast all our sins into the depths of the sea" (7:19). Discipline is a gift because it vividly demonstrates God's commitment to subdue our sin. We are unable to conquer our fleshly nature when it rises up, so God uses punishment to say: "Step aside and let Me deal with this. Sin is too ingrained in you, and your recent folly shows its ongoing power. Sit still for a while, cease your activity, and let Me work this evil out of you."

We cannot obtain the knowledge of Christ (Phil. 3:8) or be found in Him (v. 9) or know Him fully (v. 10) outside of His discipline. We do not know the joy of Jesus only through victories but also through discipline. If He is determined to punish us lovingly that we might know Him better and that He might subdue our sinful nature, we should not be reluctant to discipline the people we love in the household of faith. We have a responsibility to graciously discipline those who sin or rebel for without this they cannot know God fully or be free from sin. Through punishment God subdues both us and the sin within.

DOMARI MUSLIM GYPSIES OF IRAN (760,000; 0.0% EVANGELICAL)

PRAY THAT CHRISTIANS FROM AROUND THE WORLD WOULD WORK TOGETHER TO REACH THE DOMARI GYPSIES AND THAT THE DOMARI GYPSIES WOULD BE JOINED TO THE BODY OF CHRIST (JOHN 17:20-23).

SEPTEMBER 17: CUSTOM MERCY

PSALM 110; NAHUM 1; JOHN 14; PHILIPPIANS 4

*G*od's nature is mercy based. He is both more merciful and more terrible than we imagine. "Look upon me and be merciful to me, as Your custom is toward those who love Your name" (Ps. 119:132). He is not a tame god. He is not contained by our preferences or our comfort. He is not balanced, if balance means His mercy cancels out His wrath. God is fully merciful even as He blazes in fiery wrath against sin. He at once considers people vile (Nah. 1:14) and precious.

If God's great mercy and fierce wrath are both solid realities that stretch like railroad tracks to a point beyond our comprehension, then Nahum is like a little boy who traverses the tracks by hopping back and forth from one to the other. Nahum wrote that God is jealous, furious, an avenger, and that He reserves wrath for His enemies (1:2). He is also slow to anger (v. 3). The Lord has His way in the whirlwind and storm, the hills melt, and the earth burns at His presence (vv. 3–5); yet He is good, a stronghold in the day of trouble, knowing those who trust Him (v. 7). God will make an end of His enemies with an overflowing flood (v. 8); and He will break the yoke and bonds of our oppressors, bringing good tidings of peace (vv. 13–15). Nahum does not try to reconcile the mercy and wrath of God—he simply celebrates both.

Some aspects of God's character diminish the more we try to explain them. God is to be celebrated more than explained. He is to be experienced, not dissected. He is to be enjoyed, not catalogued. The Trinity is hard enough to explain to Christians, let alone Muslims. Yet the experience of God the Father for us, God the Son with us, God the Spirit in us is magnificent and compelling. Doctrine matters and sound teaching that is biblically based is essential, but God will not be reduced to a formula or a faulty diagram. He must be experienced and worshiped more than He must be understood.

We should celebrate God's mercy and His wrath. How wonderful that He is more merciful than we are. In His infinite mercy He gives us what we do not deserve and even gives us what we have refused to others. If God were not over-merciful there would be no hope for us. At the same time, how marvelous that God is more holy than people. He demands perfection and does not tolerate sin. We would foolishly allow sin a place in our hearts or our communities, and it would eventually destroy us. God is so committed to goodness and wholeness that He fiercely protects us from all that would corrupt us. God's wrath against sin in and around us is the purest form of mercy.

HARRATINE MUSLIMS OF MOROCCO (50,700; 0.0% EVANGELICAL)

PRAY THAT THE HEARTS OF THE HARRATINE WOULD BE LIKE GOOD SOIL,
READY TO HEAR THE GOSPEL AND TO RESPOND
(MATT. 7:1-8, 18-23).

*T*he Joy of Being Hated. Jesus wants His joy to abide in us and He wants our joy to be full (John 15:11). At the same time, He reminds us that abiding in His joy means the world will hate us (v. 19). The crucified life is not a dour "everyone is against me" martyrdom. It is a joyful "some hate me because of Jesus" celebration. We live with the twin realities of being accepted by Jesus and rejected by the world. When we are chosen, loved, and filled with Jesus we have a joy that more than compensates for the sting of rejection. We should strive neither to be accepted nor rejected by the world. We should focus on pleasing Jesus and reveling in the joy that accompanies obedience. We can rejoice that we have fellowship with Him, and let the relational chips fall where they may. Some people will hate us and some will love us. It does not matter. What does matter is that we are joyously loyal to Jesus.

The Joy of Being Patient. Paul prayed that the believers in Colosse would be "strengthened with all might, according to His glorious power, for all patience and long-suffering with joy" (Col. 1:11). Waiting is everyone's lot. What distinguishes mature believers is their ability to endure with gladness. We can have external freedoms curtailed, we can lose our possessions, we can even lose our reputations, but this cannot steal our joy—joy can only be surrendered. When followers of Jesus respond to delays, disappointments, and extended frustrations with joy, it is like fingernails screeching on the chalkboards of hell. Christians who are continually joyous are a great irritant to demonic powers—for such people keep smiling and praising no matter the prison or the problem. The continually joyous are a great delight to the heavenly hosts and to the heavenly Father for the same reason.

The Joy of Suffering. Paul went on to remind the Colossians that he rejoiced in his sufferings for them (Col. 1:24). He was willing to suffer repeatedly that Christ would be formed in their lives. Suffering is a joy when we understand that it completes others and helps them know Jesus better. Suffering for our own folly is not noble—it is deserved discipline. Suffering for the sake of other is joyous, for we see (even if by faith) that our discomfort helps Christ to grow in their hearts—and that is glorious. Followers of Jesus can cheerfully anticipate suffering, for we know that our pain is not in vain. It cultivates Christ in others. If our temporary and seasonal suffering helps Christ be magnified in our disciples, family, colleagues, and friends, it truly is a joy.

PASHTUN, SOUTHERN MUSLIMS OF AFGHANISTAN (6,952,000; 0.0% EVANGELICAL)

PRAY FOR THE PEACE THAT RESULTS WHEN MEN AND WOMEN ARE RECONCILED WITH GOD (JOHN 14:27). PRAY FOR MEN AND WOMEN OF PEACE (LUKE 10:6) AMONG THE PASHTUN.

SEPTEMBER 19: PEERLESS PRESENCE

PSALM 112; NAHUM 3; JOHN 16; COLOSSIANS 2

Presence Is Explanation. As Jesus wrapped up His earthly ministry and gave His disciples final instructions, He informed them: "These things I did not say to you at the beginning, *because I was with you*" (John 16:4, emphasis added). God's presence is our explanation! Christians, especially those from linear and direct cultures, want factual answers from God. We want to know why, what, how, and when. Jesus has a much more comprehensive and satisfying answer for us—Himself. He is the answer, an answer that addresses not only intellect and understanding but emotion, spirit, soul, and body. We need to learn not to press Jesus for details, which can only provide limited satisfaction. Rather, we need to press in for more of His presence—that is our only satisfying explanation.

Presence Is Joy. Prior to His departure, Jesus encouraged His disciples that they would see Him again in a little while and when they saw Him their sorrow would be "turned into joy" (John 16:20). When we see Jesus, we will no longer remember anguish (v. 21). Our hearts will rejoice, and no one will be able to take our joy from us (v. 22). Ultimately, eternal joy is fulfilled when Jesus comes again, but in this weary life we can experience joy explosions. Only Jesus can satisfy. It is foolish to look for satisfaction anywhere but in His presence. When Jesus instructed "ask, and you will receive, that your joy may be full" (v. 24), it was in the context of His presence. He longs to reveal Himself more fully; all we have to do is ask. There is no greater joy than the presence of Jesus.

Presence Is Peace. While joy can accelerate the pulse and quicken the body, peace tends to steady the soul and bring rest and calm. Jesus both quickens and calms. He tells us bluntly that we will have tribulation in this world but also comforts by reminding us: "In Me you may have peace" (v. 33). Peace does not come from a location or even a solution. It comes from Jesus. However, we must not confuse this promise of peace with a promise of amnesty or immunity, for Jesus also promises that we will have to go through hell on the way to heaven. The good news is that He also offers His presence on the journey.

We are doggedly fixed on having factual answers and practical solutions. Although God often provides these, Scripture teaches us that the presence of Jesus is our ultimate answer and reward—it is our explanation. When Jesus is present in power, we cannot remember our questions and they are not important anymore. The presence of Jesus is our joy. When He is present in power, we cannot remember our troubles or anguish, and they do not matter. Jesus is our peace. When He is present in power, His calm carries us through the storm.

DAROGA HINDUS OF INDIA (988,000; 0.0% EVANGELICAL)

PRAY THAT BELIEVERS AMONG THE DAROGA WOULD PROCLAIM THE MESSAGE OF THE GOSPEL CLEARLY AND WOULD MAKE THE MOST OF EVERY OPPORTUNITY GOD PLACES BEFORE THEM (COL. 4:2–5).

SEPTEMBER 20: LET US GLORIFY JESUS

PSALM 113; HABAKKUK 1; JOHN 17; COLOSSIANS 3

*O*ur work is to glorify Jesus (John 17:4). Even as He lived to glorify the Father, we live to glorify the triune God. When God is glorified to the maximum we can give, our work is finished and it is time to go home. But as long as we are not home, He calls us to manifest His character to our disciples—our children and our colleagues, those we lead, and those we follow (v. 6). It is critical to remember that Jesus is a person. We can so emphasize His deity that we forget how our emotions, longings, and desires are sourced in His. We have dignity because we bear the divine image of an eternal being. Jesus has joy and longings and in having these personal expressions, He dignifies them in us.

Jesus' Joy. Not only does Jesus have joy, He also wants us to have His joy fulfilled in us (v. 13). Both concepts are revolutionary. The great Lord of all creation has a bubbling fountain within Him that delights, celebrates, twinkles, and shines. He has the most incredible belly laugh, the keenest and gentlest sense of humor, the brightest twinkle of eye, the highest bounce of step. This divine, happy energy is available to us. Jesus wants us to be fulfilled by participating in His joy.

Jesus' Prayer. It is somewhat strange to think of Jesus praying, for we think of prayer as the petitions of the needy—and He is not needy. When Jesus prays (vv. 20–22), it is simply to communicate His will. He prays what He wants to happen, and what He wants is for multiple generations of faith to live and rejoice in unity. It should amaze us that our unity—unity across generations of faith—is important to Him, He wants us to be unified with those who have discipled us and those whom we have discipled. When generations of faith are united, powerful things happen in God's kingdom and in the spiritual realms. Jesus passionately wills this, so He prays for it.

Jesus' Longing. Jesus wants us to be with Him in heaven (v. 24). The fierce attraction Christians have for earth and for life on earth must puzzle and frustrate Him. He longs for us to be with Him in His glory, so we can be enveloped in the love of Father, Son, and Holy Spirit. Foolishly, we cling doggedly to health as we know it (delaying perfect wholeness), life as we know it (delaying complete fulfillment), and family as we experience it here on earth (delaying utter acceptance). If we realized how passionately Jesus longs for us to be with Him, we would enjoy Christian funerals more and would eagerly anticipate our own.

KARBARDIAN MUSLIMS OF SYRIA (43,400; 0.0% EVANGELICAL)

PRAY THAT THE KARBARDIAN WILL UNDERSTAND THAT HOPE FOR FORGIVENESS AND ACCEPTANCE
WITH GOD IS AVAILABLE ONLY THROUGH JESUS' WORK ON THE CROSS (1 COR. 1:18).

SEPTEMBER 21: THE JUST SHALL LIVE BY TRUST

PSALM 114; HABAKKUK 2; JOHN 18; COLOSSIANS 4

*F*aith most simply defined is trust: "Just from Jesus simply taking, life and rest, and joy and peace."[2]

We Trust Jesus to Satisfy Our Longings. Habakkuk warned against the proud person who cannot be satisfied, who enlarges desire like hell, who gathers and heaps up possessions, peoples, and conquests for himself (2:5). Good things can be perverted, and good things cannot complete or sustain us. To be completely satisfied, we must replace our longings for good things with a great passion for the greatest thing—the unspoiled presence of Jesus. "Just to trust His cleansing blood."

We Trust Jesus to Supply Our Needs. As a missionary who works and lives because of the faith pledges of generous supporters, I find it convicting that Habakkuk warned about the person who "loads himself with many pledges" (v. 6). I have seldom met a commitment of support I did not like, whether financial, emotional, or relational. Because I need to provide for myself and my family, I am hesitant to turn away such help. To be self-dependent even for finances, however, can be dangerous; it can lead us to stop trusting Jesus. That is why it is a blessing to be needy and underfunded. It keeps us trusting. "Just to rest upon His promise."

We Trust Jesus to Give Us Counsel. Habakkuk scolded the person who counseled others (and himself) poorly. He deemed it a "sin against your soul" (v. 10). We must learn to trust Jesus more than we trust ourselves. We must learn to listen to Him who is "greater than our hearts." Before our friends, more than our learning, above our intuition, beyond our experiences . . . we must learn to trust the quiet promptings of God's Spirit. He counsels us well if we commit "just from sin and self to cease."

A wonderful thing happens at levels far beyond us when we trust Jesus: "The earth will be filled with the knowledge of the glory of the LORD, as the waters cover the sea" (v. 14)! When Jesus is all our desire, all our supply and all our wisdom, and we give Him all our trust, we are well positioned to be trusted by Him. We do not want to share His glory; we want to see Him glorified. When we trust Jesus, He trusts us.

PERSIAN MUSLIMS OF TURKEY (612,000; 0.3% EVANGELICAL)

PRAY THAT BELIEVERS AMONG THE PERSIANS WILL ENDURE PERSECUTION IN A CHRISTLIKE
MANNER AND WILL GIVE THEIR LIVES FOR THE SAKE OF THE GOSPEL IF NECESSARY
(1 PETER 2:21-23).

SEPTEMBER 22: NOT TO US

PSALM 115; HABAKKUK 3; JOHN 19; 1 THESSALONIANS 1

*N*ot even our crucified life is about us. Jesus has to be the center even of our crucifixion. Yes, we must bear our own cross (John 19:17). Yes, a crucified life has implications for our loved ones (v. 25), but in the end, our crucifixion is not the main event. We are the undercard to the grandest show of history. Each of our stretched-out and pierced hands must point in one direction—to Jesus' cross and His empty tomb. If a sign is to be written above our suffering, it can only be this: "Not unto us, O LORD, not unto us, but to Your name be glory" (Ps. 115:1). We do not bring much to the redemption table. As Augustus Toplady phrased it in a wonderful hymn: "Nothing in my hand I bring, simply to the cross I cling."[3]

If we live a crucified life for the commendation of others, we have perverted the gospel and stolen what belongs to Jesus. He does not permit anyone to share in His glory. If we sense a glory-hunger creeping into our hearts, we should be horrified and terrified. We should fall prostrate and beg for mercy. If family and acquaintances, admirers and disciples contribute to our propensity toward pride, they are not friends, and we must be deaf to their siren songs. When others praise us, we smile and say, "Thank-you." Then we pray: "Not unto us, O LORD, not unto us, but to Your name be glory."

Our primary praise must always be reserved for Jesus. We must make a concerted effort to ever be praising Him. "The dead do not praise the LORD" the psalmist wrote, "but we will bless the LORD" (115:17–18). Habakkuk pointed out that we offer the purest praise when our problems are the most pressing. When the fig tree does not blossom, when there is no fruit on the vines, when the labor of the olive fails, when the fields yield no food, when the flocks are cut off from the fold and there is no herd in the stalls, then we will rejoice in the God of our salvation (Hab. 3:17–18). Praise is purest when it is not a rejoicing over the "labor of our hands" but in the goodness of God after everything we have done or tried has failed. It is one thing to praise God when He has helped us succeed. It is an entirely different matter to praise Him when everything we are responsible for has failed. It is good for us to fail periodically and to be disappointed; it is good to learn to praise God when we have done everything wrong. To give glory to God when we have succeeded is commendable. To give Him glory when we have failed miserably, or when others have failed us, is precious and priceless.

DARZI MUSLIMS OF INDIA (962,000; 0.0% EVANGELICAL)

PRAY THAT GOD WOULD RAISE UP MISSIONARIES FROM ALL OVER THE WORLD TO PLANT THE CHURCH TOGETHER AMONG THE DARZI (MATT. 9:37).

SEPTEMBER 23: WHAT SHALL WE RENDER?

PSALM 116; ZEPHANIAH 1; JOHN 20; 1 THESSALONIANS 2

*W*e imagine all kinds of ridiculous things about Jesus. We imagine He is a gardener (John 20:15) or that He is in debt to us for the labor of our hands. We think wrongly about what we can give to God and what He wants from us. Like children giving their father a tie on Father's Day, we may be well-intentioned and God is always gracious, but we tend to give Him things He does not need or cannot use. When the psalmist asked the question, "What shall I render to the LORD?" (Ps. 116:12) the answer was counterintuitive: "I will take up the cup of salvation, and call upon the name of the LORD" (v.13). The gift that pleases Jesus is not our strength and accomplishments but our need and inadequacy. What can we give God? Our need! Our dependence on Him is the great gift we give Him. We honor Him by accepting what He gives to us and by staying dependent on Him. To live in Christ without acknowledging our constant need for Him is to insult Him. The psalmist stated, "Precious in the sight of the LORD is the death of His saints" (v. 15) in the context of giving honor to God by calling on His name. Death to self-reliance is precious to God. It is something we can give Him that He values greatly.

We honor Jesus by believing in Him. We are told in John 20:31 that "believing, we may have life in His name." Belief gives us life; it is what we render to Jesus. God places high value on our belief—more than on our labor, though labor is both required and appreciated. We can labor for Him without really trusting Him. In fact, too much Christian labor is based on unbelief. We do not really believe God's promises so we take matters into our own hands and rely on human effort. Too much Christian service stems from a weak faith in God. He is most delighted in us when we fully believe and deeply trust.

As we contemplate what we can give God that delights Him, we must not overlook receiving salvation (Ps. 116:13) or calling upon Him as long as we live (v. 2). Our belief delights Jesus. Our ongoing dependency for every breath delights Him. He is delighted when we call on Him in praise and prayer. A misguided self-sufficiency causes us to think He does not want to be bothered with us. This is a subtle form of pride that offends and insults Him. He designed us to need Him. The greatest thing we can give our Lord is to receive salvation in an ongoing manner—only He can continually save us. We give to God by receiving what He has done for us. Receiving Jesus is believing Jesus—and believing Jesus delights Him.

HERKI MUSLIMS OF IRAQ (36,300; 0.0% EVANGELICAL)

PRAY THAT THE HERKI WOULD FEEL AND KNOW THE BURDEN OF SIN AND WOULD
COME TO JESUS FOR FORGIVENESS AND SALVATION
(MATT. 11:28–30).

SEPTEMBER 24: PENTECOSTAL PRIDE

PSALM 117–118; ZEPHANIAH 2; JOHN 21; 1 THESSALONIANS 3

*T*here are two equal and opposite errors about Pentecostal practice: being proud that you are Pentecostal and being proud you are not Pentecostal.

Proud of Being Pentecostal. Pride and Pentecost are mutually exclusive. Spirit empowerment is the lifeline of the weak. We seek the baptism of the Holy Spirit because we are dependent on Him. We cannot be who we need to be or do what God needs us to do without the empowerment of His Spirit. I am Pentecostal by desperation, not because I applied to join some elite fraternity. Pentecost empowers the weak to witness, so we approach it with humility. Pentecostal pride is at best pride in being humble (which is still pride) and at worst condescending and pompous. Zephaniah encouraged God's people to "seek humility" (2:3) and warned them that pride and arrogance would lead to destruction (v. 10). Proud Pentecostals are not filled with the Spirit—they are merely filled with hot air.

Proud of Not Being Pentecostal. Is it right to rejoice that we let God control our minds but not our tongues or emotions? Those who disdain Pentecostals for excessive emotion or ecstatic speech have missed the forest for the trees. The cardinal doctrine of Pentecostalism is subsequence: *more* of Jesus! It is about ongoing encounters with Jesus, repeated fillings of the Spirit, more of the Father, more of the Son, more of the Spirit. Pentecost is about hunger and desperation and being so determined to press in for more of Jesus that neither your dignity nor the scorn of others diminishes your efforts. Fillings of the Spirit always affect the tongue. The book of Acts is unrelenting on this point: bold speech, prophetic words, speaking in tongues, vigorous defense of the gospel—these are all the normal evidences of the filling of the Spirit. Who in their right mind (or spirit) would be proud of not being desperate for more of Jesus?

One of the tragedies of the Pentecostal movement is the pride on both sides that has grieved the Holy Spirit. People who have experienced ongoing fillings of the Holy Spirit should be the lowliest people on earth because those very fillings indicate an absolute human helplessness. We need the ongoing work of the Holy Spirit precisely because we are worse off than our brothers and sisters, not because we are better. Humility attracts and woos; pride repels. Pride also repels the Spirit. Let us not live unfilled with the Spirit because we are too lofty to look and live foolishly desperate.

POMAK MUSLIMS OF TURKEY (348,000; 0.4% EVANGELICAL)

PRAY THAT GOD WOULD UNVEIL THE CROSS AND WOULD TAKE AWAY THE VEIL ON THE MINDS
AND SPIRITS OF THE POMAK (2 COR. 3:16–17).

SEPTEMBER 25: SEXUAL AVENGER

PSALM 119; ZEPHANIAH 3; MATTHEW 1; 1 THESSALONIANS 4

*W*e are horrified by the honor killings in the Muslim world. It seems unfathomable that a man or woman would be killed for sexual impropriety whether based on a personal decision or someone else's decision. (By being a victim they bring shame on their family.) As we must do with all twisted actions, we determine something is perverted by measuring it against what is true.

In God's perspective, sexual purity is so important that He deals uniquely with sexual sins. Paul encouraged the Thessalonian church to abstain from sexual immorality (1 Thess. 4:3), to possess their own bodies in sanctification and honor (v. 4), and not to take advantage of or defraud their brothers in this matter—*because the Lord is the avenger of such* (v. 6). Paul dropped two large bombs on the Thessalonian Christians and on us regarding sexual sin: advantage and revenge.

Muslims have one thing right: Our bodies and our honor are not our own. When we sin against our bodies, we sin against the body of Christ. Christians in the West have reduced sin to a personal matter, while the Bible holds a much more complex understanding of sin's consequences on both the individual and the community. Every sexual sin has consequences on others. Any sexual act performed outside the willing participation of both husband and wife has consequences on others. If I engage in any sexual act (of whatever degree) with a person not my wife, I have disfigured myself, my wife, the other person, and any relatives and intimates of the other person. Muslims have it right in this regard: Sexual sin is a sin against the community. The Bible would add that sexual sin is primarily a sin against God. Privacy is no protection against consequences. Sexual sin always affects others. When we sin against God we set forces in motion to punish and purge, even when no one else knows about the sin.

The frightening thing about Paul's teaching to the Thessalonians on sexual purity and immorality is his shocking statement that God is the avenger of sexual sin (4:6). Because God has called us to holiness (v. 7), He takes drastic steps when we disfigure our temple and affect the holiness of others. My holiness is affected when I stand in the supermarket checkout line and unintentionally see a shocking headline or a sensual picture. I have not sinned, yet I am sullied by the improper sensuality of others, and God will avenge the assault on my holiness—as He will when my lust sullies others. It is fearful to realize that God will avenge all that is unholy and immoral. We must be soberly aware that our sexual sins (even private and unknown) affect others and will be avenged by God. His honor is at stake, and He will defend it.

ARUNTHATHIYAR HINDUS OF INDIA (944,000; 0.0% EVANGELICAL)

PRAY THAT BELIEVERS AMONG THE ARUNTHATHIYAR WOULD BE SET FREE FROM A SPIRIT OF FEAR OF WHAT MAY COME AND WOULD BOLDLY PROCLAIM THE TRUTH OF THE GOSPEL (2 TIM. 1:6-8).

SEPTEMBER 26: SONS OF LIGHT

PSALM 120; HAGGAI 1; MATTHEW 2; 1 THESSALONIANS 5

*T*he psalmist was not impressed with the sons of Kedar: "Woe to me that I dwell among the tents of Kedar" (Ps. 120:5). The psalmist had asked the Lord to deliver his soul from lying lips and a deceitful tongue (v. 2). In this context he bemoaned living among the proto-Arabs. Kedar was evidently the father of the Arab peoples, and Kedar's sons do not have a strong track-record of telling the truth or living in the light. It is unfair and bigoted to say that one group of people are more prone to lie than others for we all have the tendency to deceive. At the same time, if a lie will preserve honor in the Arab culture where honor is supreme, then a lie is useful.

What Lies Within. Deception lies deep within every heart. We cannot delude ourselves that we are immune to lying or that we are intrinsically truthful. I am bent to deception. I may not present myself in word or deed as blatantly different from what is true about me, but I continually present myself as better or worse than I am. I do this as much by what I say as what I do not say and by what I do not do as what I do. Misdirection is untruth. We followers of Jesus are incredibly skilled at insinuating we are better than others or that others are worse than we are. Paul reminded the Thessalonians that they were "sons of light and sons of the day," not of the "night nor of the darkness" (1 Thess. 5:5). God intends for us to be sanctified completely and preserved blameless (v. 23), and He promises that He who called us to absolute truth and light is faithful and will also do it (v. 24). We must be ruthless about what is false within us. We must be relentless that what lies within is exposed and straightened. What lies within must be truth.

What Lies Without. Deception is the order of the day in our world, as it is in all cultures. There are as many lies in secular humanist societies as there are in Islamic, Hindu, animist, or Buddhist ones. Because we live in a world that is increasingly less truthful, it is important that we live and walk in truth. Truth is essential in ministry, vitally so in Muslim lands and other contexts that do not allow overt evangelism. We cannot combat the great lies about Jesus if our methodologies or identities are deceptive. We cannot pretend to be something we are not or pretend not to be who we are. Disciples of Jesus are gospel proclaimers. We cannot allow the lies around us to woo us into deceptive behavior, methods, or speech. Sons and daughters of the Light are addicted to truth. Truth may ultimately cost us greatly but it will also reward us deeply. Only truthful sons and daughters can truly represent the Father.

BERBER, SIWA MUSLIMS OF EGYPT (32,300; 0.0% EVANGELICAL)

PRAY FOR THE WORD OF GOD IN WRITTEN, ORAL, MUSICAL, AND DRAMATIC FORMS TO BE TRANSLATED AND TO SPREAD AMONG THE BERBER, SIWA (ISA. 55:10-11).

SEPTEMBER 27: THIS DAY, THAT DAY

PSALM 121; HAGGAI 2; MATTHEW 3; 2 THESSALONIANS 1

*I*nstability is the order of our day. Shootings, bombings, attacks, violence, abuse, insecurity, and trouble are the new normal. Do not suppose that these sinful acts take the Lord by surprise. He is intentionally allowing humans to manifest what is in their evil hearts as part of the shaking process that precedes the great and terrible day of the Lord. "Once more," God promises, "I will shake heaven and earth, the sea and dry land; and I will shake all nations" (Hag. 2:6–7). The last days are upon us. Increased trouble is but a sign of Jesus' impending return. In the natural, we want to hide from the places and peoples that scare us, but in the Spirit, we must run to engage them, for time is short. The last days are upon us.

This Day. Haggai acknowledged that God's people had gone through trouble, famine, exile, and anguish but added God's encouragement: "From *this* day, I will bless you" (v. 19, emphasis added). This day (this troubled, unsettled, violent, turbulent, unsteady, precarious day that you and I live in) is the day the Lord has made; we will rejoice and be glad in it. In the midst of an upside-down world, we hold on to the promises of God's blessing moving forward. We advance with the clear-eyed realism that the day will not get better, that blessings do not mean immunity, and that the gathering clouds will yield one final storm. We also advance with the confidence that God will be with us, will be glorified by us, and, in the end, will be triumphant over all.

That Day. "In that day . . . I will take you . . . and will make you . . . for I have chosen you" (v. 23). Old Testament prophets, New Testament apostles, and Jesus Himself do not stand like naïve weather forecasters predicting a cheery *eschaton* (last days). It is going to be a time of great tribulation and great trouble. At some point, God will rapture His people out of the chaos. He instructs us to endure to the end—even as millions before us have endured unfathomable suffering up to their deaths. The promise of "that day" is not that we evade trouble, but that God has chosen us and will make us His vessels. He will use us for His glory as the world collapses around us. This is the destiny for those who live out the final moments of history—not hiding in caves cowering from the Antichrist but standing boldly for Jesus through the power of His might. We will go out with a bang . . . not a whimper!

PONTIC GREEK MUSLIMS OF TURKEY (318,000; 0.0% EVANGELICAL)

PRAY THAT GOD WOULD POUR OUT HIS SPIRIT ON THE PONTIC PEOPLE AND THAT THEY WOULD SEE DREAMS AND VISIONS OF JESUS. PRAY THAT THEY WOULD BE POWERFULLY SAVED AND EMPOWERED TO BE HIS WITNESSES (JOEL 2:28–32).

SEPTEMBER 28: HELPING GOD . . . WITH EVIL INTENT

PSALM 122; ZECHARIAH 1; MATTHEW 4; 2 THESSALONIANS 2

To my shame, there have been days when I wanted some Muslims to go to hell. My wife and I have lived in the Arab world for over twenty years, and at times I feel like every one of those years was spent banging our heads against a rock. The flesh within me says: "Fine, then! You people do not want Jesus? See how you like eternity without Him!" At times, my disappointment at their delusion and refusal of grace causes me to lose grace and graciousness toward them.

If we are not careful, we can want God to punish those who have hurt us, those who have sinned. But we sin when we are not moved at the plight of the unregenerate. The prophet Zechariah (whose name means "the Lord remembers") had an interesting dialogue with an angel. God had reviewed the ease of the nations who had punished Israel, and He was not happy that they were resting quietly (Zech. 1:11, 15). He said of them: "They helped—but with evil intent" (v. 15). It is true that Israel sinned; it is also true that God used Assyria and Babylon to teach them a lesson. What is not true is that God forgot about Israel or abandoned His people to their own folly. He did not plan to let the nations rejoice in the punishment of His people. When He observed the apathy of those nations He declared: "I am returning to Jerusalem with mercy" (v. 16).

We must beware of helping God discipline others if we have no desire to show them mercy. We must be uneasy when we rebuke others. We must long for their restoration, their "everlasting consolation and good hope by grace" (2 Thess, 2:16). This is not a difficult challenge when we have to correct people we like—it is easy to feel compassion for our friends. It is extremely difficult, however, when we must correct people we do not like or who have harmed us. The human heart is shocking. It is easy for godly people to enjoy rebuking or correcting others, to smugly think the offenders have received what they deserved. We are not exempt from "helping God, with evil intent." God not only remembers the evil ones in their time of discipline, He also notes with displeasure the righteous who rejoice when others are disciplined. It is not in the nature of God to enjoy the misery of others—even when they deserve it. When the sinful suffer, our hearts must not harbor ease and apathy.

Matthew 4:24 reveals a Jesus who delights to heal me from my torments—torments I deserve, torments that result from my own sin, my own folly, my own choices. All those who help God, including those who help Him discipline others, should agonize with the offender and rejoice that God always remembers and returns with mercy.

TILI HINDUS OF INDIA (941,000; 0.0% EVANGELICAL)

PRAY THAT CHRISTIANS FROM AROUND THE WORLD WOULD WORK TOGETHER TO REACH THE TILI AND THAT THE TILI WOULD BE JOINED TO THE BODY OF CHRIST (JOHN 17:20-23).

SEPTEMBER 29: PRAYING THROUGH AND SHUTTING UP

PSALM 123; ZECHARIAH 2; MATTHEW 5; 2 THESSALONIANS 3

The earth has always been full of bad news, but modern media makes it more immediate. People's hearts have always been vile, but now the vileness is displayed visually and graphically on a global scale. There have always been babbling, lewd, and rebellious voices, but now we hear them through more mediums of expression that have less shame. Little wonder that the Lord tells the earth to "shut up" (Zech. 2:13). The enemies of the psalmist tended to be as proud and scornful as they were violent and oppressive. For all kinds of enemies and challenges, the Bible gives good advice:

Pray through. The psalmist said that sometimes we just have to keep looking to God until He has mercy on us (Ps. 123:2). In the 1900s this concept was called "praying through." Some answers do not come after the first petition. Sometimes, like Elijah, you have to pray over and over again with your head between your knees, groaning and longing, until you see a cloud the size of a fist. Sometimes, like the importunate widow, you have to take the request back to God over and over and over and over until you receive an answer. Praying through is a commitment to pray until God has mercy.

Sing on. The psalmist said to God, "Your statutes have been my songs in the house of my pilgrimage" (Ps. 119:54). Zechariah relayed God's message in return: "Sing and rejoice. . . . For behold, I am coming and I will dwell in your midst" (Zech. 2:10). One of the best ways to abide in Jesus is by singing to Him all day long. Singing is not just for times of joy; it is also for the times when we go to battle with Jehoshaphat, when we break down walls with Joshua, and we endure prison with Paul and Silas. When the world rises against us, we fight back by singing on.

Glory in. When we pray through and sing on, we experience a marvelous intimacy with Jesus. God says that He will be a wall of fire around us and the glory in our midst (Zech. 2:5). When we pray through, sing on, and glory in God, He sends us after glory to the nations that plundered us (v. 8) and promises that "many nations shall be joined to the LORD in that day" (v. 11). Unreached peoples will be reached when we pray through, sing on, and glory in Jesus.

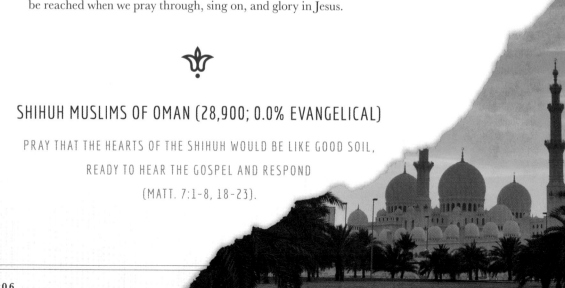

SHIHUH MUSLIMS OF OMAN (28,900; 0.0% EVANGELICAL)

PRAY THAT THE HEARTS OF THE SHIHUH WOULD BE LIKE GOOD SOIL,
READY TO HEAR THE GOSPEL AND RESPOND
(MATT. 7:1-8, 18-23).

SEPTEMBER 30: REBUKING THE DEVIL

PSALM 124; ZECHARIAH 3; MATTHEW 6; 1 TIMOTHY 1

*P*eople in ministry have some powerful enemies. Zechariah told the story of the post-exilic high priest Joshua standing before the presence of the Lord, with Satan on his right hand to oppose him (Zech. 3:1). It is interesting to note that God's chosen ones are not isolated from trouble, oppression, or resistance. If we are strolling along through our spiritual lives without any resistance, this usually signifies we are of no threat to the powers of darkness. Incredible demonic resistance and opposition are the hallmarks of those who advance God's kingdom.

Where kingdom advancers often stumble, however, is in their response to Satan's opposition. It is far too common to hear Christians try to rebuke the Devil rather than let Jesus do it. "The LORD said to Satan, 'The LORD rebuke you, Satan! The LORD who has chosen Jerusalem rebuke you!'" (3:2). Michael the archangel echoed this sentiment (Jude 9). We have no business thinking we can dominate the Devil in our own strength. If the Lord had not been on our side, we would have been swallowed alive, overwhelmed, and drowned in our souls (Ps. 124:1–5). When Satan opposes us (and he will), we must let Jesus defend us. We do this by not saying much to the Devil other than: "The Lord rebuke you!" It is easy to fall into the trap of giving too much attention to the Devil. We do not ignore him because he is insignificant; we ignore him for he is too powerful for us to deal with in our pitiful strength. The only way to deal with Satan is to refer him to a higher power: "Take your accusation to Jesus, you slimy serpent. I am under His protection, and He will answer for me!" Those who engage in a battle of wits with Satan always lose. Those who refer Satan to Jesus (for the Lord's rebuke) always win.

When we refer Satan back to the Lord, this keeps us humble. When God uses us, we too often assume it is because we are strong or capable of opposing Satan. We are not and never will be either one, which is why the strongest position in spiritual warfare is to accept that God is the One who rebukes and defeats the Devil. God uses us—and commits the glorious gospel to our trust (1 Tim. 1:11)—because we are weak. As He did with Paul, God enables us, counts us faithful, and puts us in the ministry (1 Tim. 1:12) as a pattern of grace (v. 16). For all Paul's prowess, he kept two things in perspective: God allowed him to minister, although he *formerly* was a blasphemer and insolent man (v. 13) and *presently* was the chief of sinners (v. 15).

The other reason we dare not take on Satan is because his opposing accusations are true. We cannot defend ourselves legally. We are guilty. So we must refer Satan to Jesus. Satan's rebuke is the prevailing blood of Jesus. We rebuke Satan by pleading the precious blood of Jesus.

POSHA GYPSY MUSLIMS OF TURKEY (10,000; 0.4% EVANGELICAL)

PRAY FOR THE PEACE THAT RESULTS WHEN MEN AND WOMEN ARE RECONCILED WITH GOD (JOHN 14:27). PRAY FOR MEN AND WOMEN OF PEACE (LUKE 10:6) AMONG THE POSHA.

October

"SOME WISH TO LIVE WITHIN THE SOUND OF A CHAPEL BELL.

I WANT TO RUN A RESCUE SHOP WITHIN A YARD OF HELL."

—C. T. Studd

OCTOBER 1: MOUNTAINS

PSALM 125; ZECHARIAH 4; MATTHEW 7; 1 TIMOTHY 2

Mountains Around. The Lord surrounds His people as the mountains surround Jerusalem (Ps. 125:2). As we move closer to Jesus' return, the minions of evil will move closer to us. Darkness and injustice are going to become more common, not less. If God's people do not live their faith intentionally, the fingers of fear will drive them backward and into corners of silence. On the one hand we need a clear-eyed realism to recognize the steady advance of evil; on the other hand we need the single eye of faith to recognize that we are surrounded by God. Yes, we are ringed about by many layers of enemies, but we are also surrounded by fire, angels, and almighty God. We have nothing to fear from the darkness; it cannot touch us. Evil might touch our bodies and possessions, but it will only touch our souls if we allow it to do so.

Mountains Removed. God promised Zerubbabel that the mountains before him would become a plain (Zech. 4:7). The reality of the last days is that good will increase as much as bad. The worse things get, the more people will come to Jesus. The more the church suffers, the more Jesus will be revealed. The more martyrs perish, the more persecutors will repent. Evil and gospel are rising together in a mighty titanic struggle, each growing, each swelling, each advancing ever onward. Mountains rise and loom before us. God still delights in Caleb-like men and women who believe that mountains can be removed by the Spirit of God (v. 6). God flattens incredible obstacles before us as precursors of that great day when He will finally destroy the curse.

Mountains Begun. We do not cross mountains in a single bound. We climb them slowly and steadily, beginning each climb with small steps. We dare not despise the day of small beginnings (v. 10). Many have made the five-day trek to climb Mount Kilimanjaro. (I did it with golf clubs and hit some drives off the summit.) Kilimanjaro is not climbed in a day, neither is it climbed by the swift. Those who climb too fast experience altitude sickness and falter. Slow, steady, small steps are the way to conquer mountains. There is actually nothing exotic or spectacular about mountain moving. In these last days before Jesus comes, there are mountains He wants flattened. Everybody should aim to move a mountain. If the Spirit moves mountains through days of small beginnings, then anyone is qualified to do the impossible because we are all small and we all have access to the same Spirit. If every follower of Jesus adopted a mountain, there would be one last Spirit shaking to welcome Him back. He will bring forth the capstone and we will all shout "Grace, grace!" (v. 7).

BAIRWA HINDUS OF INDIA (933,000; 0.0% EVANGELICAL)

PRAY THAT BELIEVERS AMONG THE BAIRWA WOULD PROCLAIM THE MESSAGE OF THE GOSPEL CLEARLY AND WOULD MAKE THE MOST OF EVERY OPPORTUNITY GOD PLACES BEFORE THEM (COL. 4:2-5).

OCTOBER 2: AUTHORITY TO ABSORB

*J*esus was delighted with a Roman soldier. Now consider that this is like a West Bank Palestinian thinking that an Israeli soldier is brilliant. Few in the scriptural record gave Jesus as much joy as a foreign military leader. What delighted Him was the centurion's humble understanding of authority. First, the centurion understood he was not worthy. We have lost propriety in our beseeching of heaven; we approach the throne more to demand than to plea. Sometimes our disappointment with God is an expression of hubris: He did not do what we wanted and now our feelings are hurt. The centurion demanded no rights and simply said to Jesus, "You can do this if you want to. I am at your mercy, and I wait for your command." Jesus delights to respond to those who understand and reverence Him in this way.

In quick succession, Jesus healed a leper, a servant, and a mother-in-law, and delivered a demon-possessed man (Matt. 8). That is not a list of people from the Who's Who of that culture. Matthew pointed out that Jesus did this because He had authority to heal. Matthew also described how Jesus heals: "He Himself took our infirmities and bore our sicknesses" (8:17). Jesus heals by absorption. Our sins and sicknesses end *with* and *in* Him. Jesus has the authority to be the end of sickness. In the natural world, sin and sickness pass from human to human. Child abusers tend to have been abused themselves. Viruses pass from hand to hand or from mouth to mouth. Hurts pass from generation to generation. Racism, hatred, bias, and anger pass through familial, relational, and cultural hands from grandfathers to fathers to sons. Jesus stands as the great absorber of sin and sickness. Evil is passed down the line until it is destroyed and contained by Him.

As we interact and live as broken people in a broken world, Jesus wants to give us some of His absorption authority. He wants us to be the terminal station for some of what is wrong in the world. When gossip passes down the line and reaches us, we become the gossip quencher—the great chasm into which gossip descends never to see the light again. When injustice passes through ignorant minds and hands to us, we absorb the cost, and all that we pass on is justice and mercy, truth and love. When colleagues hurl hurts at one another until unfair darts strike us, too, we absorb them and speak blessing and affirmation. God invites us to be the last in line for sin and sickness. This is not without shame or cost or crosses, and neither is it without provision. God grants us the right and power to put an end to what is wrong if we are willing to pay the cost of absorbing it *with* and *for* Him.

BERBER, SHAWIYA MUSLIMS OF MOROCCO (23,300; 0.0% EVANGELICAL)

OCTOBER 3: THE COMPASSION OF JESUS

PSALM 127; ZECHARIAH 6; MATTHEW 9; 1 TIMOTHY 4

*W*hen He saw the multitudes, He was moved with compassion for them, because they were weary and scattered, like sheep having no shepherd" (Matt. 9:36). This commentary on Jesus' compassion is preceded by His preaching, teaching, and healing (v. 35), and followed by His prayer for harvest laborers (vv. 37–38). The point is simple—for Jesus, compassion moved Him to pray that more proclaimers would be sent into the harvest field. For us, compassion moves us to send money to feed orphans or drill wells.

Jesus' Priority Is Souls. Other texts accent that God cares for body, soul, and spirit, but this text reminds us that Jesus' priority is the eternal soul. What stirs Him is that people are going to hell. This bothers Him much more than the fact that men and women are hungry. Of course, He cares about the hungry, but the unavoidable truth is that He cares much more about the lost. Jesus has enough love to care for every injustice, enough wisdom to know that the injustices in this world are not equal, and enough eternal love to allow the body to suffer if it leads to deliverance of the soul. The greatest injustice of them all is that men and women run toward hell without anyone warning them and without anyone praying for them. The masses of people who do not have eternal life are the center of His compassion. This is the priority of God, and it should be our priority as well. The compassion of Jesus moves Him to pray for laborers. The compassion of Jesus moves Him to actions that enable lost souls to hear the gospel.

Jesus' Primary Resource Is People. I suggest that Jesus is tired of seeing us throw money at problems. His answer for the problems of people is people. His response to His own stirred emotions was an action that led to gospel proclamation. He first prayed for laborers (vv. 37–8); then He called twelve to Himself and sent them out to preach, heal, and raise the dead—without taking money (10:1–8). Take our money away from us and what do we have left to give? Much—if we understand the compassion of Jesus. It is unpopular to say and it is difficult to hear, but it is what the Bible reveals about Jesus: His compassion leads Him to prioritize souls over bodies. In this life the soul and the body are not equal—not according to Scripture. Let us have the courage to admit it and live with the implications. In this life God cares for the soul more than He does for the body and is willing for the body to endure all kinds of anguish if it works to the benefit of the soul.

QASSAB MUSLIMS OF PAKISTAN (962,000; 0.0% EVANGELICAL)

PRAY THAT THE BELIEVERS AMONG THE QASSAB WILL ENDURE PERSECUTION IN A CHRISTLIKE MANNER AND WILL GIVE THEIR LIVES FOR THE SAKE OF THE GOSPEL IF NECESSARY (1 PETER 2:21-23).

*C*hristians tend to talk to God too much and listen too little. When an Arabic conversation starts to get away from me, I stop listening and trying to understand and start talking. When we talk, we tend to dominate the conversation. Sadly, prayer can be twisted from an expression of dependency to a means of control. We attempt to manipulate God by whining—and call that prayer. While God is gracious to listen to our petitions, prayer delights Him only if it expresses dependence (not demands) and a willingness to listen more than to chatter accompanied by obedience. Zechariah informed the exiles, who were diligent to fast every fifth and seventh month for seventy years (140 months of discipline), that all their effort was in vain because they did not listen carefully and obey (Zech. 7:11).

The problem is that when we do not listen to God, He stops listening to us. Zechariah 7:13 explains: "'Therefore it happened, that just as He proclaimed and they would not hear, so they called out and I would not listen,' says the LORD of Hosts." We have been deluded into thinking that God is waiting for our petitions no matter how we treat Him. We err when we suppose we can disobey and ignore the voice of the Spirit and then run to the Lord when we need help. A diminished view of God emphasizes His patience over His majestic authority. He does not loiter around waiting to serve us. We dare not think we can continually insult Him with our disobedience and expect Him to answer our summons—or even our pleas. Yes, God is merciful and compassionate, full of grace and abounding in love, but He can also be insulted and offended. We cannot treat the Lord of Hosts disrespectfully and expect Him to listen to us.

There is a confession, however, that God listens to attentively. When we confess Him before men, He confesses us before the Father (Matt. 10:32). When we obey and honor Jesus, He answers our prayers. Obedience becomes our most powerful prayer. When we obey Jesus and represent Him with honor before people, He advocates on our behalf to the Father: "I know this one. Intervene on his or her behalf!" To confess Jesus is not to confess what an individual wants Jesus to be but who He is in all His glory.

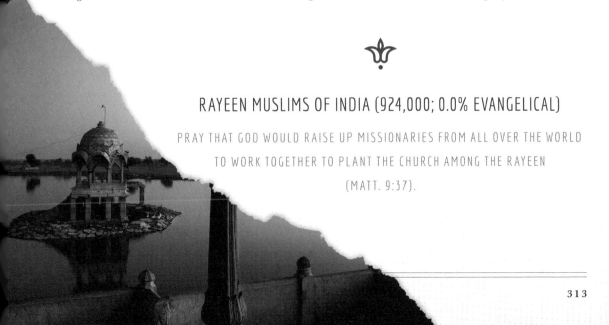

RAYEEN MUSLIMS OF INDIA (924,000; 0.0% EVANGELICAL)

PRAY THAT GOD WOULD RAISE UP MISSIONARIES FROM ALL OVER THE WORLD
TO WORK TOGETHER TO PLANT THE CHURCH AMONG THE RAYEEN
(MATT. 9:37).

OCTOBER 5: REFORM SCHOOL

PSALM 129; ZECHARIAH 8; MATTHEW 11; 2 TIMOTHY 1

*I*n our impatient moments God's restraint offends us. Like John the Baptist we are offended that Jesus does not do more with His great power (Matt. 11:6). We either do not think God is active enough in the world, or we do not like what He does or appears to leave undone. In our more lucid moments we worry less about what God is doing or not doing in the world and concentrate on what He needs to do in us (Ps. 119:35–36). We pray: "Lord, reform me! Lord, compel me. Lord, take me by force and impress your will upon me, even if I protest. Lord, in my infrequent moments of eternal clarity, I declare I need you to reform, reconstruct, purge, cleanse, and make me holy." And we find that under His yoke, learning from Him, we find rest for our souls (Matt.11:29). The Lord promised His people, "Just as you were a curse among the nations . . . so I will save you and you shall be a blessing. Do not fear, let your hands be strong" (Zech. 8:13).

Like Paul, some of us have done unimaginably hurtful things to the family of Christ. Some of us are former abusers, violent, insulting, perverted, attackers of what is holy, innocent, and pure. Some of us have been a curse to others. How amazing then the promise of God who "has abolished death and brought life and immortality to light through the gospel" (2 Tim. 1:10)! This is Paul, who had wreaked havoc on the church, testifying to the reforming power of God. For those of us who have done shameful things, God can reform and renew us and turn our curses into blessings. Do not fear—this is the power of the gospel: God takes human curses and reforms them into human blessings.

Reform school takes a while; it is not a four-year process. We do not graduate until we are elevated to glory. In the meantime, we have a responsibility to love what is true in us and to be ruthless about anything that is false. We err if we think only "obvious" sinners need reformation. Those of us who have walked with Jesus for years still need His ongoing work and loving correction in our lives. Ironically, those who have walked with Him the longest can be the most blind to their blemishes of character. We can become so familiar with grace that we no longer let it batter us.

The poet John Donne put it this way:

> *Batter my heart, three-person'd God, for you*
> *As yet but knock, breathe, shine, and seek to mend;*
> *That I may rise and stand, o'erthrow me, and bend*
> *Your force to break, blow, burn, and make me new.*[1]

BALOCH MUSLIMS OF IRAN (1,143,000; 0.0% EVANGELICAL)

PRAY THAT THE BALOCH WOULD FEEL AND KNOW THE BURDEN OF SIN AND WOULD COME TO JESUS FOR FORGIVENESS AND SALVATION (MATT. 11:28-30).

*I*f you are worried that you might have committed the "unforgivable" sin, you do not need to be. That fact that you are worried about it is proof you have not committed it.

Jesus teaches in Matthew 12:31 that all sins will be forgiven save the one of blasphemy against the Holy Spirit. The Holy Spirit is our counselor, the internal witness of God inside the believer who constantly comforts, advises, and instructs. The Holy Spirit unceasingly calls us to repentance. Working backward, the only way we will not be forgiven is if we stop repenting, and the only way we stop repenting is if we have become deaf, through sustained and repeated disobedience, to the voice of the Spirit. A single disobedience does not equate to blasphemy, but if we constantly disobey the Spirit's voice, we lose the ability to hear Him over time. When we lose the ability to hear God, we lose the desire and capacity to obey Him. As long as our hearts are tender toward Jesus (even when we sin) and our ears are open to the Spirit's voice, it is impossible for us to commit blasphemy against His Holy Spirit.

Comfort and warning go together. The warning is that we can become deaf to the Holy Spirit—and that is unpardonable. The comfort is that this is not a one-time or accidental decision; it is the result of a life of disobedience. Paul warned Timothy that some had been taken captive by the Devil to do his bidding (2 Tim. 2:26). The role of the servant of the Lord—one who is gentle, not quarrelsome, able to teach, patient, and humble (v. 24)—is to correct those who are heading down the disobedient path. Correction is another function of the Holy Spirit, and we are to pass on what we learn, at least to four generations (v. 2). As the Holy Spirit speaks to us and corrects us, we in turn are to speak and correct others so they can repent, know the truth, and escape the snare of the Devil (v. 26).

What is unforgivable for the servant of the Lord is to live in such a way as to forfeit moral authority. God's indwelling Spirit corrects us not only for our sakes but also for the sakes of others—that we might lovingly correct them. If we disobey the Holy Spirit in repeated small ways, we will have no spiritual capacity to help others. This is a double tragedy because our sin can be the catalyst for the destruction of those around us. This is why Paul urged Timothy to "depart from iniquity" so that "the solid foundation of God can stand" (v. 19). "The Lord knows those who are His" (v. 19), and the ones who are His are those who have stayed faithful through a thousand small, unnoticed acts of obedience.

TUAREG, HOGGER MUSLIMS OF LIBYA (18,500; 0.0% EVANGELICAL)

PRAY THAT GOD WOULD UNVEIL THE CROSS AND WOULD TAKE AWAY THE VEIL ON THE MINDS AND SPIRITS OF THE TUAREG, HOGGER (2 COR. 3:16-17).

OCTOBER 7: THE QUARTERMASTER OF HEAVEN

PSALM 131; ZECHARIAH 10; MATTHEW 13; 2 TIMOTHY 3

*W*hen I sit on my balcony watching and listening to the city of Cairo, I am overwhelmed. When I walk through the urban slums, the preppy Nile islands, or the Islamic quarter, I wonder how on earth we can reach this megacity and others like it around the world. No training seems adequate, no method tenable. When I am overwhelmed, the Scriptures give me hope, comfort, and songs (Ps. 119:49–56). The Scriptures teach me to wean my soul from matters that do not concern me and are beyond me (Ps. 131:2). The Scriptures make me wise and complete; they equip me (2 Tim. 3:15–17). The Scriptures remove a self-imposed pressure and remind me that all things—especially world evangelization—come from God (Zech. 10).

Rain and Showers. "Ask the LORD for rain. . . . He will give . . . showers of rain" (Zech. 10:1). Jesus restores and renews. He waters our dry places and sends blessings. He sends harvest.

Battle Capacity. God makes us like "His royal horse in battle. . . . From him the battle bow. . . . They shall fight because the LORD is with them" (vv. 3–5). Jesus gives us the appetite, capacity, and weapons for warfare. A spiritual battle lust to war for the souls of men is a divinely granted emotion.

Cornerstone. "From him comes the cornerstone" (v. 4). Missions and ministry are not built on personalities—as much as we strive to make it so. Enduring ministry is built only on Jesus. Every single one of us is dispensable and replaceable. This gives us comfort and hope when we feel small; it gives warning and pause when we feel great.

Tent Peg. "From him [comes] the tent peg" (v. 4). Even the largest tent needs the small, mostly buried stakes in the ground that keep it stable. No tent can endure buffeting winds without the humble pegs that secure it to the earth. God grants our security through a thousand little anchors unseen and invaluable. He guarantees our security and endurance.

Rule and Authority. "From him [comes] every ruler together" (v. 4). God grants authorities over us—some loving, some tyrannical. All authority is given to Jesus and granted to us from Him. Our defense comes from Him. Sometimes He defends us through wise authorities, and sometimes He forms, disciplines, and refines us by the hand of unwise authorities.

God gives me the strength to press on and the energy and passion for battle. He provides the stability and the structure upon which to build. I am not overwhelmed by the needs of the world for I am supplied and resupplied by the great quartermaster of heaven.

QIZILBASH MUSLIMS OF AFGHANISTAN (264,000; 0.0% EVANGELICAL)

PRAY THAT BELIEVERS AMONG THE QIZILBASH WOULD BE SET FREE FROM A SPIRIT OF FEAR OF WHAT MAY COME AND WOULD BOLDLY PROCLAIM THE TRUTH OF THE GOSPEL (2 TIM. 1:6–8).

OCTOBER 8: BROKEN TO BE A BLESSING

PSALM 132; ZECHARIAH 11; MATTHEW 14; 2 TIMOTHY 4

*G*od's great shepherd heart longs to care for those who are cut off. He longs to seek the young, heal the broken, and feed those who still stand (Zech. 11:16). God invites us into His passions and into the means of His provision: brokenness. When Jesus staggered from the loss of His cousin and friend and retreated to recuperate, the needy crowd denied Him even that small solace (Matt. 14). But He did not allow His personal loss and pain to blind Him to the needs of others. He took bread and "looking up to heaven, He blessed and broke and gave the loaves to the disciples; and the disciples gave to the multitudes" (v. 19). Prefiguring His own broken body, Jesus provided for people's needs.

We Are Broken to Be a Blessing. When Jesus commanded His disciples to give the crowd something to eat, this was impossible for them to do on their own initiative. Jesus was teaching them and us that our resources are not what we hold in our hands but what we have sealed in our hearts. What we have to give others is what God has steadily deposited in our spirits over time, and it can be accessed only when we are broken. Imagine that Jesus has deposited steadily into a sealed piggy bank character traits such as grace, mercy, truth, love, peace, and joy. When He wants to access those resources to help others, He must break the bank—the clay vessel that holds the treasure. The resources we have in our hands are finite; we should give them, and give them sacrificially. The resources we carry in our hearts, however, are replenished morning by morning. They are inexhaustible as long as we abide in Jesus.

It Is a Blessing to Be Broken. Jesus blesses us by breaking us. We are used to being blessed by wealth, honor, and health, and sometimes God uses those means to bless us. Other times He blesses us by breaking us. This is a blessing because it allows us to partake in the divine nature. God blessed the world by the broken body of Jesus on the cross. When He invites us into divine agony, we are also granted divine joy. There is fulfillment beyond description when He breaks us and pours us out for others (2 Tim. 4:6). Undeniably, brokenness costs something; it hurts to be broken, and to be broken repeatedly hurts repeatedly. Yet above and beyond the pain is the searing joy of having the message "preached fully through [us]" (v. 17). To be invited to share Jesus' sufferings is to be invited to share His joy. Brokenness is God's great favor to His beloved ones—it makes us like Him.

DHOBI MUSLIMS OF INDIA (911,000; 0.0% EVANGELICAL)

PRAY FOR THE WORD OF GOD IN WRITTEN, ORAL, MUSICAL, AND DRAMATIC FORMS TO BE TRANSLATED AND TO RISE AMONG THE DHOBI (ISA. 55:10-11).

OCTOBER 9: FROM MOURNING TO MORNING

PSALM 133; ZECHARIAH 12; MATTHEW 15; TITUS 1

*J*esus grants us the grace of grief over our sin, loss, and shame. Grace and prayer are gifts from God that help us realize how much of Him we are missing. Grace and supplication lead us to long for Jesus, to ache for more of Him, and to agonize over how we have treated Him in our foolish and willful hearts.

Historically, the Jewish people have for the most part rejected Jesus of Nazareth as their Messiah. Those of us who work among Arabs must diligently pray for revival among the Jewish people lest we take up the prejudices of the people we serve. Zechariah prophesied of a day when God will once more bring the Jewish people to Himself on a broad scale: "And I will pour on the house of David and on the inhabitants of Jerusalem the Spirit of grace and supplication; then they will look on Me whom they pierced. Yes, they will mourn for Him as one mourns for his only son, and grieve for Him as one grieves for a firstborn" (Zech. 12:10). A day is rapidly coming when a significant portion of the Jewish people will repent in anguish at what they have done to the Messiah. They will groan from deep within their spirits to know Him as their Savior.

What is true for the Jewish people is also true for us. God gives us grace to pray, and prayer opens our eyes to see how we have pierced Jesus, how we have wounded Him through rebellion. First, grace prayer sobers us by reminding us what is in our hearts: evil thoughts, murders, adulteries, fornications, thefts, false witness, and blasphemies (Matt. 15:19). All these things plus more are in my heart and yours. Second, grace prayer leads us to mortification: deep mourning, and wailing of soul at how disgusting, vile, and twisted we are—every one of us. Grace prayer helps us understand how little of Jesus we have apprehended, how marred His image is in our hearts, and how much more of Him there is to know. Grace prayer creates an anguished longing for what we have foolishly lost, for what we have cavalierly abandoned.

When God sends a spirit of grace and supplication upon us, the unexpected result is mourning for what we have insulted, for the One we have offended and lost. Grace not only bestows Christ's riches on us, it also opens our eyes to how deeply we have wounded Him. It reminds us how we have pierced Him with our ongoing sin. It is right that we anguish and sorrow over Him whom we have pierced. A spirit of grace and supplication leads to mourning, and mourning leads to the morning.

IZARGUIEN MUSLIMS OF MOROCCO (16,100; 0.0% EVANGELICAL)

PRAY THAT GOD WOULD POUR OUT HIS SPIRIT ON THE IZARGUIEN AND THAT THEY WOULD SEE DREAMS AND VISIONS OF JESUS. PRAY THAT THEY WOULD BE POWERFULLY SAVED AND EMPOWERED TO BE HIS WITNESSES (JOEL 2:28-32).

*M*any nomadic pastoralists across Africa surround their simple huts with a thorn-bush fence. At night they bring their cows, goats, and sheep into the enclosure for safety. Usually there is one opening that they seal at night by dragging a thorn bush into the breach. The "gate" may even be guarded. It is the gatekeeper's responsibility to keep the predators out and the vulnerable ones in. God has set up gatekeepers in His kingdom—those in spiritual authority such as parents, pastors, and leaders—who are responsible to be the first line of defense against predators. Jesus gave us the keys of the kingdom to bind and to loose (Matt. 16:19), to let the good things in and to lock the bad things out.

Spiritual authority is not for the purpose of lording it over others or dictating terms. Spiritual leadership is for the purpose of edification (2 Cor. 13:10). Gatekeepers serve those whom they protect by defending them from predatory doctrines with integrity, reverence, and incorruptibility of the truth, adorning the doctrine of God in all things (Titus 2:7, 10).

Spiritual abuse occurs when sound doctrine (v. 1) is abandoned for personal gain. Teaching the prosperity gospel is a prime example: Prosperity doctrine is nothing more than a glorified Ponzi scheme that enriches the pastor at the top of the pyramid to the lack of the trusting giver at the bottom. We sheep must beware of bad doctrine for it always leads to our hurt (Matt. 16:12).

Spiritual abandonment happens when the gatekeeper lets the enemy in to wreak havoc on the vulnerable. At the spiritual level, if I as a father or a team leader allow lust to penetrate my mind, it is as though I had opened the gate of the sheepfold to wolves. The predators can enter and massacre the sheep. "Strike the Shepherd, and the sheep will be scattered; then I will turn My hand against the little ones" (Zech. 13:7). If leaders fall, the vulnerable ones are scattered. Spiritual leadership is the first line of defense for the body of Christ. When leaders make even small concessions to evil this does immense damage within the fold. Spiritual leaders have the responsibility to guard the gates devotedly, letting in neither large lions nor small foxes. Followers have the responsibility to pray for their leaders, understanding how much demonic filth the leader can shield them from if the gate is kept firmly sealed. Small concessions by shepherds result in damaging blows to the sheep.

RAJPUT BHATTI MUSLIMS OF PAKISTAN (662,000; 0.0% EVANGELICAL)

PRAY THAT CHRISTIANS FROM AROUND THE WORLD WOULD WORK TOGETHER TO REACH THE RAJPUT BHATTI AND THAT THE RAJPUT BHATTI WOULD BE JOINED TO THE BODY OF CHRIST (JOHN 17:20-23).

OCTOBER 11: ONLY JESUS

PSALM 135; ZECHARIAH 14; MATTHEW 17; TITUS 3

Hear Only Him. Jesus took His closest disciples up the Mount of Transfiguration for a sneak preview of His glory (Matt.17:5). In the process Peter, James, and John got distracted by some of their heroes: Moses and Elijah. The Father thundered from heaven for them to have ears for Jesus alone. We are surrounded by many faithful witnesses. We read their stories, we listen to their sermons, and we profit from their wisdom. Yet every once in a while we need to be reminded to tune people out and tune Jesus in.

See Only Him. After the heavenly reminder that Jesus had better things to say than even the giants of faith, Matthew recorded that the disciples "saw no one but Jesus only" (v. 8). We, too, should have myopic vision in this regard: all other personalities and influences must fade as we see Jesus only. A great old hymn explains it well: "Since my eyes were fixed on Jesus, I've lost sight of all beside; so enchained my spirit's vision, looking at the Crucified. "All for Jesus, all for Jesus, all my days and all my hours."[2] We need to stare so fixedly at Him that we are blind to all others.

Talk Only to Him. Jesus instructed His dumbstruck disciples to tell no one what they had seen until after His resurrection (v. 9). We should not share everything He reveals to us. We need to keep some conversations confidential for a while. Some prayers should never be made prayer requests; they should be told only to Jesus. Another hymn instructs: "I must tell Jesus all of my trials; I cannot bear these burdens alone; in my distress He kindly will help me. . . . Jesus can help me, Jesus alone."[3] Some things are too precious to share with others. We hold them close to our hearts, looking only . . . listening only . . . talking only to Jesus.

Rely Only on Him. There are some things that only Jesus can do. He instructed that "some things can only come out by prayer and fasting" (v. 21). The most reliable manuscripts do not contain the word *fasting*. Most likely Jesus simply said, "Some things can only come out by prayer." Fasting has turned into a kind of magic lamp for some Christians. In order to get what they want, they deny themselves something for a period of time. Jesus undermines this subtle bribery by pointing out that in some situations there is absolutely nothing we can do but rely on Him. If some demons and sicknesses are removed only by prayer, this means only Jesus can deal with them. Prayer then is not our activity but our surrender. This type of prayer admits that only Jesus can help. We need to move away from "Jesus-plus" to "Jesus-only."

BANIA, MUHAR HINDUS OF INDIA (907,000; 0.0% EVANGELICAL)

PRAY THAT THE HEARTS OF THE BANIA, MUHAR WOULD BE LIKE GOOD SOIL, READY TO HEAR THE GOSPEL AND TO RESPOND (MATT. 7:1-8, 18-23).

OCTOBER 12: GOD'S DISPLEASURE

PSALM 136; MALACHI 1; MATTHEW 18; PHILEMON

*G*od, whose mercy endures forever (Ps.136) and whose faithfulness endures to all generations (119:90), is the same God who gets annoyed with ministers and missionaries who despise His name. He absorbs all kinds of blasphemies from the unconverted, but when His children insult Him, He tells them bluntly, "I have no pleasure in you" (Mal. 1:10). We who claim Jesus as Lord and Master tend to insult and offend Him in two primary ways: sneering at the sacraments and submitting our second-best worship.

Sneering at the Sacraments. Malachi pointed out that those appointed to represent the Lord tend to say by word and deed that "the table of the Lord is contemptible" (v. 7). When we do not sanctify the way God communicates to us, we insult Him. He has set apart His table of communion that we might reverence what He did on the cross, and He has ordained baptism to be a holy and joyous celebration. When we cavalierly approach and abuse the sacraments of the church, we despise the Lord and we offend Him. The modern Christian takes pride in an irreverent spirituality and in doing so loses a sense of the majesty of God. We have reduced Him from sovereign to sympathetic friend, and He will have none of it. He will not be reduced, even by His servants—*especially* by His servants. When we stop respecting God's means of revealing Himself to us, this is the first step toward rebellion.

Submitting Our Second Best. Malachi said that when we give lame, blind, sick, blemished sacrifices (vv. 8, 14) we despise God in a blatant evil act. When we give Him less than our best, we kindle a fire on His altar in vain (v. 10). Christian worship can be irritating to Jesus. When our worship is half-hearted, performance-oriented, and more about the show than the Savior, Jesus looks down on all the noise as evil. We no longer bring animals to the Lord for sacrifice; today we bring our energy, time, passion, zeal, intensity, enthusiasm, and devotion. When we are more exuberant about sports than praise, our praise offends God and is evil in His ears. When we are more devoted to our children than to our heavenly Father, our devotion is diminished in His sight. When we lavish our resources on retirement, comfort, clothes, or restaurants, and not on His great passion to be known in all the earth, then our token missions giving is offensive to Him. We are proud of half-hearted efforts and our blemished sacrifices, but they disgust and offend God. In order for His name is to be great among the nations (v. 11) our offerings must be pure.

MATMATA MUSLIMS OF TUNISIA (9,620; 0.0% EVANGELICAL)

PRAY FOR THE PEACE THAT RESULTS WHEN MEN AND WOMEN ARE RECONCILED WITH GOD (JOHN 14:27). PRAY FOR MEN AND WOMEN OF PEACE (LUKE 10:6) AMONG THE MATMATA.

OCTOBER 13: GODLY OFFSPRING

PSALM 137; MALACHI 2; MATTHEW 19; HEBREWS 1

*T*here is nothing so radiant as a woman who knows that her husband cherishes and adores her. There is nothing so comforting to a man as the assurance that he is the unique pride of his bride. Faithfulness between spouses is one of the most life-giving forces on earth, even as it is increasingly rare. A pure marriage is one of the best representations we have of God's love. Marriage is sacred because it reveals God's heart to all people and His power for spiritual procreation.

God brings a man and a woman together in a binding relationship that provides the best environment for raising spiritual giants. The brokenness of humanity does not limit God in His greatness. When a man and a woman are faithful to each other and to Jesus, this is the breeding ground of the saints. It is not injurious to the principle to apply it to spiritual children. A godly marriage is one of the most powerful weapons of a frontier missionary. When a man and a woman are selflessly devoted to each other under the lordship and blessings of Christ, they are a formidable force in the spirit realm. Godly marriages do more to penetrate the darkness of unreached peoples than we realize—which is one reason marriage is increasingly under satanic attack.

Spiritual warfare is more often experienced in the privacy of the home than in the marketplace. Satan, crafty as he is, knows that he can undermine the mission and ministry if he can break the marriage. Sexual sin is but the visible fruit of hidden disease; sexual faithfulness is but the minimum of our covenant promise. A darkness-devouring marriage does not simply avoid the maximum sins (Matt. 19:1–9) but is full of joy, life, truth, honesty, trust, and mutual love. God's word to those who want their marriage to endure with His endorsement is: "Take heed to your spirit, and let none deal treacherously with the wife of his youth" (Mal. 2:15).

Godly offspring—disciples from every tribe, tongue, people, and nation—depend more on healthy marriages than they do on strategy, language learning, courage, and miracles. The real miracle is a marriage that soars above all the slings and arrows of the outrageous Devil, which means that church planting is primarily done at home.

CHAUHAN MUSLIMS OF PAKISTAN (453,000; 0.0% EVANGELICAL)

PRAY THAT BELIEVERS AMONG THE CHAUHAN WOULD PROCLAIM THE MESSAGE OF THE GOSPEL CLEARLY AND WOULD MAKE THE MOST OF EVERY OPPORTUNITY GOD PLACES BEFORE THEM (COL. 4:2-5).

OCTOBER 14: ERRORS IN PRAYER

PSALM 138; MALACHI 3; MATTHEW 20; HEBREWS 2

*I*n Matthew 20, a Mediterranean mother tried to secure high office for her sons. James and John's mama approached Jesus and asked that her boys be given a leading role in the forthcoming administration. Her prayer offended the other disciples. Probably because they felt she had jumped to the head of the queue and had requested what they wanted for themselves. It was an errant prayer, but a common one. We may roll our eyes at this ambitious mother, but in an honest review of our hearts we would have to admit how many times we have prayed for what we should not receive. In prayer, we often make two equal and opposite errors: We pray for the wrong things or we do not pray for the right things.

Praying for the Wrong Things. Our ambition, greed, lust, insecurity, and fear often lead us to pray for the wrong things. It was somewhat arrogant for that mother to request that her sons have the highest office in the land, but we do the same thing through a multitude of smaller prayers. We, too, ask to be elevated over others. Jesus cannot answer our prayers for preferential treatment because it is against His nature to spoil His children, to prefer one over the other, or to grant petitions that drive us away from Him. He wants to develop character in our lives so that we serve one another, become less important, and elevate the needs of others before our own. When we ask for something that will send us in the opposite direction, He demurs. God is especially adept at recognizing prayers of false humility: "Please make us small so we can become great."

Not Praying the Right Things. If it is arrogant to ask for the wrong things, it is just as arrogant not to ask at all. We can view prayer as a nuisance to God and be so proud that in our self-sufficiency we do not want to "bother" Him. We can consider prayer as something for the weak; and be so proud that we will not ask Him for anything. The arrogance lies in thinking we are not weak, needy, and helpless. A further subtle arrogance that is often blended with self-loathing is the thought that we are unworthy of help, as if our wretchedness can trump God's mercy. Who are we to think that our wickedness is stronger than God's goodness? This is but an ironic elevation of our selves.

Prayer is like breathing for the righteous; it comes naturally to us. The prayer God created us to pray is a continual, steady dependence on Him—not for what is not ours but for the oxygen of Himself, the continual supply for our continual need.

BIND HINDUS OF INDIA (901,000; 0.0% EVANGELICAL)

PRAY THAT THE BIND WILL UNDERSTAND THAT HOPE FOR FORGIVENESS AND ACCEPTANCE WITH GOD IS ONLY AVAILABLE THROUGH JESUS' WORK ON THE CROSS (1 COR. 1:18).

OCTOBER 15: GREAT AND TERRIBLE JESUS

PSALM 139; MALACHI 4; MATTHEW 21; HEBREWS 3

The Old Testament ends with a warning about being cursed and a reminder that the day of the Lord is both great and terrible (Mal. 4:5–6). The New Testament reminds us there are only two options for people: they fall on Jesus and are broken, or Jesus falls on them and grinds them to powder (Matt. 21:44).

The God of the Old Testament and the God of the New Testament are one and the same. Covenants change but God's character does not. The God who is love and mercy is also the God of wrath and judgment. To diminish any aspect of His being is to distort His image. The prevalent picture of Jesus today is marred because it does not do justice to His anger with sin, His hatred of the evildoer, and His cursing of the disobedient and unfruitful. The gentle Jesus who scoops vulnerable children into His arms is the same Jesus who will return to earth with a robe dipped in blood to destroy wicked and disobedient people (v. 41). Those who obey Jesus encounter His love, mercy, and compassion; those who disobey inevitably face His terribleness. Unbelief is disobedience, disobedience is rebellion, and rebellion is rewarded with hell. God swears that those who do not obey will not enter His rest, and He links this disobedience to unbelief (Heb. 3:18). When we do not believe, we disobey. Unbelief is rebellion and sin that can only end with God's punishment. The Bible teaches that belief and obedience are inseparable and always end with God's pleasure and blessing. It also teaches that believing obedience is always immediate, costly, and radical.

Immediate Obedience. Matthew recorded the story of two sons, neither of whom obeyed immediately (21:28–32). One son made no pretension; the other paid lip service but never acted. Immediate obedience is the biblical standard, not the biblical norm, and God in His great patience prefers deferred obedience to no obedience at all. When He finds believers who obey immediately, He is delighted and cannot resist lavishing Himself on them. There is no other way to be happy in Jesus than to trust and obey . . . immediately.

Costly Obedience. While obedience inevitably brings joy, it is usually a deferred joy set on the other side of suffering. The most rewarding obedience costs something. Often obedience is its own joy. We do not obey to be rewarded; we obey to please Jesus. When we please Him, something divine courses through our being and gives unexplainable life.

Radical Obedience. Obedience does not have to be rational and often is not: tying sons to altars, building arks, reducing an already puny army or reducing personal resources and strength. Denying self, forgiving enemies and a thousand other "yes to the Lord" actions make no sense at all to the world. We prove our belief by our obedience. Obedient belief shields us from the wrath of God.

MANDAEAN, SABEAN MUSLIMS OF IRAQ (7,650; 0.0% EVANGELICAL)

PRAY THAT THE BELIEVERS AMONG THE MANDAEAN, SABEAN WILL ENDURE PERSECUTION IN A CHRISTLIKE MANNER AND WILL GIVE THEIR LIVES FOR THE SAKE OF THE GOSPEL IF NECESSARY (1 PETER 2:21-23).

OCTOBER 16: WORK AT RESTING

*I*t is true: there is no rest for the wicked. Hebrews 4:6 reminds us that there is no rest, either temporal or eternal, for those who disobey. No matter how educated, accomplished, or wealthy a person is, there is no lasting harbor outside of being settled in Jesus. What about the follower of Jesus? What about those who bear the name Christ who are restless? How do believers learn to live at rest?

We Must Mix the Word with Faith (Heb. 4:2). God's Word is replete with promises, but they are not formulas or magic pills. God's promises of rest, deliverance, healing, and peace can neither be bought nor worn like charms. We have to act on them in faith. Biblical faith is robust and active. Believers must actively do what the Word tells them to do in order to be at rest. The promises of the Word assume the activity of the hearer.

We Must Cease from Our Works (vv. 10–11). It seems counterintuitive that we labor to cease from working. The seeming dissonance is resolved however when we realize the difference between working to be at rest and resting to be at work. The former tries valiantly (and vainly) to earn rest and peace. The latter determinedly accepts granted rest then spends the rest of life gladly sweating for the Master. Though both require labor, the difference between the two approaches is subtle yet critical, and there is only one way to know that our labor is on the right side of rest.

We Must Let God's Word Divide and Conquer. A marvelous explanation of Scripture is found in this context of rest and labor. The Word of God is living, powerful, and sharp for the purpose of dividing the false from the true *within us* (v. 12). God's Word discerns thoughts and intents. We cannot know whether we are working to earn rest or working because we have received rest. Only God's Word can tell the difference. The Word flays open our interior thinking and motivation so we can see what God sees—"to whom all things are naked and open" (v. 13)—and make course adjustments. There is no way for us to come to a place of soul and spirit rest outside the Word of God. It reveals both our legalism and our laziness. It guides us between these equally jagged reefs and into the eternal harbor of His rest.

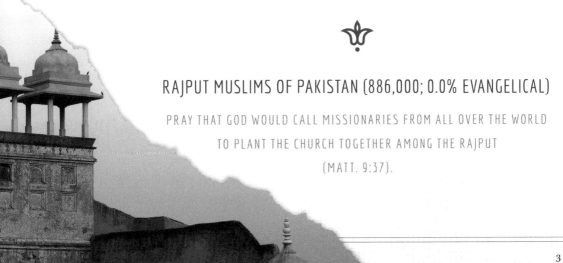

RAJPUT MUSLIMS OF PAKISTAN (886,000; 0.0% EVANGELICAL)

PRAY THAT GOD WOULD CALL MISSIONARIES FROM ALL OVER THE WORLD
TO PLANT THE CHURCH TOGETHER AMONG THE RAJPUT
(MATT. 9:37).

OCTOBER 17: STRIKES OF KINDNESS

PSALM 141; MATTHEW 23; HEBREWS 5

*U*nfortunately, those who walk with Jesus the longest are just as susceptible to becoming "dull of hearing" as the unconverted (Heb. 5:11). If we are not careful, the more we know about Jesus the harder it is for the Spirit to explain things to us. We often regress in intimacy the more we increase in head knowledge, but without intimacy there is no lasting revelation. We tend to regress from "food to milk" (v. 12). We lose our spiritual teeth and cannot "chew" on fresh revelation. We get spiritual dementia and lose a sense of discernment (v. 14). Into this malady God sends loving and wise friends to help us.

The psalmist prayed: "Let the righteous strike me; it shall be a kindness. . . . It shall be as excellent oil; let my head not refuse it" (Ps. 141:5). Though we have but one teacher, Christ (Matt. 23:8), we have many brothers and sisters, and the most loving of our siblings will tell us when we are being fools. We best humble ourselves when we accept the correction of our peers (v. 12). We best love our friends when we confront them on their folly. These are delicate matters and much abused either by too much silence or too much criticism, yet they are absolutely crucial if the family is to be healthy. Nothing can be as kind as a loving rebuke.

The image of Jesus has been so twisted that we have lost the sense of His strikes of kindness. In His incarnation He adopted human nature but never relinquished the divine. He still stands above humanity as its teacher and judge. When we refuse to be teachable, Jesus kindly hammers us. He used the following terms of endearment for the unteachable Pharisees and Sadducees: sons of hell (v. 15), fools and blind (v. 19), blind guides (v. 24), self-indulgent (v. 25), dry and dead (v. 27), hypocrites and lawless (v. 28), and serpents and brood of vipers (v. 33). He said all these niceties because those who had a knowledge of the truth refused to listen (v. 34) and, in fact, lashed out at those who spoke the truth (v. 37). Gentle Jesus is not afraid to throw around some pretty pointed descriptors for those who think they know the way of righteousness.

The wisest Christians are the ones smart enough to thank the friends who wound them. The bravest Christians are the ones brave enough to wound the ones they love. To strike with kindness is to hope, to heal, and to suffer hurt to help others.

RAIGAR HINDUS OF INDIA (886,000; 0.0% EVANGELICAL)

PRAY THAT THE RAIGAR WOULD FEEL AND KNOW THE BURDEN OF SIN AND WOULD COME TO JESUS FOR FORGIVENESS AND SALVATION (MATT. 11:28-30).

OCTOBER 18: HATED BY ALL NATIONS

PSALM 142; MATTHEW 24; HEBREWS 6

*J*esus promises that we will be hated by all nations (Matt. 24:9). The closer the approach of His second coming, the more unpopular we are going to be. It is ironic that so much mission activity is motivated by the desire to have people think well of us. This has had a negative effect our methods. For some reason we think that representing Jesus will make us popular. Obviously we have forgotten that following Jesus must include the death of our reputations. We tend to begin ministries and projects that earn us favor and shield us from hate—a fool's errand when favor becomes the goal. Our goal must ever remain to proclaim the gospel and to accept the consequence that the nations will hate us. No group of people, small or great, appreciates being told they are sinful and damned unless they repent.

Our forecast includes tribulation, being killed, being hated by all, offending many, and seeing the love of many growing cold (vv. 9–12). All these are the beginning of sorrows, and there is one primary means of navigation: endurance. Jesus tells us that "he who endures to the end will be saved" (v. 13). Not only will we be hated by all, but people from every group will resist God's work to the end and will resent the return of King Jesus. When He returns in power and great glory on the clouds of heaven "*all* the tribes of the earth will mourn" (v. 30, emphasis added). Clearly, in the last days all nations will hate missionaries and all peoples will resent the second coming of Jesus. We cannot let false optimism undermine our faith by refusing to be prepared to suffer. Faith never denies facts, and the faith that declares every nation will hear the gospel and a church will be planted among every people is the faith that acknowledges the cost: hatred of the messengers and resentment of the King.

Into this reality the writer of Hebrews interjects a precious reminder: God's purposes in Christ are infallible. We should not become sluggish (6:12); we should patiently endure with Abraham (v. 15); we should find strong consolation by fleeing to Jesus for refuge (v. 18); and we should hold on to hope as a sure and steadfast anchor for the soul (v. 19). Jesus gave His oath that our labor will not be in vain and this ends all disputes (v. 16). "The gospel of the kingdom will be preached in all the world as a witness to all the nations, and then the end will come" (Matt. 24:14). In the process, the world is going to hate us and is going to resent Jesus (vv. 9, 30). The only way this ends well is if we endure suffering. So let us determine now to suffer well, to rejoice in being rejected that the called may be accepted.

ROMANI, BALTIC MUSLIMS OF ALGERIA (3,810; 0.09% EVANGELICAL)

PRAY THAT GOD WOULD UNVEIL THE CROSS AND WOULD TAKE AWAY THE VEIL ON THE MINDS AND SPIRITS OF THE ROMANI (2 COR. 3:16–17).

OCTOBER 19: THE POWER OF AN ENDLESS LIFE

PSALM 143; MATTHEW 25; HEBREWS 7

*T*homas Obediah Chisholm penned the hymn "O to Be Like Thee": "O, to be like Thee! Lowly in spirit, holy and harmless, patient and brave."[4] This excerpt includes a phrase from Hebrews 7:26, "holy and harmless." The same verse in Hebrews defines Jesus as undefiled, separate from sinners, and higher than the heavens. What sets Christianity apart from all other faiths is the resurrection. People of other faiths who trust in their book, prophet, or ideology are wrong, not because their faith does not work but because it is temporal. It is lower than the heavens and cannot eternally endure. Many Muslims, Mormons, Hindus, and New Age adherents have testimonies. These men and women testify how their lives have changed due to the peace, discipline, or improvements resulting from their religion. We do not quibble with their testimony. We simply point out that Jesus alone has the power of an endless life.

Jesus Lives Forever. Jesus has not come according to the law of a fleshly commandment but according to the power of an endless life (Heb. 7:16). Memories and legacies and ideologies cannot compare to presence. Jesus is eternally present. His power results from His uninterrupted and eternal living presence. Because His life never ends, He crosses all time barriers and has no restrictions. No other religious figure can offer endless living.

Jesus Intercedes Forever. Because Jesus continues forever (v. 24), He is able to save to the uttermost (v. 25), always living to make intercession for those who trust in Him. This is the difference in the testimony of a Christian and a Muslim. The devotion and discipline of Muslims may positively affect their lives and families, but it cannot comprehensively save, heal, help, and cleanse—to the uttermost. Only Jesus has eternal power to intervene on our behalf. Eternity implies omnipresence. Only Jesus is there continually to save and keep. Only Jesus can cleanse the conscience. Only Jesus can forgive sin because He is its eternal conqueror.

Jesus Is Perfect Forever. God's oath appoints the Son as perfected forever (v. 28). "All may change but Jesus never! Glory to His name!"[5] Jesus is never weak, never failing, never changing. He is complete, perfect, enduring, and unblemished by the passage of time or the sins of people.

Jesus is harmless in the sense that He is gracious and forgiving, gentle in spirit, and kind to all who repent. He is also holy—impenetrable, unmovable, fixed forever, buttressed in eternal immortality, endued intrinsically with unmatched power—because of His endless life. Let us not deny the testimonies of other people. Let us simply invite them to the only One who can ensure that change and life are eternal.

SIAL MUSLIMS OF PAKISTAN (393,000; 0.0% EVANGELICAL)

PRAY THAT BELIEVERS AMONG THE SIAL WOULD BE SET FREE FROM A SPIRIT OF FEAR OF WHAT MAY COME AND WOULD BOLDLY PROCLAIM THE TRUTH OF THE GOSPEL

(2 TIM. 1:6-8).

OCTOBER 20: TO GIVE OR TO GIVE UP

PSALM 144; MATTHEW 26; HEBREWS 8

*M*atthew 26 unveils two different perspectives of giving from two different givers. One giver poured out her life savings of an alabaster flask of costly fragrant oil on Jesus (v. 7). The other gave Jesus up for thirty pieces of silver (v. 15). We face a similar choice daily: to give to Jesus extravagantly or to give Him up.

Giving to Jesus Extravagantly. To abide in Jesus we must lavish extravagant time on Him daily, both in disciplined blocks of time and in an all-day communion. Extravagant giving is not fulfilled through a one-time sacrifice but by a daily choice, a daily offering. The alabaster box was the accumulated savings of one woman and giving it to Jesus would have direct implications on her future. When Jesus is precious to us, we give Him our best, we give up other things, we prioritize Him in our schedule, and we linger in His presence, daily. Other daily choices such as when we go to bed, when we get up, how we spend our time, what we say no to, and what we prioritize undergird our responses to Jesus.

Giving Jesus Up. We criticize Judas for giving Jesus up for a sum, but we are not that different from Judas. We continually give Jesus up for truncated and rushed abiding times. We give Him up for an extra hour of sleep. We give Him up to waste time watching sports or movies that sully our souls. Most often we betray Him with the kiss of false intimacy: we pay lip service to time spent with Him but we do not live it. Pseudo-abiding is a betrayal. When we claim with our mouths that Jesus is supreme but we do not live that commitment in the moments and hours of our day, we stand with Judas and kiss the Savior. We cannot continue to hide behind the cries or worries of legalism. No lover is thought legalistic who is devoted to his bride. Another way we betray Jesus is when we use Him as a bartering chip. Judas sold Jesus cheaply. Just how much ransom is the King of Kings worth? We, too, tend to approach Jesus with the clenched fist of possession, lingering with Him for what He can give us or, worse yet, for what we can get for Him. Jim Elliot prayed: "Lord, release me from the tension of the grasping hand."[6] Abiding is not grasping Jesus to gain for self. Abiding is delighting in Jesus to the extent that we lose all sense of time and all desire for material gain, including healing or blessing. All we want is Jesus Himself. All we want to do is give to Him. This is our alabaster box: to be so delighted in Jesus that we give Him all.

JULAHA HINDUS OF INDIA (885,000; 0.0% EVANGELICAL)

PRAY FOR THE WORD OF GOD IN WRITTEN, ORAL, MUSICAL, AND DRAMATIC FORMS TO BE TRANSLATED AND TO RISE AMONG THE JULAHA (ISA. 55:10-11).

OCTOBER 21: HEAVEN IS FOR COWARDS

PSALM 145; MATTHEW 27; HEBREWS 9

*E*arth has no attraction for me outside of fighting with Christ for the souls of men and women. The writer of Hebrews declared three realities: (1) the things of earth are copies, (2) what is true awaits us in heaven, and (3) the unmitigated and uninterrupted presence of God will only be fully realized when we get to our eternal home (9:24). In this way, heaven beckons us all: rest for the weary, refuge for the innocent, deliverance for the oppressed, healing for the wounded, and peace for the warriors. Something in us should long to be in the completed presence of God. We should yearn and hope and dream and ache for heaven. Heaven is for the courageous, for the redeemed who trust in Jesus and look to Him as their forever reward.

Sometimes I rise from sleep weary, physically and spiritually exhausted at the size and difficulty of the task of world evangelism. I sit on my Cairo apartment balcony in the morning with a pounding headache after another night of bad dreams. Nursing a cup of tea, I review the day and all its demands, sigh, and wish again that I could step from earth into the arms of Jesus. Nothing is as attractive to me as heaven, for reasons both good and bad. The good reasons for heaven I listed earlier, but there is also a bad reason for wanting to go to heaven: If I am tired of fighting, if I am frustrated at the slow response, if I am angry at the unrepentant and just want to leave them to their foolish choices, if I just want to escape the unrelenting weariness of daily battle, then heaven has been reduced to a cowardly escape. It is attractive because I will not have to fight anymore.

To run from battle is both foolish and cowardly. To leave the innocent unprotected is criminal and despicable. Yet often my desire for heaven is based on these selfish ambitions. We must live with dual passions: a longing for our heavenly home and a determination to fight for our friends and lost loved ones. The only reason I am interested in one more breath on this earth is because there are more than one billion Muslims, one billion Hindus, and hundreds of millions of Buddhists, secularists, and animists who do not have the promise of God's presence ahead of them.

The best things of earth (the beauty of creation, the richness of friendship, the glory of unity and brotherhood) are only copies of the real thing. Mountains will be higher, lakes clearer, trees greener, flowers brighter, friendships deeper, music sweeter, rest purer, and joy fuller in heaven than any copies here on earth. "Oh, I want to see Him, look upon His face; there to sing forever of His saving grace."[7] There is but one reason I am at peace with that vision deferred—that my Muslim friends and neighbors might see Him, too.

SORANI MUSLIM KURDS OF IRAN (511,000; 0.0% EVANGELICAL)

PRAY THAT GOD WOULD POUR OUT HIS SPIRIT ON THE SORANI PEOPLE AND THAT THEY WOULD SEE DREAMS AND VISIONS OF JESUS. PRAY THAT THEY WOULD BE POWERFULLY SAVED AND EMPOWERED TO BE HIS WITNESSES (JOEL 2:28-32).

OCTOBER 22: THE PRECIOUS BLOOD

PSALM 146; MATTHEW 28; HEBREWS 10

*W*e Are Completed by the Blood of Jesus. The one offering of Jesus' body perfected forever "those who are being sanctified" (Heb.10:14). We sing, preach, and think about the blood of Jesus continually because it completes us. The blood of Jesus cleanses our conscience, heals our memories, removes the shame of sin, affirms our created personality, and puts us together again after sin and our natural selves have done their best to destroy us. Oh, the precious blood that completes us!

We Are Emboldened by the Blood of Jesus. The blood of Jesus gives us the spiritual courage to enter the presence of God (10:19). When the Spirit opens our eyes to the majesty of God and we realize our complete unworthiness to be near Him, the appropriate response is to fall to the ground shaking, begging for the mountains to fall on us. However, the blood stands us on our feet, gives us appropriate reverence, and walks us into the presence of glory. Oh, the precious blood that brings us near to almighty God!

We Are Protected by the Blood of Jesus. When we experience a spiritual attack, we can plead the blood of Jesus. To plead the blood is to stand in the dock while the accuser throws his most vile darts at us and we respond, "Talk to Jesus! I don't have to answer you. I have an advocate. His blood was shed for me. He is my defense and He will answer you. You have no right over me and no ability to touch me. The blood is my defense." When evil attacks us, our strongest protection is to stand under the blood and refer the Devil to the cross. Oh, the precious blood that protects us from the attacks of the enemy!

We Can Insult the Blood of Jesus. We can trample the Son of God underfoot by counting the blood of the covenant as a common thing (Heb. 10:29). If we do this, we insult the Spirit of grace. What the blood of Jesus does for us and to us is incomparably great and unfathomably costly to the Father. When we treat it lightly, we offend God. Let us live in awe of the blood of Jesus. Let us purpose to live under the blood, thankful and respectful of God's great sacrifice. Oh, the precious blood—let us never count it common!

KUMZARI MUSLIMS OF OMAN (2,430; 0.0% EVANGELICAL)

PRAY THAT CHRISTIANS FROM AROUND THE WORLD WOULD WORK TOGETHER TO REACH THE KUMZARI AND THAT THE KUMZARI WOULD BE JOINED TO THE BODY OF CHRIST (JOHN 17:20–23).

OCTOBER 23: HEALING PRAISE

PSALM 147; MARK 1; HEBREWS 11

*A*lthough we tend to approach healing as something God does in isolation, we actually partici-pate in our healing. The Scriptures are clear that faith interacts with sovereign power when the human body or emotions are restored. There is another way that we can participate in our own healing, and that is by praise. The psalmist declared praise to be beautiful and implied that it contributes to binding up the wounded (Ps. 147:1–3).

Praise is different from singing. It is wonderful to sing praise songs, but praise goes deeper than parrot-ing someone else's thoughts. Essentially, praise is our spirit's response to the Spirit of God. It includes our emotions, thoughts, and adoration of God, personally packaged and delivered to Jesus. Among the saints, personal praise begins when the prepared songs end and each individual raises his or her voice to declare the majesty of God. Praise is not contingent on our feelings, our status, our environment, or our maturity. Praise is not about us. It is about who God is despite us. When we praise God for who He is, despite how we feel or what we feel, it is pleasing to Him and healing to our wounded spirits. Praise often initiates and complements God's supernatural work in our lives.

Heaven relishes personal praise. When Jacob was dying, he blessed and worshiped, leaning on the top of his staff (Heb. 11:21). An old man with one foot in the grave opened his mouth and worshiped. This is praise worth emulating. When we are dying with Jacob, when we are in prison with Paul, when we are beaten with the apostles, when we face enemy armies with the Israelites, when our flesh is failing and we are wasting away with Job, when we have been given an impossible assignment with Mary, when all earth is shaken around us and all that we cherish is taken away and we open our mouths to speak words of adoration, this praise stirs the hosts of heaven. This praise ascends in beauty to the ears and heart of God.

When we praise despite torture, when we praise rather than accept deliverance, when we praise in trial, when we praise when mocked, when we praise in scourging, when we praise in chains, when we praise when wandering in deserts, mountains, caves, and dens (11:35–38), this praise not only moves heaven, it heals us. We can participate in our own physical and emotional healing by praising Jesus.

ROMANI, BALKAN MUSLIMS OF TURKEY (66,000; 0.0% EVANGELICAL)

PRAY THAT THE HEARTS OF THE ROMANI WOULD BE LIKE GOOD SOIL, READY TO HEAR THE GOSPEL AND TO RESPOND (MATT. 7:1-8, 18-23).

OCTOBER 24: HEAVENLY COUNSEL WITHIN

PSALM 148; MARK 2; HEBREWS 12

*G*od speaks from heaven and from within our hearts as well. The "God card" has been so over-used ("God told me such and such") that we are reluctant to admit He tells us anything unless we see it in Scripture. Without losing our devotion and adherence to Scriptural authority, we need to learn to listen to God's voice. Jesus did not receive direction from the Scriptures alone, He also "perceived in His Spirit" (Mark 2:8) what should be done and how to do it. We must learn to listen and trust what God the Spirit says to our spirits.

Not everyone has the gift of discernment. Some believers are so pastoral and kind they cannot detect anything wrong in another person. Overlooking and covering the sins of others is different from not seeing their sins or weaknesses. Christians have the Counselor within to alert them to dangers that might come through people (even well-intentioned people) and to protect them from harm. If my love for a brother or sister overcomes my good sense, I can let wolves into the sheepfold and injure the vulnerable. God warns our spirits. "The Son of Man is also Lord of the Sabbath" (Mark 2:28), Lord of all, and especially Lord over the spirits of people. We need to listen to the heavenly voice within.

"We have had human fathers who corrected us, and we paid them respect. Shall we not much more readily be in subjection to the Father of spirits and live?" (Heb. 12:9) The Father of our spirits lovingly whispers to us. He counsels us and tells us what to do about life, decisions, and other people. It is a comfort that God speaks to us through His Word, which is His general instruction to all His children. It is also a comfort that He speaks personally to our hearts. He blesses, loves, warns, directs and helps our spirits discern dangers and opportunities. We should not mock God's Spirit when He speaks either to us or to others. "See that you do not refuse Him who speaks . . . from heaven, whose voice then shook the earth" (Heb. 12:25). The God who shakes the earth also whispers to our souls. The Spirit who bypasses wind, fire, and earthquake to whisper in a still small voice, whispers still.

God has promised to remove things that can be shaken so the things that cannot be shaken may remain (v. 27). He reveals to our spirits what He wants removed. He has not forgotten how to shout and shake— "For our God is a consuming fire" (v. 29). Neither has He given up His role as Soul Whisperer.

VANJARA HINDUS OF INDIA (92,000; 0.4% EVANGELICAL)

PRAY FOR THE PEACE THAT RESULTS WHEN MEN AND WOMEN ARE RECONCILED WITH GOD (JOHN 14:27). PRAY FOR MEN AND WOMEN OF PEACE (LUKE 10:6) AMONG THE VANJARA.

OCTOBER 25: HIGH PRAISE

PSALM 149; MARK 3; HEBREWS 13

*P*raise is sourced in both the actual and the anticipated presence of Jesus. When we experience the presence of Jesus, it overwhelms us with wonder and our mouths express the joyful churning of our hearts. The anticipated presence of Jesus requires a higher praise—the praise of faith. High praise exalts Jesus for His character, whether or not the current reality is pleasurable. We read in Hebrews 13:12–15 that Jesus suffered outside the gate and we are to go there with Him, bearing His reproach for we have no continuing city here on earth. *Therefore* we continually offer a sacrifice of praise. Praise that costs something is high praise. Praise that follows Jesus, magnifying Him every difficult step of the way, is praise that delights Him

High Praise Executes Vengeance on the Nations and Punishes the Peoples (Ps. 149:7). The way of Jesus is delightfully contrary to that of the world. The people of God will suffer many injustices in the course of their lives. Our revenge is praise. In the face of great malice, we turn the other cheek by opening our mouths and declaring the preeminence of Jesus. In the spiritual realm, we strike back at our oppressors with praise. Our revenge is to ignore them and concentrate on the beauty and majesty of God. Nothing hurts a bully like being ignored. High praise turns our attention away from evil people and onto God, effectively neutralizing them by making them nonfactors.

High Praise Binds Kings and Nobles (Ps. 149:8). When we bump into officials, high and low, who make normal life difficult, it is easy to forget that God is sovereign. Little men strut around clutching their nominal authority fiercely, determined to make things difficult for God's representatives. Authorities in noncompliance with the King of Kings do all they can to frustrate His work. When we bump against the official obstacles of those who wittingly or otherwise resist what God is doing in the world, we overcome the opposition by opening our mouths and rejoicing in Jesus. When we offer high praise, we bind those who seek to bind us.

High Praise Exercises Written Judgment (Ps. 149:9). When we sense a lag between the time God issues a decree and it comes to pass, we bridge the gap with praise. God proclaims, we praise, and judgment falls. It does us no good to fret or complain during delays. This type of response is like going to war with a blunt sword. The sharp, two-edged sword of the follower of Jesus is verbalized, authentic praise—praise that precedes the realization of God's proclamations.

SUDANESE MUSLIMS OF EGYPT (4,397,000; 0.0% EVANGELICAL)

PRAY BELIEVERS AMONG THE SUDANESE WOULD PROCLAIM THE MESSAGE OF THE GOSPEL CLEARLY AND WOULD MAKE THE MOST OF EVERY OPPORTUNITY GOD PLACES BEFORE THEM (COL. 4:2–5).

OCTOBER 26: WORD PROCLAIMERS

PSALM 150, MARK 4, JAMES 1

The Word of God is central to missions. Because missions work takes place in contexts that are inherently deceptive, there must be no deception in our words or lives. We must remove all lying from our hearts (Ps. 119:29). Christians deceive themselves when they claim not to lie. We lie all the time but are clever enough to discount our lies as hyperbole or humor. God's "excellent greatness" (150:2) is sullied when it is proclaimed by two-tongued representatives.

We Are Proclaimers. Mark 4:14 states, "The sower sows the word." The missionary role, simplified to its most basic function, is to be a messenger. Before we are called to be educators, humanists, environmentalists, reformers, or spiritual SEALs (rescuing those in danger), we are called to abide in the presence of Jesus. We are called to listen to what He says and then to make it known in the world. Our gifts and service sectors vary, but the message and the source do not. The missionary is a person who lingers in God's presence, then tells the people of the world who do not have access to the gospel what God has said.

We Proclaim the Word. When missionaries traverse land and sea, it is not to make hearers in their own images but to share the words of Jesus. Missions is not about missionaries or their thoughts or ideas or opinions or words. Missions is about speaking God's truth to those who have never heard it. God wants us to elevate His Word to a high platform so it can shine (Mark 4:21). We must speak the Word so that people are "able to hear it" (v. 33). Jesus used parables to help people grapple with truth, not to disguise or veil what He wanted them to understand. The goal of the missionary is not the self-satisfaction that results from shouting parroted words to an uncomprehending audience. The goal of the missionary is to communicate God's words in such a way that all who hear will comprehend—even if they choose to reject those words. We do not confuse comprehension of the Word with acceptance of the Word. The missionary can be at peace with the rejected Word only if he or she is confident that the message was heard and understood. This is why there can be no abiding mission without linguistic and cultural fluency.

The Word Assures That We Will Have Trouble. When we are "doers" and "hearers" (James 1:22) and proclaimers of the Word, we have one guarantee: trouble. When people understand God's Word, it will offend and repulse far more of them than it will woo and please. Missionaries must come to terms with the reality that our Word-based role destines us for both joy and woe. God's Word both gives us life and leads us to our deaths.

SAYYID MUSLIMS OF PAKISTAN (1,116,000; 0.0% EVANGELICAL)

PRAY THAT THE SAYYID WILL UNDERSTAND THAT HOPE FOR FORGIVENESS AND ACCEPTANCE WITH GOD IS ONLY AVAILABLE THROUGH JESUS' WORK ON THE CROSS (1 COR. 1:18).

OCTOBER 27: CHOOSE FEAR

PROVERBS 1; MARK 5; JAMES 2

*W*e choose to fear the Lord (Prov. 1:29). Just as we can choose whether to respect our elders, so we can choose whether to honor God. We choose whether we will listen to counsel, either that of the Lord, our elders, our friends, or our followers. When we choose irreverence by refusing to listen to counsel, we will eat the fruit of our own ways. We will be filled with our own fancies and be slain and destroyed (vv. 31–32). When we choose fear (reverence), we are safe and secure "without fear of evil" (v. 33). When we choose to respect the Lord, we can disrespect evil with impunity.

Choosing to fear the Lord and to listen to Him does not allow for selective hearing. To obey some of what God instructs is a subtle form of disrespect. His law is not broken or kept piecemeal (James 2:10). We either keep the law or we do not. God's truth is not like a cluster of grapes where we can disobey one small aspect without affecting others. God's truth is like a soap bubble or a balloon—if we prick it with one pin of disobedience, we are guilty of destroying the whole thing. Thanks be to God that His mercy triumphs over judgment (v. 13), and He forgives us completely when we stumble.

If we choose to fear the Lord, we cannot believe the right things without acting on them. James wrote, "You believe that there is one God. You do well. Even the demons believe—and tremble!" (v. 19). Demons are monotheistic. The Devil knows and believes there is only one God. To believe some things about God and reject others is an irreverent insult. To believe there is one God and to reject the deity of Jesus is to choose not to fear Him but to insult Him. Islam is in direct rebellion, a flagrant disrespect of the God of heaven and earth. The monotheism of Islam is offensive to the one God who is Father, Son, and Spirit. Christians cannot gloat on this point, for those who believe without acting on their belief are as rebellious as those who believe partially. Let us not offend God by choosing to disrespect Him. Let us choose to fear the Lord, and let us express it through constant obedience, continual repentance, and complete compliance to His counsel.

KIRAR HINDUS OF INDIA (852,000; 0.0% EVANGELICAL)

PRAY THAT THE BELIEVERS AMONG THE KIRAR WILL ENDURE
PERSECUTION IN A CHRISTLIKE MANNER AND WILL GIVE THEIR
LIVES FOR THE SAKE OF THE GOSPEL IF NECESSARY
(1 PETER 2:21-23).

OCTOBER 28: AFTER WISDOM

PROVERBS 2; MARK 6; JAMES 3

*W*isdom Follows Trouble. God "stores up sound wisdom for the upright" (Prov. 2:7). We do not carry around a vast treasury of wisdom that we can draw on without prayer or reflection. Wisdom is not part of our natural being. It is available to us through the resident Holy Spirit. What is part of our natural being is the tongue, which, unfortunately, we do carry around with us. James described the tongue as a world of iniquity, a defiler of the whole body, something set on fire by hell, an unruly evil, and full of deadly poison (James 3:6–8). He also said that our self-seeking hearts often reveal a wisdom that is earthly, sensual, self-seeking, confusing, and the source of every evil thing (v. 15). As followers of Jesus, we should not rush around the world assuming we are the source of infinite wisdom, especially as our carnal wisdom so often betrays us. The normal order of things is that we get in trouble (we face a question we do not have the wisdom to answer), then we ask God to dispense divine wisdom from His inexhaustible supply.

Understanding Follows Wisdom. Understanding follows the protection of the Lord (Prov. 2:7–9). When He gives us what we need to be shielded (v. 7), guarded, and preserved (v. 8), *then* we understand "righteousness and justice, equity and every good path" (v. 9). God's wisdom does not always make sense to us nor is it always the most logical course of action, but when we obey Him and walk in His wisdom (even when it is counterintuitive), understanding is the result. We cannot wait to understand in order to act wisely. Wisdom has more to do with obedience than enlightenment, as the source of wisdom is not within us but within God. His mercies come to us with answers (Ps. 119:41–42) and, often, as we share those answers we gain understanding and wisdom.

Preservation Follows Understanding. We seek wisdom from God. Understanding follows our obedience to His wisdom, and as we understand how wise it is to walk in wisdom, we are preserved (Prov. 2:10–11). The writer of Proverbs linked wisdom to preservation from immorality. He wrote that wisdom culminates in the ability to escape the snare of seduction, specifically seduction that breaks the marriage covenant. While there is always forgiveness to the penitent, those who violate this essential wisdom of God never experience the same moral and spiritual authority (v. 19). Those who forsake wisdom and foolishly embrace immorality can no longer call others to holiness with conviction. With tears they can only warn from their self-inflicted wounds.

ARAB, CYRENAICAN MUSLIMS OF LIBYA (1,664,000; 0.1% EVANGELICAL)

PRAY THAT GOD WOULD RAISE UP MISSIONARIES FROM ALL OVER THE WORLD TO PLANT THE CHURCH TOGETHER AMONG THE ARAB, CYRENAICAN (MATT. 9:37).

OCTOBER 29: A JEALOUS SPIRIT

PROVERBS 3; MARK 7; JAMES 4

*I*n ministry and missions, most of the wounds and most of the sins come from within. Jesus said that we cannot blame devils and circumstances for what comes out of our hearts. We are soiled from the inside out, and foolishness is deep within all of us (Mark 7:15). James bluntly stated that wars and fights come from within, from the desires for pleasure that war in our members (James 4:1). We war and fight to snatch from one another what God would gladly give us if we approached Him humbly. James 4:6 is a paraphrase of Proverbs 3:34, stating that there is more God-given grace for the humble than there is for the proud. The proud get God as an enemy. The humble get Him as a friend.

James explained that "friendship with the world is enmity with God" (4:4). We cannot be friends with both, hard as we try. We have to choose between the two. It is simplistic to claim that the world is not our friend. We make friends fairly easily with materialism, prestige, acclaim, sensuality, and pride. We welcome them into our homes and our lives. We learn their jokes, know their nicknames, and feed off their energy. Anyone who claims not to be friendly with the world is self-deluded. Yet the incarnate Savior walks into this soiled peer group and bestows unexpected friendship on us. Startled and awed, we accept Him and enter into a covenant with Him, thinking we can still hang out with our former buddies once in a while. The Scripture comments on this vacillation: "The Spirit who dwells in us yearns jealously" (v. 5). God gets jealous when we spend time with our old "friends."

It seems strange to speak of the Spirit of God as jealous because we think of jealousy as petty and controlling. But He is neither petty nor controlling. Rather, He yearns for us to be devoted exclusively to Him. The Spirit is unconditionally committed to us and expects that same unreserved commitment from us. Anything less is betrayal because there is no room for third parties in the salvation covenant. The Spirit of God longs for our friendship and our fidelity. This is not the pathetic longing of the lesser for the greater. This is the unfathomable longing of the great God of all creation for reciprocal friendship with lowly, sinful people. It is a double wonder: first, that God would love and save us, and second, that His Spirit within us would jealously yearn for our exclusive friendship. Let us not be fools who choose friends who would destroy us rather than God who alone can complete us.

SHAIKH MUSLIMS OF PAKISTAN (11,675,000, 0.0% EVANGELICAL)

PRAY THAT THE SHAIKH WOULD FEEL AND KNOW THE BURDEN OF SIN AND COME TO
JESUS FOR FORGIVENESS AND SALVATION
(MATTHEW 11:28-30).

OCTOBER 30: PROGRESSIVE UNDERSTANDING

PROVERBS 4; MARK 8; JAMES 5

*W*isdom does not rush upon us like a flood, overwhelming our folly and leaving us unalterably discerning. Wisdom is a continual acquisition, and we need to be as patient with ourselves in acquiring it as Jesus is. Because we are so slow to understand, we often become discouraged and give in to the depressing thought that we are never going to learn our lessons. It seems that we will always be susceptible to the same sins and mistakes. God does not share this pessimistic view. He is committed to the process of making us wise, and He is confident of the end result—our ongoing understanding.

Mark enjoyed writing truth sandwiches. He put the meat of one truth inside complementary stories. In chapter 8 of his gospel, he told the story of a blind man whom Jesus healed progressively. After Jesus' first touch, the man could see partially: he "saw men like trees, walking" (v. 24). Jesus touched him again, and this time the man's full sight was restored. Earlier in the chapter, Mark described how the disciples were slow to understand who Jesus was. Jesus warned them about bad doctrine, and they thought He was scolding them for forgetting to bring bread. In the passage following the healing, Jesus rebuked Peter immediately after he called Jesus the Christ (vv. 29, 33). Peter's understanding was a work in progress, and so is ours. It is not realistic for us to think we will wake up wise. Wisdom happens as we walk through life, and our human limitations dictate that the accumulation of understanding will not be complete until the end of the journey. Wisdom is neither front- nor back-loaded. It is measured out steadily in daily doses.

We must be patient in the wisdom process. Our hearts need to be established over time through suffering and endurance (5:11). As we plod along the way of wisdom, we need to look in three directions: up, ahead, and down.

Look Up. We must tend our hearts with diligence for our of them spring the issues of life (Prov. 4:23). We constantly look to Jesus. The wisest thing we can do is acknowledge we are not wise and we need His help. We look to Him to keep us simple even as He makes us deep, to give us counsel even as we deliberately choose what we know is the right thing to do.

Look Ahead. Wisdom does not look through other people's windows or at other people's wives. Wisdom minds its own business, eyes straight ahead (v. 25). If we are consumed with the folly of others or their faith, we will lose momentum in our own walk.

Look Down. We must ponder the paths of our feet (v. 26), turning neither to the right nor the left (v. 27) but turning our feet to God's testimonies (Ps. 119:59). It is normal to be slow to understand. Jesus is not bothered by our slow progress, as long as we keep plodding on, daily conforming our behavior to His Word.

BANIA, OSWAL HINDUS/JAINS OF INDIA (851,000; 0.0% EVANGELICAL)

PRAY THAT GOD WOULD UNVEIL THE CROSS AND WOULD TAKE AWAY THE VEIL ON THE MINDS AND SPIRITS OF THE BANIA, OSWAL (2 COR. 3:16-17).

OCTOBER 31: TOTAL RUIN, TOTAL JOY

PROVERBS 5; MARK 9; 1 PETER 1

*T*he strongest believer is just one step away from moral disaster. The sobering reality is that one poor decision can lead to agony, for immorality is nothing less than a bitter death (Prov. 5:3). The encouraging truth is that we do not wake up one morning and decide to commit adultery. Sexual sin is the culmination of a steady inner decline. If we are purposeful in a direction of holiness, we can trust the Lord to keep us pure. The Bible gives us simple and tested means to avoid moral failure.

Run. Purity is not rocket science. If you listen to the siren song long enough, you will eventually succumb to temptation. We must remove our way far from the immoral woman and must not go near the door of her house (Prov. 5:8). Like Joseph, we must run from temptation, even if we have to leave our valuables behind. We run by not entering bookstores if we know we will flip through a novel looking for a juicy part. We run by deleting Facebook from our mobile device if we know we will search profile pictures of other users. We run by giving up Internet news if our fingers and hearts twitch to click on other things. We run by being super cautious around the opposite gender, maintaining a courteous emotional and physical distance at all times. We run by cutting good things from our daily habits, preferring to enter into life maimed rather than ride small pleasures to hell (Mark 9:43).

Rejoice. Proverbs exhorts us to revel in the wife of our youth (5:18). Joy in what we have is a choice, not a reaction. We are not craven animals who cannot control our eyes or our passions. We were created with the ability to choose faithfulness in marriage. On a grander scale, the only way to overcome lesser pleasures is with higher ones. Immorality is fun and energizing but only for a brief moment. We overcome the possible energy of sexual sin by keeping the greater joy of fidelity before us. Fidelity is sourced in God, not humanity, so the highest joys of faithfulness are available both to the single person and the married person. We overcome the temptation and pleasure of sexual dalliance by enjoying Jesus' pleasure at our faithful devotion to Him (1 Peter 1:8).

Obey. We purify our souls by "obeying the truth through the Spirit" (v. 22) because we are born again of incorruptible seed through the Word of God that endures forever (vv. 23–25). If adultery and sexual perversion are the inevitable results of a thousand little denials of the Spirit's promptings, holiness is the undeniable product of a thousand little acts of daily obedience. We stay pure ten years from now by saying yes to Jesus and His Word today. Small repeated steps of obedience produce immunity to large steps of temptation.

NAJDI BEDOUIN MUSLIMS OF IRAQ (1,466,000; 0.0% EVANGELICAL)

PRAY THAT BELIEVERS AMONG THE NAJDI WOULD BE SET FREE FROM A SPIRIT OF FEAR OF WHAT MAY COME AND WOULD BOLDLY PROCLAIM THE TRUTH OF THE GOSPEL

(2 TIM. 1:6–8).

So do not be ashamed of the testimony about our Lord or of me his prisoner. Rather, join with me in suffering for the gospel, by the power of God.

2 TIM. 1:8 NIV

November

"I HAVE FOUND THAT THERE ARE THREE STAGES IN EVERY GREAT WORK OF GOD: FIRST, IT IS IMPOSSIBLE, THEN IT IS DIFFICULT, THEN IT IS DONE."

—Hudson Taylor

NOVEMBER 1: DOES GOD HATE?

PROVERBS 6; MARK 10; 1 PETER 2

*A*ll sin is sin, and even the smallest sin separates us from God. Because we are all sinners, we cannot condemn others for their sin just because it is different from ours. It is clear that there are things that God hates (Prov. 6:16), and one of those is the person who sows discord among the brethren. It is interesting that this passage goes on to warn of adultery (vv. 20–29). Adultery is a uniquely evil way of sowing discord between those in covenant, so it is no surprise that God also hates divorce (Mal. 2:16). Jesus taught about His design for marriage: two people whom God has intentionally joined together should never be broken up (Mark 10:5, 8–9). God hates the people who sow discord in a marriage, who separate what God has joined together, including those who separate themselves.

Hate might be the most misunderstood of God's attributes since we have so often abused or misunderstood its nature. The Scripture is clear that God hates, and there are multiple citations to prove God hates certain things, even certain people. When God hates someone or something, it means He is so utterly against that person or that thing that He will destroy it. In this sense only God can hate purely because He alone has the authority to destroy a life or send a life to hell. Let us not arrogantly strip away from God what belongs to Him. Our abuse of hate does not remove God's sovereign right to destroy what is in rebellion. Granting that it is for God alone to give life or to remove it, we must still share in His passions. In order to safely do so where hate is concerned, let us turn those passions inward—not in self-loathing but in sobering self-reflection and self-correction.

We must search our hearts and lives ruthlessly for any word or action that undermines authority, assassinates character, betrays confidence, introduces suspicion, or tears down brothers and sisters. We must learn to hate and destroy anything in our hearts that hates and destroys others, especially anything that could lead to sexual sin. Sexual sin destroys the very soul of all concerned (Prov. 6:32). The warnings of God about sexual perversion and His calling to holiness and purity are incessant because the great Bishop of our souls (1 Peter 2:25) knows the powerful destruction of sexual sin. It reduces us to a crust of bread, burned and seared (Prov. 6:26–28), which is all the more reason to hate any small thing in our hearts that could make us vulnerable. It is a loving act to hate what God hates. In fear and awe let us learn to wield this dangerous sword by first hating in us what God hates.

SHUGHNI MUSLIMS OF TAJIKISTAN (98,000; 0.0% EVANGELICAL)

PRAY FOR THE WORD OF GOD IN WRITTEN, ORAL, MUSICAL, AND DRAMATIC FORMS TO BE
TRANSLATED AND TO RISE AMONG THE SHUGHNI
(ISA. 55:10-11).

*A*nswered prayer is not the same as fulfilled desire. The goal of prayer is communion with God, not granted requests. Primarily, we pray to be brought near to Jesus, not to come closer to our goals. Answers are a byproduct of the real goal of prayer: intimacy with Christ. In order to preserve this intimacy through prayer rather than turn God into our servant, His Word gives us guidelines.

We Must Believe in Order to Receive. Jesus told His disciples that doubt-free asking results in moving mountains (Mark 11:23). Faith that does impossible things is not faith in God's capacity but in His character. Muslims, for example, believe that God can do anything, but this belief does not guarantee answered prayer. We must believe that God is who He says He is if we are to receive what He wants to give.

We Must Forgive in Order to Receive. If we want to receive forgiveness (and there should not be a more common prayer), we must forgive others. It seems elementary, but this aspect of prayer is one that is often violated. We demand for ourselves what we will not give to others. Desperately in need of daily forgiveness, we daily hold others' sins and faults against them (vv. 25–26). We cannot retain hurts and anger at others and expect to receive propitiation (the appeasement of God's anger) ourselves.

We Must Submit in Order to Receive. Jesus refused to answer the questions of those who did not answer His (vv. 27–33). To me, this means we must approach prayer on God's terms, not ours. For example, we read in 1 Peter 3:5–7 that the prayers of a husband and wife who practice mutual submission will not be hindered. If we are to have our prayers answered, we must pray from a posture of submission—both to God and to one another.

We Must Love in Order to Receive. Peter also wrote that the eyes of the Lord are on the righteous and His ears open to their prayers (v. 12). Peter defined righteousness in that passage as having compassion and being tenderhearted and courteous. We cannot expect to treat others like trash and have God listen to our prayers. When we treat others well, God answers our prayers. Answered prayers bring us closer to Jesus and make us more like Him, but they do not necessarily provide what we ask for. We begin prayer by wanting things, and we end by being satisfied with Jesus.

RAJPUT, SIKHS OF INDIA (829,000; 0.0% EVANGELICAL)

PRAY THAT GOD WOULD POUR OUT HIS SPIRIT ON THE RAJPUT AND THAT THEY WOULD SEE DREAMS AND VISIONS OF JESUS. PRAY THAT THEY WOULD BE SAVED AND EMPOWERED TO BE HIS WITNESSES (JOEL 2:28–32).

NOVEMBER 3: THE FIRST COMMANDMENT

PROVERBS 8; MARK 12; 1 PETER 4

*P*roverbs refers to wisdom as pre-created, a person who existed from eternity past. This pre-figuring of Jesus opened the minds of first-century Jews to the possibility of trinitarian monotheism. Proverbs 8:34 instructs us to watch and wait for wisdom, to seek diligently for it (v. 17). First Peter 4:7 reminds us to be watchful in our prayers. When it comes to loving God, we start by listening to Him. We cannot truly love God if we have not listened carefully to what He has said and then conscientiously obeyed.

We Love God by Obeying Him. In order to love God with all our hearts, minds, and strength (Mark 12:30), we must first hear what He says. Hearing God cannot be separated from obeying what we have heard. In fact, if we do not act on what we have heard, then we have not heard and we have not loved. There is no love without obedience. The greatest commandment, by definition, demands the greatest obedience. Our love for God is not simply an internalized feeling. Great love for God happens through the energetic employment of hands, head, tongue, and feet in response to what God has told us to do. To *love* God with all our hearts, souls, minds, and strength is to *obey* God with all our hearts, souls, minds, and strength. Love is proved by obedience. Obedience is prompted by carefully listening to what God is saying. In order to listen to what God says we must quiet our souls, turn off competing voices, and wait patiently for Him to speak. The first commandment is "Hear!"

We Love Others by Preferring Them. There is an ordered sequence to love. First, we hear what God says. Second, we obey what God says, summoning every aspect of our being to attend to His desires. Third, we lay down our desires in order to serve those around us. We demonstrate that we hear, obey, and love God by hearing, serving, and loving those around us. Even as the first way we love God is by hearing Him, so the first way we love those around us is by hearing them. Too many missionaries and ministers rush by this first command of love: hearing. We serve others in the way we want to serve them. Love serves people in the way *they* want and need to be served. The rule of loving is to begin by hearing those we hope to serve and listening carefully to how they want to be helped. We do not love others when we serve them in order to feel better about ourselves.

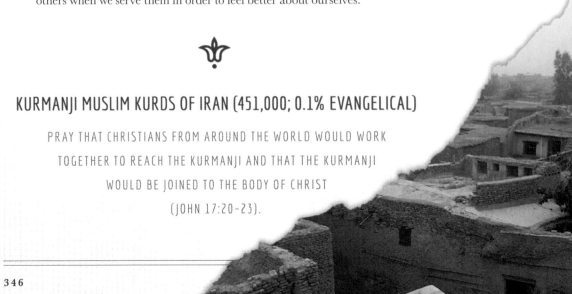

KURMANJI MUSLIM KURDS OF IRAN (451,000; 0.1% EVANGELICAL)

PRAY THAT CHRISTIANS FROM AROUND THE WORLD WOULD WORK
TOGETHER TO REACH THE KURMANJI AND THAT THE KURMANJI
WOULD BE JOINED TO THE BODY OF CHRIST
(JOHN 17:20-23).

*W*isdom or Folly. Both wisdom and folly spread an alluring banquet, and they share an identical invitation. "Whoever is simple, let him turn in here" (Prov. 9:4, 16). Both wisdom and folly offer pleasure, and both call for our indulgence. Wisdom presents relationship and knowledge of the Holy One (v. 10). It invites us to feast on Jesus. Folly offers short-term sensual revelry. The wisest thing we can do is settle into the discipline of knowing Jesus over time—a long-term joy. The most foolish thing we can do is to work toward immediate gratification, short-term joys whose price tag is long-term sorrow.

Endurance or Escape. The Spirit invites the Christian to endure suffering, and the flesh counsels to escape it. We can choose to be a witness of the sufferings of Christ and a partaker in their glory (1 Peter 5:1). We can choose to be hated by all and betrayed by our brothers (Mark 13:12–13), or we can choose to avoid persecution by refusing to allow the Holy Spirit to speak through us (v. 11). In the big scheme of things, followers of Jesus must be cautious that their eschatology is not framed by a wrongheaded theology of suffering. If we look at the rapture primarily as a means to escape suffering, we have missed a central component of the gospel—the willingness to suffer so others might be saved. The biblical norm indicates that God's primary means of deliverance is endurance. He walks with us *through* trial and trouble. Mark said it bluntly, "He who endures to the end shall be saved" (13:13)

Devoured or Delivered. Both God and Satan restlessly search the earth for opportunities. Our "adversary the devil walks about like a roaring lion, seeking whom he may devour" (1 Peter 5:9), while "the eyes of the LORD run to and fro throughout the whole earth, to show Himself strong on behalf of those whose heart is loyal to Him" (2 Chron. 16:9). Life constantly exposes us to the potential of evil. We send missionaries to areas of violence with the twin understanding that we are sending them into harm's way (the Devil's domain) at the same time we are committing them into the hands of a faithful Creator who stands strong for those who stand for Him.

Followers of Jesus are presented with choices, competing calls. Wisdom and folly issue the same invitation. Suffering offers the opportunity either to escape and be worse off for it or to endure and find unexpected joy. Daily life exposes us both to the danger of the Devil and the delight of being defended by God. Those who choose wisdom will be empowered to endure and will be marvelously delivered.

IRAQI MUSLIMS OF JORDAN (903,000; 0.3% EVANGELICAL)

PRAY THAT THE HEARTS OF THE IRAQI MUSLIMS OF JORDAN WOULD BE LIKE GOOD SOIL,
READY TO HEAR THE GOSPEL AND TO RESPOND
(MATT. 7:1-8, 18-23).

NOVEMBER 5: TURN YOUR EYES

PROVERBS 10; MARK 14; 2 PETER 1

*T*he Bible is clear about the anatomy of the soul: What goes into the heart enters by the eyes, and what comes out of the heart exits by the mouth. In order to feed our souls, we must be judicious about our eyes. The eye is the lamp of the body, and if the eye is pure and focused on the right things, then the whole body is full of light (Matt. 6:22). It is vital that we turn our eyes toward the heart of God and away from the words of people.

Turn Your Eyes to the Bible. The psalmist pleaded: "Turn away my eyes from looking at worthless things and revive me in Your way" (Ps. 119:37). We need to have an untiring eye for the Scriptures, the words and truth of Jesus. We feed our hearts and our souls by ingesting large or deep portions of Scripture on a daily basis. The Bible is like bread. Yesterday's bread does not nourish—no matter how sweet it was. We need fresh manna for our souls every morning. We need to turn our eyes to the Bible and away from our own foolish words.

Turn your eyes to the harvest. Proverbs 10 mentions the futility of empty words multiple times. Prating fools fall, and lazy sons cause shame. It annoys God when we observe the lost but do not reach out to them. "He who sleeps in harvest is a son who causes shame. . . . As vinegar to the teeth and smoke to the eyes, so is the lazy man to those who send him" (v.v. 5, 26). Missionaries are not immune to laziness or to a growing dichotomy between their rhetoric and their actions. We must continually look at what Jesus is fixed upon—and He is staring at the harvest. We turn our eyes to those who do not have access to the gospel and away from self-congratulation. We practice more weeping and less cheering.

Turn Your Eyes to God's Majesty. Peter reminds us that we are eyewitnesses of the majesty of Jesus (2 Peter 1:16). Though we are prone to darkness (not seeing well), the day dawns and the morning star rises in our hearts (v. 19), and it is not until we look at the light that we truly see the darkness. It is in looking to Jesus that words (our own and others) are purified and clarified. When we see Jesus clearly, His light goes through our eyes into our souls where it kindles a fire, and we begin to speak as we are moved by the Holy Spirit (v. 21). We turn our eyes to Jesus and away from cunning fables. The result is Spirit-empowered speech—the prophetic word on fire. The only way we escape the condemnation of our own mouths is to fix our eyes on the Bible, on the harvest, and the divine majesty of Jesus.

KHAIKHELI MUSLIMS OF PAKISTAN (369,000; 0.0% EVANGELICAL)

PRAY FOR THE PEACE THAT RESULTS WHEN MEN AND WOMEN ARE RECONCILED WITH GOD (JOHN 14:27). PRAY FOR MEN AND WOMEN OF PEACE (LUKE 10:6) AMONG THE KHAIKHELI.

NOVEMBER 6: HOLD YOUR PEACE

PROVERBS 11; MARK 15; 2 PETER 2

*I*t is both remarkable and puzzling to observe which people endure in fruitful mission and ministry. There seems to be a certain X-factor in character that aids missionaries in fruitful labor over time. It is something that defies description or even identification. Many times I have been surprised at the exceptional candidate who has faltered and the seemingly frail family who has served magnificently for decades. As we interact with people, we need to be careful not to make quick judgments that condemn or reward but to hold our peace and observe our colleagues over time. "He who is devoid of wisdom despises his neighbor, but a man of understanding holds his peace" (Prov. 11:12).

Proverbs 11 goes on to warn that failure results from a lack of counsel and encourages the safety that is found in a multitude of counselors (v. 14). My good friend Peter Njiri is an incredible African leader who differentiates between gossip and the need for leaders to evaluate their disciples. "If we were shepherds," he says, "we would talk about our animals. Since we lead men, we talk about men." It is necessary to evaluate those we are equipping for ministry, but it is important not to do this in isolation, lest our personal biases or shortcomings cloud our judgment. An important way we hold our peace is by considering the perspective of other wise and prudent counselors. Often missionaries make the mistake of listening to one cultural coach—a mistake we usually do not make in our own culture. We need to receive advice from a variety of voices, especially on the field. The majority is not always right, which means we should always consider the minority report even if we do not heed it. Our critics often have truth imbedded in their objections. Sometimes the best counsel comes not from our friendly peers but from our enemies. Let us have the humility to remember that even prophets can be overtaken by a certain kind of madness and occasionally need to hear the counsel of dumb donkeys (2 Peter 2).

Envy is the enemy of honest evaluation of others. We can cloak envy with all kinds of positive terms such as *discernment, disquiet,* and an *unsettled spirit.* Though these feelings can be genuine, we must be ruthless about the envy in our hearts for envy has consequences on Jesus and on the kingdom (Mark 15:10). Envy tends to elevate either the evil person or the benignly inadequate person to leadership roles. Envy causes us to appoint people to lead whom we would never choose otherwise. Envy destroys the just and harms the whole, for in our insecurity we restrict those who could lead best. Envy undermines good counsel and leads to disaster.

BAHNA HINDUS OF INDIA (813,000; 0.0% EVANGELICAL)

PRAY THAT BELIEVERS AMONG THE BAHNA WOULD PROCLAIM THE MESSAGE OF THE GOSPEL CLEARLY AND WOULD MAKE THE MOST OF EVERY OPPORTUNITY GOD PLACES BEFORE THEM (COL. 4:2-5).

NOVEMBER 7: SAVED BY BAPTISM

PROVERBS 12; MARK 16; 2 PETER 3

*U*nlike other rescues that prevent death, salvation is only efficacious if we die. Baptism is both a death and a resurrection, and it is only completed sequentially. We have to die with Christ if we are to be raised with Him. In this sense, belief is not enough because even the demons believe and tremble (James 2:19). Baptism must accompany belief: "He who believes and is baptized will be saved" (Mark 16:16).

We must not equate baptism with works. Salvation comes by grace through faith alone, yet faith requires baptism. In the Muslim world, the point of no return in Christian conversion is baptism. A Muslim can make a verbal profession of faith in Jesus and his friends and family will not consider it binding. However, when a Muslim is baptized this draws a clear line in the sand. It is a declaration: "I am dead to being Muslim. There is no return. Now I live only in Christ." When the Bible talks of baptism, it does not consider the symbolic act to be magical but rather binding. To be saved, we must not only believe that Jesus is Lord and Savior, we must also take irrevocable private and public steps that bind us to Him and His purposes. There is no dual citizenship spiritually; we are either all in or not in at all. Baptism demonstrates that we only have life in Christ if we have died to sin. It is a death with concrete, measurable, observable benchmarks. We do not say what we used to say, we do not do what we used to do, we do not think how we used to think, we do not react as we used to react, and we do not trust ourselves or others in the same ways.

We must be careful that we do not baptize new converts too early. Former Muslims are baptized too early if they do not understand that this act requires the death of Islam. Evangelical Christians are baptized too early if they do not understand that this act requires death to old habits, friends, behaviors, patterns, words, thoughts, and attitudes. To be truly saved, a person must nail Islam and secular humanism and any other ideology to the cross and forsake them. The symbolic act of adult baptism may only happen once (though symbolism does not suffer from repetition), but the spiritual act of baptism needs to be renewed daily. Morning by morning we need the spiritual baptism of dying and rising. When we awake from a night of sleep, let it be the renewed baptism of rising from the dead. Let our rising prayer be: "Jesus, I have died with You in baptism. Today I rise to live Your life, think Your thoughts, and do Your deeds." When the sun goes down, may its message to us be: "You must die again to the old self; you will rise to the image of Jesus." We are not saved unless we believe (turn to Jesus) and are baptized (radically turn away from sin). We die daily and we rise daily from deadly self to new life in Christ.

ASSYRIAN MUSLIMS OF IRAQ (611,000; 1.0% EVANGELICAL)

PRAY THAT ASSYRIANS WILL UNDERSTAND THAT HOPE FOR FORGIVENESS AND ACCEPTANCE WITH GOD IS ONLY AVAILABLE THROUGH JESUS' WORK ON THE CROSS (1 COR. 1:18).

*W*e have slandered John the Baptist. We present him as an antisocial, desert-dwelling, wild and wooly, locust-crunching, stern, gruff, angry prophet who did not brush his hair or teeth but yelled at people, faltered a bit at the end, then got his head chopped off. Luke presents a very different picture of John—a picture gilded with joy.

When John's birth was announced, it was framed with a prediction that he would bring joy and gladness, and many rejoiced at his birth (Luke 1:14). We are told that John was filled with the Holy Spirit in the womb (something fairly unique among humans), and that he leaped for joy in the womb when he tummy-bumped Jesus (v. 44). Elizabeth's neighbors also rejoiced at John's birth (v. 58). You cannot understand the work of the Holy Spirit in John the Baptist outside of the context of joy. The same is true of Mary: "My soul magnifies the Lord, and my spirit has rejoiced in God my Savior" (vv. 46–47). This was after the Holy Spirit had come upon her and the power of the highest had overshadowed her (v. 35). For John and for Mary, as it should be for us, the empowerment of the Spirit was evidenced by joy.

The Holy Spirit is not dour and eternally solemn. The Holy Spirit brings life, joy, light, and hope. When the Holy Spirit comes into our hearts at conversion and we are refilled again and again with the Spirit, this leads inevitably to joy. Those who claim to be Spirit-filled but live crabby, angry lives are not walking in the Spirit at all, for the Spirit of God brings joy. When we are filled with the Holy Spirit, we have joy inside of our lives and joy cascading outside of our lives. A common mark of Spirit-filled people is the joy that radiates from them, surging within them and splashing onto others. We grieve the Holy Spirit of joy when we present Him or His filling as something that makes us dour, solemn, or intimidating. The Spirit makes us winsome, approachable, gracious, joyful, and inspiring.

If the filling of the Spirit is marked by joy, so the pursuit of the Holy Spirit should be marked by joy. We have categorized a variety of litmus tests for the Spirit's filling but rarely do these include the simple joy of pursuing more of Jesus. When the soul is consumed with the joyful pursuit of magnificent Jesus, it pays no heed to what others think or what institutions demand. The soul that is most ripe for initial or repeated infillings of the Spirit is the soul that simply rejoices in God our Savior. The longing for more of Jesus is what fills us with joy so unspeakable that we must say something—even if it is ecstatic.

MOHANA MUSLIMS OF PAKISTAN (502,000; 0.0% EVANGELICAL)

PRAY THAT THE BELIEVERS AMONG THE MOHANA WILL ENDURE PERSECUTION IN A CHRISTLIKE MANNER AND WILL GIVE THEIR LIVES FOR THE SAKE OF THE GOSPEL IF NECESSARY (1 PETER 2:21-23).

NOVEMBER 9: JESUS IS NOT OUR SERVANT

PROVERBS 14; LUKE 2; 1 JOHN 2

*T*he incarnation is powerful because it was so unexpected. Who would have thought that God Almighty would come to earth as a babe wrapped in swaddling clothes (Luke 2:12)? We have become a little too comfortable with the anomalies of God—incarnation and servanthood. God is not man, and God is not a servant. The shocking fact that God became man and that He served should terrify us as much as comfort us.

It is somewhat ludicrous to call Jesus a servant-king. The danger in reducing Jesus to this hyphenated nonsense is that it leads us to consider Him a genie who exists to meet our needs and do whatever we command. This is insulting to the character of God. It does not reflect the eternity of Jesus, and it is not representative of the King of Kings and Lord of Lords.

Let us step back and examine this servant motif in the Scriptures. God does not exist in eternity past or present to serve people. The God of the Old Testament, the God who does not change, is servant to no one. The God who will come again at the trumpet blast to rule and reign will come to be served. The suffering servant of Isaiah and the proclamation that Christ "did not come to be served but to serve" are directly and *only* linked to the cross, to giving His life "as a ransom for many" (Matt. 20:28).

Even Jesus' earthly ministry was not characterized by service. He gave orders. He commanded. He did not make decisions by consensus. He demanded obedience. Girding a towel to wash His disciples' feet was alarming because it had never happened before. Jesus' disciples served Him for three years. He did not traipse around Judea and Galilee serving Judas and Peter and James; they served Him. The New Testament God is very much a God to be served and obeyed. John said that we know and love Him by obeying Him (1 John 2:3, 5). Jesus as servant hermeneutically means only one thing: The Son obeyed the Father. To consider Jesus our servant, even by expectation of the wishes He fulfills, is blasphemy.

A common error in missions is to consider our work as a continuation of what Jesus has done. It is not; we are not little messiahs. There is one Christ, and His work on the cross is done. Our work is to point others to Him. Jesus served by going to the cross. He is not a peer serving a peer, nor is He a finite human leading other humans. He is unalterably, eternally King of Kings and Lord of Lords. He is not our servant. By all means let us serve one another, but let us not demand that God serve us.

YADAV HINDUS OF INDIA (59,900,000; 0.01% EVANGELICAL)

PLEASE PRAY THAT GOD WOULD RAISE UP MISSIONARIES FROM ALL OVER THE WORLD TO PLANT THE CHURCH TOGETHER AMONG THE YADAV (MATT. 9:37).

NOVEMBER 10: BLAMELESS AND BELOVED

PROVERBS 15; LUKE 3; 1 JOHN 3

*L*et my heart be blameless regarding Your statutes," the psalmist prayed, "that I may not be ashamed" (Ps.119:80). If anything short of a blameless heart brings shame, then blamelessness must be God's minimal standard, not man's highest goal. It is staggering to think of blamelessness as the entry point, not the destination. Oh what wonder, the impossible expectations of God for us! How marvelous is God's infinite capacity to bring us to the place of blamelessness and then beyond it, how spectacular the grace that does not stop at redemption. God's unrelenting mercy presses on, past redemption, past a blameless heart, past the highest expectations of people, and presses toward His expectation for us—conformity to Himself! We can hardly bear the thought or the process.

John exclaimed in joyful wonder: "Behold what manner of love the Father has bestowed on us, that we should be called children of God" (1 John 3:1). As unbelievably blessed as we are to be God's children, it is a minimum standard. John continued to declare that "it has not yet been revealed what we shall be" (v. 2). God's goal is not just to adopt us as beloved children but to make us like Him, for "we shall see Him as He is" (v. 2). God has unimaginable goals for us. We look at becoming blameless sons and daughters as a final destination. God looks at these wondrous relational standings as portals. His destination is to stamp the divine image so deeply upon us that we become like Him.

It is difficult to believe that we will be blameless. It is even difficult for many of us to believe we are beloved. We are content to sit on the outer edges of glory. It is enough for us to be redeemed, to be one of millions who enjoy the encompassing love of the Father. We are satisfied to sense His love remotely, as one on the outer fringe of a crowd pressed in to see Jesus. We can even picture and anticipate the joy of being in heaven and looking toward the throne from a comfortable distance, where others press in around Jesus while we breathe deeply of the peripheral glow. But this is not enough for Him.

God's unrelenting passion, which does not stop at blamelessness and does not rest at becoming His children, cannot allow intimacy by proxy. God reaches into our very being and gently, firmly pulls us ever closer to Himself. It hurts, it burns, it destroys all comfort, and it is both agonizing and awesome to be brought nearer and nearer to God. We writhe and resist this infinite drawing. We feel unworthy, and that falsehood must be burned out of us. Intimacy with God scares the sin out of us. Ever deeper, ever closer, intimacy can be an uncomfortable process for those who have been twisted. But the process straightens then envelops us with sweetness.

EGYPTIAN MUSLIMS OF SAUDI ARABIA (522,000; 1.9% EVANGELICAL)

PRAY THAT THE EGYPTIANS WOULD FEEL AND KNOW THE BURDEN OF SIN AND WOULD COME TO
JESUS FOR FORGIVENESS AND SALVATION (MATT. 11:28-30).

NOVEMBER 11: TEMPTED TO PRIDE

PROVERBS 16; LUKE 4; 1 JOHN 5

*P*ride lurks in every human heart, waiting for the most damaging time to emerge. Proverbs warns us that "pride goes before destruction, and a haughty spirit before a fall" (16:18), and the destruction is not of the proud person alone. Pride destroys the innocent as often as it does the proud. When Jesus was tempted by the Devil, Luke wrote that "when the devil had ended every temptation, he departed from Him *until an opportune time*" (4:13, emphasis added). Not only did Jesus endure every form of temptation, it seems He had to overcome multiple repetitions of these temptations. The opportune time for the Devil to tempt is usually the most vulnerable time for his victims. He will tempt us to pride over and over again, and if we succumb to the repeated temptation, we will not only destroy ourselves but those around us. The goal of the Devil in tempting God's children is seldom limited to the destruction of one person. He is committed to mass slaughter.

The Pride of Thinking We Are Good. The Son of God has come and has given us understanding (1 John 5:20). Basic Christianity teaches us that we are not good, have never been good, and will never be good in our own strength. Pride repeatedly whispers otherwise and flatters us incessantly. It tells us that we are intrinsically good, we deserve exemptions, and we have innate goodness. Pride makes us feel good about ourselves; it makes us self-reliant. Humility makes us feel good about God; it makes us God-dependent.

The Pride of Thinking We Are Better. If the Devil cannot tempt us into thinking we are good, he circles around again and this time concedes: "True, you are not good, but at least you are better than those around you." To this attractive delusion we remind ourselves that "the whole world lies under the sway of the wicked one" (v. 19). We are not under the authority of the Devil, but our minds and wills are fallen and we are depraved. The biblical definition of sin does not allow for "better sin." My sin cannot be better than my neighbor's. All sin condemns. Any sin condemns. If you are a sinner (and you are), there can be no "better than."

The Pride of Thinking We Are Immune. Once more the subtle Serpent attempts to throw a coil around our spirits. "True," he says, "you are not good, and you are not better than your brother, but at least you are not vulnerable to certain sins. At least you will never do what others have done." This lie can be the most damaging of all, for the reality is that we are capable of committing any sin. The capacity for evil in our hearts knows no bounds, and a sure way to slip is to believe the lie that we are incapable of slipping. False confidence leads to moral laxity. Every wall must be shored up and defended. Nothing is as dangerous to us as an undefended strength.

SAMMA MUSLIMS OF PAKISTAN (2,063,000; 0.0% EVANGELICAL)

PRAY THAT GOD WOULD UNVEIL THE CROSS AND WOULD REMOVE THE VEIL ON THE MINDS AND SPIRITS OF THE SAMMA (2 COR. 3:16-17).

NOVEMBER 12: REACTIONARY LOVE

*I*t is humbling to realize that our love for God is reactionary. John is brutally clear that we do not initiate love for Jesus. "We love Him because He first loved us" (1 John 4:19). There is a sneaky sort of pride that is self-congratulatory about loving Jesus. It is necessary to be reminded we did not initiate love toward God. In fact, what we call love for God is not really love at all. "In this is love, *not that we love God*, but that He loved us and sent His Son to be the propitiation for our sins" (v. 10, emphasis added). Whatever love we initiate for God is inferior to the love He has for us.

Understanding the reactionary nature of our love for God is both humbling and liberating. If we are responsible to source love, what do we do when we have exhausted our meager resources? If love must originate with me, what do I offer God when I am empty of love—as I inevitably will be? People cannot manufacture unlimited anything for themselves—least of all love. But if our love is reactionary, a response to being loved, then as long as love is directed toward us we have fuel to love in return. We do not have to bear the weight or pressure of producing love for God. We have this unceasing flood of love pouring over us night and day, and love received enables us to love in return. God is the source of our love for Him! We can love God because His love enables us to love Him in return. God is the source of everything, even our love for Him. Our love for Him can be endless and eternal only when it is reactionary, and His love never fails or flags. Our love for Him is renewed morning by morning.

Our love for Jesus is in the context of propitiation—the appeasement of God's wrath. John's definition of love includes the fact that God's wrath has been appeased. This is how Jesus loved us—He placated the wrath of God by absorbing it. He bore the wrath of God by dying on a cross. Reciprocal love for Jesus is only complete when it includes wonder and horror at what He has done for us at Calvary. Love covers wrath. If we are to love God, truly love Him, then our reactionary love must include propitiation. "Beloved," said John, "if God so loved us, we also ought to love one another" (v. 11). How wonderful that we do not have to come up with the ability to love Jesus! We just respond to the way He loves us and we love others in kind.

HOLER HINDUS OF INDIA (789,000; 0.0% EVANGELICAL)

PRAY THAT BELIEVERS AMONG THE HOLER WOULD BE SET FREE FROM A SPIRIT OF FEAR OF
WHAT MAY COME AND WOULD PROCLAIM THE TRUTH OF THE GOSPEL BOLDLY
(2 TIM. 1:6–8).

NOVEMBER 13: BLESSING FOR CURSING

PROVERBS 18; LUKE 6; 2 JOHN

*W**ords Matter.*** Sticks and stones break bones, and words crush spirits. When Jesus instructed us to "bless those who curse" us (Luke 6:28), it was in the context of verbal wars. He warned that we are in danger when everyone speaks well of us, for this is what is done to false people. "Woe to you when all men speak well of you for so did their fathers to the false prophets" (v. 26). While we might enjoy the affirmation of the heathen and the hypocrite, it is actually the kiss of death. "Death and life are in the power of the tongue," says Proverbs 18:21, and we must be vigilant that the praise of the twisted does not lead to our demise. In the same vein, we must not allow the cursing of the twisted to harm us, for it can. Neither the affirmation nor the accusations we receive from people should sway us. We respond to comprehensive adulation by running from it terrified, and we respond to comprehensive cursing with verbal blessing. We affirm, encourage, and give life to those who attack us. In so doing we take their weapon from them. Words matter, both on offense and defense. Words can hurt us either by flattery or insult, and we need to be immune to both forms of poison. Words can also help us, for when we use our words to bless our enemies, it shocks and disarms them.

Truth Matters. John said that we are to love one another (2 John 5), and in the next breath he said we should have nothing to do with those who think and speak wrongly of the Savior, not even to greet them or show them hospitality (v. 10). John was not referring to people outside the household of faith. He was referring to those who claim to bear the name of Jesus but deny His deity and person. We bless them by the gift of truth. Christians tend to be too hard on the wolves and too soft on the sheep. We castigate and judge the unconverted, forgetting that sinners naturally sin, and we excuse and accommodate the redeemed, forgetting that the ransomed are supposed to cease from sin. We bless the wicked by showering them with love and we bless the righteous by pouring truth into their ears. We do the people of God no favor when we allow what is bent and twisted to have a place among us. The highest good we can do to those who claim to magnify Jesus, but in reality distort Him, is to confront them face to face (v. 12) so that ultimately, even if the journey involves pain, their joy may be full.

SUDANESE MUSLIMS OF YEMEN (474,000; 0.4% EVANGELICAL)

PRAY FOR THE WORD OF GOD IN WRITTEN, ORAL, MUSICAL, AND DRAMATIC
FORMS TO BE TRANSLATED AND TO RISE AMONG THE SUDANESE
OF YEMEN (ISA. 55:10-11).

NOVEMBER 14: SUBMITTED FAITH

PROVERBS 19; LUKE 7; 3 JOHN

*J*esus is not subject either to our authority or our expectations. John the Baptist, who knew Jesus best, was still offended or at least disappointed both by what Jesus did not do and by what He did. John did not expect Jesus to be political. After all, he prophesied that Jesus would come to baptize with the Holy Spirit and fire. However, John was disappointed in how Jesus fulfilled His spiritual ministry. Jesus' lack of spiritual ambition confused John. Often, those who know Jesus best most grievously misunderstand Him. The confusion of the righteous can be more complicated in its subtlety than the outright denial of the unconverted.

It took a Roman soldier to show real faith. This man was a foreigner. He was not a Jew, not a disciple but an oppressor, and a member of the ruling occupying class. The Roman centurion asked Jesus not to trouble Himself but to "say the word . . . for I also am a man placed under authority" (Luke 7:6–9). Jesus marveled at this "great faith" and commented that He had never seen anything like it. It took a Roman to point out that faith includes submission to authority. Faith obeys what God wants; faith does not demand God or trouble Him for what self wants. We have turned faith into a means of obtaining our will. Jesus is pleased by the type of faith that submits to His divine desires.

The faith that submits to the divine will is not a fatalistic, removed faith. Faith is not a detached belief in God's power. Faith includes intimate devotion. A known sinner came to Jesus, anointed His feet with tears and oil, and did not cease to kiss His feet (v. 45). Jesus regarded this devotion as faith, for He said to the woman: "Your faith has saved you. Go in peace" (v. 50). The faith that saves is a faith that draws near to Jesus and lavishes love, thanks, and worship on Him. We cannot worship from afar. We cannot worship with retained dignity. We cannot worship in truth if our worship is restrained or sporadic. Worship that is the fruit of faith is intimate and unceasing. The faith that saves us is the type of faith that does not cease kissing the feet of Jesus. Saving faith is not a one-time act but a lifelong obedience and submission. The faith that overcomes the world is the faith that has overcome self, cast all inhibitions aside, fallen at the feet of Jesus in unceasing devotion, and trusted that God's will and way are best.

TAJIK MUSLIMS OF TAJIKISTAN (5,329,000; 0.04% EVANGELICAL)

NOVEMBER 15: IN THE LIGHT

PROVERBS 20; LUKE 8; JUDE

*O*ur bondages cease to awe us after a while and begin to comfort us. We prefer our pigs and are afraid to be free (Luke 8:26–39). When sin settles in, it becomes bondage, and to the bound, deliverance is more intimidating than slavery. Slavery is predictable and assuring in a twisted way. Deliverance, while liberating, casts us into uncharted territory. It is often more convenient to live bound—you do not have to labor, think, risk, or care—than it is to live free. Those who seem to be free often have secret bondages. Their apparent liberty is only a façade for their addictions. Licentiousness is but the highest form of bondage. To those secretly bound, Jesus issued a warning: "Nothing is secret that will not be revealed, nor anything hidden that will not be known and come to light" (v. 17).

Jesus does not allow vice and sin to remain hidden in His servants. Because He is light and truth and is forming us into His image, anything that is not light or truth within us must be exposed and dealt with. The Devil deceives God's ministers by insinuating we are too important to be disciplined, that the ministry is too vital for God to remove us. God steadily insists that His nature is too holy to allow us to continue to represent Him when we are bound and dark within. Jesus announced that all secrets will be known, then immediately said something intriguing: "Therefore take heed how you hear!" (v. 18) Biblically, hearing is conjoined to obedience, thus Jesus is really saying, "Your obedience is going to be examined. Why and how you obey is going to be brought into the light. Your motives are going to be exposed. Your fruit is going to be examined. Your works are going to be manifest, and all will see what is real and what is false." He went on to say, "Whoever has, to him more will be given" (v. 18). This is revolutionary. Jesus said that our obedience is going to be examined—our motive, impact, effect, intensity, and alacrity. Those who have obeyed well will be given more to obey. Those who have not obeyed will not receive further assignments.

Our ongoing use in God's kingdom depends on the quality of our obedience. God is a fair but tough employer who holds us accountable. He examines our obedience and determines future assignments according to past compliance. We cannot expect to be given greater responsibilities in the kingdom if our past assignments do not pass muster under the searching light of God. It is demanding to work for Jesus. He is relentless in His requirements of obedience and quality of service. Our bondages are not an excuse He entertains. Jesus exposes our bondages and weaknesses that we might be free of them and equipped to obey freely.

BAZIGAR HINDUS OF INDIA (763,000; 0.0% EVANGELICAL)

PRAY THAT CHRISTIANS FROM AROUND THE WORLD WOULD WORK TOGETHER TO REACH THE BAZIGAR AND THAT THE BAZIGAR WOULD BE JOINED TO THE BODY OF CHRIST (JOHN 17:20-23).

*J*esus continually perplexes people, particularly the ruling class (Luke 9:7). The poor seem to have an easier time understanding Him, probably because they have the humility to accept God's self-revelation, while the rich and self-reliant have the hubris to think they can describe Him according to their whimsy. The last book of the Bible is the unveiling of Jesus. We derive the word *apocalypse* from the Greek word for "revelation." Revelation 1:1 reads: "The Revelation of Jesus Christ." In the end, every person will be aware of who God is in Christ: ruler over the kings of the earth, Alpha, Omega, Almighty, alive forevermore, and holder of the keys of hell and death. It will be tragic for those who only realize who God really is on the last day. Awareness of God and awareness of self are critical now if the future is going to be heavenly.

Self-Awareness. Ironically, the most critical thing we need to know about ourselves is that we do not know. We do not know what we should know; we do not even know how bent we are. Truth is hidden from us, we do not perceive (Luke 9:45), and we do not have the courage to ask the right questions. We do not even understand how twisted our own spirits are. Jesus told His disciples bluntly: "You do not know what manner of spirit you are of" (v. 55). The first step in self-awareness is to recognize that we are tragically flawed and desperately need help. This is not the one-time recognition of the sinner. Jesus' followers must live in constant awareness of their depravity and their need for ongoing correction. Wise people continually adjusts their ways (Prov. 21:29).

God-Awareness. While introspection is necessary, it is not about time-consuming navel-gazing. Men and women correct themselves by staring at Jesus. Only then do we realize what is wrong with us. We are at our finest when we applaud, praise, and rejoice in who God is and in what He is doing. Psalm 119:126 declares: "It is time for You to act, O LORD!" This is not a presumptuous order from servant to master. This is the anticipated praise of the slave who has finally understood the Lord's character and intention (v. 125). Intimacy with God anticipates His heart and adopts His passions. Awareness of God swells up inside our spirits and we praise, proclaim, rejoice, and shout: "Yes, God! Now it is time to reveal Yourself!" When we plea with the Lord to act, we are not ordering but praising, surging to our collective feet, roaring with our collective mouths, declaring that God is good and is at work in the earth. The stadium of heaven is giddy with delirious approval. Awareness of human depravity is inextricably linked with awareness of the majesty of God. To be God-aware is to be God-amazed and to plead with Him to act and to reveal His goodness to all.

HADARAMI MUSLIMS OF YEMEN (457,000; 0.0% EVANGELICAL)

PRAY THAT THE HEARTS OF THE HADARAMI WOULD BE LIKE GOOD SOIL, READY TO HEAR THE GOSPEL AND TO RESPOND (MATT. 7:1-8, 18-23).

NOVEMBER 17: THE PRINCIPLE OF PROMISE

PROVERBS 22; LUKE 10; REVELATION 2

We must not mistake God's principles for His guaranteed promises. Principles balance combined truths. The promises of God have to be interpreted collectively because an isolated promise that is claimed in ignorance or in isolation from other promises is distorted and leads to great harm. God promises to be merciful, and God also promises to judge the wicked with wrath. The principle is that there is forgiveness for those who repent. God promises to bless His people, and God also promises that His people will suffer. The principle is that God brings blessing through suffering. God promises His eternal presence to those who obey and His eternal absence to those who rebel. The principle is that both heaven and hell are promises of God.

Train Up a Child. Proverbs 22:6 presents the principle: "Train up a child in the way he should go, and when he is old he will not depart from it." When this verse is considered an unconditional guarantee, it leads to great pain, because many godly parents have lost wayward children, children who never repented and who died in their sins. Godly parents may have some children who end up with their promised heaven and others with their promised hell. The principle is that if we train our children in godliness, they will have every opportunity to walk with Jesus both now and eternally. The principle includes the possibility that our children will choose to rebel, choose to walk away from the Lord's protection. The promise to parents is that if they do what is right, God bears the responsibility and the burden for what happens to their children.

Nothing Shall Hurt You. Luke 10:19 presents another principle that is often misunderstood: "I give you the authority to trample on serpents and scorpions, and over all the power of the enemy, and nothing shall by any means hurt you." This verse is not a guarantee of immunity. The principle is that we are invulnerable to the attacks of the Enemy on our souls forever, as long as we stay under God's authority, and that we are invulnerable to attacks on our body until God's appointed time of suffering. Millions of Christians throughout history have been hurt painfully by the attacks of the Enemy. Christians today face unimaginable emotional and physical pain. Revelation 2:10 reminds us that the crown of life results from a faithful, painful death after great suffering. Jesus did not promise that Christians will never be hurt. He promised that we will be hurt only if He allows it and that there will be purpose in our bruising. The principle is that Jesus has all authority and nothing can happen to us outside of His will. We can live in the Arab world among insurrection and violence, assassinations and car bombings, and walk the streets confident and fearless—because we are immune to it all until it is time to suffer and hurt for Jesus' sake.

TAJIK, AFGHAN MUSLIMS OF AFGHANISTAN (8,250,000; 0.0% EVANGELICAL)

PRAY FOR THE PEACE THAT RESULTS WHEN MEN AND WOMEN ARE RECONCILED WITH GOD (JOHN 14:27). PRAY FOR MEN AND WOMEN OF PEACE (LUKE 10:6) AMONG THE TAJIK.

*Z*eal is one of those qualities that we regard with a touch of scorn. Conventional wisdom says it is the fanatic who is zealous, not the wise person. Jesus' life proved otherwise: His zeal consumed Him (John 2:17). Likewise, as His followers we are to live passionately, energetically, and zealously. The psalmist was consumed with zeal because his enemies had forgotten God's words. "My zeal has consumed me, because my enemies have forgotten Your words (Ps. 119:139). In an age when we are increasingly prone to be ashamed of the direct truths of God's Word, we would do well to remember that God's Word is sharper and wiser than ours. We may not think that the enemies of God need to hear His Word, but that sharp sword is *exactly* what they need to hear so it can pierce their hearts. It is not a waste of breath to remind the ungodly what God thinks. We must expose rebellious people to the words of God. People do not need more of other people—they need more of God.

The problem is that any light in us is susceptible to darkness (Luke 11:35). This is as true for the converted as the wicked. Christians are not immune to twisting a little bit of truth and turning it into harmful lies. After all, the best lies are based on truth. Twisted truth (dark light) is even more evil than outright lies. We do not realize that we are "miserable, poor, blind, and naked" (Rev. 3:17). In order for the wicked to be reminded of the words of God, His messengers must have "no part dark" in them (Luke 11:36). God intends to write His name on us (Rev. 3:12). In effect we become God's epistles, His letters, His mini-words. We are not the Christ; we are not even mini-Christs. We are not the Word of God. We are the stationery on which He writes, and as such we need to be clean, pure, holy, and true. Nothing must detract from the handwriting of God.

Not only should we be zealous to remind God's enemies about His words, we should also be zealous to remind ourselves. We must also be zealous to repent (v. 19), to be the clean stationery of God. Jesus knows that our works are not perfect (v. 2) and neither are our words. When we repent (v. 3) we become like a clean page that Jesus can write on to remind His enemies about Himself. He sets before us an "open door" and no one can shut it (v. 8). God's enemies best remember His words when they hear them from His announcers and read them on His announcements.

NAVITHAN HINDUS OF INDIA (747,000; 0.0% EVANGELICAL)

PRAY BELIEVERS AMONG THE NAVITHAN WOULD PROCLAIM THE MESSAGE OF THE GOSPEL CLEARLY AND WOULD MAKE THE MOST OF EVERY OPPORTUNITY THAT GOD PLACES BEFORE THEM (COL. 4:2-5).

NOVEMBER 19: THE GREAT DIVIDER

PROVERBS 24; LUKE 12; REVELATION 4

*P*eople distort Jesus into what they want Him to be: the One who unites people, makes everyone happy, and brings peace by being nonjudgmental. Yet the Prince of Peace Himself proclaimed: "Do you suppose that I came to give peace on earth? I tell you, not at all, but rather division" (Luke 12:51). Fortunately, Jesus did not come to bring peace to sinful people or to unite sinful people to God. Jesus came to war against sin and to divide it out of people at any cost, even the cost of His own blood. Jesus is the great divider.

Jesus Divides Jealousy Out of Love. It is the most natural thing in the world to rejoice when an enemy falls. This is true even for the righteous. Proverbs 24:17, however, instructs otherwise. We are not to rejoice when our enemy stumbles. The depraved human heart not only rejoices when enemies stumble, it also rejoices when competitors fail. The jealous Christian competes for prominence and position and is wickedly jealous over those who might be chosen—and rejoices over those removed from the race. Jesus does not sign peace agreements with jealousy. He goes to war with the jealousy in our hearts and cuts it out of us. Jealous love is actually fear and hate.

Jesus Divides Anxiety Out of Trust. Our Lord does not want us to live with an anxious mind (Luke 12:29). We claim to trust God, yet we have a complicated scale of trust. We trust Him to save us but not to defend our reputation. We trust Him to meet our physical needs but not our emotional ones. We trust Him to be good but not to be just. We release to Him the things we cannot control and worry about the things He leaves in our hands. Jesus does not sign peace agreements with anxiety. He goes to war with the anxiety in our hearts and cuts it out of us. Anxious trust is actually doubt.

Jesus Divides Carnality Out of the Refined. By His own admission, Jesus came to send fire on the earth (v. 49). Ultimately this fire will be physical, devastating, dissolving the elements with a fervent heat and destroying this fallen earth so that a new heaven and new earth may be created. Internally, Jesus will burn the sin out of us. Jesus does not sign peace agreements with carnality. He goes to war with the carnality in our hearts and burns it out of us. The carnal Christian is the useless Christian.

Jesus brings peace on His terms. He brings peace to the world by dividing sin out of it. He brings peace to His people by dividing the sin out of us.

SWAHILI MUSLIMS OF SAUDI ARABIA (435,000; 0.0% EVANGELICAL)

PRAY THAT THE SWAHILI WILL UNDERSTAND THAT HOPE FOR FORGIVENESS AND ACCEPTANCE WITH GOD IS ONLY AVAILABLE THROUGH JESUS' WORK ON THE CROSS (1 COR. 1:18).

NOVEMBER 20: THE SLAIN LAMB STANDS

*F*aith never denies facts. John stood in heaven and received a sealed scroll that contained the end-game of God (Rev. 5). The scroll contained the solution for a world gone mad, a world polluted and poisoned by sin and rebellion. John discerned that if the scroll could be opened, the denouement of history would unfold and all that was wrong with the twisted world and with fallen humanity would be redeemed. There was one problem—no one was found worthy to open that scroll or even to look at it, so John wept (v. 4).

It is entirely appropriate for us to weep at the sorry state of the world. When Jesus' followers lose the capacity to be brokenhearted over the state of fallen humanity and a wounded creation, we have lost something of the heart of God. The Jesus-hearted person is not someone who longs to escape a doomed planet. The Jesus-hearted person is someone who longs for all things to be restored. The effects of sin should make us mourn more than they should make us angry; we should grieve a fallen Eden. We also need to have a singular hope. The depravity of earth and the degenerate human heart have one resolution: the return of Jesus in glory.

Jesus does not necessarily fix things the way we prefer. John looked around heaven and saw "a lamb standing as if slain" (v. 6). How does a slain lamb stand? How does a butchered Savior rise in triumph over the nations and become the praise of every tongue (v. 9)? God conquered death by dying and He restores life by destroying. Neither one makes sense to us. Surely there was another way to redeem humanity. Surely God could scrub creation clean without destroying it all and starting all over again. Our limitation is that we can only see the edges of God's ways and His character. He is so much bigger, so much better, so much purer, so much deeper than we can fathom, and His ways are not our ways. Jesus fixes things, but He does not fix them in the way we desire or even approve.

If Jesus fixes cosmic problems in surprising ways, it should not surprise us that He will redeem, amend, discipline, correct, sanctify, deliver, and prepare us in ways that we neither expect nor enjoy. Great indeed are His tender mercies (Ps. 119:156), but they are linked to His judgments. God goes to great lengths to drive the sin out of us. The tender mercy of Jesus judges me. It identifies all that is unholy, divides it from what is pure, and attacks it with heavenly fire. My revival comes only after repentance and the destruction of what is offensive to God. Jesus does this for the world, He does this for the church, and He does this for me: He fixes things radically, finally, and gloriously . . . in His own wondrous way.

TALYSH MUSLIMS OF AZERBAIJAN (114,400; 0.0% EVANGELICAL)

PRAY THAT THE BELIEVERS AMONG THE TALYSH WILL ENDURE PERSECUTION IN A CHRISTLIKE MANNER AND WILL GIVE THEIR LIVES FOR THE SAKE OF THE GOSPEL IF NECESSARY (1 PETER 2:21-23).

NOVEMBER 21: NONDISCIPLESHIP

PROVERBS 26; LUKE 14; REVELATION 6

*D*allas Willard commented that if you think the cost of discipleship is high, you should consider the cost of nondiscipleship. "The cost of nondiscipleship is far greater—even when this life alone is considered—than the price paid to walk with Jesus."[1] Jesus was pretty explicit about what characterizes the nondisciple. By His definition, discipleship is not for the faint of heart or lazy in spirit. He declared that if you do not hate your own life, bear your cross, and forsake all, you cannot be His disciple.

The Nondisciple Does Not Hate His Own Life (Luke 14:26). Jesus warned that being His disciple includes hate for father, mother, wife, children, brothers, sisters, and yes, even our own lives. He meant, of course, that all other passions must pale in comparison to our passion for and allegiance to Him. When our allegiance to Jesus does not exceed all other allegiances, we are doubly deprived. Not only do we miss the completion of making Jesus our highest joy, we also miss the deepest fulfillment of all other relationships. My interaction with others is fullest when my passion for Jesus is highest.

The Nondisciple Does Not Bear His Cross (v. 27). It is one thing to embrace a stationary cross; it is another thing to bear a rugged cross on a lashed back. The friction of movement embeds splinters from the cross deep into the flesh. If we do not encounter the agony of the cross worked deep into our souls through a process of ongoing friction, the cost is unimaginable. Nondisciples do not endure the cross. They do not walk under its weight mile after unending mile, and thus are not comprehensively cured. It is a costly waste to invest in a course of treatment, begin the process, and leave prematurely. The efficacy of the cross is best applied to our lives as we walk the entire length of the Calvary road.

The Nondisciple Does Not Forsake All (v. 33). We followers of Jesus tend to excel in the selective application of Calvary. We crucify gossip and indulge in gluttony. We forsake gluttony and succumb to pride. We humble ourselves and slip into laziness. We become industrious but begin to lie. We tell the truth but without kindness. Jesus' view of discipleship demands a comprehensive abandonment of sin and self. He is neither pleased nor honored when His disciples crucify singular aspects of their flesh. Everything has to die—body, soul, mind must all be nailed to the cross. We convince ourselves that God will be satisfied with compartmentalized surrender. We laud ourselves for giving up one precious thing. Jesus remains unimpressed until we give up everything—not our worst, not even our best, simply our all.

LODHA HINDUS OF INDIA (6,630,000; 0.26% EVANGELICAL)

PRAY THAT GOD WOULD RAISE UP MISSIONARIES FROM ALL OVER THE WORLD TO PLANT
THE CHURCH TOGETHER AMONG THE LODHA (MATT. 9:37).

NOVEMBER 22: MENTORED REPENTANCE

PROVERBS 27; LUKE 15; REVELATION 7

The prodigal son teaches us to never waste an opportunity to repent. When this wayward son returned to his father, he recognized his error was first against God—"Father, I have sinned against heaven"—and then against his loved ones (Luke 15:18, 21). The prodigal son joins Joseph ("How can I do this thing and sin against God?") and David ("Against you and you only have I sinned!") in reminding us that sin first insults God, then wounds others. We are to continually turn away from sin and self and turn to Jesus. Biblical figures teach us that repentance is a posture not a proclamation. We are to be ever mindful that sin is grievous, not because it is known but because it exists. Because we continually injure God, we must continually repent. Wounds can lead us to repentance. Proverbs 27:6 reminds us: "Faithful are the wounds of a friend." Wounds are only faithful when they lead us to repentance, for repentance leads us to life. Wounds without purpose merely kill us. One of the best things friends can do for each other is to lead each other to repentance.

When I observe someone repent, my heart is stirred to do likewise. The greater the spiritual stature of the person who repents, the more influential their repentance. When a man or woman who is far more godly than I repents publicly for a sin far less egregious than mine, my spirit is slapped and I am roused to repent. Our children need to hear us repent; our colleagues need to hear us repent. Those we lead need to hear us repent often and sincerely for what is in our hearts and for what comes off our tongues. We teach others to repent by repenting. We mentor repentance by living a lifestyle that is always suspicious of self and always turns to Jesus.

We also mentor repentance by demanding it of those we love and lead. The faithful wounds of a friend must include turning the person from folly. We do not love our friends if we do not call them to repent. Jesus' true followers see the sins in their lives and turn from it. They also call others to turn from their sins. The only thing that gives us the moral authority to call others to repent is if we live repentant lives. When we rise from bed, we should repent of the carnality that has accumulated to our souls while we slept. Seven times a day or more we should turn to the Lord and ask Him for His benevolent mercy. If our hearts are always turning to Jesus, it is both ethical and powerful to ask others to turn with us. Our lives and our words must constantly be about worship characterized by of repentance.

PASHTUN, CENTRAL MUSLIMS OF UNITED ARAB EMIRATES (416,000; 0.0% EVANGELICAL)

PRAY THAT THE PASHTUN WOULD FEEL AND KNOW THE BURDEN OF SIN AND WOULD COME TO
JESUS FOR FORGIVENESS AND SALVATION (MATT. 11:28-30).

NOVEMBER 23: ABOMINABLE PRAYERS

PROVERBS 28; LUKE 16; REVELATION 8

*J*esus demands accountability for our resources. He has given us family, friends, time, and money, and He insists that we act shrewdly with what He has given (Luke 16:8). Family and friends are not resources in the sense of material to be consumed but they are God's supply to us for life and ministry. If we do not steward these gifts well, we will consume and abuse them. Consumable God-given resources are time and money. Only money is renewable; thus time is more precious. Luke wrote that both time and money are limited. Luke 16:9 refers to resources and is most properly translated "when they fail," which allows the paraphrase: Time and money are going to run out, so while you have them, use them toward everlasting ends. Mammon is usually thought of in terms of finances, but it takes time to make money and because time is not renewable it is more precious. The person who is faithful in the little moments of time will be faithful with his life. Great lives are the accumulation of innumerable, faithfully used moments.

Luke pointed out that the Pharisees were lovers of money. They loved their luxuries, and they loved spending time as it pleased them. Today, the closest equivalent to a Pharisee is a missionary or a minister. We tend to castigate the Pharisees as the worst examples of hypocrites, forgetting that we are what we despise. Because the Pharisees were brilliantly "ignorant," they knew all about God and the Scriptures but did not really understand Him. If they did understand Him, they lied to themselves long enough that their selfish and carnal interpretations of His laws no longer bothered them. Again, this is the common error of the missionary. We can be so proud of working for God that we no longer represent Him. We can become so adept at doing the right things for the wrong reasons that we lose the capacity to see how disgusting and abominable our actions are to the One we allegedly serve. We can esteem things that are abominable before God (v. 15).

The writer of Proverbs declared: "One who turns away his ear from hearing the law, even his prayer is an abomination" (28:9). This turning from hearing is not the work of the unconverted. It is more often the practice of the Christian. First, to turn away from hearing (and obeying) implies that you were once attentive and obedient. Second, the unconverted usually have no time for prayer. We can keep praying long after we have stopped obeying, and when we do, God thinks our prayers are abominable. We consistently drift toward pride in our own righteousness and constantly need to be reminded that God thinks our good works, thoughts, and nature are abominable.

TANAOLI MUSLIMS OF PAKISTAN (604,000; 0.0% EVANGELICAL)

PRAY THAT GOD WOULD UNVEIL THE CROSS AND WOULD REMOVE THE VEIL ON THE MINDS
AND SPIRITS OF THE TANAOLI (2 COR. 3:16–17).

*W*hen the disciples asked Jesus to increase their faith (Luke 17:5), He responded in two unlikely ways. First, He compared faith to a mustard seed. Second, He linked faith to doing their duty (v. 10). Jesus revealed an understanding of faith that runs counter to our perception.

Small Faith Is Big Faith. You either have faith or you do not. You either trust Jesus or you do not. When the disciples asked for increased faith, Jesus responded that that they did not need big faith to do large things, for even mustard-seed-size faith can move mulberry trees to the sea. When Jesus rebuked His disciples for having little faith, He essentially told them that they did not trust Him. When Jesus commended seekers for their great faith, He applauded the beauty of their trust. In other words, if we do not fully trust Jesus, it is as if we do not trust Him at all. He does not delight in reserved trust or qualified trust. What delights His heart is when we take Him at His word. Trust is not only sweet to us, it is sweet to Jesus. He wants us to come to the place where our little hearts trust His great heart implicitly.

God Himself Is Our Reward. Jesus' answer to the disciples request for increased faith helped to reveal their motives. It appears that they wanted great faith in order to do great miracles because great miracles would bring great attention and great reward. Jesus went right to the heart of the matter and told the disciples that they were looking for reward and gratification in the wrong place. The master does not serve his servants. He does not thank them for doing their duty. He does not even reward them for doing their duty well. This seems unfair until we realize that we are looking for reward in the wrong place. We look for reward post-service, post-obedience. Jesus taught that the reward is in the obedience itself. We look for physical rewards, and Jesus tells us that He is our reward. Faith and duty yield the same reward: Christ our Savior.

As missionaries we do not serve to be rewarded, for our service is our reward. When we serve in Jesus' name, we begin to take on His image. We become like Him as we obey Him. When we actively share in His passion, He actively conforms and chisels us to look like Him. Becoming like Jesus is a reward far greater than any material post-service benefits. He is our reward, and we find Him in our obedience.

RAJPUT, KACHHWAHA HINDUS OF INDIA (739,000; 0.05% EVANGELICAL)

PRAY THAT BELIEVERS AMONG THE RAJPUT, KACHHWAHA WOULD BE SET FREE FROM A SPIRIT OF FEAR OF WHAT MAY COME AND WOULD BOLDLY PROCLAIM THE TRUTH OF THE GOSPEL (2 TIM. 1:6-8).

NOVEMBER 25: LORD, HAVE MERCY

PROVERBS 30; LUKE 18; REVELATION 10

*J*esus loves it when we persist in prayer, when we keep coming back to Him over and over again in faith. Luke 18 tells us that if an unjust judge can be moved by the persistence of a supplicant, how much more will the Judge of all the earth do right when we keep asking Him for what He wants to do? Our "continual coming" (v. 5) delights the heart of God and our "crying out day and night" (v. 7) moves Him to action. This is not because He is slow to act. Rather, He longs for us to be like Him by sharing His passions, and the longer we desire what He wants, the more we become like Him. Part of God's delight in our persistent prayer is the effect it has on us and on the person or situation we are praying for. Prayer indeed changes the supplicant.

There is one repeated prayer that makes God's heart particularly glad: when we humbly ask Jesus to have mercy on us. When we compare ourselves to others, we can occasionally look good. When we compare ourselves to God, we can only look bad (vv. 9–14). Pure prayer views self in the light of God's character because the goal of prayer is to become like God more than to gain answers. When we approach God and compare ourselves to Him, there is but one appropriate plea: "Lord, have mercy on me, a sinner." Other prayers are self-serving. Any request or petition of God is a prayer, thus the rich young ruler prayed amiss (v. 18). The young man prayed in order to receive something, not to be transformed into God's image. Jesus shocked him by pointing out the one thing he lacked was *everything* because everything is the only thing Jesus requires. The social contract of prayer is simply this: We ask God to have mercy on us and to make us like Him as we share His passions. God agrees to answer this "prayer-at-the-root-of-all-prayers" as long as we agree to give Him everything.

If prayer has become a way to exalt ourselves (Prov. 30:32), we need to clap our hands over our mouths—for we are not praying, we are only striving. The heart of our prayer, the prayer that needs to be repeated daily if not hourly, is that of the blind man who longed to see Jesus: "Son of David, have mercy on me!" (Luke 18:38). When we pray this prayer over and over, when we cry it out, when we shout it continually, when we pray it even to the annoyance of those around us, the heart of Jesus is both thrilled and moved, for we are finally praying the one thing we lack.

PERSIAN MUSLIMS OF UNITED ARAB EMIRATES (406,000; 0.05% EVANGELICAL)

PRAY FOR THE WORD OF GOD IN WRITTEN, ORAL, MUSICAL, AND DRAMATIC FORMS TO BE TRANSLATED AND TO RISE AMONG THE PERSIANS

(ISA. 55:10-11).

NOVEMBER 26: "KINGDOM POW" THEOLOGY

PROVERBS 31; LUKE 19; REVELATION 11

*S*ome followers of Jesus, a little too full of themselves, think that Jesus needs their help. Self-important Christians think that the role of the body of Christ is to prevail in the earth and systems of men in order to present Jesus the inheritance of a redeemed earth, a reward because He is good enough to return. Even if the intentions are noble, this theology is flawed. The biblical theology of humanity is fairly pessimistic: People mess things up, rebel, and ultimately spoil everything they touch. People, even redeemed people, are fallen. Put enough fallen men and women together on a planet or in a church, and it is not long until they try to destroy each other.

No church or Christian institution has been able to avoid decay and degeneration over time. If humanity cannot rule itself, it is ludicrous to think that it can govern the earth. Revelation 11 declares that the kingdoms of this world have become the kingdoms of our Lord and of His Christ (v. 15) for one reason only: "Because *You* have taken Your great power and reigned" (v. 17, emphasis added). Lightning, noise, thunder, earthquakes, and great hail are unleashed from heaven as Jesus returns, establishes His kingdom, brings His enemies before Him, and slays them (Luke 19:27). Gentle Jesus returns to earth to establish His kingdom with His robe dipped in blood. This is what I call "Kingdom Pow" theology. Humanity does not establish the King of Kings—God comes to crown Himself.

If our role is not to overcome the injustices of earth and to present a cleaned-up planet to our returning King, what is our role? First, it is not to abandon the earth to chaos and evil. Jesus told us to "do business till I come" (v. 13). Jesus' followers should be the most energetic in the civic sphere—the best doctors, lawyers, artists, athletes, scientists, mothers, fathers, politicians, and civil servants. We live and act as signs of the coming kingdom, but we do so with the clear-eyed realism that we swim against the tide of humanity and that the world is only going to get worse. This makes our kingdom living all the more necessary, all the more noticeable, and all the more poignant. Yes, the world is self-destructing, but the King is coming.

Second, our lives and tongues must be prophetic. In the last days there will be a final outpouring of the Holy Spirit. Our role is to announce the coming King and kingdom, not to usher it in. When the Spirit is unleashed in final fullness, we will not have to preface utterances with "Thus saith the Lord." Our words to each other and to the world will be as fire out of our mouths (Rev. 11:5). God comes to crown Himself. We simply speak toward that day.

TARKHAN MUSLIMS OF PAKISTAN (2,612,000; 0.9% EVANGELICAL)

PRAY THAT GOD WOULD POUR OUT HIS SPIRIT ON THE TARKHAN AND THAT THEY WOULD SEE DREAMS AND VISIONS OF JESUS. PRAY THAT THEY WOULD BE POWERFULLY SAVED AND EMPOWERED TO BE HIS WITNESSES (JOEL 2:28-32).

NOVEMBER 27: OVERCOMING

ECCLESIASTES 1; LUKE 20; REVELATION 12

*T*he Devil is like a man-eating shark that has thrust itself onto a crowded beach—ferocious, deadly, and powerful but running out of oxygen. Revelation 12:12 assures us that though the Devil comes against us in great wrath, he knows that "he has a short time." He knows he is doomed and, in fury, wants to destroy anyone within reach. The safest thing we can do is to stay out of his vicinity and let him thrash himself to death. We do this by trusting in the blood of the Lamb, by proclaiming the victory of Jesus, and by dying to death so we might live.

Trusting. "They overcame him by the blood of the Lamb" (v. 11). We do not overcome the Devil, Jesus does. The great power encounters of God are not as minimal as healings, destruction of enemies, or miraculous provision. The majestic signs and wonders of God are these: incarnation, crucifixion, and resurrection. This is where the cosmic battle is fought and won, and none of these encounters have anything to do with us. Jesus defeats the Devil. We overcome by staying under the blood of Jesus. A person is foolish to war with the Devil but wise to shelter under the blood of Jesus. We trust Jesus to fight for us, to rebuke demons, and to triumph over evil.

Proclaiming. "They overcame him . . . by the word of their testimony" (v. 11). Our part in battling the Devil is to praise Jesus. The Devil is absolutely terrified at the presence of Jesus, so we chase the Devil away by ushering in the presence of Jesus. When God's people extol His name and ascribe worth to the Lamb, they strike blows to Satan's head, thrusting spears into his heart. We fight the Devil by ignoring him and magnifying Jesus. As we exalt and magnify Jesus, the Devil shrivels up in frustrated agony. The proclamation of Jesus' worth is all the more powerful when it costs us something. When we are sick or suffering, poor or abandoned, and we continue to praise Jesus, it is like dropping a nuclear bomb in hell.

Dying. "They did not love their lives to the death" (v. 11). Josef Ton told his communist torturers: "Your supreme weapon is killing; my supreme weapon is dying."[2] When Christians die well, they hack off the Dragon's head. When we deny ourselves, we confess our Lord. When we hold Jesus more precious than life itself, we become a powerful threat to the Devil. He often tries to remove us from this earth but only succeeds in promoting us to glory. It is good to go home.

QAZI MUSLIMS OF INDIA (725,000; 0.0% EVANGELICAL)

PRAY THAT CHRISTIANS FROM AROUND THE WORLD WOULD WORK TOGETHER TO REACH THE QAZI AND THAT THE QAZI WOULD BE JOINED TO THE BODY OF CHRIST (JOHN 17:20-23).

NOVEMBER 28: THE PATIENCE AND FAITH OF THE SAINTS

ECCLESIASTES 2; LUKE 21; REVELATION 13

*R*evelation wreaks havoc on any theology that has a high view of people. It is pretty clear that in the last days things will get rough. In fact, "it was granted to [the evil beast] to make war with the saints and to overcome them" (Rev. 13:7). The reality of the end of human history is not that the church conquers evil. It is that evil makes war on the saints and is granted the power to overcome them. There is no man-centered triumphalism in the last days—there is only disaster. In Luke 21:19 Jesus foretold the last dominance of evil before His return and instructed His disciples that by their patience they would possess their souls.

Patience of the Saints. Revelation 13:10 indicates that the saints survive the final onslaught of evil through patience and faith. We do not realize the strong weapon we have in patience. Many battles are won simply by outlasting the Enemy. The boxer Muhammad Ali was famous for his "rope a dope" strategy. He simply leaned back against the ropes of the ring and absorbed his opponent's blows, round after round, until the enemy exhausted himself. Ali would then strike at a weakened foe. Christians can overcome opposition by outlasting it. Not all opposition is evil. Sometimes good people oppose us or resist us, and often the best thing we can do is wait. Time is always on the side of the righteous, and if we have the patience to wait, God will adjudicate on our behalf. Many a Christian battle has been won by patience.

Faith of the Saints. In order to "out-wait" evil, we must have a fundamental trust that God is sovereignly good and, in the end, He will act on our behalf. Circumstances can be brutal, and as we get closer to the second coming of Christ, Christians are going to find themselves hunted and overwhelmed. Our patient endurance is possible only if we continue to trust that God will ultimately intervene. We have to hold on to the belief that we "*will* see the Son of Man coming in a cloud with power and great glory" (Luke 21:27, emphasis added). Our redemption does, in fact, draw near (v. 28), so we do not wait in cowering fear but in towering faith. Jesus Christ, Lord of Lords, very God of very God, is coming in glory, and He is going to make a final, terrible end of all evil, all demons, and the Devil himself. Battles rage around us, injustice rises, our rights are removed, and we are marginalized, imprisoned, tortured, and killed. Through it all we wait with a trusting boldness. "Strike us as much as you will," we declare to the powers of darkness in faith, "and we will absorb it by grace." For we know a final knockout punch is on the way.

TURKMEN MUSLIMS OF IRAQ (398,000; 0.0% EVANGELICAL)

PRAY THAT THE HEARTS OF THE TURKMEN WOULD BE LIKE GOOD SOIL,
READY TO HEAR THE GOSPEL AND TO RESPOND
(MATT. 7:1-8, 18-23).

NOVEMBER 29: BEAUTIFUL IN HIS TIME

ECCLESIASTES 3; LUKE 22; REVELATION 14

*R*evelation presents a beautiful picture of the effects of the everlasting gospel (Rev. 14:6). When a person accepts and embraces the gospel, that person is transformed. The gospel-centered man or woman has the Father's name written on their forehead (v. 1); their mind is sealed and controlled by God. The gospel-centered man or woman follows the Lamb wherever He goes (v. 4), their feet joyously bloody in the path of Christ. The gospel-centered man or woman has no deceit in their mouth (v. 5). There is nothing false about them, either in word or deed. The gospel-centered man or woman is without fault before the throne of God (v. 5). They are blameless and beautiful in the sight of heaven.

This profile of the person transformed by the gospel is not out of our reach. It is our destiny. God's express purpose for those who embrace His gospel is to transform them into His image. The image of God is our inheritance. God has committed it to writing through the prophetic word: "That which is written must still be accomplished in Me . . . for the things concerning Me have an end" (Luke 22:37). God's goal is to make us like Himself, and He will move heaven and earth to accomplish that goal. Nothing will deter Him from His purpose for us, not even the pain we endure in the process.

God will judge both the righteous and the wicked (Eccl. 3:17). No one escapes judgment, not even those who embrace the gospel, for judgment is a mercy that divides the evil out from the good. In order for us to come to a place where our minds are like God's, our wills (feet) follow wherever He goes, our mouths are true, and our hearts are blameless, we must first be deconstructed. God does indeed make everything beautiful in His time (v. 11), but His timing and process include a time to die, kill, break down, weep, mourn, lose, tear, hate, and war (vv. 1–8). The process of being conformed into the image of God is brutal. He takes us apart and applies judgment to every component of our character. He examines every aspect of our hearts and minds and, like a surgeon, cuts out all that does not glorify Him. We go through one agonizing cycle of the process and think we cannot bear any more. But He is mercifully relentless and steadily examines and purifies every aspect of our being. On and on it goes, daily dying, daily being killed, daily being molded into the divine image—our inflexible flesh protesting every step of the way. Beautification is agonizing. God crafts His masterpieces through seasons of great pain. It takes time to make everything beautiful.

TATAR MUSLIMS OF KAZAKHSTAN (273,000; 0.09% EVANGELICAL)

PRAY FOR THE PEACE THAT RESULTS WHEN MEN AND WOMEN ARE RECONCILED WITH GOD (JOHN 14:27). PRAY FOR MEN AND WOMEN OF PEACE (LUKE 10:6) AMONG THE TATAR.

ECCLESIASTES 4; LUKE 23; REVELATION 15

*J*esus continually did things that defied comfortable definition. His teaching did not soothe but stirred up the general population (Luke 23:5). His person separated and divided families, yet united violent Pilate and wicked Herod (v. 12). The wonders of incarnate God lavished on a tiny geographical area over a concentrated three-year span did not bring harmony between earth and heaven in the short term. They brought the cry "Away with Him!" (v. 18). In effect, humanity cried, "Away with God!" No wonder God's anger bubbles over and bowls full of His wrath are ready to be poured out (Rev. 15:7).

When Jesus came to earth to fulfill the Father's mission, He did so with a yielded spirit. He came to appease the wrath of God, and the only way to please the Father was to disappoint just about everyone else. When someone yields to God, that person cannot live to please anyone else, including self. Three times in Luke 23 Jesus was urged to save Himself (vv. 35, 37, 39), but He could not do that. He could not save Himself and still save us. He could not yield up His spirit and remain in control at the same time. Surrender of our spirits is an all-or-nothing proposition. There is no negotiation of terms.

Jesus committed His Spirit to the Father and then died (v. 46). God sends us on the same way, with the assumption that we will yield our spirits. He sends us with the understanding that we cannot save others and save ourselves. When we are not yielded, we seek to participate in the salvation of others without losing self. We agree to work in the fields of God as long as we do not lose our identity, the respect of our peers, and fair treatment by our elders and leaders. We agree to labor in the harvest, but only if we are defended by a union of other laborers who protect our rights, privileges, and guaranteed bonuses. Missionaries tend to commit themselves to the task with conditions attached: We will go to the ends of the earth to preach the gospel as long as it is a malaria-free zone, there is a school for our kids, we have a supportive team around us, we like our leadership, and there is opportunity for our gifts to be used and recognized. Missionaries never admit it—even to themselves—but many of us are trying desperately to save ourselves and others, and we cannot.

In order to be useful to God, we must have a yielded spirit. A yielded spirit has no conditions. A yielded spirit realizes it cannot save itself if it is going to participate in saving others. A person with a yielded spirit commits himself to a loving Father and then dies . . . daily.

KANDRA HINDUS OF INDIA (723,000; 0.0% EVANGELICAL)

PRAY THAT BELIEVERS AMONG THE KANDRA WOULD PROCLAIM THE MESSAGE OF THE GOSPEL CLEARLY AND WOULD MAKE THE MOST OF EVERY OPPORTUNITY GOD PLACES BEFORE THEM (COL. 4:2-5).

December

"I HAVE BUT ONE CANDLE OF LIFE TO BURN, AND I WOULD RATHER
BURN IT OUT IN A LAND FILLED WITH DARKNESS THAN IN A
LAND FLOODED WITH LIGHT."

—John Keith Falconer

DECEMBER 1: GOD'S FOOLS

ECCLESIASTES 5; LUKE 24; REVELATION 16

*G*od does not suffer fools and He has no pleasure in them (Eccl. 5:4). People with an incomplete view of God see Him as a benign, cuddly grandfather who is somewhat clueless about their sin and who completely approves of their actions. God is approachable and we should approach Him gladly, but intimacy does not mean flippancy. It is possible to abuse our places as sons and daughters of God and to approach Him cavalierly and disrespectfully. We forget that God is a righteous judge with power over plagues and punishment (Rev. 16:5–9) who does not like the actions of foolish people who talk too much, disbelieve, and refuse to repent.

Fools Talk Too Much. All too often, Christians approach the house of God to offer the sacrifice of fools, rather than to hear (Eccl. 5:1). Scripture tells us not to be rash with our mouths and to let our words be few (v. 2). God is not impressed with those who promise Him much but obey little. Much promising and scant obedience make a fool. Talk does not impress God; labor does. Hardworking, sweaty faith gains the notice of heaven. Too many Christians talk too much, work too little, and are considered foolish by God no matter how well they present themselves.

Fools Are Slow to Believe. Jesus rebuked His disciples because they had all the truth but chose not to understand. Jesus chided them as "foolish ones and slow of heart to believe" (Luke 24:25). This world has made skepticism a virtue, but doubt is never lauded in the Bible. According to the world, the wise person does not believe in anything other than himself or the work of his hands. According to the Bible, the wise person is the one with a heart to believe. The Bible often puts the center of belief in the will, not in the head. We choose to believe with our spirits when we think our way to truth. Jesus walks into our restrained reason (v. 16), and our hearts burn within us (v. 32). If we are willing, He will open our understanding (v. 45). The fool is not willing and is not able to believe.

Fools Do Not Repent. God wants men and women to turn from their folly. He woos, calls, pleads, invites, and when every other method fails, judges. His intention in trouble is that people repent and give Him glory. He wants every person to turn from folly to the protective wisdom of heaven (Rev. 16:9). Unfortunately, people usually respond to God's judgment with blasphemy. The fool gets angry at God's judgment and does not turn from sin. The wisest thing men and women can do is repent and glorify Jesus. God's fools trust Him.

SYRIAN MUSLIMS OF JORDAN (322,000; 0.0% EVANGELICAL)

PRAY THAT THE SYRIANS WILL UNDERSTAND THAT HOPE FOR FORGIVENESS AND ACCEPTANCE WITH GOD IS ONLY AVAILABLE THROUGH JESUS' WORK ON THE CROSS (1 COR. 1:18).

DECEMBER 2: ENDING WELL IN MISSIONS AND MINISTRY

ECCLESIASTES 6; JOHN 1; REVELATION 17

*W*e love Spirit-fueled beginnings. We love it when God starts something new and fresh. We love the Alpha but are not so sure what to do with the Omega. Pentecostal Christians in particular seem to have a difficult time when the Spirit of God brings something to an end. We are enthused when He initiates a work or ministry by His Spirit. We are confused when He says it is time to go or time to stop or time to die. Jesus is the Omega—the end. He stops things and He ends things. He halts ministries, the same ministries He began. He often stops things before we are ready for them to stop, and, missing the signs, we press on long after He has removed His blessing. It is tragic when God's servants try to labor on, long after He has left. In Ecclesiastes 6:3, Solomon mourned the absence of a proper burial. Closure is important on two levels: (1) it must be done in a timely fashion, and (2) it must be done well.

Ending at the Right Time. In ministry and in missions, there is a time to walk away from leadership and from responsibility. Our worth is not based on our position. I know many missionaries who stepped away from their positions at the appropriate time and went on to be more influential in their "retirement" than they were in their "career." Good missionaries never retire in the earthly sense of the word, for kingdom responsibilities never end. Good missionaries, however, realize there is a time to pass the baton of active field service and shift to an informal mentoring role. Those who have relinquished the need to stay on the front lines have found themselves invited back to influence a new generation of "generals." Sadly, those who have held on to a field position with an iron grip have often slid into marginalization. Everyone else realized they had stayed too long. Legacies can be tarnished when legends do not know how to step aside gracefully at the end of their current roles.

Ending the Right Way. Not only do we need to recognize the right time to end ministry, we also need to navigate it graciously. It is all too easy to mar a lifetime of service by foolish or petulant acts at the end. It is all too easy to launch ourselves into depression, feeding on real and imagined hurts when a valued position is removed or a ministry closes. We start ministries that come to an end. We fall in love with countries and get kicked out of them. We enter into relationships that change by distance or promotion, and a thousand things we wish would continue do not. Good things end.

The Spirit of God ends things as often as He begins things. It is just as spiritual to be halted as it is to be initiated. When we live submitted to God, completely in tune to His will, His endings are as precious and liberating as His beginnings.

TATAR, CRIMEAN MUSLIMS OF TURKEY (99,000; 0.0% EVANGELICAL)

PRAY THAT THE BELIEVERS AMONG THE TATAR WILL ENDURE PERSECUTION IN A CHRISTLIKE MANNER AND WILL GIVE THEIR LIVES FOR THE SAKE OF THE GOSPEL IF THAT IS NECESSARY (1 PETER 2:21-23).

DECEMBER 3: TONE DEAF

ECCLESIASTES 7; JOHN 2; REVELATION 18

*F*ather Macarius was a church leader in the early days of Christianity in Egypt. A young believer approached him and asked what it meant to live the crucified life, what it meant in effect to live dead. Macarius instructed the man to go to the grave of a departed Christian and speak both praise and condemnation and to record the response of the dead man. The young believer obeyed and reported: "He speaks nothing. He is dead." Macarius responded, "Praise and blame are equally nothing to him who is dead and has been buried in Christ."[1]

Solomon advised: "Do not take to heart everything people say, lest you hear your servant cursing you. For many times, also, your own heart has known that even you have cursed others" (Eccl. 7:21–22). Those who follow Jesus closely will be mocked by the world and maligned by the church. People close to us, people we work with, lead, and follow, will say condemning and critical things about us. We turn a deaf ear to them. Not because they are false, because there is usually a nugget of truth in the criticism of friends; not because they are painless but because we have done the very same thing to others. Christians can be the most vicious verbal assassins—and there is not one of us who is innocent of verbal backstabbing. When we are the victim of such things, we can ignore them, whether they are true or false, because we have done the same to others. Ironically, our guilt, not our righteousness, makes us immune to the meanness of others.

On the other hand, Jesus was completely righteous. When many believed in Him because of His miraculous signs (John 2:23), He "did not commit Himself to them because He knew all men and had no need that anyone should testify of man, for He knew what was in man" (vv. 24–25). People often praise others because they want to be praised. All too often, we compliment others from a deep longing to be recognized ourselves. Jesus does not need our praises to satisfy His ego. God was perfectly content and satisfied in the love of the Trinity before one person existed. To think that God's works are validated by the praise of people is blasphemous. In the ongoing journey of becoming like Jesus, we must become equally tone deaf to the praises of others and to the blame of others. Our validation must not come from what anyone thinks—whether saint or sinner. Our ears must be attuned to one expression of praise: "Well done, good and faithful servant" (Matt. 25:21).

RAJPUT, GAUR HINDUS OF INDIA (712,000; 0.0% EVANGELICAL)

PRAY THAT GOD WOULD RAISE UP MISSIONARIES FROM ALL OVER THE WORLD TO PLANT THE CHURCH TOGETHER AMONG THE RAJPUT, GAUR (MATT. 9:37).

DECEMBER 4: INEVITABLE DEMISE

ECCLESIASTES 8; JOHN 3; REVELATION 19

*J*esus is the only one who grows ever stronger. The rest of us decline. The eternal life we will enjoy is granted to us from the majesty of the Godhead. We participate in it, and it becomes fully ours by inheritance, with no diminishing of the Giver. If heaven means the eternal increase of God, there must be an attending decrease of people. Our greatness must increasingly be found in our smallness. We tend to think of heaven as our exaltation, but there can be only One who is exalted—all others must diminish. By His nature, God cannot increase. He has always been who He always will be, so it is our *understanding* of who He is that grows in awe and wonder. The more we understand the greatness of God, the more we see how small we are in comparison. As we decrease we do not become less valued; we simply understand that we are limited and God is not. As we become increasingly aware of who God is, the gap between God and us becomes more evident. We must decrease as He increases.

John the Baptist understood this principle well, thus Jesus considered him the greatest person born of women. John said: "He must increase, but I must decrease" (John 3:30). John understood that the rise of Christ necessitates the fall of the individual. This principle is true especially in mission and ministry. Men and women witness and minister to men and women. There is a natural attraction and trust between persons. This trust, respect, and allegiance must be transferred from the agent of reconciliation to the divine Savior. When I evangelize or disciple a Muslim or a team member, I play an influential role for a while. But I must transfer that influence to Jesus. Any process of discipleship should include the transfer of trust from the minister to the living Lord. As my disciples increasingly learn to trust Jesus and to draw life directly from Him, my influence in their lives must decrease.

Yet we struggle with the need to decrease. As mentors we want to hold on to the influence we have over our disciples. As disciples we want the unending comfort of a mentor who can help us in time of need. In Christ's kingdom, however, all mentors must inevitably decrease over time, and all disciples must learn how to go to Jesus directly for everything. People like to make heroes, and heroes love to be applauded— no matter how much they protest otherwise. But there can be only one Hero. The role of all godly men and women must diminish. Our ongoing demise is in direct proportion to the ascending glory of God.

JORDANIAN MUSLIMS OF KUWAIT (280,000; 1.0% EVANGELICAL)

PRAY THAT THE JORDANIANS WOULD FEEL AND KNOW THE BURDEN OF SIN AND WOULD
COME TO JESUS FOR FORGIVENESS AND SALVATION
(MATT. 11:28-30).

DECEMBER 5: HARD WORK IN THE HARDEST PLACES

ECCLESIASTES 9; JOHN 4; REVELATION 20

*W*herever we go in ministry and mission, we either benefit from the labor of others or we contribute to the benefit of those who will follow. "I sent you to reap that for which you have not labored; others have labored, and you have entered into their labors" (John 4:38). If we see fruit, we can be assured that it is not due solely to our dedication or vision but because others went ahead of us and did the hard work. Often prayer accomplishes this hard work. Regularly those who preceded us in ministry did this hard work. Always the Holy Spirit is brooding over the peoples and places of earth. There is nowhere that God's Spirit is not laboring over the souls of men and women.

In mission to unreached peoples there is a longstanding debate: Do we concentrate our resources where there is great response? Do we send the majority of our workers to the Muslim peoples who have been softened to the gospel by the hard work of our predecessors? Is it worthwhile to send missionaries to places where there is nothing to reap yet or do we wait until the Holy Spirit has softened hearts? Is our strategy to find where the Holy Spirit is working and then join Him there to harvest? The key in answering these questions is to understand that the Holy Spirit is at work everywhere. There is no corner of earth where the Spirit of God does not woo men and women to Himself. Our questions should not focus on where the Holy Spirit is working, because He works everywhere. Rather the questions should focus on where missionaries are not working, where the hard work is not being done, and if we are willing to do it. Jesus makes a case in John 4 that it is not a case of either/or but both/and. The harvest is ripe (v. 35), and one who sows and one who reaps may rejoice together (v. 36). Those who sow do not get to see the results of their hard work—thus, the difficulty. Reapers work just as hard as sowers with the added bonus of seeing the fruit with their eyes. The sowers must see it with their faith.

The missionary spirit of Jesus rejoices in sowing. The Holy Spirit is the Spirit of hard work. Jesus calls and sends both sowers and reapers, but there is no reaping without a generation willing to do the hard work. In these last days God still calls men and women to go to the hardest places to do the hardest work. We may never see masses of people come to Jesus, but neither will those who follow us unless we labor, sweat, cry, and beat our heads against the gates of hell day after day, year after year. It is brutal, but someone has to do it for all to rejoice. There is no ripe harvest outside of blistered hands, bloodied feet, and bruised hearts.

TELI MUSLIMS OF PAKISTAN (2,482,000; 0.0% EVANGELICAL)

PRAY THAT GOD WOULD UNVEIL THE CROSS AND WOULD REMOVE THE VEIL ON THE MINDS AND SPIRITS OF THE TELI (2 COR. 3:16-17).

*Y*esterday a colleague was shot and killed in Benghazi, Libya. This man had moved with his family to exalt Jesus among precious Libyans and was murdered as he jogged yesterday morning. He is experiencing the glorious presence of Jesus. His family and friends are experiencing the sting of death, sorrow, tears, and pain. Jesus alone has the power to kill death. The only One with the inherent power of an endless life promised that one day there will be no more death, sorrow, crying, pain, night, anything that defiles, anything that profanes, or anything that deceives (Rev. 21:4, 25, 27). We live with the tension of real pain, present death, and the promise that one day death will be vanquished. The question before the church is whether or not it has the resolve to endure enough death that death might die.

The book of Revelation makes it clear that there is an ordained amount of suffering and martyrdom. At some moment, the blood of the martyrs will accumulate to a point where God's wrath at evil will complement His forbearing mercy and He will put an end to the beginning of history. At that time, Jesus will return to kill death and usher in the fullness of life. Since Jesus has not yet returned, it is clearly (if unpleasantly) evident that not enough people have died for Jesus. This leaves two options before the church: (1) Remove our missionaries from harm's way, or (2) resolutely determine that Jesus is worth dying for and back up that belief by sending our loved ones to the peoples and lands that will slay them. We who are on the ground in volatile situations are not concerned about our safety. We understand that at any moment we may be killed. What concerns us most is how our sending base and sending churches will react. As the body of Christ, do we have the steel in our spiritual spines to respond to the death of a loved missionary by sending ten more to take his or her place? Voices of caution rise and shout: "Stop this needless waste! Deploy our workers to friendlier climes! Wait for lands to be at peace and for the peoples to cease raging!" Increasingly, our sending agencies will face scorn and lawsuits, criticism and condemnation. Will they listen to the voices of "Christian" men and women, anguished fathers and mothers who call for the removal of Christ's representatives from harm's way? Or will our leaders and our churches stand around the coffins of the men and women they have commissioned and determine in their hearts that Jesus is worthy of more martyrs?

Jesus hates death more than we do, which is why He came to destroy it. But Jesus conquered death by dying. If we really want to see the end of death and the newness of all things good, we have to be willing to die for Jesus *and* we have to be willing to send those we love to die for Him as well.

SAINI SIKHS OF INDIA (709,000; 0.0% EVANGELICAL)

PRAY THAT BELIEVERS AMONG THE SAINI WOULD BE SET FREE FROM A SPIRIT OF FEAR OF WHAT MAY COME AND WOULD BOLDLY PROCLAIM THE TRUTH OF THE GOSPEL (2 TIM. 1:6–8).

ECCLESIASTES 11; JOHN 6; REVELATION 22

*J*esus is coming soon. If this was true 2,000 years ago (Rev. 22:12), it is more true now. The day that Jesus returns will live not in infamy, but in eternity—for from that day on there will be no more curse (v. 3). Oh, what wonder! On that day I will no longer struggle with sin. On that day the virus embedded within humanity will not only be defeated, it will be completely eliminated. On that day people will no longer be at war within themselves. No wonder the Spirit, bride, and he who hears say, "Come!" (v. 17) The longing for freedom and perfect rest can only be satisfied when Jesus comes back. Personal sin may be overcome when the believer is promoted to the presence of Jesus, but communal sin continues as long as humanity inhabits earth and space. All creation groans together—including the ransomed and redeemed—for the final liberation of all things from the curse of sin and death.

The joy in heaven over each and every sinner who repents indicates the anticipation, the protracted longing of the Spirit and the saints for the final eradication of sin and death. Heavenly beings are not ignorant, nor does our awakening in glory remove our awareness of God's ambitions. Heaven itself is not fully at rest until the redemption of all things. Pilgrims plodding on earth and pilgrims in the celestial city join with the angels and the Godhead, yearning for that great and glorious day when the trumpet will sound, the Lord will descend, and all will finally be well with our souls.

The curse of sin is the issue; therefore, the issue of sin must remain the priority of both the church and missions until the day Jesus returns. Church and missions have different roles as they work toward a common goal. The mandate of missions (sodality) is the priceless vision of planting the church where it does not exist. The call of the church (modality) is to attack sin wherever it is found and to magnify Jesus in every sphere of life as a fully orbed witness to the coming kingdom. The mission sodality has one laser-like mandate. The church modality has a holistic commission. Both church and missions lose their way if they lose their focus on attacking sin. Sin is the universal and timeless malady. Jesus came to save sinners. The temporal energies and resources of church and missions *must* be concentrated on evangelism and discipleship until that great day when Jesus comes and initiates a sinless eternity.

All the cosmos longs to be free from the curse of sin. The best thing we can contribute toward ultimate liberation is to preach the gospel to every people on earth for then the end will come. Then Jesus will destroy the curse. Our going to share the gospel around the world is indelibly linked to Christ's coming. Let us go rapidly and courageously so He will come quickly and victoriously!

TALYSH MUSLIMS OF IRAN (555,000; 0.0% EVANGELICAL)

PRAY FOR THE WORD OF GOD IN WRITTEN, ORAL, MUSICAL, AND DRAMATIC FORMS TO BE
TRANSLATED AND TO RISE AMONG THE TALYSH
(ISA. 55:10-11).

DECEMBER 8: THE GLORY OF ONE

ECCLESIASTES 12; JOHN 7; JAMES 1

*I*t is all too easy to speak gospel truth for self-glorifying ends. Jesus warned, "He who speaks from himself seeks his own glory; but He who seeks the glory of the One who sent Him is true" (John 7:18). We are sent into the earth to speak and seek the glory of the One who has sent us. The Scriptures provide a simple checklist that helps us determine exactly whose glory we seek.

Is Your Doctrine Yours or God's (John 7:16)? Not even Jesus espoused His own doctrine—He spoke God's thoughts. God does not change. His essential character is without variance or shadow of turning (James 1:17). The God of the Old Testament is the God of the New Testament. Covenants come and go as they are broken by humanity, but the everlasting covenant of God's love and wrath is unaltered, eternal, fixed to His immovable nature. To speak the doctrine of God is to present God as He is, not as people want Him to be. To cite one example, being true to the doctrine of God is to tell a Muslim there is a heavenly Father whether or not the Muslim's theology allows the concept. Believability does not verify truth. Truth is sourced in the character of God and is true because He is true. Even if a Muslim verbally, viscerally, and emotionally rejects a truth about God, that truth is still effective at the spirit level, for it appeals to the God-shaped vacuum in every heart.

Do You Testify That the World's Works Are Evil (John 7:7)? This is exactly what Jesus did, and the people hated Him for it. The witness of Jesus for the glory of the Father made the hearers complain much (v. 12) and caused division (v. 43). Consciously or otherwise, those who seek their own glory tend to proclaim a popular message. It is impossible to glorify God without condemning the world. No prophet or apostle spoke only positive messages. It is incumbent on us to testify against the evil of the world and toward the righteousness of God. It is naïve folly and contrary to the gospel to remain silent about the evil works of sin. It is popular to say that we only need to speak positively about the gospel, and as much as I would like to agree, Jesus disagrees. He testified that the world's works are evil. He spoke against the religious hypocrisy of His day and the people hated Him for it. To speak only positive things about Jesus without pointing out the wickedness of idolatry and false religion is to speak half the gospel.

Our testimony must be like well-driven nails given by one Shepherd (Eccl. 12:11). We must speak as Jesus spoke. We must speak for the things He spoke for and against the things He spoke against. This will cause hatred, complaining, and division. While we do not seek the wrath of people, in seeking the glory of God, we cannot avoid it.

GYPSY, DOMARI MUSLIMS OF EGYPT (273,000; 0.2% EVANGELICAL)

PRAY THAT GOD WOULD POUR OUT HIS SPIRIT ON THE GYPSY, DOMARI AND THAT THEY WOULD SEE DREAMS AND VISIONS OF JESUS. PRAY THAT THEY WOULD BE POWERFULLY SAVED AND EMPOWERED TO BE HIS WITNESSES (JOEL 2:28-32).

DECEMBER 9: INTIMACY WITH THE KING

SONG OF SOLOMON 1; JOHN 8; JAMES 2

*F*or the most part, we are satisfied with surface intimacies. Pure, deep intimacy is rare—even in Christian marriage. The Song of Solomon unsettles us when it unashamedly calls for the rawest intimacy with God Himself. The poetic sexual imagery in the book is disturbing not because it is graphic, but because it calls us to intimacy with very God of very God. We are to be drawn away into the King's chambers (1:4). In palaces and in fields, by day or by night, we are to engage in a passionate love affair with God. It seems scandalous because it is scandalous. Intimacy with God is not scandalous because it is perverted. Remember, the emotional and physical love affair of the book is a metaphor. Intimacy with God is scandalous because of the unbridgeable distance of worth between God and us. We are not worthy to be intimate with God, and we know it.

Many believers are content with a fringe intimacy of being at the outer edge of the love of God. I have long had a picture of this settled satisfaction. I picture a great throng in heaven gathered around the hot brilliance of Jesus. This crowd extends as far as the eye can see, contained in a domed building of immeasurable size. I sit just outside the building on the doorstep. My heart is burning with the presence of Jesus. I weep and I cry. I am satisfied to sit on the outer fringe, for I can feel the love of God and am content. It is enough for me to sit there quietly, feeling the love God has for me and others, waiting for an order, eager to run at God's command.

This fringe intimacy may satisfy me, but it does not satisfy Jesus. He wants me closer, and He asks that I walk toward Him. Strangely, I do not want to. I am comfortable with my surface intimacy. To walk toward Jesus is to walk toward that searing, brilliant center, and to walk toward Jesus burns. The level of intimacy He desires and demands is uncomfortable to me. It is too raw, too close, and I fight it. I sense my unworthiness and the vast gap between my worth and God's. It seems inappropriate that I be drawn close, as if this would violate some great law of eternity. I cannot handle further intimacy. It is beyond my capacity, and I feel as if my heart might burst. Intimacy is supposed to feel good not cause discomfort. I know that Jesus loves me. Is it wrong for me to linger on the outer edges of His presence, saved, content, and comfortable? It annoys me that Jesus wants to draw me past my comfort zone to the fiery center of His love, of Himself. This then is the wonder and glad terror of heaven: God gives Himself to us in ways we cannot comprehend or even desire. He overwhelms us and burns His presence into us. Sanctification is a process of earth that burns sin out of us. Glorification is the eternal process of heaven that burns Jesus into us.

TURK MUSLIMS OF TURKEY (52,950,000; 0.0% EVANGELICAL)

PRAY THAT CHRISTIANS FROM AROUND THE WORLD WOULD WORK TOGETHER TO REACH THE TURKS
AND THAT THE TURKS WOULD BE JOINED TO THE BODY OF CHRIST
(JOHN 17:20-23).

DECEMBER 10: JUDGE JESUS

SONG OF SOLOMON 2; JOHN 9; JAMES 3

*T*he advent season provides an opportunity to consider the incarnation and to tremble. There is something horrible about God becoming human. The soft lights and gentle music of Christmas alternate with the festive side of the holidays and lead us to excise the terror of God coming to tabernacle on earth. Missing the terror of Christmas, we miss its deeper peace. God coming near is both wonderful and terrible: wonderful for it leads to our salvation, and terrible for it leads to our judgment. "For judgment I have come into this world" (John 9:39). Jesus came to earth to divide out sin and to crush it. Christmas starts a war that ends with peace, but only to those of good will, to those under the prevailing blood. Jesus' ongoing judgment divides out the evil from the good that He might destroy the evil and preserve the good. His judgment cleanses our hearts by affecting our sight, our words, and our minds.

Jesus Judges Our Sight. If we think we see, we sin (John 9:41). It took a blind, uneducated man with spunk to stand up to the religious leaders of his day and point out that for all their intelligence they were stupid. Increase in knowledge should lead to humility, and if it does not do this, it is merely an increase of information. If we think we understand all things, we have been blinded by pride. The person who sees clearly is the one who recognizes his limited knowledge and his great dependence on Jesus. When we fail to recognize our limited understanding and our increasing need for the insight of the Spirit, we are doubly blind: We do not know that we do not know. This is the most tragic blindness of all.

Jesus Judges Our Tongues. We all stumble in many things (James 3:2). If we have any doubts about our frequent failings, our tongues remind us daily. Even Christian tongues are untamable and full of deadly poison (vv. 5–12). Jesus comes to judge our words. He wants to eradicate the envy and self-seeking that lead to boasting and lying (v. 14). We all boast or lie in clever little ways. It is this self-seeking revelation of our hearts through speech that leads to confusion and every evil thing (v. 16). Jesus comes to put an end to our wicked words. If only we would give Him our tongues for Christmas, how happy He would be.

Jesus Judges Our Minds. There is an earthly, sensual, demonic form of wisdom that winds its way into our thinking and decisions, and we do not even realize it (James 3:15). Jesus came to this world to destroy evil wisdom and to replace it with wisdom that is pure, gentle, willing to yield, full of mercy, without partiality or hypocrisy. This is His Christmas gift to us if we will receive it.

CHAMAR HINDUS OF INDIA (51,798,000; 0.92% EVANGELICAL)

PRAY THAT THE HEARTS OF THE CHAMAR WOULD BE LIKE GOOD SOIL,
READY TO HEAR THE GOSPEL AND TO RESPOND
(MATT. 7:1-8, 18-23).

DECEMBER 11: NECESSARY, NOT SUFFICIENT

SONG OF SOLOMON 3; JOHN 10; JAMES 4

*C*hristians tend to be wooed by the power gifts. In ministry, and especially in frontier missions, we are tempted to put our hopes in the silver bullets of signs and wonders. We think that if God will demonstrate His power, the nations will turn to Him in mass. While we tire of various methodologies as they cycle through missions, we hold firmly to the belief that power evangelism is the one method that will never fail. If power alone were the issue, devils would have converted long ago, as they do not doubt the sovereignty of God. Scripture cannot be broken (John 10:35) nor does it speak in vain (James 4:5) when it warns that evil powers will perform spectacular signs and will deceive many in the last days. Jesus refused to go down the road of miracle provider. He told hungry eyes that they would receive no sign save the sign of the prophet Jonah—Christ's bodily death and resurrection.

Jesus declared that no one born of women was greater than John the Baptist, yet John performed no signs and wonders: "John performed no sign, but all the things that John spoke about this Man were true" (John 10:41). The great signs of Jesus are His incarnation, crucifixion, and resurrection. The great sign of men and women today is to speak about God's salvation in Christ. While signs and wonders follow the preaching of the Word and are necessary, they are not sufficient. The great traditional religions are not primarily converted by a revelation of God's power. Islam, for example, is already convinced of God's absolute dominance—God can do whatever He wants. There are examples of miracles leading Muslims to faith in Jesus, and just as many examples of miracles that lead to no change in faith. Miraculous signs and wonders are not a silver bullet in missions since the army of God is not the only army with miracles in its arsenal. But we are the only army with a God who became flesh, a God who died on the cross, and a God who rules over life and death. These are the indisputable signs we must speak about. Signs and wonders arrest our attention but they cannot transform our hearts.

Only the shed blood of the incarnate Son of God has the power to change hearts and save souls. From Adam to John the Baptist, from John the Baptist to you and me, the representatives of God have one primary mission: declare who God is and what He has done for humanity. On this side of the great signs of God (incarnation, crucifixion, resurrection), we have no excuse to be distracted or dependent on lesser signs. Let the lesser signs of God (healings, deliverance, miracles) be used to arrest the attention of rebellious and despondent people, so they might pause long enough to listen to the gospel. These lesser signs are necessary, but they never have been and never will be sufficient.

BEDOUIN, FEZZAN MUSLIMS OF LIBYA (205,000; 0.0% EVANGELICAL)

PRAY FOR THE PEACE THAT RESULTS WHEN MEN AND WOMEN ARE RECONCILED WITH GOD (JOHN 14:27). PRAY FOR MEN AND WOMEN OF PEACE (LUKE 10:6) AMONG THE BEDOUIN, FEZZAN.

*M*issionaries who live and labor in the Arab world face an ongoing tension: We desperately want to see millions of Arab Muslims come to Jesus and to be discipled and planted in churches that reproduce themselves, yet we rarely see this happen. We read the Scripture and understand that to see the glory of God we must believe (John 11:40). We know Jesus can bring life from death, that He can make dry bones live. Yet we fight an internal skepticism and unbelief for it is sheer hard work to believe that an Arab Muslim will come to faith when we witness to him. We long to see revival spread across the Arab world even as it has in Latin America, Sub-Saharan Africa, China, and Southeast Asia. We hear fantastic reports of how God has moved among Muslim peoples. We attend trainings on the latest methods, and then find that the reports are exaggerated, supported by Western funds, and the reported churches either do not exist or are syncretistic. We find ourselves torn—we would rather have five real disciples than five phantom churches, yet we have a raging agony over the millions who perish around us. We have a burning desire to see God glorified in hundreds of thousands of reproducing believers from a Muslim background.

James used a farming illustration to warn the unjust rich (James 5:1–6). In His illustration, the cries of the unpaid reapers reached the Lord of Hosts. James pivoted from that illustration to draw an application of patient perseverance, again using farming for an example of waiting for "the precious fruits of the earth," which depend on both the early and latter rains (vv. 7–8). James cited Job (v. 11) and Elijah as men who endured, and because they did, saw heaven's rain and the earth producing fruit (v. 18). If our payment is in the harvest—turning sinners from their ways and saving them from death (vv. 19–20)— then we, too, protest to the Lord of Hosts that our wages are long overdue.

The reality is that someone has to do the hard work. No one on earth reaps without someone sowing. No one on earth sows without someone reaping. It is not unfair to be the sower—it is a privilege. We sow because we believe in reaping. We sow so that someone else may reap. Ironically, the Devil uses reaping testimonies to discourage the sower and move him or her away from the critical and fatiguing work of sowing. Someone has to sow; someone has to beat his God-hardened forehead against the stone gates of hell over and over again. Someone has to exult in the privilege of being the first laborer to sweat in anonymity for years, plucking boulders out of the field, digging up stumps, sinking down wells, and planting seed in the heat of the day. While it is easier to rejoice in reaping, let us dedicate ourselves to rejoice in sowing. Our endurance prepares the ground for the latter rain.

TURKMEN MUSLIMS OF TURKMENISTAN (4,080,000; 0.0% EVANGELICAL)

PRAY THAT BELIEVERS AMONG THE TURKMEN WOULD PROCLAIM THE MESSAGE OF THE GOSPEL CLEARLY AND WOULD MAKE THE MOST OF EVERY OPPORTUNITY GOD PLACES BEFORE THEM (COL. 4:2–5).

DECEMBER 13: SURPRISING TEACHERS

SONG OF SOLOMON 5; JOHN 12; 1 PETER 1

*O**beying Makes Us Wise.*** "I understand more than the ancients, because I keep your precepts" (Ps. 119:100). Studying the Bible does not necessarily make us spiritually smart. Some of the most theologically brilliant people I know are the least submitted to Jesus and thus the greatest fools of all. Wisdom is found within the confines of obedience. We learn what Jesus is like by doing what He tells us to do. The reverent knowledge of God is apprehended through obedient service. God does not discount thinking, but thinking alone is not obedience. We cannot ponder our way to wisdom; we walk toward it. Obedience requires action, because as we obey the thoughts of God we understand them. We understand mercy by showing mercy. If you want to be wise, obey what the Scripture tells you to do.

Glorying Makes Us Remember. "When Jesus was glorified, then they remembered" (John 12:16). The disciples' understanding was limited until Jesus was glorified. Only after He was exalted did the prophecies and Scriptures make sense to them. When we obey Jesus, we magnify Him, and when we magnify Him, the world and our place in it comes into focus. Glorifying Jesus helps us to think clearly. When He is preeminent in our thoughts and lives, when we build a throne for Him through worship, these affect our minds. When He is not the center of our thoughts and lives, then our memories, thought processes, decisions, and reactions are not wise—they are often foolish. When Jesus is glorified, we not only remember who He is (Lord of all, in full control), but we see clearly who we are and what we must do or not do. When we do not know what to do, we must glorify Jesus. As we glorify Him, the confusing fog is cleared from our minds and spirits. Glorifying Jesus helps us remember what we need to do.

Dying Makes Us Bear Fruit. When a grain of wheat dies, it bears much fruit (John 12:24). One of our problems as Christians is that we think we are trees, not seeds. A tree must remain alive in order to produce fruit. Seeds have to be buried so they can burst apart. We do not have the capacity to produce life, although life is contained in us. There is a fundamental difference between being the source of life and the bearer of life. Mary carried incarnate God within her body but she did not produce Him. We are carriers of incarnate God. Although we have no capacity to produce divine life, it can be released from us if we are willing to die, to get out of the way, and to have our husks torn that divine life might emerge. The death of self, ambition, importance, and will releases God from within us. If we really want to see fruit, we must be willing to die, to get out of the way.

KUMHAR HINDUS OF INDIAH (14,487,000; 0.01% EVANGELICAL)

PRAY THAT THE KUMHAR WILL UNDERSTAND THAT HOPE FOR FORGIVENESS AND ACCEPTANCE WITH GOD IS ONLY AVAILABLE THROUGH JESUS' WORK ON THE CROSS (1 COR. 1:18).

DECEMBER 14: TROUBLED IN SPIRIT

SONG OF SOLOMON 6; JOHN 13; 1 PETER 2

*T*he Word of God provides incredible structural integrity. The Word is a lamp to our feet (Ps. 119:105), it is our revival (v. 107), it is our heritage (v. 111), and when we incline our hearts toward it forever (v. 112), we are "safe and secure from all alarms."[2] How precious the Bible is to us, and how vital that we know it, sing it, pray it, share it, and live our lives by it. The Word is both food and fodder to us, both bread to the eater and seed to the sower. However, it is not enough for the Word to be in our heads or on our tongues—it must saturate our hearts and frame our wills. It is not enough to know the Word, for even the Devil memorizes Scripture and is adept at using it against believers. The superstructure of the Word does not replace or remove the ongoing voice of the Holy Spirit within the believer—for Jesus still speaks to us: Spirit to spirit, deep unto deep.

Jesus was "troubled in spirit" and warned the disciples what the Spirit had told Him (John 13:21). We need to cultivate an ear for what the Spirit says to us. When we are uncomfortable in our spirit, it often means that the Holy Spirit is warning us. When our spirit is quickened and joyful, it often means the Holy Spirit is encouraging us. It is biblical to have ongoing conversations with the Lord in the spirit. It is biblical for us to be checked or commissioned by an inner witness. The text does not proscribe all decisions in life. We go to God's written Word for principles because He "has magnified [His] Word above all [His] name" (Ps. 138:2). Still, nothing comprehensively contains or restrains God—not even Scripture. He still speaks, and a troubled spirit is often His restraint, a gentle warning to our souls.

It is not illogical to listen to the Spirit within our hearts because the Counselor is not under the authority of His own speech. Rather, He rules over all, and His words serve Him. There are times in life when we cannot explain or defend our decisions. All we can certify is that the Spirit has not given us permission to do something or has directed us to stop doing something. God's consistency cannot be broken concerning His Word. His principles do not change; they endure as they were recorded for us. Within the structure of those principles—the big, fixed, reinforced concrete pillars of His house—God constantly talks to us about types of windows, style of carpet, and color of paint. The Spirit still speaks to our spirits, and we need to listen and obey His promptings.

SOMALI ISSA MUSLIMS OF UNITED ARAB EMIRATES (144,000; 0.0% EVANGELICAL)

PRAY THAT THE BELIEVERS AMONG THE SOMALI ISSA, LEVANTINE WILL ENDURE PERSECUTION IN A CHRISTLIKE MANNER AND WILL GIVE THEIR LIVES FOR THE SAKE OF THE GOSPEL IF NECESSARY (1 PETER 2:21-23).

DECEMBER 15: ON THE CONTRARY, BLESSING

SONG OF SOLOMON 7; JOHN 14; 1 PETER 3

*S*pirit beauty is precious in the sight of God. It is the kind of spirit we should have when we are reviled and persecuted. We should not "return evil for evil or reviling for reviling, but on the contrary blessing, knowing that you were called to this" (1 Peter 3:9). When we suffer for the sake of righteousness with a beautiful spirit (v. 14), not only are we blessed but we join with the divine long-suffering (v. 20). When we suffer and maintain a gentle spirit, we are blessed because when we suffer as Jesus did we partake of the divine nature. Yet not every Christian suffers well. The call to missions includes the call to suffering, and the call to suffering includes the call to suffer well. Suffering is not mechanically salvific, nor does the follower of Jesus automatically suffer well. Suffering makes some people bitter and other people better. There is nothing as beautiful as the Christian who suffers well, and there is nothing as disappointing and shameful as the Christian who suffers poorly. In the days to come, more and more followers of Jesus are going to suffer in frontier mission work. It will be a tragic and painful waste if we suffer poorly.

Our suffering should cause us to sing. Paul and Silas sat in jail and lifted their voices in praise. The Scripture does not indicate they were interceding for escape, nor does it imply they were strategizing or pleading for the soul of the jailer. Paul's and Silas's spirits magnified the Lord and lifted up His name. Release, witness, and conversion resulted because they suffered well. When God is the center of our suffering, the suffering makes us beautiful. When we fix our eyes on Jesus rather than on why we suffer, how long we will suffer, and who is making us suffer, then our suffering is redemptive.

All too often, Christians fall prey to the Devil's twist on suffering. We put ourselves at the center, either in self-pity or self-glorification, and both of those perspectives make us ugly. Our suffering is not about us, and it is not about our persecutors. Our suffering is about the glory of Jesus, and only when we suffer with grace and gentleness does He receive the glory He deserves. The more they beat us, the gentler we should become. The more they slander us, the more we should smile. The longer they hold us captive, the more thankful and gracious we should be. Grace and gentleness as a response to injustice both infuriate and incapacitate evil. What can the wicked do to the person who places Jesus at the center of suffering? They can either fall on their knees to join us in worship or fail miserably in their demonic task. Please, Lord, let it be the former.

UYGHUR MUSLIMS OF KAZAKHSTAN (230,000; 0.0% EVANGELICAL)

PRAY THAT GOD WOULD RAISE UP MISSIONARIES FROM ALL OVER THE WORLD
TO PLANT THE CHURCH TOGETHER AMONG THE UYGHUR
(MATT. 9:37).

DECEMBER 16: LOVE TO BE HATED

SONG OF SOLOMON 8; JOHN 15; 1 PETER 4

*W*e should love to be hated, but we should not seek to be hated. Being hated by the world brings us closer to Jesus. After all, He reminds us that "if the world hates you, you know that it hated Me before it hated you" (John 15:18). We find it odd that the world hates Jesus, but it does. When the world professes to love Jesus it is a false love, for they love a Jesus of their own making. Muslims claim they love and honor Jesus, but the Jesus they embrace is a Jesus of their own liking, not a divine sovereign. Jesus calls us from our worlds (Islam, secular humanism, nominal Christianity) and tells us that when He chooses us, the world we leave will hate us (v. 19).

It is naïve to think that if a Muslim or an atheist understood Jesus, they would love, adore, and follow Him. This is true neither for the devils nor for people. Jesus Himself said, "Now they have both seen and also hated both Me and My Father" (v. 24). It is sheer folly for the Christian to try to be liked by the world, for we cannot be respected by the world that we are called to leave *and* still be obedient to the will of the Father, even and especially when the world sees Jesus clearly. The will of God includes suffering as a normal ongoing experience for the Christian. We are to "arm ourselves with the same mind" that Jesus had (1 Peter 4:1), a predetermination to suffer unashamedly (v. 16). We should not think that suffering is strange (v. 12) but rather should rejoice in suffering because it leads us to partake in Christ (v. 13). Jesus wants us to embrace suffering for the will of God (v. 1) because we have spent enough time suffering for the foolish will of the world (v. 3).

Jesus warns that we will be hated and we will suffer, so we might as well approach hatred and suffering from a redemption perspective. This fallen world does not allow universal popularity or safety, so let us determine that we will be hated and we will suffer for the only One who can make pain redemptive. Let us be hated for Jesus' sake, not because we are selfish, foolish, violent, and mean. Let us suffer for Jesus' sake not because we are arrogant, hasty, impatient, or uncaring. Reproach for sin and stupidity is one thing; reproach for the name of Christ is blessed, for in that sting the Spirit of glory and of God rests upon us (v. 14). To suffer for self is a shame; to suffer for the Savior is a privilege. Let us then speak and live as oracles of God so He might be glorified in all things (v. 11). Let us speak and live happy to be loved or hated, caring only that we follow closely in the footsteps of Jesus: hated where He is hated, rejected where He is rejected, suffering for and with Him, loved where He is embraced, that He might be glorious in all things.

RAJPUT, GARHWALI HINDUS OF INDIA (643,000; 0.0% EVANGELICAL)

PRAY THAT THE RAJPUT, GARHWALI WOULD FEEL AND KNOW THE BURDEN OF SIN AND COME TO JESUS FOR FORGIVENESS AND SALVATION (MATT. 11:28-30).

DECEMBER 17: HELPING GOD ON HIS TERMS

ZECHARIAH 1; JOHN 16; 1 PETER 5

*J*esus is annoyingly persistent. The satisfactions of God are much more exhaustive than ours; they cost us more to attain and they satisfy us more deeply once we find them, once they find us. We set a fairly low bar for ourselves. We are pleased with ourselves when we serve God, are used by Him, speak His words, build His church, and generally make ourselves available to the divine will. God accepts these offerings but is not satisfied with performance or help and continues to go after our hearts. God says: "I am exceedingly angry with the nations at ease; for I was a little angry, and they helped but with evil intent" (Zech. 1:15). It is not enough to help God from a place of ease—it must cost us something. It is not enough to help God for our own reasons—we must share His motives.

Helping God's Way Requires God's Commitment. Revival movements tend to start, or at least flourish, among the poor. The poor are more cognizant of their need for help. Redemption lifts us. We stop sinning and wasting time and money. We start honoring God with tithes and offerings. Then God opens the windows of heaven and we are blessed. We may not become rich—Jesus stayed fairly poor all His life, as did most of the apostles—but our needs are met. Over time, Christians generally prosper and move from giving sacrificially to giving out of surplus. It does not take long for followers of Jesus to be content to help God from their ease. Jesus is not satisfied with that. He insists that we not live at ease but at war. He is angry with the nations (and churches) that live at ease when people perish under the crushing oppression and deceit of the Devil. To help God's way we must constantly give more time, love, and resources than we are comfortable with.

Helping God's Way Requires God's Motives. We should not confuse God's tools with God's friends. God called Cyrus His anointed one, His hammer. History is replete with evil people and armies that God used for His purposes. We cannot allow ourselves to think that His employment equals His favor or pleasure. He can wield any tool He wants, but He is not satisfied for us to be tools—He wants us to be His partners. We can castigate pagan forces for helping God with evil intent and overlook the evil in our own motives for service. Is it not evil to serve God for recognition? Is it not evil to help God that we might be respected and honored? Is it not evil to help God for the financial security gained from faithful support? When we help God's way we share His anguish and His joys (John 16:20–22). When we help God's way, we share His motivations—His redemptive, merciful intent.

POLISH JEWS OF ISRAEL (116,000; 0.05% EVANGELICAL)

PRAY THAT GOD WOULD UNVEIL THE CROSS AND WOULD REMOVE THE VEIL ON THE MINDS AND SPIRITS OF THE POLISH JEWS OF ISRAEL (2 COR. 3:16-17).

DECEMBER 18: SENT AFTER GLORY

*I*n Hebrew the word for *glory* is related to the word for *weight*. There is a weight to the presence of God. Zechariah noted an interesting prophetic utterance when the Messiah declared, "He sent Me after glory" (Zech. 2:8). Zechariah prophesied that the Messiah would defend God's honor among the nations and would defend the rights of God's people as "the apple of His eye." God defends humanity's honor by establishing His presence among us, by coming to dwell in our midst (v. 10). There is no greater honor to the poor peasant than for the king to visit his hovel and dignify him with His presence. If this is true for human monarchs, how much more glory is unleashed when the Lord of Creation, the King of Kings, comes to tabernacle with us!

God looks over the nations, the ethnolinguistic peoples who do not know Him. They are impoverished. They are stricken with the greatest tragedy of all time: a lack of the intimate knowledge and weighty presence of God. And God sends Jesus to set that right and to harvest glory. God joins nations to Himself (v. 11), they become His people, and He dwells in their midst. When they experience the glorious presence of God and are fulfilled, God is delighted. This transaction is so stunning and the yielded glory so significant, that all the earth falls silent before the Lord (v. 13). God is aroused from His holy habitation and collects the glory that His presence brings when He crosses the impossible divide to dignify humanity with His presence. Incarnation brings glory to God; it never glorifies humanity.

Jesus understood well that His presence in His people yielded glory. When Jesus stated that He was glorified in His disciples (John 17:10), He meant that His manifest and compelling presence in His people brought dignity to humanity and praise to God. Jesus said that as the Father had sent Him into the world, so He was sending His disciples into the world (v. 18). We, too, are sent after glory! Not only are we called by glory and virtue (2 Peter 1:3), and not only does the Father speak to us from His excellent glory (v. 17), but we are to carry the glory of God to the most remote places and to the most rebellious peoples. We are sent after the glory of God, which can only be harvested when unreached peoples experience His weighty presence. This is not a glory that humanity shares. This is a glory only God can own, for when filthy humanity embraces God, the wonder is not in the filth but in the God who saves and cleanses. Every time God ransoms a sinner from hell, every time people turn from bondage to embrace the weighty presence of God, glory is collected and laid at Jesus' feet. When unreached people turn to Jesus, there is a glory yield. We are sent after glory—His! His alone.

UZBEK, NORTHERN MUSLIMS OF UZBEKISTAN (22,404,000; 0.01% EVANGELICAL)

PRAY THAT BELIEVERS AMONG THE UZBEK WOULD BE SET FREE FROM A SPIRIT OF FEAR OF WHAT MAY COME AND WOULD BOLDLY PROCLAIM THE TRUTH OF THE GOSPEL

(2 TIM. 1:6-8).

DECEMBER 19: JESUS HELP ME

ZECHARIAH 3; JOHN 18; 2 PETER 2

*S*piritual maturity is counter to human maturity. From a human perspective, to become an adult is to be increasingly dependent on self. From the spiritual perspective, to become an adult is to be increasingly dependent on Jesus. Typically, we consider continual dependence on others to be a weakness, a sign of immaturity, but continual dependence on Jesus indicates great spiritual strength. Those who have been used greatly in God's kingdom are those who recognize their absolute need for Jesus to sustain their every breath. The psalmist said, "I rise before the dawning of the morning, and cry for help" (Ps. 119:147). There is something eternally beautiful about the person who knows deeply that without Jesus he can do nothing.

In Zechariah 3 we read the story of Joshua the high priest. In the narrative, Satan stood continually at Joshua's side to oppose him. There are two ongoing forces constantly present around us: The Accuser stands at our side opposing the work of God in and through us, and the Lord dwells within us to rebuke the lies of Satan and to repulse his attacks. The reason we need to embrace our spiritual dependence and turn to Jesus for help is because Satan stands at our side persistently waiting for moments of vulnerability. We constantly need the protection of the Lord. He rebukes Satan on our behalf and plucks us out to safety as a brand from the fire (v. 2). If the Lord did not continually keep us from evil, we would be consumed. He knows how to deliver the godly from temptations (2 Peter 2:9). Temptations can be isolated urges or they can be a sustained place of vulnerability. Jesus is able to deliver us from both if we turn to Him, if we live and breathe a "Jesus help me!" lifestyle of dependence. The godly are not delivered because they are good—for no one is good—but because they turn to Jesus for help.

Jesus defends us; we do not have to defend Him (John 18:8). When we move from a position of spiritual dependency into an arrogant assumption that Jesus needs our protection, we hurt others and we misrepresent Him. Like Peter, we chop off somebody's ear and make a mess that Jesus has to clean up. Jesus is more than capable of defending both us and His own name. If we cannot even defend ourselves without His constant intervention, how do we think we can defend Him? We are called to magnify and obey Jesus, not defend Him. He defends us, we proclaim Him. He helps us, we praise Him. He delivers us, we worship Him. It is God's responsibility to keep us from evil. It is our responsibility to turn to Him morning by morning, moment by moment, for help. Our daily dependence on Jesus makes us dominant.

RAJPUT, GARHWALI HINDUS OF INDIA (643,000; 0.0% EVANGELICAL)

PRAY FOR THE WORD OF GOD IN WRITTEN, ORAL, MUSICAL, AND DRAMATIC FORMS TO BE TRANSLATED AND RISE AMONG THE RAJPUT (ISA. 55:10-11).

DECEMBER 20: FINISHING WELL

ZECHARIAH 4; JOHN 19; 2 PETER 3

*F*inishing *Well Requires the Humility of Beginning Small.* "Who has despised the day of small things?" (Zech. 4:10) When we reflect on the life of a giant of the faith, we tend to emphasize the achievements of that person's life. Great souls build great legacies on a thousand small decisions, a thousand little acts of obedience. No man or woman starts great in the kingdom, and they do not finish well unless they start small. The foundation has to be simple, solid, and strong if the life is to speak long after it is dead. It is the subterranean start, the unseen humble beginning that supports the greatest lives, lives that end with enduring honor.

Finishing Well Requires the Power of the Holy Spirit. Sheer willpower does not get us to the end of our spiritual race. A spirit race requires Spirit fuel: "Not by might nor by power, but by My Spirit says the LORD of hosts" (v. 6). It is not our marshaled strength that gets us to the end of life blameless. It is the power of the Lord of angel armies. The forces of evil that would cause us to fail are too strong and cunning for us to escape their sinister plans unless we are surrounded by God's elite troops, unless we run the whole race on His energy.

Finishing Well Requires Mountains of Grace. The mountainous problems that surround us are made flat in the end by God's grace (4:7). Our salvation is by grace through faith, as is our completion. Only God's grace gets us through this fallen world pure. Grace never denies or circumvents our efforts and intentional discipline, but neither can we rely on our efforts to get us to the end sin-free. Those who finish well have not had more luck or been more determined than those who stumbled at the end. They have simply been graced by God. When we breathe our last breath, we should use it to shout "Grace!"

Finishing Well Requires the Centrality of Jesus. The capstone (v. 7) holds everything together. Those who finish well tend to be those who have lived a Christocentric life from beginning to end. When we determine to put Jesus at the center, and doggedly keep Him there, finishing well becomes academic. When we have fashioned our lives on the adoration of Jesus, it is not hard to be ushered into His presence at peace with Him and with all humanity. When Jesus is the center, everything fits together well. When Jesus has long been the center of our lives, we die "with Jesus at the center" (John 19:18).

ADYGHE MUSLIMS OF JORDAN (111,000; 0.02% EVANGELICAL)

PRAY THAT GOD WOULD POUR OUT HIS SPIRIT ON THE ADYGHE PEOPLE AND THAT THEY WOULD SEE DREAMS AND VISIONS OF JESUS. PRAY THAT THEY WOULD BE POWERFULLY SAVED AND EMPOWERED TO BE HIS WITNESSES (JOEL 2:28-32).

DECEMBER 21: GOD'S CURSE

ZECHARIAH 5; JOHN 20; 1 JOHN 1

*E*ither God is a liar or we are. John warned that we can make God a liar by saying we have no sin (1 John 1:10). If we say we have fellowship with God yet we walk in darkness, we lie (v. 6). It comes as a shock that we are all liars and thieves—all of us, even those who appear the most saintly. We all lie by presenting ourselves in word or posture as better than we actually are. We all steal by taking little wisps of God's glory for ourselves.

Zechariah surprises us by saying that there is a universal curse. The surprise is not in the curse, but in the originator and disseminator of the curse. "The curse that goes out over the face of the whole earth [to expel liars and thieves]," wrote Zechariah, is sent by the Lord of hosts (5:3–4). God sends this flying curse (depicted as a thirty-two-feet by sixteen-feet scroll), which shall "remain in the midst of [our] house and consume it." Evidently God does not act favorably toward thieves and liars, which includes you and me. God's curse is linked to His judgment, His dealing with what is false, and His eradication in us and the earth of what is evil. (Paul talks about the law being a curse in this sense.) God will eradicate lying and stealing in the earth. He will eradicate lying and stealing in His church. He will eradicate the lying and stealing in my heart.

We must accept that at our very best we are liars and thieves. Until we can genuinely own up to this embarrassing reality, we are yet calling God a liar. Thankfully, God is determined to burn this ugliness out of us. His law and holy wrath hammer away at the deception and idolatry in our hearts until these sins are destroyed. This process does not happen in a day or a week. This will take all our lives and will only be completed when Jesus comes again in glory. At that time He will unleash one final devastating blow against Satan and his lies and stolen glories, which are embedded in us.

God's curse in this regard is our blessing, for the sin in us is cursed but we are not. We can participate in God's intention in two primary ways. First, we can admit we are liars and thieves. We can admit this to our family and friends. We can get this shame into the light (1 John 1:7). Bringing dark things into the light breaks the back of sin and brings us into fellowship not only with God but with one another. It is our vulnerabilities that bind us together, not our strengths. Second, we can long for our freedom. A groaning to be free from our lying and stealing is a passion God uses toward our deliverance. God loves to deliver the soul who loves to be delivered.

UZBEK, SOUTHERN MUSLIMS OF AFGHANISTAN (3,103,000; 0.01% EVANGELICAL)

PRAY THAT CHRISTIANS FROM AROUND THE WORLD WOULD WORK TOGETHER TO REACH THE UZBEK AND THAT THE UZBEK WOULD BE JOINED TO THE BODY OF CHRIST (JOHN 17:20-23).

DECEMBER 22: SIGNS AND WONDERS OF GOD

ZECHARIAH 6; JOHN 21; 1 JOHN 2

*G*od scandalized the cosmos and dignified humanity forever by becoming a man. Just as we come to terms with God becoming human, the divine Son dies on a cross. Our eyes open to this wonder just in time for the resurrection to make us fall to the ground in shock. We barely recover from that bolt from heaven when Jesus ascends to the right hand of God—another unexpected masterstroke of God. Our minds reel and we are surprised once again at the triumphant and final return of the King. Our souls can hardly endure this "nibbling" at the edges of the feast of wondrous God. As the advent season approaches its zenith, we wonder again at the event that started this shocking sequence: God with us, God coming down to dwell with humanity.

Jesus Came. When humanity went astray, God came seeking (Ps. 119:176). We do not bear the sole or even the primary responsibility of finding God. He takes the initiative to find us. The incarnation is God pursuing us, pursuing us all the way to this mud hole of earth. The incarnation is God leaving what was comfortable to get down and dirty to find us. The incarnation is God leaving the sanitary zone and climbing down to swim in the sewage, looking for people of infinite less worth than He. The incarnation is wonderfully horrible. It stuns and amazes us.

Jesus Is Coming. The incarnation also gives us hope, for Jesus comes to us again and again. John wrote, "He showed Himself again" (21:1). He also noted that this was "the third time Jesus showed Himself" (v. 14). Over and over again Jesus comes to us. He carries the responsibility to find us. Yes, we seek Him, but we seek Him in response to His seeking us. He takes on the responsibility for my heart and my spirit. Oh, the holy humility of Jesus who continues to pursue us. "Oh, come to my heart, Lord Jesus! There is room in my heart for Thee!"[3]

Jesus Will Come Again. First John 2:28 encourages us to abide in Jesus that when He appears (the Greek is *phanerothe*), we might be confident and unashamed before Him "at His coming." The Greek word for appears comes from the verb to *reveal*. Jesus is coming again in glory, and He will finally, fully reveal Himself. Every time Jesus comes to us and we sense His presence, it is a foretaste of that great day "when He shall come, resplendent in His glory."[4]

MANGRIK TIBETAN BUDDHISTS OF INDIA (110,000; 0.0% EVANGELICAL)

PRAY THAT THE HEARTS OF THE MANGRIK WOULD BE LIKE GOOD SOIL, READY TO HEAR THE GOSPEL AND TO RESPOND (MATT. 7:1-8, 18-23).

DECEMBER 23: NOT FOR YOU TO KNOW

ZECHARIAH 7; ACTS 1-2; 1 JOHN 3

Followers of Jesus love His promise of empowerment. Facing overwhelming odds with underwhelming strength, we cling to the lifeline of God's promised power: "But you shall receive power when the Holy Spirit has come upon you" (Acts 1:8). We know that God's power helps us bear witness to His glory among every ethnolinguistic people. We are not so well acquainted with the preposition on the front end of that verse: *but*. But what? "It is not for you to know times or seasons," *but* it is for you to receive power to be my witnesses (vv. 7–8). We are not to know—we are to receive power.

We are preoccupied with knowing. We want to know what season we are in. We want to know how our ministry is being received. We want to know that we are significant. We want to know that our labor matters. We want to know that we are filled with the Holy Spirit. We want to know that we are bearing fruit. We want to know what God is doing. We want to know when God will fulfill His promises and complete all things. There are many good things to know, but Jesus gently reminds us that the point is not to know but to be empowered. Jesus asks us to lay aside our hunger to know and, instead, to concentrate on receiving power and disseminating witness. It is for Jesus to know and for us to obey.

"By this we know that we are of the truth, and shall assure our hearts before Him. For if our hearts condemn us, God is greater than our heart, and knows all things" (1 John 3:19–20). It is not for us to know what God is doing or how, why and why He does it. God knows all things, and that is enough for us. Any insight is a bonus. Our role is not to be the one who knows. Our role is to be the one who obeys, who believes and loves (vv. 22–23). When we obey, believe, and love, our hearts are aligned with God and He keeps us in His purposes. We find our fulfillment in empowered obedience, not in unlimited understanding.

In God's great wisdom it is often better for us not to know what season we are in and what fruit we bear. This is not mean or controlling of God, this is love and grace. Knowledge often brings more pain than power. As we allow God to bear the burden of knowledge, we can bear His glory to the ends of the earth (Zech. 6:13). Our goal is not sowing or reaping or bearing fruit. Our goal is obedience. God's goal is harvested fruit. He knows how our obedience will contribute to His fruitful harvest. That is enough for Him, and it needs to be enough for us. We need to embrace the gift of not knowing.

BEDOUIN, YAHIA MUSLIMS OF MOROCCO (101,000; 0.0% EVANGELICAL)

PRAY FOR THE PEACE THAT RESULTS WHEN MEN AND WOMEN ARE RECONCILED WITH GOD (JOHN 14:27). PRAY FOR MEN AND WOMEN OF PEACE (LUKE 10:6) AMONG THE BEDOUIN, YAHIA.

DECEMBER 24: TONGUES OF MEN AND ANGELS

ZECHARIAH 8; ACTS 3-4; 1 JOHN 4

*T*he filling of the Spirit always affects the tongue. First Corinthians 13 does not urge us to be silent but to speak from love. Love compels us to speak of Jesus. The most common hate crime committed by Christians is to not speak. Silence demonstrates a lesser love for Jesus, for if we truly love Him and experience Him, we cannot contain or restrain our mouths. When the presence of Jesus is real, the human vessel cannot contain Him. Love for Jesus and others must spill out. Peter and John explained: "We cannot but speak the things which we have seen and heard" (Acts 4:20). This is the unquestioned pattern in the book of Acts.

Jesus promised that when the Holy Spirit comes upon us, we will be His witnesses (1:8). The disciples were filled with the Spirit and began to speak with other tongues (2:4). Peter was filled with the Spirit "and said . . ." (4:8). The disciples were refilled with the Holy Spirit and "spoke the word of God with boldness" (v. 31). Stephen was full of the Holy Spirit and would not stop speaking (6:13). In fact, he saw Jesus "and said . . ." (7:55–56). The Holy Spirit was poured out on Cornelius and his household and they spoke with tongues and magnified God (10:44–46). In Ephesus, when the Holy Spirit came upon a group of believers, they spoke with tongues and prophesied (19:6).

The filling of the Holy Spirit always and immediately affects the tongue. In various ways and at various times (Heb. 1:1–2), the mouth is always involved, and the mouth always magnifies Jesus. "Holy men of God spoke as they were moved by the Holy Spirit" (2 Peter 1:21). When the Holy Spirit comes upon us, we speak, and we speak boldly of Jesus. John clarified that "by this we know the Spirit of God: every spirit that confesses Jesus Christ has come in the flesh is of God" (1 John 4:2).

If zealous Pentecostals have obfuscated the issue by overemphasizing tongues, cautious evangelicals have often excused themselves from the clear proscription of ecstatic speech in Scripture. When men and women are full of the Spirit, they immediately speak out and magnify Jesus. Fullness of the Spirit means that Jesus swells in us to the bursting and overflowing point. When Jesus invades our spirits, we cannot but open our mouths and speak in tongues, prophesy, preach boldly, witness, and exalt the magnificent Son of God. When Jesus invaded earth, angels could not contain the wonder and burst into praise over Bethlehem. The inviolable result of the Spirit's filling is a bursting heart and a speaking mouth—a mouth that super-exalts Jesus. On this the tongues of men and angels agree.

ZAZA-ALEVI MUSLIMS OF TURKEY (182,000; 0.0% EVANGELICAL)

PRAY BELIEVERS AMONG THE ZAZA-ALEVI WOULD PROCLAIM THE MESSAGE OF THE GOSPEL CLEARLY AND WOULD MAKE THE MOST OF EVERY OPPORTUNITY GOD PLACES BEFORE THEM (COL. 4:2-5).

DECEMBER 25: GOD WITH US

ZECHARIAH 9; ACTS 5-6; 1 JOHN 5

*T*here are certain things we know. We know these things because God came near and lived with us, He lives in us by His Spirit, and His Word is our counselor (Ps. 119:24). John tells us that we know we have eternal life, we know we are of God, and we know the Spirit of God has come and given us understanding (1 John 5:13–20). We have the advantage of seeing these things from this side of Bethlehem. Zechariah saw these things from the dark. He, too, knew the whole world was under the sway of the Wicked One (1 John 5:19), but in that darkness he saw a dawning light.

God looked down from heaven and observed that evil encroached everywhere. He saw and made a determination to come down and "camp around His house" (Zech. 9:8). God came near. He invaded earth and set up a perimeter defense around His people. Humanity was overwhelmed by the shadows of darkness, unable to resist the massive demonic forces pressing into heads and hearts. God came down and set up a wall. Our King came to us lowly and riding on a donkey (v. 9). Jesus, *in utero*, rode a donkey into Bethlehem and at rode one again at His triumphal entry into Jerusalem. Both were astonishingly humble rides. Jesus came to earth to defend us. Christmas is our relief and our defense. Our King comes to protect us from sin, self, and Satan. Zechariah prophesied, "The LORD their God will save them in that day. . . . They shall be like jewels of a crown" (v. 16).

In incarnation God invaded His own dark, rebellious world. Christmas represents our rescue—we know we will be delivered, but there is still a battle to fight. Christmas is knowing we are doomed, our backs to the wall, enemy hordes flowing over the gates, death only minutes away when our King in brilliant light rides over the crest of the hill and smashes through the demonic masses to stand next to us. We are yet surrounded, but now God is with us, ankle deep in blood and mud with fire in His eyes and an arm swinging His flashing sword. In this context John reminds us that faith is the victory that overcomes the world (1 John 5:4).

The world is not overcome by prayer. It is not overcome by church planting or evangelism or power encounters. The world is overcome by faith. "He who believes that Jesus is the Son of God overcomes the world" (v. 5). Christmas is about faith. It is believing that Jesus is God who came to dwell with humanity, who will defend us, who will defeat evil. We participate in the victory of Christmas by believing that God will do it again. He will come again soon to culminate His victory. On that day, not only will He be with us, we will be with Him forever. We will enjoy a second Christmas.

MAKHMI MUSLIMS OF INDIA (63,300; 0.0% EVANGELICAL)

PRAY THAT THE MAKHMI WILL UNDERSTAND THAT HOPE FOR FORGIVENESS AND ACCEPTANCE WITH GOD IS ONLY AVAILABLE THROUGH JESUS' WORK ON THE CROSS (1 COR. 1:18).

DECEMBER 26: LEAVING HOME

ZECHARIAH 10; ACTS 7-9; 2 JOHN

We have made Christmas about coming home and being comfortable. Jesus' approach to Christmas was to leave home and be uncomfortable. Christmas has become safe and cozy, a time to relax and give gifts to one another. At the original Christmas, God left the comfort of heaven to give a most precious gift to those who would largely reject it. God visited His flock (Zech. 10:3) and comforted them, but with the intention of "sowing them among the nations" (v. 9). Christmas is Christ's invitation to join Him in leaving home, to join Him in being homeless for the sake of the nations. "I will strengthen them in the LORD, and they shall walk up and down in His name" (v. 12). The *missio dei* (mission of God) is inescapable, even at Christmas, especially at Christmas. God left His heavenly home to walk the earth in discomfort so that men and women might be saved. Not much about that is "ho, ho, ho."

God also calls His sons and daughters to leave home in order to bear His glory into all the earth, into all nations. The call is relentless. God told Abraham, "Get out of your country" (Acts 7:3)! And "God spoke in this way: that his descendants would dwell in a foreign land" (v. 6). We wrongly suppose that Jesus' presence is felt most keenly at home—where we are safe and comfortable. Again and again Scripture shows just the opposite. God is most keenly experienced when we leave home and join Him in His passion to be glorified by every people on earth. God is most real to us in the challenges and trials that take place outside our comfort zones. Stephen made this point, and it was as unpopular then as it is now: "God was with [Joseph] and delivered him out of all his troubles" (v. 9). Moses was born in Egypt and was well pleasing to God (v. 20). God's voice came to Moses in the desert, and Midian was considered holy ground (vv. 29–33). God gave the living oracles at Mount Sinai, possibly in present-day Saudi Arabia (v. 38). God's presence was most powerfully revealed and His commandments most clearly given in the current-day Arab world. The teeth of Stephen's sermon (v. 54) snapped around the fact that God works outside our comfortable boundaries—both of place and perception. We are in danger of being stiff necked and rebellious against the Holy Spirit if we resist His movement, if we resist moving with Him. That is why Christmas compels us to leave home, that the nations might find Christ.

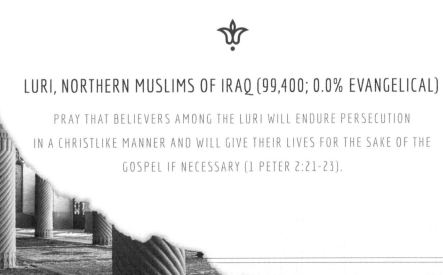

LURI, NORTHERN MUSLIMS OF IRAQ (99,400; 0.0% EVANGELICAL)

PRAY THAT BELIEVERS AMONG THE LURI WILL ENDURE PERSECUTION IN A CHRISTLIKE MANNER AND WILL GIVE THEIR LIVES FOR THE SAKE OF THE GOSPEL IF NECESSARY (1 PETER 2:21-23).

DECEMBER 27: BEAUTY AND BONDS

ZECHARIAH 11; ACTS 10-11; 3 JOHN

*G*enerosity of heart is a prayer that God answers (Acts 10:2, 4). A gracious heart takes the greatest joy when others walk and grow in the truth (3 John 4). A stingy heart restricts the ministry of others and seeks to minimize their influence. Barnabas is a classic example of the generous person whom God blesses (Acts11:22–24), while Diotrephes, who loved "to have the preeminence," is an example of a stingy shepherd (3 John 9). Zechariah described the qualities that make up the wise, generous shepherd: he seeks the young, he heals the broken, he feeds the strong sheep, he does not attack his own, and he does not abandon the flock (Zech. 11:16–17).

The wise shepherd models his life on the Good Shepherd, who carries two staffs: beauty and bonds (v. 7). The Hebrew text uses the word *grace* for "beauty" and *unity* for "bonds." The wise shepherd feeds his flock using grace and unity. We usually think of grace as something bestowed and then displayed on the wall of our hearts rather than something we feed on as fuel. Grace is what allows us to survive spiritually. To receive grace is to ingest it and be energized by it, not to display it on some interior wall. Grace has to get into our bloodstream, into our psyche, into our subconscious, into our emotions, into our innermost being. Grace must fuel how we think, react, move, and have our being. The efficacy of grace is in the consumption. Unity is not a result but an energy, a motivation. We do not reach the world to become unified; we reach the world because we are unified.

When either unity or grace is the goal rather than the love and glory of God, perversion inevitably follows our tolerance and concessions. Love and glory bring truth. Loving truth demands that unity be forged on the immovable nature of Christ and Christ alone. Truth requires that grace be given and received on God's atoning terms. Unity and grace are not the goal, attractive as those goals may be. Love and truth are the goal for the glory of God. This is why the brotherhood (v. 14) and the covenants (v. 10) sometimes need to be broken. God will give grace and unity—but not at cost to His own nature or His own glory. Grace and unity are tools, not goals. If your overarching goal is to grace people or unify them, you are in danger of corrupting both them and yourself. If your overarching goal is God's love and glory, grace and unity will feed and fuel you well.

ZAZA-DIMLI MUSLIMS OF TURKEY (1,145,000; 0.0% EVANGELICAL)

PRAY THAT GOD WOULD RAISE UP MISSIONARIES FROM ALL OVER THE WORLD TO PLANT THE CHURCH TOGETHER AMONG THE ZAZA-DIMLI (MATT. 9:37).

DECEMBER 28: PIERCING WORDS

ZECHARIAH 12; ACTS 12-13; JUDE

*T*he foolish things that come out of our mouths continually pierce God. Rather than speak grace and supplication (Zech. 12:10), we tend to speak the words of Herod: eloquent arrogance (Acts 12:23). We fall in love with the sound of our voices and believe the flatterers who tell us we speak like gods. People are fools, and God alone is wise (Jude 25). Our folly can be most evident when we open our mouths and speak. That is why God intentionally links the infilling of the Holy Spirit with divine control of the tongue. In Scripture, when a man or a woman was filled with the Spirit, this had an immediate effect on their tongue. We know God is in control of His vessels when He controls the most unruly member (James 3:1–8). God's intention for the mouth is not that it should pierce Him or others in its folly, but that it should magnify the Lord in fiery praise. The sinful tongue magnifies itself and distorts God; the holy tongue magnifies God and diminishes humanity.

To say that a Spirit-filled tongue is empowered is not to imply that it speaks only soft things. Our tongues are commissioned to proclaim the whole counsel of God. The Spirit fills us to speak God's words, and God's words pierce even to the division of soul and spirit, joints and marrow (Heb. 4:12). In Cyprus, Paul encountered the sorcerer Elymas, who withstood the words of God. Paul, "filled with the Holy Spirit, looked intently at him and said: 'O full of deceit and all fraud, you son of the devil, you enemy of all righteousness, will you not stop perverting the straight ways of the Lord?'" (Acts 13:9–10) This, too, is empowered speech, the piercing words of heaven that cut through all the fraud and lies of people and devils. The filling of the Spirit leads us to magnify God's name and to defend it. There comes a time when God's wisdom is so provoked by the foolishness of people that empowered speech issues from His vessels with the authority of the Spirit. These rebukes are witness, too, and often lead to belief. The consul Sergius Paulus (an intelligent man), believed, being astonished at the teaching of the Lord (Acts 13:7, 12).

God wants our words to pierce—but not to pierce Him. He fills us with His Spirit that our words might pierce through all the clouded confusion of humanity, cut through all the lies and deceit, and stab the heart of the matter. Because our mouths are swords, they can do great harm or great good. Only the repeated infilling of the Holy Spirit ensures that we pierce with grace for God's glory.

URDU MUSLIMS OF BAHRAIN (61,100; 0.005% EVANGELICAL)

PRAY THAT THE URDU WOULD FEEL AND KNOW THE BURDEN OF SIN AND WOULD COME
TO JESUS FOR FORGIVENESS AND SALVATION
(MATT. 11:28-30).

DECEMBER 29: TO FLEE OR NOT TO FLEE

ZECHARIAH 13; ACTS 14; REVELATION 20

*G*od's Word is both a comfort in affliction (Ps. 119:50) and a source of persecution. We read in Revelation 20:4 of the souls who were "beheaded for their witness to Jesus and for the word of God." The Word of God not only gets us into trouble but takes us through it. In these last days it is imperative that we continually point to Jesus as God and Savior, and that we continually stand on the Word of God. Neither one will endear us to the world; both will bring suffering and tribulation upon us. Those who are faithful to Jesus will face increasing pressure, and we must decide whether or not we will flee trouble when it finds us.

Paul's first missionary journey took him to places where the gospel was both welcomed and rejected. In Iconium, the city was divided (Acts 14:4). Unbelieving Jews stirred up the Gentiles and poisoned their minds against the brethren (v. 2). "*Therefore* [Paul and Barnabas] stayed there a *long time*, speaking boldly in the Lord" (v. 3, emphasis added). Paul's initial response to persecution was to endure and to respond by speaking even more boldly than before. After sustained endurance, Paul did flee and escape to Lystra (v. 6). Escape is a misleading word, perhaps, for he continued to preach boldly in Lystra: "Turn from these useless things" (v. 15)! For his effort he was stoned and dragged out of the city. Crushed by stones to the point that people thought he was dead, Paul got up—and went back into the city (v. 20). The next day he moved to Derbe to preach again.

While for both Jesus and Paul we can make a case for occasional strategic withdrawal, these cases are the exception. The rule is: stay, endure, and continue to preach the Word boldly. Further, when you do leave, you go to the next hostile place to preach boldly again. Jesus went intentionally to Jerusalem; Paul fixed his feet toward Rome. The gospel ever leads us on to danger and risk. If we leave one hot spot, it is only to enter another to proclaim the Savior there.

In this sense the ambassador of Christ never flees. We stand our ground in the face of great danger and opposition and boldly proclaim Christ. If we leave Iconium due to violent threats, it is to go to Lystra in order to be stoned. To flee or not to flee is not the question—it is our answer. Fleeing or not fleeing, we will open our mouths and boldly exalt Jesus. We purposely move from the frying pan into the fire, always at risk, always rejoicing in the bold proclamation of the gospel.

BAHRAI MUSLIMS OF EGYPT (25,000; 0.0% EVANGELICAL)

PRAY THAT GOD WOULD UNVEIL THE CROSS AND WOULD REMOVE THE
VEIL ON THE MINDS AND SPIRITS OF THE BAHRAI
(2 COR. 3:16-17).

DECEMBER 30: MYTH BUSTER

ZECHARIAH 14; ACTS 15; REVELATION 21

*W*e place too much emphasis on size and speed when it comes to church development. Church history shows it is the steady repeated truth of God that builds the enduring church. The largest church at the end of the first century was found in Rome. Most scholars estimate it had around 200 members. The churches in Ephesus, Corinth, Philippi, Colosse, and Thessalonica (among others) probably had between fifteen and fifty members. This was the normal size of the first-century church. The record of Acts takes place over about fifty years. Biblical precedent indicates that it took about one generation for a few churches to grow to what we consider a modest size. One myth is that the church has to grow quickly; another is that a big church is a strong church. The best churches tend to grow slowly and steadily.

Disciples, too, are forged over time. If a church is but a collection of disciples, then it makes sense that strong churches require time to become solid. Another common myth today in missions is that a new disciple only needs the Bible and the Holy Spirit. As appealing as this sounds, it has never been true in history, and if we are honest, it has not been true for any of us either. Consider how many books, sermons, mentors, friends, and external inputs have helped to shape and form our spirituality over time. We always need an outside catalyst to help correct our biases and heresies. A group of people studying the Scriptures can just as easily end up pooling ignorance as illumining one another. Acts 15 is a classic example of ongoing external input necessary for the formation of strong disciples and churches. The negative example of external input (requiring circumcision) does not negate the massive, ongoing positive external input.

Paul and Barnabas reported that the Gentiles were turning to Jesus. They also reported the negative external pressure. James and the council responded by correcting the error and reinforcing what was necessary. In Acts 15:20, James delineated what they should not do—former religious forms and rituals. Paul reminded the council that coming to Jesus demands conversion (v. 3), and James cited Peter when explaining that the Gentiles must come out of false religion (v. 14). In Acts 15:32, Judas and Silas exhorted and strengthened the brethren "with many words." Paul and Barnabas taught and preached to the Gentiles and committed to revisit their converts to ensure they were walking correctly (vv. 35–36). Disciples and churches are forged over time. Let us continue to believe that God will do great things and bring millions into His church. Let us continue to understand that it is slow, steady, life-on-life work to make disciples and to build churches.

BEDOUIN, KUFRA MUSLIMS OF LIBYA (26,900; 0.0% EVANGELICAL)

PRAY THAT BELIEVERS AMONG THE BEDOUIN, KUFRA WOULD BE SET FREE FROM A SPIRIT OF FEAR OF WHAT MAY COME AND WOULD BOLDLY PROCLAIM THE TRUTH OF THE GOSPEL (2 TIM. 1:6-8).

DECEMBER 31: BEGINNINGS

MALACHI 4; MATTHEW 28; MARK 16; ACTS 28; REVELATION 22

*T*he Alpha is the Omega. God does not change, and He who ends things starts things. He who is the end is the beginning. God is humanity's end. When we long for His salvation (Ps. 119:174), we are in reality longing for Him. God is humanity's eternal beginning. At the re-creation of all things, we shall see His face (Rev. 22:4). Bounded history is quite unimportant in the grand scope of things, for eternity is what matters. God was from eternity past, and He offers us the joy of eternity with Him. The entire earthly existence of humanity is but a blink when laid on the grid of God. It is difficult to grapple with eternity past, but we can easily appreciate eternity future.

Christian endings should be pure joy. Christian funerals should be the purest celebrations. When a man or woman is promoted to the presence of Jesus, our immediate response should be praise and thanks that another soul has begun a pure, curse-free eternity. When a Christian ends this blink of a breath that we know as earthly life, he drinks of the pure river of life (Rev. 22:1). He is in the unmitigated presence of Jesus (v. 3), seeing Him as He is (v. 4) with no more night or darkness (v. 5). When we cry at funerals, let it not be because we feel sorry for ourselves. Rather, let it be because a holy jealousy ignites within us to be with our loved one and the Beloved.

Jesus wants us to long for His return. The gospels end with a stirring call to preach the gospel in all the world, and embedded in that command is a longing for Jesus to return because the gospel must be preached in all the world, among every nation, before we get to go home (Matt.24:14). When Jesus' followers launch to the most difficult places on earth, it is with blended motives: We want to go home, we want to begin our curse-free eternity, and we want as many of our variegated brothers and sisters as possible to begin anew with us. We do not passively sit in this world like an infant in a crib with arms outstretched, crying in solitude for our heavenly Father to lift us from our confined space and change our defiled diaper. We rush around the nursery of earth knowing that when there are enough babies who lift their voices and cry for the coming of the Lord, He will come for us, resplendent in His glory. This nursery of fallen earth has some nice toys, but by faith we peer outside the portals of this world into the great outdoors of God's great heaven. We cry: "Come, Lord Jesus!" He replies: "Surely, I am coming quickly."

The end of each year reminds us that our ultimate beginning will soon be upon us. May we never cease to long for Jesus to come.

DRUZE MUSLIMS OF SYRIA (486,000; 0.0% EVANGELICAL)

PRAY FOR THE WORD OF GOD IN WRITTEN, ORAL, MUSICAL, AND DRAMATIC FORMS TO BE TRANSLATED AND TO RISE AMONG THE DRUZE (ISA. 55:10–11).

As the rain and the snow come down from heaven, and do not return to it without watering the earth . . . so is my word that goes out from my mouth: It will not return to me empty. . . .

ISA. 55:10-11 NIV

NOTES

January

1 John Owens, *Triumph Over Temptation* (Colorado Springs, CO: David C. Cook, 2004).

2 Ibid.

3 Rudyard Kipling, *Collected Poems of Rudyard Kipling; Wordsworth Poetry Library*, poem "If—" (London: Wordsworth Editions, 1999).

4 Owens, *Triumph Over Temptation*.

5 "Man of Sorrows." Lyrics and music by Philip Paul Bass, 1838–1876; http://cyberhymnal.org/.

6 "Under the Blood." Lyrics by Eliza Hewitt, 1801–1900; http://cyberhymnal.org/.

7 Kenneth Bailey, *Jesus Through Middle Eastern Eyes: Cultural Studies in the Gospels* (Downers Grove, IL: IVP Academic, 2008).

8 "To God Be the Glory." Lyrics by Fanny J. Crosby, 1820–1915; http://cyberhymnal.org/.

9 C. S. Lewis, *The Last Battle: Chronicles of Narnia*, Book 7 (New York: Scholastic, 1994).

10 "I'm Pressing on the Upward Way." Lyrics by Johnson Oatman, Jr., 1856–1926; http://cyberhymnal.org/.

11 John Maxwell, *The 21 Irrefutable Laws of Leadership: Follow Them and People Will Follow You* (Nashville, TN: Thomas Nelson, 2007).

12 www.sermonindex.net/modules/mydownloads/viewcat.php?cid.

13 "He Hideth My Soul." Lyrics by Fanny J. Crosby, 1820–1915; http://cyberhymnal.org/.

14 Chuck Miller, Ed. D. *The Spiritual Formation of Leaders: Integrating Spiritual Formation and Leadership Development* (Maitland, FL: Xulon Press, 2007).

15 W. H. T. Gairdner, *D. M. Thornton: A Study in Missionary Ideals and Methods* (London: Hodder and Stoughton, 1908).

16 William Blake, *The Complete Poetry and Prose of William Blake*, Ed. David Erdman (New York: Anchor Books, 1997).

February

1 Richard J. Foster, *Celebration of Discipline: The Path to Spiritual Growth*, 3rd ed. (San Francisco, CA: HarperSanFrancisco, 2002).

2 "Away in a Manger." Lyrics by John McFarland, 1851–1913; http://cyberhymnal.org/.

3 Amy Carmichael, "Hast Thou No Scar?" *Mountain Breezes: The Collected Poems of Amy Carmichael* (Fort Washington, PA: CLC Publications, 1999).

4 Westminster Shorter Catechism, http://www.shortercatechism.com/

5 Nik Ripkin, *The Insanity of God: A True Story of Faith Resurrected* (Nashville: B and H Publishing, 2013).

March

1 G. K. Chesterton, *The Ball and the Cross* (London, UK: CW Publishing, 2013), 77.

2 Eli Gautreaux, "Lost: Parable of the Father's Heart" in *The Live Dead Journal: 30 Days of Prayer for Unreached Peoples* (Springfield, MO: Influence Resources, 2012), 20–21.

3 Mrs. Howard Taylor, *Borden of Yale* (Ada, MI: Bethany House Publishers, 1988).

4 J. Hudson Taylor, *Hudson Taylor* (Ada, MI: Bethany House Publishers, 1987).

5 Gene Edwards, *A Tale of Three Kings: A Study in Brokenness* (Carol Stream, IL: Tyndale House, 1992).

NOTES

April

1 http://www.watchword.org/index.php?option=com_content&task=view&id=48&Itemid=29

2 Charles H. Spurgeon, *My Sermon-Notes: A Selection from Outlines of Discourses Delivered at the Metropolitan Tabernacle with Anecdotes and Illustrations* (China: Ulan Press, 2011).

3 Ralph Winter and Steve C. Hawthorne, Eds. *Perspectives on the World Christian Movement: A Reader,* 4th edition (Pasadena, CA: William Carey Publishers, 2009).

4 John Woolman, *The Journal and Major Essays of John Woolman* (Oxford: Oxford University Press, 1971).

5 "Rock of Ages." Lyrics by Augustus Montague Toplady, 1740–1778; http://cyberhymnal.org/.

6 A. W. Tozer, *The Knowledge of the Holy: The Attributes of God and Their Meaning in the Christian Life* (NewYork: HarperOne, 2009).

7 Elisabeth Elliot, *Through Gates of Splendor* (Carol Stream, IL: Tyndale, 1988).

8 "Who Can Cheer the Heart Like Jesus." Lyrics by Thoro Harris, 1874–1955; http://cyberhymnal.org/.

9 E. F. Harvey and L. Harvey, *They Knew Their God*, vol. 4 (Cheadle, Stoke on Trent, UK: Harvey Christian Publishers, 2004).

May

1 Frank W. Boreham, *The Golden Milestone: A Book of Essays* (Nashville, TN: Abingdon Press, 1994).

2 Albert Hibbert, *Smith Wigglesworth: The Secret of His Power* (Tulsa, OK: Harrison House, 2009).

3 "All for Jesus!" Lyrics by Mary Dagworthy James, 1810–1883; http://cyberhymnal.org/.

4 Samuel Zwemer, "The Gory of the Impossible," in *Perspectives on the World Christian Movement: A Reader*, Ralph D. Winter and Steven C. Hawthorne, eds. 4th edition (Pasadena, CA: William Carey Publishers, 2009).

5 G. K. Chesterton, *Ballad of the White Horse* (Mineola, NY: Dover Publications, 2010).

June

1 "My Faith Has Found a Resting Place." Lyrics by Eliza Edmunds Hewitt, 1851–1920; http://cyberhymnal.org/.

2 "What Can Wash Away My Sin?" Lyrics by Robert Lowry, 1826–1899; http://cyberhymnal.org/.

3 Alfred Lord Tennyson, "The Charge of the Light Brigade," in *Poems*, Ed. Hallam Lord Tennyson and annotated by Alfred Lord Tennyson (London: Macmillan, 1908), II, 369.

4 Rowan Wlliams, *Arius*, Rev. Ed. (Grand Rapids, MI: W. B. Eerdmans, 2002).

5 "Oh, Spread the Tidings 'Round." Lyrics by Frank Bottome, 1823–1894; http://cyberhymnal.org/.

6 Mark Laaser, *Healing the Wounds of Sexual Addiction* (Grand Rapids, MI: Zondervan, 2004).

7 François Fénelon, *The Seeking Heart* (Jacksonville, FL: SeedSowers, 1992), 146.

8 "Beneath the Cross of Jesus." Lyrics by Elizabeth C. Clephane, 1830–1869; http://cyberhymnal.org/.

9 http://www.iwise.com/qrPH4

10 "Turn Your Eyes Upon Jesus/" Lyrics and music by Helen H. Lemmel, 1863–1961; http://cyberhymnal.org/.

11 "And Can it Be That I Should Gain." Lyrics by Charles Wesley, 1707–1788; http://cyberhymnal.org/.

July

1 "Come Thou Fount of Every Blessing." Lyrics by Robert Robinson, 1735–1790; http://cyberhymnal.org/.

2 G. K. Chesterton, *Manalive: Complete Parts 1 and 2* (Seattle, WA: CreateSpace Independent Publishing Platform, 2014), 111.

3 "Exalt His Name Together." Lyrics by Jack Williams Hayford, 1934–present; http://cyberhymnal.org/.

4 http://www.rockfordbaptist.org/about/sermons/2005/Sermon%20-%20July%2010.pdf

5 http://quotes.liberty-tree.ca/quote_blog/Alex.Tytler.Quote.4272

6 "I Have Decided to Follow Jesus." Lyrics attributed to S. Sundar Singh, 1889–1929; http://cyberhymnal.org/.

August

1 John Nelson Wall, *George Herbert: The Country Parson and the Temple* (Mahwah, NJ: Paulist Press, 1981), 58.

2 This term is based on the practice of Zion Faith Homes and its founder Martha Wing Robinson. More information can be found in the booklet published by Zion Faith Homes titled *The Mercy Studies* by Rex Andrews.

3 "Now Rest My Long-Divided Heart." Lyrics by Philip Doddridge, 1702–1751; http://cyberhymnal.org/.

4 Warren W. Wiersbe, *The Wiersbe Bible Commentary: Old Testament* (Colorado Springs, CO: David C. Cook, 2003), 684.

September

1 "Guide Me, O Thou Great Redeemer." Lyrics by William Williams Pantycelyn, 1717–1791; http://cyberhymnal.org/.

2 "'Tis So Sweet to Trust in Jesus." Lyrics by Louisa M. R. Stead, 1850–1917; http://cyberhymnal.org/.

3 "Rock of Ages." Lyrics by Augustus Toplady, 1740–1778; http://cyberhymnal.org/.

October

1 John Donne, "Batter My Heart, Three-Person'd God" in *The Complete Poetry and Selected Prose of John Donne*, ed. Charles Coffin (New York: Random House-Modern Library Edition, 2001).

2 "All for Jesus." Lyrics by Mary Dagworthy James, 1810–1883; http://cyberhymnal.org/.

3 "I Must Tell Jesus All of My Trials." Lyrics by Elisha Albright Hoffman, 1839–1929; http://cyberhymnal.org/.

4 "O to Be Like Thee." Lyrics by Thomas Obediah Chisholm, 1886–1960; http://cyberhymnal.org/.

5 "Yesterday, Today, Forever." Lyrics by Albert Benjamin Simpson, 1843–1919; http://cyberhymnal.org/.

6 Elisabeth Elliot, *The Shadow of the Almighty: The Life and Testimony of Jim Elliot* (New York: Harper, 1958).

7 "Oh, I Want to See Him." Lyrics by Rufus H. Cornelius, 1872–1933; http://cyberhymnal.org/.

November

1 Dallas Willard, *The Spirit of the Disciplines: Understanding How God Changes Lives* (New York: HarperOne, 1999) 263.

2 Josef Ton, *Suffering, Martyrdom, and Rewards in Heaven* (Lanham, MD: University Press of America, 1997).

December

1 James O. Hannay, *The Wisdom of the Desert* (Wesport, Ireland: Metheun and Co., 1904).

2 "Leaning On the Everlasting Arms." Lyrics by Elisha A. Hoffman, 1839–1929; http://cyberhymnal.org/.

3 "Thou Didst Leave Thy Throne and Thy Kingly Crown." Lyrics by Emily Steele Elliott, 1836–1897; http://cyberhymnal.org/.

4 "When He shall Come." Lyrics by Almeda J. Pearce, 1893–1996; http://cyberhymnal.org/.

ABOUT THE AUTHOR

For the past twenty-two years, Dick has lived and worked among Muslims in Mauritania, Kenya, Sudan, and Egypt. He is the founder of Khartoum Christian Center and two initiatives to provide educational training for business development: Aslan Associates (Sudan) and iLearn (Egypt). He is also the founder of EDOSS, an NGO that helps the illiterate poor and refugees in Darfur, Sudan. He is the author of *Saharan Siftings* and *Loving Muslims* and is the editor of *Desert Rain*, *The Live Dead Journal*, and *Live Dead the Journey*.

Dick holds a PhD from the Assemblies of God Theological Seminary. He and his wife, Jennifer, have two sons, Luke and Zack. They currently reside in Cairo, Egypt.

Live Dead the Journey

The Live Dead Journal

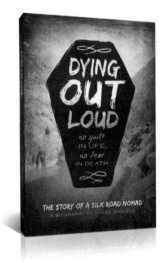

Dying Out Loud

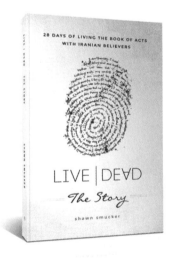

Live Dead the Story

**For more information about these resources,
visit www.influenceresources.com.**

FOR MORE INFORMATION ABOUT THIS BOOK VISIT
WWW.MYHEALTHYCHURCH.COM